AN ILLUSTRATED GUIDE TO

PERENNIALS

A unique reference guide to more than
1500 plants with comprehensive
descriptions and planting information

PROFESSOR MARSHALL CRAIGMYLE

PUBLISHED BY
SALAMANDER BOOKS LIMITED
LONDON

A Salamander Book

Published by Salamander Books Ltd.
8 Blenheim Court
Brewery Road
London N7 9NT
United Kingdom

1 3 5 7 9 8 6 4 2

Text © Salamander Books 2000

ISBN 1 84065 151 2

All correspondence concerning the content of this book should be addressed to Salamander Books Ltd.

Credits
Managing Editor: Charlotte Davies
Editor: Alison Leach
Designers: John Heritage, Mark Holt
Indexer: Amanda O'Neill
Reproduction: Studio Tec, England
Printed in Slovenia

A member of the Chrysalis Group plc

Additional Pictures
Page 1 *Physostegia* virginiana 'Alba'
Page 2 *Hemerocallis* 'Burford'
Page 4 *Rudbeckia fulgida* var. *sullivantii* 'Goldsturm' A.G.M.
Page 5 *Lobelia cardinalis* 'Cherry Ripe'

AN ILLUSTRATED GUIDE TO
PERENNIALS

CONTENTS

PERENNIALS IN THE GARDEN

❦

PERENNIALS GIVE A GARDEN ITS CHARACTER. While trees and shrubs form the permanent backbone of a garden, providing form and structure that endure for years and can not easily be changed, many of them are primarily background plants, contributing little in the way of showy flowers or extravagant foliage. At the other extreme, annuals provide seasonal color and variety but must be renewed each year, letting the gardener ring the changes but increasing the labor involved in the garden. Perennials provide color and a variety of form that last for years, and it is worth choosing them carefully. Fortunately, this is a wide and varied group of plants. While many of the world's most interesting annuals come from warm, Mediterranean-type climates, and require some help and care to grow in other conditions, perennials are well-represented in the flora of diverse habitats in all regions of the world. There is a range of perennial plants to suit every situation in the garden, from a dry stone wall to a bog garden or pond. Perennials have been important in garden design for centuries. Their influence stretches from the notorious tulip mania, in which fortunes were made and lost, to the humble cottage garden. Classic garden design featured the herbaceous border, its selection of perennials carefully graded with taller plants at the back and shorter specimens at the front, shown against the backdrop of an immaculately clipped evergreen hedge or a mellow brick wall, and appreciated from an expanse of smooth lawn. Since the end of the nineteenth century, this approach has been giving way to island beds and less regimented plantings. Increased travel means that modern gardens often show the influences of exotic locations and foreign styles. Gardens today are also often designed with concern for water conservation and other environmental issues, and so look to the natural landscape and wild plant groupings for inspiration. These considerations affect small gardens as well as great ones: even the modest size suburban plot may now revolve around a gravel garden, miniature wildflower meadow, or wildlife pond. Such gardens have the great advantage to the modern gardener of being less labor-intensive, and here the perennial comes into its own, returning to bloom again year after year.

A fine example of the traditional deep herbaceous border, here at Packwood House, in Warwickshire, England.

A PERENNIAL PLANT is one that lives for three or more years, with some perennials living for many more than that. They are distinct from annual plants, which live for one year, and biennials, which live for two, but some very beautiful perennials are short-lived (see p.473), and our gardens would be all the poorer were they restricted to plants of the long-lived variety.

Perennials have developed different strategies for surviving over winter. A perennial plant may disappear below ground completely in winter, in which case it is described as herbaceous, or it may retain some of its leaves throughout the year, in which case it is described as semi-evergreen, or all of them, in which case it is described as evergreen. The great majority of perennial plants are herbaceous. Most of them are also fibrous-rooted, but some have a swollen underground stem in the form of a bulb, a corm, a rhizome, or a tuber. These are all devices for storing energy, enabling a plant to overwinter underground, where it is protected from cold. For the average gardener, the subtle botanical differences between bulbs, corms, rhizomes, or tubers are unlikely to be important, although the particular techniques used in dividing them vary (see p.23). Subshrubs are also included in this book because they associate well with perennials in mixed borders; they produce woody mature growth that survives the cold, as well as some soft growth, which dies back in the winter.

Perennial plants come from many different regions of the world, and as a result they vary enormously in their tolerance of cold. The term "hardy" is used to describe a plant that can survive through the winter outside, and "tender" to describe a plant that requires protection under glass, but these constrictions vary from place to place. In temperate climates, many less hardy or tender perennials are treated as annuals and discarded in the autumn; conversely, in many countries of the world, plants that the Americans think of as tender can be left to overwinter in the open ground. As a result, it is necessary to define the terms whenever they are used. The Royal Horticultural Society uses a scale from H1 (needs heated protection under glass) to H4 (generally hardy in the British Isles), but its publications also give specific minimum temperatures for plants. In mainland Europe, systems with more bands, with narrower ranges, are used, but all of these remain fairly general and so provide necessarily limited help. In this book, a system of climatic zones based on minimum winter temperates has been used (see p.26), as this gives the most reliable and universal guide to a plant's needs.

How Plants Are Named

The world of plant nomenclature can be complex and may seem confusing at first. Plant names are liable to change as botanical study advances, and many out-of-date names remain in common use for some years. All plants described in the plant directory include the plant's name in binominal nomenclature – that is, a generic name followed by a specific name. The plants are listed alphabetically by species name. The authority for the terminology is *The Plant Finder*, 1999–2000 Edition, published by the Royal Horticultural Society, London, England. The terms used can be defined as follows:

Division The broadest categories, for example, Pteridophyta (ferns) or Angiospermae (flowering plants).

Order For example, Ranunculales, which includes three families. The name of an order always ends with the suffix "-ales".

Family This term is used to classify plants into groups exhibiting similar characteristics such as flower and foliage form. These names usually end

Above: *The much-hybridized genus Crocosmia has given rise to cultivars such as Crocosmia x crocosmiiflora 'Emily McKenzie', which has large, bright orange flowers with deeper-colored markings in the throats. Plants bred for the garden are often more lush in habit than the species, or have larger, bolder flowers.*

in "-aceae," for example, Liliaceae. The family name is given for every plant in the plant directory. In some cases, names have changed, and both are given, as with Asteraceae/Compositae.

Genus A genus is a group of similar species. Each genus has a Latin name, which has its first letter in capitals and which also forms the first half of the binominal nomenclature system, by which all plants are identified, and which is always written in italics, for example *Lilium formosanum*, in which *Lilium* is the genus or generic name.

Species The basic unit of plant nomenclature is a species: a group of plants with the same characteristics, interbreeding freely, usually in a distinct geographical range. The specific name forms the second word of the binominal nomenclature, and is written in italics, but without an initial capital letter. It usually indicates a characteristic of the plant, for example, *lancifolia*, meaning that the leaves are lance-shaped, or the origin of the plant, as in *formosanum*, meaning "as found in Formosa." A species grows in the wild somewhere in the world, and usually all plants are of fairly uniform appearance and habit, and can be propagated by seed. Further adaptation of the system of nomenclature divides species into lesser categories as described below.

Subspecies This denotes naturally occurring plants that have subtle differences from the species. The name is written in italics, with the word subspecies usually abbreviated as "subsp." and not given in italics, for example, *Aconitum napellus* subsp. *vulgare*.

Variety This describes a variation, between a subspecies and a form, that is sufficiently distinct to have its own name. The word variety is not written in italics, and is abbreviated to "var.," for example *Agapanthus campanulatus* var. *albidus*.

Forma This lowest of the subclassifications, is not italicized and is abbreviated to "f.," for example, *Allium carinatum* subsp. *pulchellum* f. *album*. It denotes characteristics that may be important to a gardener but which are genetically minor, such as flower color.

Hybrids These are the result of a sexual union between two species or two genera, and are distinguished by having an "x" in their name. An interspecific hybrid is expressed with the "x" before the specific name, for example, *Potentilla* x *tonguei,* while an intergeneric hybrid is expressed with the "x" before the generic name, for example, x *Solidaster luteus*. Hybrids must be propagated vegetatively from cuttings if they are to come true to type. It is possible to take seed, but only a percentage of the progeny will be true to type.

Cultivars An abbreviation of the description "cultivated variety," this is a plant raised deliberately in cultivation. Cultivar names are not given in italics, but are put in inverted commas, for example *Agapanthus* 'Bressingham Blue'. A cultivar may be a hybrid, but the name is also used generally to cover sports; these are spontaneous genetic mutations of a portion of a plant, producing atypical foliage or flowers, or both. Some sports are unstable, and revert rapidly to the parent type. Many variegated plants originated as sports. Due to their origins, most cultivars need to be propagated vegetatively, rather than from seed. The rules that govern cultivar names have been considerably tightened over the years, excluding proper names and Latin words for new cultivars. Some breeders now register trade names for their plants that are more marketable than the true cultivar names; such plants are marked "Regd." in this and other books, and the name is legally controlled.

PLANNING A PERENNIAL GARDEN

In the past, the main way in which perennials were grown was in conventional herbaceous borders. These were frequently mixed, in the sense that shrubs were included. These borders were long and needed to be deep to be effective. They usually had a high wall or hedge behind, with the result that the plants grew at an angle toward the light. Wind then tended to cascade over the wall and flatten the plants, and much time-consuming staking was required.

Island beds, pioneered by the famous nurseryman Alan Bloom in his garden in Bressingham, in Norfolk, England, have several advantages over herbaceous borders. Provided the bed is not underneath overhanging trees or in the shade of buildings, the plants grow vertically, and much less staking is required. Another great advantage of the narrow island bed is that the plants are much more accessible for general maintenance such as deadheading, cutting, or staking, and unless the bed is very large, it is not necessary to trample through it for such purposes. Shrubs are less likely to be incorporated into island beds of perennials, but it is not unusual to see subshrubs, such as *Fuchsia, Helianthemum, Phygelius,* and others included in these beds, as they are so akin to perennials in many respects, and thus many are included in this book. Island beds of shade-loving perennials can of course be created in densely shaded areas, or in dappled shade for those which prefer half-shade. Island beds are also better suited to the small garden.

Right: *A visual guide to the different leaf shapes and types of inflorescence described in the plant directory section.*

Leaf Shapes and Inflorescences

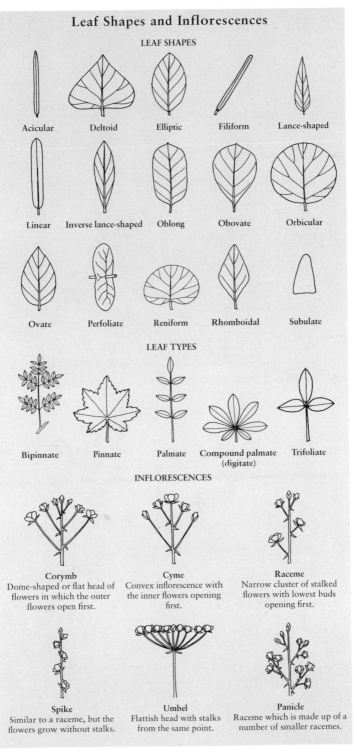

LEAF SHAPES

Acicular Deltoid Elliptic Filiform Lance-shaped

Linear Inverse lance-shaped Oblong Obovate Orbicular

Ovate Perfoliate Reniform Rhomboidal Subulate

LEAF TYPES

Bipinnate Pinnate Palmate Compound palmate (digitate) Trifoliate

INFLORESCENCES

Corymb
Dome-shaped or flat head of flowers in which the outer flowers open first.

Cyme
Convex inflorescence with the inner flowers opening first.

Raceme
Narrow cluster of stalked flowers with lowest buds opening first.

Spike
Similar to a raceme, but the flowers grow without stalks.

Umbel
Flattish head with stalks from the same point.

Panicle
Raceme which is made up of a number of smaller racemes.

11

Above: *Tender plants, such as some fuchsias, are best grown in containers that can be moved in winter. Here,* Fuchsia 'Gartenmeister Bonstedt' *grows in a sandstone basket urn.*

Left: *Exuberant planting spills onto the path from these double borders at Crathes Castle in Grampian, owned by the National Trust for Scotland.*

A development that has been spearheaded on mainland Europe is the inclusion of grasses in beds and borders, and along with this a "loosening up" of the planting, with plants of different heights being more intermingled, so that tall plants with an open, airy habit may be grown at the edge of a bed, with plants behind seen as if through a veil. Such plantings may be strongly architectural, or may tend toward a wilder, more natural look: they are perhaps not for all gardens, but they do provide a lower-maintenance option.

Conditions in the garden can affect planting as much as stylistic preferences. Containers can be used for perennial plants, and this is a useful method for gardens in temperate climes, because tender plants grown in this way can easily be brought under cover or indoors for the winter. However, it is not necessary to restrict their use to tender plants. All perennials may be grown in this way, but the containers of those that are to be left in the open garden all year round must not be small, or the plant may either dry out in summer or succumb to frost in winter because the roots are too near the cold sides of the container. For the older or wheelchair-bound gardener, containers allow plants to be raised up to levels where they can more easily be tended, smelled, and viewed close at hand. Planting in raised beds has many of the same advantages as using containers. The flowers are brought nearer and can therefore be more readily appreciated, and maintenance is easier. Raised beds have the added advantage that trailing plants can be grown on and in their walls, increasing both the selection of plant types that can be grown and the area that is available for planting, both of which are important considerations in small gardens.

Above: *Aubrieta, Alyssum, and Iberis cascading down a stone wall show the opportunity for varied planting afforded by a change in levels or a raised bed.*

You might design either part or the whole of the garden specifically to attract and support local wildlife. Labor-intensive lawns may quickly be turned into something resembling a wildflower meadow (although a true meadow takes time and care to establish), and plants chosen to feed beneficial insects incorporated (see p.470 for suitable plants). A wildlife-friendly garden will usually succeed better in its aims if it includes a pond or a bog garden. These can both be created with pond liners. In a garden that is naturally waterlogged, it is better not to fight the prevailing conditions, but to make a virtue of necessity. There are plenty of attractive, even dramatic plants that will thrive in bog conditions (see page 467).

At the opposite end of the spectrum, the need to conserve water has resulted in a rise in recent years in the popularity of gardens designed to

cope with dry summers without the need for constant watering. Thirsty lawns are replaced by paving with planting pockets or mulches of gravel, at best laid over weed-suppressing membranes, options that reduce both maintenance and evaporation. Such gravel gardens often feature tough perennials from Mediterranean climates. Perhaps the most famous gravel planting is in Beth Chatto's garden at Elmstead Market in Essex, England, a planting developed specifically to explore and show the diverse and beautiful range of plants that will survive naturally with little or no watering in a low-rainfall area (see p.466 for drought-tolerant plants).

Perennials that actively dislike wet, particularly winter wet, can be grown in scree beds. These have a covering of several inches of coarse grit, and have several advantages. They keep the neck of a plant, where it is most likely to rot in a wet winter, dry, and they provide excellent drainage, minimizing plant losses in wet winters. Scree beds are also relatively maintenance-free, and the scree garden planted up with perennials is almost totally maintenance-free.

Above: *These alpine plants growing in a scree bed were photographed in Hartpury, Gloucestershire, where they survive the winters in spite of the high level of winter wet in the area. It is necessary to plan such a bed carefully to create a natural look. Larger pieces of stone in the design here help in this. Always ensure that the stone does not come from environmentally sensitive areas.*

COMBINING PERENNIALS

There are many possible arrangements for planting perennials in any garden. The usual way of combining perennials is simply to grow all kinds – flowering, foliage, bulbs, ferns, grasses, and subshrubs – together, intermingling plants with differing contours to give a pleasant architectural outline. This has many advantages, mainly that it offers points of interest throughout the seasons. Also, since many bulbs are spring-flowering, the gaps they leave as their foliage dies down are soon filled by herbaceous perennials coming into leaf. This sort of mixed planting also helps to guard against pests or diseases associated with one plant type gaining a hold.

There are however, many other interesting possibilities for those who would like to take a more structured or thematic approach. Some gardeners prefer to create very specific mixed plantings using "companion planting," holding that certain plant combinations benefit the health of the plants; this is a subject for a specialist book.

Those with the luxury of space may plant a one-season garden or bed. There are enough perennials of interest in each season for this to be a possibility for any one of them. The drawback, especially of a summer border is that the planting lacks interest for the rest of the year. Other seasonal beds can be planted with annuals in summer.

Many gardeners combine plants on the basis of color. The all-white garden, as in the famous example at Sissinghurst, is popular, but any color can be accommodated in a planting of perennials. A scheme of two colors broadens the range of plants. Blue and gold make a very pleasing combination, as does red and yellow, but not all colors mix, so they must be chosen carefully. In a looser approach, hot-colored flowers complement each other and will have great impact, while cool-colored flowers create a restful atmosphere.

Another approach is to combine plants according to their type.

Above: *This planting of moisture-loving perennials, in Marwood Hill Garden, Barnstaple, in Devon, shows what can be achieved by gardening with the prevailing circumstances. The area, at the bottom of a slope, is a damp location that provides many bog plants with the reliably moist conditions that they require throughout the year to flourish.*

Gardeners usually have their favorite genera, and often choose to grow only these. Beds composed entirely of tulips, narcissi, irises, lilies, hostas, pinks, geraniums, columbines, cannas, campanulas, or New York daisies are all common sights. A less restrictive theme would be to use one class of plant, such as grasses, flowering plants, or ferns – ferneries were very popular in the 19th century.

Other groupings may be suggested by the area of the garden and its use. In an area directly outside a door or window, highly visible all year, a bed of evergreens (see p.465) may be appropriate. In part of the garden used mainly in fine summer weather, an abundance of flowers over a long season (see p.464) may be a priority. For a low-maintenance garden, ground-cover planting (see pp.468–469) will be essential. And in difficult, shady areas, only a grouping of shade-lovers (see p.465) will succeed.

CHOOSING PERENNIALS

When choosing perennials, whether they suit your conditions is one of the most important considerations. Do not assume that if a plant is bought locally, it will be hardy in that area: a sales center may have brought the plants from a long way off, even from another country. Many smaller nurseries do their own propagating, and so their plants may well be hardy locally; but always check first. Also, it is easiest to garden with the soil type and moisture level; there is little to be gained from trying to grow acid-loving plants in chalky soil or moisture-loving plants in a dry, free-draining soil. If some favorites must be included, be prepared to grow them in either containers or specially prepared beds, and to take extra care of them.

Another factor is the space available. The width of a plant has to be known to decide how many are needed to make a good-sized clump; for some, as many as five may be required. Also consider how far they spread. This is especially important in small gardens, and must be established beforehand. Some perennials, such as *Geranium* 'Ann Folkard', may spread several feet. Some perennials spread rapidly and invasively by underground stolons (see p.474). Even in a large garden, invasive perennials can be a nuisance: they spread through neighboring plants, grow up through them, and can cause them to die off, so are best avoided. Some perennials also seed themselves so freely that they become a nuisance (see p.473). At the other end of the scale, some perennials are short-lived, (see pp.473-474) and while there are many beautiful garden plants in this category, the gaps they leave behind need to be filled.

It is also important to look ahead to flowering time to ensure that color clashes do not occur. It is useful to draw a plan of the area in each season before planting to ensure that these points are taken into account, and when planting out, start by placing the plants on the bed in their pots to ensure they are well-spaced before planting.

There are also practical human needs to consider. Allergies and asthma are on the increase, and our understanding of which plants trigger reactions is improving. Plants in the Asteraceae/Compositae family are the worst, but by no means the only, offenders in this. Gardeners who suffer should avoid plants that cause skin irritation (see p.473), or which may trigger an allergic reaction (see p.470), and choose those plants which are least likely to cause a reaction (see pp.469-470). In gardens that will be used by young children, it is best to avoid plants that are harmful if eaten, and in particular those plants with berries or poisonous swollen roots (see p.472). Some perennials need to be lifted and divided every few years to keep them in healthy trim, (see p.474) and should be avoided by infirm gardeners, or those with little time to spare. By avoiding perennials which are likely to be troublesome to them, any gardener can plant a garden that will be a pleasure for many years.

PLANTING AND MAINTAINING PERENNIALS

Since the advent of "containerization", it has become possible to buy perennials all year round. This does not mean, however, that they can be planted all year round. Spring and autumn are good times to plant; spring is preferable in cold countries, giving the plant time to establish a root system before the onset of winter. Grasses and gray-leaved perennials transplant best in spring. Summer planting is possible, but there is the risk of the plant drying out, with disastrous results. Winter planting should be avoided if the ground is, or may become, frozen or waterlogged.

When planting perennials, keep in mind that the plants are likely to remain *in situ* for a number of years, and so thorough preparation of the ground is vital. This entails making sure that the drainage is good, removing all perennial weeds, digging over the site and incorporating as much humus as possible, and in particular, matter that is slow to disintegrate, such as bark.

Some perennials are taprooted, and resent transplantation (see p.475) so these should be placed with particular care: plant according to their needs, rather than taking a chance, and note the height when fully grown, so that it is not awkwardly placed. All plants should be allowed sufficient room for growth, and not surrounded too closely with others.

Once they are established, perennials are remarkably low-maintenance plants; nevertheless any garden requires a certain amount of

Right: *Bold red Crocosmia combines with yellow Ligularia and Kniphofia in a high-impact hot border.*

work. The following tasks will all need to be carried out on a regular basis.

Weeding It is impossible to prevent annual grasses and perennial weeds such as dandelions from seeding into beds. Weeding can be performed either by hand or by hoe. The former is preferable, because hoeing can damage root systems, but is more tiring. Some plants, such as *Eremurus,* are surface-rooting, and should never be hoed around.

Mulching The most desirable, albeit expensive, way of keeping weeds to a minimum is to mulch on a regular basis, say once or twice a season. An organic mulch will also nourish plants as it disintegrates. A mulch should be applied only when the ground is wet; if it is not possible to wait for rain, water beforehand.

Staking The most important consideration here is to provide the support early, before the plants have flopped over. After that the task is twice as difficult. Many of the commercially available staking devices are designed on the principle that the plant grows up through a circular grid, so the device should be in place early in the growth cycle. However, there are many others that are designed to be put in place only after the plant has made considerable growth; all are vastly superior to the old-fashioned bamboo cane and string method. One favored method is to use Christmas trees; the side branches of these can be cut off and put in place early, letting the plant grow up through them, or later, to provide support around the edges of the plants.

Deadheading This is a very important task for three reasons. Firstly, it

prevents energy going into the setting of seed and instead lets the plant to put its effort into building up reserves for the winter. Secondly, for some plants, it will result in a second flush of flowers later in the season. Thirdly, it will prevent many plants from self-seeding too freely.

Feeding Beds of perennials that lie undisturbed for many years will require feeding on a regular basis. The more mulching they receive, the less feeding they will require, since organic mulches decompose and feed the soil in the long run. However, nitrogen-rich fertilizers early in the growing season will help to build up a strong plant, and phosphate-rich feeds at flowering time will help to improve the quality of bloom.

Watering To water is tedious, time-consuming, and sometimes expensive, but necessary at times. The first golden rule of watering is to water thoroughly, or not at all, since repeated surface watering encourages plants to form surface roots at the expense of deep ones, which is courting disaster. The second golden rule is to do so late in the day, and not in the morning, as during the day much of the water will be lost by transpiration. It is always worth conserving water by diverting down-pipes into water butts.

Combating pests and diseases The number of pests and diseases affecting plants is extensive, but perennials suffer less than most other plants, one reason for their increasing popularity. No category of plant, how-

Below: *This well-planned combination of spires, rounded shapes, and trailing plants is at the National Trust's Packwood House, in Warwickshire.*

Above: *Careful planning has produced this spectacular flowering display in a border at Jenkyn Place, near Bentley in Hampshire. It is best to see the plants in flower and compare colors before planning such a planting: even within a single color the range of shades and tones can be surprisingly wide.*

ever, is entirely problem-free.

The major pest of perennials is the snail or slug. Common slug and snail killers contain metaldehyde, a potent poison. The dead slugs will be eaten by hedgehogs and birds (especially in suburban areas where every garden may be laced), and the poison may get into the hands of children. Slug and snail killers that are aluminum-sulphate based do not harm wildlife, but are more readily rendered ineffective by rain, needing to be renewed after each shower. Bell cloches are very useful in protecting new growth in spring, because the cloche prevents the slug killer from becoming ineffective after rain. The cloches should be removed when a healthy plant has been established. Slug traps, which are filled with beer, milk, or other suitably tempting liquids, and in which the slugs drown, are also effective: be sure to place them with the edge a little above ground level so that beneficial beetles do not fall in. Biological controls, in the form of nematodes that parasitize slugs, are a more expensive, but effective and environmentally friendly alternative. Hedgehogs are the most natural solution of all, hence the importance of not endangering them with metaldehyde.

As regards disease, the problem common to many perennials is powdery mildew, which is particularly prevalent in very wet areas. It is disfiguring, debilitating, and often fatal. Chemical fungicides barely control

it, and some plants, such as *Phlox paniculata* and *Aster novi-belgii*, are untreatable. Affected growth should be cut down and disposed of, but not composted or burned. It is often best simply to grow something else if the problem persists.

PROPAGATING PERENNIALS

Perennials can be propagated by seed, by division, and by cuttings.

Seed Species will come true from seed, but even these will show some variation in the progeny. Varieties, forms, sports, and most cultivars can not be propagated by seed if they are required to come true. The seedlings will vary widely, with only a few similar to the parent plant. Seed of *Gentiana, Helleborus,* and *Primula* must be sown fresh; be patient, as the seed will germinate the following spring, or even the spring after that. *Pulsatilla* must also be sown fresh, but germinates at once, as will seeds of the Ranunculaceae family. Most other seeds should be sown in spring. Use sterile seed compost and leave fine seeds on the surface, but lightly cover larger seeds. The largest seeds, such as *Lupinus* and *Baptisia*, have tough coats that must be chipped or abraded before sowing.

Cuttings These can be of stems or basal growth, generally taken in spring, or of roots, taken in late winter. A sandy soil should be used for rooting, preferably with bottom heat.

Division Most perennials can be increased easily by lifting and dividing established, congested plants. For herbaceous perennials, this should be

23

Above: *Division is an easy and inexpensive way to increase many herbaceous perennials. Once a border is established with these plants, it is easy to lift and divide them every three or four years. Helenium autumnale 'Pumilum magnificum', a yellow autumn daisy, offers a sunny splash of bright yellow blooms from late summer through to the end of autumn. Congested clumps should be divided by division after flowering in autumn or in spring.*

carried out during the dormant period, and as a rule, division should take place in spring or autumn. The roots of the plants determine the best method of dividing the plant. Plants with fibrous roots, such as *Aster novae-angliae* (New England daisy), *Aster novi-belgii* (New York daisy), *Leucanthemum* x *superbum* (shasta daisy), *Rudbeckia* (cone-flower), and *Helenium* (sneezeweed), can be increased by lifting and carefully dividing the complete roots. Plants with fleshy roots and woody crowns, such as *Delphinium* and *Lupinus* (lupines), can be prop-agated by lifting the crowns and using a sharp knife to cut through them, or by taking cuttings from young shoots in spring. Rhizomatous plants, such as *Iris germanica,* have thick, tough roots; these can be lifted and, using a sharp knife, the young roots around the outside of the clump divided into pieces 2–3in (5–7.5cm) long, each containing a few strong leaves. Dust the cut surfaces with fungicide, then replant them to the same depth, using the dark mark on the stem indicating the previous level as a guide. Discard the old, woody, central parts. Tuberous genera such as *Paeonia* should also be divided using a sharp knife, ensuring that each section of the tuber has good growing points. Both cormous and bulbous perennials increase freely at the root, and all that is necessary is separation of the offsets, best done when the plant is dormant. Only tap-rooted perennials can not be propagated by division and must be increased by seed or cuttings.

Most perennials are fibrous-rooted, so the method of division for these is worth describing in more detail; all fibrous-rooted plants can be increased in this way, either by pulling the outer shoots apart with roots attached, or by dividing the root ball with a spade or with garden forks held back-to-back (as opposite). They can be divided at any time between

1 Cut down all stems so that the crown of the plant can be seen. Use a garden fork to dig up the clump, taking care not to damage the roots.

2 Insert two garden forks into the clump back-to-back, and lever their handles together. Small plants are best divided with handforks.

3 Gently pull the clump into small pieces, but not very small unless a large number of plants are required. Discard the old, woody central part.

4 Replant the young pieces soon after the clump has been divided. Do not let the roots become dry; cover them with damp sacking if planting is delayed.

early autumn and midspring, as long as the soil is not frozen or water-logged. Usually this means in autumn when the weather is mild, but it is advisable to wait until spring in extremely cold and frost-prone areas.

When dividing fibrous-rooted plants, first cut down all stems to with-in a few inches of the ground. Clear these away and make sure that the soil is free from debris, including weeds. Use a garden fork to dig up the clump, taking care not to sever too many roots.

To divide the plant, push two garden forks back-to-back down through the center of the clump, then lever the handles together to force the roots apart. Ensure that the forks are both pushed in fully; otherwise the upper part of the clump will tear away from the base. Select and pull away young parts from the outside of the clump for replanting. Discard the woody, central area, which is the oldest part, and remove the roots of perennial weeds at the same time.

If the roots are extremely matted, wash them in water and part them gently with a plant label or a pointed stick. Replant the pieces before their roots become dry; if they cannot be replanted at once, wrap them in wet sacking. Ensure that the soil into which they are to be planted is also moist; water thoroughly several days before planting, so that excess moisture has time to drain away. Water again after planting and regu-larly through the growing season.

If the divided parts are particularly small, increase their size by plant-ing them in a nursery bed for one or two years before putting them in their permanent positions in a border. If the parent plant is especially fine and a large number of new plants are wanted, pot very small pieces into 3in (7.5cm) pots and place in a cold frame until they are large enough to be planted into a garden. This is most important in autumn.

HARDINESS ZONES

The first consideration when choosing a perennial to be grown in the garden all year round is whether it is hardy in your area. The United States Department of Agriculture (USDA) has developed a system of temperature zones as a basis for assessing which plants can be grown in different areas. The zones are based on the annual average minimum temperature in an area, and are illustrated on the maps below and opposite of Europe, North America, Australia, New Zealand, and South Africa. The maps have been divided into the USDA climatic zones, numbered from Zone 1, the coldest, with a winter minimum of -50°F (-44°C), up to Zone 11, the warmest, with a minimum of +40°F (+5°C). Every entry in the directory section of this book cites the plant's hardiness zone. To establish whether a perennial will be hardy in your garden, refer to the map of hardiness zones and find the rating for your area. Any plant with a zonal rating equal to or lower than the rating for

Temperature ranges

ZONE 1: Below -50°F (Below -45°C)
ZONE 2: -50 to -35°F (-45 to -37°C)
ZONE 3: -35 to -20°F (-37 to 29°C)
ZONE 4: -20 to -10°F (-29 to 23°C)
ZONE 5: -10 to-5°F (-23 to -21°C)
ZONE 6: -5 to 5°F (-21 to -15°C)
ZONE 7: 5 to 10°F (-15 to -12°C)
ZONE 8: 10 to 20°F (-12 to -7°C)
ZONE 9: 20 to 30°F (-7 to -1°C)
ZONE 10: 30 to 40°F (-I to 4°C)
ZONE 11: Above +40°F (Above +5°C)

Western Europe

your area will be hardy in your garden. Thus if your area is rated Zone 7, all plants graded from Zone 1 to Zone 7 will survive and flower at the average minimum winter temperature there and plants graded Zone 8 to Zone 11 will not. However, Zone 8 plants may be grown outside provided they are given protection in the form of a deep mulch of bracken or leaves, a pane of glass or a cloche, all of which keep the plants dry and help them substantially in surviving the winter. Zone 9 to Zone 11 plants can be grown out of doors in summer in a Zone 7 area, but will have to be lifted and kept under glass in winter or, alternatively, grown in containers and brought into a conservatory or greenhouse over winter.

Another consideration is that every garden has a number of microclimates – that is, some parts of the garden are warmer than others. It may be that the zonal rating for your area does not apply to all of your garden. So if your garden is rated Zone 7, the warmest corner, such as at the foot of a south-facing wall, may well be Zone 8. The only way to find out is to experiment by growing Zone 8-rated plants in that site.

North America

The Southern Hemisphere

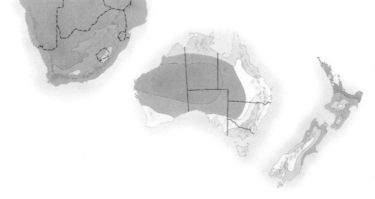

THE PLANT DIRECTORY

❦

MORE THAN 1500 plant entries are featured in the directory. Each entry is illustrated with a color picture of the plant *in situ*, and gives the botanical and common name or names; the height and spread of the plant in imperial and metric measures; the required aspect and type of soil; hardiness rating; and suitable propagation methods. There is a brief description of the plant, giving any appropriate information about the root system or the area in which the plant originated, and detailing the the form and color of the flower and the foliage. The Royal Horticultural Society in the UK carries out extensive trials of all categories of plants, and the accolade of the Award of Garden Merit is given to the most outstanding plants. A plant which has the Award of Garden Merit will have the letters A.G.M. after its name. Positive and negative attributes of each plant are given in the form of symbols, explained below.

KEY TO SYMBOLS

Positive Attribute Symbols

- Long flowering
- Repeat flowering
- Aromatic/perfumed
- Evergreen
- Architectural plant
- Good cut flower
- Good for winter drying
- Drought-tolerant
- Attracts butterflies/bees
- Attractive seedheads/berries
- Low allergen
- Attractive foliage

Negative Attribute Symbols

- Insignificant flowers
- Short-lived plant
- Requires staking
- Invasive plant
- Seeds everywhere
- Prone to slug/snail damage
- Regular lifting and dividing
- Resents disturbance
- Prone to powdery mildew
- Poisonous/skin irritant
- Highly allergenic

Herbaceous border at Bramdean House, in midsummer

Acaena caesiiglauca
(Rosaceae)

Common name: Sheepburr
Height: 5in (12cm)
Spread: To 3ft (1m)
Aspect: Sun or half-shade
Soil: Well-drained
Hardiness: Zone 6
Propagation: Seed, in
autumn; softwood cuttings,
in spring; division, in spring or
autumn

Semi-prostrate, evergreen subshrub.
Leaves glaucous, pinnate, with 7–13
obovate leaflets. Flowerheads
spherical, followed by reddish-brown
burrs in late summer.

Acaena microphylla
'Kupferteppich'
(Rosaceae)

Common name: Redspine
sheepburr
Height: 2in (5cm)
Spread 24in (60cm)
Aspect: Sun or half shade
Soil: Must not be waterlogged
Hardiness: Zone 6
Propagation: Seed, in autumn;
softwood cuttings, in spring;
division, in spring or autumn

Prostrate, evergreen subshrub. Leaves
bronze, pinnate, with 9–15 rounded
leaflets. Flowerheads spherical, small,
followed by red burrs. Good for rock
garden or wall.

Acanthus dioscoridis
var. perringii
(Acanthaceae)

Common name: Bear's-
breech
Height: 16in (40cm)
Spread: 24in (60cm)
Aspect: Sun or half shade
Soil: Well-drained
Hardiness: Zone 8
Propagation: Seed, in spring;
division, in spring or autumn;
root cuttings, in winter

Evergreen with running, fleshy
rootstalk. Leaves spiny, pinnatifid,
gray-green, rosetted. Racemes of pink
flowers with green bracts, late spring
to late summer. Shy-flowering.

Acanthus hungaricus
(Acanthaceae)

Common name: Bear's-
breech
Height: 4ft (1.2m)
Spread: 3ft (90cm)
Aspect: Sun or half shade
Soil: Well-drained
Hardiness: Zone 8
Propagation: Seed, in spring;
division, in spring or autumn;
root cuttings, in winter

Clump-forming evergreen. Leaves
oblong-obovate, dark green, deeply
lobed. Racemes of pale pink or white
flowers, bracts tinged purple, early to
midsummer.

Acanthus mollis
(**Acanthaceae**)

Common name: Bear's-
breech
Height: To 5ft (1.5m)
Spread: 3ft (90cm)
Aspect: Sun or half shade
Soil: Well-drained
Hardiness: Zone 6
Propagation: Seed, in
spring; division, in spring or
autumn; root cuttings, in winter

Clump-forming, architectural
evergreen with obovate, dark green,
deeply lobed, shiny leaves. Flowers in
racemes, white, with purple-shaded
bracts, in late summer.

Acanthus spinosus
A.G.M.
(**Acanthaceae**)

Common name: Bear's-
breech
Height: To 4ft (1.2m)
Spread: 2ft (60cm)
Aspect: Sun or half shade
Soil: Well-drained
Hardiness: Zone 6
Propagation: Seed, in spring;
division, in spring or autumn;
root cuttings, in winter

Clump-forming, architectural
evergreen. Leaves spiny, oblong,
deeply cut, arching, dark green. Tall
raceme of soft mauve flowers and
purple bracts, from late spring.

ACHILLEA (Compositae)
Yarrow • Milfoil • Sneezewort

A genus of some 80 species, from various habitats in the
temperate northern hemisphere. The daisylike flowerheads
usually lack ray petals, so have only disc florets, and are closely
packed in tight corymbs, borne on stout stems. They exhibit a
wide range of color. All are attractive to both bees and
butterflies. The foliage is feathery, save for that of *A. ptarmica*
(Zone 5), and some are evergreen. The flowerheads last a long
time, and are good for cutting and drying for the winter, and
suitable for flower arrangements in both fresh and dry states.
Achillea do best in full sun with good drainage, but they are
only reasonably tolerant of drought, so a moisture-retentive soil
is best. Drawbacks are that they are prone to powdery mildew,
and some forms require staking. *A. millefolium* (Zone 2) and
A. ptarmica, both rhizomatous, can be as invasive as weeds. All
the rest are well-behaved, except that they may die out in the
center and usually have to be lifted and divided every few years,
and the healthy outer edges replanted. Many species and
cultivars hold an Award of Garden Merit; some not illustrated
here are *A. ageratifolia* (Zone 3), *A.* x *lewisii* 'King Edward'
(Zone 5), and *A. tomentosa* (Zone 3).

Achillea 'Coronation Gold' A.G.M.
(Asteraceae/Compositae)

Common name: Yarrow
Height: 36in (90cm)
Spread: 18in (45cm)
Aspect: Sun
Soil: Humus-rich
Hardiness: Zone 6
Propagation: Division, in spring

Achillea 'Credo'
(Asteraceae/Compositae)

Common names: Milfoil; yarrow
Height: 4ft (1.2m)
Spread: 2ft (60cm)
Aspect: Sun
Soil: Humus-rich
Hardiness: Zone 6
Propagation: Division, in spring

Clump-forming evergreen with pinnatifid, oblong, gray-green leaves. Corymbs 4in (10cm) across of golden-yellow flowerheads, from midsummer. Good for small gardens.

Clump-forming perennial with feathery, pale green leaves and corymbs of pale yellow flowerheads, aging to cream, in summer.

Achillea 'Fanal'
(Asteraceae/Compositae)

Common name: Yarrow
Height: 30in (75cm)
Spread: 24in (60cm)
Aspect: Sun
Soil: Humus-rich
Hardiness: Zone 2
Propagation: Division, in spring

Achillea filipendula 'Gold Plate' A.G.M.
(Asteraceae/Compositae)

Common name: Fernleaf yarrow
Height: 4ft (1.2m)
Spread: 18in (45cm)
Aspect: Sun
Soil: Humus-rich
Hardiness: Zone 3
Propagation: Division, in spring

Mat-forming hybrid with linear, 2-pinnate, gray-green leaves. Corymbs 6in (15cm) across of bright red flowerheads with yellow discs. Flowers fade as they age.

Clump-forming evergreen. Rosettes of mid- to gray-green, oblong, 1- or 2-pinnate leaves. Bright yellow flowerheads in corymbs 6in (15cm) across, early summer to early autumn.

Achillea
'Forncett Candy'
(Asteraceae/Compositae)

Common name: Yarrow
Height: 36in (90cm)
Spread: 18in (45cm)
Aspect: Sun
Soil: Humus-rich
Hardiness: Zone 6
Propagation: Division,
in spring

Clump-forming evergreen, with
fernlike, gray-green leaves. Abundant
pale pink flowerheads, fading to
almost white in corymbs 6in (15cm)
across, in summer.

Achillea
'Huteri'
(Asteraceae/Compositae)

Common name: Yarrow
Height: 24in (60cm)
Spread: 12in (30cm)
Aspect: Sun
Soil: Humus-rich
Hardiness: Zone 6
Propagation: Division,
in spring

A bushy cultivar, with linear, pinnate
leaves of silver-gray. Flowerheads with
white ray florets are borne in corymbs
in summer.

Achillea millefolium
'Cerise Queen'
(Asteraceae/Compositae)

Common names: Yarrow;
milfoil
Height: 2ft (60cm)
Spread: 2ft (60cm)
Aspect: Sun
Soil: Humus-rich
Hardiness: Zone 2
Propagation: Division,
in spring

Rhizomatous, mat-forming cultivar.
Leaves linear to lance-shaped,
pinnatisect, dark green. Corymbs of
magenta flowerheads with white discs
in summer. Highly invasive.

Achillea
'Moonshine' A.G.M.
(Asteraceae/Compositae)

Common name: Yarrow
Height: 2ft (60cm)
Spread: 2ft (60cm)
Aspect: Sun
Soil: Humus-rich
Hardiness: Zone 7
Propagation: Division,
in spring

Clump-forming evergreen with linear
to lance-shaped, gray-green, pinnatifid
leaves. Corymbs 6in (15cm) across of
light yellow flowerheads, early
summer to early autumn.

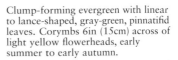

Achillea ptarmica 'Nana Compacta' (Asteraceae/Compositae)

Common name:
Sneezewort
Height: 12in (30cm)
Spread: 24in (60cm)
Aspect: Sun
Soil: Humus-rich
Hardiness: Zone 5
Propagation: Division,
in spring

Rhizomatous perennial. Leaves linear
to lance-shaped, toothed, dark green.
Corymbs of off-white flowers with
gray-green centers in summer. Too
invasive for borders.

Achillea ptarmica 'Stephanie Cohen' (Asteraceae/Compositae)

Common name:
Sneezewort
Height: 30in (75cm)
Spread: 32in (80cm)
Aspect: Sun
Soil: Any
Hardiness: Zone 5
Propagation: Division,
in spring

A handsome but invasive cultivar.
Foliage linear to lance-shaped,
toothed, green. Pale pink flowers with
darker centers, borne in corymbs from
early to late summer.

Aciphylla aurea (Apiaceae/Umbelliferae)

Common names: None
Height: 3ft (1m)
Spread: 3ft (1m)
Aspect: Full sun
Soil: Moist but well-
drained, humus-rich
Hardiness: Zone 5
Propagation: Seed, when ripe

Rosettes of straplike, 2-pinnate, gray-
green leaves with spiny tips and gold
edges. Many golden-brown, star-
shaped flowers. Needs both sexes and
warm summers to fruit.

Aciphylla glaucescens (Apiaceae/Umbelliferae)

Common names: None
Height: 3ft (1m)
Spread: 3ft (1m)
Aspect: Full sun
Soil: Moist but well-
drained, humus-rich
Hardiness: Zone 8
Propagation: Seed, when ripe

Rosettes of narrow, 3-pinnate,
straplike leaves, silver-gray, spiny-
tipped and edged. Yellow-green, star-
shaped flowers. Needs both sexes and
a warm climate to fruit.

ACONITUM (Ranunculaceae)
Monkshood • Aconite • Wolfsbane

A genus of about 100 species from woodlands, grasslands, and scrub in the northern hemisphere. They are tuberous-rooted, except for *A. lycotonum* subsp. *vulparia*. The distinctive flowers have hoods composed of sepals, so providing one of the common names, which provide the shape and color and hide the petals. They are carried in tall panicles or racemes, well above the foliage. The leaves are generally of a rich green, and ovate, round, palmately lobed, or kidney-shaped. All *Aconitum* need to be lifted and divided every few years; the taller forms, although good architectural plants for woodland or border, will also require staking. It is important to note that all parts of these plants are highly poisonous if eaten. There are no particularly tempting-looking fruits, but it is still safest to say that the genus should not be grown in a garden where there are children. Contact with the foliage may also cause skin irritation, but handled with care they make good cut flowers, and are popular with flower-arrangers. The flowers are not allergenic. Other Award of Garden Merit varieties that have not been illustrated here are *A.* 'Bressingham Spire' (Zone 4), *A. carmichaelii* 'Kelmscott' (Zone 3), and *A.* 'Spark's Variety' (Zone 4).

Aconitum × cammarum 'Bicolor' A.G.M. (Ranunculaceae)

Common name: Monkshood
Height: 4ft (1.2m)
Spread: 4ft (1.2m)
Aspect: Sun or half shade
Soil: Moist, fertile, humus-rich
Hardiness: Zone 3
Propagation: Division, in autumn

Aconitum septentrionale 'Ivorine' (Ranunculaceae)

Common name: Monkshood
Height: 36in (90cm)
Spread: 18in (45cm)
Aspect: Sun or half shade
Soil: Moist, fertile, cool
Hardiness: Zone 5
Propagation: Division, in autumn

A very hardy perennial. Foliage ovate to round, deeply lobed, glossy, dark green. Blue and white flowers in loose arching panicles from midsummer.

Very attractive perennial with deeply lobed, rounded, rich green leaves. Ivory flowers in spikelike racemes in late spring and early summer; largest in a cool, moist climate.

Aconitum lycoctonum subsp. *vulparia* (Ranunculaceae)

Common name:
Wolfsbane monkshood
Height: To 5ft (1.5m)
Spread: 1ft (30cm)
Aspect: Sun or half shade
Soil: Moist, fertile,
humus-rich
Hardiness: Zone 3
Propagation: Seed, in spring;
division, in autumn

An erect, very hardy perennial with round, lobed, rich green leaves. Panicles of hooded, pale yellow flowers are borne from mid- to late summer.

Aconitum lycoctonum, subsp. *vulparia* 'Albidum' (Ranunculaceae)

Common name:
Wolfsbane monkshood
Height: To 5ft (1.5m)
Spread: 1ft (30cm)
Aspect: Sun or half shade
Soil: Moist, fertile,
humus-rich
Hardiness: Zone 3
Propagation: Division, in autumn

A very hardy, handsome perennial. Erect stems. Leaves dark green, rounded, with 5 to 9 lobes. Flowers in panicles, hooded, pure white.

Aconitum napellus (Ranunculaceae)

Common name: Aconite
monkshood
Height: To 5ft (1.5m)
Spread: 1ft (30cm)
Aspect: Sun or half shade
Soil: Moist, fertile,
humus-rich
Hardiness: Zone 6
Propagation: Seed, in spring;
division, in autumn

Erect, with rounded, deeply lobed, often toothed, dark green leaves. Panicles of flowers are intense indigo-blue in the best forms. Very variable; buy in bloom.

Aconitum napellus subsp. *vulgare* 'Albidum' (Ranunculaceae)

Common name: Aconite
monkshood
Height: To 5ft (1.5m)
Spread: 1ft (30cm)
Aspect: Sun or half shade
Soil: Moist, fertile,
humus-rich
Hardiness: Zone 6
Propagation: Division, in autumn

Erect, with handsome foliage of rounded, deeply lobed, toothed, dark green leaves. Panicles of gray-white flowers in mid- to late summer.

Actaea alba
A.G.M.
(**Ranunculaceae**)

Common name: White
baneberry
Height: 3ft (90cm)
Spread: 2ft (60cm)
Aspect: Half shade
Soil: Cool, moist, fertile,
humus-rich
Hardiness: Zone 3
Propagation: Seed, in autumn;
division, in spring

Rhizomatous woodland plant with 2-,
3-, or 5-ternate, toothed, green leaves.
Tiny white flowers in spherical
racemes are followed by clusters of
extremely toxic white berries.

Actaea rubra
A.G.M.
(**Ranunculaceae**)

Common name: Red
baneberry
Height: 18in (45cm)
Spread: 12in (30cm)
Aspect: Half shade
Soil: Cool, moist, fertile,
humus-rich
Hardiness: Zone 3
Propagation: Seed, in autumn;
division, in spring

Woodlander with 2- or 3-pinnate
leaves of up to 15 ovate leaflets. Small
racemes of white, ovoid flowers in
spring to summer, followed by shiny,
red, highly toxic berries.

Adenophora asiatica
(Campanulaceae)

Common name: Ladybell
Height: 12in (30cm)
Spread: 6in (15cm)
Aspect: Sun or half shade
Soil: Moist, well-drained,
humus-rich
Hardiness: Zone 5
Propagation: Seed, in autumn;
cuttings in spring; no division

A charming fleshy-rooted perennial.
Leaves ovate, toothed, midgreen.
Flowers bell-shaped, pendent, pale
lavender-blue, in terminal racemes, in
mid- to late summer.

Adenophora potaninii
(Campanulaceae)

Common name: Bush
ladybell
Height: To 3ft (90cm)
Spread: 1ft (30cm)
Aspect: Sun or half shade
Soil: Moist, well-drained,
humus-rich
Hardiness: Zone 3
Propagation: Seed, in autumn;
cuttings, in spring

Reliable perennial with lax stems and
ovate to lance-shaped, toothed leaves.
Racemes of pendent, open, bell-
shaped, violet-blue flowers in mid- to
late summer.

Adiantum aleuticum
A.G.M.
(Adiantaceae/Pteridaceae)

Common name: Aleutian
maidenhair fern
Height: 30in (75cm)
Spread: 30in (75cm)
Aspect: Sun or half shade
Soil: Moist, well-drained,
humus-rich
Hardiness: Zone 4
Propagation: Spores, in warmth when
ripe; division, in spring

Rhizomatous, deciduous fern. Fronds
pale to midgreen, kidney-shaped to
broadly ovate, pedate, with oblong
segments and black stalks and
midribs.

Adiantum capillus-veneris
(Adiantaceae/Pteridaceae)

Common name: True
maidenhair fern
Height: 12in (30cm)
Spread: 18in (45cm)
Aspect: Half shade
Soil: Moist, well-drained,
alkaline, fertile
Hardiness: Zone 8
Propagation: Spores, in warmth when
ripe; division, in spring

Creeping, rhizomatous fern, evergreen
down to 28°F (-2°C). Fronds arching,
bronze-pink, turning green, 2- or 3-
pinnate, triangular. Pinnae fan-
shaped, stems black.

Adiantum pedatum
A.G.M.
(Adiantaceae/Pteridaceae)

Common name: Five-
fingered maidenhair fern
Height: 16in (40cm)
Spread: 16in (40cm)
Aspect: Half-shade
Soil: Moist, well drained,
fertile
Hardiness: Zone 5
Propagation: Spores, in warmth in
autumn; division, in spring

Deciduous, creeping, rhizomatous
fern. Fronds ovate to kidney-shaped,
pinnate, midgreen. Segments oblong
or triangular, upper edges lobed or
toothed. Stems black.

Aegopodium podagraria
'Variegatum'
(Apiaceae/Umbelliferae)

Common names:
Goutweed; Bishop's-weed
Height: 2ft (60cm)
Spread: Indefinite
Aspect: Full or half shade
Soil: Any
Hardiness: Zone 2
Propagation: Division,
in spring

Invasive rhizomatous plant. Leaves
ovate, green, cream-edged.
Insignificant white flowers. Grow in
dry shade or in a container; deadhead
before it sets seed.

Aeonium cuneatum
(Crassulaceae)

Common names: None
Height: 6ft (2m)
Spread: 20in (50cm)
Aspect: Half shade
Soil: Well-drained, fertile
Hardiness: Zone 9
Propagation: Seed, in
warmth in spring; cuttings,
in spring

Showy, evergreen succulent. Tidy
rosettes of fleshy leaves on clustered,
basal shoots. Spikelike panicle of star-
shaped, yellow flowers in spring and
summer.

Aethionema schistosum
(Brassicaceae/Cruciferae)

Common name: Stonecress
Height: 4in (10cm)
Spread: 12in (30cm)
Aspect: Sun
Soil: Well-drained
Hardiness: Zone 6
Propagation: Seed,
in spring

Upright, free-flowering; for border
front or rock garden. Narrow, linear,
acuminate, crowded leaves. Tight
raceme of 4-petalled, tiny pink flowers
in spring. From Turkey.

Aethionema
'Warley Rose' A.G.M.
(Brassicaceae/Cruciferae)

Common name: Stonecress
Height: 8in (20cm)
Spread: 8in (20cm)
Aspect: Sun
Soil: Well-drained
Hardiness: Zone 7
Propagation: Softwood
cuttings, in spring or autumn

Free-flowering but short-lived dwarf
subshrub. Leaves linear, blue-gray.
Small pink flowers in tight racemes in
spring and early summer. Good wall
plant.

Agapanthus
'Blue Imp'
(Alliaceae/Liliaceae)

Common name: African
blue lily
Height: 12in (30cm)
Spread: 8in (20cm)
Aspect: Full sun
Soil: Moist, well-drained,
fertile
Hardiness: Zone 7
Propagation: Division,
in late spring

Choice dwarf form, ideal for small
gardens. Deciduous, strap-shaped,
dark green leaves. Large umbels of
deep blue flowers in late summer.

AGAPANTHUS (Alliaceae/Liliaceae)
African blue lily

A genus of about 10 perennials from southern Africa. They are vigorous, and form large clumps. The foliage is strap-shaped, often arching, and of a deep green; some species are evergreen, but the hybrid forms are all deciduous. The inflorescence is an umbel, which may be rounded, upright, pendent, or intermediate between the two. The individual flowers may be tubular, trumpet-shaped, or bell-shaped, and are usually blue in color, although white forms exist. They are followed by attractive seed heads. The roots are very brittle, so the genus does not transplant well: they should be moved while in growth, if at all. *Agapanthus* are generally fairly hardy, but in cold areas they should be mulched over winter if left in the open ground; they make excellent container plants that can be moved under some protection in winter. The evergreen species, originating in coastal areas, are tender and should have winter protection. All make good flowers for cutting; the seed heads also dry well, and are liked by flower-arrangers. Other Award of Garden Merit forms not included in this selection are *A. africanus* and *A. africanus* 'Albus' (both Zone 9), *A. caulescens* (Zone 7), *A.* 'Loch Hope' (Zone 7), and *A. praecox* 'Variegatus' (Zone 9)

Agapanthus
'Bressingham Blue'
(Alliaceae/Liliaceae)

Common name: African blue lily
Height: 36in (90cm)
Spread: 18in (45cm)
Aspect: Full sun
Soil: Moist, well-drained, fertile
Hardiness: Zone 7
Propagation: Division, in late spring

Very robust cultivar. Trumpet-shaped, intensely amethyst-blue flowers in huge, rounded umbels in mid- to late summer. Straplike, deep green leaves.

Agapanthus
campanulatus
(Alliaceae/Liliaceae)

Common name: African blue lily
Height: 4ft (1.2m)
Spread: 18in (45cm)
Aspect: Full sun
Soil: Moist, well-drained, fertile
Hardiness: Zone 7
Propagation: Division, in late spring

Vigorous, clump-forming species. Narrow, straplike, gray-green leaves. Bell-shaped flowers of pale or dark blue in rounded umbels on strong stems.

Agapanthus campanulatus var. *albidus* (Alliaceae:Liliaceae)

Common name: African blue lily
Height: To 4ft (1.2m)
Spread: 18in (45cm)
Aspect: Full sun
Soil: Moist, well-drained, fertile
Hardiness: Zone 7
Propagation: Division, in late spring

A white-flowered form of the species. Vigorous and clump-forming, with narrow, straplike, gray-green leaves. Rounded umbels of bell-shaped flowers.

Agapanthus 'Lilliput' (Alliaceae/Liliaceae)

Common name: African blue lily
Height: 16in (40cm)
Spread: 16in (40cm)
Aspect: Full sun
Soil: Moist, well-drained, fertile
Hardiness: Zone 7
Propagation: Division, in late spring

Clump-forming dwarf form, ideal for small gardens. Umbels rounded or intermediate, flowers trumpet-shaped and deep blue, in mid- to late summer.

Agastache 'Firebird' (Labiatae/Lamiaceae)

Common name: Hyssop
Height: 2ft (60cm)
Spread: 1ft (30cm)
Aspect: Full sun
Soil: Well-drained, fertile
Hardiness: Zone 8
Propagation: Semiripe cuttings, in late summer

A short-lived cultivar with lance-shaped to ovate, gray-green, aromatic leaves. Spikes of tubular, two-lipped, long-lasting, copper-red flowers from midsummer to early autumn.

Agastache foeniculum (Labiatae/Lamiaceae)

Common names: Giant hyssop; anise hyssop
Height: 5ft (1.5m)
Spread: 1ft (30cm)
Aspect: Full sun
Soil: Well-drained, fertile
Hardiness: Zone 8
Propagation: Semiripe cuttings, in late summer

Upright, aniseed-scented plant. Veined, ovate to lance-shaped leaves, downy beneath. Blue flowers with lilac bracts and calyces, in spikes from midsummer to early autumn.

Agastache mexicana
(Labiatae/Lamiaceae)

Common name: Mexican hyssop
Height: 3ft (90cm)
Spread: 1ft (30cm)
Aspect: Full sun
Soil: Well-drained, fertile
Hardiness: Zone 9
Propagation: Semiripe cuttings, in early summer

Short-lived, bushy perennial with aromatic foliage. Ovate to lance-shaped, green leaves. Flowers rosy-red, in tall spikes, from mid- to late summer.

Agave americana
'Marginata'
(Agavaceae)

Common name: Century plant
Height: 6ft (2m)
Spread: 10ft (3m)
Aspect: Full sun
Soil: Sharply drained, acidic
Hardiness: Zone 9
Propagation: Seed, in warmth in spring; offsets, in spring or autumn

Succulent from Central America. Rosette of lance-shaped, gray-green leaves with spiny yellow edges. May produce panicles of yellow flowers in summer; monocarpic.

Ajania pacifica
(Asteraceae/Compositae)

Common names: None
Height: 1ft (30cm)
Spread: 3ft (90cm)
Aspect: Full sun
Soil: Well-drained, poor
Hardiness: Zone 6
Propagation: Seed, cuttings, or division, all in spring

Mound-forming Asian subshrub, spreading by runners. Leaves ovate, lobed, silky, gray-green, edged white. Flowers yellow buttons, in corymbs in autumn.

Ajuga reptans
'Atropurpurea' A.G.M.
(Labiatae: Lamiaceae)

Common names: Carpet bugle; Bugleweed
Height: 6in (15cm)
Spread: 36in (90cm)
Aspect: Half shade; protect from midday sun
Soil: Moist
Hardiness: Zone 6
Propagation: Softwood cuttings, in spring

Rhizomatous, creeping ground cover. Ovate to oblong-spoon-shaped, dark purple leaves. Whorled spikes of dark blue flowers in spring and early summer.

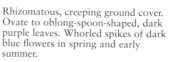

Ajuga reptans
'Burgundy Glow' A.G.M.
(Labiatae/Lamiaceae)

Common names: Carpet
bugle; Bugleweed
Height: 6in (15cm)
Spread: To 36in (90cm)
Aspect: Half shade;
protect from midday sun
Soil: Moist
Hardiness: Zone 6
Propagation: Softwood cuttings,
in spring

Rhizomatous, creeping ground cover.
Ovate to spoon-shaped leaves are
silvery green, flushed dark red. Blue
flowers in hairy-stemmed spikes in
spring to early summer.

Ajuga reptans 'Multicolor'
syn. 'Rainbow'
(Labiatae/Lamiaceae)

Common names: Carpet
bugle; Bugleweed
Height: 6in (15cm)
Spread: 3ft (1m)
Aspect: Half shade;
protect from midday sun
Soil: Moist
Hardiness: Zone 6
Propagation: Softwood cuttings,
in spring

Rhizomatous, creeping ground cover.
Ovate to spoon-shaped leaves,
reddish-bronze and green, splashed
pink and cream. Spikes of dark blue
flowers in spring to early summer.

Albuca altissima
(Hyacinthaceae/Liliaceae)

Common names: None
Height: 18in (45cm)
Spread: 12in (30cm)
Aspect: Full sun
Soil: Well-drained, fertile
Hardiness: Zone 9
Propagation: Seed, in
spring; bulbils, in autumn

Bulbous plant from South Africa.
Glabrous, green, lanceolate leaves.
Trumpet-shaped, white flowers, with
a broad green median stripe, in a
loose raceme in late summer.

Albuca humilis
(Hyacintheae/Liliaceae)

Common names: None
Height: 4in (10cm)
Spread: 2in (5cm)
Aspect: Sun
Soil: Well-drained, fertile
Hardiness: Zone 7
Propagation: Seed, in
warmth in spring; offsets,
in autumn

Bulbous perennial. Leaves narrow,
linear, green, basal. Flowers narrow,
white bells, outer tepals striped green,
inner ones tipped yellow, in late spring
and early summer.

Alcea rosea
(Malvaceae)

Common name:
Hollyhock
Height: 6ft (2m)
Spread: 3ft (1m)
Aspect: Sun
Soil: Well-drained, fertile
Hardiness: Zone 3
Propagation: Seed, *in situ*
in summer

Well-loved perennial. Leaves rounded, hairy, lobed, green. Long terminal racemes of yellow, white, pink, or purple, single flowers in early and midsummer. Dries well.

Alcea rosea
'Chater's Double'
(Malvaceae)

Common name:
Hollyhock
Height: 8ft (2.5m)
Spread: 2ft (60cm)
Aspect: Sun
Soil: Well-drained, fertile
Hardiness: Zone 3
Propagation: Seed, *in situ*
in summer

Race with fully double, peonylike flowers in many shades in early and midsummer. Leaves round, hairy, green. Grow as annuals if hollyhock rust is a problem.

Alchemilla alpina
(Rosaceae)

Common name: Mountain lady's-mantle
Height: 5in (12cm)
Spread: 20in (50cm)
Aspect: Sun or half shade
Soil: Moist, humus-rich
Hardiness: Zone 3
Propagation: Seed, in spring;
division, in spring or autumn

Creeping, mat-forming, woody perennial. Kidney-shaped or rounded, lobed, white-edged green leaves, silver beneath. Straggly cymes of tiny, yellow flowers in summer.

Alchemilla mollis
A.G.M.
(Rosaceae)

Common name: Lady's-mantle
Height: 2ft (60cm)
Spread: 3ft (90cm)
Aspect: Sun or half shade
Soil: Moist, humus-rich
Hardiness: Zone 3
Propagation: Seed, in spring;
division, in spring or autumn

Handsome, clump-forming ground cover. Leaves rounded, lobed, toothed, pale green, softly hairy. Tiny greenish-yellow flowers in lax cymes from spring to autumn.

Alisma plantago-aquatica
(Alismataceae)

Allium angulosum
(Alliaceae/Liliaceae)

Common name: Water-
plantain
Height: 30in (75cm)
Spread: 30in (75cm)
Aspect: Sun
Soil: Marginal or in water
6 12in (15–30cm) deep
Hardiness: Zone 6
Propagation: Seed, when ripe;
division, in spring

Common name: Mouse
garlic
Height: 18in (45cm)
Spread: 12in (30cm)
Aspect: Sun
Soil: Moist, fertile
Hardiness: Zone 5
Propagation: Seed, in spring;
offsets, in autumn

Rhizomatous, deciduous aquatic
marginal. Basal rosettes of elliptic to
lance-shaped, gray-green leaves. Huge,
branched panicle of tiny white flowers
in mid- and late summer.

Bulbous onion with linear to
straplike, rich, shiny, green basal
leaves, sharply keeled underneath.
Flowers are pale lilac, in
hemispherical umbels on stout stems.

ALLIUM (Liliaceae)
Onion

Huge genus of some 700 species from a wide range of habitats
in the northern hemisphere. They may be bulbous or
rhizomatous, and are grown for culinary or ornamental value,
or both. All enjoy full sun, and most prefer well-drained soil.
Hardiness varies: many are reliably hardy, but there are some
tender species. Most are deciduous. The flowerheads are
umbels, which may be ovoid, round, or pendent in shape;
individual flowers are cup-, bell-, or star-shaped. All alliums
make good cut flowers, although the onion odor may not be to
everyone's liking, and they are much used fresh and dried by
flower-arrangers. Contact with the bulbs may cause skin
irritation, or exacerbate existing allergic skin disease. Many
alliums are well-behaved garden plants, and twenty-one carry
an Award of Garden Merit as ornamental plants. Others spread
like pernicious weeds: those that carry bulbils in the flowerhead,
such as *A. carinatum* (Zone 7), *A. vineale* (Zone 5), and
A. scorodoprasum (Zone 7), should be avoided in most
situations. Other promiscuous alliums to be treated with caution
are *A. canadense* (Zone 4), *A. ampeloprasum* var. *bulbiferum*
(Zone 6), *A. paradoxum* (Zone 8), and *A. roseum* (Zone 8).

Allium carinatum subsp. *pulchellum* A.G.M. (Alliaceae/Liliaceae)

Common name: Keeled garlic
Height: 24in (60cm)
Spread: 4in (10cm)
Aspect: Sun
Soil: Well-drained, fertile
Hardiness: Zone 7
Propagation: Seed, in spring; offsets, in autumn

Bulbous evergreen perennial with midgreen, linear, basal leaves. Rich purple, bell-shaped flowers in elongated, dense umbel. Slowly forms clumps. From southern Europe.

Allium cernuum (Alliaceae/Liliaceae)

Common name: Nodding onion
Height: 24in (60cm)
Spread: 4in (10cm)
Aspect: Sun
Soil: Well-drained, fertile
Hardiness: Zone 6
Propagation: Seed, in spring; offsets, in autumn

An easy-going, vigorous, bulbous plant with deep pink, bell-shaped flowers in a drooping umbel. The leaves are narrow, dark green basal straps.

Allium cristophii A.G.M. (Alliaceae/Liliaceae)

Common name: Star-of-Persia
Height: 24in (60cm)
Spread: 8in (20cm)
Aspect: Sun
Soil: Well-drained, fertile
Hardiness: Zone 5
Propagation: Seed, in spring; offsets, in autumn

Popular bulbous perennial. Leaves basal, straplike, gray-green. Bears purplish-pink, star-shaped flowers with a metallic sheen in large, spherical umbels in early summer.

Allium flavum A.G.M. (Alliaceae/Liliaceae)

Common name: Yellow onion
Height: 16in (40cm)
Spread: 4in (10cm)
Aspect: Sun
Soil: Well-drained, fertile
Hardiness: Zone 7
Propagation: Seed, in spring; offsets, in autumn

Very variable, bulbous onion. Leaves strap-shaped, glaucous, green. Up to 60 bright yellow, bell-shaped, pendent flowers in a loose umbel in summer.

***Allium giganteum*
A.G.M.
(Alliaceae/Liliaceae)**

Common name: Giant
onion
Height: 6ft (2m)
Spread: 8in (20cm)
Aspect: Sun
Soil: Well-drained, fertile
Hardiness: Zone 5
Propagation: Seed, in spring;
offsets, in autumn

Bulbous allium with pale green,
straplike basal leaves that wither
before flowering. Large, dense umbel
of up to 60 lilac-pink, star-shaped
flowers in summer.

***Allium*
'Globemaster' A.G.M.
(Alliaceae/Liliaceae)**

Common names: None
Height: 32in (80cm)
Spread: 8in (20cm)
Aspect: Sun
Soil: Well-drained, fertile
Hardiness: Zone 7
Propagation: Offsets,
in autumn

Very desirable hybrid with strap-
shaped, gray-green basal leaves.
Numerous dark violet, star-shaped
flowers in an umbel 6–8in (15–20cm)
across, in summer.

***Allium karataviense*
A.G.M.
(Alliaceae/Liliaceae)**

Common name: Turkestan
onion
Height: 10in (25cm)
Spread: 4in (10cm)
Aspect: Sun
Soil: Well-drained, fertile
Hardiness: Zone 4
Propagation: Seed, in spring;
offsets, in autumn

Bulbous species from Central Asia.
Paired, elliptic, gray-green or gray-
purple, horizontal basal leaves. Large
umbel of many pale pink, star-shaped
flowers in summer.

***Allium moly*
A.G.M.
(Alliaceae/Liliaceae)**

Common names: Golden
garlic; lily leek
Height: 10in (25cm)
Spread: 4in (10cm)
Aspect: Sun or half shade
Soil: Well-drained, fertile
Hardiness: Zone 3
Propagation: Seed, in spring;
offsets, in autumn

Bulbous woodland plant with gray-
green, lance-shaped basal leaves. The
umbel is dense, with up to 30 star-
shaped golden-yellow flowers in
summer. From Europe.

Allium nigrum
(Alliaceae/Liliaceae)

Common names: None
Height: 14in (35cm)
Spread: 3in (8cm)
Aspect: Sun
Soil: Well-drained, fertile
Hardiness: Zone 4
Propagation: Seed, in
spring; offsets, in autumn

Bulbous Mediterranean perennial with
gray-green, lance-shaped, basal leaves.
Off-white, cup-shaped flowers with
prominent, dark green ovaries, in a
flattened umbel, summer.

Allium oreophilum
A.G.M.
(Alliaceae/Liliaceae)

Common names: None
Height: 8in (20cm)
Spread: 2in (5cm)
Aspect: Sun
Soil: Well-drained, fertile
Hardiness: Zone 4
Propagation: Seed, in
spring; offsets, in autumn

Bulbous perennial. Leaves basal,
linear, mid-green. Umbel very loose,
with some 15 long-lasting, bell-
shaped, strong pink flowers, each
tepal with a dark midrib.

Allium
'Purple Sensation' A.G.M.
(Alliaceae/Liliaceae)

Common names: None
Height: 36in (1m)
Spread: 3in (8cm)
Aspect: Sun
Soil: Well-drained, fertile
Hardiness: Zone 2
Propagation: Offsets,
in autumn

Free-flowering, bulbous hybrid of
unknown parentage. Basal, gray-green,
strap-shaped leaves. Tight, spherical
umbel of over 50 star-shaped, dark
violet flowers in summer.

Allium schoenoprasum
'Forescate'
(Alliaceae/Liliaceae)

Common name: Chives
Height: 24in (60cm)
Spread: 3in (8cm)
Aspect: Sun
Soil: Well-drained, fertile
Hardiness: Zone 1
Propagation: Offsets,
in autumn

Rhizomatous allium grown for its
edible leaves, which are hollow, dark
green cylinders, and for its dense
umbels of bright pinkish-purple
flowers in summer.

Allium schubertii
(**Alliaceae/Liliaceae**)

Common names: None
Height: 24in (60cm)
Spread: 8in (20cm)
Aspect: Sun
Soil: Well, drained, fertile
Hardiness: Zone 5
Propagation: Seed, in
spring; offsets, in autumn

Bulbous allium. The straplike, bright
green basal leaves die back before
early-summer flowering. Pale lilac
flowers have pedicels of unequal
length, so umbel appears shaggy.

Allium senescens
(**Alliaceae/Liliaceae**)

Common names: None
Height: 24in (60cm)
Spread: 2in (5cm)
Aspect: Sun
Soil: Well-drained, fertile
Hardiness: Zone 1
Propagation: Seed, in
spring; offsets, in autumn

Vigorous, bulbous perennial. Strap-
shaped, short, midgreen basal leaves.
Pink, cup-shaped, long-lasting flowers
in a dense umbel of 30 in early and
midsummer.

Allium sphaerocephalon
(**Alliaceae/Liliaceae**)

Common name: Ballhead
onion
Height: 36in (90cm)
Spread: 3in (8cm)
Aspect: Sun
Soil: well-drained, fertile
Hardiness: Zone 1
Propagation: Seed, in spring;
offsets, in autumn

Bulbous allium. Leaves arc basal,
linear, midgreen. Flowers are bell-
shaped, dark pink or red-brown, in
dense, ovoid umbel in summer;
bulbils may form in the umbel.

Allium unifolium
(**Alliaceae/Liliaceae**)

Common name: One-
leaved onion
Height: 10in (25cm)
Spread: 2in (5cm)
Aspect: Sun
Soil: Well-drained, fertile
Hardiness: Zone 4
Propagation: Seed, in spring;
offsets, in autumn

Bulbous North American perennial.
Short, linear, gray-green basal leaves
die back before flowering in spring.
Flowers clear pink, large, open, bell-
shaped, in umbels.

Aloe ferox
(Aloeaceae/Liliaceae)

Common name: Cape aloe
Height: 10ft (3m)
Spread: 5ft (1.5m)
Aspect: Full sun
Soil: Well-drained, fertile
Hardiness: Zone 9
Propagation: Seed, when
ripe: offsets, in late spring,
early summer

Evergreen succulent with a rosette of
dull-green, fleshy, lance-shaped leaves
with red teeth. Large, erect panicle of
scarlet flowers in summer.
Conservatory plant in cold areas.

Aloe tenuior
(Aloeaceae/Liliaceae)

Common names: None
Height: 10ft (3m)
Spread: 2ft (60cm)
Aspect: Full sun
Soil: Well-drained, fertile
Hardiness: Zone 9
Propagation: Seed, when
ripe; offsets in late spring to
early summer

Evergreen, succulent perennial from
South Africa. Forms a rosette of
linear, glaucous, toothed leaves. Bears
orange-yellow flowers in a panicle in
summer.

Alonsoa warscewiczii
A.G.M.
(Scrophulariaceae)

Common names: Heartleaf
muskflower
Height: 2ft (60cm)
Spread: 1ft (30cm)
Aspect: Full sun
Soil: Well-drained, fertile
Hardiness: Zone 9
Propagation: Seed, in warmth in
spring or late summer

Evergreen, bushy subshrub. Leaves
ovate to lance-shaped, toothed, dark
green. Spurred, deep pink flowers in
loose racemes, summer to autumn.
Treat as annual in cold areas.

Alopecurus pratensis
'Aureovariegatus'
(Graminae/Poaceae)

Common name: Meadow
foxtail grass
Height: 4ft (1.2m)
Spread: 2ft (60cm)
Aspect: Sun or half shade
Soil: Well-drained, fertile
Hardiness: Zone 5
Propagation: Seed, when ripe;
division, in spring or autumn

Perennial grass that clumps up
rapidly. Leaves basal, linear, striped
yellow and green. Long, dense
panicles of green or purple spikelets in
spring to midsummer.

ALSTROEMERIA (Alstroemeriaceae)
Peruvian Lily

A genus of some 50 species of perennials from South America, found in mountains and grasslands. *Alstroemeria* are tuberous, and will spread rapidly to form large clumps; they can even become invasive if the conditions suit them. The tubers should be handled carefully, and are best left undisturbed once planted. They have extremely handsome flowers, and a long flowering season, making them valuable border plants. They also make excellent cut flowers, and are popular with flower-arrangers and grown commercially for florists. A few species are tender, but many are marginally hardy in most areas, and can be grown outside if they are given a sunny spot and covered with a dry mulch through winter. Contact with the foliage may cause exacerbation of a skin allergy. The tubers should be planted 8in (20cm) deep. Thirty forms have an Award of Garden Merit, including the popular Ligtu Hybrids, a name covering many crosses, principally of *A. ligtu* and *A. haemantha*. Also holding an A.G.M. are some of the 'Princess' strain: this is a registered name, and the botanically preferred name is given as a synonym in the panel at right; the plants are most likely to be sold under the former, but may be found in books under the latter.

Alstroemeria aurea
(Alstroemeriaceae)

Common names: None
Height: 3ft (1m)
Spread: 18in (45cm)
Aspect: Sun or partial shade
Soil: Moist, well-drained, fertile
Hardiness: Zone 7
Propagation: Seed, when ripe; division, in spring or autumn

Tuberous perennial. Leaves linear to lance-shaped, midgreen. Terminal 3- to 7-rayed umbels, each with up to 3 yellow or orange flowers, in summer. Can be invasive.

Alstroemeria
Ligtu Hybrids A.G.M.
(Alstroemeriaceae)

Common name: Peruvian lily
Height: 3ft (1m)
Spread: 18in (45cm)
Aspect: Sun or half shade
Soil: Moist, well-drained, fertile
Hardiness: Zone 7
Propagation: Seed, when ripe; division, in spring or autumn

Vigorous hybrids with a wide range of colors, such as this deep red. Leaves linear to lance-shaped, midgreen. Flowers in terminal, 3- to 7-rayed racemes, summer.

51

Alstroemeria
Ligtu Hybrids A.G.M.
(Alstroemeriaceae)

Common name: Peruvian
lily
Height: 3ft (1m)
Spread: 18in (45cm)
Aspect: Sun or half shade
Soil: Moist, well-drained,
fertile
Hardiness: Zone 7
Propagation: Seed, when ripe;
division, in spring or autumn

Two-tone yellow and cream color
break in the Ligtu Hybrid range.
Leaves linear to lance-shaped,
midgreen. Terminal, 3- to
7-rayed racemes of flowers in summer.

Alstroemeria psittacina
(Alstroemeriaceae)

Common name: Peruvian
lily
Height: 3ft (1m)
Spread: 18in (45cm)
Aspect: Sun or half shade
Soil: Moist, well-drained,
fertile
Hardiness: Zone 7
Propagation: Seed, when ripe;
division, in spring or autumn

Tuberous species with gray-green,
linear to lance-shaped leaves. Flowers
in 4- to 6-rayed panicles, each ray
having up to 3 green and red flowers,
in summer.

Alstroemeria
'Solent Wings'
(Alstroemeriaceae)

Common name: Peruvian
lily
Height: 3ft (1m)
Spread: 18in (45cm)
Aspect: Sun or half shade
Soil: Moist, well-drained,
fertile
Hardiness: Zone 7
Propagation: Division,
in spring or autumn

Tuberous, hybrid Peruvian lily, with
linear to lance-shaped leaves of gray-
green. Panicles of rosy-red flowers,
edged with white, in summer.

Alstroemeria
'White Apollo'
(Alstroemeriaceae)

Common name: Peruvian
lily
Height: 3ft (1m)
Spread: 18in (45cm)
Aspect: Sun or half shade
Soil: Moist, well-drained,
fertile
Hardiness: Zone 7
Propagation: Division,
in spring or autumn

Very handsome hybrid with terminal
clusters of pure white, orange-
throated flowers, streaked brown, in
summer. Leaves linear to lance-
shaped.

Althaea cannabina
(Malvaceae)

Common name: Mallow
Height: 6ft (2m)
Spread: 30in (75cm)
Aspect: Any, but best in
sun
Soil: Moist, well-drained,
fertile
Hardiness: Zone 4
Propagation: Seed, in summer

Erect, woody-stemmed plant for the
larger garden. Leaves dark green,
paler beneath, hairy, round, lobed.
Small, pink flowers in axillary
clusters, summer to early autumn.

Althaea officinalis
(Malvaceae)

Common name:
Marshmallow
Height: 6ft (2m)
Spread: 5ft (1.5m)
Aspect: Any, but best in
sun
Soil: Moist, well-drained,
fertile
Hardiness: Zone 3
Propagation: Seed, in summer

Erect plant, sometimes grown for
culinary use. Leaves lobed, toothed,
oval, pointed, softly hairy, green.
Flowers pale pink, in terminal or
axillary clusters. From Europe.

Alyssum montanum
'Berggold'
(Brassicaceae/Cruciferae)

Common name: Madwort
Height: 6in (15cm)
Spread: 24in (60cm) or
more
Aspect: Sun
Soil: Well-drained,
humus-rich
Hardiness: Zone 6
Propagation: Seed, in spring or
autumn; cuttings, in summer

Prostrate, mat-forming evergreen with
gray, oblong-obovate leaves in
rosettes. Bears racemes of yellow,
fragrant flowerheads in early summer.
An excellent wall plant.

Alyssum spinosum
'Roseum' A.G.M.
(Brassicaceae/Cruciferae)

Common names: None
Height: 16in (40cm)
Spread: 20in (50cm)
Aspect: Sun
Soil: Well-drained,
humus-rich
Hardiness: Zone 6
Propagation: Seed, in
autumn or spring; cuttings,
in summer

Rounded, compact, evergreen
subshrub; spiny and densely branched.
Leaves small, obovate, gray-green.
Flowers cross-shaped, 4-petalled, pale
or dark pink, in racemes.

Amaryllis belladonna
(Amaryllidaceae)

Common name:
Belladonna lily
Height: 24in (60cm)
Spread: 4in (10cm)
Aspect: Full sun
Soil: Well-drained
Hardiness: Zone 9
Propagation: Seed, in warmth
when ripe; offsets, in spring

Bulbous perennial. Umbels of funnel-shaped, scented, purplish-pink flowers in autumn; strap-shaped, fleshy leaves in early winter. Protect from frost. Needs a dry dormancy.

Amicia zygomeris
(Leguminosae/
Papilionaceae)

Common names: None
Height: 6ft (2m)
Spread: 4ft (1.2m)
Aspect: Full sun
Soil: Well-drained, fertile
Hardiness: Zone 9
Propagation: Seed, in
warmth in spring; cuttings,
in spring and summer

Unusual perennial, not for a small garden. Leaves inversely heart-shaped, large, with pale green stipules. Flowers cream with purple keels, pealike, in autumn.

Amsonia
tabernaemontana
(Apocynaceae)

Common names: None
Height: 24in (60cm)
Spread: 18in (45cm)
Aspect: Sun
Soil: Moist, well-drained
Hardiness: Zone 8
Propagation: Seed or
division, in spring

Clump-forming perennial. Small, ovate or elliptic, matt, dark green leaves. Pale blue flowers in dense panicles from spring to midsummer. Milky sap may irritate skin.

Anagallis monellii
A.G.M.
(Primulaceae)

Common name: Blue
pimpernel
Height: 8in (20cm)
Spread: 16in (40cm)
Aspect: Full sun
Soil: Moist, well-drained,
fertile
Hardiness: Zone 7
Propagation: Seed or division,
both in spring

Sprawling, short-lived perennial with mid-green, lance-shaped to elliptic, stalkless leaves. Open, 5-petalled, deep blue flowers in summer. From southeast Europe.

Anaphalis triplinervis
A.G.M.
(Asteraceae/Compositae)

Common name: Pearly
everlasting
Height: 3ft (90cm)
Spread: 2ft (60cm)
Aspect: Sun or half shade
Soil: Well-drained, fertile,
humus-rich
Hardiness: Zone 5
Propagation: Seed or division,
both in spring

Perennial with spoon-shaped, pale
gray-green leaves, white-woolly
underneath. Corymbs of yellow
flowers with white bracts in summer.
From S.W. China.

Anchusa azurea
(Boraginaceae)

Common name: Alkanet
Height: 5ft (1.5m)
Spread: 2ft (60cm)
Aspect: Full sun
Soil: Moist, well-drained,
fertile
Hardiness: Zone 3
Propagation: Seed or basal
cuttings, both in spring

Clump-forming, Mediterranean
perennial. Leaves linear to lance-
shaped, hairy, dark green. Panicles of
open, gentian-blue flowers in early
summer.

Anchusa azurea
'Feltham Pride'
(Boraginaceae)

Common name: Alkanet
Height: 3ft (90cm)
Spread: 2ft (60cm)
Aspect: Full sun
Soil: Moist, well-drained,
fertile
Hardiness: Zone 3
Propagation: Basal cuttings, in
spring; root cuttings, in winter

A compact cultivar, sometimes grown
as a biennial, with linear to lance-
shaped leaves of mid- to dark green.
Clear, bright blue flowers in early
summer.

Anchusa
'Loddon Royalist' A.G.M.
(Boraginaceae)

Common name: Alkanet
Height: 3ft (90cm)
Spread: 2ft (60cm)
Aspect: Full sun
Soil: Moist, well-drained,
fertile
Hardiness: Zone 3
Propagation: Basal cuttings, in
spring; root cuttings, in winter

Sturdy hybrid, but it may still need to
be staked in exposed areas. Leaves
linear to lance-shaped, midgreen.
Panicle of deep blue flowers in early
summer.

ANEMONE (Ranunculaceae)
Windflower

This large genus contains some 120 species of perennials, with open, saucer- to cup-shaped flowers, with a prominent boss of stamens, and lobed, dissected foliage. They originate in a wide range of habitats across both the northern and southern hemispheres, and they vary widely in their character and in cultural requirements as a result. Some are good specimens for the border, others are more suitable for rock gardens or naturalizing in woodlands. For the purposes of cultivation requirements, anemones can be divided into three broad groups:

Spring-flowering, tuberous or rhizomatous species that come from Alpine or woodland areas.

Spring- or early summer-flowering, tuberous species from the Mediterranean and regions of Central Asia that have hot, dry summers.

Summer- or autumn-flowering, fibrous-rooted, tall, herbaceous species from open sites.

All these types are covered here, but the third category will form the main group. Some anemones are poisonous, and the sap of all may cause skin irritation. All are unfortunately prone to powdery mildew, and slug damage.

Anemone blanda
A.G.M.
(Ranunculaceae)

Common name:
Windflower
Height: 6in (15cm)
Spread: 6in (15cm)
Aspect: Sun or half shade
Soil: Well-drained,
humus-rich
Hardiness: Zone 5
Propagation: Seed, when ripe;
offsets, in summer

Tuberous, woodland perennial from Turkey. Leaves 3-palmate, triangular or oval, deep green. Flowers solitary, single, with deep blue tepals, in spring.

Anemone blanda
'White Splendour' A.G.M.
(Ranunculaceae)

Common name: Greek
anemone
Height: 6in (15cm)
Spread: 6in (15cm)
Aspect: Full sun or half
shade
Soil: Well-drained, humus-rich
Hardiness: Zone 5
Propagation: Seed, when ripe;
offsets, in summer

Spring flowers have pure white tepals with pinkish reverse. Leaves oval or triangular, 3-palmate, dark green. One of a few A.G.M. cultivars of this species.

Anemone coronaria
De Caen Group
(Ranunculaceae)

Common names: Florists'
poppy anemone;
windflower
Height: 18in (45cm)
Spread: 6in (15cm)
Aspect: Full sun
Soil: Porous, sandy
Hardiness: Zone 8
Propagation: Seed, when ripe;
offsets, in summer

Clones with single, long-stemmed
flowers with 5–8 tepals in a wide
range of colors. Oval, 3-palmate,
midgreen basal and stem leaves.
Tuberous; keep dry after flowering.

Anemone coronoria
St. Brigid Group
(Ranunculaceae)

Common names: Florists'
poppy anemone;
windflower
Height: 18in (45cm)
Spread: 6in (15cm)
Aspect: Full sun
Soil: Porous
Hardiness: Zone 8
Propagation: Seed, when ripe;
offsets, in summer

Leaves midgreen, 3-palmate, round or
oval. Solitary, fully double flowers in
a wide range of colors, on long stems
in spring. Tuberous; keep dry after
flowering.

Anemone cylindrica
(Ranunculaceae)

Common names: None
Height: 24in (60cm)
Spread: 4in (10cm)
Aspect: Half shade
Soil: Well-drained,
humus-rich
Hardiness: Zone 6
Propagation: Seed, when ripe

Fibrous-rooted, cushion-forming,
rosetted perennial. Leaves linear to
elliptic, glossy green. Flowers in early
spring, white with a yellow-green eye,
on long stems.

Anemone hupehensis
'Hadspen Abundance'
A.G.M. (Ranunculaceae)

Common name: Dwarf
Japanese anemone
Height: 36in (90cm)
Spread: 16in (40cm)
Aspect: Sun or half shade
Soil: Moist, fertile,
humus-rich
Hardiness: Zone 6
Propagation: Division,
in spring or autumn

Fibrous-rooted, suckering perennial.
Oval, 3-palmate, long-stalked, basal,
dark green leaves. Umbels of up to 15
flowers, each with 5 or 6 deep pink
tepals, in autumn.

57

***Anemone hupehensis* var. *japonica* 'Prinz Heinrich' A.G.M. (Ranunculaceae)**

Common name: Japanese anemone
Height: 36in (90cm)
Spread: 16in (40cm)
Aspect: Sun or half shade
Soil: Moist, fertile, humus-rich
Hardiness: Zone 6
Propagation: Division, in spring or autumn

Fibrous-rooted, suckering hybrid. Leaves oval, 3-palmate, basal, dark green. Umbels of up to 15 flowers, each with 5 or 6 dark pink tepals, in mid- to late summer.

***Anemone* × *hybrida* 'Honorine Jobert' A.G.M. (Ranunculaceae)**

Common name: Japanese anemone
Height: 4ft (1.2m)
Spread: Indefinite
Aspect: Sun or half shade
Soil: Moist, fertile, humus-rich
Hardiness: Zone 6
Propagation: Division, in spring or autumn

Vigorous, suckering, woody hybrid. Oval, 3-palmate, toothed, midgreen leaves. Umbel of up to 20 pure white flowers, the reverse pinkish, in autumn.

***Anemone* × *hybrida* 'Elegans' (Ranunculaceae)**

Common name: Japanese anemone
Height: 4ft (1.2m)
Spread: Indefinite
Aspect: Sun or half shade
Soil: Moist, well-drained, humus-rich
Hardiness: Zone 6
Propagation: Division, in spring or autumn

A cloned selection of this popular, vigorous plant. Leaves 3-palmate, oval, midgreen. Single pink flowers in umbels of up to 20 over a long period in autumn.

***Anemone* × *hybrida* 'Margarete' (Ranunculaceae)**

Common name: Japanese anemone
Height: 36in (90cm)
Spread: Indefinite
Aspect: Sun or half shade
Soil: Moist, fertile, humus-rich
Hardiness: Zone 6
Propagation: Division, in spring or autumn

A vigorous, cloned selection of this popular perennial. Umbels of semidouble, deep pink flowers in autumn. Leaves oval, 3-palmate, midgreen.

Anemone × hybrida 'Pamina'
(Ranunculaceae)

Common name: Japanese anemone
Height: 32in (80cm)
Spread: Indefinite
Aspect: Sun or half shade
Soil: Moist, fertile, humus-rich
Hardiness: Zone 6
Propagation: Division, in spring or autumn

Cloned selection, slightly smaller than most, with oval, 3-palmate, midgreen leaves and umbels of single, lilac-pink flowers with rounded tepals.

Anemone × hybrida 'Whirlwind'
(Ranunculaceae)

Common name: Japanese anemone
Height: 4ft (1.2m)
Spread: Indefinite
Aspect: Sun or half shade
Soil: Moist, fertile, humus-rich
Hardiness: Zone 6
Propagation: Division, in spring or autumn

Cloned selection of the popular Japanese anemone with umbels of semidouble, white flowers, sometimes with a center of greenish, whorled tepals.

Anemone × lesseri
(Ranunculaceae)

Common names: None
Height: 16in (40cm)
Spread: 12in (30cm)
Aspect: Sun or half shade
Soil: Well-drained, humus-rich
Hardiness: Zone 3
Propagation: Seed, when ripe

Fibrous-rooted hybrid. Large, round, 3- to 5-palmate leaves; leaflets lobed, toothed. Reddish-pink, purple, yellow, or white flowers, singly or in umbels, in summer.

Anemone leveillei
(Ranunculaceae)

Common names: None
Height: 24in (60cm)
Spread: 12in (30cm)
Aspect: Half shade
Soil: Moist, humus-rich
Hardiness: Zone 6
Propagation: Seed, when ripe

Fibrous-rooted perennial. Leaves kidney-shaped, 3-lobed, deeply divided, toothed, midgreen. Flowers white, with 8 tepals, the reverse hairy and pink, in summer.

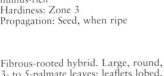

Anemone multifida
(Ranunculaceae)

Common names: None
Height: 12in (30cm)
Spread: 6in (15cm)
Aspect: Sun or half shade
Soil: Well-drained,
humus-rich
Hardiness: Zone 2
Propagation: Seed, when ripe

Sturdy, vigorous, rhizomatous
perennial. Handsome, rounded,
palmate, midgreen stem and basal
leaves. Umbels of 2 or 3 creamy
yellow flowers with 5–9 tepals.

Anemone nemorosa
A.G.M.
(Ranunculaceae)

Common names:
Windflower; wood anemone
Height: 6in (15cm)
Spread: 12in (30cm) or
more
Aspect: Half shade
Soil: Moist, well-drained,
humus-rich Hardiness: Zone 5
Propagation: Seed, when ripe;
offsets, in autumn

Creeping, rhizomatous woodlander.
Leaves round, 3-palmate; leaflets lobed
and toothed, midgreen. Flowers are
solitary, white, with 6–8 tepals, in
spring and early summer.

Anemone nemorosa
'Robinsoniana' A.G.M.
(Ranunculaceae)

Common names:
Windflower; wood anemone
Height: 6in (15cm)
Spread: 12in (30cm)
Aspect: Half shade
Soil: Well-drained,
humus-rich
Hardiness: Zone 5
Propagation: Division, in
spring or autumn

Cloned selection of the species, with
large, pale lavender-pink flowers with
creamy gray undersides. One of a few
cultivars of *A. nemorosa* to carry an
A.G.M.

Anemone rivularis
(Ranunculaceae)

Common names: None
Height: 36in (90cm)
Spread: 12in (30cm)
Aspect: Sun or half shade
Soil: Well-drained,
humus-rich
Hardiness: Zone 7
Propagation: Seed, when ripe

Fibrous-rooted, clump-forming
anemone. Long-stalked, round, 3-
palmate or 3-lobed, hairy, toothed
basal and stem leaves. Umbels of white
flowers in spring and autumn.

Anemonella thalictroides
(Ranunculaceae)

Anemonopsis
macrophylla
(Ranunculaceae)

Common name: Rue
anemone
Height: 4in (10cm)
Spread: 12in (30cm)
Aspect: Half shade
Soil: Moist, well-drained,
humus-rich
Hardiness: Zone 4
Propagation: Seed, when ripe

Common names: None
Height: 32in (80cm)
Spread: 18in (45cm)
Aspect: Half shade
Soil: Moist, acidic,
humus-rich
Hardiness: Zone 4
Propagation: Seed, when ripe;
division, in summer

Clump-forming, tuberous woodlander.
Blue-green, fernlike, 3-ternate leaves.
Pale pink, cup-shaped flowers in loose
umbels, spring to early summer. Hates
waterlogged soil.

Woodlander with glossy leaves, 3-
ternate; toothed lobes ovate-oblong.
Loose racemes of nodding, cup-
shaped flowers, sepals lilac and petals
violet, mid- to late summer.

Angelica archangelica
(Apiaceae/Umbelliferae)

Angelica gigas
(Apiaceae/Umbelliferae)

Common name: Garden
angelica
Height: 6ft (2m)
Spread: 3ft (1m)
Aspect: Full or half shade
Soil: Moist, deep, fertile,
humus-rich
Hardiness: Zone 4
Propagation: Seed, when ripe;
plant out when small

Common names: None
Height: to 6ft (2m)
Spread: 4ft (1.2m)
Aspect: Full or half shade
Soil: Moist, deep, fertile,
humus-rich
Hardiness: Zone 4
Propagation: Seed, when ripe

Herbaceous, monocarpic herb. Leaves
mid-green, 2- or 3-pinnate, with
lance-shaped, toothed leaflets. Umbels
of greenish-yellow flowers on stiff
stems, early to midsummer.

Large perennial for damp sites. Leaves
very large, 3-ternate; leaflets lobed,
diamond-ovate. Dense umbel of
purple flowers and bracts with red
stems, summer to autumn.

Anigozanthos manglesii A.G.M.
(Haemodoraceae)

Common names: None
Height: 4ft (1.2m)
Spread: 2ft (60cm)
Aspect: Full sun
Soil: Moist, well-drained, sandy, humus-rich
Hardiness: Zone 9
Propagation: Seed, in warmth when ripe

Clump-forming evergreen. Leaves lance- to strap-shaped, gray-green. Flowers 2-lipped, tubular, yellow-green, with dense, pale green hairs outside, red inside, spring to summer.

Anisodontea capensis
(Malvaceae)

Common names: None
Height: 36in (90cm)
Spread: 32in (80cm)
Aspect: Full sun
Soil: Well-drained, fertile
Hardiness: Zone 9
Propagation: Seed, in warmth in spring; semiripe cuttings, in summer

Woody evergreen. Leaves ovate-triangular, hairy, midgreen, shallowly lobed. Flowers solitary or in racemes of 2 or 3, pale pink, cup-shaped, in summer to autumn.

Anomatheca laxa var. alba
(Iridaceae)

Common names: None
Height: 12in (30cm)
Spread: 2in (5cm)
Aspect: Full sun
Soil: Sandy, fertile
Hardiness: Zone 8
Propagation: Seed, in warmth in spring; division, in spring

Cormous perennial. Leaves lance-shaped, flat, midgreen. Flowers in racemes, open, pure white, followed by brown capsules of red seeds. Self-seeds, but not invasively.

Antennaria dioica
(Asteraceae/Compositae)

Common name: Common pussy-toes
Height: 4in (10cm)
Spread: 16in (40cm)
Aspect: Full sun
Soil: Well-drained, fertile
Hardiness: Zone 5
Propagation: Seed, in spring or autumn

Mat-forming, stoloniferous ground cover. Spoon-shaped, gray-green leaves, very hairy beneath. Corymbs of fluffy, pink or white, everlasting flowers in late spring to summer.

ANTHEMIS (Asteraceae/Compositae)
Camomile

Genus of some 100 mat- or clump-forming species originating
in Europe, northern Africa, Turkey, the Caucasus, and Iran.
Anthemis make very useful border plants, with a long flowering
season extending from late spring to the end of summer, and
beautiful, filigree, aromatic, evergreen foliage when they are not
in flower. Smaller types also suit rock gardens. The flowerheads
are daisylike, with white or yellow ray florets and yellow disc
florets, and some of the species will make good cut flowers.
Although the genus as a whole is not long-lived (*A. tinctoria* in
particular is notable for this), all are easily propagated from
seed or cuttings. A plant's life can also be extended by shearing
it over in autumn just after flowering is over. This will ensure
that new basal growth is encouraged, which will take the plant
through the winter. Shearing also helps to keep the plants from
becoming mildewed, a particular problem of *Anthemis*; they
come from sunny, well-drained sites in the wild, and wet
winters are greatly disliked by all species. They do not
transplant well, but should nevertheless be divided regularly in
spring. Despite these drawbacks, these plants provide the
gardener with rewards that make them well worth all the effort.

Anthemis punctata subsp.
cupaniana A.G.M.
(Asteraceae/Compositae)

Common names: None
Height: 1ft (30cm)
Spread: 3ft (90cm)
Aspect: Full sun
Soil: Well-drained, sandy
Hardiness: Zone 6
Propagation: Seed,
division or basal cuttings,
all in spring

Evergreen with aromatic, ovate-
obovate, pinnatisect, silver-gray
leaves, gray-green in winter. Flowers
daisylike, white, long-lasting, in early
summer. From Sicily.

Anthemis tinctoria
'E.C. Buxton'
(Asteraceae/Compositae)

Common name: Golden
marguerite
Height: 28in (70cm)
Spread: 24in (60cm)
Aspect: Full sun
Soil: Well-drained, sandy
Hardiness: Zone 6
Propagation: Division or
basal cuttings, both in
spring

A selected form with lemon-yellow,
daisylike flowerheads above aromatic,
evergreen, handsome foliage. Leaves
are ovate-obovate, pinnatisect, gray-
green.

63

Anthemis 'Grallagh Gold' (Asteraceae/Compositae)

Common name: Golden marguerite
Height: 32in (80cm)
Spread: 24in (60cm)
Aspect: Full sun
Soil: Well-drained, sandy
Hardiness: Zone 6
Propagation: Division or basal cuttings, both in spring

A selected form with intense gold, daisylike flowerheads. Leaves are evergreen, aromatic, ovate-obovate, pinnatisect, and gray-green.

Anthemis tinctoria 'Sauce Hollandaise' (Asteraceae/Compositae)

Common name: Golden marguerite
Height: 2ft (60cm)
Spread: 2ft (60cm)
Aspect: Full sun
Soil: Well-drained, sandy
Hardiness: Zone 6
Propagation: Division or basal cuttings, both in spring

Cloned selection. Flowers have near-white ray petals, contrasting with yellow boss. Foliage is evergreen, ovate-obovate, aromatic, pinnatisect, and gray-green.

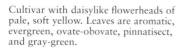

Anthemis tinctoria 'Wargrave' (Asteraceae/Compositae)

Common name: Golden marguerite
Height: 2ft (60cm)
Spread: 2ft (60cm)
Aspect: Full sun
Soil: Well-drained, sandy
Hardiness: Zone 6
Propagation: Division or basal cuttings, both in spring

Cultivar with daisylike flowerheads of pale, soft yellow. Leaves are aromatic, evergreen, ovate-obovate, pinnatisect, and gray-green.

Anthericum liliago (Anthericaceae/Liliaceae)

Common name: St. Bernard-lily
Height: 36in (90cm)
Spread: 12in (30cm)
Aspect: Full sun
Soil: Well-drained, fertile
Hardiness: Zone 7
Propagation: Seed, in spring or autumn; division, in spring

Clump-forming, rhizomatous perennial. Leaves grassy, midgreen. Panicles of open, lilylike, white flowers in late spring, early summer, followed by attractive seed heads.

Anthriscus sylvestris
(Apiaceae/Umbelliferae)

Common names: None
Height: 3ft (1m)
Spread: 1ft (30cm)
Aspect: Sun or half shade
Soil: Well-drained
Hardiness: Zone 7
Propagation: Seed, in
spring or autumn

Short-lived, clump-forming perennial.
Leaves 3-pinnate, with ovate,
pinnatifid leaflets. Umbels of tiny
white flowers from midspring to
summer.

Anthriscus sylvestris
'Ravenswing'
(Apiaceae/Umbelliferae)

Common names: None
Height: 3ft (1m)
Spread: 1ft (30cm)
Aspect: Sun or half shade
Soil: Well-drained
Hardiness: Zone 7
Propagation: Seed, in
spring or autumn

A dark-leaved form of the species.
Leaves lacy, dark purple-brown, 3-
pinnate; leaflets ovate, pinnatifid.
Loose umbels of small, white flowers
in spring to early summer.

Antirrhinum hispanicum
(Scrophulariaceae)

Common name:
Snapdragon
Height: 8in (20cm)
Spread: 12in (30cm)
Aspect: Full sun
Soil: Sharply drained,
fertile
Hardiness: Zone 7
Propagation: Softwood
cuttings, in summer

Short-lived subshrub. Leaves lance-
shaped to orbicular, green. Flowers
white or pale pink, lip streaked red,
perfumed, 2-lipped, in loose racemes,
late summer. From Spain.

Antirrhinum majus
'Taff's White'
(Scrophulariaceae)

Common name: Common
snapdragon
Height: 2ft (60cm)
Spread: 2ft (60cm)
Aspect: Full sun
Soil: Sharply drained
Hardiness: Zone 7
Propagation: Softwood
cuttings, in summer

Cloned selection of the garden
snapdragon, grown as an annual.
Leaves lance-shaped, glossy green,
edged cream. Flowers fragrant, 2-
lipped, white, in summer to autumn.

AQUILEGIA (Ranunculaceae)
Columbine

A genus of some 70 species from a wide range of habitats, from mountain to woodland, widely distributed across the northern hemisphere. The larger species and their cultivars, covered here, are popular garden plants and an almost indispensable element of the classic cottage garden. Their flowering season forms a useful bridge over the gap between the spring- and summer-flowering genera, and a wide range of colors is available. The flowers are distinctive, often bicolored, with hooked spurs, and carried either singly or in panicles. The basal leaves are also distinctive and attractive. Some enthusiasts have beds devoted entirely to columbines, and later in the season dig them out to replace them with summer bedding. They do have the drawback of being short-lived, but this is mitigated by their tendency to grow very readily from seed; they will also self-seed abundantly in the garden, and any seedling with poor flowers can be taken out, as there will be plenty of better examples. Columbines do not transplant well, so seed should be sown *in situ*, or the seedlings should be planted out when they are still small. Contact with the sap may cause skin irritation, and all members of the genus are poisonous.

Aquilegia canadensis
A.G.M.
(Ranunculaceae)

Common name: American columbine
Height: 3ft (90cm)
Spread: 1ft (30cm)
Aspect: Sun or half shade
Soil: Moist, well-drained
Hardiness: Zone 3
Propagation: Seed, when ripe or in spring

Clump-forming, with 2-ternate, fernlike, green leaves. Racemes of up to 20 nodding flowers, sepals scarlet, petals lemon, spurs red, from midspring to early summer.

Aquilegia chrysantha
'Yellow Queen'
(Ranunculaceae)

Common name: Golden columbine
Height: 3ft (90cm)
Spread: 2ft (60cm)
Aspect: Sun or half shade
Soil: Moist, well-drained
Hardiness: Zone 3
Propagation: Division, in spring

Cloned selection with fernlike, 3-ternate leaves, of ovate, green leaflets. Racemes of 4–12 flowers with pale yellow petals and golden-yellow sepals in spring to summer.

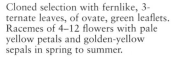

Aquilegia
Mrs Scott-Elliot Hybrids
(Ranunculaceae)

Common name:
Columbine
Height: 3ft (90cm)
Spread: 2ft (60cm)
Aspect: Sun or half shade
Soil: Moist, well-drained
Hardiness: Zone 3
Propagation: Seed, in
autumn or spring

Robust hybrid strain. Leaves 2-
ternately lobed, midgreen. Flowers in
racemes, in a range of colors and
bicolors, from spring to midsummer.

Aquilegia
Music Series A.G.M.
(Ranunculaceae)

Common name:
Columbine
Height: 18in (45cm)
Spread: 18in (45cm)
Aspect: Sun or half shade
Soil: Moist, well-drained
Hardiness: Zone 3
Propagation: Seed, in
autumn or spring

Hybrid strain of compact and robust
plants with 2-ternate, midgreen
leaves. Long-spurred flowers in a
range of colors and bicolors in spring
to summer.

Aquilegia vulgaris
(Ranunculaceae)

Common name: European
columbine
Height: 3ft (90cm)
Spread: 2ft (60cm)
Aspect: Sun or half shade
Soil: Moist, well-drained
Hardiness: Zone 3
Propagation: Seed, in spring
or autumn

Stiff, upright plant with 2-ternately
lobed, midgreen leaves. Terminal
racemes of 5–15 pendent or
horizontal, blue, pink, white, or violet
flowers in spring to early summer.

Aquilegia vulgaris var.
stellata 'Nora Barlow'
A.G.M. (Ranunculaceae)

Common name: European
columbine
Height: 3ft (90cm)
Spread: 2ft (60cm)
Aspect: Sun or half shade
Soil: Moist, well-drained
Hardiness: Zone 3
Propagation: Division,
in spring

Selected form with fully double,
pompon flowers. Tepals are red and
green, spurless, and quilted. Good
proportion of seedlings come true if
plant is grown in isolation.

Aquilegia vulgaris var. *stellata* (Ranunculaceae)

Common name: European columbine
Height: 3ft (90cm)
Spread: 2ft (60cm)
Aspect: Sun or half shade
Soil: Moist, well-drained
Hardiness: Zone 3
Propagation: Seed, in autumn or spring

Variety with spurless flowers with tepals that spread, resembling flowers of clematis (*see pp.116–117*), in shades of blue or pink. Leaves 2-ternately lobed, midgreen.

Aquilegia vulgaris 'William Guiness' (Ranunculaceae)

Common name: European columbine
Height: 28in (70cm)
Spread: 24in (60cm)
Aspect: Sun or half shade
Soil: Moist, well-drained
Hardiness: Zone 3
Propagation: Division, in spring

Selected form with dark purple to black flowers, with sepals tipped white, in terminal racemes. Leaves are midgreen and 2-ternately lobed.

Arabis blepharophylla 'Frühlingszauber' A.G.M. (Brassicaceae/Cruciferae)

Common names: None
Height: 4in (10cm)
Spread: 8in (20cm)
Aspect: Full sun
Soil: Well-drained
Hardiness: Zone 7
Propagation: Seed, in autumn

Compact, short-lived, evergreen perennial. Forms a rosette of toothed, obovate, dark green leaves. Racemes of dark pink-purple, fragrant flowers in spring to early summer.

Arabis procurrens 'Variegata' A.G.M. (Brassicaceae/Cruciferae)

Common names: None
Height: 3in (8cm)
Spread: 16in (40cm)
Aspect: Full sun
Soil: Well-drained, sandy
Hardiness: Zone 5
Propagation: Seed, in autumn

Creeping evergreen. Rosettes of oblong- to lance-shaped leaves, glossy midgreen, edged cream, sometimes tinged pink. Racemes of white flowers, in spring. Superb wall plant.

Arctotheca calendula
(Asteraceae/Compositae)

Arctotis fastuosa
'Zulu Prince'
(Asteraceae/Compositae)

Common names: None
Height: 20in (50cm)
Spread: Indefinite
Aspect: Full sun
Soil: Well-drained
Hardiness: Zone 9
Propagation: Seed, in
warmth in spring; division,
in spring

Common name: African
daisy
Height: 24in (60cm)
Spread: 16in (40cm)
Aspect: Full sun
Soil: Moist, well-drained,
sandy
Hardiness: Zone 9
Propagation: Seed, in warmth
in spring or summer

Creeping, rhizomatous, spreading
plant. Rosettes of pinnatifid, oblong,
green leaves, white-woolly beneath.
Flowers in spring or early summer,
yellow, purple-tinted beneath.

Creeping perennial often treated as
annual. Silvery white, elliptic, lobed
leaves. Solitary flowers; cream ray
florets, black triangles at the bases,
midsummer to early autumn.

Arctotis x *hybrida*
(Asteraceae/Compositae)

Arenaria montana
A.G.M.
(Caryophyllaceae)

Common name: African
daisy
Height: 2ft (60cm)
Spread: 1ft (30cm)
Aspect: Full sun
Soil: Moist, well-drained,
sandy
Hardiness: Zone 9
Propagation: Seed, in warmth
in spring or autumn

Common name: Sandwort
Height: 2in (5cm)
Spread: 12in (30cm)
Aspect: Full sun
Soil: Moist, well-drained,
gritty
Hardiness: Zone 4
Propagation: Seed, in autumn;
division, in spring

Range of hybrids. Flowers solitary,
single, in red, yellow, pink, white, or
orange; some with darker marks on
ray florets. Leaves silvery, felted,
elliptic, lobed, wavy-edged.

An evergreen, prostrate plant with
gray-green, lance-shaped leaves.
Flowers solitary or in cymes of a few
flowers, white, in late spring. Good
wall plant.

Argyranthemum frutescens subsp. *canariae* A.G.M. (Asteraceae/Compositae)

Common name: Marguerite chrysanthemum
Height: 2ft (60cm)
Spread: 2ft (60cm)
Aspect: Full sun
Soil: Well-drained
Hardiness: Zone 9
Propagation: Seed, in warmth in spring

Free-flowering subshrub with pinnatisect, dissected, green leaves. Flowers in loose corymbs, white or very pale pink, spring to autumn. From the Canary Islands.

Argyranthemum 'Jamaica Primrose' A.G.M. (Asteraceae/Compositae)

Common name: Marguerite chrysanthemum
Height: 3ft (1m)
Spread: 3ft (1m)
Aspect: Full sun
Soil: Well-drained
Hardiness: Zone 9
Propagation: Greenwood cuttings, in spring

Hybrid, evergreen subshrub, often grown as an annual. Leaves pinnatisect, toothed, gray-green. Flowers solitary, single, pale yellow, with darker disc. Long-flowering.

Argyranthemum 'Vancouver' A.G.M. (Asteraceae/Compositae)

Common name: Marguerite chrysanthemum
Height: 3ft (1m)
Spread: 32in (80cm)
Aspect: Full sun
Soil: Well-drained
Hardiness: Zone 9
Propagation: Greenwood cuttings, in spring

Handsome, evergreen, hybrid subshrub. Leaves pinnatisect, grayish-green. Solitary, double, anemone-centered flowers, spring to autumn. Ray florets pink, disc florets rose.

Arisaema amurense (Araceae)

Common names: None
Height: 18in (45cm)
Spread: 6in (15cm)
Aspect: Half shade, cool
Soil: Moist, acidic, humus-rich
Hardiness: Zone 6
Propagation: Seed, in autumn or spring; offsets, in autumn

Tuberous. Large, solitary leaf, with 5 linear to lance-shaped leaflets. Flowering spathe green, striped white and purple, may be followed by berries if both sexes grown.

Arisaema candidissimum A.G.M.
(Araceae)

Common names: None
Height: 12in (30cm)
Spread: 18in (45cm)
Aspect: Half shade, cool
Soil: Moist, humus-rich
Hardiness: Zone 6
Propagation: Seed, in autumn or spring; offsets, in autumn

Tuberous plant. Spathe white striped pink, scented; appears late, so mark position. Large, 3-palmate leaves with ovate leaflets follow. Will fruit if male and female grown.

Arisaema triphyllum
(Araceae)

Common name: Jack-in-the-pulpit
Height: 1ft (30cm)
Spread: 1ft (30cm)
Aspect: Half shade, cool
Soil: Moist, humus-rich
Hardiness: Zone 4
Propagation: Seed, in autumn or spring; offsets, in autumn

A tuberous species. Leaves three-lobed, green. Spathe hooded, green, striped purple and white, may be followed by berries if plants of both sexes are grown.

Arisarum proboscideum
(Araceae)

Common names: None
Height: 8in (20cm)
Spread: Indefinite
Aspect: Half shade, woodland
Soil: Moist, humus-rich
Hardiness: Zone 7
Propagation: Seed, in spring; division, in autumn

Rhizomatous, mat-forming perennial. Dark green, glossy, arrow-shaped leaves. Hooded, dark brown-purple spathe, with a long tip like a mouse's tail. Can be invasive.

Aristea ecklonii
(Iridaceae)

Common names: None
Height: 24in (60cm)
Spread: 18in (45cm)
Aspect: Full sun
Soil: Moist, well-drained, humus-rich
Hardiness: Zone 9
Propagation: Seed, in warmth in spring

Rhizomatous evergreen, forming tangled clumps. Lance-shaped, stem-clasping, and linear basal leaves. Panicles of lilac or blue, saucer-shaped flowers, lasting a day, summer.

71

Aristea major
(Iridaceae)

Common names: None
Height: 5ft (1.5m)
Spread: 18in (45cm)
Aspect: Full sun
Soil: Well-drained,
humus-rich
Hardiness: Zone 8
Propagation: Seed, in warmth in
spring

Handsome, rhizomatous evergreen.
Leaves both lance-shaped basal and
long, linear stem. Flowers in panicles
in summer; purple or blue, saucer-
shaped, closing at night.

Armeria maritima
(Plumbaginaceae)

Common name: Sea pink
Height: 1ft (30cm)
Spread: 1ft (30cm)
Aspect: Full sun
Soil: Well-drained
Hardiness: Zone 4
Propagation: Seed or
division, both in spring

Clump-forming evergreen, with a
cushion of linear, dark green leaves.
Red, pink, or white, cup-shaped
flowers, in spherical heads in spring
and early summer.

Armeria maritima
'Alba'
(Plumbaginaceae)

Common name: White
sea thrift
Height: 1ft (30cm)
Spread: 1ft (30cm)
Aspect: Full sun
Soil: Well-drained
Hardiness: Zone 4
Propagation: Seed or division,
both in spring

White variant of the species. Leaves in
a tight cushion, evergreen, linear, dark
green. Small, spherical heads of cup-
shaped, white flowers in early
summer.

Armeria maritima
'Vindictive' A.G.M.
(Plumbaginaceae)

Common names: None
Height: 6in (15cm)
Spread: 4in (10cm)
Aspect: Full sun
Soil: Well-drained
Hardiness: Zone 4
Propagation: Division,
in spring

Compact, dwarf selected form;
shorter stems than the species, bearing
spherical heads of rose-pink, cup-
shaped flowers. Leaves evergreen,
linear, in a cushion.

Armoracia rusticana (Brassicaceae/Cruciferae)

Common name: Horseradish
Height: 3ft (1m)
Spread: 2ft (60cm)
Aspect: Full sun
Soil: Moist, well-drained, fertile
Hardiness: Zone 5
Propagation: Division, in winter

Clump-forming perennial cultivated for the culinary use of its roots. Leaves dark green, oblong-ovate, toothed. Flowers in terminal panicles, small, white. Sap may irritate.

Artemisia lactiflora A.G.M. (Asteraceae/Compositae)

Common name: White mugwort
Height: 5ft (1.5m)
Spread: 2ft (60cm)
Aspect: Full sun
Soil: Moist, well-drained, fertile
Hardiness: Zone 4
Propagation: Seed or division, both in autumn or spring

Clump-forming culinary herb with deeply cut, pinnatisect, dark green leaves. Bears long-lasting white flowers, in panicles, from late summer to mid-autumn.

Artemisia schmidtiana 'Nana' A.G.M. (Asteraceae/Compositae)

Common names: None
Height: 4in (10cm)
Spread: 12in (30cm)
Aspect: Full sun
Soil: Well-drained, fertile
Hardiness: Zone 4
Propagation: Seed or division, both in spring or autumn

Dwarf, rhizomatous, evergreen culinary herb. Leaves pinnatisect, with linear lobes, silky-hairy, silver. Panicles of many small, yellow flowers, aging to cream, in summer.

Arthropodium candidum 'Maculatum' (Anthericaceae/Liliaceae)

Common names: None
Height: 8in (20cm)
Spread: 4in (10cm)
Aspect: Full sun
Soil: Well-drained, sandy, fertile
Hardiness: Zone 8
Propagation: Seed, in autumn or spring; division, in spring

Tuberous perennial. Leaves linear, dull flesh-pink, mottled bronze. Flowers tiny, white, in racemes or panicles, in early to midsummer. Just big enough for a border.

Arum italicum
(Araceae)

Common name: Italian arum
Height: 12in (30cm)
Spread: 6in (15cm)
Aspect: Sun or half shade
Soil: Well-drained, humus-rich
Hardiness: Zone 6
Propagation: Seed, in autumn; division, after flowering

Woodlander with large, cream spathes in early summer, then spikes of red berries. Leaves spear- to arrow-shaped, green, in late autumn. All parts toxic and irritant.

Arum italicum subsp. **italicum** 'Marmoratum' A.G.M. (Araceae)

Common name: Italian arum
Height: 12in (30cm)
Spread: 6in (15cm)
Aspect: Sun or half shade
Soil: Well-drained, humus-rich
Hardiness: Zone 6
Propagation: Seed, in autumn; division, after flowering

Variegated form of the species, with green, cream-veined, spear- to arrow-shaped leaves. Cream spathes followed by spikes of red berries. All parts toxic and irritant.

Aruncus dioicus A.G.M. (Rosaceae)

Common name: Goat's-beard
Height: 6ft (2m)
Spread: 4ft (1.2m)
Aspect: Full or half shade
Soil: Moist, fertile
Hardiness: Zone 7
Propagation: Seed or division, both in spring or autumn

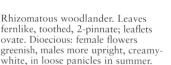

Rhizomatous woodlander. Leaves fernlike, toothed, 2-pinnate; leaflets ovate. Dioecious: female flowers greenish, males more upright, creamy-white, in loose panicles in summer.

Aruncus dioicus 'Glasnevin' (Rosaceae)

Common name: Sylvan goat's-beard
Height: 6ft (2m)
Spread: 4ft (1.2m)
Aspect: Full or half shade
Soil: Moist, fertile
Hardiness: Zone 7
Propagation: Seed or division, both in spring or autumn

Selected form with pendulous panicles, better in male plants than female. Dead-head females to prevent seeding. Leaves fernlike, toothed, 2-pinnate; leaflets ovate.

Asarina procumbens
(Scrophulariaceae)

Common name: Wild
Ginger-snapdragon
Height: 2in (5cm)
Spread: 24in (60cm)
Aspect: Half shade
Soil: Well-drained, sandy,
fertile
Hardiness: Zone 7
Propagation: Seed, in warmth
in spring

Evergreen, trailing, brittle-stemmed
plant. Leaves kidney-shaped, lobed,
hairy, dark green. Flowers
snapdragonlike, cream with yellow
throats, in summer. Good on walls.

Asclepias incarnata
(Asclepiadaceae)

Common name: Swamp
milkweed
Height: 4ft (1.2m)
Spread: 2ft (60cm)
Aspect: Full sun
Soil: Moist, humus-rich
Hardiness: Zone 3
Propagation: Seed or division,
both in spring

Good marginal plant. Leaves elliptic-
ovate, midgreen. Clustered cymes of
flowers with pink-purple, reflexed
petals and paler horns, in summer to
autumn. Silky seed heads.

Asclepias syriaca
(Asclepiadaceae)

Common names:
Milkweed; silkweed
Height: 6ft (2m)
Spread: Indefinite
Aspect: Full sun
Soil: Well-drained, fertile
Hardiness: Zone 3
Propagation: Seed or
division, both in spring

Rapidly spreading plant, not for the
border. Leaves softly hairy, ovate-
oblong, midgreen, blue-green beneath.
Flowers in cymes, pink and purple,
scented; seed heads softly spiny.

Asclepias tuberosa
(Asclepiadaceae)

Common name:
Butterfly-weed
Height: 3ft (90cm)
Spread: 1ft (30cm)
Aspect: Full sun
Soil: Well-drained, fertile,
humus-rich
Hardiness: Zone 3
Propagation: Seed or division,
both in spring

Handsome but difficult, tuberous
perennial. Leaves lance-shaped to
ovate-oblong, hairy, midgreen.
Flowers in cymes, orange, in summer
to autumn; seed heads nodding.

Asphodeline lutea
(Asphodelaceae/Liliaceae)

Common names: King's
spear; Jacob's-rod
Height: 5ft (1.5m)
Spread: 1ft (30cm)
Aspect: Full sun
Soil: Well-drained,
sandy, fertile
Hardiness: Zone 7
Propagation: Seed, in spring;
division, in autumn

Rhizomatous perennial. Leaves
narrow, grassy, gray-green. Dense
racemes of yellow flowers with large
bracts, perfumed, in late spring,
followed by attractive seed heads.

Asphodelus albus
(Asphodelaceae/Liliaceae)

Common name: Asphodel
Height: 36in (90cm)
Spread: 12in (30cm)
Aspect: Full sun
Soil: Well-drained, sandy,
humus-rich
Hardiness: Zone 6
Propagation: Seed or division,
both in spring

Clump-forming perennial. Leaves
linear, grassy, keeled, midgreen.
Flowers white, brown-veined, star-
shaped, with brownish bracts, in few-
branched racemes in spring.

Asphodelus ramosus
(Asphodelaceae/Liliaceae)

Common name: Asphodel
Height: 5ft (1.5m)
Spread: 1ft (30cm)
Aspect: Sun
Soil: Well-drained, sandy,
humus-rich
Hardiness: Zone 7
Propagation: Seed or division,
both in spring

Leaves grassy, flat, linear, keeled,
green. Flowers white with a rust
midvein and white bracts, in racemes
in summer. From southern Europe
and North Africa.

Asplenium scolopendrium
A.G.M.
(Aspleniaceae)

Common name: Hart's-
tongue fern
Height: 28in (70cm)
Spread: 24in (60cm)
Aspect: Half shade
Soil: Moist, well-drained,
sandy
Hardiness: Zone 5
Propagation: Seed, in warmth in
spring; division, in spring

Evergreen terrestrial fern. Fronds
strap-shaped, fleshy, glossy, green.
Remove old fronds in spring to allow
new to develop. Good wall plant.

ASTER (Asteraceae)

Large genus of some 150 species, including annuals, biennials, and a few subshrubs as well as perennials. They are found chiefly in the northern hemisphere, and in North America in particular, although some subshrubs originate in South Africa. Asters grow in a wide range of habitats, from woodland to mountain, and so come in all shapes and sizes; they also vary in their degrees of hardiness. Their varying cultural requirements mean that there are asters to suit a range of garden situations, from scree beds to woodlands and stream edges. They all have similar inflorescences: daisylike flowerheads with ray florets usually of white, pink, purple, or blue, and disc florets in shades of yellow. There are a few exceptions to this, with yellow ray florets or pink disc florets. All asters are prone to slug damage, and the many cultivars of *A. novi-belgii*, the New York aster, are very prone to powdery mildew; it may not be possible to grow them at all in a wet garden, even with constant care. Taller species and cultivars may need staking, and some will need to be lifted and divided every few years to maintain their vigor. Nonetheless, these are valuable late-season plants. Many of them hold an Award of Garden Merit; some that have not been profiled in detail are listed on p.58.

Aster alpinus
var. *albus*
(Asteraceae/Compositae)

Common name: White
alpine aster
Height: 25cm (10in)
Spread: 45cm (18in)
Aspect: Full sun
Soil: Well-drained, sandy
Hardiness: Zone 3
Propagation: Seed, in spring
or autumn

White form of a mostly violet species.
Midgreen, narrow, lance-shaped leaves.
Flowers solitary, single, with white
petals and yellow disc florets, spring
and early summer.

Aster amellus
'King George' A.G.M.
(Asteraceae/Compositae)

Common name: Italian
aster
Height: 18in (45cm)
Spread: 18in (45cm)
Aspect: Sun
Soil: Well-drained,
alkaline, sandy
Hardiness: Zone 5
Propagation: Division,
in spring

Clump-forming, with lance-shaped
leaves of midgreen. Flowers in late
summer to autumn, large, violet-blue
with a yellow boss. One of a few
cultivars with an A.G.M.

Aster divaricatus
(Asteraceae/Compositae)

Common names: None
Height: 2ft (60cm)
Spread: 2ft (60cm)
Aspect: Half shade
Soil: Moist
Hardiness: Zone 4
Propagation: Seed or
division, both in spring

Rhizomatous North American species.
Upper leaves ovate, lower leaves
heart-shaped, midgreen. Lax corymbs
of small white flowers, midsummer to
autumn.

Aster ericoides
(Asteraceae/Compositae)

Common names: None
Height: 3ft (1m)
Spread: 16in (40cm)
Aspect: Half shade
Soil: Moist
Hardiness: Zone 3
Propagation: Seed or
division, both in spring

Lax, freely branching, slender-
stemmed perennial. Leaves linear to
lance-shaped, green. Loose panicles of
small white flowers summer to
autumn. From North America.

Aster x frikartii
(Asteraceae/Compositae)

Common names: None
Height: 32in (80cm)
Spread: 18in (45cm)
Aspect: Full sun
Soil: Well-drained, sandy
Hardiness: Zone 4
Propagation: Division,
in spring

Hybrid of garden origin. Leaves
ovate, rough, green. Flowers in loose
corymbs, light purple-blue, with
orange discs, in late summer to
autumn.

Aster x frikartii
'Mönch' A.G.M.
(Asteraceae/Compositae)

Common names: None
Height: 28in (70cm)
Spread: 16in (40cm)
Aspect: Full sun
Soil: Well-drained, sandy
Hardiness: Zone 4
Propagation: Division,
in spring

Cloned selection, widely grown on
account of its very long flowering
season, from summer to early
autumn. The flowers are of a more
intense color than the type.

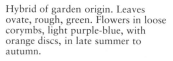

Aster lateriflorus
(Asteraceae/Compositae)

Aster macrophyllus
(Asteraceae/Compositae)

Common name: Calico
aster
Height: 3ft (1m)
Spread: 1ft (30cm)
Aspect: Half shade
Soil: Moist, good drainage
Hardiness: Zone 3
Propagation: Seed, in spring

Common names: None
Height: 3ft (1m)
Spread: 28in (80cm)
Aspect: Half or full shade
Soil: Moist
Hardiness: Zone 3
Propagation: Seed, in
spring

Clump-forming species. Leaves
midgreen, linear-oblong. Flowers
white, with pink disc florets, on
spreading, branched stems from
midsummer to autumn.

Invasive aster; good ground cover.
Large leaves, heart-shaped, toothed,
green. Flowers in corymbs, small,
starry, pale violet fading to white,
yellow disc florets, in autumn.

Aster novae-angliae 'Andenken
an Alma Pötschke' A.G.M.
(Asteraceae/Compositae)

Aster novae-angliae
'Lye End Beauty'
(Asteraceae/Compositae)

Common name: New
England aster
Height: 4ft (1.2m)
Spread: 2ft (60cm)
Aspect: Sun or half shade
Soil: Moist, fertile
Hardiness: Zone 2
Propagation: Division,
in spring

Common name: New
England aster
Height: 5½ft (1.7m)
Spread: 32in (80cm)
Aspect: Sun or half shade
Soil: Moist, fertile
Hardiness: Zone 2
Propagation: Division,
in spring

Cloned selection of a rhizomatous
aster. Leaves lance-shaped, midgreen.
Flowers in sprays, bright salmon-pink
with yellow disc florets, in autumn.
Very desirable.

Lovely clone of a rhizomatous species.
Leaves lance-shaped, midgreen.
Flowers in sprays, ray florets lilac,
disc florets yellow, in autumn. One of
many named varieties.

79

Aster novi-belgii
'Jenny'
(Asteraceae/Compositae)

Common name: New
York aster
Height: 4ft (1.2m)
Spread: 3ft (90cm)
Aspect: Full sun or half
shade
Soil: Moist, fertile
Hardiness: Zone 2
Propagation: Division,
in spring

One of many cultivars of this
rhizomatous aster, very prone to
powdery mildew. Leaves lance-shaped,
green. Double, purple-red flowers
with yellow disc florets in autumn.

Aster sedifolius
(Asteraceae/Compositae)

Common names: None
Height: 4ft (1.2m)
Spread: 2ft (60cm)
Aspect: Full sun
Soil: Well-drained, fertile
Hardiness: Zone 6
Propagation: Seed, in
spring or autumn

Leaves lance-shaped, green. Starry,
lilac flowers with yellow disc florets,
on weak stems. The form 'Nanus' is
much more compact, with flowers of
a deeper blue.

Aster thomsonii
'Nanus'
(Asteraceae/Compositae)

Common names: None
Height: 18in (45cm)
Spread: 25cm (10in)
Aspect: Half shade
Soil: Moist, fertile
Hardiness: Zone 7
Propagation: Seed, in
spring or autumn

Dwarf cultivar. Leaves elliptic to
ovate, toothed, green. Flowers in
terminal sprays, blue-lilac, star-
shaped, long-lasting, in summer to
early autumn.

Aster tongolensis
'Wartburgstern'
(Asteraceae/Compositae)

Common names: None
Height: 20in (50cm)
Spread: 20in (50cm)
Aspect: Full sun
Soil: Well-drained, fertile
Hardiness: Zone 8
Propagation: Division,
in spring

Selected form of a rhizomatous, mat-
forming species. Leaves hairy, elliptic,
dark green. Flowers solitary, single, in
summer; violet-blue ray florets,
orange disc florets.

Asteriscus maritimus
(Asteraceae)

Astilbe chinensis
var. *pumila* A.G.M.
(Saxifragaceae)

Common names: None
Height: 10in (25cm)
Spread: 8in (20cm)
Aspect: Sun
Soil: Well-drained, sandy
Hardiness: Zone 8
Propagation: Seed, in
warmth in spring

Common names: None
Height: 10in (25cm)
Spread: 8in (20cm)
Aspect: Sun or half shade
Soil: Moist or boggy
Hardiness: Zone 5
Propagation: Division,
in autumn or winter

Good wall plant from the Canary and
Cape Verde Islands. Leaves oblong to
spoon-shaped, hairy. Bears solitary,
single, orange-yellow flowers in
autumn.

Highly desirable astilbe from China,
with 3-ternate, toothed, hairy leaves
of red-green. Flowers in dense, conical
panicles of reddish-pink in late
summer.

ASTILBE (Saxifragaceae)

There are only about a dozen species in this small genus; they
are rhizomatous and clump-forming, and found in the wild in
moist areas, on stream banks, and in the woodlands of North
America and southeast Asia. The vast majority of the astilbes in
cultivation are interspecific hybrids of complex parentage,
arising from crosses between *A.* x *arendsii* (Zone 6),
A. astilboides (Zone 6), *A. chinensis* (Zone 5), *A. japonica*
(Zone 5), *A. simplicifolia* (Zone 7), and *A. thunbergii* (Zone 7).
Many deservedly hold an Award of Garden Merit. They are
easy-to-please, being fairly hardy and tolerant of sun or half
shade and of boggy or dry soil. Their divided, toothed foliage is
handsome, and they make excellent ground cover or bog or
marginal plants. Astilbes are also long-flowering, with tapering,
usually open panicles of flowers, in shades of white or cream
through pinks to rich red, in summer. These do not require staking,
and are followed by attractive seed heads, which will persist on
the plants throughout the winter. The flowers fade quickly when
cut, but the seed heads dry well. In all, they are almost exemplary
perennials. Their only drawback is that they do require regular
division and replanting if they are to stay at their best.

Astilbe x *arendsii*
'Feuer'
(Saxifragaceae)

Common name: Hybrid
astilbe
Height: 24in (60cm)
Spread: 18in (45cm)
Aspect: Sun or half shade
Soil: Moist or boggy
Hardiness: Zone 6
Propagation: Division,
in autumn or winter

A striking hybrid cultivar with flowers
of a distinctive coral-red, in open
panicles in summer. Handsome lobed,
toothed, dark green leaves.

Astilbe x *arendsii*
'Glut'
(Saxifragaceae)

Common name: Hybrid
astilbe
Height: 24in (60cm)
Spread: 18in (45cm)
Aspect: Sun or half shade
Soil: Moist or boggy
Hardiness: Zone 6
Propagation: Division,
in autumn or winter

A very desirable, compact hybrid
astilbe. Foliage deep green, lobed,
toothed. Crowded panicles of deep
crimson-red flowers in summer.

Astilbe
'Jo Ophorst'
(Saxifragaceae)

Common names: None
Height: 4ft (1.2m)
Spread: 2ft (60cm)
Aspect: Sun or half shade
Soil: Moist or boggy
Hardiness: Zone 6
Propagation: Division,
in autumn or winter

An *Astilbe* x *chinensis* var. *davidii*
hybrid, taller than most; it has
panicles of pink flowers with a hint of
lilac, in late summer. Leaves 3-ternate,
toothed.

Astilbe chinensis var.
taquetii 'Purpurlanze'
(Saxifragaceae)

Common names: None
Height: 4ft (1.2m)
Spread: 3ft (90cm)
Aspect: Half shade or sun
Soil: Prefers moist or
boggy
Hardiness: Zone 5
Propagation: Division,
in autumn or winter

An astilbe for the dry garden, as it
will tolerate this better than most.
Tall, elegant panicles of purple-red in
late summer to early autumn.

Astilbe
'Red Sentinel'
(Saxifragaceae)

Common names: None
Height: 3ft (1m)
Spread: 20in (50cm)
Aspect: Sun or half shade
Soil: Moist or boggy
Hardiness: Zone 5
Propagation: Division,
in autumn or winter

Clump-forming *A. japonica* hybrid,
with dark green, toothed leaves. Erect
panicles of dark crimson flowers are
carried above the foliage in summer.

Astilbe
'Rheinland' A.G.M.
(Saxifragaceae)

Common names: None
Height: 20in (50cm)
Spread: 18in (45cm)
Aspect: Sun or half shade
Soil: Moist or boggy
Hardiness: Zone 5
Propagation: Division,
in autumn or winter

A. japonica hybrid, clump-forming,
with midgreen foliage, and dense,
upright panicles of deep pink flowers
throughout the summer.

Astilbe
'Sprite' A.G.M.
(Saxifragaceae)

Common names: None
Height: 20in (50cm)
Spread: 3ft (1m)
Aspect: Sun or half shade
Soil: Moist or boggy
Hardiness: Zone 7
Propagation: Division, in
autumn or winter

A clump-forming *A. simplicifolia*
hybrid. Leaves midgreen, 2-ternate,
leaflets narrowly ovate. Flowers shell-
pink, in open, arching, feathery
panicles in summer.

Astrantia major
(Apiaceae/Umbelliferae)

Common name:
Masterwort
Height: 36in (90cm)
Spread: 18in (45cm)
Aspect: Sun or half shade
Soil: Moist, fertile,
humus-rich
Hardiness: Zone 6
Propagation: Seed, when ripe

Clump-forming plant. Basal rosette of
green leaves with up to 7 lobes.
Umbels of small, white flowers backed
by green-veined white bracts, in
summer, often again in autumn.

ASTRANTIA (Apiaceae/Umbelliferae)
Masterwort

This is a small genus of some ten clump-forming perennials, found across Europe and into western Asia, of which just two are in general cultivation. Their natural habitats are mountain woodlands and stream margins; they are reliably hardy, and they will grow in either sun or half shade. In the garden they will also suit a mixed border as long as it remains moist at all times. *Astrantia* form basal rosettes of handsome, palmate green leaves, but with the exception of *A. major* 'Sunningdale Variegated' they are primarily grown for their airy sprays of small flowers. These have five petals, and each is surrounded by a showy ruff of papery bracts in shades of pink and red; they are carried above the foliage on tall, wiry stems. They will self-seed freely about the garden, so if this is not desired, plants should be scrupulously deadheaded after flowering in summer: the flowers and their bracts will dry well for winter, and they are extremely popular for flower arrangements in either the fresh or the dried state. *Astrantia* will attract both bees and butterflies into the garden, but they are unfortunately also liked by slugs. Another drawback of the genus is that they are prone to powdery mildew.

Astrantia major
'Hadspen Blood'
(Apiaceae/Umbelliferae)

Common name:
Masterwort
Height: 36in (90cm)
Spread: 18in (45cm)
Aspect: Sun or half shade
Soil: Moist, fertile,
humus-rich
Hardiness: Zone 6
Propagation: Seed, when ripe

A handsome cultivar with dark red flowers, surrounded by matching dark red bracts, in summer. Species is from Central and Eastern Europe.

Astrantia major rubra
(Apiaceae/Umbelliferae)

Common name:
Masterwort
Height: 36in (90cm)
Spread: 18in (45cm)
Aspect: Sun or half shade
Soil: Moist, fertile,
humus-rich
Hardiness: Zone 6
Propagation: Division,
in spring

Handsome cultivar with plum flowers surrounded by pinkish bracts, in summer. A favorite for flower-arranging. Basal rosette of green leaves with up to 7 lobes.

Astrantia major
'Shaggy' A.G.M.
(Apiaceae/Umbelliferae)

Common name:
Masterwort
Height: 36in (90cm)
Spread: 18in (45cm)
Aspect: Sun or half shade
Soil: Moist, fertile,
humus-rich
Hardiness: Zone 6
Propagation: Division,
in spring

Extremely attractive cultivar,
sometimes sold as 'Margery Fish'.
Leaves very deeply cut. Flowers in
summer with very long and sharp-
pointed bracts, with green tips.

Astrantia major
'Ruby Wedding'
(Apiaceae/Umbelliferae)

Common name:
Masterwort
Height: 36in (90cm)
Spread: 18in (45cm)
Aspect: Sun or half shade
Soil: Moist, fertile,
humus-rich
Hardiness: Zone 6
Propagation: Division,
in spring

Handsome cultivar with particularly
attractive toothed foliage. Flowers in
summer, with plum-colored petals and
bracts. A favorite for flower
arranging.

Astrantia major
'Roma'
(Apiaceae/Umbelliferae)

Common name:
Masterwort
Height: 36in (90cm)
Spread: 18in (45cm)
Aspect: Sun or half shade
Soil: Moist, fertile,
humus-rich
Hardiness: Zone 6
Propagation: Division,
in spring

Cultivar with deep pink flowers and
bracts in summer. Very popular for
fresh or dried flower arrangements.
Leaves green, with up to 7 lobes, in
basal rosettes.

Astrantia major 'Sunningdale
Variegated' A.G.M.
(Apiaceae/Umbelliferae)

Common name:
Masterwort
Height: 36in (90cm)
Spread: 18in (45cm)
Aspect: Full sun
Soil: Moist, fertile,
humus-rich
Hardiness: Zone 6
Propagation: Division,
in spring

Cultivar grown for both flower and
foliage. Leaves have either cream
lobes or cream edges. Flowers have
bracts of pale pink. Grow in full sun
for maximum leaf color.

Astrantia maxima
A.G.M.
(Apiaceae/Umbelliferae)

Common name:
Masterwort
Height: 2ft (60cm)
Spread: 1ft (30cm)
Aspect: Sun or half shade
Soil: Moist, fertile,
humus-rich
Hardiness: Zone 6
Propagation: Seed or division,
both in spring

Clump-forming perennial. Leaves
green, with handsome, deeply divided
lobes. Flowers small, pink,
surrounded by sharp, pink bracts, in
umbels, early to midsummer.

Athyrium filix-femina
A.G.M.
(Athyriaceae)

Common name: Lady fern
Height: 4ft (1.2m)
Spread: 3ft (90cm)
Aspect: Shade
Soil: Moist, acidic, fertile,
humus-rich
Hardiness: Zone 5
Propagation: Spores in heat
when ripe; division, in spring

Rhizomatous, deciduous, variable
fern. Fronds light green, 2- or 3-
pinnate, lance-shaped. Pinnae elliptic,
segments oblong- to lance-shaped.
Stalks sometimes reddish.

Aubrieta
'Red Carpet'
(Brassicaceae/Cruciferae)

Common name: Aubrietia
Height: 2in (5cm)
Spread: 24in (60cm) or
more
Aspect: Full sun
Soil: Well-drained, neutral
or alkaline, sandy
Hardiness: Zone 7
Propagation: Softwood
cuttings, in early summer

One of several hybrid cultivars; good
wall plant or ground cover. Leaves
evergreen, oblong, hairy, midgreen.
Flowers bright scarlet, 4-petalled.
Trim after flowering.

Aurinia saxatilis
A.G.M.
(Brassicaceae/Cruciferae)

Common name: Golden-
tuft
Height: 10in (25cm)
Spread: 16in (40cm)
Aspect: Full sun
Soil: Well-drained, sandy,
fertile
Hardiness: Zone 3
Propagation: Seed,
in autumn

Mound-forming evergreen. Leaves in
rosettes, obovate, hairy, toothed,
gray-green. Flowers in panicles,
yellow, in spring and early summer.
Good in a wall.

Bacopa monnieri
(Scrophulariaceae)

Common names: None
Height: 4in (10cm)
Spread: 16in (40cm)
Aspect: Sun
Soil: Aquatic or marginal
Hardiness: Zone 8
Propagation: Division,
in spring

Aquatic or semi-aquatic, mat-forming,
creeping plant. Leaves spoon-shaped,
apex dentate. Flowers small, 5-
petalled, white or pale pink, summer.
Worldwide distribution.

Ballota
'All Hallows Green'
(Labiatae/Lamiaceae)

Common names: None
Height: 24in (60cm)
Spread: 30in (75cm)
Aspect: Full sun
Soil: Well-drained, poor,
sandy
Hardiness: Zone 8
Propagation: Softwood
cuttings, in spring

Evergreen subshrub with lime-green,
heart-shaped, aromatic, woolly leaves.
Flowers small, two-lipped, pale green,
with green calyces, in mid- to late
summer.

Ballota pseudodictamnus
A.G.M.
(Labiatae/Lamiaceae)

Common names: None
Height: 20in (50cm)
Spread: 24in (60cm)
Aspect: Full sun
Soil: Well-drained, poor,
sandy
Hardiness: Zone 8
Propagation: Softwood
cuttings, in spring

Evergreen subshrub. Leaves ovate,
grayish- to yellowish-green. Flowers
on white-woolly stems, white or
pinkish-white with pale green calyces.
Dislikes winter wet.

Baptisia australis
A.G.M.
(Leguminosae/Papilionaceae)

Common name: False or
wild indigo
Height: 5ft (1.5m)
Spread: 2ft (60cm)
Aspect: Full sun
Soil: Sharply drained,
sandy
Hardiness: Zone 5
Propagation: Seed, when
ripe; division, in spring

Erect or spreading plant. Leaves
palmate, with inversely lance-shaped
leaflets, deep green. Flowers in
racemes, pea-like, indigo-blue,
followed by inflated seed heads.

87

Begonia grandis subsp. *evansiana* (Begoniaceae)

Common names: None
Height: 32in (80cm)
Spread: 12in (30cm)
Aspect: Full sun or half shade
Soil: Moist, fertile, humus-rich
Hardiness: Zone 8
Propagation: Bulbils, in autumn

Tuberous begonia with ovate, olive-green leaves. Pendent cymes of perfumed, bright pink flowers on tallish, branched stems in summer. Produces plenty of bulbils.

Belamcanda chinensis (Iridaceae)

Common name: Blackberry-lily
Height: 36in (90cm)
Spread: 8in (20cm)
Aspect: Sun or half shade
Soil: Moisture-retentive, but well-drained
Hardiness: Zone 8
Propagation: Seed or division, in spring

Rhizomatous, short-lived perennial. Leaves sword-shaped, green. Flowers orange, with maroon spots, in summer, followed by handsome, open seed heads; seeds black.

Bellis perennis (Asteraceae/Compositae)

Common name: English daisy
Height: 8in (20cm)
Spread: 8in (20cm)
Aspect: Sun or half shade
Soil: Well-drained, fertile
Hardiness: Zone 4
Propagation: Seed or division, both in spring

Well-known evergreen. Leaves obovate to spoon-shaped, green. Flowers solitary, single or double; disc florets yellow, ray florets white, red, or pink. Good ground cover.

Bellis perennis 'Pomponette' A.G.M. (Asteraceae/Compositae)

Common name: English daisy
Height: 8in (20cm)
Spread: 8in (20cm)
Aspect: Sun or half shade
Soil: Well-drained, fertile
Hardiness: Zone 4
Propagation: Seed or division, both in spring

Cloned selection. Leaves spoon-shaped to obovate, green. Flowerheads fully double, with quilled petals. Evergreen ground cover. Treat as a biennial in cold areas.

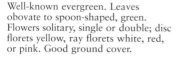

Bellium crassifolium canescens
(Asteraceae/Compositae)

Common names: None
Height: 6in (15cm)
Spread: 8in (20cm)
Aspect: Half shade
Soil: Well-drained, fertile
Hardiness: Zone 8
Propagation: Seed, in spring

Mediterranean species, at home in coastal gardens. Leaves elliptic to spoon-shaped, fleshy, green. Flowers solitary, white, with yellow discs, in summer.

Bergenia cordifolia
(Saxifragaceae)

Common name: Heartleaf bergenia
Height: 24in (60cm)
Spread: 32in (80cm)
Aspect: Sun or half shade
Soil: Moist, well-drained, humus-rich
Hardiness: Zone 3
Propagation: Division, in spring or autumn

Evergreen from Siberia. Leaves round or heart-shaped, midgreen, flushed purple in winter. Panicles of pink flowers on long, strong, red stems, late winter to early spring.

BERGENIA (Saxifragaceae)

This genus from the moorlands, woodlands, and meadows of Central and East Asia, contains only some half dozen or so species; however, these hybridize very readily and so have given rise to a large number of named-variety hybrids. They are all evergreen and rhizomatous, and generally hardy. Elephant's ears are extremely useful perennials, as they will grow in sun or shade and in dry or wet soil. The leaves are distinctive: large, round, glossy, and leathery, in rosettes, and coloring up well in winter, particularly in poor soil. They make excellent ground cover, and are good in a woodland situation. The flowering cymes are also handsome, and provide particularly welcome color when they appear in winter and early spring. The flowers last well in water, and the leaves will last for weeks, which gives them great appeal for flower-arrangers. They are suitable plants for those with allergies. They do benefit from regular lifting and dividing, but this is also the best way to propagate, as plants in gardens where more than one type is growing will produce hybrid seeds. Slugs can be a problem. Other cultivars with an Award of Garden Merit are 'Bressingham White' (Zone 4) and *B. cordifolia* 'Purpurea' (Zone 3).

Bergenia 'Silberlicht'
A.G.M.
(Saxifragaceae)

Common names: None
Height: 18in (45cm)
Spread: 24in (60cm)
Aspect: Sun or half shade
Soil: Moist, well-drained,
humus-rich
Hardiness: Zone 6
Propagation: Division,
in autumn or spring

Hybrid with large, broad, obovate
green leaves with scalloped edges.
White flowers in early and midspring
age to pink, and have pink sepals.

Bergenia 'Sunningdale'
(Saxifragaceae)

Common names: None
Height: 18in (45cm)
Spread: 24in (60cm)
Aspect: Sun or half shade
Soil: Moist, well-drained,
humus-rich
Hardiness: Zone 3
Propagation: Division,
in autumn or spring

Clump-forming hybrid with large,
round or obovate leaves, deep green
turning red in winter. Flowers rich
lilac-magenta, on long red stems in
early and midwinter.

Blechnum spicant
A.G.M.
(Blechnaceae)

Common name: Hard fern
Height: 20in (50cm)
Spread: 24in (60cm)
Aspect: Half or deep shade
Soil: Moist, acidic,
humus-rich
Hardiness: Zone 5
Propagation: Spores,
in late summer

Evergreen, rhizomatous fern. Lance-
shaped, sterile, dark green fronds,
pinnate and pinnatifid with oblong
pinnae, surround taller, fertile fronds
with linear pinnae.

Bletilla striata
(Orchidaceae)

Common names: None
Height: 2ft (60cm)
Spread: 2ft (60cm)
Aspect: Half shade
Soil: Moist, well-drained,
humus-rich
Hardiness: Zone 7
Propagation: Division,
in spring

Terrestrial, deciduous orchid.
Pseudobulbs flattened, each producing
3 or 4 oblong to lance-shaped green
leaves. Terminal racemes of magenta
flowers, spring to early summer.

Bletilla striata
'Albostriata'
(Orchidaceae)

Common names: None
Height: 2ft (60cm)
Spread: 2ft (60cm)
Aspect: Half shade;
protect from midday
summer sun
Soil: Moist, well-drained,
humus-rich
Hardiness: Zone 7
Propagation: Division, in spring

A selected form with white flowers,
flushed pink, in spring to summer.
Leaves oblong to lance-shaped, green.
Grow in a peat bed or a woodland
garden.

Brunnera macrophylla
A.G.M.
(Boraginaceae)

Common name: Heartleaf
brunnera
Height: 2ft (60cm)
Spread: 2ft (60cm)
Aspect: Half or full shade
Soil: Moist, well-drained,
humus-rich
Hardiness: Zone 3
Propagation: Seed or division,
both in spring

Rhizomatous woodland or ground-
cover plant. Leaves large and green;
basal leaves heart-shaped, stem leaves
elliptic. Flowers in panicles, bright
blue, in spring.

Brunnera macrophylla
'Dawson's White'
(Boraginaceae)

Common name: Heartleaf
brunnera
Height: 2ft (60cm)
Spread: 2ft (60cm)
Aspect: Half or full shade
Soil: Moist, well-drained,
humus-rich
Hardiness: Zone 3
Propagation: Division,
in spring

Handsome variegated cultivar, good
in woodland. Leaves large, elliptic
and heart-shaped with wide cream
margins. Flowers blue. Will not come
true from seed.

Brunnera macrophylla
'Hadspen Cream' A.G.M.
(Boraginaceae)

Common name: Heartleaf
brunnera
Height: 2ft (60cm)
Spread: 2ft (60cm)
Aspect: Half or full shade
Soil: Moist, well-drained,
humus-rich
Hardiness: Zone 3
Propagation: Division,
in spring

Variegated clone, with large, cream-
edged, elliptic and heart-shaped leaves,
contrasting well with the bright blue
flowers. Suits a woodland setting, and
good for cutting.

Brunsvigia subacaulis
(Amaryllidaceae/Liliaceae)

**Buglossoides
purpurocaerulea**
(Boraginaceae)

Common names: None
Height: 18in (45cm)
Spread: 8in (20cm)
Aspect: Full sun
Soil: Sharply drained,
sandy
Hardiness: Zone 9
Propagation: Seed, in warmth
in spring; offsets, in autumn

Common names: None
Height: 2ft (60cm)
Spread: Indefinite
Aspect: Full sun; protect
from midday sun
Soil: Well-drained, fertile
Hardiness: Zone 6
Propagation: Division,
in spring

Bulbous perennial. Bright crimson
flowers should appear before leaves,
but may not do so for years. Leaves
long, strap-shaped, dark green. From
South Africa.

Rhizomatous ground cover;
nonflowering shoots root as they run,
spreading rapidly. Leaves dark green,
lance-shaped. Flowers are small,
purple, in erect cymes.

Bulbine alooides
(Asphodelaceae/Liliaceae)

Bulbinella hookeri
(Asphodelaceae/Liliaceae)

Common names: None
Height: 12in (30cm)
Spread: 6in (15cm)
Aspect: Full sun
Soil: Well-drained, sandy
Hardiness: Zone 9
Propagation: Seed, in
warmth in spring; division,
in spring

Common names: None
Height: 24in (60cm)
Spread: 18in (30cm)
Aspect: Sun or half shade
Soil: Well-drained, neutral
or acidic
Hardiness: Zone 8
Propagation: Seed, when
ripe; division, in autumn

Clump-forming perennial from South
Africa, with compact rosettes of
green, fleshy, lance-shaped leaves.
Racemes of yellow, star-shaped
flowers in spring.

Fleshy-rooted perennial from South
Africa with rosettes of grasslike,
succulent leaves. Flowers star-shaped,
yellow, in dense racemes, in spring to
summer.

Buphthalmum salicifolium
(Asteraceae/Compositae)

Common name:
Willowleaf-oxeye
Height: 24in (60cm)
Spread: 18in (45cm)
Aspect: Full sun
Soil: Dry, sandy, poor
Hardiness: Zone 4
Propagation: Seed or division,
both in spring

Leaves narrow, lance-shaped or
obovate, dark green. Flowers yellow,
inulalike daisies on erect stems all
summer long, especially if deadheaded
regularly.

Bupleurum falcatum
(Apiaceae/Umbelliferae)

Common names: None
Height: 3ft (90cm)
Spread: 2ft (60cm)
Aspect: Full sun
Soil: Well-drained
Hardiness: Zone 3
Propagation: Seed or
division, both in spring

Leaves narrow, linear, green. Yellow
flowers in umbels, similar to the
familiar *Gypsophila paniculata* (*see
p.216*), not spectacular, but lasting for
many weeks.

Bupleurum fruticosum
(Apiaceae/Umbelliferae)

Common name: Shrubby
hare's ear
Height: 6ft (2m)
Spread: 9ft (3m)
Aspect: Full sun
Soil: Any, well-drained
Hardiness: Zone 7
Propagation: Seed or
division, both in spring

Dense, evergreen subshrub, too large
for the small garden. Leaves obovate,
blue-green. Flowers starry, yellow, in
umbels, summer to autumn. Good
seaside plant.

Butomus umbellatus
A.G.M.
(Butomaceae)

Common name:
Flowering-rush
Height: 4ft (1.2m)
Spread: 18in (45cm)
Aspect: Full sun
Soil: Marginal, or aquatic
to 35cm (10in) deep
Hardiness: Zone 5
Propagation: Seed, in mud
in spring; division, in spring

Rhizomatous aquatic perennial.
Leaves long, radical, green, turning
bronze. Flowers numerous, perfumed,
pink, in umbels in late summer.

Cacalia glabra
(Asteraceae)

Common names: None
Height: 32in (80cm)
Spread: 18in (45cm)
Aspect: Sun
Soil: Well-drained
Hardiness: Zone 6
Propagation: Seed, in
spring

Calamintha grandiflora 'Variegata'
(Labiatae/Lamiaceae)

Common name: Calamint
Height: 18in (45cm)
Spread: 18in (45cm)
Aspect: Sun or half shade
Soil: Moist, well-drained
Hardiness: Zone 5
Propagation: Seed or
division, both in spring

Leaves kidney-shaped, coarse, pale green, with glabrous undersides. Flattish corymbs of small, pink flowers in spring. European member of a widely distributed genus.

Rhizomatous culinary herb; good ground cover. Leaves aromatic, ovate, toothed, variegated green and cream. Pink flowers in lax cymes, in summer.

Calamintha nepeta
(Labiatae/Lamiaceae)

Common name: Lesser
calamint
Height: 18in (45cm)
Spread: 32in (80cm)
Aspect: Sun or half shade
Soil: Moist, well-drained
Hardiness: Zone 6
Propagation: Seed or division,
both in spring

Calamintha nepeta subsp. *glandulosa* 'White Cloud'
(Labiatae/Lamiaceae)

Common name: Lesser
calamint
Height: 18in (45cm)
Spread: 32in (80cm)
Aspect: Sun or half shade
Soil: Moist, well-drained
Hardiness: Zone 6
Propagation: Seed or
division, both in spring

Aromatic culinary herb; good ground cover. Leaves ovate, hairy, green. Pink flowers in branching cymes of up to 15, in summer. From Eurasia and N. Africa.

Long-flowering, cloned selection; good for culinary use or ground cover. Flowers white, in branching cymes, spring and summer. Leaves aromatic, ovate, hairy, green.

Calandrinia grandiflora
(Portulacaceae)

Calanthe discolor
(Orchidaceae)

Common names: None
Height: 36in (90cm)
Spread: 18in (45cm)
Aspect: Full sun
Soil: Sharply drained,
acidic, humus-rich
Hardiness: Zone 7
Propagation: Seed, in spring; stem
cuttings, in spring

Common names: None
Height: 8in (20cm)
Spread: 8in (20cm)
Aspect: Half shade
Soil: Well-drained, sandy,
humus-rich
Hardiness: Zone 8
Propagation: Division, after
flowering

An evergreen species from Chile,
often grown as an annual in cold
areas. Leaves fleshy, elliptic, green.
Flowers in racemes, cup-shaped,
magenta, in summer.

Evergreen terrestrial orchid from
Korea, Japan, and Taiwan. Leaves
oblong, green. Flowers in erect
racemes of up to 10, purplish with
pink lips.

Calceolaria biflora
(Scrophulariaceae)

Calceolaria integrifolia
A.G.M.
(Scrophulariaceae)

Common names: Slipper
flower; slipperwort
Height: 8in (20cm)
Spread: 8in (20cm)
Aspect: Sun or half shade
Soil: Porous, acidic, fertile
Hardiness: Zone 6
Propagation: Seed, in autumn
or spring; division, in spring

Common names: Slipper
flower; slipperwort
Height: 3ft (1m)
Spread: 1ft (30cm)
Aspect: Sun or half shade
Soil: Porous, acidic, fertile
Hardiness: Zone 9
Propagation: Seed, in autumn
or spring; division, in spring

Rhizomatous evergreen from South
America. Leaves in rosettes, oblong,
toothed, dark green. Flowers yellow,
2-lipped, in loose racemes of up to 8,
all summer long.

Lax subshrub. Leaves gray-green,
ovate to lance-shaped, toothed.
Flowers in cymes of as many as 35,
yellow, all summer long. Usually
treated as an annual in cold areas.

Calceolaria polyrhiza
(Scrophulariaceae)

Calceolaria tenella
(Scrophulariaceae)

Common names: Slipper
flower; slipperwort
Height: 3in (8cm)
Spread: 8in (20cm)
Aspect: Sun or half shade
Soil: Sandy, acidic, fertile
Hardiness: Zone 9
Propagation: Seed, in autumn
or spring; division, in spring

Common names: Slipper
flower; slipperwort
Height: 3in (8cm)
Spread: 18in (45cm)
Aspect: Sun or half shade
Soil: Sandy, acidic, fertile
Hardiness: Zone 9
Propagation: Seed, in autumn
or spring; division, in spring

Rhizomatous, dwarf evergreen from
Chile and Argentina. Leaves ovate,
toothed, green. Cymes of up to 6
yellow flowers, spotted red, in
summer. Good for an alpine house.

An evergreen, creeping perennial from
Chile. Leaves ovate, toothed, light
green. Three-flowered cymes of
pouched, yellow, red-spotted blooms,
in summer.

Caltha palustris
'Flore Pleno' A.G.M.
(Ranunculaceae)

Camassia leichtlinii
subsp. *leichtlinii* A.G.M.
(Hyacinthaceae/Liliaceae)

Common names: Kingcup;
marsh marigold
Height: 10in (25cm)
Spread: 10in (25cm)
Aspect: Full sun
Soil: Marginal aquatic
Hardiness: Zone 3
Propagation: Division,
in autumn or spring

Common name: Quamash
Height: 4ft (1.2m)
Spread: 4in (10cm)
Aspect: Sun or half shade
Soil: Moist, well-drained,
humus-rich
Hardiness: Zone 3
Propagation: Seed, when
ripe; offsets, in summer

Rhizomatous marginal plant for
temperate climates. Leaves kidney-
shaped, toothed, deep green. Flowers
in corymbs, yellow, waxy, fully
double.

Bulbous perennial from the western
U.S.A. Leaves linear, green. Flowers in
racemes, star-shaped, off-white, in late
spring. The flowering season is very
short.

***Camassia leichtlinii*
'Semiplena'
(Hyacinthaceae/Liliaceae)**

Common name: Quamash
Height: 4ft (1.2m)
Spread: 4in (10cm)
Aspect: Sun or half shade
Soil: Moist, well-drained,
humus-rich
Hardiness: Zone 3
Propagation: Offsets,
in summer

Semidouble, sterile form (so cannot be raised from seed). Flowers in dense racemes, star-shaped, cream; short season in spring. Bulbs become crowded very quickly.

Camassia quamash
(Hyacinthaceae/Liliaceae)

Common name: Quamash
Height: 36in (90cm)
Spread: 2in (5cm)
Aspect: Sun or half shade
Soil: Moist, well-drained,
humus-rich
Hardiness: Zone 5
Propagation: Seed, when
ripe; offsets, in summer

Edible, bulbous plant from North America. Leaves linear, green. Flowers starry, cup-shaped, blue, in racemes; short season in late spring. Can be naturalized in grass.

CAMPANULA (Campanulaceae)
Bellflower

This is a very large genus, containing some 300 species, including annuals and biennials as well as perennials. They are found in very diverse habitats in temperate southern Europe, Turkey, and Asia. The species therefore have differing cultivation requirements, but as a whole they are fairly undemanding, and will grow in sun or dappled shade if given a soil that is well-drained and fertile. There is a campanula to suit most situations in a garden, from wall plants to borders, as the habits vary from trailing or spreading to clump-forming or upright; the taller varieties of the latter may require staking. Campanula flowers also show a wide variety of shapes, from tubular and bell-shaped to star-shaped, and intermediates between these. The flowering season is long, from late spring through the summer. Some species are rampant and invasive, and to be avoided unless you have plenty of room for them to spread or are willing to confine them to a container. Species that fall into this category are *C. persicifolia*, *C. pulla*, and *C. takesimana*; *C. persicifolia* will also self-seed liberally around the garden unless it is deadheaded. The only other disadvantage is that they are prone to attack by slugs and snails.

Campanula barbata
(Campanulaceae)

Common name: Bearded
bellflower
Height: 12in (30cm)
Spread: 8in (20cm)
Aspect: Sun or half shade
Soil: Moist, well-drained
Hardiness: Zone 6
Propagation: Seed, in autumn

Campanula
'Burghaltii' AG.M.
(Campanulaceae)

Common name: Bellflower
Height: 2ft (60cm)
Spread: 1ft (30cm)
Aspect: Sun or half shade
Soil: Moist, well-drained,
alkaline, fertile
Hardiness: Zone 7
Propagation: Division,
in spring or autumn

Short-lived perennial from the Alps
and Norway. Leaves oblong, hairy,
toothed, green. Flowers in one-sided
racemes, pendent, blue, bell-shaped,
in late spring.

Hybrid between *C. punctata* and
C. latifolia. Basal leaves heart-shaped,
stem leaves ovate, green. Pendent,
tubular, lavender flowers, in racemes
in summer.

Campanula carpatica
A.G.M.
(Campanulaceae)

Common name:
Carpathian bellflower
Height: 8in (20cm)
Spread: 24in (60cm)
Aspect: Sun or half shade
Soil: Moist, well-drained
Hardiness: Zone 3
Propagation: Seed, in autumn

Campanula carpatica
'Blaue Clips'
(Campanulaceae)

Common name:
Carpathian bellflower
Height: 1ft (30cm)
Spread: 1ft (30cm)
Aspect: Sun or half shade
Soil: Moist, well-drained
Hardiness: Zone 3
Propagation: Division,
in spring or autumn

Clump-forming plant from the
Carpathians. Leaves basal, ovate,
toothed, green. Flowers solitary,
upturned, open bells, blue, white, or
violet, over a long period in summer.

Compact hybrid; comes almost true
from seed. Very free-flowering;
remontant if sheared after flowering.
Flowers light sky blue, in summer.
May need staking.

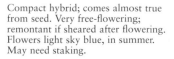

Campanula carpatica
'Weisse Clips'
(Campanulaceae)

Common name:
Carpathian bellflower
Height: 1ft (30cm)
Spread: 1ft (30cm)
Aspect: Sun or half shade
Soil: Moist, well-drained
Hardiness: Zone 3
Propagation: Division,
in spring or autumn

Campanula
cochleariifolia A.G.M.
(Campanulaceae)

Common names: None
Height: 4in (10cm)
Spread: 12in (30cm)
Aspect: Sun or half shade
Soil: Moist, well-drained
Hardiness: Zone 6
Propagation: Seed, in
autumn

Compact hybrid, with flowers of pure
white, over a long period; blooms
again if sheared over after first flush.
May need staking. Comes almost true
from seed.

Rhizomatous, rosette-forming,
miniature. Leaves round, toothed,
green. Flowers solitary, blue, pendent,
bells, in summer. Charming plant
from the Alps.

Campanula
'Elizabeth'
(Campanulaceae)

Common name: Bellflower
Height: 16in (40cm)
Spread: 16in (40cm)
Aspect: Sun or half shade
Soil: Moist, well-drained
Hardiness: Zone 7
Propagation: Division,
in spring or autumn

Campanula garganica
'Dickson's Gold'
(Campanulaceae)

Common name: Bellflower
Height: 2in (5cm)
Spread: 12in (30cm)
Aspect: Sun or half shade
Soil: Moist, well-drained
Hardiness: Zone 5
Propagation: Division,
in spring or autumn

A rhizomatous hybrid from *C.
takesimana*. Leaves in rosettes, heart-
shaped. Flowers in racemes, pendent
bells, reddish, cream inside; late
summer. Good ground cover.

Attractive *C. garganica* hybrid. Leaves
ovate to heart-shaped, toothed; the
yellow color is a striking contrast to
the blue of the upward-facing, starry
flowers.

Campanula glomerata 'Superba' A.G.M. (Campanulaceae)

Common name: Clustered bellflower
Height: 2ft (60cm)
Spread: Indefinite
Aspect: Sun or half shade
Soil: Moist, well-drained, alkaline
Hardiness: Zone 2
Propagation: Seed, in spring

Leaves ovate to lance-shaped, toothed, deep green. Flowers in dense racemes, tubular, violet-purple. Flowers again if sheared after first flush. From Europe and Asia.

Campanula glomerata var. *alba* (Campanulaceae)

Common names: Clustered bellflower
Height: 2ft (60cm)
Spread: Indefinite
Aspect: Sun or half shade
Soil: Moist, well-drained, alkaline
Hardiness: Zone 2
Propagation: Division, in spring or autumn

Pure white sport of a purplish-flowered species. Leaves ovate to lance-shaped, round-toothed. May need staking. Will flower twice if sheared after first flush.

Campanula 'Kent Belle' (Campanulaceae)

Common name: Canterbury bells
Height: 30in (75cm)
Spread: 12in (30cm)
Aspect: Sun or half shade
Soil: Moist, well-drained
Hardiness: Zone 3
Propagation: Division, in spring or autumn

This very handsome hybrid is a recent introduction. Tall stems bear large, silky, shining bells, deep violet in color. Leaves ovate, toothed, green.

Campanula lactiflora 'Loddon Anna' A.G.M. (Campanulaceae)

Common name: Milky bellflower
Height: 3ft (90cm)
Spread: 2ft (60cm)
Aspect: Sun or half shade
Soil: Moist, well-drained, alkaline, fertile
Hardiness: Zone 5
Propagation: Division, in spring or autumn

Cloned cultivar of an undemanding species. Leaves ovate, toothed, green. Flowers lilac-pink bells in conical panicles, early summer to autumn. Flowers twice if deadheaded.

Campanula lactiflora 'Pritchard's Variety.' A.G.M. (Campanulaceae)

Common name: Milky bellflower
Height: 30in (75cm)
Spread: 24in (60cm)
Aspect: Sun or half shade
Soil: Moist, well-drained, alkaline, fertile
Hardiness: Zone 5
Propagation: Division, in spring or autumn

Handsome cloned cultivar. Flowers deep purple, over a long period, early summer to early autumn. Flowers twice if deadheaded. Needs staking, but grows virtually anywhere.

Campanula latifolia 'Alba' (Campanulaceae)

Common name: Great bellflower
Height: 4ft (1.2m)
Spread: 2ft (60cm)
Aspect: Sun or half shade
Soil: Moist, well-drained, alkaline, fertile
Hardiness: Zone 3
Propagation: Seed, in spring; division, in spring or autumn

Vigorous perennial. Basal leaves toothed, ovate-oblong, rough-surfaced, green; stem leaves similar, pointed. Flowers in spiky racemes, open, tubular, white, in summer.

Campanula latiloba 'Hidcote Amethyst' A.G.M. (Campanulaceae)

Common name: Bellflower
Height: 36in (90cm)
Spread: 18in (45cm)
Aspect: Sun or half shade
Soil: Moist, well-drained, alkaline, fertile
Hardiness: Zone 3
Propagation: Division, in spring or autumn

Handsome clone of a species from Turkey. Leaves basal, lance-shaped, toothed, green. Flowers cup-shaped, pale amethyst, shaded purple, in racemes, in mid- and late summer.

Campanula persicifolia 'Alba' (Campanulaceae)

Common name: Peach-leaved bellflower
Height: 36in (90cm)
Spread: 18in (45cm)
Aspect: Sun or half shade
Soil: Moist, well-drained, alkaline, fertile
Hardiness: Zone 3
Propagation: Seed, in spring; division, in spring or autumn

Evergreen (rare in campanulas), rhizomatous plant. Rosettes of basal, narrow, toothed, green leaves. Racemes of cup-shaped, pure white flowers in early and midsummer.

Campanula persicifolia
'Chettle Charm'
(Campanulaceae)

Common name: Peach-
leaved bellflower
Height: 3ft (90cm)
Spread: 1ft (30cm)
Aspect: Sun or half shade
Soil: Moist, well-drained,
alkaline, fertile
Hardiness: Zone 3
Propagation: Division,
in spring or autumn

Cloned cultivar of rhizomatous,
unusual evergreen species. Leaves
lance-shaped to oblong-ovate,
toothed. Racemes of creamy-white
flowers, tinted blue, in summer.

Campanula persicifolia
'Telham Beauty'
(Campanulaceae)

Common name: Peach-
leaved bellflower
Height: 3ft (90cm)
Spread: 1ft (30cm)
Aspect: Sun or half shade
Soil: Moist, well-drained,
alkaline, fertile
Hardiness: Zone 3
Propagation: Division, spring
or autumn

Cloned cultivar; rhizomatous,
evergreen. Leaves basal, toothed,
lance-shaped to oblong-obovate.
Flowers very large, blue, in summer
and again in autumn.

Campanula pulla
(Campanulaceae)

Common name: Bellflower
Height: 8in (20cm)
Spread: 12in (30cm)
Aspect: Sun or half shade
Soil: Moist, well-drained
Hardiness: Zone 6
Propagation: Seed in
autumn

An invasive perennial from the Alps.
Leaves in basal rosettes, spoon-
shaped, toothed, green, shiny. Flowers
solitary, bell-shaped, pendent, deep
purple, in spring to summer.

Campanula pyramidalis
(Campanulaceae)

Common name: Chimney
bellflower
Height: To 6ft (3m)
Spread: 2ft (60cm)
Aspect: Sun or half shade
Soil: Moist, well-drained,
alkaline, fertile
Hardiness: Zone 8
Propagation: Seed, in spring;
division, spring or autumn

A short-lived perennial often treated
as a biennial. Leaves in rosettes,
ovate, toothed, green. Flowers in
racemes, cup-shaped, fragrant, blue,
from late spring to summer.

Campanula rotundifolia
(Campanulaceae)

Common names: Harebell;
Scottish bluebell
Height: 1ft (30cm)
Spread: 1ft (30cm)
Aspect: Sun or half shade
Soil: Moist, well-drained
Hardiness: Zone 3
Propagation: Seed in spring

Spreads by underground runners.
Leaves basal, round, toothed, green.
Flowers fragrant, cup-shaped, pale
blue or white,
in racemes in late spring to summer.

Campanula takesimana
(Campanulaceae)

Common names: None
Height: 32in (80cm)
Spread: Indefinite
Aspect: Sun or half shade
Soil: Well-drained
Hardiness: Zone 7
Propagation: Seed, in
spring; division, in spring
or autumn

Highly invasive rhizomatous species.
Leaves glossy, heart-shaped, green.
Flowers in arching sprays, off-white,
flushed pink or brown, pendent, bell-
shaped, in summer.

Campanula trachelium
(Campanulaceae)

Common name: Coventry-
bells
Height: 3ft (90cm)
Spread: 1ft (30cm)
Aspect: Sun or half shade
Soil: Well-drained,
alkaline, fertile
Hardiness: Zone 3
Propagation: Seed, in spring;
division, in spring or autumn

Woody-based Mediterranean species.
Leaves nettlelike, ovate, toothed, midgreen. Flowers tubular, blue or white,
in short racemes in mid- to late
summer.

Canna indica
(Cannaceae)

Common name: Indian
shot
Height: To 6ft (2m)
Spread: 2ft (60cm)
Aspect: Sun
Soil: Well-drained, fertile,
humus-rich
Hardiness: Zone 8
Propagation: Seed, in warmth
in spring; division, in spring

Rhizomatous South American plant.
Leaves broad, elliptic, large, bronze-
green. Flowers in racemes to panicles,
irislike, orange or red, summer to
autumn; best deadheaded.

Canna
'King Midas'
(Cannaceae)

Common names: None
Height: 5ft (1.5m)
Spread: 2ft (60cm)
Aspect: Sun
Soil: Well-drained, fertile, humus-rich
Hardiness: Zone 8
Propagation: Division, in spring

Rhizomatous hybrid of complex origin. Leaves, large, broad, dark green. Flowers in raceme, gladiolus-like, yellow with orange markings, midsummer to early autumn.

Canna
'Striata'
(Cannaceae)

Common names: None
Height: 5ft (1.5m)
Spread: 20in (50cm)
Aspect: Sun
Soil: Well-drained, fertile, humus-rich
Hardiness: Zone 8
Propagation: Division, in spring

Handsome perennial of uncertain origins. Leaves large, broad, pale green with bright yellow veins. Flowers gladioluslike, orange, in racemes, midsummer to early autumn.

Cardamine pentaphyllos
(Brassicaceae/Cruciferae)

Common name: Bittercress
Height: 2ft (60cm)
Spread: 1ft (30cm)
Aspect: Half or full shade
Soil: Moist, humus-rich
Hardiness: Zone 6
Propagation: Seed or division, both in spring

Clump-forming, rhizomatous perennial. Leaves 5-palmate, leaflets green, toothed, lance-shaped. Flowers in lax racemes, pink, white, or lilac, late spring and early summer.

Cardamine pratensis
'Flore Pleno' A.G.M.
(Brassicaceae/Cruciferae)

Common name: Cuckoo bittercress
Height: 8in (20cm)
Spread: 12in (30cm)
Aspect: Half or full shade
Soil: Moist, humus-rich
Hardiness: Zone 4
Propagation: Seed, in autumn or spring; division, in spring

Rhizomatous perennial. Leaves in rosettes, pinnate; leaflets ovate-round, deep green, glossy. Flowers in panicles, lilac-pink, double. Produces plantlets in leaf clusters.

Cardiocrinum giganteum
A.G.M.
(Liliaceae)

Common name: Giant-lily
Height: To 12ft (4m)
Spread: 18in (45cm)
Aspect: Half shade
Soil: Moist, well-drained,
humus-rich
Hardiness: Zone 7
Propagation: Seed, when ripe;
offsets, after flowering

Bulbous perennial, forming rosettes of
large, broad, ovate, glossy leaves.
Flowers large, trumpet-shaped,
nodding, perfumed, white, in racemes
of up to 20 in summer.

Carex comans
(Cyperaceae)

Common name: Sedge
Height: 16in (40cm)
Spread: 30in (75cm)
Aspect: Sun or half shade
Soil: Moist; dislikes
extreme wet or dry
conditions
Hardiness: Zone 7
Propagation: Seed, in warmth in
spring; division, in early summer

An evergreen, rhizomatous, tufted
sedge from New Zealand. Leaves 10in
(25cm) long, arching, red-brown.
Flowers, in summer, are
inconspicuous.

CAREX (Cyperaceae)
Sedge

This is an extremely large genus, containing some 1,500 or
more rhizomatous or tufted species, most of which are
evergreen, but some of which are herbaceous. Sedges are found
naturally in a very wide range of habitats, and spread all over
the world, so it is impossible to generalize about their cultural
requirements as a genus; this also means that it is possible to
find a sedge to suit every situation in every garden. They are
generally hardy, but there are a few that are not. Large numbers
of species and selections are in cultivation; however, many of
these have little or no garden value. Out of all of them, two
cultivars alone, *C. elata* 'Aurea' and *C. oshimensis* 'Evergold'
(Zone 7); have achieved an Award of Garden Merit. For the
most part, sedges are grown for their foliage, which is linear
and grasslike, and may be flushed yellow or variegated. Flowers
are grasslike, mostly in shades of brown and often
inconspicuous, but a few sedges do also have attractive
inflorescences. They are carried in panicles, generally short and
spiked, sometimes longer or drooping, as in *C. pendula*.
Without exception, sedges should be avoided by anyone who is
seeking to create a low-allergen garden.

Carex elata 'Aurea' A.G.M. (Cyperaceae)

Common name: Tufted sedge
Height: 28in (70cm)
Spread: 18in (45cm)
Aspect: Sun or half shade
Soil: Moist to wet
Hardiness: Zone 7
Propagation: Division, in late spring

Deciduous, rhizomatous species. Leaves to 24in (60cm), golden-yellow, green-edged. Insignificant flowers in spring to summer; males are tall, above leaves, females shorter.

Carex pendula (Cyperaceae)

Common names: Drooping, pendulous, or weeping sedge
Height: 5ft (1.5m)
Spread: 5ft (1.5m)
Aspect: Sun or half shade
Soil: Moist to wet, fertile
Hardiness: Zone 8
Propagation: Division, in late spring

Evergreen, tufted sedge. Leaves 3ft (90cm), keeled, shiny, green, blue-green beneath. Flowers in catkinlike cylinders, dark brown, spring to summer. Stems upright or arching.

Carex testacea (Cyperaceae)

Common names: None
Height: 5ft (1.5m)
Spread: 5ft (1.5m)
Aspect: Sun or half shade
Soil: Moist; dislikes extreme wet or dry conditions
Hardiness: Zone 7
Propagation: Seed, in warmth in spring

Tufted evergreen species. Leaves arching, 2ft (60cm), pale green, orange-brown in full sun. Flower spikes brown, cylindrical, 2ft (60cm), in summer; seed heads longer.

Carlina acaulis (Asteraceae/Compositae)

Common name: Smooth carlina
Height: 4in (10cm)
Spread: 10in (25cm)
Aspect: Sun
Soil: Very well-drained, poor
Hardiness: Zone 4
Propagation: Seed in autumn

Short-lived perennial from the Alps. Leaves in rosettes, pinnatisect, oblong, spiny. Flowers stemless, spiky, silvery, off-white bracts around a brown disc in summer.

Catananche caerulea 'Major' A.G.M. (Asteraceae/Compositae)

Common name: Blue
Cupid's-dart
Height: 3ft (90cm)
Spread: 1ft (30cm)
Aspect: Full sun
Soil: Well-drained
Hardiness: Zone 7
Propagation: Seed or
division, both in spring

Handsome cultivar of a plant from
S.W. Europe. Leaves linear, grassy,
hairy, gray-green. Flowers solitary,
dark-centered, lilac-blue, surrounded
by bracts to match.

Catananche caerulea 'Alba' (Asteraceae/Compositae)

Common name: White
Cupid's-dart
Height: 3ft (90cm)
Spread: 1ft (30cm)
Aspect: Full sun
Soil: Well-drained
Hardiness: Zone 7
Propagation: Seed or
division, both in spring

White cultivar, often treated as a
biennial. Solitary flowers have lilac-
blue centers, pure white ray florets
and bracts. Linear, grassy, hairy leaves
are gray-green.

Cautleya gracilis (Zingiberaceae)

Common names: None
Height: 18in (45cm)
Spread: 10in (25cm)
Aspect: Half shade
Soil: Moist, humus-rich
Hardiness: Zone 8
Propagation: Seed, in
warmth in spring;
division, in spring

Woodlander; plant rhizomes 6in
(15cm) deep. Leaves broad, lance-
shaped, glossy, green, reddish-gray
beneath. Flowers yellow, bracts red-
brown, in spikes in late summer.

Cautleya spicata (Zingiberaceae)

Common names: None
Height: 24in (60cm)
Spread: 18in (45cm)
Aspect: Half shade
Soil: Moist, humus-rich
Hardiness: Zone 8
Propagation: Seed, in
warmth in spring;
division, in spring

Rhizomatous Himalayan species.
Leaves broad, lance-shaped, shiny,
midgreen. Flowers yellow, two-lipped,
with orange bracts, in stiff spikes in
late summer.

107

Cedronella canariensis
(Labiatae/Lamiaceae)

Common names: None
Height: 3ft (1m)
Spread: 2ft (60cm)
Aspect: Full sun
Soil: Well-drained, fertile
Hardiness: Zone 9
Propagation: Seed, in
warmth in spring; softwood
cuttings, in spring

Short-lived plant from the Canary
Islands. Leaves aromatic, 3-palmate,
green, used in herb teas and potpourri.
Two-lipped, pink, white, or lilac
flowers, in whorls in summer.

Celmisia coriacea
(Asteraceae/Compositae)

Common name: New
Zealand daisy
Height: 24in (60cm)
Spread: 18in (30cm)
Aspect: Sun or half shade
Soil: Moist, well-drained,
humus-rich
Hardiness: Zone 7
Propagation: Seed, when ripe;
division, in spring

Rhizomatous evergreen; tricky in dry,
warm areas. Leaves lance-shaped,
gray-green, silky, hairy. Flowers late
spring to summer, solitary; ray florets
white, disc yellow.

Celmisia hookeri
(Asteraceae/Compositae)

Common name: New
Zealand daisy
Height: 1ft (30cm)
Spread: 2ft (60cm)
Aspect: Sun or half shade
Soil: Moist, well-drained,
acidic, humus-rich
Hardiness: Zone 7
Propagation: Seed, when ripe;
division, in spring

Tufted evergreen from New Zealand.
Good seaside plant; not for hot, dry
areas. Leaves broad, oblong, glossy,
deep green, felty white beneath.
Solitary flowers; white, yellow disc.

Celmisia spectabilis
(Asteraceae/Compositae)

Common name: New
Zealand daisy
Height: 1ft (30cm)
Spread: 1ft (30cm)
Aspect: Sun or half shade
Soil: Moist, well-drained,
acidic, humus-rich
Hardiness: Zone 7
Propagation: Seed, when ripe;
division, in spring

Clump-forming, rhizomatous
evergreen, not for hot, dry sites. Leaves
glossy, silvery green above, felty white
beneath, oblong. Flowers solitary, ray
florets white, disc florets yellow.

Centaurea bella
(Asteraceae/Compositae)

Common name:
Knapweed
Height: 12in (30cm)
Spread: 18in (45cm)
Aspect: Sun
Soil: Well-drained
Hardiness: Zone 6
Propagation: Seed, in spring;
division, in spring or autumn

Clump-forming plant from the
Caucasus. Leaves obovate, pinnatifid,
feathery, green, hairy beneath.
Flowers solitary, florets lobed, purple-
pink, in summer.

Centaurea dealbata
'Steenbergii'
(Asteraceae/Compositae)

Common name: Persian
centaurea
Height: 2ft (60cm)
Spread: 2ft (60cm)
Aspect: Sun
Soil: Well-drained
Hardiness: Zone 3
Propagation: Seed, in spring;
division, in spring or autumn

Undemanding, clump-forming
perennial from the Caucasus. Leaves
obovate, pinnatisect, green, with gray-
green undersides. Flowers pink, in
midsummer.

Centaurea hypoleuca
'John Coutts'
(Asteraceae/Compositae)

Common name:
Knapweed
Height: 24in (60cm)
Spread: 18in (45cm)
Aspect: Sun
Soil: Well-drained
Hardiness: Zone 5
Propagation: Seed, in spring;
division, in spring or autumn

Cultivar of a species from the
Caucasus. Leaves lance-shaped,
pinnatifid, wavy-edged, green, white
beneath. Flowers rose-pink, solitary,
fragrant, long-lasting, in summer.

Centaurea macrocephala
(Asteraceae/Compositae)

Common name: Globe
centaurea
Height: 6ft (1.5m)
Spread: 2ft (60cm)
Aspect: Sun
Soil: Well-drained
Hardiness: Zone 3
Propagation: Seed, in spring;
division, in spring or autumn

Vigorous perennial from the Caucasus
and Turkey. Leaves green, broad,
lance-shaped, pinnatifid. Flowers
large, yellow, with a basal support of
brown, papery bracts.

Centaurea montana
(Asteraceae/Compositae)

Common name: Mountain
bluet
Height: 18in (45cm)
Spread: 24in (60cm)
Aspect: Sun
Soil: Well-drained
Hardiness: Zone 3
Propagation: Seed, in spring;
division, in spring or autumn

Rhizomatous perennial. Leaves ovate,
green, woolly beneath. Widely spaced
florets give red-violet flowers a lacy
look. Deadhead for more flowers and
to prevent self-seeding.

Centaurea montana alba
(Asteraceae/Compositae)

Common name: White
mountain bluet
Height: 18in (45cm)
Spread: 24in (60cm)
Aspect: Sun
Soil: Well-drained
Hardiness: Zone 3
Propagation: Seed, in spring;
division, in spring or autumn

Rhizomatous perennial. Leaves lance-
shaped to ovate, pinnatifid, green,
woolly beneath. Flowers solitary,
white, lacy. Deadhead for more
flowers and to prevent self-seeding.

Centaurium erythraea
(Gentianaceae)

Common name: Common
centaury
Height: 4in (10cm)
Spread: 2in (5cm)
Aspect: Sun or half shade
Soil: Moist, well-drained
Hardiness: Zone 8
Propagation: Seed, when ripe;
division, in spring

Short-lived perennial from Europe
and Weste Asia. Leaves basal,
obovate, gray-green, prominently
veined. Flowers in flat-topped cymes,
pink, in summer.

Centranthus ruber
(Valerianaceae)

Common name: Red
valerian
Height: 3ft (1m)
Spread: 3ft (1m)
Aspect: Sun
Soil: Well-drained, poor,
alkaline
Hardiness: Zone 7
Propagation: Seed, in spring

Woody, much-branched perennial.
Leaves fleshy, glaucous, ovate to
lance-shaped. Dense cymes, of small,
pink or red, fragrant flowers all
summer; cut back after flowering.

Centranthus ruber 'Albus' (Valerianaceae)

Common name: Red valerian
Height: 3ft (1m)
Spread: 3ft (1m)
Aspect: Sun
Soil: Well-drained, poor, alkaline
Hardiness: Zone 7
Propagation: Seed, in spring

Woody, branching plant. Leaves ovate to lance-shaped, fleshy, green, glaucous. White, fragrant, in dense cymes. Cut after flowering for more flowers and to prevent self-seeding.

Cephalaria gigantea (Dipsacaceae)

Common name: Tatarian cephalaria
Height: 6ft (2m)
Spread: 32in (80cm)
Aspect: Sun or half shade
Soil: Moist, well-drained, fertile
Hardiness: Zone 6
Propagation: Seed or division, both in spring

Clump-forming perennial. Leaves toothed, pinnatifid-pinnatisect, lobes oblong, toothed, green. Flowers on branching stems, solitary, scabiouslike, primrose, in summer.

Cerastium tomentosum (Caryophyllaceae)

Common name: Snow-in-summer
Height: 3in (8cm)
Spread: Indefinite
Aspect: Sun
Soil: Well-drained
Hardiness: Zone 4
Propagation: Seed, in autumn; division, in spring

Rampant, invasive perennial from Italy and Sicily. Leaves lance-shaped to linear, white-woolly. Flowers star-shaped, white, in cymes, all summer. Superb wall plant.

Chaerophyllum hirsutum 'Roseum' (Apiaceae/Umbelliferae)

Common names: None
Height: 24in (60cm)
Spread: 18in (30cm)
Aspect: Sun or half shade
Soil: Moist, fertile
Hardiness: Zone 6
Propagation: Seed, when ripe

Tap-rooted perennial. Leaves aromatic, 2- or 3-pinnate; lobes ovate, toothed. Pink flowers in compound umbels, late spring to early summer. Flowers again if deadheaded.

111

Chamaemelum nobile 'Flore Pleno' (Asteraceae/Compositae)

Common name: Double Roman camomile
Height: 12in (30cm)
Spread: 18in (45cm)
Aspect: Sun
Soil: Sandy, well-drained
Hardiness: Zone 4
Propagation: Seed, *in situ* in spring

Mat-forming, aromatic herb. Leaves fresh green, pinnate, feathery. Flowers double, ray florets cream, disc florets yellow, in summer. Highly allergenic, skin irritant.

Chelidonium majus (Papaveraceae)

Common name: Greater celandine
Height: 24in (60cm)
Spread: 8in (20cm)
Aspect: Any, but best in half shade
Soil: Any
Hardiness: Zone 6
Propagation: Seed in spring

Clump-forming, woodland plant. Leaves lobed-pinnatisect, scalloped, green. Small, yellow, 4-petalled flowers in umbels, in summer. Highly allergenic and skin irritant.

Chelidonium majus 'Flore Pleno' (Papaveraceae)

Common name: Double greater celandine
Height: 24in (60cm)
Spread: 8in (20cm)
Aspect: Any
Soil: Any
Hardiness: Zone 6
Propagation: Seed, in spring

Cultivar with double flowers, larger than in the species. Leaves green, lobed-pinnatisect, scalloped. Will grow anywhere, self-seeds freely. Skin irritant and very allergenic.

Chelone glabra (Scrophulariaceae)

Common name: White turtle-head
Height: 3ft (1m)
Spread: 18in (45cm)
Aspect: Sun or half shade
Soil: Moist, fertile, deep
Hardiness: Zone 3
Propagation: Seed or division, both in spring

Sturdy perennial from the U.S.A. Leaves ovate to lance-shaped, green. White flowers, tinged pink, 2-lipped, very weather-resistant, in dense terminal racemes in autumn.

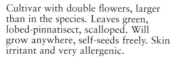

Chelone obliqua
(Scrophulariaceae)

Common name: Rose
turtle-head
Height: 2ft (60cm)
Spread: 1ft (30cm)
Aspect: Sun or half shade
Soil: Moist, fertile, deep
Hardiness: Zone 3
Propagation: Seed or division,
both in spring

Erect, sturdy plant from the U.S.A.
Leaves lance-shaped to elliptic,
toothed, green, boldly veined. Flowers
in terminal racemes, deep pink,
resembling turtle heads, autumn.

Chiastophyllum
oppositifolium A.G.M.
(Crassulaceae)

Common names: None
Height: 8in (20cm)
Spread: 6in (15cm)
Aspect: Half shade
Soil: Moist, well-drained
Hardiness: Zone 7
Propagation: Seed, in
autumn; cuttings, in summer

Rhizomatous, mat-forming evergreen.
Leaves ovate-round, wavy-edged,
fleshy, green. Arching, branched
racemes of bell-shaped yellow flowers,
spring to summer.

Chrysanthemum weyrichii
(Asteraceae/Compositae)

Common names: None
Height: 12in (30cm)
Spread: 18in (45cm)
Aspect: Sun
Soil: Moist, well-drained,
fertile
Hardiness: Zone 4
Propagation: Seed, in autumn;
division, in spring
or autumn

Rhizomatous, mat-forming perennial
from Russia. Leaves aromatic, 5-
lobed, round, green. Flowers
daisylike, ray florets pink and disc
florets yellow, in autumn.

Chrysanthemum yezoense
A.G.M.
(Asteraceae/Compositae)

Common names: None
Height: 12in (30cm)
Spread: 18in (45cm)
Aspect: Sun
Soil: Moist, well-drained
Hardiness: Zone 3
Propagation: Seed, in
autumn; division in spring
or autumn

Perennial from Japan. Leaves fleshy,
ovate, pinnate, lobes oblong. Flowers
single, ray florets white, disc florets
yellow, weather-resistant, in branching
sprays, in autumn.

Chrysogonum virginianum
(Asteraceae/Compositae)

Common name: Golden star
Height: 10in (25cm)
Spread: 10in (25cm)
Aspect: Sun or half shade
Soil: Moist, well-drained, humus-rich
Hardiness: Zone 5
Propagation: Seed, when ripe; division, in spring or autumn

Rhizomatous, evergreen woodland ground cover. Leaves ovate, hairy, green. Flowers solitary, star-shaped, 5-petalled, yellow, from early spring to late summer.

Cicerbita plumieri
(Asteraceae/Compositae)

Common names: None
Height: 4ft (1.2m)
Spread: 18in (45cm)
Aspect: Sun or half shade
Soil: Moist, acidic, fertile, humus-rich
Hardiness: Zone 5
Propagation: Seed or division, both in spring

Perennial from N. Europe. Leaves basal, green, pinnatifid-pinnatisect. Flowers in erect panicles, florets strap-shaped, lilac, from summer to early autumn.

Cichorium intybus
A.G.M.
(Asteraceae/Compositae)

Common name: Chicory
Height: 4ft (1.2m)
Spread: 2ft (60cm)
Aspect: Sun
Soil: Well-drained, fertile
Hardiness: Zone 3
Propagation: Seed, in autumn or spring

Clump-forming, taprooted, culinary herb. Leaves basal, inverse lance-shaped, toothed, green. Flowers on branched stems, florets strap-shaped, blue, closed by midday.

Cimicifuga racemosa
A.G.M.
(Ranunculaceae)

Common names: Cohash bugbane; snakeroot
Height: 6ft (2m)
Spread: 2ft (60cm)
Aspect: Half shade
Soil: Moist, fertile, humus-rich
Hardiness: Zone 4
Propagation: Seed, when ripe; division, in spring

Clump-forming perennial. Leaves basal, green, 2- or 3-ternate; lobes oblong, toothed. Racemes, sometimes arched, of offensive-smelling white flowers, in summer.

Cimicifuga simplex
(**Ranunculaceae**)

Common name: Bugbane
Height: 4ft (1.2m)
Spread: 2ft (60cm)
Aspect: Half shade
Soil: Moist, well-drained,
fertile
Hardiness: Zone 5
Propagation: Seed, when ripe;
division, in spring

Clump-forming woodlander. Leaves
basal, 3-ternate; leaflets ovate,
purplish-green. Malodorous white
flowers in bottle-brush racemes white,
in autumn. No staking.

Cimicifuga simplex
var. *simplex* 'Atropurpurea'
(**Ranunculaceae**)

Common name: Bugbane
Height: 4ft (1.2m)
Spread: 2ft (60cm)
Aspect: Half shade
Soil: Moist, well-drained,
fertile
Hardiness: Zone 5
Propagation: Seed, when ripe;
division, in spring

Cloned form with purple foliage, stems,
and buds. Leaves basal, 3-ternate;
leaflets ovate. White, malodorous
flowers in bottle-brush racemes in
autumn. No staking needed.

Cirsium rivulare
'Atropurpureum'
(**Asteraceae/Compositae**)

Common name: Plume
thistle
Height: 4ft (1.2m)
Spread: 2ft (60cm)
Aspect: Sun
Soil: Moist, well-drained
Hardiness: Zone 5
Propagation: Seed or division,
both in spring

Leaves prickly, green, elliptic to lance-
shaped, entire-pinnatifid. Flowers on
erect stems, spherical, crimson-purple,
early and midsummer. Deadhead to
stop self-seeding.

Cirsium spinosissimum
(**Asteraceae/Compositae**)

Common names: None
Height: 4ft (1.2m)
Spread: 28in (70cm)
Aspect: Sun
Soil: Moist, sandy, humus-
rich
Hardiness: Zone 5
Propagation: Seed or division,
both in spring

Alpine species. Leaves whitish-green,
oblong to lance-shaped, pinnatifid;
lobes ovate, spiny. Flowerheads
cream-white, backed by narrow,
prickly bracts, mid- to late summer.

Claytonia megarhiza
(Portulacaceae)

Claytonia virginica
(Portulacaceae)

Common name: Spring
beauty
Height: 2in (5cm)
Spread: 6in (15cm)
Aspect: Sun
Soil: Well-drained, sandy,
humus-rich
Hardiness: Zone 4
Propagation: Seed, in autumn

Common name: Virginia
spring beauty
Height: 12in (30cm)
Spread: 8in (20cm)
Aspect: Half shade
Soil: Well-drained, sandy,
humus-rich
Hardiness: Zone 6
Propagation: Seed, in autumn

Short-lived, tap-rooted evergreen from
the Rocky Mountains. Leaves fleshy,
spoon-shaped, deep green. Flowers
cup-shaped, white, in racemes on
short stems in spring.

Cormous perennial from eastern
North America. Leaves basal, linear,
fleshy, green. Small flowers in
racemes, pink with red veins, in
spring.

Clematis × eriostemon
'Hendersonii'
(Ranunculaceae)

Clematis heracleifolia
(Ranunculaceae)

Common names: None
Height: To 15ft (5m)
Spread: 3ft (1m)
Aspect: Sun or half shade
Soil: Well-drained, fertile,
humus-rich
Hardiness: Zone 4
Propagation: Division,
in spring

Common name: Tube
clematis
Height: 3ft (90cm)
Spread: 4ft (1.2m)
Aspect: Sun
Soil: Well-drained, fertile,
humus-rich
Hardiness: Zone 3
Propagation: Division,
in spring

Hybrid herbaceous clematis; suits a
mixed border. Flowers solitary, bell-
shaped, blue, tinted indigo, with
recurved tips and cream anthers. Only
for the large garden.

Herbaceous clematis from China.
Leaves 3-lobed, toothed, green.
Flowers scented, in racemes, blue, in
summer, followed by good seed heads.
Not for the small garden.

Clematis heracleifolia var. *davidiana* (Ranunculaceae)

Common name: Tube clematis
Height: 3ft (90cm)
Spread: 4ft (1.2m)
Aspect: Sun
Soil: Well-drained, fertile, humus-rich
Hardiness: Zone 3
Propagation: Division, in spring

A form of this late, large-flowered species with rich blue flowers. The sepals are more spreading and less reflexed than in the species, giving a more substantial flower.

Clematis integrifolia (Ranunculaceae)

Common name: Solitary clematis
Height: 2ft (60cm)
Spread: 5ft (1.5m)
Aspect: Sun
Soil: Well-drained, fertile, humus-rich
Hardiness: Zone 3
Propagation: Division in spring

Herbaceous clematis from C. Europe. Leaves inversely lance-shaped to elliptic, downy. Flowers solitary, midblue bells, in summer, followed by silvery seed heads.

Clematis integrifolia 'Rosea' A.G.M. (Ranunculaceae)

Common name: Solitary clematis
Height: 2ft (60cm)
Spread: 3ft (1m)
Aspect: Sun
Soil: Well-drained, fertile, humus-rich
Hardiness: Zone 3
Propagation: Division, in spring

Cloned cultivar with perfumed, sugar-pink flowers with darker undersides, in summer. Leaves inversely lance-shaped to elliptic, downy. Suitable for the small garden.

Clintonia umbellulata (Convallariaceae/Liliaceae)

Common name: Speckled wood-lily
Height: 12in (30cm)
Spread: 6in (15cm)
Aspect: Half or full shade
Soil: Acid, moist, fertile, humus-rich
Hardiness: Zone 4
Propagation: Seed or division, both in autumn

Rhizomatous, hardy perennial. Bright green, glossy, oblong-oblanceolate leaves. White flowers, spotted green and purple, in dense umbels, late spring to summer. Seeds black.

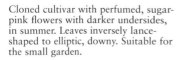

Clivia nobilis
(Amaryllidaceae)

Common name: Green-tip
kafir-lily
Height 16in (40cm)
Spread: 12in (30cm)
Aspect: Half shade
Soil: Well-drained, fertile,
humus-rich
Hardiness: Zone 10
Propagation: Seed, in warmth when
ripe; division, in winter or spring

Bulbous evergreen from South Africa.
Strap-shaped, basal, bright green
leaves. Flowers narrow trumpets,
scarlet with green mouths, in pendent
umbels, spring and summer.

Codonopsis clematidea
(Campanulaceae)

Common name: Clematis
Asia-bell
Height: 2ft (60cm)
Spread: 2ft (60cm)
Aspect: Sun or half shade
Soil: Moist, well-drained,
humus-rich
Hardiness: Zone 4
Propagation: Seed, in autumn
or spring

Branched, scrambling plant from
C. Asia. Leaves ovate-acuminate.
Flowers solitary, nodding, bell-shaped,
pale blue; beautiful black, yellow, and
blue marks inside.

Colchicum autumnale
(Colchicaceae/Liliaceae)

Common names: Autumn
crocus; meadow saffron
Height: 6in (15cm)
Spread: 3in (8cm)
Aspect: Sun
Soil: Well-drained, fertile,
humus-rich
Hardiness: Zone 5
Propagation: Offsets, in summer

European species of cormous
perennial. Flowers lavender-pink
goblets, in autumn, before erect,
lance-shaped, green leaves. All parts
are poisonous and irritate skin.

Colchicum bivonae
(Colchicaceae/Liliaceae)

Common names: Autumn
crocus; meadow saffron
Height: 6in (15cm)
Spread: 4in (10cm)
Aspect: Sun
Soil: Well-drained, fertile,
humus-rich
Hardiness: Zone 6
Propagation: Seed, when ripe;
offsets, in summer

Cormous perennial from Italy and
Turkey. Flowers perfumed, tasselated,
purplish-pink goblets with cream
centers, before strap-shaped leaves,
autumn. All parts poisonous.

Colchicum byzantinum
A.G.M.
(Colchicaceae/Liliaceae)

Common name: Byzantine
autumn crocus
Height: 5in (12cm)
Spread: 4in (10cm)
Aspect: Sun
Soil: Well-drained, fertile,
humus-rich
Hardiness: Zone 6
Propagation: Seed, when ripe;
offsets, in summer

Vigorous, probably hybrid, cormous
plant. Flowers open funnels, lilac, in
autumn, before elliptic to lance-
shaped, ribbed leaves. All parts
poisonous and irritant.

Commelina coelestis
(Commelinaceae)

Common name: Mexican
dayflower
Height: 36in (90cm)
Spread: 18in (45cm)
Aspect: Sun or half shade
Soil: Well-drained, fertile
Hardiness: Zone 8
Propagation: Seed, in warmth in
spring; division, in spring

Clump-forming, erect tuberous plant
from Central and South America.
Leaves lance-shaped to oblong,
midgreen. Flowers in cymes, vivid
blue, late summer to autumn.

Convallaria majalis
A.G.M.
(Convallariaceae/Liliaceae)

Common name: Lily-of-
the-valley
Height: 10in (25cm)
Spread: 18in (45cm)
Aspect: Half or full shade
Soil: Moist, fertile,
humus-rich
Hardiness: Zone 3
Propagation: Flesh-free seeds, when
ripe; division, in autumn

Rhizomatous, woodland ground
cover. Leaves basal, elliptic, smooth,
midgreen. Arching racemes of
perfumed, spherical, white bells, late
spring. Seeds mildly toxic.

Convolvulus althaeoides
subsp. *tenuissimus*
(Convolvulaceae)

Common name: Bindweed
Height: 6in (15cm)
Spread: Indefinite
Aspect: Sun
Soil: Well-drained, sandy
Hardiness: Zone 8
Propagation: Seed, in
warmth in spring

Invasive, trailing or climbing perennial
from S. Europe. Leaves ovate, lobed,
silver-green. Flowers open funnels,
clear pink, in mid- to late summer.
Best confined in a tub.

Convolvulus sabatius
A.G.M.
(Convolvulaceae)

Common name: Bindweed
Height: 6in (15cm)
Spread: 20in (50cm)
Aspect: Sun
Soil: Well-drained, sandy
Hardiness: Zone 8
Propagation: Seed, in
warmth in spring

Coreopsis grandiflora
(Asteraceae/Compositae)

Common name: Tickseed
Height: 36in (90cm)
Spread: 18in (45cm)
Aspect: Sun or half shade
Soil: Well-drained, fertile
Hardiness: Zone 7
Propagation: Seed, in
spring; division, in autumn

Trailing perennial from Italy, Spain, and N. Africa. Leaves oblong to broadly ovate, midgreen. Flowers open cups, lavender-blue, from summer to early autumn.

Clump-forming perennial from the U.S.A. Leaves lance-shaped to palmately lobed. Flowers solitary, single, yellow; ray florets have jagged edges. Spring to late summer.

COREOPSIS (Asteraceae/Compositae)
Tickseed

The 100 or so annual and perennial species in this genus all originate in Mexico and Central and North America. All the perennials are fairly hardy, in spite of the generally southerly bias in the distribution of the genus in the wild. *Coreopsis* are found naturally in woodlands and open grasslands; in the garden, their daisylike, usually bright yellow flowerheads make an eye-catching addition to an annual or perennial border. Many species, such as *C. grandiflora* (Zone 7) and *C. verticillata* (Zone 6), can be short-lived; because of this tendency, and the ability of most species to flower well in their first year when grown from seed, some are more commonly cultivated as annuals. Perennial *Coreopsis* are easy-going spreaders, so if they are not grown as annuals, they must be lifted and divided every few years to keep them vigorous. Although they are upright in habit, *Coreopsis* do not, as a rule, require staking; some of the taller cultivars may, however, benefit from support. All will repeat-flower if deadheaded. The flowerheads are attractive to both bees and butterflies; they also make good cut flowers for arrangements, as they last well in water. Unfotunately, they are without exception highly allergenic.

Coreopsis grandiflora 'Early Sunrise' (Asteraceae/Compositae)

Common name: Tickseed
Height: 18in (45cm)
Spread: 18in (45cm)
Aspect: Sun or half shade
Soil: Well-drained, fertile
Hardiness: Zone 7
Propagation: Division,
in spring

Selected, double-flowered form, with
jagged ray florets of golden yellow,
flushed orange near the center, in late
spring to summer. Leaves lance-
shaped or palmately lobed.

Coreopsis grandiflora 'Sunray' (Asteraceae/Compositae)

Common name: Tickseed
Height: 30in (75cm)
Spread: 18in (45cm)
Aspect: Sun or half shade
Soil: Well-drained, fertile
Hardiness: Zone 7
Propagation: Division,
in spring

A selected form, often treated as an
annual, with semidouble, deep yellow
flowers in late spring to summer.
Leaves lance-shaped or palmately
lobed.

Coreopsis rosea 'American Dream' (Asteraceae/Compositae)

Common name: Rose
tickseed
Height: 24in (60cm)
Spread: 18in (30cm)
Aspect: Sun or half shade
Soil: Well-drained, fertile
Hardiness: Zone 4
Propagation: Division,
in spring

A selected form of a species from
North America. Leaves linear, bright
green. Flowers solitary, single, in
midsummer; ray florets deep pink,
disc florets yellow.

Coreopsis verticillata 'Grandiflora' A.G.M. (Asteraceae/Compositae)

Common name:
Threadleaf coreopsis
Height: 32in (80cm)
Spread: 18in (45cm)
Aspect: Sun or half shade
Soil: Well-drained, fertile
Hardiness: Zone 6
Propagation: Seed or division,
both in spring

Bushy, rhizomatous perennial. Leaves
are midgreen, deeply incised, 3-
pinnate; lobes filamentous, linear.
Yellow flowers in loose corymbs, early
summer to early autumn.

Coreopsis verticillata 'Moonbeam' (Asteraceae/Compositae)

Common name: Threadleaf coreopsis
Height: 20in (50cm)
Spread: 18in (45cm)
Aspect: Sun or half shade
Soil: Well-drained, fertile
Hardiness: Zone 6
Propagation: Division, in spring

A selected form of the species with flowers of lemon-yellow, all summer long. Leaves are midgreen, deeply incised, 3-pinnate; lobes linear, filamentous.

Coreopsis verticillata 'Zagreb' (Asteraceae/Compositae)

Common name: Threadleaf coreopsis
Height: 1ft (30cm)
Spread: 1ft (30cm)
Aspect: Sun or half shade
Soil: Well-drained, fertile
Hardiness: Zone 6
Propagation: Division, in spring

Drought-resistant, cloned cultivar, with flowers of golden-yellow all summer. Midgreen leaves are deeply incised, 3-pinnate, with linear, filamentous lobes.

Coriaria terminalis (Coriariaceae)

Common names: None
Height: 3ft (1m)
Spread: 6ft (2m)
Aspect: Sun
Soil: Well-drained, fertile
Hardiness: Zone 8
Propagation: Seed, in warmth in spring; division, in spring

Rhizomatous, deciduous subshrub. Leaves alternate, lance-shaped, glossy-green. Insignificant flowers are followed by black berries with poisonous seeds.

Coriaria terminalis var. *xanthocarpa* (Coriariaceae)

Common names: None
Height: 3ft (90cm)
Spread: 5ft (1.5m)
Aspect: Sun
Soil: Well-drained, fertile
Hardiness: Zone 8
Propagation: Seed, in warmth in spring; division, in spring

Rhizomatous, deciduous subshrub. Shoots arching, leaves lance-shaped, bright green. Insignificant flowers, followed by berries of translucent yellow with poisonous seeds.

Cornus canadensis A.G.M. (Cornaceae)

Common names:
Bunchberry; dwarf cornel
Height: 6in (15cm)
Spread: Indefinite
Aspect: Sun or half shade
Soil: Moist, acidic
Hardiness: Zone 2
Propagation: Division,
in spring or autumn

Highly invasive plant. Leaves lance-shaped to oval, midgreen. Flowers tiny, green, with large, white, pink-tinted bracts, spring and early summer, followed by red berries.

Cortaderia selloana 'Pumila' A.G.M. (Poaceae/Bambusoideae)

Common name: Pampas grass
Height: To 5ft (1.5m)
Spread: 3ft (90cm)
Aspect: Sun
Soil: Well-drained, fertile
Hardiness: Zone 8
Propagation: Seed, in warmth in spring; division, in spring

Dwarf clone of a tall species; the only form for small gardens. Leaves long, razor-edged (wear gloves), arching, glaucous. Flowering panicles erect, silvery-yellow, in autumn.

Cortaderia selloana 'Rendatleri' (Poaceae/Bambusoideae)

Common name: Pampas grass
Height: 8ft (2.5m)
Spread: 6ft (2m)
Aspect: Sun
Soil: Well-drained, fertile
Hardiness: Zone 8
Propagation: Seed, in warmth in spring; division, in spring

Pampas grass with most attractive pinkish-purple panicles. Place at the back of the border: razor-sharp leaf-blades will cut nearby plants in a wind. Wear gloves.

Cortusa matthiolii (Primulaceae)

Common names: None
Height: 12in (30cm)
Spread: 6in (15cm)
Aspect: Half shade
Soil: Moist, well-drained, fertile, humus-rich
Hardiness: Zone 7
Propagation: Seed, when ripe; division, in spring

European woodlander, for cool, moist sites. Leaves basal, round- or heart-shaped, midgreen. Flowers in one-sided umbels, bell-shaped, pink, late spring and early summer.

Corydalis cheilanthifolia
(Papaveraceae)

Common name:
Fernleaved corydalis
Height: 12in (30cm)
Spread: 10in (25cm)
Aspect: Sun or half shade
Soil: Well-drained, fertile
Hardiness: Zone 6
Propagation: Seed, when ripe;
division, in autumn

Fibrous-rooted evergreen. Leaves fern-like, 2- or 3-pinnate, leaflets lance-shaped to linear, tinted bronze. Deep yellow flowers in racemes, spring to summer. Good wall plant.

Corydalis flexuosa
(Papaveraceae)

Common names: None
Height: 12in (30cm)
Spread: 8in (20cm)
Aspect: Half shade
Soil: Moist, well-drained,
humus-rich
Hardiness: Zone 7
Propagation: Seed, when ripe;
division, in autumn

Woodlander from China. Leaves 2-ternate, leaflets ovate, glaucous green. Brilliant blue flowers in terminal and axillary racemes, late spring to summer. Summer dormant.

Corydalis lutea
(Papaveraceae)

Common name: Yellow
corydalis
Height: 16in (40cm)
Spread: 12in (30cm)
Aspect: Sun or half shade
Soil: Moist, well-drained,
fertile, humus-rich
Hardiness: Zone 6
Propagation: Seed, when ripe;
division, in autumn

Rhizomatous, mound-forming, evergreen woodlander. Leaves midgreen, fernlike, 2- or 3-pinnate; leaflets obovate, 3-lobed. Flowers yellow, in racemes, all summer.

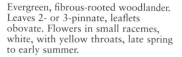

Corydalis ochroleuca
(Papaveraceae)

Common names: None
Height: 12in (30cm)
Spread: 12in (30cm)
Aspect: Sun or half shade
Soil: Moist, well-drained,
fertile
Hardiness: Zone 5
Propagation: Seed, when ripe;
division, in autumn

Evergreen, fibrous-rooted woodlander. Leaves 2- or 3-pinnate, leaflets obovate. Flowers in small racemes, white, with yellow throats, late spring to early summer.

Corydalis ophiocarpa
(Papaveraceae)

Common names: None
Height: 30in (75cm)
Spread: 12in (30cm)
Aspect: Sun or half shade
Soil: Moist, well-drained,
fertile, humus-rich
Hardiness: Zone 6
Propagation: Seed, when ripe;
division, in autumn

Perennial from the E. Himalayas.
Leaves in a dense rosette, 2-pinnate,
gray-green. Flowers in a crowded
terminal raceme, ivory, the inner
petals tipped red, in spring.

Corydalis solida
A.G.M.
(Papaveraceae)

Common names: None
Height: 12in (30cm)
Spread: 6in (15cm)
Aspect: Sun or half shade
Soil: Sharply drained,
sandy
Hardiness: Zone 6
Propagation: Seed, when ripe;
division, in autumn

Tuberous perennial from N. Europe.
Leaves gray-green, 2- or 3-ternate;
leaflets ovate, deeply dissected.
Flowers pale lilac-pink, red or white,
in dense spiky racemes, in spring.

Cosmos atrosanguineus
(Asteraceae/Compositae)

Common name: Chocolate
cosmos
Height: 30in (75cm)
Spread: 18in (45cm)
Aspect: Sun
Soil: Moist, well-drained,
fertile
Hardiness: Zone 8
Propagation: Seed, in
warmth in late spring

Spreading, with pinnate or 2-pinnate
leaves; lobes ovate to diamond-
shaped. Solitary, single, velvety,
chocolate-scented, maroon flowers,
summer to autumn.

Crambe cordifolia
A.G.M.
(Brassicaceae/Cruciferae)

Common name: Greater
sea-kale
Height: 6ft (2m)
Spread: 5ft (1.5m)
Aspect: Sun
Soil: Well-drained, fertile
Hardiness: Zone 6
Propagation: Seed or
division, both in spring

Coastal plant. Leaves large, ovate to
kidney-shaped, toothed, deep green.
Flowers tiny, perfumed, cross-shaped,
white, in branched panicles, in late
spring and early summer.

Crambe maritima
(Brassicaceae/Cruciferae)

Common name: Sea-kale
Height: 32in (80cm)
Spread: 24in (60cm)
Aspect: Sun
Soil: Well-drained, fertile
Hardiness: Zone 5
Propagation: Seed or
division, both in spring

Culinary herb from coastal Europe
and the Black Sea. Leaves glaucous
green, large, ovate, twisted. Flowers
in dense racemes, small, perfumed,
white, from late spring.

Crepis incana
A.G.M.
(Asteraceae/Compositae)

Common name: Pink
dandelion
Height: 1ft (30cm)
Spread: 1ft (30cm)
Aspect: Full sun
Soil: Any well-drained
Hardiness: Zone 8
Propagation: Seed, when ripe

Perennial from Greece. Leaves
dandelion-like, inverse lance-shaped,
pinnatifid, gray-green. Corymbs of
dandelion-like, bright pink flowers.
Flowers well if deadheaded.

Crinum macowanii
(Amaryllidaceae)

Common names: None
Height: 24in (60cm)
Spread: 6in (15cm)
Aspect: Sun
Soil: Moist, well-drained,
fertile, humus-rich
Hardiness: Zone 9
Propagation: Seed, in warmth when
ripe; offsets, in spring

Bulbous plant from South Africa.
Leaves basal straps, wavy-edged,
green. Flowers in umbels, perfumed,
white or pink, with a red stripe on
each tepal. All parts toxic.

Crinum × powellii
A.G.M.
(Amaryllidaceae)

Common names: None
Height: 4ft (1.2m)
Spread: 1ft (30cm)
Aspect: Sun
Soil: Moist, well-drained,
fertile, humus-rich
Hardiness: Zone 6
Propagation: Seed or offsets,
both in spring

Deciduous, bulbous hybrid of garden
origin. Leaves long, arching, green
straps. Flowers perfumed, flared, pink
trumpets, in umbels late summer to
autumn. All parts toxic.

Crinum x *powellii*
'Album' A.G.M.
(Amaryllidaceae)

Common names: None
Height: 4ft (1.2m)
Spread: 1ft (30cm)
Aspect: Sun
Soil: Moist, well-drained,
fertile, humus-rich
Hardiness: Zone 6
Propagation: Seed or offsets,
both in spring

Crocosmia x *crocosmiiflora*
'Citronella' (Iridaceae)

Common name:
Montbretia
Height: 24in (60cm)
Spread: 4in (10cm)
Aspect: Sun or half shade
Soil: Moist, well-drained,
fertile, humus-rich
Hardiness: Zone 7
Propagation: Division, in spring

White form of deciduous, bulbous
hybrid. Flared, scented trumpet
flowers marginally bigger than the
pink form. Leaves long, arching,
green straps. All parts toxic.

A hybrid cultivar with flowers of
pale yellow in upright to slightly
arched, branching spikes, in late
summer. Leaves are pale green.

CROCOSMIA (Iridaceae)
Montbretia

This genus of cormous perennials consists of some half a dozen
species from South Africa, which have been hybridized
extensively since the end of the 19th century. The original cross
was made in 1882, in France, between *C. pottsii* and *C. aurea*,
and given the unwieldy label *C.* x *crocosmiiflora*. The
terminology has become very complex, and is often given only
in part; here, they are dealt with in alphabetical order of the
cultivar name, as is common practice. The hybrids are extremely
handsome and useful plants, generally a great improvement on
the wild forms. Their degree of hardiness varies, but most are
fairly hardy. The corms form "chains" in time, with new corms
growing on old corms, and must be lifted and divided when the
clumps become too dense; the old corms should not be detached
in the process, as they are stores of nourishment for the new
ones. The leaves are erect, linear to lance-shaped, pleated or
ribbed, and green or brownish-green. The flowers are in spikes,
which may be branched or unbranched, carried on wiry stems,
and are followed by attractive seed capsules. Both the leaves
and the flowering spikes last well in water, and montbretias are
popular for flower-arranging; they are low-allergen plants.

Crocosmia
'Emberglow'
(Iridaceae)

Common name:
Montbretia
Height: 30in (75cm)
Spread: 4in (10cm)
Aspect: Sun or half shade
Soil: Moist, well-drained,
humus-rich, fertile
Hardiness: Zone 7
Propagation: Division in spring

A hybrid with midgreen foliage and flowers of dark red, arranged in 2 neat rows along arching, branching spikes, in late summer.

Crocosmia x *crocosmiiflora*
'Emily McKenzie'
(Iridaceae)

Common name:
Montbretia
Height: 24in (60cm)
Spread: 4in (10cm)
Aspect: Sun or half shade
Soil: Moist, well-drained,
fertile, humus-rich
Hardiness: Zone 7
Propagation: Division, in spring

A hybrid with midgreen foliage and large, downward-facing flowers of bright orange, with mahogany markings in the throat, in late summer.

Crocosmia
'Firebird'
(Iridaceae)

Common name:
Montbretia
Height: 32in (80cm)
Spread: 4in (10cm)
Aspect: Sun or half shade
Soil: Moist, well-drained,
fertile, humus-rich
Hardiness: Zone 7
Propagation: Division, in spring

Robust hybrid bearing vibrant orange-red, upward-facing flowers in late summer, in generally unbranched spikes. Leaves are midgreen.

Crocosmia x *crocosmiiflora*
'Jackanapes'
(Iridaceae)

Common name:
Montbretia
Height: 24in (60cm)
Spread: 4in (10cm)
Aspect: Sun or half shade
Soil: Moist, well-drained,
fertile, humus-rich
Hardiness: Zone 7
Propagation: Division, in spring

Striking hybrid with large, bicolored flowers of red and orange in late summer, on freely branching, arching stems above midgreen foliage.

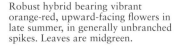

**Crocosmia x crocosmiiflora
'Lady Hamilton'
(Iridaceae)**

Common name:
Montbretia
Height: 32in (80cm)
Spread: 4in (10cm)
Aspect: Sun or half shade
Soil: Moist, well-drained,
fertile, humus-rich
Hardiness: Zone 9
Propagation: Division, in spring

A hybrid with leaves of mid-green
and flowers of rich yellow with
apricot centers. Flowers are borne on
upright, branching stems, in late
summer.

**Crocosmia
'Lucifer' A.G.M.
(Iridaceae)**

Common name:
Montbretia
Height: 3ft (1m)
Spread: 4in (10cm)
Aspect: Sun or half shade
Soil: Moist, well-drained,
fertile, humus-rich
Hardiness: Zone 7
Propagation: Division, in spring

Very popular, dependable hybrid with
flowers of intense, deep tomato-red in
late summer, on branching, slightly
arched spikes. Leaves are pleated,
midgreen.

**Crocosmia masoniorum
AG.M.
(Iridaceae)**

Common name:
Montbretia
Height: 4ft (1.2m)
Spread: 4in (10cm)
Aspect: Sun or half shade
Soil: Moist, well-drained,
fertile, humus-rich
Hardiness: Zone 7
Propagation: Seed, when ripe;
division, in spring

Large, robust species from South
Africa. Leaves long, pleated,
midgreen. Flowers upward-facing,
orange-red, in arching spikes, in
summer.

**Crocosmia paniculata
(Iridaceae)**

Common name:
Montbretia
Height: 4ft (1.2m)
Spread: 4in (10cm)
Aspect: Sun or half shade
Soil: Moist, well-drained,
fertile, humus-rich
Hardiness: Zone 8
Propagation: Seed, when ripe;
division, in spring

Large species from South Africa, with
pleated leaves of olive-green.
Flowering spike branched, flowers
orange-red, downturned, in late
summer.

Crocosmia
'Severn Sunrise'
(Iridaceae)

Common name:
Montbretia
Height: 32in (80cm)
Spread: 4in (10cm)
Aspect: Sun or half shade
Soil: Moist, well-drained,
fertile, humus-rich
Hardiness: Zone 7
Propagation: Division, in spring

A hybrid with flowers of glowing
orange with lighter throats, in
generally upright, branching spikes,
above leaves of midgreen, in late
summer.

Crocosmia × *crocosmiiflora*
'Solfaterre' A.G.M.
(Iridaceae)

Common name:
Montbretia
Height: 32in (80cm)
Spread: 4in (10cm)
Aspect: Sun or half shade
Soil: Moist, well-drained,
fertile, humus-rich
Hardiness: Zone 8
Propagation: Division, in spring

Very old hybrid with unusual,
bronze-colored leaves. Bears flowers
of apricot-yellow in late summer.
Excellent for flower arrangements.

Crocosmia
'Vulcan'
(Iridaceae)

Common name:
Montbretia
Height: 32in (80cm)
Spread: 4in (10cm)
Aspect: Sun or half shade
Soil: Moist, well-drained,
fertile, humus-rich
Hardiness: Zone 7
Propagation: Division, in spring

A hybrid with midgreen leaves, and
spikes of plentiful, outward-facing
flowers of vibrant orange-red color,
borne in late summer.

Crocosmia
'Walburton Yellow'
(Iridaceae)

Common name:
Montbretia
Height: 32in (80cm)
Spread: 4in (10cm)
Aspect: Sun or half shade
Soil: Moist, well-drained,
fertile, humus-rich
Hardiness: Zone
Propagation: Division, in spring

Modern hybrid with typical large,
upward-facing flowers of clear yellow
color, carried in spikes above
midgreen foliage, in late summer.

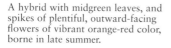

CROCUS (Iridacae)
Crocus

These cormous perennials of varying hardiness are found naturally in Europe, North Africa, and through the Middle East to China. They are suitable for planting at the edges of beds or borders, and flower in spring or autumn. Their flowers are goblets, formed by six tepals, the outer three opening to reveal the inner three, which may be of a different color. Some are perfumed. The foliage is linear, semierect, midgreen, with a silver or pale green central stripe. In the spring-flowering types, the foliage appears with, or just after the flowers; in some of the autumn-flowering types it may appear before the flowers. Crocuses are universally deciduous. An Award of Garden Merit has been bestowed on no fewer than 39 crocuses, and it is for the specialist book to cover them in detail. The representatives of the genus here with one exception are all spring-flowering, and all but one hold an A.G.M. Those which require a dry summer dormancy are not covered here, since they need an alpine house or bulb frame; other types are easy to grow. All they ask is sun and good drainage, and they will increase and will require regular division. Wildlife can be a problem: sparrows pull the flowers apart, and garden rodents eat the corms.

Crocus chrysanthus 'Blue Pearl' A.G.M. (Iridaceae)

Common names: None
Height: 3in (7cm)
Spread: 2in (5cm)
Aspect: Sun
Soil: Well-drained, sandy, fertile
Hardiness: Zone 4
Propagation: Offsets, in summer

A hybrid cultivar of a species from S.E. Europe and Turkey. Flowers perfumed, white, with yellow throats, and outer tepals of lilac-blue, in spring.

Crocus chrysanthus 'Cream Beauty' A.G.M. (Iridaceae)

Common names: None
Height: 3in (7cm)
Spread: 2in (5cm)
Aspect: Sun
Soil: Moist, well-drained, sandy
Hardiness: Zone 4
Propagation: Offsets, in summer

A hybrid cultivar, with perfumed, cream flowers with brownish-green bases, and yellow throats, in spring. Leaves mid- to gray-green, appearing with or after flowers.

Crocus kotschyanus A.G.M. (Iridaceae)

Common names: None
Height: 4in (10cm)
Spread: 3in (6cm)
Aspect: Sun
Soil: Dry in summer, sandy
Hardiness: Zone 5
Propagation: Seed, when
ripe; offsets, in summer

Vigorous crocus species found in
Syria, Lebanon, and Turkey. Pale lilac
flowers with cream stamens appear in
autumn, before the leaves.

Crocus x luteus 'Golden Yellow' A.G.M. (Iridaceae)

Common names: None
Height: 4in (10cm)
Spread: 2in (5cm)
Aspect: Sun
Soil: Well-drained, sandy
Hardiness: Zone 4
Propagation: Offsets,
in summer

Vigorous hybrid, with golden yellow
flowers, the outer tepals marked with
darker stripes on the back, in spring.
Naturalizes well.

Crocus tomassinianus 'Ruby Giant' (Iridaceae)

Common names: None
Height: 4in (10cm)
Spread: 1in (3cm)
Aspect: Sun
Soil: Well-drained, sandy
Hardiness: Zone 5
Propagation: Offsets,
in summer

Clump-forming, vigorous crocus that
naturalizes well. Bears rich reddish-
pink flowers in spring. A sterile
hybrid cultivar, so does not set seed.

Crocus chrysanthus 'Snow Bunting' A.G.M. (Iridaceae)

Common names: None
Height: 3in (8cm)
Spread: 2in (5cm)
Aspect: Sun
Soil: Well-drained, sandy
Hardiness: Zone 4
Propagation: Offsets,
in summer

A vigorous hybrid cultivar, flowering
in spring. White flowers may have
faint, feathery bluish markings. Mid-
to gray-green leaves with or after the
flowers.

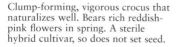

Cuphea cyanea
(Lythraceae)

Common names: None
Height: 4ft (1.2m)
Spread: 3ft (1m)
Aspect: Sun or half shade
Soil: Well-drained, fertile
Hardiness: Zone 9
Propagation: Seed, in
warmth in spring; division,
in spring

Evergreen subshrub from Mexico.
Leaves ovate; shoots sticky, glandular-
hairy. Flowers tubular, orange-red,
tipped green, with 2 violet petals, in
racemes, summer.

Cuphea hyssopifolia
A.G.M.
(Lythraceae)

Common names: None
Height: 24in (60cm)
Spread: 32in (80cm)
Aspect: Sun or half shade
Soil: Well-drained, fertile
Hardiness: Zone 10
Propagation: Seed, in
warmth in spring; division,
in spring

Evergreen subshrub. Leaves lance-
shaped, dark green. Flowers in short
racemes on downy stems, purple-pink,
from summer to autumn. From
Mexico and Guatemala.

CYCLAMEN (Primulaceae)
Sowbread

This genus is found over a wide diversity of habitat and terrain.
Cyclamen grow in the Mediterranean region, Iran, and Somalia;
not surprisingly, they have varying degrees of hardiness, from
Zone 6 to Zone 9. The less hardy species are not included here;
they prefer a dry summer dormancy, and are most suitable for
alpine house or conservatory. There are some 20 species, all
tuberous, and ten have an Award of Garden Merit. Cyclamen
grow in any soil type. Mostly, they are woodlanders, but some
are found in dry areas, and so their cultural requirements are
not easy to summarize. They are usually spring- or autumn-
flowering, but may flower at other times. The flowers are highly
distinctive, with five reflexed petals ranging in color from white
through shades of pink to red. Some are scented. After the
flowers fade, the stalks of many cyclamen coil down among the
leaves to release the seed as close to the ground as possible. The
foliage, often marked with silver, is handsome in all species, and
some are evergreen. The one constant rule when buying
cyclamen is to buy them while in growth, and not as dry
shrivelled tubers. Planting is best done in autumn, and the
tubers should be planted just below the soil surface.

133

Cyclamen coum
A.G.M.
(Primulaceae)

Common name: Sowbread
Height: 3in (8cm)
Spread: 4in (10cm)
Aspect: Half shade
Soil: Well-drained, fertile,
humus-rich
Hardiness: Zone 6
Propagation: Seed, in darkness
when ripe

Tuberous plant from the Black Sea
region. Leaves round, shiny, plain
green, or marked silver. Flowers pink,
red, or white, in early autumn, with
the leaves.

Cyclamen coum subsp.
coum f. ***albissimum***
(Primulaceae)

Common name: Sowbread
Height: 3in (8cm)
Spread: 4in (10cm)
Aspect: Half shade
Soil: Well-drained, fertile,
humus-rich
Hardiness: Zone 6
Propagation: Seed, in darkness
when ripe

Charming, white-flowered form of the
species. The clear white flowers are
marked dark red at the mouth,
appearing in early autumn with the
leaves.

Cyclamen repandum
(Primulaceae)

Common name: Sowbread
Height: 6in (15cm)
Spread: 5in (12cm)
Aspect: Half shade
Soil: Well-drained, fertile,
humus-rich
Hardiness: Zone 7
Propagation: Seed, in darkness
when ripe

Perennial from N. Mediterranean.
Leaves triangular, green, speckled, or
marbled silver. Flowers red, perfumed,
appearing with the leaves in mid- to
late spring.

Cyclamen repandum
subsp. ***peloponnesiacum***
A.G.M. (Primulaceae)

Common name: Sowbread
Height: 6in (15cm)
Spread: 5in (12cm)
Aspect: Half shade
Soil: Well-drained, fertile,
humus-rich
Hardiness: Zone 7
Propagation: Seed, in darkness
when ripe

A form of *C. repandum* from the
Peloponnese peninsula. Leaves
scalloped, more heavily marked silver
than the type, flowers pale pink; both
in spring.

Cynara cardunculus A.G.M.
(Asteraceae/Compositae)

Common name: Cardoon
Height: 5ft (1.5m)
Spread: 4ft (1.2m)
Aspect: Sun
Soil: Well-drained, fertile
Hardiness: Zone 6
Propagation: Seed or division, both in spring

Clump-forming perennial from Morocco and the S.W. Mediterranean. Leaves silver, spiny, pinnatifid; blanched midribs edible. Flowers huge thistles, on woolly stems.

Cynara baetica subsp. maroccana
(Asteraceae/Compositae)

Common names: None
Height: 3ft (1m)
Spread: 2ft (60cm)
Aspect: Sun
Soil: Well-drained, sandy, fertile
Hardiness: Zone 8
Propagation: Seed or division, both in spring

Clump-forming perennial from Morocco. Leaves pinnatisect; lobes linear, toothed, spiny, with white woolly undersides. Flower purple, thistlelike, good for drying.

Cynara scolymus
(Asteraceae/Compositae)

Common name: Globe artichoke
Height: 6ft (2m)
Spread: 4ft (1.2m)
Aspect: Sun
Soil: Well-drained, fertile
Hardiness: Zone 6
Propagation: Seed or division, both in spring

Culinary plant from the N. Mediterranean. Leaves pinnatifid, gray-green, pointed, white-woolly underneath. Flower purple, with big bracts, in autumn, edible as a bud.

Cynoglossum nervosum
(Boraginaceae)

Common names: Chinese forget-me-not; hound's tongue
Height: 32in (80cm)
Spread: 24in (60cm)
Aspect: Sun or half shade
Soil: Well-drained, moist
Hardiness: Zone 5
Propagation: Seed or division, both in spring

Perennial from N. India and W. Pakistan. Leaves lance-shaped to oblong, hairy, bright green. Cymes of intense blue, forget-me-not flowers, spring to summer. Feed sparingly.

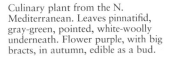

135

Cypella herbertii
(Iridaceae)

Cypripedium acaule
(Orchidaceae)

Common names: None
Height: 24in (60cm)
Spread: 4in (10cm)
Aspect: Sun
Soil: Well-drained, sandy,
humus-rich
Hardiness: Zone 9
Propagation: Seed, in warmth
when ripe

Common name: Pink
moccasin-flower
Height: 10in (25cm)
Spread: 10in (25cm)
Aspect: Half shade
Soil: Moist, acidic, fertile,
humus-rich
Hardiness: Zone 5
Propagation: Division, in spring

Bulbous perennial from South
America. Lance-shaped to linear,
pleated leaves. Outer tepals of flowers
mustard, inner tepals brown, spotted
or streaked purple, summer.

Terrestrial, rhizomatous orchid from
North America. Leaves paired,
elliptic. Flower solitary, nodding,
brown-green, with pink lips, in
summer. Extremely difficult to grow.

Cypripedium calceolus
(Orchidaceae)

Cypripedium reginae
(Orchidaceae)

Common name: Yellow
lady's-slipper
Height: 16in (40cm)
Spread: 16in (40cm)
Aspect: Half shade
Soil: Moist, acidic, fertile,
humus-rich
Hardiness: Zone 5
Propagation: Division, in spring

Common name: Showy
lady's-slipper
Height: 30in (75cm)
Spread: 12in (30cm)
Aspect: Half shade
Soil: Moist, acidic, fertile,
humus-rich
Hardiness: Zone 4
Propagation: Division, in spring

Terrestrial rhizomatous orchid. Leaves
ovate-elliptic, dark green. Flower
single or paired, brown-purple, petals
twisted, lips large, yellow. Very
difficult in cultivation.

Terrestrial rhizomatous orchid from
North America. Leaves ovate to
lance-shaped. Flowers single or
paired, white, with rose-pink lips, in
summer. Very difficult to grow.

Cyrtanthus
brachyscyphus
(**Amaryllidaceae**)

Common name: Fire lily
Height 12in (30cm)
Spread: 4in (10cm)
Aspect: Sun
Soil: Well-drained, fertile,
humus-rich
Hardiness: Zone 9
Propagation: Seed, in warmth
when ripe; offsets, in spring

Deciduous, bulbous perennial from
South Africa. Leaves lance-shaped,
semierect, green. Flowers in umbels,
tubular, red, in spring to summer.

Dactylis glomerata
'Variegata'
(**Graminae/Poaceae**)

Common names: None
Height: 18in (45cm)
Spread: 10in (25cm)
Aspect: Sun or half shade
Soil: Well-drained, fertile
Hardiness: Zone 5
Propagation: Division,
in spring

Clump-forming, evergreen, perennial
grass from Eurasia and North Africa.
Leaves linear, variegated cream.
Flowering spike one-sided, pale green.

Dactylorhiza elata
A.G.M.
(**Orchidaceae**)

Common name: Robust
marsh orchid
Height: 24in (60cm)
Spread: 6in (15cm)
Aspect: Half shade
Soil: Well-drained, moist,
humus-rich
Hardiness: Zone 6
Propagation: Division, in spring

Tuberous, terrestrial orchid. Leaves
linear to lance-shaped, green, may be
spotted brown. Flowers in dense
terminal racemes, purple, with bracts,
late spring. Easy in right place.

Dactylorhiza foliosa
A.G.M.
(**Orchidaceae**)

Common name: Madeiran
orchid
Height: 60cm (24in)
Spread: 15cm (6in)
Aspect: Half shade
Soil: Well-drained, moist,
humus-rich
Hardiness: Zone 7
Propagation: Division, in spring

Terrestrial, tuberous orchid. Lance-
shaped, green leaves, can be spotted
brown. Flowers in racemes, pink or
purple, with bracts, late spring to
early summer. Easy in right place.

137

Dactylorhiza fuchsii
(Orchidaceae)

Common name: Common
spotted orchid
Height: 24in (60cm)
Spread: 6in (15cm)
Aspect: Half shade
Soil: Moist, well-drained,
humus-rich
Hardiness: Zone 6
Propagation: Division, in spring

Terrestrial, tuberous, deciduous
orchid. Leaves lance-shaped, spotted
purple. Dense terminal umbels of
flowers, late spring and early summer,
mauve. Easy in right place.

Dactylorhiza praetermissa
(Orchidaceae)

Common name: Southern
marsh orchid
Height: 24in (60cm)
Spread: 6in (15cm)
Aspect: Half shade
Soil: Moist, well-drained,
humus-rich
Hardiness: Zone 6
Propagation: Division, in spring

Tuberous, terrestrial, deciduous orchid
from N. Europe. Leaves lance-shaped,
can be spotted. Flowers in dense
umbel, pale garnet, with bracts. Easy
in right conditions.

Dahlia 'Bishop of
Llandaff' A.G.M.
(Asteraceae/Compositae)

Common names: None
Height: 4ft (1.2m)
Spread: 18in (45cm)
Aspect: Sun
Soil: Well-drained, fertile,
humus-rich
Hardiness: Zone 10
Propagation: Division,
in spring

Hybrid dahlia in the "miscellaneous"
classification. Leaves pinnate, lobes
oval, toothed, black-red. Peony-
flowered, blooms semidouble, bright
red.

Dahlia merckii
(Asteraceae/Compositae)

Common names: None
Height: 6ft (2m)
Spread: 3ft (1m)
Aspect: Sun
Soil: Well-drained, fertile,
humus-rich
Hardiness: Zone 9
Propagation: Division,
in spring

Tuberous perennial from Mexico.
Leaves pinnate, green. Flowers on
many-branched stems, single pink,
purple, or white, with yellow disc
florets.

Darmera peltata
A.G.M.
(Saxifragaceae)

Common name: Umbrella
plant
Height: 6ft (2m)
Spread: 5ft (1.5m)
Aspect: Sun or half shade
Soil: Marginal aquatic
Hardiness: Zone 6
Propagation: Seed or division,
both in spring

Rhizomatous marginal plant from the
U.S.A. Leaves large, peltate, round,
deeply lobed, toothed, veined, deep
green. Flowers on tall stems in large
cymes, pink, in spring.

Davallia mariesii
A.G.M.
(Davalliaceae)

Common name: Hare's-
foot fern
Height: 6in (15cm)
Spread: Indefinite
Aspect: Half shade
Soil: Moist, sandy, humus-
rich
Hardiness: Zone 9
Propagation: Spores, in warmth
when ripe; division, in spring

Rhizomatous, deciduous, creeping
fern from East Asia. Fronds 3- to 4-
pinnate, finely cut, broad, midgreen.
Segments linear or triangular.

DELPHINIUM (Ranunculaceae)
Delphinium • Larkspur

Genus of some 250 species, from all parts of the world except
the Arctic, Australia, and Antarctica. Most are fibrous-rooted; a
few are tuberous. The best-known delphiniums are the tall
hybrids with dense spires of flowers, but some species are small
enough for the rock garden. The leaves are toothed and 3-, 5-,
or 7-lobed. Tall hybrids almost always need staking. They make
excellent cut flowers, and are prized by flower-arrangers.
Delphiniums are low in allergens, but all parts are poisonous
and skin irritant. They are prone to powdery mildew, slugs, and
snails. They are classified in three groups.
Belladonna Group Upright, to 4ft (1.2m), branching, with
palmately lobed leaves and loose spikes of elfin-caplike single
flowers with spurs up to 1¼in (3cm), in early and late summer.
Elatum Group: Clump-forming, to over 5½ft (1.7m), with
tapering flower spikes and similar smaller, later-flowering lateral
shoots in late spring to early summer, again in autumn if cut
back; flowers single to double, with 5 large outer sepals and an
"eye" of 8 inner sepals. The most popular type.
Pacific Hybrids Short-lived, grown as annuals or biennials. Over
5½ft (1.7m) tall, and bloom in spring and early summer.

Delphinium beesianum
'Cliveden Beauty'
(Ranunculaceae)

Common name: Larkspur
Height: 4ft (1.2m)
Spread: 18in (45cm)
Aspect: Sun
Soil: Well-drained, fertile
Hardiness: Zone 3
Propagation: Heeled basal
cuttings, in spring

Belladonna Group delphinium:
upright, suits a border. Branching
stems bear flowers of sky blue in very
loose, open spikes, early and late
summer.

Delphinium beesianum
'Peace'
(Ranunculaceae)

Common name: Larkspur
Height: 4ft (1.2m)
Spread: 18in (45cm)
Aspect: Sun
Soil: Well-drained, fertile
Hardiness: Zone 3
Propagation: Heeled basal
cuttings, in spring

Belladonna Group delphinium with
flowers of intense blue, borne in open
spikes in early and late summer. Suits
a border or island bed.

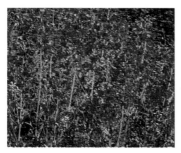

Delphinium beesianum
'Volkerfrieden'
(Ranunculaceae)

Common name: Larkspur
Height: 4ft (1.2m)
Spread: 18in (45cm)
Aspect: Sun
Soil: Well-drained, fertile
Hardiness: Zone 3
Propagation: Heeled basal
cuttings, in spring

Vigorous Belladonna Group
delphinium: upright, suitable for a
border or island bed. Bears flowers of
deep blue in early and late summer.

Delphinium
Blue Jade Group
(Ranunculaceae)

Common name: Larkspur
Height: 5ft (1.5m)
Spread: 2ft (60cm)
Aspect: Sun
Soil: Well-drained, fertile
Hardiness: Zone 3
Propagation: Heeled basal
cuttings, in spring

Clump-forming Elatum group
delphinium, with large flowers of
mid-blue with darker eyes, borne in
dense spikes. Among the shorter
examples of this group.

Delphinium cashmerianum
(Ranunculaceae)

Common name: Larkspur
Height: 16in (40cm)
Spread: 6in (15cm)
Aspect: Sun
Soil: Well-drained, fertile
Hardiness: Zone 5
Propagation: Seed, in
spring

Perennial from the W. Himalayas.
Leaves round, toothed, 5- to 7-lobed,
green. Dark blue-purple, single flowers
in open panicles, in early and again in
late summer.

Delphinium
'Galahad'
(Ranunculaceae)

Common name: Larkspur
Height: 5½ft (1.7m)
Spread: 30in (75cm)
Aspect: Sun
Soil: Well-drained, fertile
Hardiness: Zone 3
Propagation: Seed, in
spring

Pacific Hybrid delphinium, grown as
an annual or biennial. Large, short-
lived flowers of pure white. Suits a
border or island bed.

Delphinium grandiflorum
'Blue Butterfly'
(Ranunculaceae)

Common name: Siberian
larkspur
Height: 16in (40cm)
Spread: 8in (20cm)
Aspect: Sun
Soil: Well-drained, fertile
Hardiness: Zone 3
Propagation: Seed, in spring

Selected form of a short-lived perennial
from Japan and China to Siberia.
Leaves 5-lobed, lobes narrowly
divided. Flowers in open panicles,
single, bright blue, early summer.

Delphinium
Magic Fountain Series
(Ranunculaceae)

Common name: Larkspur
Height: 5ft (1.5m)
Spread: 2ft (60cm)
Aspect: Sun
Soil: Well-drained, fertile
Hardiness: Zone 3
Propagation: Seed, in
spring

Series with flowers in a range of
colors, from the Elatum Group. One
of the shorter examples of the group;
suits a border or an island bed.

Delphinium nudicaule
(Ranunculaceae)

Common name: Orange larkspur
Height: 24in (60cm)
Spread: 8in (20cm)
Aspect: Sun
Soil: Well-drained, fertile
Hardiness: Zone 8
Propagation: Seed, in spring

Short-lived perennial from California. Leaves 3- to 5-lobed, fleshy, green. Flowers in open panicles, single, funnel-shaped, vermilion with yellow throats, in summer.

Delphinium speciosum
(Ranunculaceae)

Common name: Larkspur
Height: 30in (75cm)
Spread: 12in (30cm)
Aspect: Sun
Soil: Well-drained, fertile
Hardiness: Zone 6
Propagation: Seed, in spring

Perennial from the Caucasus and C. Asia. Leaves 3- to 5-lobed, segments broad, toothed, subdivided further. Flowers in racemes, intense blue, in summer.

Desmodium elegans
(Leguminosae/Papilionaceae)

Common name: Beggarweed
Height: 5ft (1.5m)
Spread: 5ft (1.5m)
Aspect: Sun
Soil: Well-drained
Hardiness: Zone 6
Propagation: Seed, in autumn; softwood cuttings, in spring

Deciduous subshrub. Leaves long, 3-pinnate, leaflets obovate, green above, gray below. Flowers in terminal panicles, pealike, pink, from late summer to autumn.

Dianella nigra
(Liliaceae/Phormiaceae)

Common name: New Zealand blueberry
Height: 24in (60cm)
Spread: 18in (45cm)
Aspect: Sun or half shade
Soil: Well-drained, acidic, fertile, humus-rich
Hardiness: Zone 9
Propagation: Seed, in warmth in spring; division, in spring

Evergreen woodlander from New Zealand. Leaves grassy, linear to lance-shaped, dark green. Loose panicles of small, off-white flowers in summer, then black berries.

Dianella tasmanica
(Liliaceae/Phormiaceae)

Common name:
Tasmanian blueberry
Height: 4ft (1.2m)
Spread: 18in (45cm)
Aspect: Sun or half shade
Soil: Well-drained, acidic,
fertile, humus-rich
Hardiness: Zone 9
Propagation: Seed, in warmth in
spring; division, in spring

Rhizomatous evergreen from
Tasmania and S.E. Australia. Leaves
stiff, rough-edged, straplike. Lavender
flowers in branching panicles in
summer, then blue berries.

Dianthus callizonus
(Caryophyllaceae)

Common name: Pink
Height: 8in (20cm)
Spread: 12in (30cm)
Aspect: Sun
Soil: Well-drained
Hardiness: Zone 5
Propagation: Cuttings of
non-flowering shoots,
in summer

Mat-forming species from the
Carpathians. Leaves linear to lance-
shaped, gray-green. Flowers solitary,
single, petals toothed, lavender-pink
with a purple eye, summer.

DIANTHUS (Caryophyllaceae)
Carnation • Pink

Widely grown genus of some 300 species from Eurasia and
Africa, with one from arctic America.They are evergreen and
long-flowering, with perfumed flowers, excellent for cutting. All
Dianthus ask is a sandy, well-drained soil, in sun. They may
flower themselves to death, but are generally short-lived and
must be replaced on a regular basis, from cuttings in late
summer. They are also loved by pigeons and rabbits. All are
highly allergenic. There are four major categories, of which only
the last is included here.

Perpetual-flowering Carnations: Grown under glass for
exhibition or the cut-flower trade.

Malmaison Carnations: Grown under glass for exhibition or the
cut-flower trade.

Border Carnations: Summer-flowering, sometimes clove-scented,
fully double garden plants in a range of colors and fancy or
picotee-edged. They were derived initially from
D. plumarius.**Pinks:** Summer-flowering garden plants, grouped
into alpine, old-fashioned, or modern. They may be single or
double, clove-scented or not. Sterile "mule" pinks are crosses
between border carnations and sweet william (*D. barbatus*).

Dianthus
'Cranmere Pool' A.G.M.
(Caryophyllaceae)

Common name: Pink
Height: 18in (45cm)
Spread: 12in (30cm)
Aspect: Sun
Soil: Well-drained
Hardiness: Zone 3
Propagation: Cuttings of
non-flowering shoots,
in summer

Hybrid garden pink cultivar, with
double flowers which are off-white
with a rich magenta center, slightly
toothed, and scented, in summer.

Dianthus
'Dainty Dame'
(Caryophyllaceae)

Common name: Pink
Height: 6in (15cm)
Spread: 8in (20cm)
Aspect: Sun
Soil: Well-drained
Hardiness: Zone 3
Propagation: Cuttings of
non-flowering shoots,
in summer

A compact, hybrid pink cultivar with
perfumed, single, white flowers with a
deep maroon eye, the petals slightly
toothed, in summer.

Dianthus deltoides
A.G.M.
(Caryophyllaceae)

Common name:
Maiden pink
Height: 8in (20cm)
Spread: 12in (30cm)
Aspect: Sun
Soil: Well-drained
Hardiness: Zone 3
Propagation: Cuttings of non-
flowering shoots, in summer

Mat-forming pink species widespread
in Europe and Asia. Leaves dark
green. Flowers solitary, single,
toothed, bearded, white, pink, or red,
in summer.

Dianthus deltoides
'Leuchtfunk'
(Caryophyllaceae)

Common name:
Maiden pink
Height: 8in (20cm)
Spread: 12in (30cm)
Aspect: Sun
Soil: Well-drained
Hardiness: Zone 3
Propagation: Cuttings of non-
flowering shoots, in summer

A cloned selection of the mat-forming
maiden pink species, bearing
abundant flowers of intense cerise, in
summer. Leaves dark green.

Dianthus
'Devon Dove'® A.G.M.
(Caryophyllaceae)

Common name: Pink
Height: 18in (45cm)
Spread: 12in (30cm)
Aspect: Sun
Soil: Well-drained
Hardiness: Zone 3
Propagation: Cuttings of
non-flowering shoots,
in summer

A hybrid pink cultivar bearing double
flowers of pure white, petals toothed,
bearded, in summer. Leaves and stems
a bloomy blue-green.

Dianthus
'Dewdrop'
(Caryophyllaceae)

Common name: Pink
Height: 18in (45cm)
Spread: 12in (30cm)
Aspect: Sun
Soil: Well-drained
Hardiness: Zone 3
Propagation: Cuttings of
non-flowering shoots,
n summer

Hybrid pink cultivar with semidouble
white flowers, with dark markings at
the center, petals toothed, in summer.
Leaves are linear.

Dianthus
'Doris' A.G.M.
(Caryophyllaceae)

Common name: Pink
Height: 18in (45cm)
Spread: 12in (30cm)
Aspect: Sun
Soil: Any, well-drained
Hardiness: Zone 3
Propagation: Cuttings of
non-flowering shoots,
in summer

Modern hybrid pink with perfumed,
double, bicolored flowers of pale pink
with a dark pink center, petals
toothed, in summer.

Dianthus
'Gran's Favourite' A.G.M.
(Caryophyllaceae)

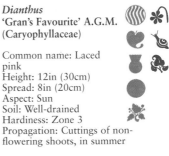

Common name: Laced
pink
Height: 12in (30cm)
Spread: 8in (20cm)
Aspect: Sun
Soil: Well-drained
Hardiness: Zone 3
Propagation: Cuttings of non-
flowering shoots, in summer

Popular, mound-forming, laced,
modern pink with clove-scented,
double white flowers, with pink
centers and edges, in summer.

Dianthus gratianopolitanus A.G.M. (Caryophyllaceae)

Common name: Cheddar pink
Height: 6in (15cm)
Spread: 15in (35cm)
Aspect: Sun
Soil: Well-drained
Hardiness: Zone 3
Propagation: Cuttings of non-flowering shoots, in summer

A mat-forming species from N.W. and C. Europe. Leaves gray-green. Flowers single, solitary, intensely perfumed, deep pink, in summer. Petals toothed, bearded.

Dianthus 'Haytor Rock' A.G.M. (Caryophyllaceae)

Common name: Modern clove pink
Height: 18in (45cm)
Spread: 12in (30cm)
Aspect: Sun
Soil: Any, well-drained
Hardiness: Zone 3
Propagation: Cuttings of non-flowering shoots, in summer

Excellent modern hybrid pink bearing flushes of clove-scented, double, pink flowers, streaked red, in summer. Leaves gray-green.

Dianthus 'Houndspool Ruby' A.G.M. (Caryophyllaceae)

Common name: Modern pink
Height: 18in (45cm)
Spread: 8in (20cm)
Aspect: Sun
Soil: Any well-drained
Hardiness: Zone 3
Propagation: Cuttings of non-flowering shoots, in summer

Clump-forming modern pink with double, bicolored flowers of ruby-red with currant-red centers, in flushes through summer. Leaves gray-green.

Dianthus 'Inshriach Dazzler' A.G.M. (Caryophyllaceae)

Common name: Alpine pink
Height: 4in (10cm)
Spread: 6in (15cm)
Aspect: Sun
Soil: Well-drained
Hardiness: Zone 3
Propagation: Cuttings of non-flowering shoots, in summer

An alpine pink with solitary, single flowers of deep carmine-red with fringed petals, carried on short stems, in summer. Good for border edge or rock garden.

Dianthus knappii
(Caryophyllaceae)

Common name: Pink
Height: 16in (40cm)
Spread: 12in (30cm)
Aspect: Sun
Soil: Well-drained
Hardiness: Zone 3
Propagation: Seed, in
spring or autumn

The only yellow-flowered species.
Flowers on long stems, in few-
flowered clusters, yellow, with a
purple spot near the base,
in summer. From the W. Balkans.

Dianthus
'Mrs. Sinkins'
(Caryophyllaceae)

Common name: Old-
fashioned pink
Height: 18in (45cm)
Spread: 12in (30cm)
Aspect: Sun
Soil: Well-drained
Hardiness: Zone 3
Propagation: Cuttings of non-
flowering shoots, in summer

A popular, old-fashioned self with one
flush of flowers, in summer. Flowers
are shaggy, double, fringed, white,
and strongly perfumed; calyces tend
to split.

Dianthus myrtinervius
(Caryophyllaceae)

Common name: Pink
Height: 2in (5cm)
Spread: 8in (20cm)
Aspect: Sun
Soil: Well-drained
Hardiness: Zone 7
Propagation: Seed, in
autumn or spring

Mat-forming species from the Balkans
and Greece. Leaves lance, bright
green. Flowers solitary, single, deep
pink, with a pale eye, in summer.

Dianthus pavonius
A.G.M.
(Caryophyllaceae)

Common name: Pink
Height: 3in (8cm)
Spread: 8in (20cm)
Aspect: Sun
Soil: Well-drained
Hardiness: Zone 4
Propagation: Seed, in
autumn or spring

Mat-forming perennial from the Alps.
Leaves linear, gray-green. Flowers
solitary, single, toothed, bearded, deep
pink in summer. Good for border or
rock garden.

147

Dianthus
'Prince Charming'
(Caryophyllaceae)

Common name: Pink
Height: 4in (10cm)
Spread: 8in (20cm)
Aspect: Sun
Soil: Well-drained
Hardiness: Zone 3
Propagation: Seed, in
autumn or spring

Dianthus
'Queen of Henri'
(Caryophyllaceae)

Common name: Pink
Height: 18in (45cm)
Spread: 8in (20cm)
Aspect: Sun
Soil: Well-drained
Hardiness: Zone 3
Propagation: Cuttings of
non-flowering shoots, in
summer

A small pink with single flowers, of a
washed-out pink in color. Leaves are
linear and green. Suitable for the edge
of a border or for a rock garden.

Modern pink with patterned,
perfumed flowers. The centers of the
petals are white, their edges laced
with pink. Leaves are gray-green.

Dianthus
'Rose Joy' A.G.M.
(Caryophyllaceae)

Common name: Pink
Height: 18in (45cm)
Spread: 8in (20cm)
Aspect: Sun
Soil: Well-drained
Hardiness: Zone 3
Propagation: Cuttings of
non-flowering shoots, in
summer

Dianthus
'Royal Velvet'
(Caryophyllaceae)

Common name: Pink
Height: 18in (45cm)
Spread: 8in (20cm)
Aspect: Sun
Soil: Well-drained
Hardiness: Zone 3
Propagation: Cuttings of
non-flowering shoots, in
summer

Dependable modern pink with
double, toothed, pink-purple flowers,
in clusters of 2–3, in flushes through
summer. Foliage is gray-green.

A modern hybrid pink, with single,
laced, pink flowers, blotched white, in
flushes through summer. Foliage is
linear and gray-green.

Dianthus superbus
(Caryophyllaceae)

Common name: Superb
pink
Height: 8in (20cm)
Spread: 8in (20cm)
Aspect: Sun
Soil: Well-drained
Hardiness: Zone 4
Propagation: Seed, in
autumn or spring

Species from the mountains of
Eurasia. Leaves linear, green. Flowers
single, solitary or in pairs, perfumed,
purple-pink, with deeply fringed
petals, in summer.

Dianthus
'Valda Wyatt' A.G.M.
(Caryophyllaceae)

Common name: Modern
pink
Height: 1ft (30cm)
Spread: 1ft (30cm)
Aspect: Sun
Soil: Well-drained
Hardiness: Zone 3
Propagation: Cuttings of
nonflowering shoots, in
summer

Modern bicolored pink with double,
clove-scented flowers of lavender-
pink, with deeper pink centers, in
flushes through summer.

Dianthus
'Waithman Beauty'
(Caryophyllaceae)

Common name: Modern
pink
Height: 12in (30cm)
Spread: 8in (20cm)
Aspect: Sun
Soil: Well-drained
Hardiness: Zone 3
Propagation: Cuttings of
nonflowering shoots, in
summer

A modern hybrid pink with flowers of
deep pink, blotched white and with
white centers, in flushes in summer.
Leaves are linear, gray-green.

Dianthus
'Whatfield Joy'
(Caryophyllaceae)

Common name: Modern
pink
Height: 8in (20cm)
Spread: 4in (10cm)
Aspect: Sun
Soil: Well-drained
Hardiness: Zone 3
Propagation: Cuttings of
nonflowering shoots, in
summer

A modern hybrid pink with single,
small flowers of rose pink, with a
paler center, borne in flushes in
summer. Leaves are linear and green.

Dianthus
'Widecombe Fair'
(Caryophyllaceae)

Common name: Modern
pink
Height: 12in (30cm)
Spread: 8in (20cm)
Aspect: Sun
Soil: Well-drained
Hardiness: Zone 3
Propagation: Cuttings of
nonflowering shoots, in
summer

Diascia
'Coral Belle'®, syn. 'Hecbel'
(Scrophulariaceae)

Common name: Twinspur
Height: 12in (30cm)
Spread: 8in (20cm)
Aspect: Sun
Soil: Moist, well-drained,
fertile
Hardiness: Zone 8
Propagation: Cuttings,
spring or summer

Modern hybrid pink with double,
clove-scented, peach flowers, which
open to blush pink, in flushes through
summer. Leaves are linear, gray-green.

A hybrid *Diascia*. Leaves ovate to
lance-shaped, midgreen. Racemes of
flowers, coral-pink in color, all
summer long. Good for the front of a
border.

DIASCIA (Scrophulariaceae)
Twinspur

There are some 50 or so erect to creeping or trailing, annual
and short-lived perennial species in this genus. They originate in
the southern regions of the African continent, and
consequentially they are for the most part not very hardy. They
are, however, relatively recent arrivals, and some are proving
hardier than at first thought, surviving in Zone 9 or even into
Zone 8, provided they are given protection from excessive
winter wet. They prefer moist soil, but do not tolerate
waterlogged conditions. Diascias are chiefly valued for their
long flowering season. The flowers are invariably pink or
salmon-colored, and borne in racemes on stems that range from
erect to prostrate. They are tubular and five-lobed; the two
upper lobes are spurred and have curious sacs marked with
yellow and purple patches, known as "windows," at the base.
They should be deadheaded regularly to prolong flowering. The
foliage is midgreen, linear to ovate, and toothed, and sometimes
evergreen. Diascias also benefit from a shearing-over in late
summer, and this provides a useful source of cuttings for
propagation, either to safeguard in case of winter losses or to
replace plants that have passed their best, every few years.

Diascia fetcaniensis
(Scrophulariaceae)

Common name: Twinspur
Height: 10in (25cm)
Spread: 12in (30cm)
Aspect: Sun
Soil: Moist, well-drained,
fertile
Hardiness: Zone 8
Propagation: Seed, in warmth
in spring; cuttings, in spring

Species from the Drakensberg
mountains of southern Africa. Leaves
ovate, hairy, green. Flowers in loose
racemes, rose-pink, spurs downturned,
summer and early autumn.

Diascia
'Joyce's Choice' A.G.M.
(Scrophulariaceae)

Common name: Twinspur
Height: 12in (30cm)
Spread: 8in (20cm)
Aspect: Sun
Soil: Moist, well-drained,
fertile
Hardiness: Zone 8
Propagation: Cuttings,
in spring or summer

Reliable hybrid *Diascia*. Leaves ovate-
linear, midgreen. Flowers in loose
racemes, bicolored light and dark
yellowish-pink, all summer.

Diascia
'Lady Valerie' A.G.M.
(Scrophulariaceae)

Common name: Twinspur
Height: 12in (30cm)
Spread: 8in (20cm)
Aspect: Sun
Soil: Moist, well-drained,
fertile
Hardiness: Zone 8
Propagation: Cuttings,
in spring or summer

A hybrid *Diascia*. Leaves ovate to
heart-shaped, midgreen. Flowers of a
strong yellowish-pink are carried in
loose racemes all summer.

Diascia rigescens
A.G.M.
(Scrophulariaceae)

Common name: Twinspur
Height: 12in (30cm)
Spread: 16in (40cm)
Aspect: Sun
Soil: Moist, well-drained,
fertile
Hardiness: Zone 8
Propagation: Seed or
cuttings, both in spring

Trailing species from South Africa.
Leaves heart-shaped, toothed,
midgreen. Flowers in dense racemes,
deep pink, in summer. Flops over if
not staked.

151

Diascia
'Rose Queen'
(Scrophulariaceae)

Common name: Twinspur
Height: 18in (45cm)
Spread: 12in (30cm)
Aspect: Sun
Soil: Moist, well-drained,
fertile
Hardiness: Zone 8
Propagation: Cuttings,
in spring or summer

A very floriferous and handsome
hybrid *Diascia* cultivar with flowers
of a most intense pink, borne in loose
racemes all summer long.

Diascia
'Ruby Field' A.G.M.
(Scrophulariaceae)

Common name: Twinspur
Height: 10in (25cm)
Spread: 18in (45cm)
Aspect: Sun
Soil: Moist, well-drained,
fertile
Hardiness: Zone 8
Propagation: Cuttings,
in spring or summer

An early hybrid *Diascia* cultivar.
Leaves heart-shaped, midgreen. Very
prolific in flowering, bearing masses
of salmon-pink flowers all summer.

Diascia vigilis
A.G.M.
(Scrophulariaceae)

Common name: Twinspur
Height: 12in (30cm)
Spread: 18in (45cm)
Aspect: Sun
Soil: Moist, well-drained,
fertile
Hardiness: Zone 8
Propagation: Seed or
cuttings, both in spring

Species from the Drakensberg
mountains of southern Africa. Leaves
ovate to lance-shaped, toothed, fleshy.
Flowers in loose racemes, clear pink,
all summer.

Dicentra
'Adrian Bloom'
(Fumariaceae/Papaveraceae)

Common name: Bleeding-
heart
Height: 16in (40cm)
Spread: 18in (45cm)
Aspect: Half shade
Soil: Moist, well-drained,
fertile
Hardiness: Zone 5
Propagation: Division, in spring
or just after the leaves die down

Clump-forming, rhizomatous hybrid.
Leaves pinnate, lobes long, gray-
green. Flowers in narrow racemes,
carmine, in late spring and
sporadically to autumn.

DICENTRA (Fumariaceae/Papaveraceae)
Bleeding-heart

A genus of some 20 or so annuals and perennials found in both Asia and North America, originating for the most part in moist woodland habitats. They may be rhizomatous, tuberous, or have fleshy tap roots. All are reliably hardy. The foliage is much-divided, fernlike, and silver-gray; some species are evergreen, but most are deciduous. The flowers are pendent, carried in arching panicles or racemes. They are highly distinctive: the two outer petals are pouched, giving a generally heart-shaped outline, while the two inner petals form a hood over the anthers. This curious appearance has earned the plants in the genus a variety of common names, from bleeding-heart (most often used for *D. spectabilis*) to Dutchman's breeches. They last well in water, and make excellent and unusual cut flowers; they and the foliage are valuable for flower arrangements. Most of the perennials in the genus make good border plants, but one or two are simply too invasive and better placed in a woodland garden. *D. spectabilis* is not long-lived. *Dicentra* are low in allergens, but all parts of the plants are poisonous and skin irritant. Their preferred conditions are half shade and moist, fertile soil, but they are drought-tolerant.

Dicentra
'Pearl Drops'
(Fumariaceae/Papaveraceae)

Common name: Bleeding-heart
Height: 12in (30cm)
Spread: 18in (45cm)
Aspect: Half shade
Soil: Moist, well-drained, fertile
Hardiness: Zone 5
Propagation: Division, in spring or just after the leaves die down

Rhizomatous, invasive, hybrid cultivar. Leaves lobed, glaucous blue-green. Flowers white, tinted pink, in racemes from mid-spring to summer.

Dicentra scandens
(Fumariaceae/Papaveraceae)

Common name: Bleeding-heart
Height: 5ft (1.5m)
Spread: 18in (45cm)
Aspect: Half shade
Soil: Moist, well-drained, fertile
Hardiness: Zone 6
Propagation: Seed, when ripe or in spring

Scrambling or climbing species. Leaves deeply lobed, segments ovate to lance-shaped, midgreen. Long racemes of yellow flowers, on leafy, wiry stems, in summer.

Dicentra spectabilis
A.G.M.
(Fumariaceae/Papaveraceae)

Common name: Bleeding-heart
Height: 3ft (1m)
Spread: 18in (45cm)
Aspect: Half shade
Soil: Moist, well-drained, fertile
Hardiness: Zone 6
Propagation: Seed, when ripe or in spring

Clump-forming species. Leaves 2-ternate, lobes ovate to cut, midgreen. Flowers in arching racemes, outer petals rose-pink, inner ones white, spring to early summer.

Dicentra spectabilis
'Alba' A.G.M.
(Papaveraceae)

Common name: Bleeding-heart
Height: 4ft (1.2m)
Spread: 18in (45cm)
Aspect: Half shade
Soil: Moist, well-drained, fertile
Hardiness: Zone 6
Propagation: Seed, when ripe or in spring

Pure white form of the species, and more robust and longer-lived. Late spring to midsummer. Woodlander from Siberia, China, and Korea.

Dicentra
'Spring Morning'
(Fumariaceae/Papaveraceae)

Common name: Bleeding-heart
Height: 18in (45cm)
Spread: 18in (45cm)
Aspect: Half shade
Soil: Moist, well-drained, fertile
Hardiness: Zone 5
Propagation: Division, in spring or just after the leaves die down

Clump-forming, rhizomatous hybrid, with finely divided, dark green leaves, which contrast well with the racemes of pale pink, nodding flowers.

Dicksonia antarctica
A.G.M.
(Cyathaceae/Dicksoniaceae)

Common name: Tree fern
Height: To 15ft (5m)
Spread: To 12ft (4m)
Aspect: Half or full shade
Soil: Acidic, humus-rich
Hardiness: Zone 8
Propagation: Spores, when ripe

Rhizomatous, treelike fern from Australia and Tasmania. Fronds 2- to 3-pinnate, pale green, darkening with age, evergreen in mild climates. Trunk up to 2ft (60cm) across.

Dictamnus albus
A.G.M.
(Rutaceae)

Common names: Dittany;
gasplant
Height: 36in (90cm)
Spread: 24in (60cm)
Aspect: Sun or half shade
Soil: Dry, well-drained
Hardiness: Zone 3
Propagation: Seed, when
ripe; division, in spring or
autumn

Leaves pinnate, spiny, lemon-scented,
green. Flowers in long, open racemes,
white. Oil in flowers and fruit
aromatic; can be ignited on hot days.
Toxic, skin irritant, allergenic.

Dictamnus albus
var. *purpureus* A.G.M.
(Rutaceae)

Common name: Dittany;
gasplant
Height: 36in (90cm)
Spread: 24in (60cm)
Aspect: Sun or half shade
Soil: Dry, well-drained
Hardiness: Zone 3
Propagation: Seed, when
ripe; division, in spring or
autumn

Purple-flowered form. Leaves pinnate,
spiny, lemon-scented, green. Flowers in
long, open racemes. On hot days oil in
flowers and fruit can be ignited. Toxic,
irritant, allergenic.

Dierama pendulum
(Iridaceae)

Common names: None
Height: 6ft (2m)
Spread: 2ft (60cm)
Aspect: Sun
Soil: Well-drained, humus-
rich
Hardiness: Zone 7
Propagation: Seed, when
ripe; division, in spring

Cormous evergreen from South
Africa. Leaves basal, arching, grasslike,
gray-green. Flowers bell-shaped,
pendent, pink, on arching stems in
summer. Seed heads good.

Dierama pulcherrimum
(Iridaceae)

Common names: None
Height: 5ft (1.5m)
Spread: 2ft (60cm)
Aspect: Sun
Soil: Well-drained,
humus-rich
Hardiness: Zone 7
Propagation: Seed, when
ripe; division, in spring

Cormous evergreen from South Africa
and Zimbabwe. Leaves basal, grassy,
green. Flowers tubular to bell-shaped,
white or pink, pendent, on arching
stems, summer.

Dietes bicolor
(Iridaceae)

Common name: Wild iris
Height: 3ft (1m)
Spread: 1ft (30cm)
Aspect: Sun or half shade
Soil: Moist, well-drained
Hardiness: Zone 9
Propagation: Seed, in
autumn or spring

Rhizomatous evergreen from Africa.
Leaves basal, erect, leathery, sword-shaped, pale green. Flowers flat; 3
cream tepals have a brown spot at the
base, spring to summer.

Dietes grandiflora
(Iridaceae)

Common name: Wild iris
Height: 3ft (1m)
Spread: 1ft (30cm)
Aspect: Sun or half shade
Soil: Moist, well-drained
Hardiness: Zone 9
Propagation: Seed, in
autumn or spring

Rhizomatous plant from South Africa.
Erect, linear, leathery, pale green, basal
leaves. Flat, evanescent flowers; 3 white
tepals marked mauve and yellow,
spring and early summer.

DIGITALIS (Scrophulariaceae)
Foxglove

There are 20 or so biennial and short-lived perennial species
from Eurasia and North Africa in this genus. They are tall,
architectural plants which do not require staking except in very
exposed situations. They are fine woodland plants. Most are
perennial, but in Britain they all tend to be thought of as
biennial because the native _D. purpurea_ is that; this species, too,
can be perennial, but the flowers deteriorate markedly in later
years. Foxgloves self-seed, so the fact that they are short-lived is
not really a problem. Their self-seeding is not invasive, with the
seedlings appearing around the base of the parent plant, but if it
is a problem, deadheading will cure it. They are very drought-tolerant, but they are prone to powdery mildew. The foliage is
handsome, oblong to obovate, toothed or entire, midgreen,
growing in basal rosettes. The flowers are in upright racemes,
which are usually one-sided, and are open bells or tubules in a
range of golden or purple shades, often marked with spots or
veins inside. They are very attractive to bees, and an imposing
addition to flower arrangements. They are low in allergens, so
suitable for the gardener with allergies, but all parts of the plant
are poisonous and contact can irritate skin.

Digitalis ferruginea
(Scrophulariaceae)

Common name: Rusty
foxglove
Height: 4ft (1.2m)
Spread: 18in (45cm)
Aspect: Half shade
Soil: Moist, avoiding
extremes of wet or dry,
humus-rich
Hardiness: Zone 7
Propagation: Seed, in spring

Tall woodlander. Dark green, oblong,
entire leaves in rosettes. Flowers in
long narrow spikes, golden-brown,
veined red-brown inside, in summer.
Toxic and skin irritant.

Digitalis
'Glory of Roundway'
(Scrophulariaceae)

Common name: Foxglove
Height: 36in (90cm)
Spread: 12in (30cm)
Aspect: Half shade
Soil: Moist, avoiding wet
or dry extremes, humus-
rich
Hardiness: Zone 5
Propagation: Division,
in spring

Hybrid foxglove cultivar with tall
racemes of funnel-shaped, flowers of
pale yellow, tinted pink, in summer.
Good woodland plant. All parts toxic
and skin irritant.

Digitalis grandiflora
A.G.M.
(Scrophulariaceae)

Common name: Yellow
foxglove
Height: 3ft (1m)
Spread: 18in (45cm)
Aspect: Half shade
Soil: Humus-rich
Hardiness: Zone 4
Propagation: Seed, in spring

Woodlander from Europe to Siberia.
Leaves ovate-oblong, toothed, veined,
midgreen. Raceme of pale yellow
tubular flowers in early to midsummer. Toxic and irritant.

Digitalis
'John Innes Tetra'
(Scrophulariaceae)

Common name: Foxglove
Height: 36in (90cm)
Spread: 12in (30cm)
Aspect: Half shade
Soil: Humus-rich
Hardiness: Zone 6
Propagation: Division,
in spring

A hybrid foxglove cultivar with
racemes of tubular, orange, yellow-
lipped flowers in summer. Good for a
woodland garden. All parts toxic and
skin irritant.

Digitalis lanata
A.G.M.
(Scrophulariaceae)

Common name: Grecian foxglove
Height: 24in (60cm)
Spread: 12in (30cm)
Aspect: Half shade
Soil: Humus-rich
Hardiness: Zone 7
Propagation: Seed, in spring

Digitalis lutea
(Scrophulariaceae)

Common name: Straw foxglove
Height: 24in (60cm)
Spread: 12in (30cm)
Aspect: Half shade
Soil: Humus-rich
Hardiness: Zone 4
Propagation: Seed, in spring

Woodland species. Leaves oblong to lance-shaped, midgreen. Dense raceme of cream to fawn flowers, veined brown, pale lower lip, in midsummer. Toxic and skin irritant.

Woodland species. Leaves glossy, green, inverse-lance-shaped to oblong, toothed. Slim raceme of pale yellow flowers, early- to midsummer. Toxic and skin irritant.

Digitalis × mertonensis
A.G.M.
(Scrophulariaceae)

Common names: None
Height: 36in (90cm)
Spread: 12in (30cm)
Aspect: Half shade
Soil: Humus-rich
Hardiness: Zone 5
Propagation: Division, in spring

Digitalis purpurea
(Scrophulariaceae)

Common name: Biennial foxglove
Height: To 6ft (2m)
Spread: 2ft (60cm)
Aspect: Half shade
Soil: Humus-rich
Hardiness: Zone 6
Propagation: Seed, in spring

Tetraploid hybrid; comes true from seed. Leaves toothed, veined, glossy, lance-shaped to ovate. Racemes of pinkish-buff flowers, spring to early summer. Toxic and irritant.

Biennial or short-lived perennial European species. Leaves lance-shaped, toothed, deep green. Flowers in one-sided racemes, pink, purple, or white. Toxic and skin irritant.

Dionaea muscipula
(Droseraceae)

Diphylleia cymosa
(Berberidaceae)

Common name: Venus
flytrap
Height: 12in (30cm)
Spread: 6in (15cm)
Aspect: Sun
Soil: Moist, acidic
Hardiness: Zone 8
Propagation: Seed, in
warmth in spring

Common names: None
Height: 3ft (1m)
Spread: 1ft (30cm)
Aspect: Full or half shade
Soil: Moist, humus-rich
Hardiness: Zone 7
Propagation: Seed or
division, both in spring

Rosette-forming, insectivorous species
from North America. Leaves yellow-
green, stalks winged, spiny-edged.
Flowers in umbels on bare stalks,
white, early to midsummer.

Rhizomatous woodlander. Leaves
large, peltate, toothed, dark green.
Flowers in terminal cymes, white,
bowl-shaped, in late spring to early
summer; blue berries follow.

Diplarrhena moraea
(Iridaceae)

Disa uniflora
(Orchidaceae)

Common names: None
Height: 24in (60cm)
Spread: 10in (25cm)
Aspect: Sun or half shade
Soil: Moist, well-drained,
sandy, acidic
Hardiness: Zone 7
Propagation: Seed or
division, both in spring

Common names: None
Height: 24in (60cm)
Spread: 8in (20cm)
Aspect: Half shade
Soil: Peaty, mossy, sandy
Hardiness: Zone 10
Propagation: Division,
after growth starts

Rhizomatous plant from Australia.
Leaves basal, long, linear, dark green.
Flowers scented, white; purple and
yellow marks on inner tepals, in late
spring to early summer.

Terrestrial orchid from South Africa.
Leaves lance-shaped, green. Short
raceme of up to 10 flowers in summer,
red with gold veins. Not easy; keep
cool and shaded in summer.

Disporum smithii
(Convallariaceae/Liliaceae)

Common names: None
Height: 2ft (60cm)
Spread: 1ft (30cm)
Aspect: Half shade
Soil: Moist, well-drained,
humus-rich
Hardiness: Zone 6
Propagation: Seed, in
autumn; division, in spring

Rhizomatous woodlander. Leaves
ovate to lance-shaped, scalloped,
green. Flowers in umbels, pendent,
tubular, greenish-white, in spring;
orange berries in late summer.

Dodecatheon meadia
A.G.M.
(Primulaceae)

Common name: Common
shooting-star
Height: 16in (40cm)
Spread: 10in (25cm)
Aspect: Sun or half shade
Soil: Moist, well-drained,
acidic, humus-rich
Hardiness: Zone 3
Propagation: Seed, when ripe, after
cold exposure; division, in spring

Clump-forming woodlander from the
U.S.A. Leaves ovate to spoon-shaped,
midgreen. Flowers in umbels,
magenta, in spring. *D. meadia* f.
album also has an A.G.M.

Dodecatheon pulchellum
A.G.M.
(Primulaceae)

Common name: Southern
shooting-star
Height: 14in (35cm)
Spread: 6in (15cm)
Aspect: Sun or half shade
Soil: Moist, well-drained,
acidic, humus-rich
Hardiness: Zone 5
Propagation: Seed, when ripe, after
cold exposure; division, in spring

Clump-forming woodlander from
western North America. Leaves
spoon-shaped to ovate, midgreen.
Flowers in umbels of up to 20, cerise,
in spring.

Doronicum orientale
'Magnificum'
(Asteraceae/Compositae)

Common name: Oriental
leopard's-bane
Height: 20in (50cm)
Spread: 36in (90cm)
Aspect: Half shade
Soil: Moist, humus-rich
Hardiness: Zone 5
Propagation: Seed, in
spring; division, in autumn

Spreading, rhizomatous woodlander
from Europe and the near East.
Leaves basal, ovate, scalloped,
midgreen. Flowers large, solitary,
yellow daisies, mid- to late spring.

Doronicum pardalianches
(Asteraceae Compositae)

Common names: None
Height: 36in (90cm)
Spread: 36in (90cm)
Aspect: Half shade
Soil: Moist, humus-rich
Hardiness: Zone 6
Propagation: Seed, in
spring; division, in autumn

Spreading, rhizomatous woodlander
from Europe. Leaves basal, ovate,
toothed, hairy, midgreen. Flowers
yellow, daisylike, in corymbs, spring
to midsummer.

Doronicum plantagineum
(Asteraceae/Compositae)

Common name: Plantain
leopard's-bane
Height: 32in (80cm)
Spread: 18in (45cm)
Aspect: Half shade
Soil: Moist, humus-rich
Hardiness: Zone 6
Propagation: Seed, in spring; division,
in autumn

Rhizomatous woodlander from W.
Europe. Leaves basal, ovate, hairy,
midgreen; die down soon after
flowering. Flowers on branching
stems, yellow, in late spring.

Draba longisiliqua
A.G.M.
(Brassicaceae/Cruciferae)

Common names: None
Height: 4in (10cm)
Spread: 8in (20cm)
Aspect: Sun; protect
against winter wet
Soil: Sharply drained,
gritty
Hardiness: Zone 6
Propagation: Seed, after cold
exposure, in autumn

Cushion-forming evergreen. Rosettes
of leaves, obovate, gray-hairy. Flowers
yellow, in dense, short racemes, in
spring. Grow in alpine house or cover
with glass in winter.

Dracunculus vulgaris
(Araceae)

Common name: Dragon
arum
Height: 5ft (1.5m)
Spread: 2ft (60cm)
Aspect: Sun, but tolerates
half shade
Soil: Well-drained, dry in
summer, humus-rich
Hardiness: Zone 9
Propagation: Offsets, in autumn or
spring
Tuberous Mediterranean woodlander.
Basal, pedate, deep green leaves;
brownish marks. Flowers spring to
summer; maroon spathe, black spadix,
malodorous. May bear berries.

161

Dryas octopetala
A.G.M.
(Rosaceae)

Common name: Mt.
Washington dryad
Height: 4in (10cm)
Spread: 3ft (1m)
Aspect: Sun or half shade
Soil: Well-drained, gritty,
humus-rich
Hardiness: Zone 2
Propagation: Seed, when ripe;
softwood cuttings, in summer

Subshrub from Europe. Leaves ovate,
scalloped, green. Flowers almost
stemless, upward-facing, white with
yellow stamens, in late spring to early
summer.

Dryopteris affinis
A.G.M. (Aspidiaceae/
Dryopteridaceae)

Common name: Golden
male fern
Height: 3ft (90cm)
Spread: 3ft (90cm)
Aspect: Half shade
Soil: Moist, humus-rich
Hardiness: Zone 6
Propagation: Spores, in
warmth when ripe

Evergreen, rhizomatous, terrestrial
fern. Fronds lance-shaped, 2-pinnate,
pale green, turning dark green, with a
dark spot where each pinna joins the
brown midrib.

Echinacea pallida
(Asteraceae/Compositae)

Common name: Pink
coneflower
Height: 4ft (1.2m)
Spread: 18in (45cm)
Aspect: Sun
Soil: Well-drained,
humus-rich
Hardiness: Zone 5
Propagation: Seed, in spring;
division, in autumn or spring

Rhizomatous perennial from the
U.S.A. Leaves linear to lance-shaped,
bristly, dark green. Flowers daisylike,
disc florets brown, ray florets
drooping, pale pink, late summer.

Echinacea purpurea
(Asteraceae/Compositae)

Common name: Purple
coneflower
Height: 5ft (1.5m)
Spread: 18in (45cm)
Aspect: Sun
Soil: Well-drained,
humus-rich
Hardiness: Zone 3
Propagation: Seed, in spring;
division, in spring or autumn

Rhizomatous perennial from the
U.S.A. Leaves ovate, toothed, smooth,
green. Flowers solitary, single, ray
florets reflexed, purple, disc florets
golden-brown.

Echinacea purpurea
'Robert Bloom'
(Asteraceae/Compositae)

Common name: Purple
coneflower
Height: 5ft (1.5m)
Spread: 18in (45cm)
Aspect: Sun
Soil: Well-drained,
humus-rich
Hardiness: Zone 3
Propagation: Seed, in spring;
division, in spring or autumn

A selected form of *E. purpurea*.
Flowers mauve-crimson, reflexed ray
florets, with prominent discs of
orange-brown. Leaves ovate, toothed,
smooth, green.

Echinacea purpurea
'Magnus'
(Asteraceae/Compositae)

Common name: Great
purple coneflower
Height: 5ft (1.5m)
Spread: 18in (45cm)
Aspect: Sun
Soil: Well-drained,
humus-rich
Hardiness: Zone 3
Propagation: Seed, in spring;
division, in spring or autumn

Large-flowered form of *E. purpurea*,
in which the flowerheads are 7in
(18cm) across. Ray florets held almost
horizontal. Leaves ovate, toothed,
smooth, green.

Echinacea purpurea
'White Lustre'
(Asteraceae/Compositae)

Common name: White
coneflower
Height: 5ft (1.5m)
Spread: 18in (45cm)
Aspect: Sun
Soil: Well-drained,
humus-rich
Hardiness: Zone 3
Propagation: Seed, in spring;
division, in spring or autumn

White form of *E. purpurea*. Flowers
have creamy-white, reflexed ray
florets, and orange-brown disc florets.
Leaves ovate, toothed, smooth, green.

Echinacea purpurea
'White Swan'
(Asteraceae/Compositae)

Common name: White
coneflower
Height: 5ft (1.5m)
Spread: 18in (45cm)
Aspect: Sun
Soil: Well-drained,
humus-rich
Hardiness: Zone 3
Propagation: Seed, in spring;
division, in spring or autumn

Selected white form of *E. purpurea*.
Flowers are large, with white ray
florets and orange-brown disc florets.
Leaves are ovate, toothed, smooth,
green.

Echinops bannaticus
(Asteraceae/Compositae)

Common name: Globe-thistle
Height: 4ft (1.2m)
Spread: 2ft (60cm)
Aspect: Sun
Soil: Well-drained, poor
Hardiness: Zone 3
Propagation: Seed, in midspring; division, in spring or autumn

Clump-forming perennial from S.E. Europe. Leaves ovate, spiny, hairy, pinnatisect, gray-green. Flowers terminal, spherical, blue-gray, with bristly bracts, late summer.

Echinops ritro
A.G.M.
(Asteraceae/Compositae)

Common name: Small globe-thistle
Height: 24in (60cm)
Spread: 18in (45cm)
Aspect: Sun
Soil: Well-drained, poor
Hardiness: Zone 3
Propagation: Seed, in midspring; division, in spring or autumn

Clump-forming plant. Leaves oblong, pinnatisect, spiny, dark green, cobwebby above, white-downy beneath. Flowerhead spherical, bright blue, in late summer.

Echium pininana
(Boraginaceae)

Common name: Bugloss
Height: 12ft (4m)
Spread: 3ft (1m)
Aspect: Sun
Soil: Well-drained, fertile
Hardiness: Zone 9
Propagation: Seed, in warmth in summer

Echium wildpretii
(Boraginaceae)

Common names: Bugloss
Height: 6ft (2m)
Spread: 2ft (60cm)
Aspect: Sun
Soil: Well-drained, fertile
Hardiness: Zone 9
Propagation: Seed, in warmth in summer

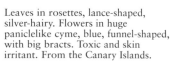

Leaves in rosettes, lance-shaped, silver-hairy. Flowers in huge paniclelike cyme, blue, funnel-shaped, with big bracts. Toxic and skin irritant. From the Canary Islands.

Perennial from the Canary Islands. Leaves in a basal rosette, narrow, lance-shaped, hairy, pale green. Flowers in dense cymes, funnel-shaped, red, late spring to summer.

Edraianthus pumilio
A.G.M.
(Campanulaceae)

Common names: None
Height: 1in (3cm)
Spread: 6in (15cm)
Aspect: Sun
Soil: Sharply drained,
sandy, chalky
Hardiness: Zone 6
Propagation: Seed, in
autumn; softwood cuttings,
in summer

Dwarf, cushion-forming perennial
from Dalmatia. Leaves linear, hairy,
silver-green. Flowers solitary, stemless,
upturned bells, deep purple-blue, in
early summer.

Elsholtzia stauntonii
(Labiatae/Lamiaceae)

Common name: Staunton
elsholtzia
Height: 4ft (1.2m)
Spread: 3ft (1m)
Aspect: Sun
Soil: Well-drained, fertile
Hardiness: Zone 4
Propagation: Seed, in
warmth when ripe; softwood
cuttings, in summer

Deciduous subshrub with toothed,
lance-shaped, midgreen leaves, aging
red, mint-scented. Flowers small,
purple-pink; dense panicles or
racemes, late summer to autumn.

Elymus hispidus
(Graminae/Poaceae)

Common name: Blue wild
rye
Height: 30in (75cm)
Spread: 16in (40cm)
Aspect: Sun
Soil: Moist, well-drained,
fertile
Hardiness: Zone 5
Propagation: Seed, *in situ*
in autumn or spring

Noninvasive evergreen grass from
Eurasia. Leaves silvery blue, ridged
below, upright, then arching. Dense,
wheatlike flower panicle in summer,
silver-blue turning beige.

Elymus magellanicus
(Graminae/Poaceae)

Common name: Wild rye
Height: 6in (15cm)
Spread: 12in (30cm)
Aspect: Sun
Soil: Moist, well-drained,
fertile
Hardiness: Zone 5
Propagation: Seed, *in situ*
in autumn or spring

Mound-forming, tufted grass from
South America. Leaves linear, folded,
blue. Flower spike lax or prostrate,
bearing up to 7 flowers, all summer
long.

165

Eomecon chionantha
(Papaveraceae)

Common names: None
Height: 16in (40 cm)
Spread: Indefinite
Aspect: Half shade
Soil: Moist, well-drained,
humus-rich
Hardiness: Zone 7
Propagation: Seed or
division, both in spring

Invasive woodlander from eastern
China. Leaves handsome, leathery,
kidney-shaped, green. Flowers like
white poppies, in loose panicles, from
late spring to midsummer.

Epilobium angustifolium
(Onagraceae)

Common name: Fireweed;
rosebay
Height: 5ft (1.5m)
Spread: 3ft (1m)
Aspect: Sun or half shade
Soil: Moist, well-drained,
humus-rich
Hardiness: Zone 3
Propagation: Seed, when ripe;
division, in spring or autumn

Highly invasive, rhizomatous plant.
Leaves lance-shaped, midgreen.
Flowers in racemes, pink saucers,
from summer to early autumn. Self-
seeds very prolifically.

Epilobium angustifolium
var. album
(Onagraceae)

Common name: White
rosebay
Height: 5ft (1.5m)
Spread: 3ft (1m)
Aspect: Sun or half shade
Soil: Moist, well-drained,
humus-rich
Hardiness: Zone 3
Propagation: Seed, when ripe;
division, in spring or autumn

White-flowered form; flowers in
racemes from summer to early
autumn. Claimed to be less invasive
than the usual form of the species, but
still a liberal self-seeder.

Epilobium dodonaei
(Onagraceae)

Common name: Willow-
weed
Height: 36in (90cm)
Spread: 8in (20cm)
Aspect: Sun or half shade
Soil: Moist, well-drained,
humus-rich
Hardiness: Zone 6
Propagation: Seed, when ripe;
division, in spring or autumn

An invasive perennial from C. Europe
to W. Asia. Leaves linear, toothed,
hairy, midgreen. Flowers in loose
terminal racemes, dark pink-purple,
all summer.

Epilobium glabellum
(Onagraceae)

Epimedium davidii
(Berberidaceae)

Common name: Willow-
weed
Height: 8in (20cm)
Spread: 8in (20cm)
Aspect: Half shade
Soil: Moist, well-drained,
humus-rich
Hardiness: Zone 8
Propagation: Seed, when ripe;
division, in spring or autumn

Common names: None
Height: 12in (30cm)
Spread: 18in (45cm)
Aspect: Half shade
Soil: Moist, well-drained,
fertile, humus-rich
Hardiness: Zone 7
Propagation: Seed, when
ripe; division, in autumn

Clump-forming woodland ground
cover. Leaves elliptic-ovate, toothed,
dark green. Flowers solitary, on
branching stems, white or pink,
summer. Evergreen in mild areas.

Clump-forming evergreen from W
China. Leaves bronze aging to green,
3-palmate, lobes ovate to lance-
shaped. Flowers yellow, with curved
spurs, spring to early summer.

EPIMEDIUM (Berberidaceae)
Bishop's-hat

A genus of some 40 rhizomatous, clump-forming, perennial
species, of varying hardiness, found from the Mediterranean
across to temperate regions of East Asia. Their natural habitat
is woodland or shady scrub, and they all prefer a sheltered and
partly shaded site. Some species are evergreen, others
semievergreen, yet others deciduous. All have handsome, mainly
basal foliage, and will make excellent ground cover, especially in
a woodland or other partly shaded situation; smaller types are
suitable for a rock garden. New growth in spring may be tinted
bronze, and the leaves of many deciduous species color
attractively in autumn. The foliage of the semi-evergreen and
deciduous types should be sheared over in late winter before
new growth begins, to show the flowers to their best. Although
Epimedium are not spectacular when in bloom, they have a
quiet charm. The individual flowers are delicate in appearance.
They are mainly cup- or saucer-shaped and composed of two
sets of four tepals surrounding four petals; these often have
elongated spurs. They are nodding, in shades of pink, purple,
buff, white, or yellow, and carried in erect to arching racemes
or panicles on slender stems. *Epimedium* are low in allergens.

**Epimedium grandiflorum
A.G.M.
(Berberidaceae)**

Common name: Bishop's-
hat
Height: 1ft (30cm)
Spread: 1ft (30cm)
Aspect: Half shade,
Soil: Moist, well-drained,
fertile, humus-rich
Hardiness: Zone 5
Propagation: Seed, when
ripe; division, in autumn

Rhizomatous, deciduous plant. Leaves
lobed, leaflets ovate to heart-shaped,
spiny-edged, bronze turning green.
Flowers pink, white, purple, or
yellow, spurred, in spring.

**Epimedium x rubrum
A.G.M.
(Berberidaceae)**

Common names: None
Height: 1ft (30cm)
Spread: 1ft (30cm)
Aspect: Half shade
Soil: Moist, well-drained,
fertile, humus-rich
Hardiness: Zone 5
Propagation: Seed, when
ripe; division, in autumn

Rhizomatous, semievergreen perennial
of garden origin. Leaves 2-ternate,
lobes spiny, ovate, pointed, red
turning brown, lasting over winter.
Flowers red and cream, spring.

**Epimedium x versicolor
'Sulphureum' A.G.M.
(Berberidaceae)**

Common names: None
Height: 1ft (30cm)
Spread: 3ft (1m)
Aspect: Half shade
Soil: Moist, well-drained,
fertile, humus-rich
Hardiness: Zone 5
Propagation: Seed, when
ripe; division, in autumn

Rhizomatous, evergreen perennial of
garden origin. Leaves lobed, 5-11
ovate, spiny leaflets, red-brown
turning green. Flowers deep yellow,
spurs long, in spring.

**Epimedium x youngianum
'Roseum'
(Berberidaceae)**

Common names: None
Height: 1ft (30cm)
Spread: 1ft (30cm)
Aspect: Half shade
Soil: Moist, well-drained,
humus-rich, fertile
Hardiness: Zone 5
Propagation: Seed, when
ripe; division, in autumn

Deciduous rhizomatous perennial
with ovate leaves, sometimes spotted
or with pale green centers and dark
green edges. Flowers dusky pink, in
spring.

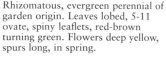

Epipactis gigantea
(Orchidaceae)

Common name: Giant
helleborine
Height: 16in (40cm)
Spread: To 3ft (1m)
Aspect: Half or full shade
Soil: Moist, well-drained,
humus-rich
Hardiness: Zone 6
Propagation: Division, such that
each piece has an eye, in spring

Rhizomatous terrestrial orchid. Ovate
to lance-shaped, green leaves. Flowers
nodding, in spikes, greenish-yellow,
veined maroon and brown. Spreads
rapidly in ideal sites.

Eranthis hyemalis
A.G.M
(Ranunculaceae)

Common name: Winter
aconite
Height: 3in (8cm)
Spread: 2in (5cm)
Aspect: Sun or half shade
Soil: Reliably moist through
summer, fertile, humus-rich
Hardiness: Zone 5
Propagation: Seed or division,
both in spring

Tuberous perennial from S. Europe.
Basal leaves lobed-pinnate, green.
Stem leaves in a ruff below flower,
dissected, bright green. Flowers
yellow cups. All parts poisonous.

Eremurus himalaicus
(Asphodelaceae/Liliaceae)

Common name:
Himalayan desert-candle
Height: 6ft (2m)
Spread: 2ft (60cm)
Aspect: Sun
Soil: Sandy, well-drained,
fertile
Hardiness: Zone 3
Propagation: Seed, in autumn;
division, after flowering

Fleshy-rooted perennial. Leaves in
rosettes, linear, green. Flowers in tall
racemes, white, spring to early
summer. Must have winter cold to
flower. Do not dig near base.

Eremurus robustus
(Asphodelaceae/Liliaceae)

Common name: Giant
desert-candle
Height: 10ft (3m)
Spread: 3ft (1m)
Aspect: Sun
Soil: Well-drained, sandy,
fertile
Hardiness: Zone 6
Propagation: Seed, in autumn;
division, after flowering

Perennial from C. Asia. Leaves blue-
green, strap-shaped, rough-edged.
Flowers pink, in racemes, in early to
midsummer. Needs winter cold to
flower. Do not dig near base.

Eremurus stenophyllus
(Asphodelaceae/Liliaceae)

Common name: Bunge
Desert-candle
Height: 3ft (1m)
Spread: 2ft (60cm)
Aspect: Sun
Soil: Well-drained, sandy,
fertile
Hardiness: Zone 5
Propagation: Seed, in autumn;
division, after flowering

Perennial from W. Asia, Iran, and
Pakistan. Leaves linear, hairy, gray-
green. Flowers in racemes, yellow,
fading to orange, early to midsummer.
Do not dig or hoe near base.

Erigeron aurantiacus
(Asteraceae/Compositae)

Common name: Daisy
fleabane
Height: 1ft (30cm)
Spread: 1ft (30cm)
Aspect: Sun
Soil: Well-drained, fertile,
humus-rich
Hardiness: Zone 6
Propagation: Seed or division,
both in spring

Clump-forming perennial from
Turkestan. Leaves spoon-shaped to
elliptic, velvety, green. Flowerheads
solitary, single, bright orange with
yellow discs, in summer.

ERIGERON (Asteraceae/Compositae)
Fleabane

There are over 200 species in this genus, most of them
perennials; their main distribution in the wild is in North
America. They range from mat- or mound-forming alpines to
taller, clump-forming border types. They are invaluable border
perennials, with several excellent characteristics. They have a
long flowering season: *Erigeron karvinskianus* is the longest-
flowering of all hardy perennials, blooming nonstop for up to
six months; few gardeners could ask for more.

They are easy-going, requiring only sun and reasonably fertile,
well-drained soil; some of the alpines benefit from protection
against excessive winter wet. Almost all are reliably hardy, and
they are excellent for coastal gardens, *E. glaucus* especially so.
They are much appreciated by bees and butterflies in the
garden, and also by flower arrangers, as they last very well in
water if picked when open. There have to be disadvantages, and
as a genus they need to be lifted and divided every few years.
Some of the taller hybrids do require staking, and slugs are fond
of the new growth in spring. All *Erigeron* are unfortunately
highly allergenic, and so should be avoided by allergic gardeners
(note that this is not the only genus commonly called fleabane).

Erigeron 'Charity' (Asteraceae/Compositae)

Common name: Fleabane
Height: 24in (60cm)
Spread: 18in (45cm)
Aspect: Sun
Soil: Well-drained, fertile, humus-rich
Hardiness: Zone 5
Propagation: Division, in spring

Clump-forming hybrid cultivar. Leaves midgreen, lance-shaped. Flowerheads lilac-pink with yellow discs, semidouble, in early and midsummer.

Erigeron compositus (Asteraceae/Compositae)

Common name: Fernleaf fleabane
Height: 6in (15cm)
Spread: 4in (10cm)
Aspect: Sun
Soil: Well-drained, fertile, humus-rich
Hardiness: Zone 5
Propagation: Seed or division, both in spring

Cushion-forming perennial. Leaves 3- or 4-ternate, lobed, hairy, gray-green. Yellow-centered, pale blue, white, or pink, solitary, single flowerheads, in summer. Self-seeds.

Erigeron 'Dignity' (Asteraceae/Compositae)

Common name: Fleabane
Height: 20in (50cm)
Spread: 18in (45cm)
Aspect: Sun
Soil: Well-drained, fertile, humus-rich
Hardiness: Zone 5
Propagation: Division, in spring

Hybrid fleabane cultivar with lance- to spoon-shaped leaves, and violet-mauve flowerheads with yellow centers in early and midsummer.

Erigeron 'Four Winds' (Asteraceae/Compositae)

Common name: Fleabane
Height: 20in (50cm)
Spread: 18in (45cm)
Aspect: Sun
Soil: Well-drained, fertile, humus-rich
Hardiness: Zone 5
Propagation: Division, in spring

Hybrid cultivar with lance-shaped, midgreen leaves, and solitary, single flowerheads of strong pink with yellow centers, in early and midsummer.

Erigeron glaucus
(Asteraceae/Compositae)

Common name: Beach
fleabane
Height: 12in (30cm)
Spread: 18in (45cm)
Aspect: Sun
Soil: Well-drained, fertile,
humus-rich
Hardiness: Zone 3
Propagation: Seed or
division, both in spring

Coastal species. Leaves lance-shaped
to obovate, glaucous green.
Flowerheads solitary, semidouble, pale
mauve with yellow discs, late spring
to midsummer.

Erigeron karvinskianus
A.G.M.
(Asteraceae/Compositae)

Common name: Bonytip
fleabane
Height: 1ft (30cm)
Spread: 3ft (1m)
Aspect: Sun
Soil: Well-drained, fertile,
humus-rich
Hardiness: Zone 7
Propagation: Seed or
division, both in spring

Vigorous, spreading; excellent wall
plant. Leaves hairy, gray-green, lance-
shaped. Flowerheads single, small,
white turning pink, summer to early
winter in mild areas.

Erigeron philadelphicus
(Asteraceae/Compositae)

Common name:
Philadelphia fleabane
Height: 2ft (60cm)
Spread: 1ft (30cm)
Aspect: Sun
Soil: Well-drained, moist
Hardiness: Zone 2
Propagation: Seed or
division, both in spring

Species from northern U.S.A. and
Canada. Leaves obovate, hairy,
scalloped, green. Flowerheads solitary,
single, rose-lilac, with a yellow disc.

Erigeron
'Rotes Meer'
(Asteraceae/Compositae)

Common name: Fleabane
Height: 2ft (60cm)
Spread: 2ft (60cm)
Aspect: Sun
Soil: Well-drained, fertile,
humus-rich
Hardiness: Zone 5
Propagation: Division,
in autumn

Hybrid fleabane cultivar with
semidouble flowerheads of a deep red
with yellow centers, borne in summer.
Leaves are spoon-shaped.

Erigeron 'Schneewitschen' (Asteraceae/Compositae)

Common name: Fleabane
Height: 28in (70cm)
Spread: 24in (60cm)
Aspect: Sun
Soil: Well-drained, fertile, humus-rich
Hardiness: Zone 3
Propagation: Division, in spring

A hybrid garden cultivar bearing single flowerheads of purest white, with yellow centers, in summer. Good in a herbaceous or a mixed border.

Erigeron 'Serenity' (Asteraceae/Compositae)

Common name: Fleabane
Height: 30in (75cm)
Spread: 18in (45cm)
Aspect: Sun
Soil: Well-drained, fertile, humus-rich
Hardiness: Zone 5
Propagation: Division, in spring

Hybrid cultivar of lax habit, bearing semidouble flowerheads of violet-mauve, in corymbs, in early and midsummer. Leaves are lance-shaped.

Erinus alpinus A.G.M. (Scrophulariaceae)

Common name: Alpine liverbalsam
Height: 4in (10cm)
Spread: 4in (10cm)
Aspect: Sun or half shade
Soil: Well-drained
Hardiness: Zone 6
Propagation: Seed, in autumn

Semievergreen. Inverse-lance-shaped, sticky leaves. Flowers 2-lipped, pink, purple, or white in short racemes, late spring to early summer. May repeat-flower if deadheaded.

Eriogonum umbellatum (Polygonaceae)

Common name: Sulfur-flower
Height: 1ft (30cm)
Spread: 1m (3ft)
Aspect: Sun
Soil: Well-drained, sandy
Hardiness: Zone 7
Propagation: Seed, in autumn; cuttings, in spring

Leaves in rosettes, ovate, midgreen, white undersides. Yellow flowers turning red, in umbels, in summer. Hates winter wet. Not always free-flowering. Trim after flowering.

**Eriogonum umbellatum
var. torreyanum**
(Polygonaceae)

Eriophyllum lanatum
(Asteraceae/Compositae)

Common name:
Sulfur-flower
Height: 1ft (30cm)
Spread: 3ft (1m)
Aspect: Sun
Soil: Well-drained, sandy
Hardiness: Zone 7
Propagation: Seed, in
autumn; cuttings, in spring

Common name: Woolly
eriophyllum
Height: 2ft (60 cm)
Spread: 2ft (60cm)
Aspect: Sun
Soil: Well-drained, sandy
Hardiness: Zone 5
Propagation: Seed, in
autumn; division, in spring

Subshrub from U.S.A. Leaves ovate,
shiny, dark green. Flowers in umbels,
yellow, with pronounced bracts, in
summer. Free-flowering, in contrast to
the species.

Perennial from W. North America.
Leaves divided, white-woolly, silver-
gray. Flowers solitary or in corymbs,
yellow, spring to summer. Can be
invasive.

ERODIUM (Geraniaceae)
Heronbill

A genus of some 60 species distributed across Europe, Asia,
North Africa, North and South America, and Australia. Most
are perennials, but the genus also includes annuals and both
deciduous and evergreen subshrubs. Most are reliably hardy,
but one or two are less so; all are drought-tolerant. *Erodium* are
invaluable garden plants, on account of their long flowering
season, which stretches from spring to late summer, and their
handsome foliage. The leaves may be lobed, pinnatisect, or
pinnate. The flowers are usually borne in umbels, but sometimes
singly, and range in color from pink to purple, often with
darker veins or markings, as well as some yellow or white
examples. They are five-petalled and geraniumlike, but can be
distinguished by their stamens: *Erodium* have five stamens,
whereas geraniums have ten. Some types are too small for a
border and are best grown in a rock garden, but others are
excellent plants for the front of the border. All make good
plants for coastal gardens. They are easy to cultivate, provided
they have a sunny position and good drainage, and they do not
require staking. They do have a tendency to self-seed, so should
be cut back after flowering if this is not desired.

Erodium carvifolium
(Geraniaceae)

Common name: Heronbill
Height: 14in (35cm)
Spread: 8in (20cm)
Aspect: Sun
Soil: Well-drained, sandy,
humus-rich
Hardiness: Zone 7
Propagation: Seed, when
ripe; division, in spring

Long-flowering plant from Spain.
Leaves basal, 2-pinnate, green with
white midrib. Flowers in umbels of up
to 10, deep pink, over a long period
in spring and summer.

Erodium
'Fran's Choice'
(Geraniaceae)

Common name: Heronbill
Height: 8in (20cm)
Spread: 8in (20cm)
Aspect: Sun
Soil: Well-drained, sandy,
humus-rich
Hardiness: Zone 7
Propagation: Seed, when
ripe; division, in spring

Hybrid, clump-forming cultivar.
Leaves pinnatisect, toothed, midgreen.
Flowers borne in short terminal
umbels, pink, in summer.

Erodium manescaui
(Geraniaceae)

Common name: Pyrenees
heronbill
Height: 18in (45cm)
Spread: 8in (20cm)
Aspect: Sun
Soil: Well-drained, sandy,
humus-rich
Hardiness: Zone 6
Propagation: Seed, when
ripe; division, in spring

Clump-forming. Leaves toothed,
hairy, midgreen, pinnate; lobes ovate.
Flowers in long-stemmed umbels,
magenta, upper two petals spotted,
spring to summer.

Erodium
'Merstham Pink'
(Geraniaceae)

Common name: Heronbill
Height: 9in (22cm)
Spread: 10in (25cm)
Aspect: Sun
Soil: Well-drained, sandy,
humus-rich
Hardiness: Zone 6
Propagation: Division,
in spring

Hybrid cultivar; superb wall plant.
Leaves fernlike or carrotlike, dark
green. Flowers in umbels, pink, over a
long period, in summer to autumn.

Erodium pelargoniiflorum
(Geraniaceae)

Eryngium agavifolium
(Apiaceae/Umbelliferae)

Common name: Geranium
heronbill
Height: 1ft (30cm)
Spread: 1ft (30cm)
Aspect: Sun
Soil: Well-drained, sandy,
humus-rich
Hardiness: Zone 6
Propagation: Seed, when
ripe; division, in spring

Common name: Sea holly
Height: 5ft (1.5m)
Spread: 2ft (60cm)
Aspect: Sun
Soil: Moist, well-drained,
fertile
Hardiness: Zone 7
Propagation: Seed, when
ripe; division, in spring

Species from Anatolia. Leaves
midgreen, geraniumlike, ovate-
cordate, lobed. Flowers in umbels,
white, upper two petals spotted
purple, over a long period, summer.

Rosette-forming evergreen from
Argentina. Leaves sword-shaped,
toothed, glossy. Flowers in cylindrical
umbels, greenish-white, bracts spiny
or entire, late summer.

ERYNGIUM (Apiaceae/Umbelliferae)
Sea holly

A genus of over 200 species, which can be split into "oldworld" and "new-world." The species from dry regions of
North Africa, Turkey, Asia, China, and Korea are usually
taprooted, and have rounded leaves and congested, white or
blue flowerheads with conspicuous bracts. Those from wet
regions of South America and warm regions of Central and
North America are usually fibrous-rooted and evergreen, with
long, narrow leaves and flowers of greenish-white or purple.
They are excellent border plants, especially for coastal gardens,
and can be long-flowering. Eryngiums usually have spiny, silver-
veined leaves in basal rosettes; wear gloves when handling. The
flowerhead is a rounded, crowded head of small, stalkless
flowers, like that of a thistle. Flowers dry well, and are useful
for flower-arranging, either fresh or dry. Eryngiums like a
position in sun and well-drained soil, which should not be too
rich, or they will make soft growth and suffer from powdery
mildew. They attract bees and butterflies, and are low in
allergens. They dislike transplantation, so should be sited
carefully in the first instance. Some will self-seed, especially
E. giganteum, and some require staking.

Eryngium alpinum
A.G.M.
(Apiaceae/Umbelliferae)

Common name: Sea holly
Height: 28in (70cm)
Spread: 18in (45cm)
Aspect: Sun
Soil: Well-drained to dry,
poor, humus-rich
Hardiness: Zone 5
Propagation: Seed, when
ripe; division, in spring

Tap-rooted European species. Basal
leaves spiny and heart-shaped; stem,
3-lobed. Flowers in cylindrical
umbels, steely-blue or white, with
bracts, summer to autumn.

Eryngium alpinum
'Amethyst'
(Apiaceae/Umbelliferae)

Common name: Sea holly
Height: 28in (70cm)
Spread: 18in (45cm)
Aspect: Sun
Soil: Well-drained to dry,
poor, humus-rich
Hardiness: Zone 5
Propagation: Seed, when
ripe; division, in spring

Cloned selection of E. alpinum, in
which the flowers are smaller and
violet-blue. Is tap-rooted, so resents
disturbance. Basal leaves spiny, heart-
shaped; stem, 3-lobed.

Eryngium alpinum
'Slieve Donard'
(Apiaceae/Umbelliferae)

Common name: Sea holly
Height: 28in (70cm)
Spread: 18in (45cm)
Aspect: Sun
Soil: Well-drained to dry,
poor, humus-rich
Hardiness: Zone 5
Propagation: Seed, when
ripe; division, in spring

Cloned selection of E. alpinum, with
flowers and bracts of creamy-green, in
summer to autumn. Basal leaves
spiny, heart-shaped; stem leaves, 3-
lobed.

Eryngium bourgatii
(Apiaceae/Umbelliferae)

Common name: Sea holly
Height: 18in (45cm)
Spread: 12in (30cm)
Aspect: Sun
Soil: Well-drained to dry,
poor, humus-rich
Hardiness: Zone 5
Propagation: Seed, when
ripe; division, in spring

Tap-rooted species from the Pyrenees.
Dark green, silver-veined, rounded,
pinnatifid, spiny leaves. Flowers in
cylindrical umbels, blue with silver
bracts, mid- to late summer.

Eryngium bourgatii 'Picos'
(Apiaceae/Umbelliferae)

Common name: Sea holly
Height: 18in (45cm)
Spread: 12in (30cm)
Aspect: Sun
Soil: Well-drained to dry, poor, humus-rich
Hardiness: Zone 5
Propagation: Division, in spring

Cloned selection of *E. bourgatii*, with bright blue flowers and silver bracts in summer. Rounded, pinnatifid, spiny, dark green, silver-veined leaves. Very desirable.

Eryngium eburneum
(Apiaceae/Umbelliferae)

Common name: Sea holly
Height: 4ft (1.2m)
Spread: 1ft (30cm)
Aspect: Sun
Soil: Moist but well-drained, humus-rich, fertile
Hardiness: Zone 5
Propagation: Seed, when ripe; division, in spring

Evergreen from South America. Leaves in a rosette, narrow, linear, spiny, midgreen. Spherical umbels of gray-green flowers and bracts on branched stems, late summer.

Eryngium giganteum A.G.M.
(Apiaceae/Umbelliferae)

Common name: Sea holly
Height: 3ft (90cm)
Spread: 1ft (30cm)
Aspect: Sun
Soil: Well-drained to dry, poor, humus-rich
Hardiness: Zone 5
Propagation: Seed when ripe

Short-lived or monocarpic species. Leaves heart-shaped, basal, and stem, ovate, spiny, silver-veined, midgreen. Branched umbels of steel-blue flowers with silver-gray bracts.

Eryngium horridum
(Apiaceae/Umbelliferae)

Common name: Sea holly
Height: 10ft (3m)
Spread: 3ft (1m)
Aspect: Sun
Soil: Moist but well-drained, fertile
Hardiness: Zone 5
Propagation: Seed, when ripe; division, in spring

Species from Brazil and Argentina. Leaves linear, arched, midgreen. Flowerheads spherical, on branching stems, in summer. Unspectacular, but unusual.

Eryngium x oliverianum A.G.M.
(Apiaceae/Umbelliferae)

Common name: Sea holly
Height: 36in (90cm)
Spread: 18in (45cm)
Aspect: Sun
Soil: Well-drained to dry, poor
Hardiness: Zone 5
Propagation: Division, in autumn

Tap-rooted, deciduous garden hybrid. Basal leaves ovate, 3-lobed, spiny, dark green; stem leaves 4- to 5-palmately lobed. Flowers and bracts silver-blue, summer to autumn.

Eryngium pandanifolium
(Apiaceae/Umbelliferae)

Common name: Sea holly
Height: 12ft (4m)
Spread: 6ft (2m)
Aspect: Sun
Soil: Moist, well-drained, fertile
Hardiness: Zone 8
Propagation: Seed when ripe; division in spring

Clump-forming species from Argentina and Brazil. Leaves linear, spiny, silver-green. Flowers brown-purple with dark bracts, in cylindrical umbels, late summer to autumn.

Eryngium proteiflorum
(Apiaceae/Umbelliferae)

Common name: Sea holly
Height: 3ft (90cm)
Spread: 2ft (60cm)
Aspect: Sun
Soil: Well-drained to dry, poor
Hardiness: Zone 8
Propagation: Seed, when ripe; division, in autumn

Tap-rooted evergreen from Mexico. Leaves in rosettes, linear, spiny-edged, silvery green. Flowers in cylindrical umbels, gray-blue, with spiny bracts, in spring.

Eryngium x tripartitum A.G.M.
(Apiaceae/Umbelliferae)

Common name: Sea holly
Height: 36in (90cm)
Spread: 20in (50cm)
Aspect: Sun
Soil: Well-drained, poor
Hardiness: Zone 5
Propagation: Seed, when ripe; division, in spring

Tap-rooted Mediterranean species. Leaves ovate, 3-lobed, toothed, dark green. Violet-blue flowers with blue-gray bracts, in spherical umbels, in summer to autumn.

Erysimum alpinum syn.
E. heiraciifolium
(Brassicaceae/Cruciferae)

Common name: Alpine
wallflower
Height: 6in (15cm)
Spread: 6in (15cm)
Aspect: Sun
Soil: Well-drained, fertile
Hardiness: Zone 6
Propagation: Seed, in
spring

Dwarf wallflower from Scandinavia,
with lance-shaped, midgreen leaves
and perfumed, sulfur-yellow flowers,
borne in racemes in summer.

Erysimum
'Bowles Mauve' A.G.M.
(Brassicaceae/Cruciferae)

Common name:
Wallflower
Height: 30in (75cm)
Spread: 24in (60cm)
Aspect: Sun
Soil: Well-drained, fertile
Hardiness: Zone 7
Propagation: Heeled
softwood cuttings, in
spring or summer

Strong, evergreen, hybrid, woody
subshrub. Leaves lance-shaped, gray-
green. Mauve flowers in racemes on
long stems, over a long period from
early spring to summer.

Erysimum linifolium
'Variegatum'
(Brassicaceae/Cruciferae)

Common name: Alpine
wallflower
Height: 28in (70cm)
Spread: 10in (25cm)
Aspect: Sun
Soil: Well-drained, fertile
Hardiness: Zone 6
Propagation: Heeled
softwood cuttings, in
spring or summer

Mat-forming, woody evergreen with
gray-green, white-variegated, narrow,
linear to lance-shaped leaves. Lilac
flowers in long racemes on long
stems, spring to autumn.

Erysimum
'Orange Flame'
(Brassicaceae/Cruciferae)

Common name:
Wallflower
Height: 4in (10cm)
Spread: 12in (30cm)
Aspect: Sun
Soil: Well-drained, fertile
Hardiness: Zone 7
Propagation: Heeled
softwood cuttings, in
spring or summer

Mat-forming, creeping, evergreen,
hybrid perennial. Leaves inverse
lance-shaped, dark green. Flowers in
lax racemes, orange, from spring to
autumn.

ERYTHRONIUM (Liliaceae)
Dogtooth fawn-lily

There are some 22 clump-forming, bulbous species in this genus. They are found in open meadow and deciduous woodland habitats, distributed across Eurasia and North America, and as a consequence they are suited to a range of garden situations, from a rock garden or mixed border to a woodland planting. They are hardy, and grow well in acidic, moisture-retentive but well-drained conditions, in dappled half shade. The bulbs are toothlike, with long points, and should be planted vertically in the autumn, quite deeply; there should be 5in (12cm) of soil above the top of the bulb. Bulbs should never be bought in the dry state, nor allowed to dry out when dividing established clumps, as they will give you only limited success at best, and they may not recover at all. The leaves are basal and invariably handsome, being glossy, green, and often mottled, marbled, or otherwise marked with bronze, maroon, or white. The nodding, bell- to hat-shaped flowers are borne singly or in clusters of up to ten, at the tops of erect, leafless stems. They have a delicate, charming appearance, with recurved tepals in shades of white, yellow, pink, or purple, and prominent stamens. The only significant problem is attack by slugs and snails.

Erythronium californicum 'White Beauty' A.G.M. (Liliaceae)

Common name: California fawn-lily
Height: 35cm (14in)
Spread: 10cm (4in)
Aspect: Half shade
Soil: Well-drained, acidic, humus-rich
Hardiness: Zone 5
Propagation: Division, after flowering

Cloned selection of a bulbous woodlander. Leaves elliptic, deep green, mottled cream. Flowers 1–3 per stem, pendent, cream, with white anthers and prominent stamens.

Erythronium dens-canis A.G.M. (Liliaceae)

Common name: Dogtooth fawn-lily
Height: 6in (15cm)
Spread: 4in (10cm)
Aspect: Sun or half shade
Soil: Well-drained, acidic, humus-rich
Hardiness: Zone 3
Propagation: Division, after flowering

Eurasian species. Leaves elliptic-oblong, midgreen, marbled brown. Flowers downturned, solitary, pink, white, or lilac with purple anthers, in spring.

Erythronium grandiflorum
(Liliaceae)

Common name: Avalanche
fawn-lily
Height: 12in (30cm)
Spread: 4in (10cm)
Aspect: Half shade
Soil: Well-drained, acidic,
humus-rich
Hardiness: Zone 3
Propagation: Division,
after flowering

Species from the western U.S.A.
Leaves elliptic, bright green. Flowers
1–3 per stem, golden-yellow, with
distinctive stigmas and anthers, in
spring.

Erythronium helenae
(Liliaceae)

Common names: None
Height: 14in (35cm)
Spread: 6in (15cm)
Aspect: Half shade
Soil: Well-drained, acidic,
humus-rich
Hardiness: Zone 5
Propagation: Division,
after flowering

A species from California, closely
related to *E. oregonum* and
E. californicum. Leaves elliptic, bright
green. Flowers cream, with yellow
centers, in spring.

Erythronium 'Pagoda' A.G.M.
(Liliaceae)

Common names: None
Height: 14in (35cm)
Spread: 4in (10cm)
Aspect: Half shade
Soil: Well-drained, acidic,
humus-rich
Hardiness: Zone 5
Propagation: Division,
after flowering

A vigorous hybrid cultivar. Leaves
elliptic, deep green, mottled. Flowers,
up to 10 per stem, are yellow, with
dark yellow anthers, in spring.

Erythronium tuolumnense A.G.M.
(Liliaceae)

Common name: Tuolumne
fawn-lily
Height: 14in (35cm)
Spread: 3in (8cm)
Aspect: Half shade
Soil: Well-drained, acidic,
humus-rich
Hardiness: Zone 5
Propagation: Division,
after flowering

Vigorous species from C. California.
Leaves elliptic, pale green. Flowers
bright yellow, strongly recurved, with
yellow anthers, up to 7 on a stem, in
spring.

Eucomis autumnalis
(Hyacinthaceae/Liliaceae)

Common names: None
Height: 12in (30cm)
Spread: 8in (20cm)
Aspect: Sun
Soil: Well-drained, dry in
winter, fertile
Hardiness: Zone 8
Propagation: Offsets in spring

Eucomis bicolor
(Hyacinthaceae/Liliaceae)

Common names: None
Height: 24in (60cm)
Spread: 8in (20cm)
Aspect: Sun
Soil: Well-drained, fertile
Hardiness: Zone 8
Propagation: Offsets in
spring

Bulbous, with a basal rosette of
straplike, broad, wavy-edged leaves.
Small, starry, greenish-white flowers
in racemes topped by spiky bracts,
late summer to autumn.

Bulbous plant. Leaves broad straps,
wavy-edged, bright green. Flowers in
racemes, topped by pineapplelike,
pink-edged green bracts, in late
summer and autumn.

Eucomis pallidiflora
(Hyacithaceae/Liliaceae)

Common names: None
Height: 28in (70cm)
Spread: 8in (20cm)
Aspect: Sun
Soil: Well-drained, fertile
Hardiness: Zone 8
Propagation: Offsets in
spring

Eupatorium album
(Asteraceae/Compositae)

Common name: Hemp
agrimony
Height: 3ft (1m)
Spread: 1ft (30cm)
Aspect: Sun or half shade
Soil: Moist
Hardiness: Zone 4
Propagation: Seed or
division, both in spring

Vigorous, bulbous plant from South
Africa. Leaves semierect, strap-
shaped, wavy-edged, green. Flowers in
racemes, greenish-white, in late
summer.

Coarse woodland or waterside plant
from the eastern U.S.A. Leaves oblong
to lance-shaped, toothed, midgreen.
Tubular, white flowers in corymbs.

Eupatorium purpureum
(Asteraceae/Compositae)

Common name: Bluestem
Joe-Pye-weed
Height: 6ft (2m)
Spread: 3ft (1m)
Aspect: Sun or half shade
Soil: Moist
Hardiness: Zone 4
Propagation: Seed or
division, both in spring

Clump-forming plant. Leaves lance-
shaped, toothed, midgreen tinged
purple. Tubular flowers in terminal
panicles, pink, from midsummer to
early autumn.

Euphorbia amygdaloides
(Euphorbiaceae)

Common name: Wood
spurge
Height: 32in (80cm)
Spread: 12in (30cm)
Aspect: Half shade
Soil: Moist, humus-rich
Hardiness: Zone 7
Propagation: Seed or
division, both in spring

Evergreen from Europe, Turkey, and
the Caucasus. Leaves obovate, matt,
green. Cymes of green-yellow
involucres and cyathia from
midspring to early summer.

EUPHORBIA (Euphorbiaceae)
Spurge

A vast genus containing over 2,000 species, from annuals and
perennials to succulents and shrubs, from many habitats in
many parts of the world. As a consequence, their cultural
requirements differ widely. They range from extremely hardy to
tender, and may be evergreen, semievergreen, or deciduous.
Nearly all bear highly characteristic "cyathia," small cups of
long-lasting bracts that may be green, yellow, red, brown, or
purple, cupping nectaries and insignificant flowers with much-
reduced parts. In the perennial and shrubby species, these are
carried in dense clusters. The leaves are very varied, and often
ephemeral. Gardeners tend to be polarized into enthusiasm or
antipathy toward this genus. Some species are too invasive to be
included in the garden, especially *E. cyparissias* (Zone 4) and
E. pseudovirgata (Zone 6). Others, such as *E. lathyris* (Zone 6),
E. hybernia (Zone 9), *E. coralloides* (Zone 8), and *E. wallichii*
(Zone 7) will self-seed prolifically. All euphorbias resent
disturbance, so site them carefully at the outset. All are useful for
flower-arranging, in the fresh and the dry state, but it must be
noted that all parts of euphorbias are poisonous and bleed a skin-
irritant milky sap, and the flowers are also highly allergenic.

Euphorbia amygdaloides 'Purpurea' (Euphorbiaceae)

Common name: Wood spurge
Height: 32in (80cm)
Spread: 12in (30cm)
Aspect: Half shade
Soil: Moist, humus-rich
Hardiness: Zone 7
Propagation: Seed or division, both in spring

A variant of the species with obovate, purple leaves. Involucres and cyathia are acid yellow, in cymes from midspring to early summer.

Euphorbia amygdaloides var. _robbiae_ A.G.M. (Euphorbiaceae)

Common name: Wood spurge
Height: 32in (80cm)
Spread: 12in (30cm)
Aspect: Sun or half shade
Soil: Moist
Hardiness: Zone 7
Propagation: Division, in spring

A select form of _E. amygdaloides_. Spreads by rhizomes, and may be invasive. Leaves broad, leathery, shiny green. Cymes to 7in (18cm) tall, less dense than in the species.

Euphorbia characias (Euphorbiaceae)

Common name: Wood spurge
Height: 4ft (1.2m)
Spread: 3ft (1m)
Aspect: Sun
Soil: Well-drained, sandy
Hardiness: Zone 8
Propagation: Seed or division, both in spring

Evergreen Mediterranean subshrub. Leaves linear, gray-green. Cyathia yellow-green, cupped by green involucres, in dense terminal cymes in spring and summer.

Euphorbia characias subsp. _characias_ A.G.M. (Euphorbiaceae)

Common name: Wood spurge
Height: 4ft (1.2m)
Spread: 3ft (1m)
Aspect: Sun
Soil: Well-drained, sandy
Hardiness: Zone 8
Propagation: Division, in spring

A variant of _E. characias_ in which the nectaries in the cyathia are dark reddish-brown, with notched or short horns. Leaves are linear, gray-green.

***Euphorbia characias*
subsp. *wulfenii* A.G.M.**
(Euphorbiaceae)

Common names: None
Height: 4ft (1.2m)
Spread: 3ft (1m)
Aspect: Sun
Soil: Well-drained, sandy
Hardiness: Zone 7
Propagation: Division,
in spring

***Euphorbia characias*
subsp. *wulfenii* 'Variegata'**
(Euphorbiaceae)

Common names: None
Height: 4ft (1.2m)
Spread: 3ft (1m)
Aspect: Sun
Soil: Well-drained, sandy
Hardiness: Zone 7
Propagation: Division,
in spring

Popular variant of *E. characias* in
which the cyathia and nectaries are
yellow-green. The leaves are linear
and gray-green, as in the species.

Cultivar of *E. characias* subsp.
wulfenii, in which the leaves are
edged with cream. The cyathia and
nectaries are yellow-green, the
involucres green.

***Euphorbia cyparissias*
'Fens Ruby'**
(Euphorbiaceae)

Common name: Cypress
spurge
Height: 16in (40cm)
Spread: 16in (40cm)
Aspect: Sun
Soil: Well-drained
Hardiness: Zone 4
Propagation: Division,
in spring

***Euphorbia dulcis*
'Chameleon'**
(Euphorbiaceae)

Common name: Spurge
Height: 1ft (30cm)
Spread: 1ft (30cm)
Aspect: Shade
Soil: Moist, humus-rich
Hardiness: Zone 5
Propagation: Division,
in spring

Selected form of a rhizomatous,
invasive species from Europe. Leaves
feathery, linear, blue-green. Cyathia
and involucres yellow-green, in
terminal cymes.

Form of a rhizomatous species from
Europe. Leaves inverse lance-shaped,
purple. Cyathia and involucres
yellow-green, tinted purple.

Euphorbia griffithii
'Fireglow'
(Euphorbiaceae)

Common name: Spurge
Height: 3ft (90cm)
Spread: 2ft (60cm)
Aspect: Half shade
Soil: Moist, humus-rich
Hardiness: Zone 5
Propagation: Division,
in spring

Selected form of a rhizomatous
species. Leaves lance-shaped, dark
green, midribs red; good in autumn.
Flowers, early summer in cymes;
involucres red, cyathia yellow.

Euphorbia polychroma
A.G.M.
(Euphorbiaceae)

Common name: Cushion
euphorbia
Height: 16in (40cm)
Spread: 24in (60cm)
Aspect: Sun or half shade
Soil: Well-drained,
humus-rich
Hardiness: Zone 6
Propagation: Seed or
division, both in spring

Herbaceous species from Europe to
Turkey. Leaves obovate, dark green.
Flowers in terminal cymes, cyathia
yellow, involucres yellow-green,
midspring to midsummer.

Euphorbia polychroma
'Candy'
(Euphorbiaceae)

Common name: Cushion
euphorbia
Height: 16in (40cm)
Spread: 24in (60cm)
Aspect: Sun or half shade
Soil: Well-drained,
humus-rich
Hardiness: Zone 6
Propagation: Seed or
division, both in spring

A variant of the species with stems
and obovate leaves of dark purple.
Cyathia and involucres a paler yellow.
Flowers in terminal cymes, midspring
to midsummer.

Fascicularia bicolor
(Bromeliaceae)

Common names: None
Height: 18in (45cm)
Spread: 24in (60cm)
Aspect: Sun
Soil: Sharply drained, poor
Hardiness: Zone 8
Propagation: Seed or
division, both in spring

Rosetted, evergreen, terrestrial
bromeliad. Leaves arching, long,
tough, spiny, green; inner leaves turn
red as corymb of blue flowers and
white bracts appears in summer.

Felicia petiolata
(Asteraceae/Compositae)

Ferula communis
(Apiaceae/Umbelliferae)

Common name: Blue daisy
Height: 3ft (1m)
Spread: 3ft (1m)
Aspect: Sun
Soil: Sharply drained,
fertile
Hardiness: Zone 9
Propagation: Stem-tip
cuttings, in autumn

Common name: Common
giant fennel
Height: To 10ft (3m)
Spread: 2ft (60cm)
Aspect: Sun
Soil: Well-drained, fertile
Hardiness: Zone 8
Propagation: Seed, when
ripe

Prostrate plant from South Africa.
Leaves lanceolate, green. Flowers
daisylike, pink or white, with yellow
centers, over long periods in summer.
Not for damp climates.

Tap-rooted, inedible plant. Leaves
green, malodorous, finely divided.
Slow to flower; umbels of yellow,
white, or purple in summer. _(See also_
Foeniculum _p.189.)_

Festuca glauca
'Elijah Blue'
(Graminae/Poaceae)

Festuca ovina
'Tetra Gold'
(Graminae/Poaceae)

Common name: Blue
fescue
Height: 12in (30cm)
Spread: 10in (25cm)
Aspect: Sun
Soil: Well-drained to dry
Hardiness: Zone 5
Propagation: Division,
in spring

Common name: Sheep's
fescue
Height: 12in (30cm)
Spread: 10in (25cm)
Aspect: Sun
Soil: Dry, well-drained
Hardiness: Zone 5
Propagation: Division,
in spring

Evergreen grass. Leaves blue-green,
narrow, linear. Flowers brownish-
green, in dense panicles, in early and
midsummer. Regular division keeps
foliage color good.

Hybrid evergreen grass. Leaves
narrow, linear, yellow-green. Dense
panicle of brown flowers, in early and
midsummer. Regular division keeps
leaf color brilliant.

Filipendula purpurea A.G.M. (Rosaceae)

Common name: Japanese meadowsweet
Height: 4ft (1.2m)
Spread: 2ft (60cm)
Aspect: Sun or half shade
Soil: Moist, well-drained, fertile, humus-rich
Hardiness: Zone 6
Propagation: Seed or division, both in autumn or spring

Perennial from Japan. Leaves toothed, pinnate, leaflets 5- to 7-lobed, green. Flowers perfumed, red fading to pink, in crowded corymbs, in mid- to late summer.

Filipendula ulmaria 'Variegata' (Rosaceae)

Common name: Queen-of-the-meadow
Height: 3ft (90cm)
Spread: 2ft (60cm)
Aspect: Sun or half shade
Soil: Moist, well-drained, fertile, humus-rich
Hardiness: Zone 2
Propagation: Seed or division, both in autumn or spring

Species from Europe and W. Asia. Leaves pinnate, veined, inverse lance-shaped, green, striped or marked yellow. Flowers in dense, branching corymbs, creamy-white, summer.

Filipendula vulgaris (Rosaceae)

Common name: Double dropwort
Height: 24in (60cm)
Spread: 18in (45cm)
Aspect: Sun
Soil: Dry, well-drained
Hardiness: Zone 3
Propagation: Seed or division, both in autumn or spring

Rhizomatous species from Eurasia. Leaves pinnate, fernlike, toothed, dark green. Flowers perfumed, in loose corymbs, white, in early and midsummer.

Foeniculum vulgare 'Purpureum' (Apiaceae/Umbelliferae)

Common name: Fennel (edible)
Height: 6ft (1.8m)
Spread: 2ft (60cm)
Aspect: Sun
Soil: Moist, well-drained, fertile
Hardiness: Zone 5
Propagation: Seed, in warmth or *in situ*, in spring

Deep-rooting herb from S. Europe. Leaves aromatic, bronze-purple, hairlike, finely cut. Flowers tiny, yellow, on branching stems, in compound umbels, mid- to late summer.

Fragaria
'Lipstick'
(Rosaceae)

Common name:
Strawberry
Height: 6in (15cm)
Spread: Indefinite
Aspect: Sun or half shade
Soil: Moist, well-drained,
fertile
Hardiness: Zone 5
Propagation: Plantlets
from runners, at any time

Sterile, stoloniferous ground cover.
Leaves 3-palmate, lobes toothed,
broad, ovate. Flowers single, in
cymes, cerise, spring to autumn.
Evergreen in mild areas.

Fragaria
'Pink Panda'®
(Rosaceae)

Common name:
Strawberry
Height: 6in (15cm)
Spread: Indefinite
Aspect: Sun or half shade
Soil: Moist, well-drained,
fertile
Hardiness: Zone 5
Propagation: Plantlets from
runners, at any time

Stoloniferous, sterile ground cover.
Leaves 3-palmate, lobes broad, ovate,
toothed, bright green, evergreen in
mild areas. Pink, single flowers in
cymes, spring to autumn.

Fragaria vesca
(Rosaceae)

Common name: European
strawberry
Height: 8in (20cm)
Spread: Indefinite
Aspect: Sun or half shade
Soil: Moist, well-drained,
fertile
Hardiness: Zone 5
Propagation: Plantlets from
runners, at any time

Stoloniferous ground cover species.
Leaves 3-palmate, lobes ovate,
toothed, bright green. Flowers in
cymes, white, followed by small, red,
edible fruits.

Francoa sonchifolia
(Saxifragaceae)

Common names: None
Height: 3ft (1m)
Spread: 18in (45cm)
Aspect: Sun or half shade
Soil: Moist, well-drained,
humus-rich
Hardiness: Zone 7
Propagation: Seed or
division, both in spring

Evergreen perennial from Chile.
Leaves in a basal rosette, hairy, broad,
deeply lobed, green. Flowers in tall,
compact racemes, pink, with deep
pink marks, in summer.

Francoa sonchifolia
Rodgerson's form
(Saxifragaceae)

Common names: None
Height: 3ft (1m)
Spread: 18in (45cm)
Aspect: Sun or half shade
Soil: Moist, well-drained,
humus-rich
Hardiness: Zone 7
Propagation: Seed or
division, both in spring

Fritillaria acmopetala
A.G.M.
(Liliaceae)

Common name: Fritillary
Height: 16in (40cm)
Spread: 3in (8cm)
Aspect: Sun
Soil: Well-drained, fertile
Hardiness: Zone 7
Propagation: Offsets, in
summer; seed, gathered in
autumn, kept cold until spring,
then sown in warmth

Selected form of this evergreen
woodlander from Chile. Basal rosette
of hairy, broad, deeply lobed leaves.
Tall flowering raceme of dark pink
flowers.

Bulbous perennial from E.
Mediterranean. Leaves linear, blue-
green. Flowers bell-shaped, pendent,
pale green to brown, in late spring.

FRITILLARIA (Liliaceae)
Fritillary

A genus of some 100 species, all of which are bulbous
perennials, distributed across temperate regions of the northern
hemisphere. They are found especially in southwestern Asia, the
Mediterranean area, and western North America, and come
from a wide range of habitats, and consequently vary in their
cultural requirements, but all are hardy. Fritillaries range in size
from diminutive species, suitable only for the rock garden, to
tall plants, eminently suitable for beds or borders, and
woodland species. However, some species require more
particular conditions, which in wet regions can be met only by
growing them in a bulb frame or alpine house; the smaller
species are for the dedicated exhibitor. The fragile bulbs require
careful handling. The leaves are for the greater part lance-
shaped or linear. The flowers are usually pendulous, and tubular
to bell- or saucer-shaped, with 6 tepals. They are often marked
with a distinctive checked, or "tessellated," pattern. Flowers are
borne singly or in terminal racemes or umbels; in some types,
most notably *F. imperialis*, there is a cluster of leaflike bracts
above the flowers. Unfortunately, nearly all fritillaries have a
distinctly unpleasant smell.

Fritillaria hermonis
subsp. *amana*
(Liliaceae)

Common name: Fritillary
Height: 12in (30cm)
Spread: 3in (7cm)
Aspect: Sun
Soil: Sharply drained,
fertile
Hardiness: Zone 8
Propagation: Offsets, in summer;
seed, gathered in autumn, kept cold
until spring, then sown in warmth

Bulbous plant from the Lebanon to
Turkey. Leaves lance-shaped, glaucous
gray-green. Flowers single or paired,
pendent bells, green, tessellated
brown, or purple, spring.

Fritillaria imperialis
(Liliaceae)

Common name: Crown
imperial
Height: 4ft (1.2m)
Spread: 1ft (30cm)
Aspect: Sun
Soil: Well-drained, dry in
summer, limy, fertile
Hardiness: Zone 4
Propagation: Offsets, after
foliage dies down

Handsome, bulbous species. Leaves
lance-shaped, in whorls. Flowers in
umbels, pendent, orange, crowned by
leaflike bracts, late spring. Plant 8in
(20cm) deep.

Fritillaria imperialis
'Maxima Lutea' A.G.M.
(Liliaceae)

Common name: Yellow
crown imperial
Height: 4ft (1.2m)
Spread: 1ft (30cm)
Aspect: Sun
Soil: Well-drained, dry in
summer, limy, fertile
Hardiness: Zone 4
Propagation: Offsets, after
foliage dies down

Variant of the species with yellow
flowers, pendent, in umbels, crowned
by leaflike bracts, late spring. Leaves
lance-shaped, in whorls. Plant 8in
(20cm) deep.

Fritillaria imperialis
'Rubra'
(Liliaceae)

Common name: Crown
imperial
Height: 4ft (1.2m)
Spread: 1ft (30cm)
Aspect: Sun
Soil: Well-drained, limy,
fertile
Hardiness: Zone 4
Propagation: Offsets, after
foliage dies down

Very handsome, a crown of leaflike
bracts on top of the red flower, but
demanding; given sun, lime, potash,
and deep planting, it may flower.
Leaves lance-shaped.

Fritillaria meleagris
A.G.M.
(Liliaceae)

Common name: Guinea-
hen fritillary
Height: 12in (30cm)
Spread: 4in (10cm)
Aspect: Sun or half shade
Soil: Humus-rich
Hardiness: Zone 4
Propagation: Offsets, after
foliage dies down

Bulbous Eurasian species. Leaves gray-
green, linear. Flowers pendent, solitary
or paired bells, white or purple, with
bold tessellation, spring. Also shown is
F. *alba*, A.G.M.

Fritillaria michailovskyi
A.G.M.
(Liliaceae)

Common name: Fritillary
Height: 6in (15cm)
Spread: 2in (5cm)
Aspect: Sun
Soil: Sharply drained, dry
during dormancy, fertile
Hardiness: Zone 7
Propagation: Offsets, after
foliage dies down

Handsome species from Turkey.
Leaves lance-shaped, midgreen.
Flowers pendent bells, purple-brown,
yellow-edged tepals, in umbels in late
spring.

Fritillaria persica
(Liliaceae)

Common name: Persian
fritillary
Height: 3ft (1m)
Spread: 4in (10cm)
Aspect: Sun
Soil: Well-drained, sandy,
fertile
Hardiness: Zone 5
Propagation: Offsets, after
foliage dies down

Robust bulbous species from Turkey,
best in hot, dry areas. Leaves lance-
shaped, glaucous green. Flowers
purple or brown-green, pendent bells,
in racemes, in spring.

Fritillaria pudica
(Liliaceae)

Common name: Yellow
fritillary
Height: 6in (15cm)
Spread: 2in (5cm)
Aspect: Sun
Soil: Well-drained, dry
during dormancy, fertile
Hardiness: Zone 6
Propagation: Offsets, after
foliage has died down

Bulbous species from North America.
Mid-green, lance-shaped leaves.
Flowers solitary or paired, pendent
bells, yellow or orange-yellow, in
early spring. Dislikes wet.

193

FUCHSIA (Onagraceae)
Fuchsia

A genus of subshrubs from Central and South America and New Zealand, of only 100 or so species, but with over 8,000 hybrids in cultivation. They are mostly deciduous and mostly tender, but some are hardy, and some are evergreen, especially in warm regions. They are happy in any soil that is reliably moist, and have a flowering season from midsummer to autumn. The flowers are handsome, and unique. They are pendent, in terminal clusters, and tubular or bell-shaped, with long tubes, widely spread sepals, and below these a skirt of petals; these may be of a similar color, or of different colors. The number of petals varies; 4 in single-flowered types, between 5 and 7 in semidouble varieties, and more than 8 in fully double varieties. The group derived from *Fuchsia triphylla* is single-flowered, with very long tubes. Fuchsias in cold areas need the warmest corner of the garden; even then, frost will kill off much of the top growth in winter. In very cold areas, give them a winter mulch to protect from frost. They are excellent plants for mixed beds or borders, or hanging baskets, but will not grow under trees. Trailing types are good for baskets. A few are grown for their foliage value, rather than their flowers; all have berries after flowering.

Fuchsia
'Bicentennial'
(Onagraceae)

Common names: None
Height: 18in (45cm)
Spread: 24in (60cm)
Aspect: Sun or half shade
Soil: Moist, well-drained
Hardiness: Zone 9
Propagation: Softwood
cuttings, in spring

Hybrid fuchsia, with arching stems bearing an abundance of fully double flowers with sepals of pale orange-pink and petals of magenta-pink.

Fuchsia
'Genii' A.G.M.
(Onagraceae)

Common names: None
Height: 36in (90cm)
Spread: 36in (90cm)
Aspect: Sun or half shade
Soil: Moist, well-drained
Hardiness: Zone 9
Propagation: Softwood
cuttings, in spring

Hybrid fuchsia grown principally for its foliage value. Leaves broadly ovate, lime-green. Flowers small, single, tubes and sepals red, corolla purple.

Fuchsia
'Coralle' A.G.M.
(Onagraceae)

Common names: None
Height: 36in (90cm)
Spread: 24in (60cm)
Aspect: Sun or half shade
Soil: Well-drained, moist
Hardiness: Zone 9
Propagation: Softwood
cuttings, in spring

Fuchsia magellanica
'Versicolor' A.G.M.
(Onagraceae)

Common name: Magellan
fuchsia
Height: 3ft (1m)
Spread: 5ft (1.5m)
Aspect: Sun or half shade
Soil: Moist, well-drained
Hardiness: Zone 6
Propagation: Softwood
cuttings, in spring

Upright Triphylla group hybrid. Olive-green leaves. Flowers in terminal clusters on strong stems; long, tapering orange tubes, salmon-pink sepals and corolla.

Species fuchsia. Leaves copper in the early season, gray-green with pink tips later. Flowers small, with red tubes, red, wide-spreading sepals, and purple corollas.

Fuchsia
'Madame Cornélissen'
A.G.M. (Onagraceae)

Common names: None
Height: 36in (90cm)
Spread: 12in (30cm)
Aspect: Sun or half shade
Soil: Moist, well-drained
Hardiness: Zone 6
Propagation: Softwood
cuttings, in spring

Fuchsia
'Phénoménal'
(Onagraceae)

Common names: None
Height: 1ft (30cm)
Spread: 1ft (30cm)
Aspect: Sun or half shade
Soil: Moist, well-drained
Hardiness: Zone 8
Propagation: Softwood
cuttings, in spring

Strong, upright hybrid fuchsia. Medium-sized, semidouble or double flowers have red tubes, recurved red sepals, and a white corolla, from midsummer to late autumn.

Hybrid fuchsia with very large, double flowers. Tube and sepals red, corolla mauve-purple. Long flowering, from summer to late autumn.

Fuchsia
'Reading Show'
(Onagraceae)

Common names: None
Height: 1ft (30cm)
Spread: 1ft (30cm)
Aspect: Sun or half shade
Soil: Moist, well-drained
Hardiness: Zone 8
Propagation: Softwood
cuttings, in spring

Fuchsia splendens
A.G.M.
(Onagraceae)

Common names: None
Height: 6ft (2m)
Spread: 3ft (1m)
Aspect: Sun or half shade
Soil: Moist, well-drained
Hardiness: Zone 9
Propagation: Seed, in
warmth in spring; softwood
cuttings, in spring

Long-flowering hybrid fuchsia. Very
large, double flowers, with red tube
and sepals and a deep blue corolla
with a red base, from summer to late
autumn.

Species from Mexico and Costa Rica.
Ovate, toothed, hairy, green leaves.
Small, solitary flowers; tubes broad
and orange, sepals green with a red
base, petals green.

Fuchsia
'Thalia' A.G.M.
(Onagraceae)

Common names: None
Height: 36in (90cm)
Spread: 36in (90cm)
Aspect: Sun
Soil: Moist, well-drained
Hardiness: Zone 9
Propagation: Softwood
cuttings, in spring

Fuchsia
'Thornley's Hardy'
(Onagraceae)

Common names: None
Height: 12in (30cm)
Spread: 8in (20cm)
Aspect: Sun or half shade
Soil: Moist, well-drained
Hardiness: Zone 5
Propagation: Softwood
cuttings, in spring

Triphylla group fuchsia. Leaves deep
olive-green, velvety. Flowers in
terminal clusters, long, slim, red;
tubes and sepals red, petals orange-
red, in summer.

Hybrid fuchsia, with a sprawling
habit. Flowers pendent, small. Tube
creamy-white, sepals spreading and
creamy-white, corolla deep rose-pink.

Fuchsia
'Tom West'
(Onagraceae)

Common names: None
Height: 2ft (60cm)
Spread: 2ft (60cm)
Aspect: Sun or half shade
Soil: Moist, well-drained
Hardiness: Zone 9
Propagation: Softwood
cuttings, in spring

Hybrid fuchsia, grown principally for its foliage. Leaves variegated green and cream, and veined pink. Flowers small, single; tubes and sepals red, corolla purple.

Gaillardia
'Burgunder'
(Asteraceae/Compositae)

Common name: Blanket-flower
Height: 24in (60cm)
Spread: 18in (45cm)
Aspect: Sun
Soil: Well-drained, sandy, poor
Hardiness: Zone 4
Propagation: Softwood cuttings, in spring

Hybrid of garden origin. Leaves basal, in rosettes, inverse lance-shaped, gray or green. Flowers daisylike, single, dark wine-red, from summer to early autumn.

Gaillardia
'Kobold'
(Asteraceae/Compositae)

Common name: Blanket-flower
Height: 12in (30cm)
Spread: 18in (45cm)
Aspect: Sun
Soil: Well-drained, sandy, poor
Hardiness: Zone 4
Propagation: Softwood cuttings, in spring

Hybrid, known also as 'Goblin'. Leaves basal, in rosettes, green. Flowers single, ray florets red with yellow tips, disc florets deep red, summer to early autumn.

Galanthus nivalis
A.G.M.
(Amaryllidaceae)

Common name: Snowdrop
Height: 4in (10cm)
Spread: 4in (10cm)
Aspect: Half shade
Soil: Moist, well-drained, humus-rich
Hardiness: Zone 4
Propagation: Division, after flowering

Bulbous woodlander from N. Europe. Leaves narrow, glaucous. Flowers solitary, scented, white; inner tepals marked green at tip, late winter. All parts toxic and irritant.

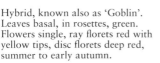

Galega x hartlandii 'Alba' A.G.M.
(Leguminosae/Papilionaceae)

Common name: Goat's-rue
Height: 5ft (1.5m)
Spread: 3ft (90cm)
Aspect: Sun or half shade
Soil: Moist
Hardiness: Zone 4
Propagation: Seed, in spring; division, in autumn or spring

Clump-forming perennial. Leaves pinnate, leaflets oval, green. Flowers in erect axillary racemes, pealike, white, from early summer to early autumn.

Galega officinalis
(Leguminosae/Papilionaceae)

Common name: Common goat's-rue
Height: 1.5m (5ft)
Spread: 90cm (3ft)
Aspect: Sun or half shade
Soil: Moist
Hardiness: Zone 4
Propagation: Seed, in spring; division in early or late winter

Species from S.E. Europe to Pakistan. Soft green, pinnate leaves, leaflets lance-shaped. Flowers in racemes, white, mauve, or bicolored, early summer to early autumn.

Galium odoratum
(Rubiaceae)

Common name: Sweet woodruff
Height: 18in (45cm)
Spread: Indefinite
Aspect: Sun or half shade
Soil: Moist, humus-rich
Hardiness: Zone 5
Propagation: Seed, when ripe; division, in spring or autumn

Rhizomatous plant from N. Africa, Europe, and Siberia. Leaves lance-shaped, emerald green, whorled. Small, starry, scented, white flowers in cymes, late spring to midsummer.

Galtonia candicans
(Hyacinthaceae/Liliaceae)

Common name: Giant summer hyacinth
Height: 4ft (1.2m)
Spread: 4in (10cm)
Aspect: Sun
Soil: Moist, well-drained, fertile
Hardiness: Zone 6
Propagation: Seed or offsets, both in spring

Bulbous, moist-grassland plant from South Africa. Leaves lance-shaped, gray-green. Flowers in tall slim racemes, pendent, scented, tubular, white, in late summer.

Galtonia princeps
(Hyacinthaceae/Liliaceae)

Common name: Summer
hyacinth
Height: 36in (90cm)
Spread: 4in (10cm)
Aspect: Sun
Soil: Moist, well-drained,
fertile
Hardiness: Zone 8
Propagation: Seed or
offsets, both in spring

Bulbous species from southern Africa.
Flowers rather smaller than those of
G. candicans, and tinted green, in
late summer. Leaves lance-shaped,
green.

Galtonia viridiflora
A.G.M.
(Hyacinthaceae/Liliaceae)

Common name: Summer
hyacinth
Height: 36in (1m)
Spread: 4in (10cm)
Aspect: Sun
Soil: Moist, well-drained,
fertile
Hardiness: Zone 8
Propagation: Seed or
offsets, both in spring

Bulbous perennial from southern
Africa. Leaves lance-shaped, gray-
green. Flowers in tallish, compact
racemes of up to 30, trumpet-shaped,
pendent, pale green.

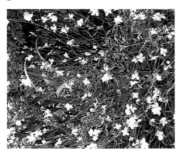

Gaura lindheimeri
A.G.M.
(Onagraceae)

Common name: White
gaura
Height: 5ft (1.5m)
Spread: 3ft (1m)
Aspect: Sun
Soil: Well-drained, sandy
Hardiness: Zone 4
Propagation: Seed or
division, both in spring

Clump-forming plant from Louisiana
and Texas. Flowers in loose panicles,
white, summer to autumn. Graceful in
a wind. Leaves lance- to spoon-
shaped, toothed.

Gaura lindheimeri
'Siskiyou Pink'
(Onagraceae)

Common name: Pink
gaura
Height: 5ft (1.5m)
Spread: 3ft (1m)
Aspect: Sun
Soil: Well-drained, sandy
Hardiness: Zone 4
Propagation: Seed or
division, both in spring

Delightful form of the species.
Flowers in loose panicles, pale and
deep pink, over a long period from
summer to autumn. Leaves lance- to
spoon-shaped, toothed.

Gazania
Chansonette Series A.G.M.
(Asteraceae/Compositae)

Common name: Treasure
flower
Height: 8in (20cm)
Spread: 8in (20cm)
Aspect: Sun
Soil: Well-drained, sandy
Hardiness: Zone 9
Propagation: Seed, in
warmth in spring; cuttings,
in autumn

Selected hybrids of evergreens from
tropical Africa. Leaves basal, lance-
shaped, glossy green above, gray-
felted below. Single pink, yellow,
orange, or bronze flowers, summer.

Gazania
Daybreak Series A.G.M.
(Asteraceae /Compositae)

Common name: Treasure
flower
Height: 8in (20cm)
Spread: 8in (20cm)
Aspect: Sun
Soil: Well-drained, sandy
Hardiness: Zone 9
Propagation: Seed, in
warmth in spring; cuttings,
in autumn

Hybrids of evergreens from tropical
Africa. Leaves lance-shaped, green
above, white-felted below. Flowers
single, solitary, white, orange, yellow,
or pink, spring and summer.

Gazania
Talent Series A.G.M.
(Asteraceae/Compositae)

Common name: Treasure
flower
Height: 8in (20cm)
Spread: 8in (20cm)
Aspect: Sun
Soil: Well-drained, sandy
Hardiness: Zone 9
Propagation: Seed, in
warmth in spring; cuttings,
in autumn

Selected hybrids of evergreens from
tropical Africa. Leaves lance-shaped,
gray-felted above and below. Flowers
single, solitary, yellow, brown, orange,
or pink, in summer.

Gentiana angustifolia
(Gentianaceae)

Common names: Gentian
Height: 4in (10cm)
Spread: 12in (30cm)
Aspect: Sun
Soil: Well-drained, light,
humus-rich
Hardiness: Zone 7
Propagation: Seed or
division, both in spring

Evergreen perennial from the Pyrenees,
Alps, and Jura mountains. Leaves
lance-shaped, in rosettes. Flowers on
short stems, deep blue, single,
trumpet-shaped, early summer.

Gentiana asclepiadea
A.G.M.
(Gentianaceae)

Common name: Willow
gentian
Height: 36in (90cm)
Spread: 18in (45cm)
Aspect: Half shade
Soil: Moist, well-drained,
acidic, humus-rich
Hardiness: Zone 6
Propagation: Seed, when
ripe; division, in spring

Clump-forming herbaceous species
from C. and S. Europe. Leaves
willowlike, lance-shaped to ovate,
pointed. Axillary clusters of flowers
on arching stems, blue trumpets.

Gentiana asclepiadea
var. *alba*
(Gentianaceae)

Common name: White
willow gentian
Height: 36in (90cm)
Spread: 18in (45cm)
Aspect: Sun
Soil: Well-drained, light,
humus-rich
Hardiness: Zone 6
Propagation: Seed or
division, both in spring

Naturally occuring form of the
species, bearing white flowers on
more upright stems. Leaves lance-
shaped to ovate, pointed, willowlike.

Gentiana lutea
(Gentianaceae)

Common name: Yellow
gentian
Height: 6ft (2m)
Spread: 2ft (60cm)
Aspect: Sun
Soil: Well-drained,
humus-rich
Hardiness: Zone 4
Propagation: Seed or
division, both in spring

Robust, fleshy-rooted mountain
species. Basal leaves blue-green, ovate,
ribbed; stem leaves paired, ovate,
green. Flowers yellow, star-shaped, in
clusters of up to 10, summer.

Gentiana septemfida
A.G.M.
(Gentianaceae)

Common names: None
Height: 8in (20cm)
Spread: 12in (30cm)
Aspect: Sun
Soil: Moist, well-drained,
humus-rich
Hardiness: Zone 3
Propagation: Seed or
division, both in spring

Spreading, herbaceous species from
Turkey to C. Asia. Leaves ovate,
pointed, paired. Flowers in terminal
clusters, narrow bells, bright blue,
white throats, in summer.

Gentiana tibetica
(Gentianaceae)

Common name: Tibetan
gentian
Height: 24in (60cm)
Spread: 8in (20cm)
Aspect: Sun
Soil: Well-drained,
humus-rich
Hardiness: Zone 6
Propagation: Seed or
division, both in spring

Species from Tibet. Basal leaves
broad, lance, green; stem leaves linear.
Flowers in dense terminal racemes,
white, surrounded by apical leaves, in
summer.

Geranium
'Ann Folkard' A.G.M.
(Geraniaceae)

Common names: None
Height: 2ft (60cm)
Spread: 5ft (1.5m)
Aspect: Sun or half shade
Soil: Well-drained
Hardiness: Zone 7
Propagation: Division,
in spring

Hybrid, scrambling ground cover.
Leaves 5-lobed, toothed, yellow at
first, turning green. Flowers saucer-
shaped, magenta with dark centers
and veining, all summer.

GERANIUM (Geraniaceae)
Cranesbill

A genus of over 300 species from temperate regions of both
hemispheres. The perennial species are indispensable for beds
and borders: they have beautiful flowers, make excellent ground
cover, and are easy to grow and long-lived. They dislike
waterlogged soil: this is reflected in their distribution in the wild,
where they are found in all habitats except boggy ones. They are
a diverse group, and vary in both their degree of hardiness and
their cultural requirements. *G. malviflorum* (Zone 8) is unusual
in that it makes top-growth over winter, flowers in spring, and
disappears till winter. Geranium flowers are mostly saucer-
shaped, but may be flat or stellate; they may be borne in umbels,
panicles, or cymes. The leaves are basal and stem, palmately
lobed, and often deeply divided and toothed; some species are
evergreen. Many geranium species are floppy or scramble, and
most need support of some kind to make them look reasonable.
All should be sheared over in the autumn to encourage new
basal growth. All are low-allergen plants, and most are drought-
tolerant. *G. nodosum* (Zone 6) and *G. procurrens* (Zone 7)
root as they touch the soil, and *G. thunbergii* (Zone 7) self-
seeds to an unacceptable degree, so must be deadheaded.

**Geranium cinereum
'Ballerina' A.G.M.
(Geraniaceae)**

Common names: None
Height: 6in (15cm)
Spread: 12in (30cm)
Aspect: Sun or half shade
Soil: Well-drained
Hardiness: Zone 5
Propagation: Division,
in spring

Long-flowering hybrid evergreen.
Leaves 5- to 7-lobed, divisions 3-
lobed, gray-green. Flowers cup-
shaped, upward-facing, pale pink
veined dark pink, spring to summer.

**Geranium cinereum
var. *subcaulescens* A.G.M.
(Geraniaceae)**

Common names: None
Height: 6in (15cm)
Spread: 12in (30cm)
Aspect: Sun or half shade
Soil: Well-drained
Hardiness: Zone 5
Propagation: Seed or
division, both in spring

Species from Italy, the Balkans, and
Turkey. Leaves deeply lobed, deep
green. Flowers on longish stems,
brilliant magenta with black centers,
in summer.

**Geranium himalayense
(Geraniaceae)**

Common names: None
Height: 18in (45cm)
Spread: 24in (60cm)
Aspect: Any
Soil: Well-drained
Hardiness: Zone 4
Propagation: Seed or
division, both in spring

Rhizomatous species. Leaves basal, 7-
lobed, veined, green, colorful in
autumn. Loose cymes of flowers,
saucer-shaped, deep blue, in flushes
from early summer to autumn.

**Geranium himalayense
'Plenum'
(Geraniaceae)**

Common names: None
Height: 10in (25cm)
Spread: 24in (60cm)
Aspect: Any
Soil: Well-drained
Hardiness: Zone 4
Propagation: Seed or
division, both in spring

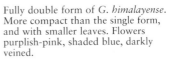

Fully double form of G. *himalayense*.
More compact than the single form,
and with smaller leaves. Flowers
purplish-pink, shaded blue, darkly
veined.

203

Geranium ibericum
subsp. *jubatum*
(Geraniaceae)

Common name: Caucasus
geranium
Height: 20in (50cm)
Spread: 24in (60cm)
Aspect: Sun or half shade
Soil: Well-drained
Hardiness: Zone 6
Propagation: Seed or
division, both in spring

Clump-forming; 9- to 11-lobed, basal,
hairy, leaves. Cymes of violet-blue,
cup-shaped, upward-facing flowers in
flushes from early summer. From
Turkey, Iran, the Caucasus.

Geranium incanum
(Geraniaceae)

Common names: None
Height: 16in (40cm)
Spread: 24in (60cm)
Aspect: Sun
Soil: Well-drained
Hardiness: Zone 9
Propagation: Seed or
division, both in spring

Evergreen from South Africa. Leaves
basal, filigree, aromatic, deeply cut into
5-toothed, lobed, gray-green segments.
Loose cymes of dark pink flowers,
summer to autumn.

Geranium
'Johnson's Blue' A.G.M.
(Geraniaceae)

Common names: None
Height: 18in (45cm)
Spread: 30in (75cm)
Aspect: Sun or half shade
Soil: Well-drained
Hardiness: Zone 4
Propagation: Division,
in spring

Rhizomatous hybrid. Leaves 7-lobed,
basal; leaflets further lobed, toothed,
mid-green. Flowers in loose cymes,
blue saucers with pink centers, in
summer.

Geranium macrorrhizum
'Ingwersen's Variety'
A.G.M. (Geraniaceae)

Common names: None
Height: 1ft (30cm)
Spread: 2ft (60cm)
Aspect: Sun or half shade
Soil: Well-drained
Hardiness: Zone 4
Propagation: Division,
in spring

Cloned selection of a rhizomatous
species. Leaves 7-lobed, toothed,
aromatic, sticky, light green. Flowers
flat, pale pink, calyx inflated, stamens
prominent, early summer.

Geranium maculatum
(Geraniaceae)

Common names:
Cranesbill; wild geranium
Height: 24in (60cm)
Spread: 18in (45cm)
Aspect: Sun
Soil: Moist, well-drained
Hardiness: Zone 4
Propagation: Seed or
division, both in spring

Tuberous species from eastern North
America. Leaves basal, 5- to 7-lobed,
glossy, green. Flowers in loose cymes,
lilac saucers, from late spring for
many weeks.

Geranium maderense
A.G.M.
(Geraniaceae)

Common names: None
Height: 5ft (1.5m)
Spread: 5ft (1.5m)
Aspect: Sun
Soil: Well-drained
Hardiness: Zone 9
Propagation: Seed or
division, both in spring

Species from Madeira. Bright green,
basal, 5- to 7-lobed, toothed leaves.
Panicles of flat, pale-veined magenta
flowers on purple-hairy stems, spring
to late summer.

Geranium x oxonianum
'Rose Clair'
(Geraniaceae)

Common names: None
Height: 3ft (90cm)
Spread: 2ft (60cm)
Aspect: Sun or half shade
Soil: Well-drained
Hardiness: Zone 5
Propagation: Division,
in spring

Clump-forming, robust hybrid. Leaves
basal, 5-lobed, each with 5 leaflets,
green, toothed, veined. Flowers in
loose cymes, pink, fading to white,
spring to autumn.

Geranium phaeum
(Geraniaceae)

Common names: None
Height: 2ft (60cm)
Spread: 18in (45cm)
Aspect: Half or full shade
Soil: Moist, well-drained
Hardiness: Zone 5
Propagation: Seed or
division, both in spring

Herbaceous species from the
mountains of Eurasia. Leaves basal,
7- to 9-lobed, green. Flowers in cymes,
violet-blue, black, white, or maroon
in late spring and early summer.

Geranium 'Phillippe Vapelle' (Geraniaceae)

Common names: None
Height: 16in (40cm)
Spread: 12in (30cm)
Aspect: Sun or half shade
Soil: Well-drained
Hardiness: Zone 7
Propagation: Division, in spring

A hybrid of *G. renardii* x *G. platypetalum*. Leaves basal, lobed, softly hairy, blue-gray. Flowers large, blue-purple, with bold, dark veins, long period from spring to summer.

Geranium pratense (Geraniaceae)

Common name: Meadow geranium
Height: 3ft (90cm)
Spread: 2ft (60cm)
Aspect: Sun or half shade
Soil: Well-drained
Hardiness: Zone 5
Propagation: Seed or division, both in spring

Herbaceous species from Europe to China. Leaves basal, 7 to 9 deeply divided lobes, toothed, green. Flowers in dense cymes, blue, violet, or white saucers, in summer.

Geranium pratense 'Mrs. Kendall Clark' A.G.M. (Geraniaceae)

Common name: Meadow geranium
Height: 3ft (90cm)
Spread: 2ft (60cm)
Aspect: Sun or half shade
Soil: Well-drained
Hardiness: Zone 5
Propagation: Division, in spring

Cloned selection of the species. Leaves basal, 7- to 9-lobed, toothed, midgreen. Flowers in umbels, saucer-shaped, pearl-gray, over a long period in summer.

Geranium pratense 'Plenum Violaceum' A.G.M. (Geraniaceae)

Common name: Meadow geranium
Height: 3ft (90cm)
Spread: 2ft (60cm)
Aspect: Sun or half shade
Soil: Well-drained
Hardiness: Zone 5
Propagation: Division, in spring

Double-flowered form. Leaves basal, lobed, toothed, midgreen. Flowers in dense cymes, rich, deep violet-blue saucers, tinged purple in the center, over a long period in summer.

Geranium psilostemon
A.G.M.
(Geraniaceae)

Common names: None
Height: 4ft (1.2m)
Spread: 4ft (1.2m)
Aspect: Sun or half shade
Soil: Well-drained
Hardiness: Zone 6
Propagation: Seed or
division, both in spring

Clump-forming; leaves basal, lobed, toothed, green, red in spring and autumn. Flowers large, deep purple, black centers and veins, in loose cymes; very long period in summer.

Geranium pyrenaicum
'Bill Wallis'
(Geraniaceae)

Common names: None
Height: 2ft (60cm)
Spread: 1ft (30cm)
Aspect: Sun or half shade
Soil: Well-drained
Hardiness: Zone 7
Propagation: Seed, in
spring

Cultivar of an evergreen species. Leaves small, lobed, midgreen. Flowers small, in loose cymes, rich purple; long period in summer. Self-seeds; comes true from seed.

Geranium x
riversleaianum 'Mavis
Simpson' (Geraniaceae)

Common names: None
Height: 1ft (30cm)
Spread: 4ft (1.2m)
Aspect: Sun or half shade
Soil: Well-drained
Hardiness: Zone 7
Propagation: Division, in
spring

Cultivar of a hybrid of garden origin. Leaves basal, 7-lobed, blunt-toothed, gray-green. Flowers in loose cymes, clear pink, nonstop all summer. Superb ground cover.

Geranium x riversleaianum
'Russell Pritchard' A.G.M.
(Geraniaceae)

Common names: None
Height: 1ft (30cm)
Spread: 3ft (1m)
Aspect: Sun or half shade
Soil: Well-drained
Hardiness: Zone 7
Propagation: Division, in
spring

Cultivar of a garden hybrid. Leaves basal, 7-lobed, toothed, gray-green. Flowers in loose cymes, dark magenta, over long periods in summer. Excellent ground cover.

Geranium sanguineum 'Elsbeth' (Geraniaceae)

Common name: Blood-red geranium
Height: 8in (20cm)
Spread: 12in (30cm)
Aspect: Sun or half shade
Soil: Well-drained
Hardiness: Zone 5
Propagation: Division, in spring

Cloned selection of a rhizomatous European species. Leaves stem, 5- to 7-lobed, toothed, mid-green. Flowers in loose cymes, large, bright purple saucers, spring to summer.

Geranium sanguineum 'Shepherd's Warning' A.G.M. (Geraniaceae)

Common name: Blood-red geranium
Height: 6in (15cm)
Spread: 6in (15cm)
Aspect: Sun or half shade
Soil: Well-drained
Hardiness: Zone 5
Propagation: Division, in spring

Cultivar of a rhizomatous species, low-growing, mat-forming, and with flowers of deep pink which fade to white, in summer. Excellent ground cover.

Geranium sanguineum var. *striatum* A.G.M. (Geraniaceae)

Common name: Blood-red geranium
Height: 4in (10cm)
Spread: 6in (15cm)
Aspect: Sun or half shade
Soil: Well-drained
Hardiness: Zone 5
Propagation: Seed or division, both in spring

Form from Walney Island, off the coast of Cumbria. Leaves stem, 5- to 7-lobed. Large flowers in loose cymes, pale pink with dark pink veins, for many weeks in summer.

Geranium sanguineum var. *striatum* 'Splendens' (Geraniaceae)

Common name: Blood-red geranium
Height: 18in (45cm)
Spread: 12in (30cm)
Aspect: Sun or half shade
Soil: Well-drained
Hardiness: Zone 5
Propagation: Seed or division, both in spring

One of the taller cultivars of the species. Leaves stem, 5- to 7-lobed, midgreen. Flowers large, deep pink with darker veins, in summer.

Geranium
'Stanhoe'
(Geraniaceae)

Common names: None
Height: 8in (20cm)
Spread: 8in (20cm)
Aspect: Sun or half shade
Soil: Well-drained
Hardiness: Zone 7
Propagation: Division, in
spring

A hybrid of garden origin, between
G. sessiliflorum and *G. traversii*.
Leaves small, round, hairy, gray-
green. Flowers delicate pink, from
midsummer to autumn.

Geranium sylvaticum
'Album' A.G.M.
(Geraniaceae)

Common name: Forest-
loving cranesbill
Height: 30in (75cm)
Spread: 24in (60cm)
Aspect: Sun or half shade
Soil: Moist, well-drained
Hardiness: Zone 4
Propagation: Seed or
division, both in spring

Clump-forming geranium. Leaves
basal, 7-lobed, lobes deeply cut,
toothed. Flowers in dense cymes,
white, blue or pink saucers, in spring
and early summer.

Geranium sylvaticum
'Amy Doncaster'
(Geraniaceae)

Common names: Forest-
loving cranesbill
Height: 30in (75cm)
Spread: 24in (60cm)
Aspect: Sun or half shade
Soil: Moist, well-drained
Hardiness: Zone 4
Propagation: Division, in
spring

Cloned cultivar of the woodland
geranium, with flowers of deep blue
with white eyes, in spring and
summer. Leaves basal,
7-lobed, lobes deeply cut, toothed.

Geranium tuberosum
(Geraniaceae)

Common names: None
Height: 12in (30cm)
Spread: 10in (25cm)
Aspect: Sun or half shade
Soil: Well-drained
Hardiness: Zone 8
Propagation: Seed or
division, both in spring

Mediterranean species. Summer-
dormant; makes deeply cut, toothed,
midgreen leaves over winter and bears
loose cymes of bright pink flowers
with dark veins in spring.

Geranium wallichianum
'Buxton's Variety' A.G.M.
(Geraniaceae)

Common name: Wallich
geranium
Height: 1ft (30cm)
Spread: 1m (3ft)
Aspect: Sun or half shade
Soil: Well-drained
Hardiness: Zone 7
Propagation: Division, in
spring

Gerbera jamesonii
(Asteraceae/Compositae)

Common name: Transvaal
daisy
Height: 18in (45cm)
Spread: 24in (60cm)
Aspect: Sun
Soil: Well-drained, fertile
Hardiness: Zone 8
Propagation: Seed in
warmth or division, both
in spring

Cultivar of a trailing species from
Kashmir and Afghanistan. Leaves 3-
to 5-lobed, toothed. Flowers in loose
cymes, large, sky-blue saucers, from
midsummer to autumn.

From Indonesia, Madagascar and
South Africa. Leaves inverse lance-
shaped, lobed, woolly below. Flowers
solitary, single, red with yellow
centers, spring to late summer.

GEUM (Rosaceae)
Avens

A genus of some 50 species, all perennial and hardy, from
temperate and polar regions of both hemispheres, with the
exception of Australia. Their natural habitats range from
mountainsides to woodlands and damp meadows, and they will
grow in just about any soil as long as it is not waterlogged.
They prefer full sun, but will tolerate light or dappled shade.
Avens have handsome, evergreen foliage, mainly borne in basal
rosettes. They are very useful border plants, since they bloom in
early summer before the main summer flowering season, and
can be persuaded to repeat-flower by deadheading. The flowers,
in pink, red, orange, yellow or cream, are open and bowl- to
saucer-shaped. In the garden they are much appreciated by bees,
and they are also excellent for cutting and low in allergens. One
drawback of this genus is that they do begin to flower less well
after a few years, and will become free-flowering again only if
they are lifted and divided, with the old, woody growth being
discarded, and only the soft, new growth replanted. By far the
best time to do this is in late spring; division at other times will
mean losing a year's flowering. They can be grown from seed,
but tend to hybridize readily.

Geum
'Dolly North'
(Rosaceae)

Common name: Avens
Height: 2ft (60cm)
Spread: 2ft (60cm)
Aspect: Sun or half shade
Soil: Well-drained, fertile
Hardiness: Zone 5
Propagation: Seed or
division, both in autumn
or spring

A *Geum chiloense* hybrid. Leaves
basal, in rosettes, pinnate, leaflets
heart- to kidney-shaped, wrinkled.
Flowers glowing orange, in cymes on
branched stems, early summer.

Geum coccineum
(Rosaceae)

Common name: Avens
Height: 20in (50cm)
Spread: 12in (30cm)
Aspect: Sun or half shade
Soil: Well-drained, fertile
Hardiness: Zone 4
Propagation: Seed or
division, both in spring or
autumn

An evergreen perennial from the
Balkans. Leaves basal, pinnate, hairy,
and stem, entire, toothed. Flowers in
cymes, brick-red with yellow stamens,
in early summer.

Geum
'Lady Stratheden' A.G.M.
(Rosaceae)

Common name: Avens
Height: 2ft (60cm)
Spread: 2ft (60cm)
Aspect: Sun or half shade
Soil: Well-drained, fertile
Hardiness: Zone 6
Propagation: Seed or
division, both in spring or
autumn

A *Geum chiloense* hybrid. Leaves
pinnate, hairy, lobes kidney-shaped to
ovate. Flowers semi-double, in cymes
of up to 5, yellow, all summer.

Geum
'Mrs J. Bradshaw' A.G.M.
(Rosaceae)

Common name: Avens
Height: 2ft (60cm)
Spread: 2ft (60cm)
Aspect: Sun or half shade
Soil: Well-drained, fertile
Hardiness: Zone 6
Propagation: Seed or
division, both in spring or
autumn

A *Geum chiloense* hybrid. Leaves
pinnate, hairy, lobes ovate to heart-
shaped, mid-green. Flowers in cymes
of up to 5, semi-double, red, from
early to late summer.

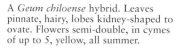

211

Geum 'Princess Juliana' (Rosaceae)

Common name: Avens
Height: 2ft (60cm)
Spread: 2ft (60cm)
Aspect: Sun or half shade
Soil: Well-drained, fertile
Hardiness: Zone 5
Propagation: Seed or division, both in spring or autumn

A *Geum chiloense* hybrid. Leaves pinnate, hairy, lobes ovate to heart-shaped, mid-green. Flowers in cymes of up to 5, semi-double, strong yellow, early and midsummer.

Geum rivale (Rosaceae)

Common name: Water avens
Height: 2ft (60cm)
Spread: 18in (45cm)
Aspect: Sun or half shade
Soil: Wet or marginal aquatic, humus-rich
Hardiness: Zone 3
Propagation: Seed or division, both in spring or autumn

European species. Leaves in basal rosettes, pinnate, obovate, veined, scalloped. Cymes of flowers, pendent, orange-yellow or pink bells, from late spring to midsummer.

Geum 'Tangerine' (Rosaceae)

Common name: Avens
Height: 1ft (30cm)
Spread: 1ft (30cm)
Aspect: Sun or half shade
Soil: Moist, fertile
Hardiness: Zone 3
Propagation: Division, in spring or autumn

Geum rivale hybrid. Leaves in basal rosettes, pinnate, obovate to wedge-shaped, dark green, scalloped. Flowers in cymes, orange, pendent saucers, late spring to midsummer.

Gillenia trifoliata A.G.M. (Rosaceae)

Common name: Bowman's-root
Height: 3ft (1m)
Spread: 2ft (60cm)
Aspect: Half shade
Soil: Moist, well-drained, acidic
Hardiness: Zone 4
Propagation: Seed or division, both in spring or autumn

Rhizomatous woodlander. Leaves 3-palmate, toothed, veined, leaflets ovoid, bronze-green. Flowers asymmetric, starry, white; long period from spring to late summer.

GLADIOLUS (Iridaceae)
Gladiolus

A genus of almost 200 species of cormous perennials from many countries, especially Africa, and South Africa in particular, Madagascar, the Arabian peninsula and western Asia. Some are hardy, but others are half-hardy or tender. All like sun and well-drained, fertile soil. The genus has been hybridized extensively for the flower trade and exhibition: over 10,000 cultivars and hybrids exist, and new ones are produced continually. There are different ways of classifying them; of most use to the gardener is the grouping of most into Grandiflorus, Nanus and Primulinus. Grandiflorus are tall, with a single, long, dense spike of many large flowers. Nanus are shorter, with 2 or 3 dense spikes of small flowers. Both of these groups are tender and need lifting each year. Primulinus, with a single loose spike of many flowers, contain some that can be left in the ground all year round in warmer areas. For the greater part, they do not need staking. Some species, *G. papilio* and *G. communis* subsp. *byzantinus* for example, are invasive; in transplanting them, make sure that all the tiny cormlets are moved as well, or they will make plants of flowering size by the next season. They make excellent cut flowers, and are low in allergens.

Gladiolus callianthus
A.G.M.
(Iridaceae)

Classification: Species
Height: 3ft (1m)
Spread: 4in (10cm)
Aspect: Sun
Soil: Well-drained, fertile
Hardiness: Zone 9
Propagation: Seed, in warmth in spring; offsets when dormant

Tender species, formerly *Acidanthera*. Leaves basal, erect, linear, green. Flowers in arching spikes, scented, white with a purple throat, in late summer and early autumn.

Gladiolus cardinalis
(Iridaceae)

Classification: Species
Height: 3ft (90cm)
Spread: 4in (10cm)
Aspect: Sun
Soil: Well-drained, fertile
Hardiness: Zone 9
Propagation: Seed, in warmth in spring; offsets, when dormant

A tender, cormous perennial from South Africa. Leaves basal, erect, linear, green. Flowers in spikes of up to 12, funnel-shaped, bright red with white flash on each tepal.

Gladiolus communis subsp. *byzantinus* A.G.M. (Iridaceae)

Classification: Species
Height: 1m (3ft)
Spread: 4in (10cm)
Aspect: Sun
Soil: Well-drained, fertile
Hardiness: Zone 6
Propagation: Seed, in spring; offsets, when dormant

Invasive type. Leaves basal, erect, linear, green. Flowers in spikes of up to 20, funnel-shaped, magenta with pale streaks on the lower tepal. Divide regularly.

Gladiolus 'Green Woodpecker' A.G.M. (Iridaceae)

Classification: Grandiflorus
Height: 5ft (1.5m)
Spread: 5in (12cm)
Aspect: Sun
Soil: Well-drained, fertile
Hardiness: Zone 9
Propagation: Offsets, when dormant

Leaves basal, erect, linear, green. Flowers in spikes of up to 25, ruffled, green-yellow with red marks on the throat, in mid- and late summer.

Gladiolus papilio (Iridaceae)

Classification: Species
Height: 3ft (90cm)
Spread: 3in (8cm)
Aspect: Sum
Soil: Well-drained, fertile
Hardiness: Zone 8
Propagation: Offsets, when dormant

Highly invasive species from South Africa. Leaves basal, erect to arching, linear, mid-green. Flowers in spikes of up to 5, hooded, gray-green with red internal marks.

Gladiolus 'The Bride' A.G.M. (Iridaceae)

Classification: Cardinalis hybrid
Height: 2ft (60cm)
Spread: 2in (5cm)
Aspect: Sun
Soil: Well-drained, fertile
Hardiness: Zone 8
Propagation: Offsets, when dormant

Hybrid cultivar. Leaves basal, erect, linear, midgreen. Flowering spike of up to 6 white flowers, marked pink on the lower tepal, from early spring to early summer.

Gladiolus tristis
(Iridaceae)

Classification: Species
Height: 5ft (1.5m)
Spread: 2in (5cm)
Aspect: Sun
Soil: Well-drained, fertile
Hardiness: Zone 7
Propagation: Seed, in
spring; offsets, when
dormant

South African species. Leaves basal,
erect, linear. Tall spike of up to 20
open funnel-shaped, scented flowers,
creamy-white, with dark flushing or
dots, in spring.

Glaucium flavum
(Papaveraceae)

Common name: Yellow
horned poppy
Height: 3ft (90cm)
Spread: 18in (45cm)
Aspect: Sun
Soil: Well-drained, fertile
Hardiness: Zone 7
Propagation: Seed, sown
in situ in spring or autumn

Rosette-forming, short-lived, coastal
plant. Leaves pinnatifid, lobes
toothed, rough, glaucous blue-green.
Flowers single, yellow, in summer,
followed by good seed heads.

Glaucium flavum
f. *fulvum*
(Papaveraceae)

Common name: Horned
poppy
Height: 36in (90cm)
Spread: 18in (45cm)
Aspect: Sun
Soil: Well-drained, fertile
Hardiness: Zone 7
Propagation: Seed, sown
in situ in spring or autumn

Form of the species with flowers of
bright orange, in summer, followed by
long, curved seed pods. Short-lived,
but self-seeds; resents disturbance.

Glyceria maxima
var. *variegata*
(Graminae/Poaceae)

Common names: None
Height: 28in (70cm)
Spread: Indefinite
Aspect: Sun
Soil: Water to 15cm (6in)
deep
Hardiness: Zone 5
Propagation: Division,
in spring

Rhizomatous, aquatic grass from
Europe and Asia. Leaves narrow
straps, striped cream, white and green.
Flowers in panicles, purplish-green, in
mid- to late summer.

Glycyrrhiza glabra
(Leguminosae/Papilionaceae)

Common name: Licorice
Height: 3ft (1m)
Spread: 18in (45cm)
Aspect: Sun
Soil: Moist, deep, fertile
Hardiness: Zone 8
Propagation: Seed or
division, both in spring

Tap-rooted plant from the
Mediterranean to SW Asia. Leaves
pinnate, leaflets ovate, sticky, glandular,
pale green. Flowers in racemes, pale
blue and white, late summer.

Goniolimon tataricum
(Plumbaginaceae)

Common name: Tatarian
sea-lavender
Height: 1ft (30cm)
Spread: 1ft (30cm)
Aspect: Sun
Soil: Well-drained, gritty
Hardiness: Zone 4
Propagation: Seed, in
spring

Rosette-forming plant. Leaves inverse
lance-shaped, smooth, leathery, pale
green. Wide panicles of tubular
flowers, white sepals and red petals.
Excellent for cutting and drying.

Grindelia chiloensis
(Asteraceae/Compositae)

Common name: Gumweed
Height: 3ft (1m)
Spread: 3ft (1m)
Aspect: Sun
Soil: Well-drained
Hardiness: Zone 6
Propagation: Seed, in
spring; semi-ripe cuttings,
in summer

Evergreen subshrub from Argentina
and Chile. Leaves basal, inverse lance-
shaped, gray-green. Flowers solitary,
semi-double, yellow, on long stalks,
over summer.

Gypsophila paniculata
(Caryophyllaceae)

Common name: Baby's-
breath
Height: 4ft (1.2m)
Spread: 4ft (1.2m)
Aspect: Sun
Soil: Well-drained, sandy
Hardiness: Zone 4
Propagation: Seed, in
warmth in winter to spring

Taprooted plant. Leaves lance-shaped
to linear, glaucous-green. Loose
panicles of many small, white,
trumpet flowers, over a long period in
mid- to late summer.

Gypsophila repens
A.G.M.
(Caryophyllaceae)

Common name: Creeping
gypsophila
Height: 8in (20cm)
Spread: 12in (30cm)
Aspect: Sun
Soil: Well-drained, sandy
Hardiness: Zone 4
Propagation: Seed, in
warmth in winter to spring

Mat-forming perennial from the
mountains of S Europe. Leaves linear,
midgreen. Flowers in loose panicles,
white or pink, over a long period in
summer.

Gypsophila
'Rosenschleier' A.G.M.
(Caryophyllaceae)

Common name: Baby's-
breath
Height: 18in (45cm)
Spread: 18in (45cm)
Aspect: Sun
Soil: Well-drained, sandy
Hardiness: Zone 4
Propagation: Seed, in
warmth in winter to spring

A robust, semi-evergreen hybrid.
Leaves lance-shaped to linear, blue-
green. Flowers in loose, many-
flowered panicles, double, white,
turning pink, mid- to late summer.

Hacquetia epipactis
A.G.M.
(Apiaceae/Umbelliferae)

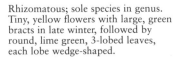

Common names: None
Height: 2in (5cm)
Spread: 8in (20cm)
Aspect: Half shade
Soil: Moist, well-drained,
acidic, humus-rich
Hardiness: Zone 7
Propagation: Seed, when
ripe; division, in spring

Rhizomatous; sole species in genus.
Tiny, yellow flowers with large, green
bracts in late winter, followed by
round, lime green, 3-lobed leaves,
each lobe wedge-shaped.

Hakonechloa macra
'Mediovariegata'
(Graminae/Poaceae)

Common names: None
Height: 18in (45cm)
Spread: 18in (45cm)
Aspect: Sun or half shade
Soil: Moist, well-drained,
humus-rich
Hardiness: Zone 5
Propagation: Division,
in spring

Leaves arching, linear, green, with
median stripes and asymmetric
narrow margins of pale yellow.
Panicles of pale green spikelets, late
summer to midautumn.

217

Haplopappus glutinosus
(Asteraceae/Compositae)

Common names: None
Height: 6in (15cm)
Spread: 12in (30cm)
Aspect: Sun
Soil: Sharply drained,
fertile, protected from
winter wet
Hardiness: Zone 9
Propagation: Seed, when
ripe or in spring

An evergreen, tender perennial from
Chile and Argentina. Leaves in dense
cushions, oblong, lobed or
pinnatisect, sticky, green. Flowers
solitary, single, yellow, in summer.

Hedychium densiflorum
(Zingiberaceae)

Common name: Ginger-
lily
Height: 15ft (5m)
Spread: 6ft (2m)
Aspect: Sun or half shade
Soil: Moist, well-drained,
humus-rich
Hardiness: Zone 8
Propagation: Seed, in warmth
when ripe; division, in spring

Rhizomatous Himalayan plant.
Leaves oblong, pointed, shiny green.
Flowers in dense, cylindrical racemes,
tubular, scented, orange or yellow, in
late summer.

Hedychium forrestii
(Zingiberaceae)

Common name: Ginger-
lily
Height: 5ft (1.5m)
Spread: 2ft (60cm)
Aspect: Sun or half shade
Soil: Moist, well-drained,
humus-rich
Hardiness: Zone 9
Propagation: Seed, in warmth
when ripe; division, in spring

Tender, rhizomatous perennial from
China. Leaves narrow, lance-shaped,
veined, green. Flowers in racemes,
white, in late summer and early
autumn. Excellent for cutting.

Hedychium yunnanense
(Zingiberaceae)

Common name: Ginger-
lily
Height: 3ft (1m)
Spread: 2ft (60cm)
Aspect: Sun or half shade
Soil: Moist, well-drained,
humus-rich
Hardiness: Zone 9
Propagation: Seed, in warmth
when ripe; division, in spring

Tender, rhizomatous species from
Yunnan. Leaves broad obovate, shiny
green. Raceme of white, deeply
divided flowers with orange bracts;
attractive seed heads.

Hedysarum coronarium
(Leguminosae/Papilionaceae)

Helenium autumnale
(Asteraceae/Compositae)

Common name: Sulla
sweetvetch
Height: 3ft (1m)
Spread: 2ft (60cm)
Aspect: Sun
Soil: Well-drained, gritty
Hardiness: Zone 3
Propagation: Seed, when
ripe or in spring

Common name: Common
sneezeweed
Height: 5ft (1.5m)
Spread: 18in (45cm)
Aspect: Sun
Soil: Moist, well-drained,
fertile
Hardiness: Zone 3
Propagation: Seed, in spring;
division, in spring or autumn

Perennial from the Mediterranean.
Leaves pinnate, with up to 15 obovate
leaflets, midgreen. Flowers in racemes,
perfumed, deep red, pealike, on erect
stems in spring.

A perennial from North America.
Leaves lance-shaped, toothed,
midgreen. Flowers solitary, ray florets
yellow, disc florets brown, from late
summer to midautumn.

HELENIUM (Asteraceae/Compositae)
Sneezeweed

A genus of 40 or so species of generally clump-forming annuals,
biennials and perennials from Central and North America.
Their natural habitats are woodland edges or grasslands and are
usually damp, and they will do well in a sunny position. The
genus has been much hybridized, such that there is a large
number of hybrids of uncertain parentage, but of great value in
the garden. Sneezeweeds flower over long periods in late
summer and autumn, and the earlier-flowering types can be
persuaded to flower again if deadheaded. The flowers are
daisylike, with prominent discs of yellow or brown, and ray
florets of yellow, orange, and red, bringing rich autumn tints in
the border. They are much-visited by bees and butterflies,
providing valuable late food. The foliage is midgreen, lance-
shaped, and unspectacular. The taller species and cultivars
usually need to be staked, and all become congested fairly
rapidly, so it is necessary to lift and divide them every few years
or so. The flowers are excellent for cutting, and are popular for
flower-arranging, but they are named sneezeweed for a reason,
being highly allergic. The plants are also poisonous, and
contact with the foliage can cause skin irritation.

Helenium
'Crimson Beauty'
(Asteraceae/Compositae)

Common name: Common
sneezeweed
Height: 4ft (1.2m)
Spread: 2ft (60cm)
Aspect: Sun
Soil: Moist, well-drained,
humus-rich
Hardiness: Zone 3
Propagation: Seed, in spring;
division, in spring or autumn

Very hardy hybrid cultivar. Leaves
ovate, midgreen. Flowers solitary, ray
florets bright red, disc florets brown,
from late summer to midautumn.

Helenium
'Goldene Jugend'
(Asteraceae/Compositae)

Common name: Common
sneezeweed
Height: 32in (80cm)
Spread: 24in (60cm)
Aspect: Sun
Soil: Moist, well-drained,
humus-rich
Hardiness: Zone 5
Propagation: Seed, in spring;
division, in spring or autumn

A hybrid cultivar. Leaves ovate,
midgreen. Flowers solitary, ray florets
yellow, disc florets pale brown, over a
long period in early and midsummer.

Helenium
'Moerheim Beauty'
(Asteraceae/Compositae)

Common name: Common
sneezeweed
Height: 3ft (90cm)
Spread: 2ft (60cm)
Aspect: Sun
Soil: Moist, well-drained,
humus-rich
Hardiness: Zone 3
Propagation: Seed, in spring;
division, in spring or autumn

Very hardy hybrid Helenium. Leaves
ovate, midgreen. Flowers solitary, ray
florets dark, coppery-red, disc florets
brown, over a long period from early
to late summer.

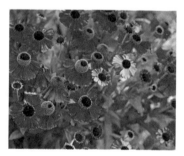

Helenium
'Sahin's Early Flowerer'
(Asteraceae/Compositae)

Common name: Common
sneezeweed
Height: 3ft (90cm)
Spread: 2ft (60cm)
Aspect: Sun
Soil: Moist, well-drained,
humus-rich
Hardiness: Zone 5
Propagation: Seed, in spring;
division, in spring or autumn

A hybrid Helenium. Leaves ovate,
midgreen. Flowers single, ray florets
bright red, disc florets dark brown, in
late spring to midsummer.

Helenium
'Waldtraut'
(Asteraceae/Compositae)

Common name: Common sneezeweed
Height: 3ft (90cm)
Spread: 2ft (60cm)
Aspect: Sun
Soil: Moist, well-drained, humus-rich
Hardiness: Zone 3
Propagation: Seed, in spring; division, in spring or autumn

Very hardy hybrid *Helenium*. Leaves ovate, midgreen. Flowers single, ray florets orange, disc florets brown, over a long period in late summer and early autumn.

Helianthemum
'Ben Fhada'
(Cistaceae)

Common name: Sunrose
Height: 8in (20cm)
Spread: 8in (20cm)
Aspect: Sun
Soil: Well-drained, fertile
Hardiness: Zone 6
Propagation: Softwood cuttings, in spring to early summer

Subshrub, evergreen in mild areas. Leaves oblong to linear, gray-green. Flowers yellow with an orange center, 5-petalled saucers, in cymes; long period in late spring to summer.

Helianthemum
'Fireball'
(Cistaceae)

Common name: Sunrose
Height: 8in (20cm)
Spread: 12in (30cm)
Aspect: Sun
Soil: Well-drained, fertile
Hardiness: Zone 6
Propagation: Softwood cuttings, in spring to early summer

Hybrid, evergreen or semi-evergreen subshrub. Leaves oblong, gray-green. Flowers in cymes, double, bright scarlet, over a long period in late spring to summer.

Helianthemum
'Laurenson's Pink'
(Cistaceae)

Common name: Sunrose
Height: 8in (20cm)
Spread: 12in (30cm)
Aspect: Sun
Soil: Well-drained, fertile
Hardiness: Zone 6
Propagation: Softwood cuttings, in spring to s ummer

A hybrid subshrub. Leaves linear, mid-green. Flowers in cymes, single, pale pink with an orange center, over a long period in spring to midsummer.

**Helianthemum
nummularium**
(Cistaceae)

Common name: Sunrose
Height: 8in (20cm)
Spread: 12in (30cm)
Aspect: Sun
Soil: Well-drained, fertile
Hardiness: Zone 6
Propagation: Seed, when
ripe or in spring

Subshrub from mainland Europe.
Leaves ovate to lance-shaped, gray-
green. Flowers in cymes, single, petals
deep pink, paler at base; long period
from spring to summer.

Helianthus decapetalus
(Asteraceae/Compositae)

Common name: Thinleaf
sunflower
Height: 4ft (1.2m)
Spread: Indefinite
Aspect: Sun
Soil: Moist, well-drained,
humus-rich
Hardiness: Zone 5
Propagation: Division, in
spring or autumn

Rampant, rhizomatous species. Leaves
ovate to lance-shaped, smooth above,
hairy-rough below. Flowers single,
daisylike, yellow with brown centers,
late summer to autumn.

HELIANTHUS (Asteraceae/Compositae)
Sunflower

A genus of some 80 species, annual and perennial, from North,
Central and South America. They are generally tall, coarse plants
demanding quite a bit of space; the taller, spreading types are
best in a wild garden. They require full sun and good drainage,
and should not be overfed, as this will result in more foliage
than flowers. There are many cultivars and hybrids, and the
nomenclature of these is highly confused and liable to change
frequently. Sunflowers are grown for their large, daisylike
flowers with usually yellow ray florets and brown, purple or
yellow disc florets; these are borne over lengthy periods in
summer, and long, hot summers are needed for good flowering.
The flowers of perennial species are generally smaller than those
of the annuals. They attract bees and are excellent for cutting;
unfortunately they are also highly allergenic. Sunflowers are
prone to powdery mildew, and so should not be allowed to dry
out in summer. Slugs are fond of their new growth in spring.
Some will spread aggressively, and it is necessary to dig around
them annually to sever the spreading roots. They need to be
staked, and they must be lifted and divided every few years.
Contact with the foliage may cause skin irritation.

Helianthus doronicoides
(Asteraceae/Compositae)

Common name: Sunflower
Height: 5ft (1.5m)
Spread: 2ft (60cm)
Aspect: Sun
Soil: Moist, well-drained,
humus-rich
Hardiness: Zone 4
Propagation: Division, in
spring or autumn

Invasive herbaceous species from the
U.S.A. Leaves ovate to lance-shaped,
large, bristly. Flowers single, daisylike,
lemon, over a long period from
summer to autumn.

Helianthus
'Lemon Queen'
(Asteraceae/Compositae)

Common name: Sunflower
Height: 6ft (1.8m)
Spread: 4ft (1.2)
Aspect: Sun
Soil: Moist, well-drained,
humus-rich
Hardiness: Zone 5
Propagation: Division, in
spring or autumn

Hybrid sunflower. Leaves ovate,
veined, dark green. Flowers pale
yellow, daisylike, with darker yellow
centers, over a long period in late
summer to autumn.

Helianthus x *multiflorus*
(Asteraceae/Compositae)

Common name: Sunflower
Height: 6ft (2m)
Spread: 3ft (1m)
Aspect: Sun
Soil: Moist, well-drained,
humus-rich
Hardiness: Zone 5
Propagation: Division, in
spring or autumn

Clump-forming garden hybrid. Leaves
ovate to lance-shaped, hairy, deep
green. Flowers with yellow ray florets
and brown disc florets, over a long
period from late summer.

Helianthus x *multiflorus*
'Loddon Gold' A.G.M.
(Asteraceae/Compositae)

Common name: Sunflower
Height: 5ft (1.5m)
Spread: 3ft (90cm)
Aspect: Sun
Soil: Moist, well-drained
humus-rich
Hardiness: Zone 5
Propagation: Division, in
spring or autumn

Hybrid, also called *Helianthus*
'Loddon Gold'. Leaves lance-shaped
to ovate, hairy, dark green. Flowers
double, rich yellow; long period from
late summer onward.

223

Helianthus × *multiflorus* 'Triomphe de Gand' (Asteraceae/Compositae)

Common name: Sunflower
Height: 4ft (1.2m)
Spread: 3ft (90cm)
Aspect: Sun
Soil: Moist, well-drained, humus-rich
Hardiness: Zone 5
Propagation: Division, in spring or autumn

Hybrid, also called *Helianthus* 'Triomphe de Gand'. Leaves ovate to lance-shaped, hairy, dark green. Flowers large, single, yellow, disc florets quilled, in late summer.

Helianthus salicifolius (Asteraceae/Compositae)

Common name: Willowleaved sunflower
Height: 8ft (2.5m)
Spread: 3ft (90cm)
Aspect: Sun
Soil: Moist, well-drained, humus-rich
Hardiness: Zone 4
Propagation: Division, in spring or autumn

Rhizomatous species from the U.S.A. Very handsome foliage, arching, linear to lance-shaped, bright green. Flowers single, yellow, over a long period from early autumn.

Helichrysum italicum A.G.M. (Asteraceae/Compositae)

Common name: Straw-flower
Height: 2ft (60cm)
Spread: 3ft (90cm)
Aspect: Sun
Soil: Well-drained, protected from winter wet
Hardiness: Zone 8
Propagation: Seed or division, both in spring

Evergreen subshrub from S Europe. Leaves linear, aromatic, silver-gray. Flowers dark yellow, "everlasting" in corymbs on long stems; long period from summer to autumn.

Helichrysum 'Schwefellicht' (Asteraceae/Compositae)

Common name: Straw-flower
Height: 16in (40cm)
Spread: 12in (30cm)
Aspect: Sun
Soil: Well-drained, protected from winter wet
Hardiness: Zone 6
Propagation: Seed or division, both in spring

A hybrid herbaceous perennial. Leaves lance-shaped, woolly, silver-white. Flowers "everlasting," fluffy, yellow, in tight corymbs, in late summer.

Helictotrichon
sempervirens A.G.M.
(Graminae/Poaceae)

Common names: None
Height: 4ft (1.2m)
Spread: 2ft (60cm)
Aspect: Sun
Soil: Well-drained
Hardiness: Zone 5
Propagation: Seed or
division, both in spring

Evergreen perennial grass from
Europe. Leaves linear, flat or rolled,
blue-gray. Flowers in stiff spikelets,
straw-colored, shiny, in panicles in
early to midsummer.

Heliopsis helianthoides
'Ballerina'
(Asteraceae/Compositae)

Common name: Sunflower
heliopsis
Height: 3ft (1m)
Spread: 2ft (60cm)
Aspect: Sun
Soil: Moist, well-drained,
fertile, humus-rich
Hardiness: Zone 4
Propagation: Division, in
spring or autumn

Hybrid cultivar. Leaves ovate to
lance-shaped, toothed, midgreen.
Flowers semi-double, yellow with
orange discs, on branching stems,
summer to early autumn.

Heliopsis helianthoides
'Canary Bird'
(Asteraceae/Compositae)

Common name: Sunflower
heliopsis
Height: 1m (3ft)
Spread: 60cm (2ft)
Aspect: Sun
Soil: Moist, well-drained,
fertile, humus-rich
Hardiness: Zone 4
Propagation: Division, in
spring or autumn

Hybrid cultivar. Leaves ovate to
lance-shaped, toothed, midgreen.
Flowers semi-double, yellow with
dark centers, from midsummer to
early autumn.

Heliopsis helianthoides
'Gigantea'
(Asteraceae/Compositae)

Common name: Sunflower
heliopsis
Height: 4ft (1.2m)
Spread: 2ft (60cm)
Aspect: Sun
Soil: Well-drained, fertile,
humus-rich
Hardiness: Zone 4
Propagation: Division, in
spring or autumn

Hardy cultivar. Leaves ovate to lance-
shaped, toothed, midgreen. Flowers
semidouble, yellow with dark centers,
from midsummer to early autumn.

225

Heliopsis helianthoides var. *scabra* 'Light of Loddon' (Asteraceae/Compositae)

Common name: Sunflower heliopsis
Height: 4ft (1.2m)
Spread: 2ft (60cm)
Aspect: Sun
Soil: Well-drained, fertile, humus-rich
Hardiness: Zone 4
Propagation: Division, in spring or autumn

Hardy cultivar. Leaves lance-shaped to ovate, toothed, dark green. Flowers semi-double, with yellow ray florets and brown disc florets, midsummer to early autumn.

Helleborus argutifolius A.G.M. (Ranunculaceae)

Common names: None
Height: 4ft (1.2m)
Spread: 3ft (90cm)
Aspect: Sun or half shade
Soil: Alkaline, humus-rich
Hardiness: Zone 7
Propagation: Seed, when ripe; division, in spring or autumn

Species from Corsica and Sardinia. Leaves 3-lobed, leaflets elliptic, spiny-toothed, dark green, leathery. Pendent, pale green flowers in dense cymes, late winter to early spring.

HELLEBORUS (Ranunculaceae)
Hellebore

A small genus of only 15 or so rhizomatous species, but one that gives the gardener some handsome weather-resistant winter flowers of excellent quality and form. They are native to central and eastern Europe and western Asia. Their natural habitats vary quite considerably, from rocky scrub and grassland to woodland, and so their cultural requirements also vary; some do well in full sun, and are good in a sunny border, while others enjoy dappled shade, and are excellent for naturalizing in a woodland garden. Some species perform best if their soil is acidic, but others prefer alkaline conditions; what they all have in common is a dislike of soils with extremes of wetness or dryness. All hellebores are reliably hardy. The flowers appear in late winter and spring and vary from open saucer-shaped to bell-shaped and tubular; each has 5 tepals, numerous stamens, and leafy bracts. They range in color from pure white through to deep purple, with some spotted and green types. The foliage may be evergreen or deciduous, and is leathery, toothed, and dark green. Hellebores are high-allergen plants, and all parts are poisonous and may also cause skin irritation on contact, so they are best avoided by the allergic gardener.

Helleborus argutifolius
'Pacific Frost'
(Ranunculaceae)

Common names: None
Height: 4ft (1.2m)
Spread: 3ft (90cm)
Aspect: Half shade
Soil: Alkaline, humus-rich
Hardiness: Zone 7
Propagation: Division, in
spring or autumn

Grown for its outstanding leaves,
blotched pale green and silver, ovate.
Flowers in many-flowered cymes,
pendent, pale green, in late winter to
early spring.

Helleborus niger
A.G.M.
(Ranunculaceae)

Common name:
Christmas-rose
Height: 12in (30cm)
Spread: 18 in (45cm)
Aspect: Half shade
Soil: Alkaline, humus-rich
Hardiness: Zone 3
Propagation: Seed, when
ripe; division, in spring or
autumn

Species from central Europe. Leaves
dark green, oblong to lance-shaped,
apex toothed. Flowers solitary or
paired, white saucers, pink-flushed, in
late winter to early spring.

Helleborus odorus
(Ranunculaceae)

Common name: Hellebore
Height: 20in (50cm)
Spread: 20in (50cm)
Aspect: Sun or half shade
Soil: Alkaline, humus-rich
Hardiness: Zone 6
Propagation: Seed, when
ripe; division, in spring or
autumn

Leaves dark green, basal, pedate, 3
lateral leaflets, each divided into 3–5
toothed lobes. Cymes of up to 5
green, fragrant, saucer-shaped flowers,
late winter to early spring.

Helleborus orientalis
hybrid
(Ranunculaceae)

Common name: Lenten-
rose
Height: 20in (50cm)
Spread: 18in (45cm)
Aspect: Sun or half shade
Soil: Alkaline, humus-rich
Hardiness: Zone 6
Propagation: Division, in
spring or autumn

Leaves leathery, basal, pedate, deep
green, with 7 to 9 elliptic leaflets.
Flowers deep pink, outward-facing
saucers, midwinter to midspring. One
of many cultivars.

Helleborus orientalis hybrid
(Ranunculaceae)

Common name: Lenten-rose
Height: 20in (50cm)
Spread: 18in (45cm)
Aspect: Sun or half shade
Soil: Alkaline, humus-rich
Hardiness: Zone 6
Propagation: Division, in spring or autumn

Leaves basal, leathery, pedate, deep green, with 7 to 9 elliptic leaflets. Flowers pale pink, downward-facing saucers, midwinter to midspring. One of many cultivars.

Helleborus x sternyii
Blackthorn Group
A.G.M. (Ranunculaceae)

Common name: Hellebore
Height: 14in (35cm)
Spread: 12in (30cm)
Aspect: Sun or half shade
Soil: Alkaline, humus-rich
Hardiness: Zone 7
Propagation: Seed, when ripe; division, in spring or autumn

Hybrid evergreen hellebore. Leaves with 3 elliptic leaflets, boldly veined, grayish-green. Flowers in many-flowered cymes, green, suffused pink, from midwinter to spring.

Helleborus viridis
(Ranunculaceae)

Common name: Green hellebore
Height: 16in (40cm)
Spread: 18in (45cm)
Aspect: Sun or half shade
Soil: Alkaline, humus-rich
Hardiness: Zone 6
Propagation: Seed, when ripe; division, in spring or autumn

Evergreen species. Leaves basal, with up to 13 oblong leaflets, midgreen. Flowers in cymes of up to 4, pendent, green, in winter or early spring.

Heloniopsis orientalis
(Liliaceae/Melanthiaceae)

Common names: None
Height: 8in (20cm)
Spread: 8in (20cm)
Aspect: Half shade
Soil: Moist, well-drained, acidic, humus-rich
Hardiness: Zone 7
Propagation: Seed, in spring or autumn; division, in spring

Rhizomatous, evergreen woodlander. Leaves broad, lance-shaped, leathery, pale green. Flowers pink, nodding funnels, in racemes of up to 10.

HEMEROCALLIS (Hemerocallidaceae/Liliaceae)
Day-lily

A genus of about 15 perennials from Japan, China, and Korea. They have been extensively hybridized, however, to the extent that 30,000 hybrids are in cultivation. They are clump-forming, and need to be lifted and divided every few years. *Hemerocallis fulva* and *H. lilio-asphodelus* are as invasive as weeds, however, and should not be admitted to the small garden. They will thrive in sun or light shade, and are not demanding as to soil type, so long as it is not too dry. The foliage is grassy, arching, and bright green; it may be evergreen or semievergreen, and disguises the fading leaves of spring-flowering bulbs well. The flowering stems are stout, and staking is not usually required. The flowers may be circular, triangular, stellate, or spider-shaped in outline, and may be single or double. They are summer-flowering. Each flower lasts for just one day (or one night in the case of the nocturnal varieties, which open in the late afternoon), but is usually followed by a succession of others. Some are perfumed. Day-lilies are indispensable plants for the mixed border, and are good for ground cover. They make excellent cut flowers, and are cherished by flower-arrangers. They are low in allergens, and suitable for allergic gardeners.

Hemerocallis
'Amersham'
(Hemerocallidaceae/Liliaceae)

Common name: Day-lily
Height: 28in (70 cm)
Spread: 26in (65cm)
Aspect: Sun
Soil: Moist, well-drained, fertile
Hardiness: Zone 4
Propagation: Division, in spring or autumn

Hemerocallis
'Bette Davis Eyes'
(Hemerocallidaceae/Liliaceae)

Common name: Day-lily
Height: 26in (65cm)
Spread: 26in (65cm)
Aspect: Sun
Soil: Moist, well-drained, fertile
Hardiness: Zone 4
Propagation: Division, in spring or autumn

A deciduous, hybrid day-lily bearing a succession of single, star-shaped flowers of striking dark red with a contrasting yellow throat.

A hardy, hybrid *Hemerocallis* cultivar with a succession of circular flowers of a delicate, peach-pink color, with a dark magenta throat.

Hemerocallis
'Black Magic'
(Hemerocallidaceae/Liliacea)

Common name: Day-lily
Height: 2ft (60cm)
Spread: 2ft (60cm)
Aspect: Sun
Soil: Moist, well-drained, fertile
Hardiness: Zone 4
Propagation: Division, in spring or autumn

A hardy, hybrid *Hemerocallis* with star-shaped flowers of rich maroon, with a central pale stripe on each petal, and a yellow throat.

Hemerocallis
'Cartwheels' A.G.M.
(Hemerocallidaceae/Liliaceae)

Common name: Day-lily
Height: 30in (75cm)
Spread: 30in (75cm)
Aspect: Sun
Soil: Moist, well-drained, fertile
Hardiness: Zone 4
Propagation: Division, in spring

A hardy, evergreen, nocturnal-flowering hybrid day-lily. A free-flowering cultivar, with star-shaped flowers of clear, unmarked yellow.

Hemerocallis
'Chemistry'
(Hemerocallidaceae/Liliaceae)

Common name: Day-lily
Height: 28in (70cm)
Spread: 28in (70cm)
Aspect: Sun
Soil: Moist, well-drained, fertile
Hardiness: Zone 4
Propagation: Division, in spring or autumn

A hardy, hybrid dayliliy with a succession of star-shaped flowers of amber, marked with a brown ring near the center and an orange throat.

Hemerocallis
'Chicago Royal Robe'
(Hemerocallidaceae/Liliaceae)

Common name: Day-lily
Height: 24in (60cm)
Spread: 6in (15cm)
Aspect: Sun
Soil: Moist, well-drained, humus-rich
Hardiness: Zone 4
Propagation: Division, in spring or autumn

A hardy, semievergreen, hybrid day-lily with a succession of large, perfumed, circular flowers of dark purple with a yellow-green throat.

Hemerocallis
'Chicago Sunrise'
(Hemerocallidaceae/Liliaceae)

Common name: Day-lily
Height: 28in (70cm)
Spread: 6in (15cm)
Aspect: Sun
Soil: Moist, well-drained,
humus-rich
Hardiness: Zone 4
Propagation: Division, in
spring or autumn

Freeflowering, hardy, semievergreen
hybrid day-lily, with a succession of
circular, clear yellow flowers with a
darker throat, from midsummer.

Hemerocallis
'Corky' A.G.M.
(Hemerocallidaceae/Liliaceae)

Common name: Daylily
Height: 32in (80cm)
Spread: 3½in (9cm)
Aspect: Sun
Soil: Moist, well-drained,
humus-rich
Hardiness: Zone 4
Propagation: Division, in
spring

Very freeflowering, evergreen, hardy
hybrid day-lily, with black stems,
mahogany buds, and small, star-
shaped flowers of lemon-yellow, in
midsummer.

Hemerocallis.
'Golden Scroll'
(Hemerocallidaceae/Liliaceae)

Common name: Daylily
Height: 19in (48cm)
Spread: 6in (15cm)
Aspect: Sun
Soil: Moist, well-drained,
humus-rich
Hardiness: Zone 4
Propagation: Division, in
spring or autumn

A hybrid day-lily with lush foliage
and ruffled, circular, muted tangerine-
orange to deep peach flowers, with a
green throat, in late summer.

Hemerocallis
'King Haiglar'
(Hemerocallidaceae/Liliaceae)

Common name: Day-lily
Height: 28in (70cm)
Spread: 5in (13cm)
Aspect: Sun
Soil: Moist, well-drained,
humus-rich
Hardiness: Zone 4
Propagation: Division, in
spring or autumn

A very freeflowering, hybrid day-lily
cultivar bearing large flowers of rich
scarlet, with a small yellow throat, in
midsummer.

231

Hemerocallis 'Lady Neva'
(Hemerocallidaceae/Liliaceae)

Common name: Day-lily
Height: 36in (90cm)
Spread: 9in (22cm)
Aspect: Sun
Soil: Moist, well-drained, humus-rich
Hardiness: Zone 4
Propagation: Division, in spring or autumn

A hybrid day-lily with ruffled flowers of buff to bright yellow, marked maroon; throat flared, yellow, filaments yellow, anthers gray.

Hemerocallis 'Little Grapette'
(Hemerocallidaceae/Liliaceae)

Common name: Day-lily
Height: 12in (30cm)
Spread: 18in (45cm)
Aspect: Sun
Soil: Moist, well-drained, fertile
Hardiness: Zone 4
Propagation: Division, in spring or autumn

A hybrid day-lily with star-shaped flowers of deep purple with a green throat, in midsummer. Shorter daylilies such as this are excellent for containers.

Hemerocallis 'Mighty Mogul'
(Hemerocallidaceae/Liliaceae)

Common name: Day-lily
Height: 36in (90cm)
Spread: 18in (45cm)
Aspect: Sun
Soil: Moist, well-drained, humus-rich
Hardiness: Zone 4
Propagation: Division, in spring

A hybrid day-lily with a succession of bright scarlet flowers with a yellow throat. The petals are reflexed and have slightly ruffled edges.

Hemerocallis 'Stella de Oro' A.G.M.
(Hemerocallidaceae/Liliaceae)

Common name: Day-lily
Height: 12in (30cm)
Spread: 18in (45cm)
Aspect: Sun
Soil: Moist, well-drained, humus-rich
Hardiness: Zone 4
Propagation: Division, in spring

A vigorous, freeflowering, hybrid evergreen day-lily, with a succession of circular, bright yellow flowers on slender stems in early summer.

Hesperis matronalis
(Brassicaceae/Cruciferae)

Common name: Dame's
rocket
Height: 36in (90cm)
Spread: 18in (45cm)
Aspect: Sun or half shade
Soil: Moist, well-drained,
fertile
Hardiness: Zone 3
Propagation: Seed, sown
in situ in spring

Short-lived, rosette-forming plant
from Asia and Europe. Leaves dark
green, ovate, toothed, hairy. Flowers
perfumed, lilac-purple, in panicles,
spring to midsummer.

Heuchera cylindrica
'Greenfinch'
(Saxifragaceae)

Common name: Coral-
bells
Height: 3ft (90cm)
Spread: 2ft (60cm)
Aspect: Any
Soil: Moist, well-drained,
fertile
Hardiness: Zone 4
Propagation: Division, in
autumn

Cloned cultivar. Leaves round,
scalloped, dark green, mottled pale
green. Flowers in panicles on tall
spikes, green, from mid-spring to
midsummer. Good ground cover.

Heuchera micrantha
var. *diversifolia*
'Palace Purple' A.G.M.

Common name: Coral-
bells
Height: 2ft (60cm)
Spread: 2ft (60cm)
Aspect: Any
Soil: Moist, well-drained,
fertile
Hardiness: Zone 5
Propagation: Division, in
autumn

Leaves large, shiny, jagged, metallic
bronze. Flowers in very tall, loose
panicles, cream, anthers red, followed
by good seed heads in early summer.
Good ground cover.

Heuchera
'Persian Carpet'
(Saxifragaceae)

Common name: Coral-
bells
Height: 14in (35cm)
Spread: 24in (60cm)
Aspect: Any
Soil: Moist, well-drained,
fertile
Hardiness: Zone 7
Propagation: Division, in
autumn

Hybrid with large, round, metallic,
silvery red-purple leaves. Flowers on
tall spikes in panicles, greenish, in
early summer. Handsome ground
cover. Liked by bees.

233

Heuchera
'Pewter Moon'
(Saxifragaceae)

Common name: Coral-
bells
Height: 16in (40cm)
Spread: 12in (30cm)
Aspect: Any
Soil: Moist, well-drained,
fertile
Hardiness: Zone 7
Propagation: Division, in
autumn

Hybrid with ovate to heart-shaped
leaves, bronze-purple, marbled gray.
Flowers in panicles, ice-pink, in early
summer. A good evergreen ground
cover for shade.

Heuchera
'Rachel'
(Saxifragaceae)

Common name: Coral-
bells
Height: 1ft (30cm)
Spread: 1ft (30cm)
Aspect: Any
Soil: Moist, well-drained,
fertile
Hardiness: Zone 7
Propagation: Division, in
autumn

Hybrid with rounded, lobed, toothed
leaves of dark green with bronzed
edges. Flowers in erect panicles, pale
pink, in early summer. Evergreen
ground cover for shade.

Heuchera
'Red Spangles' A.G.M.
(Saxifragaceae)

Common name: Coral-
bells
Height: 20in (50cm)
Spread: 10in (25cm)
Aspect: Any
Soil: Moist, well-drained,
fertile
Hardiness: Zone 4
Propagation: Division, in
autumn

Hybrid with round, lobed, toothed
leaves of dark green, marbled pale
green. Flowers in short, open panicles,
scarlet, all summer. Evergreen ground
cover for shade.

x *Heucherella alba*
'Bridget Bloom'
(Saxifragaceae)

Common names: None
Height: 16in (40cm)
Spread: 12in (30cm)
Aspect: Any
Soil: Moist, well-drained,
fertile, acidic
Hardiness: Zone 5
Propagation: Division, in
autumn or spring

Evergreen hybrid of *Heuchera* and
Tiarella. Leaves ovate, 7- to 9-lobed,
toothed, green. Panicles of tiny, pink
flowers in late spring and again in
autumn. Ground cover.

**x *Heucherella alba*
'Rosalie'
(Saxifragaceae)**

Common names: None
Height: 16in (40cm)
Spread: 8in (20cm)
Aspect: Any
Soil: Moist, well-drained,
fertile, acidic
Hardiness: Zone 5
Propagation: Division, in
spring or autumn

Hybrid of *Heuchera* and *Tiarella*.
Leaves ovate, 7- to 9-lobed, toothed,
green, veined brown. Flowers in
panicles, tiny, pale pink, in spring and
again in autumn.

**Hieracium lanatum
(Asteraceae/Compositae)**

Common name:
Hawkweed
Height: 18in (45cm)
Spread: 8in (20cm)
Aspect: Sun
Soil: Well-drained, poor
Hardiness: Zone 7
Propagation: Seed, in
autumn or spring; division,
in spring

Clump-forming. Leaves linear to
lance-shaped, densely white-hairy,
gray-green, margined white. Loose
panicles of semi-double, chrome-
yellow flowers, in summer.

**Hieracium maculatum
(Asteraceae/Compositae)**

Common name:
Hawkweed
Height: 32in (80cm)
Spread: 8in (20cm)
Aspect: Sun
Soil: Well-drained, poor
Hardiness: Zone 6
Propagation: Seed, in
autumn or spring; division,
in spring

Leaves ovate to lance-shaped,
toothed, dark green, spotted brown-
purple. Flowers in corymbs, yellow
daisies. Seeds everywhere, so
deadhead after flowering.

**Hordeum jubatum
(Graminae/Poaceae)**

Common name: Squirrel-
tail grass
Height: 20in (50cm)
Spread: 12in (30cm)
Aspect: Sun
Soil: Well-drained, fertile
Hardiness: Zone 5
Propagation: Seed, sown
in situ in spring or autumn

Grass from Asia and North America.
Leaves erect to arching, linear, pale
green. Dense, broad panicles of
arched, silky, bristled spikelets in early
and midsummer.

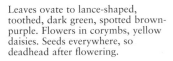

235

HOSTA (Hostaceae/Liliaceae)
Plantain-lily

A genus of some 70 species from eastern Russia, China, Japan, and Korea. They are soundly perennial, and are grown principally for their foliage value. Some of them have very nice flowers, and therefore qualify on both accounts. Some give a second, albeit brief, display in autumn. The leaves may be round, ovate, or lance- or heart-shaped, 5–20in (12–50cm) in length, and come in all shades of green, solid or with margins or centers marked with variegation in shades from white to rich yellow. The flowers are in one-sided racemes, and may be bell- or trumpet-shaped. Hostas will grow in sun or full shade, but flower better in sun; the yellow-foliaged types do best in sun. They demand moisture at the roots, and more so when in full sun, so must be watered in dry spells; the foliage will wilt as a warning. They respond readily to division at almost any time of year. The great scourge of the genus is the attention of the slug and snail families; should they nibble the emergent shoots, the leaves will be scarred for the rest of the season, so take preventative measures early in spring. Hostas are good plants for the allergic gardener, since they are low in allergens.The foliage and flowers are very useful in flower-arranging.

Hosta crispula
A.G.M.
(Hostaceae/Liliaceae)

Common name: Plantain-lily
Height: 3ft (90cm)
Spread: 3ft (90cm)
Aspect: Full shade
Soil: Moist, well-drained, fertile
Hardiness: Zone 5
Propagation: Division, in autumn or spring

Leaves lance- to heart-shaped, edges scalloped, deep green margined irregularly in white. Flowers lavender-white, funnel-shaped, on scapes in summer.

Hosta
'Eric Smith'
(Hostaceae/Liliaceae)

Common name: Plantain-lily
Height: 4ft (1.2m)
Spread: 2ft (60cm)
Aspect: Any
Soil: Moist, well-drained, fertile
Hardiness: Zone 5
Propagation: Division, in autumn or spring

A hardy hybrid in the Tardiana Group. Leaves large, rounded, bluish-green. Flowers lilac-pink funnels on tall scapes, in midsummer.

Hosta
'Frances Williams' A.G.M.
(Hostaceae/Liliaceae)

Common name: Plantain-
lily
Height: 26in (65cm)
Spread: 36in (1m)
Aspect: Full or half shade
Soil: Moist, well-drained,
fertile
Hardiness: Zone 5
Propagation: Division, in
spring or autumn

Clump-forming hybrid. Leaves
glaucous blue-green, margined yellow-
green, heart-shaped. Flowers gray-
white bells on scapes, in early
summer. Relatively slug-resistant.

Hosta
'Ground Master'
(Hostaceae/Liliaceae)

Common name: Plantain-
lily
Height: 20in (50cm)
Spread: 22in (55cm)
Aspect: Full or half shade
Soil: Moist, well-drained,
fertile
Hardiness: Zone 5
Propagation: Division, in
autumn or spring

Hybrid cultivar. Leaves ovate to
lance-shaped, matt green, with
irregular wavy margins of cream,
fading to white. Flowers on scapes,
purple funnels, in summer.

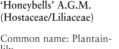

Hosta
'Honeybells' A.G.M.
(Hostaceae/Liliaceae)

Common name: Plantain-
lily
Height: 3ft (90cm)
Spread: 4ft (1.2m)
Aspect: Half shade or sun
Soil: Moist, well-drained,
fertile
Hardiness: Zone 5
Propagation: Division, in
autumn or spring

A robust hybrid. Leaves ovate or
heart-shaped, wavy-edged, strongly
veined, luminous pale green. Flowers
perfumed, white bells, on scapes in
late summer.

Hosta plantaginea
(Hostaceae/Liliaceae)

Common name: Fragrant
plantain-lily
Height: 75cm (30in)
Spread: 1m (3ft)
Aspect: Half shade or sun
Soil: Moist, well-drained,
fertile
Hardiness: Zone 5
Propagation: Division, in
autumn or spring

Leaves glossy pale green, ovate to
heart-shaped, veins prominent.
Flowers scented, white trumpets, on
scapes, late summer to autumn. Shy-
flowering in cold areas.

237

Hosta rohdeifolia
(Hostaceae/Liliaceae)

Common name: Plantain-lily
Height: 3ft (1m)
Spread: 18in (45cm)
Aspect: Full or half shade
Soil: Moist, well-drained, fertile
Hardiness: Zone 5
Propagation: Division, in autumn or spring

A species from Japan. Leaves lance- to inverse-lance-shaped, olive-green. Flowers on leafy scapes, purple funnels, with dark purple stripes, in summer.

Hosta
'Royal Standard' A.G.M.
(Hostaceae/Liliaceae)

Common name: Plantain-lily
Height: 3ft (1m)
Spread: 4ft (1.2m)
Aspect: Any
Soil: Moist, well-drained, fertile
Hardiness: Zone 5
Propagation: Division, in autumn or spring

Robust, hybrid perennial. Leaves ovate to heart-shaped, ribbed, shiny pale green. Flowers white, perfumed funnels on scapes in late summer.

Hosta sieboldiana
(Hostaceae/Liliaceae)

Common name: Siebold plantain-lily
Height: 3ft (1m)
Spread: 4ft (1.2m)
Aspect: Half shade or sun
Soil: Moist, well-drained, fertile
Hardiness: Zone 5
Propagation: Division, in autumn or spring

Species from Japan. Leaves large, ovate to heart-shaped, thick, gray-green, green, or blue. Flowers in scapes, pale lilac-gray bells, in early summer.

Hosta
'So Sweet'
(Hostaceae/Liliaceae)

Common name: Plantain-lily
Height: 24in (60cm)
Spread: 22in (55cm)
Aspect: Half shade or sun
Soil: Moist, well-drained, fertile
Hardiness: Zone 5
Propagation: Division, in autumn or spring

Hybrid with ovate to lance-shaped, glossy, midgreen leaves, margined creamy-white. Flowers white, purple-striped, fragrant, funnel-shaped, in mid- and late summer.

Hosta
'Sun Power'
(Hostaceae/Liliaceae)

Common name: Plantain-
lily
Height: 4ft (1.2m)
Spread: 3ft (1m)
Aspect: Full or half shade
Soil: Moist, well-drained,
fertile
Hardiness: Zone 5
Propagation: Division, in
autumn or spring

A hybrid perennial. Leaves ovate to
heart-shaped, bright yellow or yellow-
green. Flowers pale lavender or white,
on scapes in summer.

Hosta
'Sweet Susan'
(Hostaceae/Liliaceae)

Common name: Plantain-
lily
Height: 18in (45cm)
Spread: 28in (70cm)
Aspect: Half shade or sun
Soil: Moist, well-drained
Hardiness: Zone 5
Propagation: Division, in
autumn or spring

Hybrid with large, heart-shaped,
midgreen leaves. Flowers funnel-
shaped, perfumed, white, edged
purple, on scapes in early and again
in late summer.

Hosta
'Tall Boy'
(Hostaceae/Liliaceae)

Common name: Plantain-
lily
Height: 3ft (1m)
Spread: 3ft (1m)
Aspect: Any
Soil: Moist, well-drained,
fertile
Hardiness: Zone 5
Propagation: Division, in
autumn or spring

A hybrid perennial. Leaves ovate,
green. Flowers funnel-shaped, purple,
in dense racemes on scapes well above
the leaves, in late summer.

Hosta undulata
var. *undulata* A.G.M.
(Hostaceae/Liliaceae)

Common name: Wavy-
leaved plantain-lily
Height: 32in (80cm)
Spread: 18in (45cm)
Aspect: Any
Soil: Moist, well-drained,
fertile
Hardiness: Zone 5
Propagation: Division, in
autumn or spring

Leaves lance-shaped to elliptic,
twisted, green with pronounced
central white band. Flowers on
arching scapes, mauve, funnel-shaped,
in early and midsummer.

Hosta
'Wide Brim' A.G.M.
(Hostaceae/Liliaceae)

Common name: Plantain-lily
Height: 22in (55cm)
Spread: 3ft (1m)
Aspect: Any
Soil: Moist, well-drained, fertile
Hardiness: Zone 5
Propagation: Division, in autumn or spring

Clump-forming hybrid. Leaves relatively small, heart-shaped, puckered, dark green, margined cream. Flowers pale lavender funnels, in summer.

Houttuynia cordata
'Chameleon'
(Saururaceae)

Common names: None
Height: 1ft (30cm)
Spread: Indefinite
Aspect: Sun
Soil: Moist, humus-rich, fertile
Hardiness: Zone 5
Propagation: Division in spring

Rampant ground cover. Leaves aromatic, ovate or heart-shaped, heavily variegated in red, yellow, and green. Flowers tiny, green-yellow, with white bracts, in spring.

Houttuynia cordata
'Flore Pleno'
(Saururaceae)

Common names: None
Height: 1ft (30cm)
Spread: Indefinite
Aspect: Sun or half shade
Soil: Moist, humus-rich, fertile
Hardiness: Zone 5
Propagation: Division, in spring

Highly invasive, rhizomatous woodlander. Leaves aromatic, ovate or heart-shaped, gray-green. Flowers tiny, green-yellow, with pure white bracts. Ground cover in shade.

Hyacinthoides non-scripta
var. alba
(Hyacinthaceae/Liliaceae)

Common names: None
Height: 16in (40cm)
Spread: 4in (10cm)
Aspect: Half shade
Soil: Moist, well-drained, fertile, humus-rich
Hardiness: Zone 5
Propagation: Offsets, in summer

Vigorous, bulbous, woodlander. Leaves linear, glossy, dark green. Flowers in one-sided, arched racemes, pendent, perfumed, bell-shaped, white. Spreads rapidly.

Hyacinthoides non-scripta
var. _rosea_
(Hyacinthaceae/Liliaceae)

Common names: None
Height: 16in (40cm)
Spread: 4in (10cm)
Aspect: Half shade
Soil: Moist, well-drained,
fertile, humus-rich
Hardiness: Zone 5
Propagation: Offsets, in
summer

Vigorous, bulbous woodlander.
Leaves linear, glossy-green. Flowers in
one-sided, arching racemes, lilac-pink,
perfumed, bell-shaped. Excellent in
half shade.

Hyacinthus orientalis
'Blue Jacket' A.G.M.
(Hyacinthaceae/Liliaceae)

Common name: Common
hyacinth
Height: 12in (30cm)
Spread: 3in (8cm)
Aspect: Sun or half shade
Soil: Well-drained, fertile
Hardiness: Zone 5
Propagation: Offsets, in
summer

Hybrid of a bulbous plant from the
Middle East. Leaves linear,
channelled, green. Flowers in dense,
erect racemes, perfumed, single,
tubular, navy blue, in early spring.

Hyacinthus orientalis
'City of Haarlem' A.G.M.
(Hyacinthaceae/Liliaceae)

Common name: Common
hyacinth
Height: 12in (30cm)
Spread: 3in (8cm)
Aspect: Sun or half shade
Soil: Well-drained, fertile
Hardiness: Zone 5
Propagation: Offsets, in
summer

Hybrid cultivar. Leaves linear,
channelled, green. Flowers in erect,
dense racemes of up to 40, perfumed,
tubular, primrose, in early spring.

Hyacinthus orientalis
'Gipsy Queen' A.G.M.
(Hyacinthaceae/Liliaceae)

Common name: Common
hyacinth
Height: 12in (30cm)
Spread: 3in (8cm)
Aspect: Sun or half shade
Soil: Well-drained, fertile
Hardiness: Zone 5
Propagation: Offsets, in
summer

Hybrid cultivar. Leaves linear,
channelled, green. Flowers in erect
racemes of up to 40, perfumed,
tubular, single, salmon-pink, in early
spring.

241

Hyacinthus orientalis
'L'Innocence' A.G.M.
(Hyacinthaceae/Liliaceae)

Common name: Common
hyacinth
Height: 12in (30cm)
Spread: 3in (8cm)
Aspect: Sun or half shade
Soil: Well-drained, fertile
Hardiness: Zone 5
Propagation: Offsets, in
summer

Hybrid cultivar. Leaves linear,
channelled, green. Flowers in erect
racemes of up to 40, single, perfumed,
tubular, pure white, in early spring.

Hylomecon japonica
(Papaveraceae)

Common names: None
Height: 8in (20cm)
Spread: 18in (45cm)
Aspect: Half or full shade
Soil: Moist, well-drained,
acidic, humus-rich
Hardiness: Zone 7
Propagation: Seed, when
ripe; division, in spring

Rhizomatous woodlander. Leaves
pinnate, lobes ovate, toothed, pale
green. Flowers solitary, single, 4-
petalled cups, chrome yellow, from
spring to summer.

Hymenocallis × festalis
(Amaryllidaceae)

Common name: Spider-lily
Height: 32in (80cm)
Spread: 12in (30cm)
Aspect: Sun or half shade
Soil: Moist, well-drained,
fertile
Hardiness: Zone 9
Propagation: Seed, in
warmth when ripe; offsets,
in summer

Evergreen, tender, bulbous garden
hybrid. Leaves basal, oblong, shiny,
green. Flowers in umbels on erect
stems, white, perfumed, central cup,
petals long and twisted.

Hypericum cerastioides
(Clusiaceae/Guttiferae)

Common name: Rhodope
St. John's-wort
Height: 8in (20cm)
Spread: 18in (45cm)
Aspect: Sun
Soil: Well-drained, sandy
Hardiness: Zone 7
Propagation: Division,
in spring or autumn

A herb from Greece, Turkey and
Bulgaria. Leaves ovate, downy gray-
green. Flowers in cymes of up to 5,
star-shaped, golden yellow, late spring
and early summer.

Hypericum olympicum A.G.M. (Clusiaceae/Guttiferae)

Common name: Olympia
St. John's-wort
Height: 1ft (30cm)
Spread: 1ft (30cm)
Aspect: Sun
Soil: Well-drained, sandy
Hardiness: Zone 6
Propagation: Greenwood
cuttings, in summer

A subshrub from Greece and Turkey.
Leaves oblong, pointed, gray-green.
Flowers in cymes of up to 5, star-shaped, deep yellow, in summer.

Hypericum perforatum (Clusiaceae/Guttiferae)

Common name: Common
St. John's-wort
Height: 4ft (1.2m)
Spread: 2ft (60cm)
Aspect: Sun
Soil: Well-drained, sandy
Hardiness: Zone 3
Propagation: Division,
in spring or autumn

A hardy perennial from Europe and
Asia. Leaves ovate, midgreen, with
large, opaque spots. Flowers in cymes,
star-shaped, bright yellow, in summer.

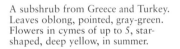

Hyssopus officinalis f. *albus* (Labiatae/Lamiaceae)

Common name: Hyssop
Height: 2ft (60cm)
Spread: 3ft (90cm)
Aspect: Sun
Soil: Well-drained, fertile
Hardiness: Zone 3
Propagation: Seed, in
autumn

Hardy, aromatic subshrub. Leaves
linear, midgreen. Flowers funnel-shaped, scented, whorled, white (deep
blue in the species), in spikes, from
midsummer to autumn.

Iberis sempervirens 'Pinky Perpetual' (Brassicaceae/Cruciferae)

Common name: Evergreen
candytuft
Height: 12in (30cm)
Spread: 16in (40cm)
Aspect: Sun
Soil: Moist, well-drained,
fertile
Hardiness: Zone 4
Propagation: Softwood
cuttings, in late spring

Hardy, evergreen subshrub from
Europe. Leaves linear, short, dark
green. Flowers pink, in racemes, in
late spring and early summer. The
species has white flowers.

Iberis sempervirens
'Weisser Zwerg'
(Brassicaceae/Cruciferae)

Common name: Evergreen
candytuft
Height: 4in (10cm)
Spread: 8in (20cm)
Aspect: Sun
Soil: Moist, well-drained,
fertile
Hardiness: Zone 4
Propagation: Softwood
cuttings, in late spring

A very compact cloned selection.
Leaves are short, linear, dark green.
Bears a profusion of white, stemless
flowers in spring.

Impatiens tinctoria
(Balsaminaceae)

Common name: Balsam
Height: 7ft (2.2m)
Spread: 3ft (1m)
Aspect: Half shade
Soil: Moist, well-drained,
humus-rich
Hardiness: Zone 10
Propagation: Seed, in
warmth in early spring

Robust, tuberous plant. Leaves
oblong to lance-shaped, toothed,
spirally arranged, green. Flowers in
racemes, white, scented, with a violet
throat, summer to autumn.

Imperata cylindrica
'Rubra'
(Graminae/Poaceae)

Common names: None
Height: 2ft (60cm)
Spread: 1ft (30cm)
Aspect: Sun or half shade
Soil: Moist, well-drained,
humus-rich
Hardiness: Zone 8
Propagation: Division,
in spring

Half-hardy grass from Japan. Leaves
linear, flat, pale green, turning bright
red from the tips downward. Panicles
of fluffy, silvery spikelets in late
summer in warm areas.

Incarvillea arguta
(Bignoniaceae)

Common names: None
Height: 3ft (90cm)
Spread: 1ft (30cm)
Aspect: Sun, shade in
summer
Soil: Moist, well-drained,
fertile
Hardiness: Zone 8
Propagation: Seed, in
spring or autumn

Leaves pinnate, deep green, leaflets
lance-shaped, toothed. Flowers in
racemes of up to 20, pendent, tubular,
pink or white, in early and
midsummer.

INCARVILLEA (Bignoniaceae)

A genus of some 15 or so annuals and taprooted perennials from rocky mountains and high-altitude grasslands of central and eastern Asia. The flowers are held high, singly or in panicles or racemes, on stiff stems, and are tubular to trumpet-shaped, with 5 petals. They are mostly purple or pink in color, but white forms exist; flowering time is early or midsummer. The foliage is dark green, and the alternate leaves pinnate or pinnatisect. *Incarvillea* would be worth taking some time over, but in fact they are easy and accommodating plants; the delicate, exotic look of the flowers belies the fact that these plants are hardy or half-hardy. They are suitable for either a rock garden or a mixed border. They have carrot-like roots, and so resent disturbance once they have become established. They should be planted with their crowns 3–4in (8–10cm) below the soil surface, and damage to the fleshy roots should be avoided at all costs. Some protection should be given from very high levels of wet in winter, and a mulch protection used in prolonged frosts. *Incarvillea* are easy to grow from seed, but they will take three years to flower, except for *I. arguta*, which may well flower in its first season.

Incarvillea delavayi
(Bignoniaceae)

Common names: None
Height: 2ft (60cm)
Spread: 1ft (30cm)
Aspect: Sun, shade in summer
Soil: Moist, well-drained, fertile
Hardiness: Zone 6
Propagation: Seed, in spring or autumn

Taprooted plant from China. Leaves dark green, pinnate, leaflets lance-shaped, toothed. Flowers in racemes of up to 10, purple-pink, in early and midsummer.

Incarvillea delavayi f. *alba* (Bignoniaceae)

Common names: None
Height: 2ft (60cm)
Spread: 1ft (30cm)
Aspect: Sun, shade in summer
Soil: Moist, well-drained, fertile
Hardiness: Zone 6
Propagation: Seed, in pring or autumn

Leaves dark green, pinnate, leaflets lance-shaped, toothed, terminal segment large. Flowers in racemes of up to 10, white with a yellow throat, in early and midsummer.

Incarvillea delavayi 'Bees Pink' (Bignoniaceae)

Common names: None
Height: 2ft (60cm)
Spread: 1ft (30cm)
Aspect: Sun, shade in summer
Soil: Moist, well-drained, fertile
Hardiness: Zone 6
Propagation: Division, in spring

Selected form of the species. Leaves dark green, pinnate, leaflets lance-shaped, toothed. Flowers in racemes of up to 10, pink trumpets, in early and midsummer.

Incarvillea mairei (Bignoniaceae)

Common names: None
Height: 20in (50cm)
Spread: 12in (30cm)
Aspect: Sun, shade in summer
Soil: Moist, well-drained, fertile
Hardiness: Zone 4
Propagation: Seed, in spring or autumn

Leaves dark green, pinnate, leaflets ovate, toothed. Few-flowered racemes of purple-crimson trumpets with a yellow throat, in early summer.

Incarvillea sinensis 'Alba' (Bignoniaceae)

Common names: None
Height: 34in (85cm)
Spread: 12in (30cm)
Aspect: Sun
Soil: Moist, well-drained, fertile
Hardiness: Zone 4
Propagation: Seed, in spring or autumn

Taprooted plant from China and Nepal. Leaves dark green, pinnatisect, pinnae linear to lance-shaped. Tall, few-flowered racemes of white trumpets, in late summer.

Incarvillea 'Snowtop' (Bignoniaceae)

Common names: None
Height: 2ft (60cm)
Spread: 1ft (30cm)
Aspect: Sun
Soil: Moist, well-drained, fertile
Hardiness: Zone 6
Propagation: Division, in spring, with care

Hardy hybrid. Pure white flowers in summer. Dies down very early, so mark the position well, to prevent damaging the roots of the dormant plant.

Incarvillea zhongdianensis
(Bignoniaceae)

Common names: None
Height: 16in (40cm)
Spread: 8in (20cm)
Aspect: Sun
Soil: Moist, well-drained,
fertile
Hardiness: Zone 7
Propagation: Seed, in
autumn or spring

Recent introduction (as *I. compacta*)
from China. Foliage dark glossy-
green. Flowers of a glorious purplish-
pink, with a yellow throat. Should
become very popular.

Inula acaulis
(Asteraceae/Compositae)

Common name: Stemless
inula
Height: 4in (10cm)
Spread: 1ft (30cm)
Aspect: Sun
Soil: Moist, well-drained,
Hardiness: Zone 6
Propagation: Seed or
division, both in spring or
autumn

Choice, compact, rhizomatous species
from Asia. Leaves inversely lance-
shaped, midgreen. Flowers solitary,
single, ray florets yellow, disc florets
brown, in summer.

INULA (Asteraceae/Compositae)

A genus of some 100 species, mostly perennial, but including
some annuals and biennials; all the perennial species are hardy,
easy to grow, and some (for example, *Inula hookeri* and
I. racemosa) are frankly invasive. Their native habitats, ranging
across temperate and tropical regions of Asia, Africa, and Europe,
range from moist, shady lowlands to sunny and mountainous
areas. They will grow in any soil, but prefer a moisture-retentive
one; if they become too dry, they are prone to powdery mildew.
I. magnifica will even grow in boggy soil. All species suit a sunny
position, but *I. ensifolia* will tolerate light shade, and *I. hookeri*
prefers half shade. In general, the robust, taller species naturalize
well in wildflower gardens, although some need to be staked if
they are not supported by other plants, and the smaller types are
a good choice for growing in rock gardens. *I. helenium* has been
cultivated as a medicinal herb. The flowers, borne singly or in
corymbs in summer, are yellow or orange and daisylike, and are
much visited by bees and butterflies. Some are good for cutting.
The foliage is unremarkable; the basal leaves are large,
sometimes toothed or hairy, and the stem leaves are
progressively smaller as they ascend.

Inula ensifolia
(Asteraceae/Compositae)

Inula helenium
(Asteraceae/Compositae)

Common name: Swordleaf
inula
Height: 2ft (60cm)
Spread: 1ft (30cm)
Aspect: Sun or half shade
Soil: Moist, well-drained,
fertile
Hardiness: Zone 5
Propagation: Seed or division,
both in spring or autumn

Rhizomatous, free-flowering species.
Leaves stemless, linear, midgreen.
Flowers in corymbs or solitary, single,
daisylike, golden-yellow, in mid- to
late summer.

Common name:
Elecampane
Height: 5ft (1.5m)
Spread: 3ft (90cm)
Aspect: Sun
Soil: Moist, well-drained,
fertile
Hardiness: Zone 5
Propagation: Seed or division,
both in spring or autumn

A medicinal rhizomatous plant.
Leaves in basal rosette, ovate,
toothed, midgreen. Flowers in
corymbs or solitary, single, daisylike,
yellow, in mid- and late summer.

Inula hookeri
(Asteraceae/Compositae)

Inula magnifica
(Asteraceae/Compositae)

Common names: None
Height: 32in (80cm)
Spread: Indefinite
Aspect: Half shade
Soil: Moist, well-drained,
fertile
Hardiness: Zone 6
Propagation: Seed or
division, both in spring or
autumn

Invasive species. Leaves ovate,
toothed, hairy, green. Flowers solitary
or in heads of 2 or 3, single, ray
florets thin, pale yellow, in late
summer to midautumn.

Common names: None
Height: 6ft (1.8m)
Spread: 3ft (90cm)
Aspect: Sun
Soil: Moist, well-drained,
fertile
Hardiness: Zone 6
Propagation: Seed or
division, both in spring or
autumn

Species from the Caucasus. Leaves
very large, elliptic-ovate, dark green.
Single, daisylike flowers in corymbs of
up to 20, golden-yellow, in late
summer.

Inula orientalis
(Asteraceae/Compositae)

Common name: Caucasian
inula
Height: 3ft (1m)
Spread: 2ft (60cm)
Aspect: Sun
Soil: Moist, well-drained,
fertile
Hardiness: Zone 6
Propagation: Seed or division,
both in spring or autumn

Rhizomatous species. Leaves ovate-
elliptic, toothed, hairy, midgreen.
Solitary, yellow daisylike flowers, with
reflexed and incurved ray florets, in
summer.

Inula royleana
(Asteraceae/Compositae)

Common name:
Himalayan elecampene
Height: 32in (80cm)
Spread: 18in (45cm)
Aspect: Sun
Soil: Moist, well-drained,
fertile
Hardiness: Zone 6
Propagation: Seed or division,
both in spring or autumn

A hardy species from the Himalayas.
Leaves ovate, hairy, toothed, veined,
green. Flowers solitary, single, yellow,
daisylike, from midsummer to
autumn.

Ipheion
'Alberto Castillo'
(Alliaceae/Liliaceae)

Common names: None
Height: 8in (20cm)
Spread: 2in (5cm)
Aspect: Sun
Soil: Moist, well-drained,
humus-rich
Hardiness: Zone 6
Propagation: Offsets, in
summer

Selected form of a bulbous
Argentinian plant. Leaves straplike,
narrow, blue-green. Flowers upward-
facing, larger than the type, solitary,
scented, white, in spring.

Ipheion uniflorum
(Alliaceae/Liliaceae)

Common names: None
Height: 8in (20cm)
Spread: 2in (5cm)
Aspect: Sun
Soil: Moist, well-drained,
humus-rich
Hardiness: Zone 6
Propagation: Offsets, in
summer

A hardy bulbous perennial from
Argentina. Leaves narrow, straplike,
blue-green. Flowers solitary, upward-
facing, perfumed, pale silvery blue
stars, in spring.

249

Ipheion uniflorum
'Froyle Mill' A.G.M.
(Alliaceae/Liliaceae)

Common names: None
Height: 12in (30cm)
Spread: 2in (5cm)
Aspect: Sun
Soil: Moist, well-drained,
humus-rich
Hardiness: Zone 6
Propagation: Offsets, in
summer

Selected form of a bulbous hardy
perennial from Argentina. Leaves
narrow, straplike, blue-green. Flowers
solitary, perfumed, dusky violet stars,
in spring.

Iris
'Brighteyes'
(Iridaceae)

Classification: Bearded iris
Height: 16in (40cm)
Spread: Indefinite
Aspect: Sun
Soil: Well-drained, fertile,
acidic
Hardiness: Zone 6
Propagation: Division, in
summer to autumn

An intermediate, rhizomatous iris.
Leaves narrow, green. Pale yellow
flowers with distinctive brown
markings on the falls, hence its name.

IRIS (Iridaceae)
Flag • Fleur de Lis • Sword lily

A genus of some 300 species from very diverse and scattered
habitats in the northern hemisphere. They can be bulbous,
rhizomatous, or fleshy-rooted, evergreen or deciduous, and vary
widely in their cultural requirements. The classification by the
American Iris Society (*see right*) will be used here. An iris flower
has three outer and three inner tepals. The outer three bend
back, and may also hang down, and so are called "falls"; they
are usually the most colorfully marked part of the flower. The
falls are especially large and colorful in the bearded irises,
which have white or colored hairs, like a beard, in the center of
each fall. Crested irises have a ridge, or crest, on each fall. The
three inner tepals are called "standards," since they generally
stand upright in the center of the flower, but they may lie
horizontal, as in *I. tectorum*; droop, as in *I. bucharica*; or be
much reduced, as in *I. danfordiae*. Three modified styles called
stigma flaps reach out over the falls from the middle of the
flower and can form an important element. All parts of the
plant are poisonous, and contact with the sap may cause skin
irritation. Iris are low-allergen plants, however. The flowers and
foliage are much used by flower-arrangers.

Iris bucharica A.G.M. (Iridaceae)

Classification: Bulbous iris
Height: 16in (40cm)
Spread: 4in (10cm)
Aspect: Sun
Soil: Well-drained, neutral
to alkaline
Hardiness: Zone 5
Propagation: Seed, in
autumn or spring; division,
in summer or autumn

A Juno iris from Central Asia. Leaves glossy, green. Flowers have standards below falls; standards yellow, falls white with a yellow spot.

Iris chrysographes (Iridaceae)

Classification: Beardless
iris
Height: 20in (50cm)
Spread: Indefinite
Aspect: Sun or half shade
Soil: Well-drained, acidic
Hardiness: Zone 5
Propagation: Seed, in
autumn or spring; division,
in summer or autumn

A rhizomatous Siberian iris from China. Leaves linear, grey-green. Flowers perfumed, dark violet-red, with silver stripes on the falls.

Iris cristata (Iridaceae)

Classification: Crested iris
Height: 4in (10cm)
Spread: Indefinite
Aspect: Sun or half shade
Soil; Moist, humus-rich
Hardiness: Zone 4
Propagation: Seed, in
autumn or spring; division,
in summer or autumn

A crested iris species from eastern United States. Leaves lance-shaped, green. Flowers lilac-blue, with an orange patch on each fall, in late spring.

CLASSIFICATION of IRIS by the R.H.S.

Bearded species and cultivars, in various sizes from miniature dwarf to tall, form the most widely cultivated group of irises. They are rhizomatous, and prefer well-drained conditions.

Aril irises are a group of bearded irises that includes the Oncocyclus, Regelia, Regeliocyclus, and Arilbred types. These become dormant in summer after flowering, and should be kept dry while dormant.

Beardless irises generally have more flowers per stem than bearded types. They include Pacific Coast Native, Siberian, Spuria, Laevigatae, Louisiana and Unguiculares, and are rhizomatous. They prefer well-drained conditions, apart from the Laevigatae, which need damp soil.

Crested irises are rhizomatous and spread freely. They prefer moist soil.

Bulbous irises, grouped as Juno, Reticulata, or Xiphium, are beardless and summer dormant. They prefer well-drained soil.

Iris danfordiae
(Iridaceae)

Classification: Bulbous iris
Height: 6in (15cm)
Spread: 2in (5cm)
Aspect: Sun
Soil: Well-drained, alkaline
Hardiness: Zone 5
Propagation: Seed, in
autumn or spring; division,
in summer or autumn

A Reticulata species from Turkey.
Leaves paired, narrow, green. Flowers
have much-reduced standards. Falls
bright yellow, speckled green.

Iris douglasiana
A.G.M.
(Iridaceae)

Classification: Beardless
iris
Height: 28in (70cm)
Spread: Indefinite
Aspect: Sun or half shade
Soil: Well-drained, acidic
Hardiness: Zone 7
Propagation: Seed, in
autumn or spring; division,
in summer or autumn

An evergreen Pacific Coast iris. Leaves
stiff, glossy, green. Flowers lavender-
blue, white, or cream on branched
stems, in late spring and early
summer.

Iris ensata
A.G.M. (Iridaceae)

Classification: Beardless
iris
Height: 3ft (90cm)
Spread: Indefinite
Aspect: Sun
Soil: Moist to wet, deep,
acidic, humus-rich
Hardiness: Zone 5
Propagation: Seed, in autumn or
spring; division, in summer or autumn

A Laevigatae beardless iris. Leaves
long straps, green. Flowers lilac,
purple, or red on branching stems, in
midsummer. Marginal aquatic.

Iris ensata
'Freckled Geisha'
(Iridaceae)

Classification: Beardless
iris
Height: 3ft (90cm)
Spread: Indefinite
Aspect: Sun
Soil: Moist to wet, deep,
acidic, humus-rich
Hardiness: Zone 5
Propagation: Division, in
summer or autumn

A hybrid, rhizomatous Laevigatae iris
with very large flowers of lilac and
white, with yellow bases on the falls.
Marginal aquatic plant.

Iris ensata
'Galatea Marx'
(Iridaceae)

Classification: Beardless
iris
Height: 3ft (90cm)
Spread: Indefinite
Aspect: Sun
Soil: Moist to wet, deep,
acidic, humus-rich
Hardiness: Zone 5
Propagation: Division, in
summer or autumn

A hybrid Laevigatae iris cultivar.
Single, sometimes branched stems
bear flowers with pale blue falls and
purple standards. Marginal aquatic.

Iris ensata
'Moonlight Waves'
(Iridaceae)

Classification: Beardless
iris
Height: 3ft (90cm)
Spread: Indefinite
Aspect: Sun
Soil: Moist to wet, deep,
acidic, humus-rich
Hardiness: Zone 5
Propagation: Division, in
summer or autumn

A hybrid Laevigatae iris cultivar, each
stem bearing 3 or 4 large flowers of a
rich, deep, purple-blue in midsummer.
Marginal aquatic.

Iris graminea
A.G.M. (Iridaceae)

Classification: Beardless iris
Common name: Plum tart
iris
Height: 16in (40cm)
Spread: Indefinite
Aspect: Sun or half shade
Soil: Well-drained, acidic
Hardiness: Zone 5
Propagation: Seed, in autumn or
spring; division, in summer or autumn

A Spuria iris from Spain and across
Europe to Russia. Leaves linear, flat,
bright green. Flowers perfumed, of
purple or violet color, falls have white
tips, veined violet.

Iris
'Holden Clough' A.G.M.
(Iridaceae)

Classification: Beardless
iris
Height: 3ft (90cm)
Spread: Indefinite
Aspect: Sun or half shade
Soil: Moist, deep, acidic,
humus-rich
Hardiness: Zone 6
Propagation: Division, in
summer or autumn

A hybrid Laevigatae iris. Leaves
angled outward, so plant takes up a
lot of room; evergreen in warm areas.
Flowers pale brown, veined purple.
Marginal aquatic.

Iris innominata
(Iridaceae)

Classification: Beardless
iris
Height: 8in (20cm)
Spread: Indefinite
Aspect: Sun or half shade
Soil: Well-drained, acidic
Hardiness: Zone 7
Propagation: Seed, in
autumn or spring; division,
in summer or autumn

An evergreen Pacific Coast iris, from
the southwestern U.S.A. Leaves
narrow, green. Flowers pale lavender-
blue, purple, yellow, or cream, in
early summer.

Iris japonica
A.G.M. (Iridaceae)

Classification: Crested iris
Height: 18in (45cm)
Spread: Indefinite
Aspect: Sun or half shade
Soil: Moist, humus-rich
Hardiness: Zone 7
Propagation: Seed, in
autumn or spring; division,
in summer or autumn

Leaves glossy, straplike. Flowers white
or lavender, frilly; falls have orange
crests and purple patches. Long-
flowering. Rhizomes lie on soil surface
and spread slowly.

Iris laevigata
A.G.M.
(Iridaceae)

Classification: Beardless
iris
Height: 2ft (60cm)
Spread: Indefinite
Aspect: Sun or half shade
Soil: Moist to wet, deep,
acidic, humus-rich
Hardiness: Zone 4
Propagation: Seed, in autumn or
spring; division, in summer or autumn

A Laevigatae iris from Russia and the
Far East. Leaves broad, green straps.
Flowers purple-blue, with a yellow
patch on the falls. Marginal aquatic.

Iris latifolia
A.G.M.
(Iridaceae)

Classification: Bulbous iris
Height: 2ft (60cm)
Spread: 8in (20cm)
Aspect: Sun
Soil: Well-drained, alkaline
Hardiness: Zone 5
Propagation: Seed, in
autumn or spring; division,
in summer or autumn

A Xiphium iris from Spain. Leaves
narrow, green, lance-shaped. Flowers
white, blue, or violet, with a yellow
spot on the falls, in early summer.

Iris missouriensis
(Iridaceae)

Classification: Beardless
iris
Height: 20in (50cm)
Spread: Indefinite
Aspect: Sun or half shade
Soil: Well-drained, acidic
Hardiness: Zone 9
Propagation: Seed, in
autumn or spring

Tender iris from western and central
North America. Leaves narrow, taller
than flowers, which have short, blue
standards and larger blue falls, veined
purple, in summer.

Iris pallida
'Argentea Variegata'
(Iridaceae)

Classification: Bearded iris
Height: 3ft (90cm)
Spread: Indefinite
Aspect: Sun
Soil: Well-drained, fertile,
acidic
Hardiness: Zone 6
Propagation: Division, in
summer or autumn

From Croatia. Leaves short, bright
green, silver-striped, straplike,
evergreen. Tall spikes of scented
flowers, blue with yellow beards, in
late spring and early summer.

Iris pseudacorus
(Iridaceae)

Classification: Beardless
iris
Height: 4ft (1.2m)
Spread: Indefinite
Aspect: Sun
Soil: Moist to wet, deep,
acidic, humus-rich
Hardiness: Zone 6
Propagation: Seed, in autumn or
spring; division, in summer or autumn

A robust Laevigatae iris from Europe,
Asia, and North Africa. Leaves ribbed,
straplike, gray-green. Flowers yellow,
with brown markings on standards.
Marginal aquatic.

Iris pumila
(Iridaceae)

Classification: Miniature
dwarf bearded iris
Height: 4in (15cm)
Spread: Indefinite
Aspect: Sun
Soil: Well-drained, fertile,
acidic
Hardiness: Zone 4
Propagation: Seed, in autumn or
spring; division, in summer or autumn

A miniature dwarf bearded iris from
Europe and the Urals. Leaves
straplike, green. Flowers solitary,
perfumed, purple, blue or yellow, in
spring.

Iris reticulata
A.G.M.
(Iridaceae)

Classification: Bulbous iris
Height: 6in (15cm)
Spread: 2in (5cm)
Aspect: Sun
Soil: Moist, well-drained,
alkaline
Hardiness: Zone 5
Propagation: Seed, in
autumn or spring; division,
in summer or autumn

Reticulata from Turkey and the
Caucasus. Leaves linear. Flowers
solitary, scented, deep purple with
yellow ridge on falls. Bulb may split
into tiny, slow-to-flower bulbils.

Iris sibirica
A.G.M.
(Iridaceae)

Classification: Beardless
iris
Height: 3ft (1m)
Spread: Indefinite
Aspect: Sun or half shade
Soil: Acid, moist
Hardiness: Zone 4
Propagation: Seed in
autumn or spring; division
in summer or autumn

From East Europe, Turkey, and
Russia. Leaves grasslike, green.
Flowers violet-blue, falls white next to
the hafts, and darkly veined.

Iris sibirica
'Limeheart'
(Iridaceae)

Classification: Beardless
iris
Height: 4ft (1.2m)
Spread: Indefinite
Aspect: Sun or half shade
Soil: Moist, acidic
Hardiness: Zone 4
Propagation: Division, in
summer or autumn

A hybrid Siberian iris, one of a large
number of cultivars from this species.
Leaves are grasslike, flowers are white
with greenish hafts.

Iris sibirica
'Wisley White' **A.G.M.**
(Iridaceae)

Classification: Beardless
iris
Height: 4ft (1.2m)
Spread: Indefinite
Aspect: Sun or half shade
Soil: Moist, acidic
Hardiness: Zone 4
Propagation: Division, in
summer or autumn

A handsome and hardy hybrid
cultivar of the Siberian iris. Leaves
narrow, grasslike. Flowers white, with
yellow markings on the falls.

Iris spuria
'Destination'
(Iridaceae)

Classification: Beardless
iris
Height: 3ft (1m)
Spread: Indefinite
Aspect: Sun or half shade
Soil: Well-drained, acidic
Hardiness: Zone 5
Propagation: Division, in
summer or autumn

A rhizomatous, hybrid Spuria iris
cultivar. The species originates in
Eurasia. Leaves broad, tough, green.
Flowers clear golden-yellow.

Iris tenax
(Iridaceae)

Classification: Beardless
iris
Height: 14in (35cm)
Spread: Indefinite
Aspect: Sun or half shade
Soil: Well-drained, acidic
Hardiness: Zone 7
Propagation: Seed, in
autumn or spring; division,
in summer or autumn

A Pacific Coast iris from the
northwestern U.S.A. Leaves narrow,
dark green. Flowers blue, white,
cream, or yellow, from mid-spring to
early summer.

Iris
'Three Cherries'
(Iridaceae)

Classification: Bearded iris
Height: 8in (20cm)
Spread: Indefinite
Aspect: Sun
Soil: Acid, well-drained
Hardiness: Zone 6
Propagation: Division, in
summer or autumn

A rhizomatous, hybrid, miniature
dwarf bearded iris with yellow
flowers. The falls have bands of
brown and cream toward the tip.

Iris
'Tinkerbell'
(Iridaceae)

Classification: Bearded iris
Height: 8in (20cm)
Spread: Indefinite
Aspect: Sun
Soil: Well-drained, fertile,
acidic
Hardiness: Zone 6
Propagation: Division, in
autumn or spring

A rhizomatous, standard dwarf
bearded hybrid iris cultivar. Leaves
lance-shaped, green. Flowers pale
blue, with a darker blue center.

Iris tridentata
(Iridaceae)

Classification: Beardless
iris
Height: 28in (70cm)
Spread: Indefinite
Aspect: Half shade
Soil: Moist, acidic
Hardiness: Zone 5
Propagation: Seed, in
autumn or spring; division,
in summer or autumn

A rhizomatous speacies from the
eastern U.S.A. Leaves linear, dull
green. Flowers purple-blue, with
white basal spots, in early summer.
Tricky to cultivate.

Iris uromovii
(Iridaceae)

Classification: Beardless
iris
Height: 1ft (30cm)
Spread: Indefinite
Aspect: Sun or half shade
Soil: Well-drained, acidic
Hardiness: Zone 6
Propagation: Seed, in
autumn or spring; division,
in summer or autumn

A rhizomatous Spuria iris originating
in Bulgaria. Leaves linear, sharp,
green. Flowers strong violet-blue, with
white falls veined violet-blue.

Isatis tinctoria
(Brassicaceae/Cruciferae)

Common name: Woad
Height: 4ft (1.2m)
Spread: 18in (45cm)
Aspect: Sun
Soil: Moist, well-drained
Hardiness: Zone 7
Propagation: Seed or
division, both in spring

Short-lived, taprooted plant from
Europe. Leaves in basal rosettes,
oblong to lance-shaped, gray-green.
Flowers on branched stems, in
panicles, yellow, in early summer.

Jasione laevis
(Campanulaceae)

Common names: None
Height: 12in (30cm)
Spread: 8in (20cm)
Aspect: Sun
Soil: Well-drained, sandy
Hardiness: Zone 5
Propagation: Seed, when
ripe; division, in spring or
autumn

A perennial from Europe, including
Britain. Leaves in basal rosettes,
narrow, oblong, green. Solitary,
spherical heads of blue flowers, in
summer.

Jeffersonia diphylla
(Berberidaceae)

Common name: American
twinleaf
Height: 8in (20cm)
Spread: 6in (15cm)
Aspect: Full or half shade
Soil: Moist, humus-rich
Hardiness: Zone 5
Propagation: Seed, when
ripe; division, in spring

Choice woodlander from the U.S.A.
Leaves kidney-shaped, cleft, gray-
green, with glaucous undersides.
Flowers cup-shaped, starry, white in
late spring.

Kirengeshoma palmata
A.G.M. (Hydrangeaceae)

Common names: None
Height: 4ft (1.2m)
Spread: 6ft (2m)
Aspect: Half shade
Soil: Moist, acidic,
humus-rich
Hardiness: Zone 5
Propagation: Seed or
division, both in spring

Distinctive rhizomatous woodlander.
Leaves very large, broad, ovate, pale
gray-green. Terminal cymes of 3
nodding flowers, broad yellow tubes,
late summer to early autumn.

Juncus effusus
'Spiralis'
(Juncaceae)

Common names:
Corkscrew rush, spiral
rush
Height: 1ft (30cm)
Spread: Indefinite
Aspect: Sun or half shade
Soil: Moist, acidic
Hardiness: Zone 4
Propagation: Seed or
division, both in spring

Invasive, leafless, marginal aquatic.
Stems shiny, spiraled, dark green,
forming a tangle. Flowers small,
brown, on short stalks in cymes, all
summer.

Knautia arvensis
(Dipsacaceae)

Common names: None
Height: 5ft (1.5m)
Spread: 18in (45cm)
Aspect: Sun
Soil: Well-drained, fertile
Hardiness: Zone 6
Propagation: Seed or basal
cuttings, both in spring

Taprooted perennial from Eurasia.
Leaves pinnatifid or simple, dull
green. Flowers flat, lilac-blue, with
involucral bracts, from midsummer to
autumn.

Knautia macedonica
(Dipsacaceae)

Common names: None
Height: 32in (80cm)
Spread: 18in (45cm)
Aspect: Sun
Soil: Well-drained, fertile
Hardiness: Zone 6
Propagation: Seed or basal
cuttings, both in spring

Kniphofia
'Atlanta'
(Asphodelaceae/Liliaceae)

Common name: Red hot
poker
Height: 4ft (1.2m)
Spread: 32in (80cm)
Aspect: Sun or half shade
Soil: Moist, well-drained,
humus-rich
Hardiness: Zone 5
Propagation: Division, in
spring

Clump-forming perennial from
Macedonia. Leaves basal and stem,
pinnatifid, mid-green. Flowers purple-
red, with involucral bracts, in mid-
and late summer.

Rhizomatous, evergreen hybrid.
Leaves strap-shaped, gray-green.
Flowers orange-red, in racemes,
fading to yellow from base of spike,
in late spring to early summer.

KNIPHOFIA (Asphodelaceae/Liliaceae)
Red hot poker

This genus contains some 70 or so species of rhizomatous
perennials from central and southern Africa. Their native
habitats are usually moist places, often along the banks of rivers
or in grasslands on mountainsides. They will thrive in any soil
as long as it is moisture-retentive, and they prefer sun but will
take light shade; they vary from tender to fully hardy. Many
will tolerate coastal conditions. Red hot pokers are mostly
clump-forming, with arching, linear to strap-shaped leaves, and
may be evergreen or deciduous; leaves of the deciduous types
tend to be narrow, those of the evergreens both longer and
broader. The flowers are cylindrical or tubular and usually
pendent, but upright in some types. They are borne well above
the leaves in spikelike racemes, usually dense. There are various
colors, including green and toffee, but the most commonly seen
are those that open red and then turn yellow, giving a
characteristic, bicolored inflorescence. Red hot pokers make
good cut flowers, and are popular with flower-arrangers. Bees
and butterflies are attracted to them, and they are low-allergen
plants. Cultivars ranging in height from 20in (50cm) to 6ft (2m)
are available; the taller varieties may require staking.

Kniphofia
'Bees Sunset' A.G.M.
(Asphodelaceae/Liliaceae)

Common name: Red hot poker
Height: 3ft (90cm)
Spread: 2ft (60cm)
Aspect: Sun or half shade
Soil: Moist, well-drained, humus-rich
Hardiness: Zone 5
Propagation: Division, in spring

A hardy, deciduous red hot poker. Leaves linear, toothed, midgreen. Flowers in racemes, yellow-orange, borne from early to late summer.

Kniphofia caulescens
A.G.M.
(Asphodelaceae/Liliaceae)

Common name: Red hot poker
Height: 4ft (1.2m)
Spread: 2ft (60cm)
Aspect: Sun or half shade
Soil: Moist, well-drained, humus-rich
Hardiness: Zone 7
Propagation: Seed or division, both in spring

Evergreen hardy species. Leaves linear, arched, glaucous, toothed, keeled. Flowers in short racemes, coral-red fading to cream, from late summer to midautumn.

Kniphofia
'Fiery Fred'
(Asphodelaceae/Liliaceae)

Common name: Red hot poker
Height: 4ft (1.2m)
Spread: 2ft (60cm)
Aspect: Sun or half shade
Soil: Moist, well-drained, humus-rich, fertile
Hardiness: Zone 6
Propagation: Division, in spring

A hardy herbaceous perennial. Leaves linear, midgreen. Flowers in racemes, orange-red fading to light brown, from early to late summer.

Kniphofia
'Green Jade'
(Asphodelaceae/Liliaceae)

Common name: Red hot poker
Height: 5ft (1.5m)
Spread: 30in (75cm)
Aspect: Sun or half shade
Soil: Moist, well-drained, humus-rich, fertile
Hardiness: Zone 5
Propagation: Division, in spring

A hardy, evergreen perennial. Leaves linear, keeled, green. Flowers green fading to cream, in dense racemes in late summer and early autumn.

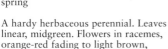

Kniphofia
'Shining Sceptre'
(Asphodelaceae/Liliaceae)

Common name: Red hot poker
Height: 4ft (1.2m)
Spread: 2ft (60cm)
Aspect: Sun or half shade
Soil: Moist, well-drained, humus-rich, fertile
Hardiness: Zone 5
Propagation: Division, in spring

A hardy, deciduous perennial. Leaves linear, midgreen. Flowers in racemes, opening clear yellow and fading to ivory, in summer.

Kniphofia 'Sunningdale Yellow' A.G.M.
(Asphodelaceae/Liliaceae)

Common name: Red hot poker
Height: 4ft (1.2m)
Spread: 2ft (60cm)
Aspect: Sun or half shade
Soil: Moist, well-drained, humus-rich, fertile
Hardiness: Zone 5
Propagation: Division, in spring

A hardy, deciduous perennial cultivar. Leaves linear, midgreen. Long-lasting flowers in racemes, clear yellow, in mid- and late summer.

Kniphofia thompsonii
var. *snowdenii*
(Asphodelaceae/Liliaceae)

Common name: Red hot poker
Height: 36in (90cm)
Spread: 18in (45cm)
Aspect: Sun or half shade
Soil: Moist, well-drained, humus-rich, fertile
Hardiness: Zone 8
Propagation: Seed or division, both in spring

Rhizomatous species from Kenya and Uganda. Leaves linear, upright, midgreen. Flowers in very open few-flowered racemes, coral-pink, midsummer to late autumn.

Kniphofia triangularis
A.G.M.
(Asphodelaceae/Liliaceae)

Common name: Red hot poker
Height: 36in (90cm)
Spread: 18in (45cm)
Aspect: Sun or half shade
Soil: Moist, well-drained, humus-rich, fertile
Hardiness: Zone 6
Propagation: Seed or division, both in spring

A hardy species, known also as *K. galpinii*. Leaves grassy, arching, linear, green. Flowers in dense racemes, reddish-orange, in early and midsummer.

Lamium galeobdolon
(Labiatae/Lamiaceae)

Common names: Golden
dead nettle; jellow
archangel
Height: 2ft (60cm)
Spread: Indefinite
Aspect: Half or full shade
Soil: Moist, well-drained
Hardiness: Zone 6
Propagation: Division, in
spring or autumn

Highly invasive rhizomatous plant.
Leaves ovate to heart-shaped,
toothed, midgreen, may be silver-
marked. Flowers 2-lipped, yellow,
spotted brown, in spikes in summer.

Lamium galeobdolon
'Hermann's Pride'
(Labiatae/Lamiaceae)

Common name: Golden
dead nettle
Height: 18in (45cm)
Spread: Indefinite
Aspect: Full or half shade
Soil: Moist, well-drained
Hardiness: Zone 6
Propagation: Division, in
spring or autumn

More compact and marginally less
invasive form of the species. Grown
primarily for its small, ovate leaves,
heavily streaked silver. Good ground
cover in shade.

Lamium maculatum
(Labiatae/Lamiaceae)

Common name: Spotted
dead nettle
Height: 8in (20cm)
Spread: 4ft (1.2m)
Aspect: Half or full shade
Soil: Moist, well-drained
Hardiness: Zone 4
Propagation: Division, in
spring or autumn

Rhizomatous, creeping plant. Leaves
ovate, toothed, matt-green, often
marked silver. Flowers in spikes, pink,
purple, or white, in early summer.
Good ground cover.

Lamium maculatum
f. album
(Labiatae/Lamiaceae)

Common name: Dead
nettle
Height: 8in (20cm)
Spread: 4ft (1.2m)
Aspect: Full or half shade
Soil: Moist, well-drained
Hardiness: Zone 4
Propagation: Division, in
spring or autumn

White form of the species. Ovate,
toothed leaves silver-gray, flowers
pure white; a pleasing combination. A
good ground cover plant for shady
areas.

Lamium maculatum 'Aureum' (Labiatae/Lamiaceae)

Common name: Dead
nettle
Height: 8in (20cm)
Spread: 36in (90cm)
Aspect: Full or half shade
Soil: Moist, well-drained
Hardiness: Zone 4
Propagation: Division, in
spring or autumn

A cultivar of the species with pink
flowers that contrast with the yellow
of the toothed, ovate leaves. Makes a
colorful ground cover.

Lamium maculatum 'Ickwell Beauty' (Labiatae/Lamiaceae)

Common name: Dead
nettle
Height: 8in (20cm)
Spread: 36in (90cm)
Aspect: Full or half shade
Soil: Moist, well-drained
Hardiness: Zone 4
Propagation: Division, in
spring or autumn

A form with toothed, ovate leaves
that all have some variegation, but in
differing degrees and in different
colors. Unique ground cover.

Lamium orvala (Labiatae/Lamiaceae)

Common name: Dead
nettle
Height: 2ft (60cm)
Spread: 1ft (30cm)
Aspect: Full or half shade
Soil: Moist, well-drained
Hardiness: Zone 6
Propagation: Seed or
division, spring or autumn.

A hardy perennial from Europe.
Leaves large, broad, ovate, toothed,
hairy, green. Flowers in spikes,
purplish-pink, from late spring to
summer. Non-invasive.

Lathyrus vernus A.G.M. (Leguminosae/Papilionaceae)

Common name: Spring
vetchling
Height: 18in (45cm)
Spread: 18in (45cm)
Aspect: Sun or half shade
Soil: Well-drained, humus-
rich, fertile
Hardiness: Zone 4
Propagation: Seed (after
soaking) in spring

A hardy herbaceous plant. Leaves
paired, ovate, pointed, midgreen.
Flowers pea-like, in one-sided
racemes, blue-purple, in spring,
followed by purple seed pods.

Lavandula stoechas
A.G.M
(Labiatae/Lamiaceae)

Common name: Lavender
Height: 2ft (60cm)
Spread: 2ft (60cm)
Aspect: Sun
Soil: Well-drained, fertile
Hardiness: Zone 8
Propagation: Seed, in
spring; semiripe cuttings,
in summer

Evergreen Mediterranean subshrub.
Leaves linear, aromatic, gray-green.
Flowers purple, perfumed, in dense
spikes topped by purple bracts, from
late spring to summer.

Lavatera
'Barnsley' A.G.M.
(Malvaceae)

Common name: Herb tree-
mallow
Height: 6ft (2m)
Spread: 4ft (1.2m)
Aspect: Sun
Soil: Well-drained, fertile
Hardiness: Zone 7
Propagation: Softwood
cuttings, in early summer

Robust, architectural, hybrid
subshrub. Leaves palmate, gray-green.
Flowers open funnels, white with a
red eye, in racemes all summer long.

Lavatera
'Bredon Springs'
(Malvaceae)

Common name: Herb tree-
mallow
Height: 6ft (2m)
Spread: 4ft (1.2m)
Aspect: Sun
Soil: Well-drained, fertile
Hardiness: Zone 8
Propagation: Softwood
cuttings, in early summer

Architectural, hybrid subshrub.
Leaves palmate, 3- to 5-lobed, gray-
green. Flowers in racemes, open
funnels, dusky pink flushed mauve, all
summer.

Lavatera
'Burgundy Wine'
(Malvaceae)

Common name: Herb tree-
mallow
Height: 4ft (1.2m)
Spread: 3ft (90cm)
Aspect: Sun
Soil: Well-drained, fertile
Hardiness: Zone 7
Propagation: Softwood
cuttings, in summer

Robust, hybrid subshrub. Leaves
palmate, 3- to 5-lobed, gray-green.
Flowers deep pink, darker-veined, in
racemes all summer. The best mallow
for the small garden.

Lavatera 'Candy Floss' (Malvaceae)

Common name: Herb tree-mallow
Height: 6ft (2m)
Spread: 4ft (1.2m)
Aspect: Sun
Soil: Well-drained, fertile
Hardiness: Zone 8
Propagation: Softwood cuttings, in summer

Robust, architectural, hybrid subshrub. Leaves palmate, 3- to 5-lobed, gray-green. Flowers in racemes, open, pale pink funnels, all summer.

Leontopodium alpinum (Asteraceae/Compositae)

Common name: Edelweiss
Height: 6in (15cm)
Spread: 6in (15cm)
Aspect: Sun
Soil: Sharply drained, alkaline
Hardiness: Zone 4
Propagation: Seed, in spring

Clump-forming alpine for a scree bed. Leaves linear to lance-shaped, basal, gray-green. Flowers white, surrounded by gray-white, woolly bracts, in spring.

Leonotis dysophylla (Labiatae/Lamiaceae)

Common names: None
Height: 10ft (3m)
Spread: 3ft (1m)
Aspect: Sun
Soil: Well-drained, fertile
Hardiness: Zone 9
Propagation: Seed, in warmth in spring

A tall, tender, architectural perennial from South Africa. Leaves inversely lance-shaped, midgreen. Flowers in whorls, tubular, brilliant orange, in autumn.

Leonotis leonurus (Labiatae/Lamiaceae)

Common name: Lion's-ear
Height: 8ft (2.5m)
Spread: 3ft (1m)
Aspect: Sun
Soil: Well-drained, fertile
Hardiness: Zone 9
Propagation: Seed, in warmth in spring

A tall, unusual, tender perennial from South Africa. Leaves are inversely lance-shaped, midgreen. Flowers in whorls, tubular, two-lipped, scarlet, in late autumn.

Leptinella dendyi
(Asteraceae/Compositae)

Leucanthemopsis alpina
(Asteraceae/Compositae)

Common names: None
Height: 16in (40cm)
Spread: 4in (10cm)
Aspect: Sun
Soil: Sharply drained,
gritty
Hardiness: Zone 8
Propagation: Seed, when
ripe; division, in spring

Common names: None
Height: 4in (10cm)
Spread: 6in (15cm)
Aspect: Sun
Soil: Sharply drained
Hardiness: Zone 6
Propagation: Seed, when
ripe

Compact, cushion-forming scree plant
from New Zealand. Leaves 2-
pinnatifid, leathery, aromatic, gray-
green. Flowers solitary, semi-double,
cream, from late spring to summer.

Mat-forming, rhizomatous plant.
Silver-gray leaves, from ovate- to
spoon-shaped to pinnatisect or
pinnatifid. Flowers solitary, ray florets
white, disc florets yellow.

LEUCANTHEMUM (Asteraceae/Compositae)
Shasta daisy

A genus of about 26 annual and perennial species from a range
of habitats in temperate Asia and Europe, and previously
included under *Chrysanthemum*. The plants in the genus that
are of prime importance for perennial beds are *Leucanthemum*
x *superbum*, the shasta daisy, a hybrid strain of garden origin,
still also known as *Chrysanthemum maximum*. This group
provides us with an invaluable set of robust, soundly perennial,
easy-going plants, which will grow in sun or half shade in any
good soil; in heavy clay soils they have a reputation for giving
up the fight. They are inclined to be lax plants, and some form
of support is required. The foliage is handsome, but it will be
attacked by slugs as the plants break ground in spring, and will
not reappear unless the plants are protected. The flowers are
solitary and may be single or double. Although other species in
the genus have yellow flowers, the flowers of these hybrids had
been exclusively white, with yellow discs (which tend to be
paler in double-flowered types), until the cultivar 'Sonnenschein'
made its appearance; it has yellow buds that open to cream
flowers. The flowers are excellent for cutting, and are liked by
flower-arrangers.

Leucanthemum × superbum 'Aglaia' A.G.M. (Asteraceae/Compositae)

Common name: Shasta daisy
Height: 2ft (60cm)
Spread: 2ft (60cm)
Aspect: Sun or half shade
Soil: Moist, well-drained, fertile
Hardiness: Zone 5
Propagation: Division, in spring or autumn

One of the very best shasta daisies, with inversely lance-shaped, glossy, dark green leaves. Flowers semidouble, white, shaggy, all summer.

Leucanthemum × superbum 'Beauté Nivelloise' (Asteraceae/Compositae)

Common name: Shasta daisy
Height: 34in (85cm)
Spread: 2ft (60cm)
Aspect: Sun or half shade
Soil: Moist, well-drained, fertile
Hardiness: Zone 5
Propagation: Division, in spring or autumn

Leaves inversely lance-shaped, glossy, dark green. Flowers single, ray florets twisted and irregularly incurved or reflexed, white, disc florets yellow, all summer.

Leucanthemum × superbum 'Droitwich Beauty' (Asteraceae/Compositae)

Common name: Shasta daisy
Height: 3ft (90cm)
Spread: 2ft (60cm)
Aspect: Sun or half shade
Soil: Moist, well-drained, fertile
Hardiness: Zone 5
Propagation: Division, in spring or autumn

Leaves inversely lance-shaped, shiny, dark green. Flowers semidouble, shaggy, with white ray florets and pale yellow disc florets, all summer.

Leucanthemum × superbum 'Phyllis Smith' (Asteraceae/Compositae)

Common name: Shasta daisy
Height: 3ft (90cm)
Spread: 2ft (60cm)
Aspect: Sun or half shade
Soil: Moist, well-drained, fertile
Hardiness: Zone 5
Propagation: Division, in spring or autumn

Leaves inversely lance-shaped, glossy, dark green. Flowers single, ray florets white, twisted, reflexed, and incurved, disc florets yellow, all summer.

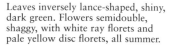

Leucanthemum x *superbum*
'Snowcap'
(Asteraceae/Compositae)

Common name: Shasta
daisy
Height: 18in (45cm)
Spread: 18in (45cm)
Aspect: Sun or half shade
Soil: Moist, well-drained,
fertile
Hardiness: Zone 5
Propagation: Division, in
spring or autumn

Leaves inversely lance-shaped, glossy,
dark green. Flowers single, ray florets
white, disc florets yellow, all summer.
The best dwarf form may not need
staking.

Leucanthemum x *superbum*
'Sonnenschein'
(Asteraceae/Compositae)

Common name: Shasta
daisy
Height: 3ft (90cm)
Spread: 2ft (60cm)
Aspect: Sun or half shade
Soil: Moist, well-drained,
fertile
Hardiness: Zone 5
Propagation: Division, in
spring or autumn

Very desirable shasta daisy. Leaves
inversely lance-shaped, glossy, dark
green. Flowers single, ray florets
cream, disc florets yellow, all summer.

Leucanthemum x *superbum*
'White Iceberg'
(Asteraceae/Compositae)

Common name: Shasta
daisy
Height: 3ft (90cm)
Spread: 2ft (60cm)
Aspect: Sun or half shade
Soil: Moist, well-drained,
fertile
Hardiness: Zone 5
Propagation: Division, in
spring or autumn

Leaves inversely lance-shaped, glossy
dark green. Flowers single, ray florets
white, incurved and reflexed, disc
florets yellow, all summer.

Leucanthemum x *superbum*
'Wirral Supreme' A.G.M.
(Asteraceae/Compositae)

Common name: Shasta
daisy
Height: 32in (80cm)
Spread: 24in (60cm)
Aspect: Sun or half shade
Soil: Moist, well-drained
Hardiness: Zone 5
Propagation: Division, in
spring or autumn

Leaves inversely lance-shaped, glossy,
dark green. Flowers double, ray
florets white, long on the periphery,
short in the center, disc florets yellow,
all summer.

269

Leucojum aestivum
(Amaryllidaceae)

Common name: Summer snowflake
Height: 24in (60cm)
Spread: 4in (10cm)
Aspect: Sun
Soil: Moist to wet, humus-rich
Hardiness: Zone 4
Propagation: Offsets, after foliage dies down

Bulbous plant from Eurasia and the Near East. Leaves strap-shaped, dark glossy green. Up to 8 flowers per leafless stem, white bells with green tips, chocolate-scented, in spring.

Leucojum vernum
A.G.M.
(Amaryllidaceae)

Common name: Spring snowflake
Height: 12in (30cm)
Spread: 3in (8cm)
Aspect: Sun
Soil: Moist to wet, humus-rich
Hardiness: Zone 5
Propagation: Offsets, after foliage dies down

Bulbous plant from Europe. Leaves strap-shaped, glossy-green. Flowers 1 or 2 on each stem, white bells with green tips, in early spring.

Levisticum officinale
(Apiaceae/Umbelliferae)

Common name: Lovage
Height: 6ft (2m)
Spread: 3ft (1m)
Aspect: Sun
Soil: Moist, well-drained, fertile
Hardiness: Zone 4
Propagation: Seed, when ripe; division, in spring

Vigorous Mediterranean herb. Dark green leaves in rosettes, 2- or 3-pinnate, lobes ovate, toothed. Flowers starry, in umbels, yellow, in summer; good seed heads.

Lewisia
Cotyledon Hybrids
(Portulacaceae)

Common names: None
Height: 1ft (30cm)
Spread: 16in (40cm)
Aspect: Half shade
Soil: Sharply drained, acidic, humus-rich, fertile
Hardiness: Zone 6
Propagation: Seed, in autumn; division, in early summer

Hybrid evergreen. Leaves in rosettes, dark green, fleshy. Flowers in compact panicles, funnel-shaped, pink, orange, yellow, or magenta, spring to summer. Keep neck dry.

Liatris spicata
(Asteraceae/Compositae)

Common name: Spike
Height: 4ft (1.2m)
Spread: 18in (45cm)
Aspect: Sun
Soil: Moist, well-drained,
fertile
Hardiness: Zone 3
Propagation: Seed in
autumn; division in spring

Tuberous or cormous plant. Leaves basal, linear to lance-shaped, and stem, green. Flowers pink in dense spikes open from the top down, late summer and early autumn.

Liatris spicata 'Alba'
(Asteraceae/Compositae)

Common name: Spike
Height: 4ft (1.2m)
Spread: 18in (45cm)
Aspect: Sun
Soil: Moist, well-drained,
fertile
Hardiness: Zone 3
Propagation: Seed, in
autumn; division, in spring

White-flowered form of the species. Flowers in dense spikes, opening from the top downward, white, in late summer to early autumn. Attracts bees.

Libertia formosa
(Iridaceae)

Common name: Showy
libertia
Height: 3ft (90cm)
Spread: 2ft (60cm)
Aspect: Sun
Soil: Moist, well-drained,
humus-rich, fertile
Hardiness: Zone 8
Propagation: Seed, when
ripe; division, in spring

Rhizomatous evergreen from Chile. Leaves linear, rigid, leathery, midgreen. Flowers in clustered panicles, white or cream from late spring to midsummer; good seed heads.

Libertia grandiflora
(Iridaceae)

Common names: None
Height: 3ft (90cm)
Spread: 2ft (60cm)
Aspect: Sun
Soil: Moist, well-drained,
humus-rich, fertile
Hardiness: Zone 8
Propagation: Seed, when
ripe; division, in spring

Rhizomatous evergreen from New Zealand. Leaves linear, leathery, dark green. Flowers in panicles, in clusters of up to 6, white, in late spring and early summer.

LIGULARIA (Asteraceae/Compositae)

A genus of some 150 species of perennials, mostly from Asia, with a few examples from Europe. Their natural habitats are moist areas, from the banks of mountain streams to damp grasslands and woodlands. As a consequence, they like a moisture-retaining or even a wet soil in the garden, and are not happy in dry climates unless the soil is kept reliably moist; their leaves droop obviously when they need to be watered. They prefer light shade, or at least shade from the midday sun, and are hardy. *Ligularia* are universally large and fairly coarse in appearance, and so are not for the very small garden; if you have the room for them, they will naturalize well in a moist wildflower garden, and make an impressive picture beside water. Despite being tall, they have stiff stems and do not need to be staked except in exposed areas. As with so many plants with daisylike flowers, they are highly allergenic, and should be avoided by the allergic gardener; aside from this consideration, some of them do make good cut flowers. All are visited by bees. Unfortunately, the plants are also liked by slugs, which eat the emergent shoots in spring; the leaves will never recover fully from this, so as ever with slug control, take preventative measures early in the season, before growth begins.

Ligularia dentata
(Asteraceae/Compositae)

Common name: Bigleaf golden-ray
Height: 5ft (1.5m)
Spread: 3ft (1m)
Aspect: Half shade
Soil: Moist, deep, fertile, humus-rich
Hardiness: Zone 4
Propagation: Seed, in autumn or spring; division, in spring

Clump-forming plant. Leaves rounded, toothed, midgreen. Flowers orange-yellow with brown centers, in flat corymbs, from midsummer to early autumn.

Ligularia dentata
'Othello'
(Asteraceae/Compositae)

Common name: Bigleaf golden-ray
Height: 3ft (1m)
Spread: 2ft (60cm)
Aspect: Half shade
Soil: Moist, deep, fertile, humus-rich
Hardiness: Zone 4
Propagation: Division, in spring or autumn

A selected form of *L. dentata* with leaves of dark brownish color, and corymbs of deep orange flowers. A striking plant, one of the best forms.

Ligularia x _hessei_
(Asteraceae/Compositae)

Common names: None
Height: 6ft (2m)
Spread: 3ft (1m)
Aspect: Half shade
Soil: Moist, humus-rich,
deep, fertile
Hardiness: Zone 5
Propagation: Division, in
spring or autumn

An interspecific hybrid plant of
garden origin. Leaves oblong to heart-
shaped, midgreen. Flowers in upright
panicles, orange-yellow.

Ligularia hodgsonii
(Asteraceae/Compositae)

Common names: None
Height: 3ft (90cm)
Spread: 2ft (60cm)
Aspect: Half shade
Soil: Moist, humus-rich,
deep, fertile
Hardiness: Zone 5
Propagation: Seed, in
autumn or spring; division,
in spring

Clump-forming species from Japan.
Leaves kidney-shaped, toothed,
midgreen. Flowers in many-flowered
corymbs, yellow-orange, disc brown,
in summer to early autumn.

Ligularia japonica
(Asteraceae/Compositae)

Common names: None
Height: 6ft (2m)
Spread: 3ft (1m)
Aspect: Half shade
Soil: Moist, humus-rich,
deep, fertile
Hardiness: Zone 5
Propagation: Seed, in
autumn or spring; division,
in spring

Clump-forming species. Leaves basal,
heart-shaped, lobed, toothed,
midgreen. Flowers in racemes of 8 or
more, orange-yellow, in early summer.

Ligularia przewalskii
(Asteraceae/Compositae)

Common names: None
Height: 6ft (2m)
Spread: 3ft (1m)
Aspect: Half shade
Soil: Moist, deep, humus-
rich, fertile
Hardiness: Zone 5
Propagation: Seed, in
spring; division, in spring
or autumn

Species from China. Leaves palmate,
lobed, deeply cut, toothed, midgreen.
Flowers in dense, slender racemes, on
purple stems, yellow, in mid- to late
summer.

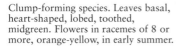

Ligularia
'The Rocket' A.G.M.
(Asteraceae/Compositae)

Common names: None
Height: 6ft (1.8m)
Spread: 3ft (1m)
Aspect: Half shade
Soil: Moist, deep, humus-
rich, fertile
Hardiness: Zone 4
Propagation: Division, in
spring or autumn

Hybrid cultivar, and the best of all.
Leaves triangular, deep-cut, toothed,
midgreen. Flowers on branched black
stems, in compact panicles, yellow.

Ligularia
'Wiehenstephan'
(Asteraceae/Compositae)

Common names: None
Height: 6ft (1.8m)
Spread: 3ft (1m)
Aspect: Half shade
Soil: Moist, humus-rich,
deep, fertile
Hardiness: Zone 5
Propagation: Division, in
spring or autumn

A chance seedling in the
Weihenstephan garden in Germany.
Leaves triangular, deep-cut, toothed,
midgreen. Flowers in dense racemes,
bright yellow.

LILIUM (Liliaceae)
Lily

Genus of some 100 mostly bulbous species from the northern
hemisphere, mostly Eurasia and North America, with a few
from the Philippines. Many are beautiful and easily grown; as
with most popular garden plants, there are many cultivars. The
habitats of the genus vary, and so cultural requirements vary,
but the great majority have one basic need: drainage. Most lilies
will not thrive in heavy clay soil; raised beds or planters are the
simple answer in such circumstances. Some, however, like moist
soil, and some also prefer the soil to be slightly acidic. Moving
and division are best done while the plants are still in active
growth after flowering in summer, so that they have a spell of
warm weather to settle before winter. Most lilies do not spread;
plant the bulbs 3 times their own width apart. They may require
staking. The flowers have six tepals, and may be bell-, bowl-,
star-, trumpet-, Turk's-cap- or funnel-shaped; are classified as
being small, medium or large; and may be upward- or outward-
facing or pendent. They may be hardy or tender, fragrant or not,
and of any color except blue. They make excellent cut flowers,
and are prized by flower-arrangers, but are highly allergenic, with
sticky, staining pollen: florists often remove anthers as buds open.

Lilium
'African Queen' (Div. 6)
(Liliaceae)

Common names: None
Height: 6ft (2m)
Spread: Nil
Aspect: Sun or half shade
Soil: Sharply drained,
moisture-retentive
Hardiness: Zone 8
Propagation: Scales, offsets,
or bulbils in late summer

Hybrid strain. Leaves lance-shaped,
glossy green. Flowers perfumed, large,
in racemes of up to 12, outward-
facing, outside purple-brown, inside
apricot, mid- and late summer.

Lilium candidum
A.G.M. (Div. 9)
(Liliaceae)

Common name:
Madonna lily
Height: 6ft (1.8m)
Spread: Nil
Aspect: Sun or half shade
Soil: Sharply drained,
moisture-retentive
Hardiness: Zone 6
Propagation: Scales, offsets
or bulbils, all in late summer

Leaves spirally-arranged, lance-
shaped, midgreen. Flowers in racemes
of up to 20, perfumed, trumpet-
shaped, white with yellow bases, in
summer.

Lilium bulbiferum
(Div. 9)
(Liliaceae)

Common name: Bulbil lily
Height: 5ft (1.5m)
Spread: Indefinite
Aspect: Sun or half shade
Soil: Sharply drained,
moisture-retentive
Hardiness: Zone 7
Propagation: Scales, offsets
or bulbils, all in late summer

Invasive species once satisfied. Leaves
lance-shaped, hairy-edged, green.
Flowers in umbels, of up to 5, bright
orange-red bowls, in early to
midsummer.

**Classification according to the
International Lily register, 1982,
with amendments by the Royal
Horticultural Society, 1992**

Division 1 Asiatic hybrids, with
racemes or umbels of usually
unscented flowers.

Division 2 Martagon hybrids, with
racemes of Turk's-cap, sometimes
scented flowers.

Division 3 Candidum hybrids,
with usually Turk's-cap, sometimes
scented flowers, solitary or in
umbels or racemes.

Division 4 American hybrids, with
racemes of mostly Turk's-cap,
sometimes scented flowers.

Division 5 Longiflorum hybrids,
with umbels of large, often scented,
trumpet- or funnel-shaped flowers.

Division 6 Trumpet and Aurelian
hybrids, with racemes or umbels
of usually scented flowers of
various shapes.

Division 7 Oriental hybrids, with
racemes or panicles of often
scented flowers of various shapes.

Division 8 Other hybrids

Division 9 All true species

Lilium formosanum
(Div. 9)
(Liliaceae)

Common name:
Formosa lily
Height: 5ft (1.5m)
Spread: Nil
Aspect: Sun or half shade
Soil: Moist, acidic
Hardiness: Zone 5
Propagation: Scales, in late
summer

Rhizomatous species. Leaves linear,
dark green. Flowers scented, paired or
solitary trumpets in umbels of up to
10, white flushed red-purple outside,
in late summer.

Lilium formosanum
var. *pricei* A.G.M. (Div. 9)
(Liliaceae)

Common name: Formosa
lily
Height: 1ft (30cm)
Spread: Nil
Aspect: Sun or half shade
Soil: Moist, acidic
Hardiness: Zone
Propagation: Scales, in late
summer

A very dwarf form of *Lilium
formosanum*, making it suitable for
rock gardens, the front of the border
or containers. Flowers earlier and
deeper flushed than the species.

Lilium grayi
(Div. 9)
(Liliaceae)

Common name: Gray's lily
Height: 5ft (1.5m)
Spread: Nil
Aspect: Sun or half shade
Soil: Moist, acidic
Hardiness: Zone 5
Propagation: Scales,
offsets, or bulbils, all in late
summer

A species from the eastern U.S.A.
Leaves lance-shaped, whorled, green.
Flowers in umbels of up to 10,
perfumed, funnel-shaped to tubular,
red.

Lilium henryi
A.G.M. (Div. 9)
(Liliaceae)

Common name: Henry lily
Height: 10ft (3m)
Spread: Indefinite
Aspect: Sun or half shade
Soil: Well-drained,
alkaline, humus-rich
Hardiness: Zone 5
Propagation: Scales, offsets
or bulbils, all in late summer

Vigorous, easy species. Leaves lance-
shaped to ovate. Flowers perfumed,
Turk's-cap, orange, spotted black, in
racemes of up to 10, in late summer.
Good beginner's lily.

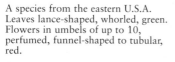

Lilium lancifolium
(Div. 9)
(Liliaceae)

Common names: None
Height: 5ft (1.5m)
Spread: Nil
Aspect: Sun or half shade
Soil: Moist, acidic
Hardiness: Zone 4
Propagation: Scales,
offsets or bulbils, all in late
summer

Species from the Far East. Leaves
narrow, lance-shaped, green. Flowers
in racemes of up to 40, nodding,
Turk's-cap, orange, in late summer
and early autumn.

Lilium martagon
(Div. 9)
(Liliaceae)

Common name: Martagon
lily; Turk's-cap lily
Height: 6ft (2m)
Spread: Nil
Aspect: Sun or half shade
Soil: Any, well-drained
Hardiness: Zone 4
Propagation: Scales, offsets
or bulbils, all in late
summer

A species from Europe across to
Mongolia. Leaves stem, inversely
lance-shaped, green. Flowers
unpleasantly scented, in racemes of up
to 50, nodding, Turk's-cap, pink.

Lilium martagon
var. *album* A.G.M. (Div. 9)
(Liliaceae)

Common name: White
martagon lily
Height: 6ft (2m)
Spread: Nil
Aspect: Sun or half shade
Soil: Well-drained
Hardiness: Zone 4
Propagation: Scales, offsets
or bulbils, all in late
summer

White-flowered form of the species.
Flowers smaller than the species, pure
white, downturned Turk's-caps, with
the same offensive smell.

Lilium monadelphum
A.G.M. (Div. 9)
(Liliaceae)

Common name:
Caucasian lily
Height: 5ft (1.5m)
Spread: Nil
Aspect: Sun
Soil: Fertile
Hardiness: Zone 5
Propagation: Scales, offsets
or bulbils, all in late
summer

Leaves inverse-lance-shaped, bright
green. Flowers in racemes of up to 30,
perfumed, nodding trumpets, yellow,
flushed brown outside. From Turkey
and the Caucasus.

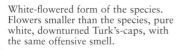

Lilium
Pink Perfection Group
A.G.M. (Div. 6) (Liliaceae)

Common names: None
Height: 6ft (2m)
Spread: Nil
Aspect: Sun or half shade
Soil: Well-drained,
moisture-retentive
Hardiness: Zone 7
Propagation: Seed, in
warmth when ripe

A hybrid group derived from Asiatic species. Leaves linear, green. Flowers in racemes or umbels, perfumed, nodding trumpets, purple-pink, in summer.

Lilium pumilum
A.G.M. (Div. 9)
(Liliaceae)

Common name: Coral lily
Height: 18in (45cm)
Spread: Nil
Aspect: Sun or half shade
Soil: Well-drained, acidic
Hardiness: Zone 5
Propagation: Scales,
offsets or bulbils, all in late
summer

A species from Russia and the Far East. Leaves linear, scattered, green. Flowers in racemes of up to 30, perfumed, nodding, Turk's-cap, scarlet, in early summer.

Lilium regale
A.G.M. (Div. 9)
(Liliaceae)

Common name: Regal lily
Height: 6ft (2m)
Spread: Nil
Aspect: Sun
Soil: Moist, well-drained
Hardiness: Zone 5
Propagation: Scales,
offsets or bulbils, all in late
summer

A species from China. Leaves linear, glossy, dark green. Flowers in umbels of up to 25, perfumed trumpets, white with yellow throats, in summer.

Lilium speciosum
var. *album* (Div. 9)
(Liliaceae)

Common names:
Speciosum lily
Height: 5ft (1.5m)
Spread: Nil
Aspect: Half shade
Soil: Moist, acidic
Hardiness: Zone 8
Propagation: Scales, offsets
or bulbils, all in late
summer

A species from the Far East. Leaves lance-shaped, scattered, green. Racemes of up to 12, large, perfumed, pendent, white flowers, in late summer to early autumn.

Limonium latifolium
(Plumbaginaceae)

Common name: Wide-leaf
sea lavender
Height: 36in (90cm)
Spread: 18in (45cm)
Aspect: Sun
Soil: Sandy, well-drained
Hardiness: Zone 5
Propagation: Seed, in spring

Evergreen seaside plant. Leaves in
rosettes, dark green spoons. Flowers
in open panicles, dense spikes of
minute, blue-violet trumpets, in early
summer.

Linaria purpurea
(Scrophulariaceae)

Common name: Purple
toadflax
Height: 3ft (90cm)
Spread: 1ft (30cm)
Aspect: Sun
Soil: Well-drained, sandy
Hardiness: Zone 6
Propagation: Seed or
division, both in spring

Leaves linear, midgreen. Flowers in
dense, slender racemes, pink, violet,
or purple, snapdragonlike, with
curved spurs, from early summer to
early autumn.

Linaria purpurea
'Canon Went'
(Scrophulariaceae)

Common name: Purple
toadflax
Height: 3ft (90cm)
Spread: 1ft (30cm)
Aspect: Sun
Soil: Well-drained, sandy
Hardiness: Zone 6
Propagation: Seed or
division, both in spring

Selected form that comes true from
seed. Leaves linear, midgreen. Slender,
dense racemes of pink,
snapdragonlike flowers, from early
summer to early autumn.

Linaria purpurea
'Springside White'
(Scrophulariaceae)

Common name: Purple
toadflax
Height: 3ft (90cm)
Spread: 1ft (30cm)
Aspect: Sun
Soil: Well-drained, sandy
Hardiness: Zone 6
Propagation: Seed or
division, both in spring

A selected form of the species that
comes true from seed, with white
flowers appearing over a long period
from early summer to early autumn.

279

Linaria triornithophora
(Scrophulariaceae)

Common name: Three
birds flying
Height: 4ft (1.2m)
Spread: 2ft (60cm)
Aspect: Sun
Soil: Well-drained, sandy
Hardiness: Zone 7
Propagation: Seed or
division, both in spring

Invasive species. Leaves lance-shaped,
mid-green, in whorls. Flowers in loose
racemes, purple and yellow,
snapdragonlike, in whorls of 3, from
summer to autumn.

Linum flavum
'Compactum'
(Linaceae)

Common name: Golden
flax
Height: 6in (15cm)
Spread: 8in (20cm)
Aspect: Sun
Soil: Sharply drained,
humus-rich, with protection
from winter wet
Hardiness: Zone 5
Propagation: Seed, in spring or autumn

Compact form of a European plant.
Leaves lance-shaped, deep green.
Flowers many-branched cymes of
upward-facing, golden cups, opening
only in sun, in summer.

Linum monogynum
(Linaceae)

Common name: Flax
Height: 2ft (60cm)
Spread: 1ft (30cm)
Aspect: Sun
Soil: Well-drained, sandy
Hardiness: Zone 8
Propagation: Seed, in
spring or autumn

A perennial flax from New Zealand.
Leaves narrow, gray-green. Flowers in
corymbs, white, upward-facing, in
terminal clusters.

Linum narbonense
(Linaceae)

Common name: Narbonne
flax
Height: 24in (60cm)
Spread: 18in (45cm)
Aspect: Sun
Soil: Well-drained, sandy
Hardiness: Zone 5
Propagation: Seed, in spring
or autumn

Short-lived Mediterranean species.
Leaves narrow, lance-shaped,
glaucous green. Few-flowered cymes
of rich blue saucers with white eyes,
in early to midsummer.

Linum perenne
(Linaceae)

Common name:
Perennial flax
Height: 2ft (60cm)
Spread: 1ft (30cm)
Aspect: Sun
Soil: Well-drained, sandy
Hardiness: Zone 5
Propagation: Seed, in spring
or autumn

Lax, straggly species. Leaves narrow,
lance-shaped, glaucous. Flowers in
terminal panicles, blue cups, fading
over the day, over a long period in
early to midsummer.

Liriope muscari
A.G.M.
(Convallariaceae/Liliaceae)

Common name: Big blue
lily-turf
Height: 12in (30cm)
Spread: 18in (45cm)
Aspect: Full or half shade
Soil: Moist, well-drained,
sandy, fertile
Hardiness: Zone 6
Propagation: Seed or
division, both in spring

An evergreen, robust perennial from
China. Leaves linear to straplike, dark
green. Flowers in dense spikes, violet-
mauve, from early to late autumn.

Lithodora diffusa
'Heavenly Blue' A.G.M.
(Boraginaceae)

Common names: None
Height: 6in (15cm)
Spread: 32in (80cm)
Aspect: Sun
Soil: Acidic, humus-rich
Hardiness: Zone 7
Propagation: Semiripe
cuttings, in summer

Selected form of an evergreen
subshrub from Europe. Leaves elliptic,
deep green. Flowers in terminal
cymes, blue, over a long period in late
spring and early summer.

Lobelia
'Butterfly Rose'
(Campanulaceae/Lobeliaceae)

Common names: None
Height: 36in (90cm)
Spread: 12in (30cm)
Aspect: Sun or half shade
Soil: Moist, deep, humus-
rich
Hardiness: Zone 7
Propagation: Seed, when
ripe; division, in spring

A hybrid, clump-forming perennial.
Leaves inversely lance-shaped, shiny,
green. Flowers in racemes, pale pink,
some dark pink appearing in them, in
summer.

LOBELIA (Campanulaceae/Lobeliaceae)
Lobelia

A genus of some 370 species of annuals, perennials, and shrubs with a worldwide distribution, but from South, Central, and North America in particular. They are found in a wide variety of habitats from marshlands to mountainsides, and range from hardy through half-hardy to tender. In general lobelias prefer a sunny position, but will tolerate light shade, and like moisture at the roots; some, indeed, are happiest as marginal aquatics, particularly if the soil is acid. The species vary widely in appearance, but all have alternate, simple leaves, and two-lipped, tubular flowers. The lips are divided into lobes: the upper lip into a pair of usually upright lobes, and the lower lip into three spreading lobes. The calyx tubes are sometimes swollen. In most species, the flowers are borne in terminal panicles or racemes, but in others they may be solitary. The foliage is handsome, and darkly colored in some types. Their main drawback is that they are short-lived in the garden, and some need to be lifted and divided regularly to keep them at their best. Lobelias make good cut flowers, and are much used by flower-arrangers, but care should be taken in handling them, as contact with the sap may cause skin irritation.

Lobelia cardinalis
A.G.M.
(Campanulaceae/Lobeliaceae)

Common name: Cardinal-flower
Height: 36in (90cm)
Spread: 12in (30cm)
Aspect: Sun or half shade
Soil: Moist, humus rich, fertile
Hardiness: Zone 3
Propagation: Seed, when ripe; bud cuttings, in summer

Short-lived, rhizomatous species. Leaves ovate, toothed, bronze-green. Flowers in racemes, tubular, scarlet; purplish bracts. Will grow in a bog or marginal aquatic site.

Lobelia
'Eulalia Berrige'
(Campanulaceae/Lobeliaceae)

Common names: None
Height: 30in (75cm)
Spread: 12in (30cm)
Aspect: Sun or half shade
Soil: Moist, deep, humus-rich
Hardiness: Zone 8
Propagation: Division, in spring

A hybrid perennial lobelia. Leaves ovate, midgreen. Flowers in open, upright racemes, cerise-mauve. Good for growing in a border.

Lobelia
'Fan Zinnoberrosa' A.G.M.
(Campanulaceae/Lobeliaceae)

Common names: None
Height: 24in (60cm)
Spread: 10in (25cm)
Aspect: Sun or half shade
Soil: Moist, deep, humus-rich
Hardiness: Zone 8
Propagation: Division, in spring

A reliable hybrid perennial lobelia. Leaves ovate, bronze-green. Flowers borne in dense, upright racemes, cinnabar rose, in summer.

Lobelia × *gerardii*
'Vedrariensis'
(Campanulaceae/Lobeliaceae)

Common names: None
Height: 4ft (1.2m)
Spread: 1ft (30cm)
Aspect: Sun or half shade
Soil: Moist, deep, humus-rich
Hardiness: Zone 7
Propagation: Division, in spring

A rhizomatous hybrid lobelia. Leaves basal, in rosettes, lance-shaped to elliptic, dark green. Flowers in racemes, tubular, violet, all summer.

Lobelia 'Kompliment
Scharlach' A.G.M.
(Campanulaceae/Lobeliaceae)

Common names: None
Height: 36in (90cm)
Spread: 12in (30cm)
Aspect: Sun or half shade
Soil: Moist, deep, humus-rich
Hardiness: Zone 7
Propagation: Division in spring

A clump-forming, hybrid perennial lobelia. Leaves elliptic, dark green. Flowers in loose racemes, tubular, scarlet, borne in summer.

Lobelia siphilitica
(Campanulaceae/Lobeliaceae)

Common name: Big blue lobelia
Height: 4ft (1.2m)
Spread: 1ft (30cm)
Aspect: Sun or half shade
Soil: Moist, deep, humus-rich
Hardiness: Zone 5
Propagation: Seed, when ripe; division, in spring

A hardy, clump-forming species. Leaves ovate, toothed, hairy, pale green. Flowers in dense racemes, bright blue, with leafy bracts, in late summer to autumn.

Lobelia siphilitica
'Alba'
(Campanulaceae/Lobeliaceae)

Common name: Big white
lobelia
Height: 4ft (1.2m)
Spread: 1ft (30cm)
Aspect: Sun or half shade
Soil: Moist, deep, humus-
rich
Hardiness: Zone 5
Propagation: Seed, when
ripe; division, in spring

The white form of the species. Leaves
ovate, toothed, hairy, light green.
Flowers in dense racemes, white, from
late summer to midautumn.

Lobelia tupa
(Campanulaceae/Lobeliaceae)

Common names: None
Height: 36in (90cm)
Spread: 12in (30cm)
Aspect: Sun or half shade
Soil: Moist, deep, humus-
rich
Hardiness: Zone 8
Propagation: Seed, when
ripe; division, in spring

A clump-forming perennial from
Chile. Leaves ovate, downy green.
Flowers in racemes, brick-red, with
reddish-purple calyces, in late
summer.

Lobelia
'Will Scarlet'
(Campanulaceae/Lobeliaceae)

Common names: None
Height: 36in (90cm)
Spread: 12in (30cm)
Aspect: Sun or half shade
Soil: Moist, deep, humus-
rich
Hardiness: Zone 7
Propagation: Division, in
spring

A hybrid lobelia. Leaves ovate,
greenish-blue or greenish-maroon.
Flowers in racemes, bright red, from
midsummer to early autumn.

Lotus corniculatus
(Leguminosae/Papilionaceae)

Common name: Bird's-
foot trefoil
Height: 12in (30cm)
Spread: 18in (45cm)
Aspect: Sun
Soil: Well-drained, fertile
Hardiness: Zone 5
Propagation: Seed, in
autumn or spring

A spreading perennial of worldwide
distribution. Leaves pinnate, leaflets
obovate, blue-green. Flowers in
racemes, clear yellow.

Lotus maculatus
A.G.M.
(Leguminosae/papilionaceae)

Common names: None
Height: 8in (20cm)
Spread: Indefinite
Aspect: Sun
Soil: Well-drained, fertile
Hardiness: Zone 10
Propagation: Seed, in
warmth in spring

Creeping plant. Leaves palmate,
leaflets linear, midgreen. "Lobster-
claw" flowers, solitary or in small
clusters, yellow, tipped orange or red,
in spring and early summer.

Lunaria rediviva
(Cruciferae)

Common name: Perennial
honesty
Height: 3ft (90cm)
Spread: 1ft (30cm)
Aspect: Sun or half shade
Soil: Moist, well-drained,
fertile
Hardiness: Zone 8
Propagation: Seed, in spring

Perennial from Eurasia. Leaves dark
green, large, triangular, toothed.
Flowers scented, lilac-white, in
racemes in late spring and early
summer, followed by flat seed pods.

LUPINUS (Leguminosae/Papilionaceae)
Lupine

A genus of some 200 species, including annuals, perennials, and
both semievergreen and evergreen subshrubs or shrubs, from
North Africa, southern Europe, and the Americas. Their native
habitats range from dry uplands to woodlands, riverbanks, and
coastal situations. Lupines are an invaluable genus of repeat-
flowering, handsome plants with attractive leaves for the border.
The flowers are pealike, and are borne in long, upright terminal
racemes or spikes; they are scented, and attract bees. They are
also, unfortunately, highly allergenic. There is a very large
number of hybrids in cultivation, and many are derived from
crosses with *Lupinus polyphyllus*, from western North America,
as one parent; many hybrids have bicolored flowers. Lupines
will grow in sun or half shade, and tolerate a range of soils
except alkaline or waterlogged ones. Their drawbacks are that
they are prey to slugs and prone to powdery mildew. They are
also short-lived, and resent disturbance, but they are easy to
propagate. The seeds of lupines are poisonous, so children
should be warned. The flowers last well in water provided that
they are inverted and the hollow stem is filled with water and
plugged with cotton wool before they are put in the vase.

Lupinus 'Band of Nobles' Series A.G.M.
(Leguminosae/Papilionaceae)

Common name: Lupine
Height: 5ft (1.5m)
Spread: 30in (75cm)
Aspect: Sun or half shade
Soil: Well-drained, sandy, acidic, fertile
Hardiness: Zone 5
Propagation: Seed, after soaking, in spring or autumn

Strain of hybrid lupines. Leaves basal, hairy, palmate, midgreen. Flowers in racemes, perfumed, in colors from red, pink, yellow, white, or blue to bicolored.

Lupinus 'Chandelier'
(Leguminosae/Papilionaceae)

Common name: Lupine
Height: 36in (90cm)
Spread: 30in (75cm)
Aspect: Sun or half shade
Soil: Well-drained, sandy, acidic, fertile
Hardiness: Zone 5
Propagation: Basal cuttings, in midspring

A hybrid perennial lupine. Leaves basal, palmate, hairy, midgreen. Scented flowers in racemes, bright yellow, in early and midsummer.

Lupinus 'My Castle'
(Leguminosae/Papilionaceae)

Common name: Lupine
Height: 36in (90cm)
Spread: 30in (75cm)
Aspect: Sun or half shade
Soil: Well-drained, sandy, acidic, fertile
Hardiness: Zone 5
Propagation: Basal cuttings, in midspring

A hybrid, clump-forming perennial lupine. Leaves basal, palmate, hairy, midgreen. Flowers in racemes, deep pink, in early and midsummer.

Lupinus 'Noble Maiden'
(Leguminosae/Papilionaceae)

Common name: Lupine
Height: 36in (90cm)
Spread: 30in (75cm)
Aspect: Sun or half shade
Soil: Well-drained, sandy, acidic, fertile
Hardiness: Zone 5
Propagation: Basal cuttings, in midspring

A clump-forming, hybrid lupine cultivar. Leaves basal, palmate, hairy, midgreen. Flowers in racemes, creamy-white, in early and midsummer.

Lupinus
'The Chatelaine'
(Leguminosae/Papilionaceae)

Common name: Lupine
Height: 36in (90cm)
Spread: 30in (75cm)
Aspect: Sun or half shade
Soil: Well-drained, sandy
acidic, fertile
Hardiness: Zone 5
Propagation: Basal cuttings,
in midspring

A clump-forming, hybrid lupine.
Leaves basal, palmate, hairy,
midgreen. Flowers in racemes,
bicolored, pink and white, in early
and midsummer.

Lupinus
'The Governor'
(Leguminosae/Papilionaceae)

Common name: Lupine
Height: 36in (90cm)
Spread: 30in (75cm)
Aspect: Sun or half shade
Soil: Well-drained, sandy,
fertile
Hardiness: Zone 5
Propagation: Basal cuttings,
in midspring

A hybrid, clump-forming cultivar.
Leaves basal, palmate, hairy,
midgreen. Flowers in racemes,
bicolored, blue and white, in early
and midsummer.

Lupinus
'The Page'
(Leguminosae/Papilionaceae)

Common name: Lupine
Height: 36in (90cm)
Spread: 30in (75cm)
Aspect: Sun or half shade
Soil: Well-drained, sandy,
fertile
Hardiness: Zone 5
Propagation: Basal cuttings,
in midspring

A hybrid, clump-forming lupine
cultivar. Leaves basal, palmate, hairy,
midgreen. Flowers in panicles,
carmine red, in early and midsummer.

Luzula sylvatica
'Aurea'
(Juncaceae)

Common names: None
Height: 32in (80cm)
Spread: 18in (45cm)
Aspect: Full or half shade
Soil: Moist, well-drained,
humus-rich, fertile
Hardiness: Zone 6
Propagation: Seed, in spring
or autumn; division, in
spring

A tufted, evergreen grass. Leaves
linear, channelled, shiny yellow.
Flowers in open panicles, small,
chestnut-brown, from mid-spring to
early summer.

LYCHNIS (Caryophyllaceae)
Campion • Catchfly

A genus of some 20 species of biennials and perennials from arctic and northern temperate regions; they are reliably hardy. Their natural habitats range from alpine conditions to damp woodlands and grasslands, and they will grow in sun or partial shade, and in any soil as long as it is well-drained and fertile. *Lychnis flos-cuculi* is even happy in bog conditions. *Lychnis* are upright, generally with branching stems, and bear tubular to salverform or star-shaped flowers in terminal cymes or panicles. The flowers come in a range of colors from purple through scarlet to pink or white, and some types make good cut flowers. The smaller, alpine types are most suitable for a rock or alpine garden, while the taller forms will do well in a sunny border or naturalized in a wildflower garden. Some species, most notably *L.* x *arkwrightii, L. coronaria,* and *L.* x *haageana,* are short-lived, but the others are soundly perennial. The taller varieties need to be staked. *L. flos-jovis* and *L. chalcedonica* attract both bees and butterflies, while *L. flos-cuculi* is loved by bees. All are prone to damage by slugs in spring, so preventative action must be taken early. All seem to self-seed prolifically; deadhead after flowering to avoid this if it is not wanted.

Lychnis alpina
(Caryophyllaceae)

Common names: Alpine campion; alpine catchfly
Height: 6in (15cm)
Spread: 6in (15cm)
Aspect: Sun or half shade
Soil: Well-drained, fertile
Hardiness: Zone 5
Propagation: Seed, when ripe or in spring

A mountain perennial. Leaves in rosettes, lance-shaped, dark green. Flowers in terminal cymes of up to 20, pink, petals 2-lobed, frilled, in summer.

Lychnis x *arkwrightii*
'Vesuvius'
(Caryophyllaceae)

Common name:
Arkwright campion
Height: 18in (45cm)
Spread: 12in (30cm)
Aspect: Sun or half shade
Soil: Well-drained, fertile
Hardiness: Zone 5
Propagation: Basal cuttings or division, both in spring

Short-lived, hybrid, clump-forming plant. Leaves lance-shaped, hairy, dark green-brown. Flowers in terminal cymes of up to 10, star-shaped, scarlet-orange, in summer.

Lychnis chalcedonica
(Caryophyllacae)

Common name: Maltese cross
Height: 4ft (1.2m)
Spread: 1ft (30cm)
Aspect: Sun or half shade
Soil: Moist, fertile
Hardiness: Zone 4
Propagation: Seed or division, both in spring

Leaves basal, ovate, midgreen. Flowers in terminal, rounded cymes, vermilion, petals deeply notched, double, in early and midsummer. From European Russia.

Lychnis chalcedonica
'Rosea'
(Caryophyllaceae)

Common name: Pink Maltese cross
Height: 4ft (1.2m)
Spread: 30cm (1ft)
Aspect: Sun or half shade
Soil: Moist, fertile
Hardiness: Zone 5
Propagation: Seed or division, both in spring

Single-flowered, pink form of the species. Leaves basal, ovate, midgreen. Flowers in terminal cymes, single, star-shaped, pink, in early and midsummer.

Lychnis coronaria
(Caryophyllaceae)

Common name: Rose campion
Height: 32in (80cm)
Spread: 18in (45cm)
Aspect: Sun
Soil: Dry, well-drained, fertile
Hardiness: Zone 4
Propagation: Seed or division, both in spring

Short-lived species. Leaves ovate to lance-shaped, woolly silver-gray. Flowers in few-flowered, terminal racemes, single, scarlet or purple, over a long period in late summer.

Lychnis coronaria
'Alba' A.G.M.
(Caryophyllaceae)

Common name: White rose campion
Height: 32in (80cm)
Spread: 18in (45cm)
Aspect: Sun
Soil: Dry, well-drained
Hardiness: Zone 4
Propagation: Seed or division, both in spring

White form of the species. Leaves ovate to lance-shaped, silver-gray, woolly. Flowers in few-flowered terminal cymes, single, white, over a long period in late summer.

Lychnis coronaria
Oculata Group
(Caryophyllaceae)

Common name: Rose
campion
Height: 32in (80cm)
Spread: 18in (45cm)
Aspect: Sun
Soil: Dry, well-drained,
fertile
Hardiness: Zone 4
Propagation: Seed or
division, both in spring

A free-flowering cultivar. Leaves ovate
to lance-shaped, silver-gray, woolly.
Flowers in terminal cymes, white with
a cherry-pink eye, over a long period
in late summer.

Lychnis flos-cuculi
var. albiflora
(Caryophyllaceae)

Common name: White
ragged robin
Height: 30in (75cm)
Spread: 36in (90cm)
Aspect: Sun or half shade
Soil: Moist, well-drained,
fertile
Hardiness: Zone 6
Propagation: Seed or
division, both in spring

White form of a rampant species.
Leaves basal, inversely lance-shaped;
stem, oblong, bluish-green. Flowers in
terminal cymes, star-shaped, in late
spring and early summer.

Lychnis flos-jovis
(Caryophyllaceae)

Common name: Flower-
of-love
Height: 24in (60cm)
Spread: 18in (45cm)
Aspect: Sun
Soil: Dry, well-drained,
fertile
Hardiness: Zone 5
Propagation: Seed or
division, both in spring

Mat-forming species from the Alps.
Leaves basal and stem, spoon- to
lance-shaped, gray-green. Flowers in
cymes, single, pink, white, or scarlet,
early to late summer.

Lychnis miqueliana
(Caryophyllaceae)

Common names: None
Height: 2ft (60cm)
Spread: 1ft (30cm)
Aspect: Sun or half shade
Soil: Well-drained, fertile
Hardiness: Zone 6
Propagation: Seed or
division, both in spring

A hardy species from Japan. Leaves
oblong to ovate, midgreen. Flowers
single, large, petals toothed,
vermilion, in few-flowered cymes, in
summer.

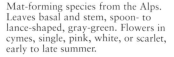

LYSIMACHIA (Primulaceae)
Loosestrife

A genus of some 150 species of evergreen and herbaceous
perennials and shrubs from northern temperate and southern
subtropical regions; they vary from hardy to half-hardy, as a
consequence. Their natural habitats are damp woodlands and
grasslands, often near water; in the garden, they prefer a soil
which is moist, and moisture-retentive, especially in summer,
but also like good drainage. If they are given the moist root run
they enjoy, they can be invasive (except *Lysimachia ephemerum*),
so they are best used as water marginals, or in a bog garden or
wild or woodland garden. Many make large plants, and some
of the taller types may require staking. Slugs also enjoy the moist
conditions preferred by these plants, and measures to protect the
foliage from attack should be taken early. Some species, however,
are low-growing, and make good ground cover. They will grow
in sun or part-shade. Leaf shapes and arrangements vary,
although the leaves are generally simple. All bear 5-petalled
flowers, ranging from cup- or saucer-shaped to star-shaped,
which are either solitary and axillary or carried in terminal
panicles or racemes. The flowers are usually yellow in color, but
there are also white-, pink-, or purple-flowered types.

Lysimachia ciliata
(Primulaceae)

Common name: Fringed
loosestrife
Height: 4ft (1.2m)
Spread: 2ft (60cm)
Aspect: Sun or half shade
Soil: Moist, humus-rich
Hardiness: Zone 4
Propagation: Seed or
division, both in spring

Invasive, rhizomatous species from
North America. Leaves ovate to
lance-shaped, midgreen. Flowers on
slim stems, single or paired, pendent,
yellow stars, in summer.

Lysimachia ciliata
'Firecracker' A.G.M.
(Primulaceae)

Common name: Fringed
loosestrife
Height: 4ft (1.2m)
Spread: 2ft (60cm)
Aspect: Sun or half shade
Soil: Moist, humus-rich
Hardiness: Zone 4
Propagation: Division, in
spring

A form of the species with purple
foliage, which contrasts well with the
yellow flowers. This is also known as
Lysimachia ciliata 'Purpurea'.

Lysimachia clethroides
A.G.M.
(Primulaceae)

Common name: Japanese
loosestrife
Height: 3ft (90cm)
Spread: 2ft (60cm)
Aspect: Sun or half shade
Soil: Moist, humus-rich
Hardiness: Zone 4
Propagation: Seed or
division, both in spring

Invasive rhizomatous species. Leaves
lance-shaped, pointed, midgreen,
paler beneath. Flowers in dense,
tapering, arching racemes, white,
single, starry, mid- and late summer.

Lysimachia ephemerum
(Primulaceae)

Common name:
Loosestrife
Height: 3ft (90cm)
Spread: 1ft (30cm)
Aspect: Sun or half shade
Soil: Moist, humus-rich
Hardiness: Zone 7
Propagation: Seed or
division, both in spring

Non-spreading species. Leaves linear
to lance-shaped, glaucous gray-green.
Flowers white saucers, in dense,
upright, terminal racemes, in early
and midsummer.

Lysimachia nummularia
'Aurea' A.G.M.
(Primulaceae)

Common names: Creeping
Jenny; moneywort;
creeping Charlie
Height: 2in (5cm)
Spread: Indefinite
Aspect: Sun or half shade
Soil: Moist, humus-rich
Hardiness: Zone 5
Propagation: Seed or
division, both in spring

Golden form of a rampant, evergreen
species from Europe. Leaves ovate to
round, golden-yellow. Flowers
solitary, single, cup-shaped, upturned,
yellow.

Lysimachia punctata
(Primulaceae)

Common name: Yellow
loosestrife
Height: 3ft (90cm)
Spread: 2ft (60cm)
Aspect: Sun or half shade
Soil: Moist, humus-rich
Hardiness: Zone 5
Propagation: Seed or
division, both in spring

An invasive, rhizomatous species.
Leaves elliptic- to lance-shaped, dark
green. Yellow flowers in whorls from
the leaf axils, in mid- and late
summer.

Lysimachia punctata 'Alexander' (Primulaceae)

Common name: Yellow
loosestrife
Height: 3ft (90cm)
Spread: 2ft (60cm)
Aspect: Sun or half shade
Soil: Moist, humus-rich
Hardiness: Zone 5
Propagation: Division, in
spring

A selected cultivar of the species.
Leaves elliptic- to lance-shaped, dark
green edged cream or white. Flowers
yellow, in whorls in the leaf axils,
mid- and late summer.

Lythrum salicaria (Lythraceae)

Common name: Purple
loosestrife
Height: 4ft (1.2m)
Spread: 18in (45cm)
Aspect: Sun
Soil: Wet to marginal
aquatic, fertile
Hardiness: Zone 3
Propagation: Seed, in warmth
in spring; division, in spring

Clump-forming plant. Leaves lance-
shaped, downy, green. Flowers bright
purple-red stars in spiky racemes,
midsummer to early autumn.
Deadhead to prevent self-seeding.

Lythrum salicaria 'Blush' (Lythraceae)

Common name: Pink
loosestrife
Height: 4ft (1.2m)
Spread: 18in (45cm)
Aspect: Sun
Soil: Wet to marginal
aquatic, fertile
Hardiness: Zone 3
Propagation: Division, in
spring

Selected form of the species. Leaves
lance-shaped, downy, green. Flowers
blush-pink stars in spiky racemes,
midsummer to early autumn.
Deadhead to prevent self-seeding.

Lythrum salicaria 'Robert' (Lythraceae)

Common name: Pink
loosestrife
Height: 4ft (1.2m)
Spread: 18in (45cm)
Aspect: Sun
Soil: Wet to marginal
aquatic, fertile
Hardiness: Zone 3
Propagation: Division, in
spring

A selected form with bright pink,
starry flowers in spiky racemes,
midsummer to early autumn. Leaves
lance-shaped, downy, green.
Deadhead to prevent self-seeding.

Lythrum virgatum 'The Rocket' (Lythraceae)

Common name: Pink loosestrife
Height: 36in (90cm)
Spread: 18in (45cm)
Aspect: Sun
Soil: Moist, fertile
Hardiness: Zone 4
Propagation: Seed or division, both in spring

A clump-forming perennial from Europe, Asia, and China. Leaves linearly lance-shaped, midgreen. Flowers in slim, spiky racemes, deep pink, all summer.

Macleaya cordata A.G.M. (Papaveraceae)

Common name: Plume-poppy
Height: 8ft (2.5m)
Spread: 3ft (90cm)
Aspect: Sun or half shade
Soil: Moist, well-drained, fertile
Hardiness: Zone 3
Propagation: Seed, in spring; division, in spring or autumn

Rhizomatous plant from the Far East. Leaves handsome, 5- to 7-lobed, gray-green, white-downy below. Flowers creamy-white, tubular, in panicles, mid- and late summer.

Maianthemum bifolium (Convallariaceae/Liliaceae)

Common name: Wild lily-of-the-valley
Height: 6in (15cm)
Spread: Indefinite
Aspect: Full or half shade
Soil: Moist, well-drained, acidic, humus-rich
Hardiness: Zone 3
Propagation: Seed, when ripe; division of runners, in spring

Invasive ground cover. Leaves ovate to heart-shaped, glossy deep green. Flowers in racemes of up to 20, perfumed, white, in early summer, followed by small, red berries.

Malva moschata (Malvaceae)

Common name: Musk mallow
Height: 3ft (90cm)
Spread: 2ft (60cm)
Aspect: Sun
Soil: Moist, well-drained, fertile
Hardiness: Zone 3
Propagation: Seed or basal cuttings, both in spring

A short-lived perennial from Africa. Leaves heart-shaped and pinnatisect, midgreen. Flowers in axillary clusters, pink saucers, early summer to early autumn.

Malva moschata
f. *alba* A.G.M.
(**Malvaceae**)

Common name: White
musk mallow
Height: 3ft (90cm)
Spread: 2ft (60cm)
Aspect: Sun
Soil: Moist, well-drained,
fertile
Hardiness: Zone 3
Propagation: Seed or basal
cuttings, both in spring

A white form of the species. Leaves
heart-shaped and pinnatisect,
midgreen, musk-scented. Flowers in
axillary clusters, white saucers, early
summer to early autumn.

Malva sylvestris
(**Malvaceae**)

Common name: Mallow
Height: 4ft (1.2m)
Spread: 2ft (60cm)
Aspect: Sun
Soil: Moist, well-drained,
fertile
Hardiness: Zone 5
Propagation: Seed or basal
cuttings, both in spring

Leaves round to heart-shaped, light
green. Flowers in axillary clusters,
purplish-pink, with dark veins, from
late spring to mid-autumn. From
Eurasia and North Africa.

Malva sylvestris
'Primley Blue'
(**Malvaceae**)

Common name: Mallow
Height 8in (20cm)
Spread: 24in (60cm)
Aspect: Sun
Soil: Moist, well-drained,
fertile
Hardiness: Zone 5
Propagation: Basal cuttings,
in spring

Desirable, prostrate, hybrid. Leaves
heart-shaped, midgreen. Flowers pale
blue, with darker blue veining, in
axillary clusters, from late spring to
midautumn.

Malvastrum lateritium
(**Malvaceae**)

Common name: False
mallow
Height: 6in (15cm)
Spread: Indefinite
Aspect: Sun
Soil: Well-drained
Hardiness: Zone 8
Propagation: Seed or
softwood cuttings, both
in spring

A prostrate perennial from South
America. Leaves rounded, lobed,
rough, dark green. Flowers solitary,
peach-colored, yellow-centered,
sporadically throughout summer.

Marrubium peregrinum
(Labiatae/Lamiaceae)

Common name:
Horehound
Height: 2ft (60cm)
Spread: 1ft (30cm)
Aspect: Sun
Soil: Well-drained, poor
Hardiness: Zone 8
Propagation: Seed or
softwood cuttings, both
in spring

Leaves aromatic, obovate, hairy,
crenate, dark green. Flowers tubular,
2-lipped, pale pink, in whorls, in early
summer. Deadhead to prevent self-
seeding. From Eurasia.

Matthiola
pink perennial
(Brassicaceae/Cruciferae)

Common name: Perennial
common stock
Height: 18in (45cm)
Spread: 12in (30cm)
Aspect: Sun
Soil: Moist, well-drained,
fertile
Hardiness: Zone 7
Propagation: Seed, in spring
or autumn

Short-lived plant, probably of garden
origin. Leaves linear-ovate, gray-
green. Flowers in terminal spikes,
cruciform, pink, double, scented, over
a long period in summer.

Matthiola
white perennial
(Brassicaceae/Cruciferae)

Common name: Perennial
common stock
Height: 18in (45cm)
Spread: 12in (30cm)
Aspect: Sun
Soil: Moist, well-drained,
fertile
Hardiness: Zone 7
Propagation: Seed, in spring
or autumn

Short-lived plant, of garden origin.
Leaves linear-ovate, gray-green.
Flowers in terminal spikes, perfumed,
cruciform, white, over a long period
in summer.

Mazus reptans
'Albus'
(Scrophulariaceae)

Common names: None
Height: 2in (5cm)
Spread: 18in (45cm)
Aspect: Sun
Soil: Moist, well-drained,
fertile
Hardiness: Zone 3
Propagation: Seed or
division, both in spring

Woodlander ground cover. Leaves
lance-shaped, toothed, midgreen.
Flowers in short racemes of up to 5,
white, narrow, tubular, in late spring
to summer.

MECONOPSIS (Papaveraceae)
Poppy

A genus of some 45 species of annuals, biennials, and deciduous or evergreen, often monocarpic or short-lived perennials. Most originate in the Himalayas, Burma, and China. One, *Meconopsis cambrica*, is native to western Europe; this species will grow anywhere, and is exempt from the cultural guidance below, which applies to species from the Far East. *Meconopsis* have handsome foliage in basal rosettes, and striking seed heads, but it is for quality of flower that they are best loved. The flowers are single, open cups, usually pendent, and may be solitary (usually on leafless stems) or in short panicles or racemes (usually on leafy stems), which open from above. *M. cambrica* is yellow or orange, but the coloring of the blue species is quite exquisite, and worth any effort. These come from a range of habitats, from moist, shady woodlands to mountain screes and meadows; some are very hardy, others much less so. They like some degree of shade, and the soil should be acid, humus-rich to a degree, moist, but well-drained and never waterlogged; in dry summers they must be watered. They do best in cooler climates, especially those with cool, damp summers. They may need staking in exposed areas.

Meconopsis betonicifolia
A.G.M.
(Papaveraceae)

Common name: Blue-poppy
Height: 4ft (1.2m)
Spread: 18in (45cm)
Aspect: Half shade
Soil: Moist, well-drained, acidic, humus-rich
Hardiness: Zone 7
Propagation: Seed, when ripe

Meconopsis betonicifolia
var. *alba*
(Papaveraceae)

Common name: White-poppy
Height: 4ft (1.2m)
Spread: 18in (45cm)
Aspect: Half shade
Soil: Moist, well-drained, acidic, humus-rich
Hardiness: Zone 7
Propagation: Seed, when ripe

Deciduous, short-lived species. Leaves in basal rosettes, ovate, toothed, light blue-green. Flowers solitary, pendent or horizontal, blue saucers, in early summer.

Leaves in basal rosettes, blue-green, rusty-hairy, ovate, toothed. Flowers single, white, pendent, in early summer. Prevent flowering for a year or two to improve longevity.

Meconopsis cambrica
(Papaveraceae)

Common name: Welsh-poppy
Height: 18in (45cm)
Spread: 12in (30cm)
Aspect: Any
Soil: Any
Hardiness: Zone 6
Propagation: Seed, when ripe

Taprooted perennial from Europe. Leaves stem and basal, pinnatisect, fernlike, fresh green. Flowers solitary, single, yellow cups, from spring to autumn. Seeds prolifically.

Meconopsis cambrica
var. *aurantiaca* 'Flore Pleno' (Papaveraceae)

Common name: Orange Welsh-poppy
Height: 18in (45cm)
Spread: 12in (30cm)
Aspect: Any
Soil: Any
Hardiness: Zone 6
Propagation: Seed, when ripe

A double-flowered form of the orange variety of Welsh poppy. It does not self-seed prolifically, and so is not the nuisance that the single form can represent.

Meconopsis cambrica
'Flore Pleno'
(Papaveraceae)

Common name: Double Welsh-poppy
Height: 18in (45cm)
Spread: 12in (30cm)
Aspect: Any
Soil: Any
Hardiness: Zone 6
Propagation: Division, in spring

The double yellow form of the Welsh poppy, perhaps less graceful than the single form, but having the virtue of not self-seeding everywhere.

Meconopsis
chelidoniifolia
(Papaveraceae)

Common names: None
Height: 3ft (1m)
Spread: 2ft (60cm)
Aspect: Half shade
Soil: Moist, well-drained, acidic, humus-rich
Hardiness: Zone 8
Propagation: Seed, when ripe

A species from China. Leaves pinnatisect, lobes pinnatifid, hairy, pale green. Flowers on upper leaf stalks, single, pendent or horizontal, yellow.

Meconopsis grandis A.G.M.
(Papaveraceae)

Common names: None
Height: 4ft (1.2m)
Spread: 2ft (60cm)
Aspect: Half shade
Soil: Moist, well-drained, acidic, humus-rich
Hardiness: Zone 5
Propagation: Seed, when ripe

Clump-forming species; monocarpic in dry conditions. Leaves basal rosette and stem, elliptic, toothed, brown-hairy. Flowers blue, solitary, single, shallow cups, early summer.

Meconopsis napaulensis
(Papaveraceae)

Common names: None
Height: 8ft (2.5m)
Spread: 3ft (90cm)
Aspect: Half shade
Soil: Moist, well-drained, acidic, humus-rich
Hardiness: Zone 8
Propagation: Seed, when ripe

Monocarpic species. Leaves in rosettes, pinnatisect, yellow-green, red-hairy, lobes oblong. Flowers in racemes of up to 17, pendent bowls, late spring to midsummer.

Meconopsis paniculata
(Papaveraceae)

Common names: None
Height: 6ft (2m)
Spread: 2ft (60cm)
Aspect: Half shade
Soil: Moist, well-drained, acidic, humus-rich
Hardiness: Zone 8
Propagation: Seed, when ripe

Monocarpic evergreen. Leaves in rosettes, pinnatisect, yellow-hairy, gray-green. Flowers in racemes, cup-shaped, pendent pale yellow, late spring to summer.

Meconopsis punicea
(Papaveraceae)

Common names: None
Height: 30in (75cm)
Spread: 12in (30cm)
Aspect: Half shade
Soil: Moist, well-drained, acidic, humus-rich
Hardiness: Zone 7
Propagation: Seed, when ripe

Taprooted species. Leaves in rosettes, inversely lance-shaped, gray-hairy, midgreen. Flowers on scapes, pendent, crimson, petals flared, summer to autumn.

Meconopsis quintuplinervia A.G.M. (Papaveraceae)

Common names: None
Height: 18in (45cm)
Spread: 12in (30cm)
Aspect: Half shade
Soil: Moist, well-drained, acidic, humus-rich
Hardiness: Zone 8
Propagation: Seed, when ripe

Clump-forming species. Leaves in rosettes, lance-shaped, golden-hairy, midgreen. Flowers solitary, pendent, lavender cups, from early to late summer.

Meconopsis regia (Papaveraceae)

Common names: None
Height: 6ft (2m)
Spread: 3ft (1m)
Aspect: Half shade
Soil: Moist, well-drained, acidic, humus-rich
Hardiness: Zone 8
Propagation: Seed, when ripe

Monocarpic evergreen from Nepal. Leaves in rosettes, elliptic, silver-hairy, midgreen. Flowers outward-facing on branched stems, red cups, from late spring to midsummer.

Meconopsis x sheldonii A.G.M. (Papaveraceae)

Common names: None
Height: 5ft (1.5m)
Spread: 2ft (60cm)
Aspect: Half shade
Soil: Moist, well-drained, acidic, humus-rich
Hardiness: Zone 6
Propagation: Division, after flowering

Hybrid perennial of garden origin. Leaves in rosettes, lance-shaped, hairy, dark green. Flowers solitary, cup-shaped, deep rich blue, in late spring and early summer.

Meconopsis x sheldonii 'Slieve Donard' A.G.M. (Papaveraceae)

Common names: None
Height: 5ft (1.5m)
Spread: 2ft (60cm)
Aspect: Half shade
Soil: Moist, well-drained, acidic, humus-rich
Hardiness: Zone 6
Propagation: Division, after flowering

A selected form of this garden hybrid, with flowers of brilliant, rich blue in late spring and early summer. Leaves in rosettes, dark green, lance-shaped, hairy.

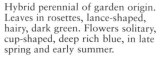

Megacarpaea polyandra
(Brassicaceae/Cruciferae)

Common names: None
Height: 6ft (2m)
Spread: 2ft (60cm)
Aspect: Sun
Soil: Well-drained, fertile
Hardiness: Zone 7
Propagation: Seed, when
ripe

Taprooted perennial from the
Himalayas. Leaves pinnate, lobes
ovate, toothed, mid-green. Flowers in
dense racemes, off-white, in spring
and summer.

Melianthus major
A.G.M.
(Melianthaceae)

Common name: Large
honey-bush
Height: 10ft (3m)
Spread: 10ft (3m)
Aspect: Sun
Soil: Well-drained, fertile
Hardiness: Zone 9
Propagation: Seed in
warmth, suckers or softwood
cuttings, all in spring

Tender perennial, evergreen in warm
areas, from South Africa. Leaves
pinnate, leaflets ovate, toothed, gray-
green. Flowers in racemes, red, from
late spring to summer.

Melissa officinalis
'Aurea'
(Labiatae/Lamiaceae)

Common name: Lemon
balm
Height: 4ft (1.2m)
Spread: 18in (45cm)
Aspect: Sun
Soil: Poor, well-drained
Hardiness: Zone 4
Propagation: Seed or
division, both in spring

Bushy perennial. Leaves aromatic,
ovate, wrinkled, dark green, splashed
gold. Flowers small, in spikes, pale
yellow, all summer. Liked by bees and
butterflies.

Mellitis melissophyllum
(Labiatae/Lamiaceae)

Common names: None
Height: 28in (70cm)
Spread: 20in (50cm)
Aspect: Half shade
Soil: Moist, well-drained,
fertile
Hardiness: Zone 6
Propagation: Seed, when
ripe; division, in spring

Woodlander. Leaves honey-scented,
oval, scalloped, veined, hairy,
wrinkled, green. Flowers in whorls, 2-
lipped, tubular, white, pink-lipped, in
spring and early summer.

**Mentha × gracilis
'Variegata'
(Labiatae/Lamiaceae)**

Common name: Ginger
mint
Height: 18in (45cm)
Spread: Indefinite
Aspect: Sun
Soil: Moist, poor
Hardiness: Zone 7
Propagation: Division, in
spring or autumn

A very invasive perennial from
Europe. Leaves aromatic, ginger-
flavored, ovate, flecked or striped
yellow. Flowers in whorls, lilac, in
summer. Ground cover.

**Mertensia pulmonarioides
A.G.M.
(Boraginaceae)**

Common name: Bluebells
Height: 18in (45cm)
Spread: 10in (25cm)
Aspect: Half shade
Soil: Sharply drained, poor
Hardiness: Zone 3
Propagation: Seed or root
cuttings, both in autumn;
division, in spring

A clump-forming woodlander from
North America. Leaves ovate, blue-
green. Flowers in terminal cymes,
tubular, blue, in mid- and late spring.

**Mertensia simplicissima
(Boraginaceae)**

Common names: None
Height: 3ft (90cm)
Spread: 1ft (30cm)
Aspect: Half shade
Soil: Sharply drained, poor
Hardiness: Zone 6
Propagation: Seed or root
cuttings, both in autumn;
division, in spring

Prostrate plant from Russia to the Far
East. Leaves ovate, glaucous, blue-
green. Flowers tubular, turquoise, in
terminal cymes on prostrate stems,
spring to early autumn.

**Microseris ringens
(Asteraceae/Compositae)**

Common names: None
Height: 2ft (60cm)
Spread: 1ft (30cm)
Aspect: Sun
Soil: Well-drained, humus-
rich
Hardiness: Zone 8
Propagation: Seed, in
spring or autumn

Australian perennial. Leaves ovate,
hairy, rough, soft green. Flowers
single, yellow, daisylike, in large, flat-
topped racemes in early summer and
again in late summer.

Milium effusum
'Aureum'
(Graminae/Poaceae)

Common names: None
Height: 2ft (60cm)
Spread: 1ft (30cm)
Aspect: Half shade or sun
Soil: Moist, well-drained,
humus-rich
Hardiness: Zone 6
Propagation: Seed, *in situ*
in spring; division, in spring

A spreading grass from Eurasia and
North America. Leaves flat, linear,
yellow-green. Flowers in open
panicles, single-flowered spikes from
late spring to midsummer.

Mimulus
'Andean Nymph' A.G.M.
(Scrophulariaceae)

Common name: Monkey-
flower
Height: 8in (20cm)
Spread: 12in (30cm)
Aspect: Wet, humus-rich,
fertile
Soil: Sun or half shade
Hardiness: Zone 6
Propagation: Division, in spring;
softwood cuttings, in early summer

Short-lived, rhizomatous hybrid
aquatic marginal. Leaves ovate, hairy,
toothed, light green. Flowers in
racemes, white with pink throats,
over a long period in summer.

Mimulus aurantiacus
A.G.M.
(Scrophulariaceae)

Common name: Monkey-
flower
Height: 3ft (1m)
Spread: 3ft (1m)
Aspect: Sun or half shade
Soil: Moist, humus-rich,
fertile
Hardiness: Zone 8
Propagation: Seed in autumn
or spring; division in spring

Subshrub from the U.S.A. Leaves
oblong, toothed, sticky, glossy green.
Flowers in leafy racemes, red, orange,
or yellow trumpets, in late summer to
autumn.

Mimulus cardinalis
A.G.M.
(Scrophulariaceae)

Common name: Scarlet
monkey-flower
Height: 36in (90cm)
Spread: 24in (60cm)
Aspect: Sun or half shade
Soil: Wet, humus-rich,
fertile
Hardiness: Zone 7
Propagation: Seed, in autumn
or spring; division, in spring

A creeping perennial from the western
U.S.A. and Mexico. Leaves ovate,
toothed, downy, green. Flowers on
erect stems, solitary, tubular, scarlet,
all summer long.

303

Mimulus luteus
(Scrophulariaceae)

Common name: Yellow
monkey-flower
Height: 1ft (30cm)
Spread: 2ft (60cm)
Aspect: Sun or half shade
Soil: Wet, humus-rich,
fertile
Hardiness: Zone 7
Propagation: Seed, in spring
or autumn; division, in spring

Invasive species from Chile. Leaves
ovate-oblong, midgreen. Flowers on
upright or decumbent stems, yellow,
spotted red-purple, from late spring to
summer.

Mirabilis jalapa
(Nyctaginaceae)

Common name: Common
four-o'clock flower
Height: 2ft (60cm)
Spread: 2ft (60cm)
Aspect: Sun
Soil: Well-drained, fertile,
protected from winter wet
Hardiness: Zone 8
Propagation: Seed, in warmth in
spring; division, in spring

Tuberous perennial. Leaves ovate,
midgreen. Flowers perfumed, pink,
red, yellow, white, or magenta open
in late afternoon, and die next
morning. Blooms all summer.

Mitchella repens
(Rubiaceae)

Common names:
Creeping-box; partridge-
berry
Height: 2in (5cm)
Spread: 12in (30cm)
Aspect: Half shade
Soil: Moist, well-drained,
acidic, humus-rich
Hardiness: Zone 3
Propagation: Seed, in autumn;
division of runners, in spring

A creeping, evergreen perennial from
the U.S.A. Leaves ovate, green.
Flowers white, perfumed, in summer,
followed by red berries.

Monarda
'Aquarius'
(Labiatae/Lamiaceae)

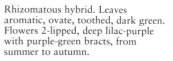

Common name: Bergamot
Height: 36in (1m)
Spread: 18in (45cm)
Aspect: Sun or half shade
Soil: Moist, well-drained,
humus-rich, fertile
Hardiness: Zone 4
Propagation: Division or
basal cuttings, both in
spring

Rhizomatous hybrid. Leaves
aromatic, ovate, toothed, dark green.
Flowers 2-lipped, deep lilac-purple
with purple-green bracts, from
summer to autumn.

MONARDA *(Labiatae/Lamiaceae)*
Bee-balm • Bergamot

A genus of only some 15 species of annuals and rhizomatous, clump-forming, herbaceous perennials from North America, but one which has been hybridized extensively to produce many very garden-worthy, hardy herbaceous perennials. Most hybrids derive from *Monarda didyma* or *M. fistulosa*. They like sun, but will grow in dappled shade. Their natural habitats include both dry prairie and woodlands, so they vary in that some like drier soils while others prefer them moist, but the soil must be moisture-retentive for all; in dry spells they are very prone to mildew. The flowers are in whorls, sagelike, tubular, 2-lipped, with a hooded upper lip and a spreading lower lip, and often have colored bracts. Bergamots are long-flowering, make excellent cut flowers, and are often used for flower arrangements, in both the fresh and dried state. Bees also like the flowers, but only bumblebees can gain direct access; honey bees can reach the pollen only after other insects have made holes. The stems are distinctive in that they are square; in the taller varieties they require staking. The foliage is unspectacular, but aromatic. Slugs attack the young growth in spring. Bergamots are low-allergen plants, so suit the allergic gardener.

Monarda
'Balance'
(Labiatae/Lamiaceae)

Common name: Bergamot
Height: 36in (1m)
Spread: 18in (45cm)
Aspect: Sun or half shade
Soil: Moist, humus-rich, well-drained, fertile
Hardiness: Zone 4
Propagation: Division basal or cuttings in spring

A rhizomatous hybrid cultivar. Leaves aromatic, ovate, toothed, dark green. Flowers 2-lipped, brick-red, from summer to autumn.

Monarda
'Cambridge Scarlet'
(Labiatae/Lamiaceae)

Common name: Bergamot
Height: 36in (1m)
Spread: 18in (45cm)
Aspect: Sun or half shade
Soil: Moist, well-drained, humus-rich, fertile
Hardiness: Zone 4
Propagation: Division or basal cuttings, both in spring

Hybrid, rhizomatous cultivar. Leaves aromatic, ovate, toothed, dark green. Flowers 2-lipped, scarlet with brown bracts, from summer to autumn.

Monarda
'Croftway Pink'
(Labiatae/Lamiaceae)

Common name: Bergamot
Height: 36in (1m)
Spread: 18in (45cm)
Aspect: Sun or half shade
Soil: Moist, well-drained,
humus-rich, fertile
Hardiness: Zone 4
Propagation: Division or
basal cuttings, both in
spring

Rhizomatous, hybrid cultivar. Leaves
aromatic, ovate, toothed, dark green.
Flowers 2-lipped, pink with pink-
tinged bracts, from summer to
autumn.

Monarda didyma
(Labiatae/Lamiaceae)

Common names: Bee-
balm; Oswego-tea
Height: 36in (1m)
Spread: 18in (45cm)
Aspect: Sun or half shade
Soil: Moist, well-drained,
humus-rich, fertile
Hardiness: Zone 4
Propagation: Seed, in spring
or autumn; division, in spring

Rhizomatous species from the eastern
U.S.A. Leaves aromatic, ovate,
toothed, dull green. Flowers pink with
red-tinted bracts, from mid- to late
summer.

Monarda fistulosa
(Labiatae/Lamiaceae)

Common name: Wild
bergamot
Height: 4ft (1.2m)
Spread: 18in (45cm)
Aspect: Sun
Soil: Moist, well-drained,
humus-rich, fertile
Hardiness: Zone 4
Propagation: Seed, in spring or
autumn; division, in spring

A rhizomatous perennial. Leaves
aromatic, ovate, toothed, dull green.
Flowers sage-like, 2-lipped, pale pink
with purple bracts, from summer to
autumn.

Monarda
'Gardenview Scarlet'
(Labiatae/Lamiaceae)

Common name: Bergamot
Height: 3ft (1m)
Spread: 18in (45cm)
Aspect: Sun or half shade
Soil: Moist, well-drained,
humus-rich, fertile
Hardiness: Zone 4
Propagation: Division or
basal cuttings, both in
spring

A hybrid, rhizomatous bergamot.
Leaves aromatic, ovate, toothed, dark
green. Flowers 2-lipped, scarlet with
dark bracts, from summer to autumn.

Monarda
'Isla'
(Labiatae/Lamiaceae)

Common name: Bergamot
Height: 3ft (1m)
Spread: 18in (45cm)
Aspect: Sun or half shade
Soil: Moist, well-drained,
humus-rich, fertile
Hardiness: Zone 4
Propagation: Division or
basal cuttings, both in
spring

A rhizomatous, hybrid cultivar.
Leaves aromatic, ovate, toothed, dark
green. Flowers sagelike, 2-lipped, pink
with pinkish bracts, from summer to
autumn.

Monarda
'Prärienacht'
(Labiatae/Lamiaceae)

Common name: Bergamot
Height: 3ft (1m)
Spread: 18in (45cm)
Aspect: Sun or half shade
Soil: Moist, well-drained,
humus-rich, fertile
Hardiness: Zone 4
Propagation: Division or
basal cuttings, both in
spring

A rhizomatous, hybrid bergamot.
Leaves aromatic, ovate, toothed, dark
green. Flowers 2-lipped, purple-lilac
with red-green bracts, from
midsummer to autumn.

Monarda punctata
(Labiatae/Lamiaceae)

Common name: Horse-mint
Height: 3ft (1m)
Spread: 18in (45cm)
Aspect: Sun or half shade
Soil: Moist, well-drained,
humus-rich, fertile
Hardiness: Zone 4
Propagation: Division or
basal cuttings, both in
spring; seed, in autumn

A species from the U.S.A. Leaves
aromatic, toothed, pale green. Flowers
in whorls, sagelike, 2-lipped, pink,
spotted purple, bracts green, tinged
pink, in summer.

Monarda
'Scorpion'
(Labiatae/Lamiaceae)

Common name: Bergamot
Height: 3ft (1m)
Spread: 18in (45cm)
Aspect: Sun or half shade
Soil: Moist, well-drained,
humus-rich, fertile
Hardiness: Zone 4
Propagation: Division or
basal cuttings, both in
spring

A hybrid, rhizomatous cultivar.
Leaves aromatic, ovate, toothed, dark
green, Flowers in whorls, 2-lipped,
hooded, deep pink, from summer to
autumn.

307

Monarda 'Squaw'
(Labiatae/Lamiaceae)

Common name: Bergamot
Height: 3ft (1m)
Spread: 18in (45cm)
Aspect: Sun or half shade
Soil: Moist, well-drained,
humus-rich, fertile
Hardiness: Zone 4
Propagation: Division or
basal cuttings, both in
spring

A rhizomatous, hybrid bergamot.
Leaves aromatic, ovate, toothed, dark
green. Flowers in whorls, sagelike,
hooded, bright crimson, from summer
to autumn.

Monarda 'Twins'
(Labiatae/Lamiaceae)

Common name: Bergamot
Height: 3ft (1m)
Spread: 18in (45cm)
Aspect: Sun or half shade
Soil: Moist, well-drained,
humus-rich, fertile
Hardiness: Zone 4
Propagation: Division or
basal cuttings, both in
spring

A hybrid, rhizomatous bergamot.
Leaves aromatic, toothed, dark green.
Flowers in whorls, sagelike, hooded,
lilac-pink, from summer to autumn.

Moraea spathulata
(Iridaceae)

Common names: None
Height: 3ft (90cm)
Spread: 3in (8cm)
Aspect: Sun
Soil: Well-drained, humus-
rich, fertile
Hardiness: Zone 8
Propagation: Seed, in
warmth in autumn; offsets,
when dormant

A cormous perennial from Africa.
Leaves basal, narrowly linear, flat,
green. Flowers in succession, in
clusters, each short-lived, irislike,
from spring to summer.

Morina longifolia
(Morinaceae)

Common name: Whorlflower
Height: 3ft (90cm)
Spread: 1ft (30cm)
Aspect: Sun
Soil: Sharply drained,
humus-rich, protected from
winter wet
Hardiness: Zone 6
Propagation: Seed, when
ripe; root cuttings, in winter

Evergreen with leaves in a basal
rosette, lance-shaped, spiny, dark
green. Flowers in tiered whorls, with
spiny bracts, white, becoming pink,
then red, in summer.

Muscari armeniacum
A.G.M.
(Hyacinthaceae/Liliaceae)

Common name: American
grape-hyacinth
Height: 8in (20cm)
Spread: 2in (5cm)
Aspect: Sun
Soil: Moist, well-drained,
fertile
Hardiness: Zone 4
Propagation: Offsets, in
summer

A vigorous, bulbous perennial from
the Caucasus. Leaves linear, midgreen,
after the flowers. Flowers in dense
racemes, bright blue with white
mouths, in spring.

Muscari azureum
A.G.M.
(Hyacinthaceae/Liliaceae)

Common name: Grape-
hyacinth
Height: 4in (10cm)
Spread: 2in (5cm)
Aspect: Sun
Soil: Moist, well-drained,
fertile
Hardiness: Zone 8
Propagation: Offsets, in
summer

A bulbous perennial from Turkey.
Leaves inverse lance-shaped, gray-
green. Flowers in dense racemes, sky-
blue bells with a dark stripe on each
lobe, in spring.

Muscari comosum
'Plumosum'
(Hyacinthaceae/Liliaceae)

Common name: Feather-
hyacinth
Height: 24in (60cm)
Spread: 2in (5cm)
Aspect: Sun
Soil: Moist, well-drained,
fertile
Hardiness: Zone 4
Propagation: Offsets, in
summer

Bulbous perennial from Europe and
Turkey. Leaves linear, spreading,
midgreen. Flowers are absent; heads
are composed of sterile, purple
threads.

Muscari latifolium
(Hyacinthaceae/Liliaceae)

Common name: Grape-
hyacinth
Height: 8in (20cm)
Spread: 2in (5cm)
Aspect: Sun
Soil: Moist, well-drained,
fertile
Hardiness: Zone 4
Propagation: Offsets, in
summer

Bulbous perennial. Leaves midgreen,
semi-erect, inverse lance-shaped.
Dense racemes of purple-black, urn-
shaped flowers are crowned by sterile,
blue flowers.

Myosotidium hortensia
(Boraginaceae)

Common names: None
Height: 2ft (60cm)
Spread: 3ft (90cm)
Aspect: Half shade
Soil: Moist, well-drained, sandy
Hardiness: Zone 8
Propagation: Seed, when ripe; division, in spring

Leaves large, ovate to heart-shaped, with conspicuous veins, glossy green. Flowers in cymes, blue bells with white margins, in early summer. Not for a hot, dry garden.

Myosotis scorpioides
(Boraginaceae)

Common names: True forget-me-not
Height: 1ft (30cm)
Spread: 1ft (30cm)
Aspect: Sun or half shade
Soil: Marginal aquatic
Hardiness: Zone 5
Propagation: Seed or division, both in spring

A rampant, rhizomatous perennial from Eurasia and North America. Leaves ovate, midgreen. Flowers in open cymes, small, blue, salverform, in early summer.

Myrrhis odorata
(Apiaceae/Umbelliferae)

Common names: Myrrh; sweet Cicely
Height: 6ft (2m)
Spread: 5ft (1.5m)
Aspect: Half shade
Soil: Moist, well-drained, fertile
Hardiness: Zone 5
Propagation: Seed, in spring; division, in spring or autumn

Aniseed-flavored culinary herb. Leaves 2- or 3-pinnate, lobes lance-shaped, toothed, bright green. Flowers in compound umbels, small, star-shaped, white; fruits brown.

Narcissus
'Actaea' A.G.M. (Div. 9)
(Amaryllidaceae)

Common name: Daffodil
Height: 18in (45cm)
Spread: 6in (15cm)
Aspect: Sun or half shade
Soil: Well-drained, fertile, humus-rich
Hardiness: Zone 4
Propagation: Offsets, in summer or autumn

A reliable hybrid with perfumed flowers. Flowers with white, wavy, open perianth and low, bowl-shaped, red-rimmed, yellow corona, in late spring.

NARCISSUS (Amaryllidaceae)
Daffodil

A genus of some 50 species of bulbous perennials from varied habitats in Europe and North Africa; the genus has been hybridized extensively, and several thousand cultivars have been developed. Daffodils are an excellent garden plant, suitable for naturalizing, growing in a border, or planting in containers. They will grow in sun or half-shade, although the former is preferred. They like the soil to be moist during the growing season but dry during the dormant period, and so a humus-rich but sharply drained soil is best. The flowers are borne on leafless stems, which may carry anything from one to 20 blooms. The flower has a perianth and a corona: the perianth is made up of six petals, spreading or reflexed, and the corona may be any shape between a shallow cup and a long trumpet. The leaves are basal, and usually strap-shaped, sometimes cylindrical; they should be left to die down, not cut back, or flowering will be poorer the following year. Daffodils benefit from lifting and dividing every few years, and as this is best done during the summer dormancy, it is advisable to mark the positions of the clumps while the foliage is there to guide you. The bulbs are poisonous, and contact with the sap may cause skin irritation.

Narcissus
'Baby Moon' (Div. 7)
(Amaryllidaceae)

Common name: Daffodil
Height: 10in (25cm)
Spread: 3in (8cm)
Aspect: Sun or half shade
Soil: Well-drained,
alkaline, humus-rich,
fertile
Hardiness: Zone 4
Propagation: Offsets, in
summer or autumn

A hybrid Jonquilla narcissus. Flowers small, perfumed, with the perianth and small-cupped corona both yellow, in midspring.

Narcissus
'Bantam' A.G.M. (Div. 2)
(Amaryllidaceae)

Common name: Daffodil
Height: 10in (25cm)
Spread: 6in (15cm)
Aspect: Sun or half shade
Soil: Well-drained, fertile,
humus-rich
Hardiness: Zone 4
Propagation: Offsets, in
summer or autumn

A good hybrid narcissus. Flowers with short, golden yellow perianth segments and short, flared, orange, cup-shaped, red-rimmed corona, in midspring.

Narcissus
'Bravoure' A.G.M. (Div. 1)
(Amaryllidaceae)

Common name: Daffodil
Height: 18in (45cm)
Spread: 6in (15cm)
Aspect: Sun or half shade
Soil: Moist, well-drained,
humus-rich
Hardiness: Zone 4
Propagation: Offsets, in
summer or autumn

A robust Trumpet daffodil. Flowers
with pointed, overlapping, white
perianth segments and a long, yellow,
trumpet-shaped corona, in midspring.

**DIVISIONS OF NARCISSUS by
the American Daffodil Society**

1) Trumpet

2) Large-cupped

3) Small-cupped

4) Double

5) Triandrus

6) Cyclamineus

7) Jonquilla

8) Tazetta

9) Poeticus

10) Species, wild forms, and
hybrids

11) Miscellaneous

Each daffodil illustrated will have
a division number.

Narcissus bulbocodium
(Div. 10)
(Amaryllidaceae)

Common name: Petticoat
daffodil
Height: 6in (15cm)
Spread: 3in (8cm)
Aspect: Sun or half shade
Soil: Well-drained, acidic,
humus-rich
Hardiness: Zone 6
Propagation: Seed, when ripe;
offsets, in summer or autumn

A species from Europe and North
Africa. Flowers small, yellow, with
reduced, pointed perianth segments
and an expanded, megaphone-shaped
corona, in midspring.

Narcissus
'Canaliculatus' (Div. 8)
(Amaryllidaceae)

Common name: Daffodil
Height: 5in (12cm)
Spread: 6in (16cm)
Aspect: Sun or half shade
Soil: Well drained,
alkaline, humus-rich
Hardiness: Zone 8
Propagation: Offsets, in
summer or autumn

A perfumed, cluster-headed, Tazetta
narcissus. Flower with reflexed, white
perianth and a yellow, barrel-shaped
corona, in midspring.

Narcissus cyclamineus
A.G.M. (Div. 10)
(Amaryllidaceae)

Common name: Daffodil
Height: 8in (20cm)
Spread: 3in (8cm)
Aspect: Sun or half shade
Soil: Well-drained, acidic,
humus-rich
Hardiness: Zone 5
Propagation: Seed, when
ripe; offsets, in summer or
autumn

Species from Spain and Portugal.
Leaves narrow, keeled, spreading.
Flowers small, nodding, yellow.
Perianth totally reflexed, corona long
and narrow, in early spring.

Narcissus
'February Gold' A.G.M.
(Div. 6) (Amaryllidaceae)

Common name: Daffodil
Height: 12in (30cm)
Spread: 3in (8cm)
Aspect: Sun or half shade
Soil: Well-drained, acidic,
humus-rich, fertile
Hardiness: Zone 6
Propagation: Offsets, in
summer or autumn

A robust, hybrid, Cyclamineus
narcissus. Flowers with golden-yellow,
reflexed perianth and long, trumpet-
shaped corona of deeper yellow, in
early spring

Narcissus
'Hawera' A.G.M. (Div. 5)
(Amaryllidaceae)

Common name: Daffodil
Height: 7in (18cm)
Spread: 3in (8cm)
Aspect: Sun or half shade
Soil: Well-drained, acidic,
humus-rich, fertile
Hardiness: Zone 4
Propagation: Offsets, in
summer or autumn

A Triandrus hybrid with many
flowers on each stem. Perianth
segments reflexed, canary yellow;
corona a shallow cup of paler yellow.
Flowers in late spring.

Narcissus
'Ice Follies' A.G.M. (Div. 2)
(Amaryllidaceae)

Common name: Daffodil
Height: 16in (40cm)
Spread: 6in (16cm)
Aspect: Sun or half shade
Soil: Well-drained, fertile,
humus-rich
Hardiness: Zone 6
Propagation: Offsets, in
summer or autumn

A prolific daffodil, with large, cream
perianth segments and a wide, frilly-
edged, cup-shaped corona, lemon
fading to almost white, in midspring.

Narcissus
'Jack Snipe' A.G.M. (Div. 6)
(Amaryllidaceae)

Common name: Daffodil
Height: 8in (20cm)
Spread: 3in (8cm)
Aspect: Sun or half shade
Soil: Well-drained, acidic,
humus-rich
Hardiness: Zone 6
Propagation: Offsets, in
summer or autumn

A robust, hybrid, Cyclamineus
daffodil. Flowers with reflexed, white
perianth segments and a yellow,
trumpet-shaped corona, in early to
midspring.

Narcissus
'Jetfire' A.G.M. (Div. 6)
(Amaryllidacae)

Common name: Daffodil
Height: 8in (20cm)
Spread: 6in (15cm)
Aspect: Sun or half shade
Soil: Well-drained, acidic,
humus-rich, fertile
Hardiness: Zone 6
Propagation: Offsets, in
summer or autumn

A robust, hybrid, Cyclamineus
daffodil. Flowers with reflexed,
golden-yellow perianth and a long,
orange, trumpet-shaped corona in
early spring.

Narcissus jonquilla
A.G.M. (Div. 10)
(Amaryllidaceae)

Common name: Jonquil
Height: 12in (30cm)
Spread: 3in (8cm)
Aspect: Sun or half shade
Soil: Well-drained, acidic,
humus-rich, fertile
Hardiness: Zone 4
Propagation: Seed, when
ripe; offsets, in summer or
autumn

A species from Spain. Leaves narrow,
erect to spreading, midgreen. Flowers
strongly scented, yellow; perianth
segments pointed, corona a small, flat
cup, in late spring.

Narcissus
'Minnow' A.G.M. (Div. 8)
(Amaryllidaceae)

Common name: Daffodil
Height: 7in (18cm)
Spread: 3in (8cm)
Aspect: Sun or half shade
Soil: Well-drained, acidic,
humus-rich, fertile
Hardiness: Zone 8
Propagation: Offsets, in
summer or autumn

A robust, hybrid Tazetta daffodil.
Flowers with cream perianth segments
fading to white and a yellow, cup-
shaped corona,
in midspring.

Narcissus obvallaris
A.G.M. (Div. 10)
(Amaryllidaceae)

Common name: Daffodil
Height: 12in (30cm)
Spread: 6in (16cm)
Aspect: Sun or half shade
Soil: Well-drained, humus-rich, fertile
Hardiness: Zone 4
Propagation: Seed, when ripe; offsets, in summer or autumn

A species found in South Wales and across W Europe. Leaves erect, glaucous green. Flowers golden-yellow, with spreading perianth segments and a long corona.

Narcissus
'Peeping Tom' A.G.M.
(Div. 6) (Amaryllidaceae)

Common name: Daffodil
Height: 8in (20cm)
Spread: 3in (8cm)
Aspect: Sun or half shade
Soil: Well-drained, acidic, humus-rich, fertile
Hardiness: Zone 6
Propagation: Offsets, in summer or autumn

A robust, hybrid, Cyclamineus daffodil. Flowers yellow, with strongly reflexed perianth segments, and a long, trumpet-shaped corona, in midspring.

Narcissus
'Pipit' (Div. 7)
(Amaryllidaceae)

Common name: Daffodil
Height: 10in (25cm)
Spread: 3in (8cm)
Aspect: Sun or half shade
Soil: Well-drained, acidic, humus-rich, fertile
Hardiness: Zone 4
Propagation: Offsets, in summer or autumn

A perfumed, hybrid, Jonquilla daffodil. Flowers with recurved, lemon perianth segments and a yellow, cup-shaped corona, in mid- to late spring.

Narcissus
'Rippling Waters' A.G.M.
(Div. 5) (Amaryllidaceae)

Common name: Daffodil
Height: 8in (20cm)
Spread: 3in (8cm)
Aspect: Sun or half shade
Soil: Well-drained, acidic, humus-rich, fertile
Hardiness: Zone 4
Propagation: Offsets, in summer or autumn

Hybrid with multiflowered stems. Flowers with large, reflexed, white perianth segments and a pale yellow, cup-shaped, shallow corona, in mid- and late spring.

Narcissus
'Rip van Winkle' (Div. 4)
(Amaryllidaceae)

Common name: Daffodil
Height: 6in (15cm)
Spread: 6in (15cm)
Aspect: Sun or half shade
Soil: Well-drained, humus-rich, fertile
Hardiness: Zone 4
Propagation: Offsets, in summer or autumn

A hybrid with double flowers. Perianth segments narrow, pointed, cream. Corona divided, segments doubled into irregular central mass, yellow, in early spring.

Narcissus
'Salomé' (Div. 2)
(Amaryllidaceae)

Common name: Daffodil
Height: 18in (45cm)
Spread: 6in (15cm)
Aspect: Sun or half shade
Soil: Well-drained, humus-rich, fertile
Hardiness: Zone 4
Propagation: Offsets, in summer or autumn

Large-cupped, hybrid daffodil. Flowers with pale cream perianth segments and a large, peach, cup-shaped, almost trumpet-shaped corona, in midspring.

Narcissus
'Sundial' (Div. 7)
(Amaryllidaceae)

Common name: Daffodil
Height: 8in (20cm)
Spread: 3in (8cm)
Aspect: Sun or half shade
Soil: Well-drained, acidic, humus-rich, fertile
Hardiness: Zone 4
Propagation: Offsets, in summer or autumn

A small, hybrid Jonquilla daffodil. Flowers with perianth segments of cream, and a small, golden-yellow, cup-shaped corona, in midspring.

Narcissus
'Tête-à-tête' A.G.M. (Div. 11) (Amaryllidaceae)

Common name: Daffodil
Height: 6in (15cm)
Spread: 6in (15cm)
Aspect: Sun or half shade
Soil: Well-drained, humus-rich, fertile
Hardiness: Zone 4
Propagation: Offsets, in summer or autumn

A vigorous, Miscellaneous section daffodil. Flowers with golden-yellow, reflexed perianth segments and a yellow, cup-shaped corona, in early spring.

Narcissus
'Thalia' (Div. 5)
(Amaryllidaceae)

Common name: Daffodil
Height: 14in (35cm)
Spread: 3in (8cm)
Aspect: Sun or half shade
Soil: Well-drained, acidic,
humus-rich, fertile
Hardiness: Zone 4
Propagation: Offsets, in
summer or autumn

A Triandrus daffodil. Flowers milk-
white, in pairs, with twisted, reflexed,
narrow perianth segments and an
open, cup-shaped corona, in
midspring.

Nectaroscordum siculum
(Alliaceae/Liliaceae)

Common names: None
Height: 5ft (1.5m)
Spread: 4in (10cm)
Aspect: Sun or half shade
Soil: Well-drained, fertile
Hardiness: Zone 6
Propagation: Seed, in
autumn or spring; offsets,
in summer

A vigorous, bulbous plant from Italy
and France. Leaves basal, linear,
keeled, mid-green. Flowers in umbels
of up to 30, open, pendulous, plum-
colored bells, in summer.

Nemesia denticulata
(Scrophulariaceae)

Common names: None
Height: 16in (40cm)
Spread: 8in (20cm)
Aspect: Sun
Soil: Moist, well-drained,
acidic, fertile
Hardiness: Zone 8
Propagation: Seed, in
warmth in spring or
autumn

A neat, compact, mound-forming
perennial from South Africa. Leaves
lance-shaped, toothed. Flowers large,
flattish, lilac, from spring to autumn.

Nepeta govaniana
(Labiatae/Lamiaceae)

Common name: Catmint
Height: 36in (90cm)
Spread: 24in (60cm)
Aspect: Sun or half shade
Soil: Well-drained
Hardiness: Zone 5
Propagation: Division, in
spring or autumn; seed, in
autumn

A clump-forming Himalayan plant.
Leaves aromatic, ovate, hairy,
pointed, scalloped, midgreen. Flowers
in panicles, pale yellow, from
midsummer to early autumn.

Nepeta sibirica
(Labiatae/Lamiceae)

Common names: Catmint;
catnip
Height: 36in (90cm)
Spread: 18in (45cm)
Aspect: Sun
Soil: Well-drained
Hardiness: Zone 3
Propagation: Division, in
spring or autumn; seed, in
autumn

Species from Russia and Asia. Leaves
aromatic, lance-shaped, toothed, dark
green. Flowers in whorled cymes,
blue, in mid- and late summer.

Nepeta subsessilis
(Labiatae/Lamiaceae)

Common names:
Catmints; catnip
Height: 36in (90cm)
Spread: 12in (30cm)
Aspect: Sun
Soil: Well-drained
Hardiness: Zone 7
Propagation: Division, in
spring or autumn; seed, in
autumn

A clump-forming perennial from
Japan. Leaves aromatic, ovate,
toothed, dark green. Flowers in
upright, whorled cymes, from
midsummer to early autumn.

Nerine bowdenii
A.G.M.
(Amaryllidaceae)

Common name: Cape
Colony nerine
Height: 18in (45cm)
Spread: 3in (8cm)
Aspect: Sun
Soil: Well-drained
Hardiness: Zone 8
Propagation: Seed, in
warmth when ripe; division,
after flowering

A bulbous perennial from Africa.
Leaves broad straps, midgreen.
Flowers in open umbels of up to 7,
perfumed, pink funnels with recurved
tepals, in late autumn.

Nierembergia repens
(Solanaceae)

Common name: White
cupflower
Height: 2in (5cm)
Spread: 18in (45cm)
Aspect: Sun
Soil: Moist, well-drained
Hardiness: Zone 8
Propagation: Seed or
division, both in spring

A prostrate perennial from the Andes.
Leaves spoon-shaped, bright green.
Flowers open, upward-facing cups,
white, over long periods in summer.

Nomocharis pardanthina
(Liliaceae)

Nymphaea alba
(Nymphaeaceae)

Common names: None
Height: 36in (90cm)
Spread: 4in (10cm)
Aspect: Half shade, or sun
in cool areas
Soil: Moist in summer,
acidic, humus-rich
Hardiness: Zone 7
Propagation: Seed, in
warmth in autumn or spring

A woodlander from China. Leaves
lance-shaped, midgreen. Flowers in
racemes of up to 6, nodding, saucer-
shaped, pink, spotted purple, in early
summer.

Common name: European
white water-lily
Height: Surface
Spread: 5ft (1.5m)
Aspect: Sun
Soil: Undisturbed water
Hardiness: Zone 5
Propagation: Seed, covered
by an inch of water, in
warmth when ripe

A rhizomatous, aquatic perennial
from Eurasia and North Africa.
Leaves round, deep green. Flowers
perfumed, star-shaped, yellow-
centered, in summer.

Nymphaea
'James Brydon' A.G.M.
(Nymphaeaceae)

Nymphoides peltata
(Menyanthaceae)

Common name: Water-lily
Height: Surface
Spread: 4ft (1.2m)
Aspect: Sun
Soil: Still water
Hardiness: Zone 4
Propagation: Division of
rhizomes or separated
offsets, both in summer

A rhizomatous, hybrid, aquatic
perennial. Leaves rounded, bronze-
green. Flowers cup-shaped, vivid rose-
red with yellow stamens, in summer.

Common name: Floating-
heart
Height: 3in (8cm)
Spread: Indefinite
Aspect: Sun
Soil: Still water
Hardiness: Zone 6
Propagation: Separated
runners, in summer

A rhizomatous, herbaceous perennial
from Eurasia. Leaves ovate, mottled,
green. Flowers on long stems, yellow,
funnel-shaped, in summer.

OENOTHERA (Onagraceae)
Evening-primrose • Sundrops

A genus of some 125 species of annuals, biennials, and perennials from North America in particular, but also distributed in Central and South America. The perennial members of the genus are mostly short-lived. Their natural habitats are often on mountainsides, and in the garden they prefer a position in sun in a well-drained soil; small types such as *Oenothera macrocarpa* are suitable for a rock garden. Some evening-primroses are taprooted, and resent disturbance, so these should be sited carefully when they are first planted. The individual flowers are often short-lived, but they are borne in succession over a long period throughout the summer. The flowers are cup- or saucer-shaped, sometimes trumpet-shaped, white, yellow, or pink, and often perfumed. They are borne either singly in the axils or in terminal racemes. All are attractive to bees. The taller forms of evening-primrose require staking. Many of them seed around to an unacceptable degree; deadheading to prevent self-seeding is not easy in this genus, since ripened seed pods and unopened flower buds are found on the same stem, so naturalizing them in a wild garden may be a preferred option for these types.

Oenothera deltoides
(Onagraceae)

Common name: Desert evening-primrose
Height: 12in (30cm)
Spread: 8in (20cm)
Aspect: Sun
Soil: Sharply drained
Hardiness: Zone 9
Propagation: Seed, in early spring

A perennial from Arizona; Baja California, and Mexico. Leaves ovate, midgreen. Flowers solitary, white bowls, on erect and decumbent stems, in summer.

Oenothera fruticosa
(Onagraceae)

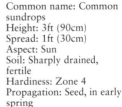

Common name: Common sundrops
Height: 3ft (90cm)
Spread: 1ft (30cm)
Aspect: Sun
Soil: Sharply drained, fertile
Hardiness: Zone 4
Propagation: Seed, in early spring

A short-lived species from North America. Leaves ovate, toothed, midgreen. Flowers in racemes of up to 10, deep yellow cups, from late spring to late summer.

Oenothera fruticosa
'Fyrverkeri' A.G.M.
(Onagraceae)

Common name: Common
sundrops
Height: 3ft (90cm)
Spread: 1ft (30cm)
Aspect: Sun
Soil: Sharply drained,
fertile
Hardiness: Zone 4
Propagation: Division, in
early spring

A selected form of the species, with
purple-brown-flushed leaves, and red
buds opening to chrome-yellow
flowers, from late spring for many
weeks.

Oenothera macrocarpa
A.G.M.
(Onagraceae)

Common name: Ozark
sundrops
Height: 6in (15cm)
Spread: 18in (45cm)
Aspect: Sun
Soil: Sharply drained
Hardiness: Zone 5
Propagation: Seed, in early
spring

A robust perennial from the southern
U.S.A. Leaves lance-shaped, toothed,
mid-green. Flowers solitary, golden
cups, over a long period from spring
to autumn.

Oenothera nuttallii
(Onagraceae)

Common name: Sundrops
Height: 3ft (90cm)
Spread: 2ft (60cm)
Aspect: Sun
Soil: Sharply drained
Hardiness: Zone 5
Propagation: Seed, in early
spring

North American species. Leaves
oblong, dull green. Flowers on
straggly stems, large, creamy-white, in
summer. Long-lived. Very late to
reappear, so mark position.

Oenothera rosea
(Onagraceae)

Common name: Rose
sundrops
Height: 2ft (60cm)
Spread: 1ft (30cm)
Aspect: Sun
Soil: Sharply drained
Hardiness: Zone 6
Propagation: Seed, in early
spring

A species from the Americas. Leaves
oblong, midgreen. Flowers small,
pink, diurnal cups. Not to be
confused with *O. speciosa* 'Rosea', a
superior plant.

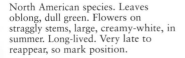

321

Oenothera speciosa
(Onagraceae)

Common name: Showy
evening-primrose
Height: 1ft (30cm)
Spread: 1ft (30cm)
Aspect: Sun
Soil: Sharply drained
Hardiness: Zone 5
Propagation: Seed, in early
spring

Species from the southwest U.S.A.
Leaves basal, in rosettes, oblong,
midgreen. Flowers solitary, single
white cups, aging to pink, over a long
period in summer.

Oenothera speciosa
'Rosea'
(Onagraceae)

Common name: Showy
evening-primrose
Height: 1ft (30cm)
Spread: 1ft (30cm)
Aspect: Sun
Soil: Sharply drained
Hardiness: Zone 5
Propagation: Seed, in early
spring

A form of the species with yellow-
centered flowers that have white
petals suffused pink towards the
periphery. Long-flowering, but can be
invasive.

Oenothera speciosa
'Siskiyou'
(Onagraceae)

Common name: Showy
evening-primrose
Height: 1ft (30cm)
Spread: 1ft (30cm)
Aspect: Sun
Soil: Sharply drained
Hardiness: Zone 5
Propagation: Division, in
early spring

A selected form of the species with
yellow-centered flowers that have
white petals suffused pink around the
perimeter. Can be invasive.

Oenothera stubbei
(Onagraceae)

Common name: Evening-
primrose
Height: 4ft (1.2m)
Spread: 1ft (30cm)
Aspect: Sun
Soil: Sharply drained
Hardiness: Zone 8
Propagation: Seed, in early
spring

A perennial from Mexico. Leaves in a
basal rosette, and stem, elliptic to
lance-shaped, midgreen. Flowers
yellow aging to orange, then red, in
summer.

Olsynium douglasii album
(Iridaceae)

Common names: None
Height: 12in (30cm)
Spread: 4in (10cm)
Aspect: Half shade
Soil: Moist, humus-rich,
fertile
Hardiness: Zone 9
Propagation: Seed, in
autumn

A tender, clump-forming perennial
from North America. Leaves linear,
gray-green. Flowers nodding, bell-
shaped, in spathes of up to 4, white,
in early spring.

Omphalodes cappadocica
'Cherry Ingram' A.G.M.
(Boraginaceae)

Common name: Navel-
seed
Height: 1ft (30cm)
Spread: 1ft (30cm)
Aspect: Half shade
Soil: Moist, humus-rich,
fertile
Hardiness: Zone 6
Propagation: Division, in
early spring

An evergreen, clump-forming,
woodland ground cover. Leaves basal,
ovate, veined, pointed, dull green.
Flowers deep blue, in racemes, in
spring, intermittently thereafter.

Omphalodes cappadocica
'Starry Eyes'
(Boraginaceae)

Common name: Navel-
seed
Height: 12in (30cm)
Spread: 18in (45cm)
Aspect: Half shade
Soil: Moist, humus-rich,
fertile
Hardiness: Zone 6
Propagation: Division, in
early spring

Evergreen woodland ground cover.
Leaves ovate, green. Flowers pale blue
with a central white stripe on each
petal, in loose racemes in spring,
intermittently thereafter.

Onoclea sensibilis
A.G.M.
(Aspidiaceae)

Common name: Sensitive
fern
Height: 2ft (60cm)
Spread: Indefinite
Aspect: Half shade
Soil: Moist, acidic, fertile,
humus-rich
Hardiness: Zone 4
Propagation: Spores, in warmth
when ripe; division, in spring

A deciduous fern from North America
and Asia. Spring fronds sterile,
pinnate, lobes lance-shaped, pale
green. Autumn fronds fertile, erect, 2-
pinnate; pinnate black lobes.

Onosma alborosea
(Boraginaceae)

Common names: None
Height: 10in (25cm)
Spread: 10in (25cm)
Aspect: Sun
Soil: Dry, sharply drained
Hardiness: Zone 7
Propagation: Seed in
autumn

Clump-forming evergreen from Asia.
Leaves obovate, white-hairy, gray-green. Flowers in terminal, congested
cymes, narrow, white, tubular, tips
turning pink with age.

Ophiopogon planiscapus
'Nigrescens' A.G.M.
(Convallariaceae/Liliaceae)

Common name: Lily-turf
Height: 8in (20cm)
Spread: 12in (30cm)
Aspect: Sun or half shade
Soil: Acidic, humus-rich,
fertile
Hardiness: Zone 6
Propagation: Seed, when
ripe; division, in spring

A stoloniferous, evergreen ground
cover from Japan. Leaves near-black
straps. Flowers in racemes, pinkish-white, in summer, followed by black
berries.

Orchis mascula
(Orchidaceae)

Common name: Early
purple orchid
Height: 12in (30cm)
Spread: 6in (15cm)
Aspect: Half shade
Soil: Sharply drained,
humus-rich, fertile
Hardiness: Zone 5
Propagation: Offsets, in
spring

A terrestrial orchid from Europe.
Leaves long, pointed, purple-spotted,
midgreen. Flowers in erect racemes,
pale or dark purple, in spring and
summer.

Origanum amanum
A.G.M.
(Labiatae/Lamiaceae)

Common names:
Marjoram; oregano
Height: 8in (20cm)
Spread: 12in (30cm)
Aspect: Sun
Soil: Well-drained,
alkaline, fertile
Hardiness: Zone 8
Propagation: Seed, division
or basal cuttings, all in spring

Evergreen subshrub from Turkey.
Leaves aromatic, ovate, bright green.
Flowers in terminal whorls, pink
surrounded by green bracts, in
summer and autumn.

Origanum
'Buckland'
(Labiatae/Laamiaceae)

Common names:
Marjoram; oregano
Height: 8in (20cm)
Spread: 6in (15cm)
Aspect: Sun
Soil: Well-drained,
alkaline, fertile
Hardiness: Zone 7
Propagation: Division or
basal cuttings, both in spring

A hybrid marjoram. Leaves aromatic,
rounded, hairy, gray-green. Flowers in
whorls, pink, tubular, surrounded by
pink bracts, in summer and autumn.

Origanum laevigatum
A.G.M.
(Labiatae/Lamiaceae)

Common names:
Marjoram; oregano
Height: 24in (60cm)
Spread: 18in (45cm)
Aspect: Sun
Soil: Well-drained,
alkaline, fertile
Hardiness: Zone 8
Propagation: Seed, division
or basal cuttings, all in spring

A perennial from Turkey and Cyprus.
Leaves aromatic, ovate, dark green.
Flowers in whorls, tubular, purple-
pink, from spring to autumn.

Origanum laevigatum
'Herrenhausen' A.G.M.
(Labiatae/Lamiaceae)

Common names:
Marjoram; oregano
Height: 18in (45cm)
Spread: 18in (45cm)
Aspect: Sun
Soil: Well-drained,
alkaline, fertile
Hardiness: Zone 8
Propagation: Division or
basal cuttings, both in spring

A hybrid evergreen perennial. Leaves
aromatic, ovate, purple-green.
Flowers in whorls, denser form than
the species, deep pink, from spring to
autumn.

Origanum vulgare
'Aureum' A.G.M.
(Labiatae/Lamiaceae)

Common name: Wild
marjoram
Height: 2ft (60cm)
Spread: 1ft (30cm)
Aspect: Sun
Soil: Well-drained,
alkaline, fertile
Hardiness: Zone 5
Propagation: Division or
basal cuttings, both in spring

A rhizomatous perennial from
Europe. Leaves aromatic, ovate,
golden. Flowers in whorls, tubular,
pink, midsummer to early autumn.
Less invasive than the species.

Ornithogalum arabicum
(Hyacinthaceae/Liliaceae)

Common name: Arabian
star-of-Bethlehem
Height: 32in (80cm)
Spread: 4in (10cm)
Aspect: Sun
Soil: Well-drained, fertile
Hardiness: Zone 9
Propagation: Seed, in
autumn or spring; offsets,
when dormant

Bulbous Mediterranean plant. Leaves
dark green, linear, broad, arching.
Flowers cup-shaped, in corymbs of up
to 25, perfumed, white with a black
ovary, in early summer.

Ornithogalum narbonense
(Hyacinthaceae/Liliaceae)

Common name: Star-of-
Bethlehem
Height: 36in (90cm)
Spread: 8in (20cm)
Aspect: Sun
Soil: Well-drained, fertile
Hardiness: Zone 7
Propagation: Seed, in
autumn or spring; offsets,
when dormant

A bulbous perennial from Turkey and
Iran. Leaves basal, linear, arching,
gray-green. Flowers starry, white, in
narrow, tapering racemes, in late
spring and early summer.

Ornithogalum nutans
A.G.M.
(Hyacinthaceae/Liliaceae)

Common name: Nodding
star-of-Bethlehem
Height: 24in (60cm)
Spread: 2in (5cm)
Aspect: Sun
Soil: Well-drained, fertile
Hardiness: Zone 6
Propagation: Seed, autumn
or spring; offsets, when
dormant

Bulbous plant from Eurasia. Leaves
semi-erect, strap-shaped, green with a
central silver stripe. Flowers in one-
sided racemes of up to 20, silver-white
funnels, in spring.

Ornithogalum thyrsoides
(Hyacinthaceae/Liliaceae)

Common name: Cape
chinkerichee
Height: 32in (80cm)
Spread: 4in (10cm)
Aspect: Sun
Soil: Well-drained, fertile
Hardiness: Zone 9
Propagation: Seed, in
autumn or spring; offsets,
when dormant

A bulbous plant from South Africa.
Leaves basal, narrow, lance-shaped,
midgreen, before the many-flowered,
dense racemes of white cups, in spring
and early summer.

Ornithogalum umbellatum
(Hyacinthaceae/Liliaceae)

Common name: Star-of-Bethlehem
Height: 12in (30cm)
Spread: 4in (10cm)
Aspect: Sun
Soil: Well-drained, fertile
Hardiness: Zone 5
Propagation: Seed, in autumn or spring; offsets, when dormant

A robust, bulbous perennial from Europe to the Middle East. Leaves basal, linear, veined silver, green. Flowers in racemes of up to 20, starry, white, in early summer.

Orthrosanthus chimboracensis
(Iridaceae)

Common names: None
Height: 24in (60cm)
Spread: 8in (20cm)
Aspect: Sun
Soil: Well-drained, fertile, humus-rich
Hardiness: Zone 9
Propagation: Seed, in warmth in spring; division, in spring

A tender, rhizomatous, evergreen perennial from Mexico to Peru. Leaves basal, linear, rough, green. Flowers in loose panicles, lavender bowls, in summer.

Osmunda cinnamomea
(Osmundaceae)

Common name: Cinnamon fern
Height: 3ft (90cm)
Spread: 2ft (60cm)
Aspect: Half shade
Soil: Moist, acidic, fertile, humus-rich
Hardiness: Zone 3
Propagation: Spores, in summer; division, in autumn or spring

Deciduous fern. Sterile, blue-green, ovate to lance-shaped, pinnate fronds, segments pinnatifid, surround erect, narrow, fertile fronds topped by cinnamon sporangia.

Osteospermum 'Buttermilk' A.G.M.
(Asteraceae/Compositae)

Common name: Veldt daisy
Height: 2ft (60cm)
Spread: 2ft (60cm)
Aspect: Sun
Soil: Well-drained, fertile
Hardiness: Zone 9
Propagation: Softwood cuttings, in spring; semiripe cuttings, in summer

Evergreen subshrub. Leaves inverse lance-shaped, midgreen. Flowers solitary, single, daisylike, ray florets primrose, disc florets mauve, from late spring to autumn.

OSTEOSPERMUM (Asteraceae/Compositae)
Veldt daisy

A genus of some 70 species of annuals, perennials, and evergreen subshrubs from mountainous, forest edge, or grassland habitats in southern Africa and the Arabian Peninsula. They are mostly tender or half-hardy, but a few are reliably hardy, and hybrids are being produced from these which are also hardy. In frost-prone areas the more tender types can be treated as annuals. *Osteospermum* have three features that commend them to the gardener: they have a very long flowering season, stretching from late spring to autumn, they are evergreen, and they make excellent ground cover, so are worth taking some trouble over. Their daisylike flowerheads have ray florets of pink, white, or yellow, with a wider range of shades available in the cultivars, and often contrasting, darker disc florets. They require little more than a position in full sun (the flowers of many will close in shade or dull weather) and well-drained soil; a sunny bank is an ideal situation. Deadheading will improve and prolong flowering. They make good cut flowers. Regrettably, like most daisylike flowers, they are highly allergenic, so best avoided by the allergic gardener. They are prone to downy mildew in wet areas.

Osteospermum caulescens syn. *O.* 'White Pim' A.G.M. (Asteraceae/Compositae)

Common name: Veldt daisy
Height: 4in (10cm)
Spread: 24in (60cm)
Aspect: Sun
Soil: Well-drained, fertile
Hardiness: Zone 8
Propagation: Seed, in warmth in spring

Subshrub from South Africa. Leaves inverse lance-shaped, toothed, midgreen. Flowers solitary, single, ray florets white, disc florets blue, from late spring to autumn.

Osteospermum jucundum A.G.M. (Asteraceae/Compositae)

Common name: Veldt daisy
Height: 20in (50cm)
Spread: 36in (90cm)
Aspect: Sun
Soil: Well-drained, fertile
Hardiness: Zone 7
Propagation: Seed, in warmth in spring

Rhizomatous subshrub. Leaves inverse lance-shaped, grayish-green. Flowers single, solitary, ray florets mauve, disc florets purple, from late spring to autumn.

Osteospermum
'Nairobi Purple'
(Asteraceae/Compositae)

Common name: Veldt
daisy
Height: 6in (15cm)
Spread: 36in (90cm)
Aspect: Sun
Soil: Well-drained, fertile
Hardiness: Zone 9
Propagation: Softwood
cuttings, in spring; semiripe
cuttings, in summer

Tender, evergreen hybrid subshrub.
Leaves ovate to spoon-shaped, bright
green. Flowers solitary, single, ray
florets purple, disc florets black, from
late spring to autumn.

Osteospermum
'Silver Sparkler' A.G.M.
(Asteraceae/Compositae)

Common names: Veldt
daisy
Height: 18in (45cm)
Spread: 36in (90cm)
Aspect: Sun
Soil: Well-drained, fertile
Hardiness: Zone 8
Propagation: Softwood
cuttings, in spring; semiripe
cuttings, in summer

Evergreen subshrub. Leaves inverse
lance-shaped, gray-green, edged
white. Flowers solitary, single, ray
florets steely-white, disc florets brown,
late spring to autumn.

Osteospermum
'Sirius'
(Asteraceae/Compositae)

Common name: Veldt
daisy
Height: 1ft (30cm)
Spread: 1ft (30cm)
Aspect: Sun
Soil: Well-drained, fertile
Hardiness: Zone 8
Propagation: Softwood
cuttings, in spring; semiripe
cuttings, in summer

Hybrid, evergreen subshrub. Leaves
ovate to spoon-shaped, dull green.
Flowers single, solitary, ray florets
cerise, aging to pink, disc florets
green, late spring to autumn.

Osteospermum
'Sunny Alex'
(Asteraceae/Compositae)

Common name: Veldt
daisy
Height: 1ft (30cm)
Spread: 1ft (30cm)
Aspect: Sun
Soil: Well-drained, fertile
Hardiness: Zone 8
Propagation: Softwood
cuttings, in spring; semiripe
cuttings, in summer

Evergreen subshrub. Leaves inverse
lance-shaped, toothed, dull green.
Flowers single, solitary, ray florets
bright yellow, disc florets orange,
from late spring to autumn.

329

Ostrowskia magnifica
(Campanulaceae)

Common names: None
Height: 5ft (1.5m)
Spread: 18in (45cm)
Aspect: Sun
Soil: Moist, well-drained,
deep, fertile
Hardiness: Zone 7
Propagation: Seed, when
ripe

Leaves in whorls, ovate, toothed.
Flowers in racemes, outward-facing,
milky-blue or white, open bells, in
early and midsummer. Taproot is
easily damaged; avoid moving it.

Othonna cheirifolia
(Asteraceae/Compositae)

Common names: None
Height: 12in (30cm)
Spread: 18in (45cm)
Aspect: Sun
Soil: Sharply drained,
fertile
Hardiness: Zone 8
Propagation: Seed, in
warmth in spring; basal
cuttings, in summer

An evergreen, spreading subshrub
from North Africa. Leaves spoon-
shaped, fleshy, gray-green. Flowers in
corymbs, daisylike, yellow, in late
autumn and early winter.

Ourisia coccinea
(Scrophulariaceae)

Common names: None
Height: 8in (20cm)
Spread: 16in (40cm)
Aspect: Half shade
Soil: Moist, humus-rich,
fertile
Hardiness: Zone 7
Propagation: Seed, when
ripe or in spring

Mat-forming evergreen from the
Andes. Leaves in rosettes, oblong,
veined, toothed, pale green. Flowers
tubular, 2-lipped, pendent, scarlet, in
racemes, all summer.

Oxalis acetosella
(Oxalidaceae)

Common names:
Shamrock; sorrel
Height: 2in (5cm)
Spread: Indefinite
Aspect: Full or half shade
Soil: Moist, humus-rich,
fertile
Hardiness: Zone 3
Propagation: Division, in
spring

Hardy, highly invasive woodland
plant. Leaves 3-lobed, leaflets inverse
heart-shaped, pale green. Flowers
solitary, dark-veined pink cups, in
spring.

Oxalis hedysariodes
(Oxalidaceae)

Oxalis pes-caprae
(Oxalidaceae)

Common names:
Shamrock; sorrel
Height: 36in (1m)
Spread: 18in (45cm)
Aspect: Full or half shade
Soil: Sharply drained,
fertile
Hardiness: Zone 9
Propagation: Seed, in
warmth in late winter to spring

Common name: Buttercup
oxalis
Height: 5in (12cm)
Spread: Indefinite
Aspect: Shade
Soil: Moist, humus-rich
Hardiness: Zone 9
Propagation: Seed, in
warmth in late winter to
spring

A tender subshrub from Central
America. Leaves 3-lobed, leaflets
ovate, light green. Flowers in axillary
cymes, funnel-shaped, yellow, in
summer.

Rampant, bulbous plant. Leaves 3-
lobed, leaflets inverse heart-shaped,
bright green. Flowers in umbellate
cymes, solitary, deep golden-yellow, in
spring and early summer.

Oxalis tetraphylla
'Iron Cross'
(Oxalidaceae)

Pachyphragma
macrophyllum
(Brassicaceae/Cruciferae)

Common name: Four-leaf
oxalis
Height: 6in (15cm)
Spread: 6in (15cm)
Aspect: Full or half shade
Soil: Moist, humus-rich,
fertile
Hardiness: Zone 8
Propagation: Seed or
offsets, both in spring

Common names: None
Height: 16in (40cm)
Spread: 90cm (36in)
Aspect: Half shade
Soil: Humus-rich, fertile
Hardiness: Zone 7
Propagation: Seed, in
autumn; division, in spring

Invasive, bulbous plant. Leaves 4-
lobed, each leaflet inversely triangular,
midgreen, with a purple basal band.
Flowers in cymes of up to 12, funnel-
shaped, pink, in summer.

Woodland plant. Leaves large, basal,
rounded, scalloped, some
overwintering. Flowers in flat corymbs,
cruciform, white, malodorous, in
spring, followed by berries.

PAEONIA (Paeoniaceae)
Peony

A genus of some 30 or so species from rocky scrubland and meadows across Eurasia and western North America. There are two types of plant in the genus: the herbaceous, tuberous perennials, and the shrubs that are known as tree peonies; only one of the latter will be included here. The perennial peonies are long-lived and easy to grow in sun or part-shade, and in any soil provided that it is not waterlogged. They do not take kindly to root disturbance, so site them carefully when first planting them; they can become large in time, so leave them plenty of room. Most peonies flower in early summer. The flowers are large, often brightly colored, showy, and sometimes perfumed; they may be single, semi-double, double, or anemone-form, and are followed by attractive, lobed seed pods containing red or black seeds. The foliage is dissected and handsome. Some species are invasive, notably *P. mascula* subsp. *arietiana* (Zone 8), *P. mollis* (Zone 6), *P. officinalis*, *P. peregrina* (Zone 8), and *P. tenuifolia*, but the rest are well-behaved. They may require staking in exposed areas, especially those with large and double flowers. They are low-allergen, and suit the allergic gardener. All parts of the plants are poisonous, however.

Paeonia lactiflora 'Bowl of Beauty' A.G.M. (Paeoniaceae)

Common name: Chinese peony
Height: 3ft (1m)
Spread: 3ft (1m)
Aspect: Sun or half shade
Soil: Moist, well-drained, fertile, humus-rich
Hardiness: Zone 6
Propagation: Division, in spring or autumn

A herbaceous perennial. Leaves 2-ternate, lobes obovate, midgreen. Flowers large, anemone-form, carmine red with a cream center, in early summer.

Paeonia broteroi (Paeoniaceae)

Common name: Peony
Height: 20in (50cm)
Spread: 20in (50cm)
Aspect: Sun or half shade
Soil: Moist, well-drained, fertile, humus-rich
Hardiness: Zone 7
Propagation: Seed, in autumn to early winter

A herbaceous perennial from Spain and Portugal. Leaves divided, glossy, mid-green. Flowers single, pink cups, in late spring and early summer.

Paeonia delavayi
A.G.M.
(Paeoniaceae)

Common name: Tree peony
Height: 6ft (2m)
Spread: 4ft (1.2m)
Aspect: Sun or half shade
Soil: Moist, well-drained, fertile, humus-rich
Hardiness: Zone 6
Propagation: Seed, in autumn or spring; semiripe cuttings, in summer

A robust tree peony from China. Leaves 2-pinnate, lobes deeply cut, dark green. Flowers single, cup-shaped, rich, dark red, in early summer.

Paeonia lactiflora
'Lady Alexandra Duff'
A.G.M. (Paeoniaceae)

Common name: Chinese peony
Height: 28in (70cm)
Spread: 28in (70cm)
Aspect: Sun or half shade
Soil: Moist, well-drained, fertile, humus-rich
Hardiness: Zone 6
Propagation: Division, in spring or autumn

One of many cultivars of this species. Leaves divided, leaflets elliptic to lance-shaped. Flowers double, pale pink, in midsummer.

Paeonia mascula
subsp. *arietina*
(Paeoniaceae)

Common name: Peony
Height: 3ft (1m)
Spread: 3ft (1m)
Aspect: Sun or half shade
Soil: Moist, well-drained, fertile, humus-rich
Hardiness: Zone 8
Propagation: Seed in autumn or winter; division, in spring or autumn

A herbaceous perennial. Leaves divided into 9 ovate leaflets, bluish-green. Flowers single, rose-pink cups with yellow stamens, in early summer.

Paeonia mascula
subsp. *russii*
(Paeoniaceae)

Common name: Peony
Height: 18in (45cm)
Spread: 18in (45cm)
Aspect: Sun or half shade
Soil: Moist, well-drained, fertile, humus-rich
Hardiness: Zone 8
Propagation: Seed, in autumn or winter; division, in spring or autumn

A very compact form of the species, found in Greece, Corsica, Sicily, and Sardinia. Leaves tinged purple. Flowers single, rose-pink with yellow stamens, in early summer.

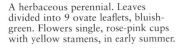

Paeonia mascula
subsp. *triternata*
(Paeoniaceae)

Common name: Peony
Height: 18in (45cm)
Spread: 18in (45cm)
Aspect: Sun or half shade
Soil: Moist, well-drained,
fertile, humus-rich
Hardiness: Zone 8
Propagation: Seed, in
autumn or winter; division,
in spring or autumn

A form of the species from Asia
Minor and the Balkans. Flowers
single, pink; the bright red seed heads
found in this and many other peonies
are shown here.

Paeonia mlokosewitschii
A.G.M.
(Paeoniaceae)

Common name: Peony
Height: 3ft (90cm)
Spread: 3ft (90cm)
Aspect: Sun or half shade
Soil: Moist, well-drained,
fertile, humus-rich
Hardiness: Zone 6
Propagation: Seed, in
autumn or early winter;
division, in spring or autumn

Leaves divided into 9 ovate leaflets,
bluish-green. Flowers short-lived,
single, bowl-shaped, petals broad,
lemon-yellow, in late spring and early
summer.

Paeonia obovata
var. *alba* A.G.M.
(Paeoniaceae)

Common name: Peony
Height: 28in (70cm)
Spread: 28in (70cm)
Aspect: Sun or half shade
Soil: Moist, well-drained,
fertile, humus-rich
Hardiness: Zone 7
Propagation: Seed, in
autumn or early winter;
division, in spring or autumn

Peony from China. Leaves divided
into 9 leaflets, with elliptic lobes, dark
green. Flowers single, cup-shaped,
white, with yellow anthers and purple
filaments.

Paeonia officinalis
(Paeoniaceae)

Common name: Common
peony
Height: 28in (70cm)
Spread: 28in (70cm)
Aspect: Sun or half shade
Soil: Moist, well-drained,
humus-rich, fertile
Hardiness: Zone 8
Propagation: Seed, in autumn or early
winter; division, in spring or autumn

A species from Europe. Leaves
divided into 9 leaflets, with oblong
lobes, dark green. Flowers single, cup-
shaped, rose-pink with yellow
stamens, in early to midsummer.

Paeonia officinalis
'Anemoniflora Rosea'
A.G.M. (Paeoniaceae)

Common name: Anemone-
flowered peony
Height: 28in (70cm)
Spread: 28in (70cm)
Aspect: Sun or half shade
Soil: Moist, well-drained,
humus-rich, fertile
Hardiness: Zone 8
Propagation: Seed, in autumn or early
winter; division, in spring or autumn

A form of the European common
peony with anemone-centered flowers
of pale pink. Leaves dark green,
divided into 9 leaflets with oblong
lobes.

Paeonia tenuifolia
(Paeoniaceae)

Common name: Fern-
leaved peony
Height: 28in (70cm)
Spread: 28in (70cm)
Aspect: Sun or half shade
Soil: Moist, well-drained,
humus-rich, fertile
Hardiness: Zone 8
Propagation: Seed, in autumn or early
winter; division, in spring or autumn

Leaves many-segmented, segments
linear, dark green. Flowers single,
cup-shaped, deep red with yellow
stamens, late spring to early summer.
From Europe and Russia.

Paeonia lactiflora
'White Wings'
(Paeoniaceae)

Common name: Chinese
peony
Height: 35in (85cm)
Spread: 35in (85cm)
Aspect: Sun or half shade
Soil: Moist, well-drained,
humus-rich, fertile
Hardiness: Zone 7
Propagation: Seed, in autumn or early
winter; division, in spring or autumn

A hardy perennial cultivar. Leaves
dark, glossy green. Flowers single,
cup-shaped, perfumed, white, with
ruffled petals, in early summer.

Papaver anomalum album
(Papaveraceae)

Common names: None
Height: 16in (40cm)
Spread: 6in (15cm)
Aspect: Sun
Soil: Well-drained, deep,
fertile
Hardiness: Zone 7
Propagation: Seed, in spring

A perennial poppy from China.
Leaves basal, 2-pinnatisect, glabrous,
blue-green. Flowers solitary, single,
white (yellow in type) with yellow
centers, in late spring.

335

PAPAVER (Papaveraceae)
Poppy

A genus of some 70 species of annuals, biennials, and perennials from many parts of the world, including Europe, Asia, South Africa, North America, Australia, and some subarctic areas. The perennial members of the genus are easy to grow. All are sun-lovers, and will grow well so long as they are in sun and their soil is not waterlogged; they do best in poor but deeply cultivated, well-drained soil, or even sharply drained in the case of the *Papaver alpinum* and its forms. Poppies are taprooted and do not transplant well, so should be sited carefully when they are first planted. The flowers are short-lived but beautiful, being brightly colored and silky, and are followed by decorative, distinctively shaped "pepper-pot" seed capsules. These are best removed if abundant self-seeding is not desired, but if seed is wanted they must ripen on the plant. The flowers are low-allergen. They are good for arrangements, but they need to be picked at night before the bud opens, and the bottom of the stem dipped in very hot water, kept cool overnight, then arranged in the morning. The seed pods are also good, either fresh or dried. The only drawbacks of poppies are that they often need to be staked, and they are prone to downy mildew.

Papaver atlanticum
(Papaveraceae)

Common names: None
Height: 12in (30cm)
Spread: 6in (15cm)
Aspect: Sun
Soil: Well-drained, deep, fertile
Hardiness: Zone 6
Propagation: Seed, in spring

A short-lived, clump-forming perennial from Morocco. Leaves oblong, toothed, midgreen. Flowers solitary, single, orange saucers, in summer.

Papaver nudicaule
(Papaveraceae)

Common name: Iceland poppy
Height: 12in (30cm)
Spread: 6in (15cm)
Aspect: Sun
Soil: Well-drained, deep, fertile
Hardiness: Zone 3
Propagation: Seed, in spring

A hardy plant derived from the sub-arctic *P. croceum*. Dense tuft of oval, pinnatisect, hairy, gray-green leaves. Flowers scented, in all colors, solitary, single bowls, summer.

Papaver fauriei
(Papaveraceae)

Common names: None
Height: 4in (10cm)
Spread: 4in (10cm)
Aspect: Sun
Soil: Well-drained, deep,
fertile
Hardiness: Zone 2
Propagation: Seed, in spring

A hardy, mound-forming, short-lived
plant from Japan and Russia. Leaves
pinnate, lobes lance-shaped, deep-cut,
gray-green. Flowers solitary, single
yellow in summer.

Papaver
'Fireball'
(Papaveraceae)

Common names: None
Height: 1ft (30cm)
Spread: Indefinite
Aspect: Sun
Soil: Well-drained, deep,
fertile
Hardiness: Zone 7
Propagation: Seed, in spring

An invasive perennial of uncertain
origin. Leaves lance-shaped, toothed,
midgreen. Flowers semidouble,
solitary, scarlet-orange, from late
spring to summer.

Papaver orientale
'Allegro'
(Papaveraceae)

Common name: Oriental
poppy
Height: 36in (90cm)
Spread: 75cm (30in)
Aspect: Sun
Soil: Well-drained
Hardiness: Zone 3
Propagation: Division, in
spring

Spreading, clump-forming cultivar.
Leaves pinnatisect, leaflets lance-
shaped, toothed. Flowers solitary
cups, scarlet-orange with black basal
spots, late spring to midsummer.

Papaver orientale
'Beauty of Livermere'
A.G.M. (Papaveraceae)

Common name: Oriental
poppy
Height: 4ft (1.2m)
Spread: 3ft (90cm)
Aspect: Sun
Soil: Well-drained, deep,
fertile
Hardiness: Zone 3
Propagation: Division, in
spring

Clump-forming, spreading cultivar.
Leaves pinnatisect, leaflets lance-
shaped, toothed. Flowers solitary,
single cups, scarlet with black basal
marks, spring to midsummer.

337

Papaver orientale
'Black and White' A.G.M.
(Papaveraceae)

Common name: Oriental
poppy
Height: 3ft (90cm)
Spread: 3ft (90cm)
Aspect: Sun
Soil: Well-drained, deep,
fertile
Hardiness: Zone 3
Propagation: Division, in
spring

Clump-forming cultivar. Leaves
pinnatisect, leaflets lance-shaped,
toothed, midgreen. Flowers solitary,
single cups, white with red or black
basal marks, spring to midsummer.

Papaver orientale
'Charming'
(Papaveraceae)

Common name: Oriental
poppy
Height: 3ft (90cm)
Spread: 3ft (90cm)
Aspect: Sun
Soil: Well-drained, deep,
fertile
Hardiness: Zone 3
Propagation: Division, in
spring

Leaves pinnatisect, leaflets lance-
shaped, toothed, midgreen. Flowers
solitary, single cups, blush pink with
plum-colored basal marks, late spring
to midsummer.

Papaver orientale
'Harvest Moon'
(Papaveraceae)

Common name: Oriental
poppy
Height: 3ft (90cm)
Spread: 3ft (90cm)
Aspect: Sun
Soil: Well-drained, deep,
fertile
Hardiness: Zone 3
Propagation: Division, in
spring

Hybrid oriental poppy. Leaves
pinnatisect, leaflets lance-shaped,
toothed, midgreen. Flowers solitary,
single cups, burnt orange, from late
spring to midsummer.

Papaver orientale
'Patty's Plum'
(Papaveraceae)

Common name: Oriental
poppy
Height: 3ft (90cm)
Spread: 3ft (90cm)
Aspect: Sun
Soil: Well-drained, deep,
fertile
Hardiness: Zone 3
Propagation: Division, in
spring

Hybrid oriental poppy. Leaves
pinnatisect, leaflets lance-shaped,
toothed, midgreen. Flowers solitary,
single, plum-colored cups, from late
spring to midsummer.

Papaver rupifragum
(Papaveraceae)

Common name: Spanish poppy
Height: 18in (45cm)
Spread: 8in (20cm)
Aspect: Sun
Soil: Well-drained, deep, fertile
Hardiness: Zone 7
Propagation: Seed, in spring

A short-lived perennial species from Spain. Leaves obovate, toothed, midgreen. Flowers solitary, single, dark orange bowls, in summer.

Papaver spicatum
(Papaveraceae)

Common names: None
Height: 24in (60cm)
Spread: 6in (15cm)
Aspect: Sun
Soil: Well-drained, deep, fertile
Hardiness: Zone 8
Propagation: Seed, in spring

A species from Turkey. Leaves in a basal rosette, oblong-elliptic, toothed, pale green. Flowers pale orange, outward-facing, in a slender raceme, in succession, in summer.

Paradisea liliastrum
A.G.M.
(Asphodelaceae/Liliaceae)

Common name: St-Bruno-lily
Height: 2ft (60cm)
Spread: 1ft (30cm)
Aspect: Sun or half shade
Soil: Moist, well-drained, fertile
Hardiness: Zone 7
Propagation: Seed, when ripe or in spring; division, in spring

A rhizomatous, clump-forming perennial. Leaves grassy. Flowers white with large yellow anthers, strongly scented, in one-sided racemes, late spring or early summer.

Paradisea lusitanicum
(Asphodelaceae/Liliaceae)

Common names: None
Height: 4ft (1.2m)
Spread: 16in (40cm)
Aspect: Sun or half shade
Soil: Moist, well-drained, fertile
Hardiness: Zone 8
Propagation: Seed, when ripe or in spring; division, in spring

A rhizomatous perennial from Spain and Portugal. Leaves in basal rosettes, linear, green. Flowers in racemes of up to 25, white, perfumed trumpets, in summer.

Parahebe perfoliata A.G.M.
(Scrophulariaceae)

Common names: None
Height: 32in (80cm)
Spread: 18in (45cm)
Aspect: Sun
Soil: Well-drained, fertile
Hardiness: Zone 9
Propagation: Seed, when ripe or in spring

Tender, evergreen perennial from Australia. Leaves in perfoliate pairs, toothed, leathery, glaucous, blue-green. Flowers in racemes, blue saucers, in late summer.

Paraquilegia anemonoides
(Scrophulariaceae)

Common names: None
Height: 4in (10cm)
Spread: 4in (10cm)
Aspect: Sun
Soil: Sharply drained, alkaline, poor, protected from winter wet
Hardiness: Zone 5
Propagation: Seed, when ripe

A perennial from Asia. Leaves ferny, 2- or 3-ternate, segments blue-green, deeply lobed. Flowers nodding, lilac, in late spring. For cool summers; best in a raised bed.

Paris polyphylla
(Trilliaceae)

Common names: None
Height: 3ft (90cm)
Spread: 1ft (30cm)
Aspect: Full or half shade
Soil: Moist, humus-rich
Hardiness: Zone 7
Propagation: Seed, in autumn; division, after foliage dies down

Rhizomatous woodlander. Bare stems topped with whorls of oval, green leaves, then of greenish sepals, then of greenish-yellow petals. Violet stigma.

Parnassia nubicola
(Parnassiaceae/Saxifragaceae)

Common name: Grass of Parnassus
Height: 12in (30cm)
Spread: 6in (15cm)
Aspect: Sun
Soil: Wet, humus-rich, fertile
Hardiness: Zone 4
Propagation: Seed, in autumn; division, in spring or autumn

A hardy, waterside perennial from the Himalayas. Leaves elliptic, matt green. Flowers open saucers, white with yellow staminodes, in late summer.

Pelargonium crispum 'Variegatum' A.G.M. (Geraniaceae)

Common name: Finger pelargonium
Height: 18in (45cm)
Spread: 6in (15cm)
Aspect: Sun
Soil: Well-drained, fertile
Hardiness: Zone 10
Propagation: Softwood cuttings, in spring, summer, or autumn

An upright, tender perennial subshrub from South Africa. Leaves pale green, margined cream, aromatic. Flowers pale mauve, in spring and summer.

Pelargonium endlicherianum (Geraniaceae)

Common names: None
Height: 10in (25cm)
Spread: 6in (15cm)
Aspect: Sun
Soil: Sharply drained, alkaline, fertile, protected from winter wet
Hardiness: Zone 7
Propagation: Seed, in spring

A hardy perennial from Asia Minor, Syria, and Armenia. Leaves basal, rounded, crenate, hairy, dark green. Flowers deep pink, veined purple, in scapes, in summer.

Pelargonium peltatum hybrids (Geraniaceae)

Common name: Ivy-leaved geraniums
Height: 8in (20cm)
Spread: 18in (45cm)
Aspect: Sun
Soil: Well-drained, fertile
Hardiness: Zone 10
Propagation: Softwood cuttings, in spring, summer, or autumn

Tender, trailing evergreens. Leaves peltate, fleshy, bright green. Flowers purple, pink, red, white, or mauve, single or double, over a long period in spring and summer.

Pelargonium zonale hybrids (Geraniaceae)

Common name: Zonal geraniums
Height: 2ft (60cm)
Spread: 1ft (30cm)
Aspect: Sun or half shade
Soil: Well-drained, fertile
Hardiness: Zone 10
Propagation: Softwood cuttings, in spring, summer, or autumn

Bushy evergreens. Leaves rounded, green, edged or zoned maroon or bronze. Flowers single or double, red, purple, pink, or orange, in spring and summer.

PENSTEMON (Scrophulariaceae)
Penstemon

A genus of about 250 species of evergreen to deciduous perennials and subshrubs from North and Central America, and one which has been hybridized comprehensively. They come from a wide range of habitats, from mountain areas to plains, and as a result the genus varies in hardiness. The majority of species are half-hardy, with just a few tender or reliably hardy types. They are most likely to remain evergreen in mild areas. Penstemons prefer a sunny position, but they will tolerate light shade. The soil should be well-drained, and not too fertile; otherwise they become lush, flower less freely, and are less likely to survive the winter. A dry winter mulch is advisable in frost-prone areas. They are long-flowering, with a season lasting from early summer until well into autumn if deadheaded. The flowers are tubular, funnel-shaped, or bell-shaped, and 2-lipped, the upper lip usually 2-lobed and the lower lip usually 3-lobed. They are borne in upright panicles or racemes, and the colors range from deep purple through reds and pinks to white, with rare yellows. Penstemons are low-allergen plants. Their drawbacks are that they are prey to slugs and susceptible to powdery mildew. Some of the taller varieties need to be staked.

***Penstemon* 'Andenken an Friedrich Hahn' A.G.M. (Scrophulariaceae)**

Common names: None
Height: 30in (75cm)
Spread: 24in (60cm)
Aspect: Sun or half shade
Soil: Well-drained, fertile
Hardiness: Zone 7
Propagation: Division, in spring

Hybrid cultivar. Leaves linear to lance-shaped, midgreen. Flowers tubular, deep wine red, in racemes, from midsummer to midautumn. Has also been called 'Garnet'.

***Penstemon barbatus* (Scrophulariaceae)**

Common name: Bearlip penstemon
Height: 6ft (1.8m)
Spread: 20in (50cm)
Aspect: Sun or half shade
Soil: Well-drained, fertile
Hardiness: Zone 3
Propagation: Seed, in late winter or spring; division, in spring

A tall penstemon species. Leaves in basal rosettes, lance-shaped, midgreen. Flowers in panicles, pendent, tubular, red, from early summer to early autumn.

Penstemon cardwellii
f. *albus*
(Scrophulariaceae)

Common names: None
Height: 8in (20cm)
Spread: 12in (30cm)
Aspect: Sun or half shade
Soil: Well-drained, fertile
Hardiness: Zone 8
Propagation: Seed, in late
winter or spring; division,
in spring

A dwarf, evergreen subshrub. Leaves
elliptic, toothed, midgreen. Flowers in
few-flowered panicles, tubular, white,
(deep purple in type) in early summer.

Penstemon
'Charles Rudd'
(Scrophulariaceae)

Common names: None
Height: 24in (60cm)
Spread: 18in (45cm)
Aspect: Sun or half shade
Soil: Well-drained, fertile
Hardiness: Zone 7
Propagation: Division, in
spring

A hybrid penstemon. Leaves lance-
shaped to linear, midgreen. Flowers in
racemes, small, tubular, magenta with
a white throat, from midsummer to
midautumn.

Penstemon
'Cherry Ripe' A.G.M.
(Scrophulariaceae)

Common names: None
Height: 3ft (1m)
Spread: 18in (45cm)
Aspect: Sun or half shade
Soil: Well-drained, fertile
Hardiness: Zone 7
Propagation: Division, in
spring

Short-lived cultivar. Leaves linear to
lance-shaped, bluish-green. Flowers
rose-pink with a white throat,
nodding, tubular, in open panicles,
midsummer to autumn.

Penstemon
'Chester Scarlet' A.G.M.
(Scrophulariaceae)

Common names: None
Height: 24in (60cm)
Spread: 18in (45cm)
Aspect: Sun or half shade
Soil: Well-drained, fertile
Hardiness: Zone 7
Propagation: Division, in
spring

A hybrid penstemon. Leaves elliptic,
mid-green. Flowers in panicles, large,
tubular to bell-shaped, scarlet, with a
white throat, from midsummer to
midautumn.

Penstemon digitalis
(Scrophulariaceae)

Common name: White
penstemon
Height: 36in (1m)
Spread: 18in (45cm)
Aspect: Sun or half shade
Soil: Well-drained, fertile
Hardiness: Zone 3
Propagation: Seed, in late
winter or spring; division,
in spring

Hardy species. Leaves in basal
rosettes, inverse lance-shaped,
midgreen. Flowers in panicles, tubular
to bell-shaped, white, interior striped
purple, all summer.

Penstemon digitalis
'Husker's Red'
(Scrophulariaceae)

Common names: None
Height: 30in (75cm)
Spread: 12in (30cm)
Aspect: Sun or half shade
Soil: Well-drained, fertile
Hardiness: Zone 3
Propagation: Division, in
spring

A selected form of the species. Leaves
in basal rosettes, inverse lance-shaped,
maroon-red. Flowers white, tinted
pink, from early to late summer.

Penstemon
'Drinkstone'
(Scrophulariaceae)

Common names: None
Height: 32in (80cm)
Spread: 18in (45cm)
Aspect: Sun or half shade
Soil: Well-drained, fertile
Hardiness: Zone 7
Propagation: Division, in
spring

Also called 'Drinkstone Red'. Leaves
ovate-elliptic, midgreen. Flowers
tubular to bell-shaped, scarlet-
vermilion, streaked magenta inside,
early to late summer.

Penstemon heterophyllus
(Scrophulariaceae)

Common name: Chaparral
penstemon
Height: 20in (50cm)
Spread: 20in (50cm)
Aspect: Sun or half shade
Soil: Well-drained, fertile
Hardiness: Zone 8
Propagation: Seed, in late
winter to early spring;
division, in spring

An evergreen subshrub from
California. Leaves linear to lance-
shaped, midgreen. Flowers in racemes,
tubular to bell-shaped, blue, lobes
lilac, in summer.

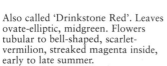

Penstemon
'Modesty'
(Scrophulariaceae)

Common names: None
Height: 32in (80cm)
Spread: 18in (45cm)
Aspect: Sun or half shade
Soil: Well-drained, fertile
Hardiness: Zone 7
Propagation: Division, in
spring

A hybrid penstemon. Leaves lance-shaped to linear, midgreen. Flowers in racemes, tubular to bell-shaped, pink with a white throat, from summer to autumn.

Penstemon
'Osprey' A.G.M.
(Scrophulariaceae)

Common names: None
Height: 36in (1m)
Spread: 18in (45cm)
Aspect: Sun or half shade
Soil: Well-drained, fertile
Hardiness: Zone 7
Propagation: Division, in
spring

Tall hybrid. Leaves linear to lance-shaped, midgreen. Flowers in racemes, tubular to bell-shaped, rose-carmine, throat white, in summer to autumn.

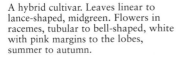

Penstemon
'Peace'
(Scrophulariaceae)

Common names: None
Height: 24in (60cm)
Spread: 18in (45cm)
Aspect: Sun or half shade
Soil: Moist, well-drained
Hardiness: Zone 7
Propagation: Division, in
spring

A hybrid cultivar. Leaves linear to lance-shaped, midgreen. Flowers in racemes, tubular to bell-shaped, white with pink margins to the lobes, summer to autumn.

Penstemon
'Pennington Gem' A.G.M.
(Scrophulariaceae)

Common names: None
Height: 30in (75cm)
Spread: 18in (45cm)
Aspect: Sun or half shade
Soil: Well-drained, fertile
Hardiness: Zone 7
Propagation: Division, in
spring

A hybrid penstemon. Leaves lance-shaped to linear, midgreen. Flowers in racemes, tubular to bell-shaped, pink with white throats, from midsummer to midautumn.

Penstemon pinifolius A.G.M. (Scrophulariaceae)

Common names: None
Height: 16in (40cm)
Spread: 10in (25cm)
Aspect: Sun or half shade
Soil: Moist, well-drained
Hardiness: Zone 8
Propagation: Seed, in late winter to spring; division, in spring

An evergreen species from Mexico and the southern U.S.A. Leaves needlelike, mid-green. Flowers in terminal racemes, tubular, scarlet, in summer.

Penstemon pinifolius 'Mersea Yellow' (Scrophulariaceae)

Common names: None
Height: 16in (40cm)
Spread: 10in (25cm)
Aspect: Sun or half shade
Soil: Well-drained, fertile
Hardiness: Zone 8
Propagation: Seed, in late winter to spring; division, in spring

A yellow-flowered form of the species. Leaves needlelike, pale green. Flowers in racemes, tubular, yellow, in summer. The best of the yellow penstemons.

Penstemon 'Pershore Pink Necklace' (Scrophulariaceae)

Common names: None·
Height: 3ft (1m)
Spread: 18in (45cm)
Aspect: Sun or half shade
Soil: Moist, well-drained
Hardiness: Zone 7
Propagation: Division, in spring

Leaves lance-shaped to linear, midgreen. Flowers in racemes, pink with white throat and carmine band at base of lower lobes, tubular to bell-shaped, in summer.

Penstemon 'Port Wine' A.G.M. (Scrophulariaceae)

Common names: None
Height: 36in (90cm)
Spread: 18in (45cm)
Aspect: Sun or half shade
Soil: Well-drained, fertile
Hardiness: Zone 7
Propagation: Division, in spring

A hybrid penstemon. Leaves linear to lance-shaped, midgreen. Flowers in racemes, tubular to bell-shaped, claret with white throat, from early to late summer.

Penstemon
'Red Emperor'
(Scrophulariaceae)

Common names: None
Height: 36in (90cm)
Spread: 18in (45cm)
Aspect: Sun or half shade
Soil: Well-drained, fertile
Hardiness: Zone 7
Propagation: Division, in
spring

A hybrid cultivar. Leaves linear to
lance-shaped, midgreen. Flowers in
racemes, tubular to bell-shaped, deep
red with a white ring around mouth,
in summer.

Penstemon
'Rubicundus' A.G.M.
(Scrophulariaceae)

Common names: None
Height: 4ft (1.2m)
Spread: 18in (45cm)
Aspect: Sun or half shade
Soil: Well-drained, fertile
Hardiness: Zone 7
Propagation: Division, in
spring

Short-lived hybrid. Leaves lance-
shaped to linear, light green. Flowers
in racemes, tubular to bell-shaped,
red, mouth white, streaked red, in
summer to autumn.

Penstemon rupicola
'Diamond Lake'
(Scrophulariaceae)

Common names: None
Height: 8in (20cm)
Spread: 18in (45cm)
Aspect: Sun or half shade
Soil: Moist, well-drained
Hardiness: Zone 8
Propagation: Division in
spring

Selected form of evergreen species.
Leaves elliptic-round, toothed, thick,
blue-green. Flowers pink with white
mouths, tubular to funnel-shaped, in
racemes, early summer.

Penstemon
'Sour Grapes'
(Scrophulariaceae)

Common names: None
Height: 24in (60cm)
Spread: 18in (45cm)
Aspect: Sun or half shade
Soil: Well-drained, fertile
Hardiness: Zone 8
Propagation: Division, in
spring

A hybrid penstemon. Leaves elliptic-
ovate, midgreen. Flowers in racemes,
tubular to bell-shaped, dull lilac-blue,
with white throats, from midsummer
to midautumn.

Penstemon
'White Bedder' A.G.M.
(Scrophulariaceae)

Common names: None
Height: 28in (70cm)
Spread: 12in (30cm)
Aspect: Sun or half shade
Soil: Well-drained, fertile
Hardiness: Zone 7
Propagation: Division, in
spring

A hybrid penstemon. Leaves elliptic-
ovate, bright green. Flowers tubular
to bell-shaped, pure white, in
racemes, from midsummer to early
autumn.

Penstemon
'Whitethroat'
(Scrophulariaceae)

Common names: None
Height: 36in (90cm)
Spread: 18in (45cm)
Aspect: Sun or half shade
Soil: Well-drained, fertile
Hardiness: Zone 7
Propagation: Division, in
spring

A hybrid penstemon. Leaves lance-
shaped to linear, midgreen. Flowers in
racemes, tubular to bell-shaped,
cerise, throat pure white, from
summer to autumn.

Pentaglottis sempervirens
(Boraginaceae)

Common names: None
Height: 3ft (1m)
Spread: 3ft (1m)
Aspect: Full or half shade
Soil: Moist, humus-rich
Hardiness: Zone 7
Propagation: Seed, when
ripe or in spring; division,
in spring

Taprooted perennial. Basal leaves in
rosette, large, ovate; stem leaves
smaller, midgreen. Flowers in leafy
cymes, small, bright blue, from spring
to early summer.

Pentas lanceolata
(Rubiaceae)

Common name: Egyptian
star-clusters
Height: 6ft (2m)
Spread: 3ft (1m)
Aspect: Sun
Soil: Well-drained, fertile
Hardiness: Zone 10
Propagation: Seed, in
warmth in spring; softwood
cuttings, at any time

Evergreen from the Arabian Peninsula
and Africa. Leaves hairy, midgreen,
ovate to lance-shaped. Flowers in
domed corymbs, long-tubed, starry,
pink, spring to autumn.

Perovskia atriplicifolia
(Labiatae/Lamiaceae)

Common names: None
Height: 4ft (1.2m)
Spread: 3ft (1m)
Aspect: Sun
Soil: Well-drained, fertile
Hardiness: Zone 6
Propagation: Softwood
cuttings, in late spring; semi-ripe
cuttings, in summer

A subshrub from Afghanistan. Leaves
ovate, deeply cut, gray-green. Flowers
in tall panicles, small, tubular, lilac-
blue, from late summer to early
autumn.

Perovskia
'Blue Spire' A.G.M.
(Labiatae/Lamiaceae)

Common names: None
Height: 4ft (1.2m)
Spread: 3ft (1m)
Aspect: Sun
Soil: Well-drained, fertile
Hardiness: Zone 6
Propagation: Softwood
cuttings, in late spring; semi-ripe
cuttings, in summer

An upright subshrub, with ovate,
deeply divided, silver-gray leaves.
Flowers in panicles, tubular, violet-
blue, in late summer and early
autumn.

PERSICARIA (Polygonaceae)
Mountain fleece • Snakeweed

A genus of around 80 species of annuals, stoloniferous or
rhizomatous perennials, and a few subshrubs, from very varied
habitats worldwide. They may be hardy or half-hardy, and
deciduous to evergreen. *Persicaria* like growing in sun, as long
as they are in a moisture-retentive soil, but tolerate light shade;
some species, such as *P. bistorta,* will even tolerate dry soil.
Some members of the genus, most notably *P. affinis,*
P. cuspidatum (Zone 4), and *P. sachalinense* (Zone 4), are
rampant invaders, and best avoided in a small garden. Most
species are undemanding, easy-going plants, however, and make
excellent ground cover, or can be naturalized in a wild garden.
Some have a long flowering season. They bear small, cup-, bell-,
or funnel-shaped flowers, in densely packed spikes or racemes.
The flowers are usually long-lasting and may be red, pink, or
white; they are followed by distinctive, ovoid or 3-angled fruits,
usually brownish in color. Many of the members of the genus
were, until very recently, classified under *Polygonum,* and may
still be found under that name in old catalogs and books. The
main drawbacks of these plants are that all members of the
genus are highly allergenic, poisonous, and skin-irritant.

349

Persicaria affinis
(Polygonaceae)

Common name:
Himalayan fleece-flower
Height: 10in (25cm)
Spread: Indefinite
Aspect: Sun or half shade
Soil: Moist
Hardiness: Zone 3
Propagation: Division, in
spring or autumn

A vigorous, evergreen ground cover.
Leaves dark green, lance-shaped to
elliptic. Flowers in spikes, bright rose-
red cups, fading to pink, then brown,
midsummer to autumn.

Persicaria amplexicaulis
(Polygonaceae)

Common name: Mountain
fleece
Height: 4ft (1.2m)
Spread: 1.2m (4ft)
Aspect: Sun or half shade
Soil: Moist
Hardiness: Zone 5
Propagation: Division, in
spring or autumn

Vigorous, clump-forming perennial.
Leaves lance-shaped to ovate, pointed,
midgreen. Flowers in narrow spikes,
bright red bells, from midsummer to
early autumn.

Persicaria amplexicaulis
'Firetail' A.G.M.
(Polygonaceae)

Common name: Mountain
fleece
Height: 4ft (1.2m)
Spread: 4ft (1.2m)
Aspect: Sun or half shade
Soil: Moist
Hardiness: Zone 5
Propagation: Division, in
spring or autumn

A selected form of the species, with
flowers of larger size and brighter red,
from midsummer to early autumn.
Leaves ovate to lance-shaped, pointed,
midgreen.

Persicaria amplexicaulis
var. *pendula*
(Polygonaceae)

Common names: None
Height: 4ft (1.2m)
Spread: 4ft (1.2m)
Aspect: Sun or half shade
Soil: Moist
Hardiness: Zone 6
Propagation: Division, in
spring or autumn

A form of this vigorous, clump-
forming species, with narrow, arching
spikes of red flowers, and pale green,
ovate to lance-shaped, pointed leaves.

Persicaria bistorta subsp. *carnea* (Polygonaceae)

Common name: Snakeweed
Height: 28in (70cm)
Spread: 18in (45cm)
Aspect: Sun or half shade
Soil: Moist
Hardiness: Zone 4
Propagation: Division, in spring or autumn

A robust, clump-forming perennial. Leaves broad, ovate, pointed, veined, midgreen. Flowers in spherical spikes, deep pink, from early summer to midautumn.

Persicaria bistorta 'Superba' A.G.M. (Polygonaceae)

Common name: Snakeweed
Height: 3ft (90cm)
Spread: 3ft (90cm)
Aspect: Sun or half shade
Soil: Moist
Hardiness: Zone 4
Propagation: Division, in spring or autumn

A robust perennial from Eurasia. Leaves broad, ovate, pointed, veined, midgreen. Flowers in dense, cylindrical spikes, pink bells, over a long period in summer.

Persicaria campanulata (Polygonaceae)

Common names: None
Height: 3ft (90cm)
Spread: 3ft (90cm)
Aspect: Sun or half shade
Soil: Moist
Hardiness: Zone 8
Propagation: Division, in spring or autumn

Stoloniferous perennial. Leaves basal and stem, elliptic, hairy, veined, midgreen, white below. Flowers scented, pink bells, in loose panicles, midsummer to autumn.

Persicaria campanulata 'Rosenrot' (Polygonaceae)

Common names: None
Height: 3ft (90cm)
Spread: 3ft (90cm)
Aspect: Sun or half shade
Soil: Moist
Hardiness: Zone 8
Propagation: Division, in spring

Selected form of the species with rosy red flowers, in loose panicles, midsummer to autumn. Leaves basal and stem, elliptic, hairy, veined, midgreen, white below.

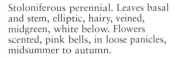

Persicaria capitata
(Polygonaceae)

Common name: Pinkhead
knotweed
Height: 3in (8cm)
Spread: Indefinite
Aspect: Sun or half shade
Soil: Moist
Hardiness: Zone 8
Propagation: Division, in
spring or autumn

Creeping, stem-rooting ground cover
from the Himalayas. Leaves ovate,
dark green, with a purple "V."
Flowers pink bells, in short-stemmed,
dense panicles, in summer.

Persicaria virginiana
'Painter's Palette'
(Polygonaceae)

Common names: None
Height: 4ft (1.2m)
Spread: 4ft (1.2m)
Aspect: Sun or half shade
Soil: Moist
Hardiness: Zone 5
Propagation: Division, in
spring or autumn

A selected form of a herbaceous
species. Leaves ovate-elliptic, with a
central "V," and variegated red,
yellow, and green. Flowers
insignificant.

Petasites japonicus
var. *giganteus* 'Variegatus'
(Asteraceae/Compositae)

Common name: Japanese
butterbur
Height: 4ft (1.2m)
Spread: 5ft (1.5m)
Aspect: Full or half shade
Soil: Moist, humus-rich,
fertile, deep
Hardiness: Zone 5
Propagation: Division, in
spring or autumn

Rhizomatous perennial. Leaves basal,
huge, reniform, toothed, green and
cream. Flowers scented, in dense
corymbs, yellowish-white, in late
winter to spring.

Phaenosperma globosa
(Poaceae)

Common names: None
Height: 5ft (1.5m)
Spread: 2ft (60cm)
Aspect: Sun
Soil: Well-drained
Hardiness: Zone 7
Propagation: Seed, in
autumn or spring

A deciduous grass. Leaves broad,
linear, long, light green with darker
ribs. Flower stems tall, with
pyramidal panicles of pale brown
flowers.

Phlomis fruticosa
AG.M.
(Labiatae/Lamiaceae)

Common names: None
Height: 3ft (1m)
Spread: 5ft (1.5m)
Aspect: Sun
Soil: Well-drained, fertile
Hardiness: Zone 7
Propagation: Seed, in
warmth in spring; softwood
cuttings, in summer

Phlomis italica
(Labiatae/Lamiaceae)

Common names: None
Height: 1ft (30cm)
Spread: 2ft (60cm)
Aspect: Sun
Soil: Well-drained, fertile
Hardiness: Zone 8
Propagation: Seed, in
warmth in spring; softwood
cuttings, in summer

Evergreen, Mediterranean subshrub.
Leaves ovate to lance-shaped, sagelike,
gray-green, wrinkled. Flowers in
whorls, dead-nettle-like, yellow, in
early and midsummer.

An evergreen subshrub from the
Balearic islands. Leaves lance-shaped
to oblong, gray-woolly. Flowers in
whorls, tubular, dead-nettlelike, lilac,
in summer.

PHLOX (Polemoniaceae)
Phlox

A genus of over 60 species, all North American except one from
Siberia. They come from three types of habitat: alpine phloxes
need a sharply drained soil and sun; woodlanders, represented
by *Phlox divaricata* and its cultivars, require a humus-rich soil
in part shade; waterside species, most notably *P. paniculata*,
have given us the modern, hybrid, border phloxes, which need a
moist, fertile soil, in sun or half shade. This group has been
hybridized extensively; some of the hybrids have large, colorful
flowers, but are shorter-lived than one might hope, given that
P. paniculata is soundly perennial; their survival depends on
their having moisture and nutrients at the roots at all times, so
they require annual top-dressing, but they dislike waterlogged
soil. They have a rich fragrance and attract bees and butterflies.
Phlox are low-allergen plants. They benefit from being lifted
and divided every few years, keeping the young growths and
discarding the woody center. Some taller varieties may need
staking. All can be devoured by slugs in spring, especially the
woodland types, so one must take action early. All are also prone
to powdery mildew in some degree; border phloxes must never
be allowed to dry out, or be enclosed closely by other plants.

Phlox adsurgens
'Wagon Wheel'
(Polemoniaceae)

Common name:
Periwinkle phlox
Height: 1ft (30cm)
Spread: 1ft (30cm)
Aspect: Half shade
Soil: Moist, well-drained,
fertile, humus-rich
Hardiness: Zone 6
Propagation: Softwood cuttings
of blind shoots, in spring

A prostrate woodlander from the
U.S.A. Leaves ovate, midgreen.
Flowers salmon-pink, salverform,
narrow-petalled, in open cymes, in
late spring and early summer.

Phlox
'Chattahoochee' A.G.M.
(Polemoniaceae)

Common names: None
Height: 6in (15cm)
Spread: 12in (30cm)
Aspect: Half shade
Soil: Moist, well-drained,
fertile, humus-rich
Hardiness: Zone 4
Propagation: Softwood
cuttings of blind shoots,
in spring

Short-lived, prostrate hybrid. Leaves
lance-shaped, purple becoming
midgreen. Flowers in cymes,
salverform, lavender-blue with a red
eye, long periods in summer to autumn.

Phlox divaricata
'Blue Dreams'
(Polemoniaceae)

Common name: Wild blue
phlox
Height: 14in (35cm)
Spread: 20in (50cm)
Aspect: Half shade
Soil: Moist, well-drained,
humus-rich, fertile
Hardiness: Zone 4
Propagation: Softwood cuttings
of blind shoots, in spring

A spreading, hybrid perennial. Leaves
ovate, hairy, midgreen. Flowers in
open cymes salverform, lavender-blue
with a dark eye, in early summer.

Phlox maculata
(Polemoniaceae)

Common name: Wild
sweet William
Height: 36in (1m)
Spread: 18in (45cm)
Aspect: Sun or half shade
Soil: Moist, fertile
Hardiness: Zone 5
Propagation: Division, in
spring or autumn

A herbaceous perennial from the
eastern U.S.A. Leaves linear,
midgreen. Flowers in cymes,
perfumed, salverform, violet, white,
or pink, in early and midsummer.

Phlox paniculata
'Fujiyama' A.G.M.
(Polemoniaceae)

Phlox paniculata
'Harlequin'
(Polemoniaceae)

Common name: Garden
phlox
Height: 30in (75cm)
Spread: 36in (90cm)
Aspect: Sun or half shade
Soil: Moist, fertile
Hardiness: Zone 4
Propagation: Division, in
spring or autumn

Common name: Garden
phlox
Height: 3ft (1m)
Spread: 3ft (1m)
Aspect: Sun or half shade
Soil: Moist, fertile
Hardiness: Zone 4
Propagation: Division, in
spring or autumn

A hybrid perennial. Leaves thin,
ovate, toothed, midgreen. Flowers
white, perfumed, salverform, in
cymes, from summer to midautumn.

A hybrid perennial. Leaves thin,
ovate, toothed, pale green, margined
ivory. Flowers in cymes, perfumed,
red-purple, from summer to early
autumn.

Phlox paniculata
'Magnificence'
(Polemoniaceae)

Phlox paniculata
'Norah Leigh'
(Polemoniaceae)

Common name: Garden
phlox
Height: 3ft (1m)
Spread: 3ft (1m)
Aspect: Sun or half shade
Soil: Moist, fertile
Hardiness: Zone 4
Propagation: Division, in
spring or autumn

Common name: Garden
phlox
Height: 3ft (1m)
Spread: 3ft (1m)
Aspect: Sun or half shade
Soil: Moist, fertile
Hardiness: Zone 4
Propagation: Division, in
spring or autumn

A hybrid perennial. Leaves thin,
ovate, toothed, midgreen. Flowers in
cymes, scented, salverform, bright,
clear pink, from summer to autumn.

A hybrid perennial. Leaves thin,
ovate, toothed, variegated pale green
and cream. Flowers in small cymes,
perfumed, pale lilac, from summer to
autumn.

Phlox paniculata 'Otley Choice' (Polemoniaceae)

Common name: Garden phlox
Height: 3ft (1m)
Spread: 3ft (1m)
Aspect: Sun or half shade
Soil: Moist, fertile
Hardiness: Zone 4
Propagation: Division, in spring or autumn

A hybrid perennial. Leaves thin, ovate, toothed, midgreen. Flowers in cymes, scented, salverform, cerise, from midsummer to autumn.

Phlox paniculata 'Starfire' (Polygonaceae)

Common name: Garden phlox
Height: 4ft (1.2m)
Spread: 3ft (90cm)
Aspect: Sun or half shade
Soil: Moist, fertile
Hardiness: Zone 4
Propagation: Division in spring or autumn

A hybrid perennial. Leaves ovate, toothed, dark green. Flowers in cymes, perfumed, salverform, deep crimson-red, from midsummer to early autumn.

Phormium cookianum 'Jester' (Agavaceae/Phormiaceae)

Common name: Fiber-lily
Height: 6ft (2m)
Spread: 10ft (3m)
Aspect: Sun
Soil: Moist, well-drained
Hardiness: Zone 8
Propagation: Division, in spring

Hybrid evergreen. Leaves linear, keeled, arching to erect, bronze and green. Flowers in panicles, tubular, green, in summer. Foliage very good for flower arrangements.

Phormium 'Sundowner' A.G.M. (Agavaceae/Phormiaceae)

Common name: Fiber-lily
Height: 6ft (2m)
Spread: 10ft (3m)
Aspect: Sun
Soil: Moist, well-drained
Hardiness: Zone 8
Propagation: Division, in spring

Evergreen hybrid. Leaves linear, keeled, arching to erect, long, bronze-green with pink margins. Flowers green-yellow, in tall panicles, in summer; good seed heads.

Phormium tenax
A.G.M.
(Agavaceae/Phormiaceae)

Common name: New
Zealand fiber-lily
Height: 12ft (4m)
Spread: 6ft (2m)
Aspect: Sun
Soil: Moist, well-drained
Hardiness: Zone 8
Propagation: Seed or
division, both in spring

A tall, evergreen perennial from New
Zealand. Leaves stiff, linear, dark
green above, blue-green below.
Flowers in tall panicles, dull red, in
summer.

Phuopsis stylosa
(Rubiaceae)

Common names: None
Height: 6in (15cm)
Spread: 30in (75cm)
Aspect: Sun or half shade
Soil: Moist, sharply
drained, fertile
Hardiness: Zone 7
Propagation: Seed, in
autumn; division, in spring

Trailing, mat-forming perennial.
Leaves in whorls, musk-scented, pale
green, elliptic, pointed. Flowers in
globular heads, tubular, small, pink,
over a long period in summer.

Phygelius aequalis
(Scrophulariaceae)

Common names: None
Height: 3ft (1m)
Spread: 3ft (1m)
Aspect: Sun
Soil: Moist, well-drained,
fertile
Hardiness: Zone 8
Propagation: Seed,
softwood cuttings or
separated suckers, all in spring

A subshrub from South Africa. Leaves
ovate, dark green. Flowers in panicles,
long, pendent, dusky pink with yellow
throats, in summer.

Phygelius aequalis
'Yellow Trumpet' A.G.M.
(Scrophulariaceae)

Common names: None
Height: 3ft (1m)
Spread: 3ft (1m)
Aspect: Sun
Soil: Moist, well-drained,
fertile
Hardiness: Zone 8
Propagation: Softwood
cuttings or separated suckers,
both in spring

A yellow sport of the species;
suckering subshrub with a long
flowering season in summer. Flowers
creamy-yellow, leaves pale green.

Phygelius × *rectus* 'Moonraker' (Scrophulariaceae)

Common names: None
Height: 5ft (1.5m)
Spread: 5ft (1.5m)
Aspect: Sun
Soil: Moist, well-drained, fertile
Hardiness: Zone 8
Propagation: Softwood cuttings or separated suckers, both in spring

An evergreen, suckering subshrub of garden origin. Leaves ovate, dark green. Flowers in panicles, tubular, curved, pale yellow, over a long period in summer.

Phygelius × *rectus* 'Salmon Leap' (Scrophulariaceae)

Common names: None
Height: 4ft (1.2m)
Spread: 5ft (1.5m)
Aspect: Sun
Soil: Moist, well-drained, fertile
Hardiness: Zone 8
Propagation: Softwood cuttings or separated suckers, both in spring

Evergreen, suckering subshrub of garden origin. Leaves ovate, dark green. Flowers in panicles, tubular, curved, deeply lobed, orange, over a long period in summer.

Phygelius × *rectus* 'Winchester Fanfare' (Scrophulariaceae)

Common names: None
Height: 5ft (1.5m)
Spread: 5ft (1.5m)
Aspect: Sun
Soil: Moist, well-drained, fertile
Hardiness: Zone 8
Propagation: Softwood cuttings or separated suckers, both in spring

An evergreen, suckering subshrub of garden origin. Leaves ovate, dark green. Flowers in panicles, pendent, tubular, dusky pink, over a long period in summer.

Physalis alkekengi var. *franchettii* (Solanaceae)

Common names: Chinese-lantern; strawberry ground-cherry
Height: 30in (75cm)
Spread: Indefinite
Aspect: Sun or half shade
Soil: Well-drained
Hardiness: Zone 6
Propagation: Seed or division, both in spring

Rhizomatous perennial from Europe and Asia. Leaves broad, ovate, bright green. Flowers solitary, white, in summer, then orange berries inside papery, red calyces.

Physostegia virginiana
(Labiatae/Lamiaceae)

Common name: Virginia
lion's-heart
Height: 4ft (1.2m)
Spread: Indefinite
Aspect: Sun or half shade
Soil: Moist, humus-rich,
fertile
Hardiness: Zone 4
Propagation: Seed, in autumn;
division, in early spring

Invasive rhizomatous ground cover.
Leaves ovate to lance-shaped,
toothed, midgreen. Flowers in
racemes, bright pink, from
midsummer to early autumn.

Physostegia virginiana
'Alba'
(Labiatae/Lamiaceae)

Common names: Virginia
lion's-heart
Height: 4ft (1.2m)
Spread: Indefinite
Aspect: Sun or half shade
Soil: Moist, humus-rich,
fertile
Hardiness: Zone 4
Propagation: Seed, in autumn;
division, in early spring

White-flowered form of the species;
invasive ground cover. Leaves ovate,
toothed, midgreen. Flowers in
racemes, white, from midsummer to
early autumn.

Physostegia virginiana
subsp. *speciosa* 'Bouquet
Rose' (Labiatae/Lamiaceae)

Common name: Virginia
lion's-heart
Height: 4ft (1.2m)
Spread: Indefinite
Aspect: Sun or half shade
Soil: Moist, humus-rich,
fertile
Hardiness: Zone 4
Propagation: Division, in
early spring

A selected form of the species, with
racemes of pale lilac-pink flowers
from midsummer to early autumn.
Leaves ovate, toothed, midgreen.
Good ground cover.

Physostegia virginiana
'Summer Snow'
(Labiatae/Lamiaceae)

Common name: Virginia
lion's-heart
Height: 4ft (1.2m)
Spread: Indefinite
Aspect: Sun or half shade
Soil: Moist, well-drained,
fertile
Hardiness: Zone 4
Propagation: Division, in
early spring

A selected form; invasive ground
cover. Leaves ovate, toothed,
midgreen. Flowers white with green
calyces, in racemes, midsummer to
early autumn.

Physostegia virginiana
subsp. *speciosa* 'Variegata'
(Labiatae/Lamiaceae)

Phyteuma orbiculare
(Campanulaceae)

Common name: Virginia
lion's-heart
Height: 4ft (1.2m)
Spread: Indefinite
Aspect: Sun or half shade
Soil: Moist, well-drained,
fertile
Hardiness: Zone 4
Propagation: Division, in
early spring

Invasive ground cover. Grown for its
ovate, toothed, grayish-green, white-
margined leaves. Racemes of purple
flowers from midsummer to early
autumn.

Common name: Ballhead
rampion
Height: 20in (50cm)
Spread: 18in (45cm)
Aspect: Sun
Soil: Well-drained, fertile
Hardiness: Zone 6
Propagation: Seed, in
autumn

A perennial from Eurasia. Leaves
elliptic to lance-shaped, toothed,
midgreen. Flowers in terminal dense
spherical clusters, blue, with
acuminate bracts, in summer.

Phytolacca americana
(Phytolaccaceae)

Phytolacca polyandra
(Phytolaccaceae)

Common name: Common
poke-berry
Height: 12ft (4m)
Spread: 3ft (1m)
Aspect: Sun or half shade
Soil: Moist, fertile
Hardiness: Zone 4
Propagation: Seed, in
warmth in early spring

A foul-smelling North American
perennial. Leaves ovate, midgreen.
Flowers white or pink, in racemes,
from midsummer to early autumn;
maroon berries extremely toxic.

Common names: None
Height: 6ft (2m)
Spread: 2ft (60cm)
Aspect: Sun or half shade
Soil: Moist, fertile
Hardiness: Zone 6
Propagation: Seed, in
warmth in early spring

Perennial from China. Leaves elliptic-
ovate, midgreen, yellow in autumn.
Pink flowers in compact racemes on
red stems in late summer, followed by
toxic, black berries.

Pilosella aurantiaca
(Asteraceae/Compositae)

Common names: None
Height: 12in (30cm)
Spread: 30in (75cm)
Aspect: Sun or half shade
Soil: Sharply drained,
fertile
Hardiness: Zone 5
Propagation: Seed or
division, in autumn or
spring

A stoloniferous perennial. Leaves in
basal rosettes, lance-shaped to elliptic,
bluish-green. Flowers in clusters of up
to 10, orange-red, daisylike, in summer.

Pimpinella major
'Rosea'
(Apiaceae/Umbelliferae)

Common names: None
Height: 3ft (90cm)
Spread: 2ft (60cm)
Aspect: Sun or half shade
Soil: Moist, fertile
Hardiness: Zone 5
Propagation: Seed, when
ripe

A taprooted perennial from Eurasia.
Leaves basal and stem, pinnate,
leaflets ovate, midgreen. Flowers
small, pink, in compound, flat
umbels, in spring.

Plantago major
'Rosularis'
(Plantaginaceae)

Common name: Broad-
leaved plantain
Height: 1ft (30cm)
Spread: 1ft (30cm)
Aspect: Sun
Soil: Sharply drained,
acidic, fertile
Hardiness: Zone 5
Propagation: Division, in
spring

Invasive perennial from Europe.
Leaves in basal rosettes, ovate, light
green. Flowering spike a scape
reduced to a rosette of green leaves,
said to resemble a rose flower.

Plantago major
'Rubrifolia'
(Plantaginaceae)

Common name: Broad-
leaved plantain
Height: 1ft (30cm)
Spread: 1ft (30cm)
Aspect: Sun
Soil: Sharply drained,
acidic, fertile
Hardiness: Zone 5
Propagation: Seed, in
autumn; division, in spring

A hardy European perennial, a weed
of lawns. Leaves in basal rosettes,
ovate, purple and green. Flowers in
slender spikes, brownish-green, in
summer.

Platycodon grandiflorus A.G.M.
(Campanulaceae)

Common name: Balloon-flower
Height: 2ft (60cm)
Spread: 1ft (30cm)
Aspect: Sun or half shade
Soil: Moist, well-drained, humus-rich, fertile
Hardiness: Zone 4
Propagation: Seed, *in situ* in spring; division or separation, in summer

Perennial from Asia. Leaves ovate, toothed, bluish-green. Flowers in clusters, open, purple-blue, 5-petalled saucers, in late summer. Late to appear, so mark position.

Platycodon grandiflorus f. albus
(Campanulaceae)

Common name: Balloon-flower
Height: 2ft (60cm)
Spread: 1ft (30cm)
Aspect: Sun or half shade
Soil: Moist, well-drained, humus-rich, fertile
Hardiness: Zone 4
Propagation: Seed, *in situ* in spring; division or separation, in summer

White-flowered form. Leaves ovate, toothed, bluish-green. Flowers pure white saucers, in late summer. Late to reappear in spring, so mark its position.

Platycodon grandiflorus 'Fuji Pink'
(Campanulaceae)

Common name: Balloon-flower
Height: 2ft (60cm)
Spread: 1ft (30cm)
Aspect: Sun or half shade
Soil: Moist, well-drained, humus-rich, fertile
Hardiness: Zone 4
Propagation: Division or separation of rooted basal shoots, both in summer

A form of the species with flowers of lilac-pink, in late summer. Leaves ovate, toothed, bluish-green. Is late to emerge in spring, so mark its position.

Plectranthus ciliatus
(Labiatae/Lamiaceae)

Common names: None
Height: 18in (45cm)
Spread: Indefinite
Aspect: Full or half shade
Soil: Any
Hardiness: Zone 9
Propagation: Seed, when ripe; division, in spring

A tender, invasive, evergreen ground cover from South Africa. Leaves ovate, toothed, bright green. Flowers in short sprays, starry, mauve, in summer to autumn.

Pleione formosana
A.G.M.
(Orchidaceae)

Common names: None
Height: 6in (15cm)
Spread: 12in (30cm)
Aspect: Half shade
Soil: Sharply drained,
humus-rich, fertile
Hardiness: Zone 8
Propagation: Division, in
spring

Terrestrial or lithophytic orchid. Single,
mid-green, lance-shaped to elliptic,
folded leaf from each pseudobulb.
Flowers pale pink, white lips spotted
brown, solitary, spring.

Pleione speciosa
(Orchidaceae)

Common names: None
Height: 3in (7cm)
Spread: 4in (10cm)
Aspect: Half shade
Soil: Sharply drained,
humus-rich, fertile
Hardiness: Zone 8
Propagation: Division, in
spring

Terrestrial or lithophytic orchid.
Single leaf from each pseudobulb,
lance-shaped, mid-green. Flowers
solitary, bright magenta with peach-
blotched lip, in spring.

Podophyllum hexandrum
(Berberidaceae)

Common names: None
Height: 18in (45cm)
Spread: 12in (30cm)
Aspect: Full or half shade
Soil: Moist, humus-rich,
fertile
Hardiness: Zone 6
Propagation: Seed, when
ripe; division, in spring or
autumn

Leaves 3- to 5-lobed, purple-blotched,
toothed. Flower solitary, single, open
cups, white with yellow anthers, in
spring to summer; edible red fruit.
Plant poisonous.

Polemonium caeruleum
(Polemoniaceae)

Common name: Jacob's-
ladder
Height: 3ft (90cm)
Spread: 1ft (30cm)
Aspect: Sun or half shade
Soil: Moist, well-drained,
fertile
Hardiness: Zone 2
Propagation: Seed or
division, both in spring

A clump-forming perennial from
Eurasia and North America. Leaves 2-
pinnate, with up to 27 oblong leaflets,
midgreen. Flowers in cymes, open,
blue bells, in early summer.

Polemonium caeruleum
subsp. *caeruleaum*
var. *album* (Polemoniaceae)

Common name: Jacob's-
ladder
Height: 3ft (90cm)
Spread: 1ft (30cm)
Aspect: Sun or half shade
Soil: Moist, well-drained,
fertile
Hardiness: Zone 2
Propagation: Seed or
division, both in spring

White form of a good low-allergen
plant. Flowers in cymes, open white
bells in early summer. Leaves 2-
pinnate, with up to 27 oblong leaflets,
midgreen.

Polemonium caeruleum
'Brise d'Anjou'
(Polemoniaceae)

Common name: Jacob's-
ladder
Height: 30in (75cm)
Spread: 12in (30cm)
Aspect: Sun or half shade
Soil: Moist, well-drained,
fertile
Hardiness: Zone 2
Propagation: Division, in
spring or autumn

A form of Jacob's ladder with
midgreen, cream-margined, 2-pinnate
leaves with up to 27 oblong leaflets.
Flowers pink, in cymes, in early
summer.

Polemonium carneum
(Polemoniaceae)

Common name: Salmon
polemonium
Height: 16in (40cm)
Spread: 8in (20cm)
Aspect: Sun or half shade
Soil: Moist, well-drained,
fertile
Hardiness: Zone 6
Propagation: Seed, in autumn
or spring; division, in spring

A hardy, clump-forming perennial
from the western U.S.A. Leaves
pinnate, leaflets ovate-elliptic,
midgreen. Flowers in cymes, pale pink
saucers, in early summer.

Polemonium carneum
'Apricot Delight'
(Polemoniaceae)

Common name: Salmon
polemonium
Height: 16in (40cm)
Spread: 8in (20cm)
Aspect: Sun or half shade
Soil: Moist, well-drained,
fertile
Hardiness: Zone 6
Propagation: Division, in
spring

A selected form of the species. Leaves
pinnate, leaflets elliptic-ovate. Flowers
large, apricot, borne over a rather
longer season than the type.

Polygala chamaebuxus A.G.M.
(Polygalaceae)

Common names:
Groundbox polygala
Height: 6in (15cm)
Spread: 12in (30cm)
Aspect: Sun or half shade
Soil: Sharply drained,
fertile, humus-rich
Hardiness: Zone 6
Propagation: Seed, in autumn;
softwood cuttings, in early summer

Dwarf, evergreen subshrub. Leaves
leathery, lance-shaped, dark green.
Flowers with yellow lips and wings,
yellow keel aging to purple, in late
spring and early summer.

Polygonatum x hybridum A.G.M.
(Convallariaceae/Liliaceae)

Common name: Common
Solomon's seal
Height: 5ft (1.5m)
Spread: 1ft (30cm)
Aspect: Sun or half shade
Soil: Moist, well-drained,
fertile, humus-rich
Hardiness: Zone 6
Propagation: Seed, in
autumn; division, in spring

Rhizomatous woodlander. Leaves
ovate to lance-shaped, midgreen.
Flowers pendent, tubular, creamy-
white, axillary, in late spring. May
bear berries. All parts toxic.

Polygonatum x hybridum 'Striatum'
(Convallariaceae/Liliaceae)

Common name: Common
Solomon's seal
Height: 5ft (1.5m)
Spread: 1ft (30cm)
Aspect: Sun or half shade
Soil: Moist, well-drained,
fertile, humus-rich
Hardiness: Zone 6
Propagation: Division, in
spring

Form of Solomon's seal with leaves
striped green and creamy-white.
Flowers pendent, tubular, creamy-
white, axillary, in late spring. May
bear berries. All parts toxic.

Polygonatum stewartianum
(Convallariaceae/Liliaceae)

Common names: None
Height: 36in (90cm)
Spread: 10in (25cm)
Aspect: Sun or half shade
Soil: Moist, well-drained,
humus-rich, fertile
Hardiness: Zone 6
Propagation: Seed, in
autumn; division, in spring

A rhizomatous perennial. Leaves in
whorls, linear to lance-shaped,
midgreen. Flowers in clusters,
pendent, tubular, pink, spring to
midsummer. May have red berries.

POLYPODIUM (Polypodaceae)
Polypody

A genus of some 75 species of evergreen and decidous ferns. They originate mainly in the tropical areas of North, Central, and South America, with a few distributed in more temperate regions, in Africa and in western Europe, including Britain with *P. cambricum*, the Welsh polypody. The majority of the species are evergreen. They vary from tender to hardy; the hardier types are terrestrial, but the more numerous tropical types are epiphytic. In moist, frost-free areas, they can be found growing on trees and damp walls, and at the other extreme on sand dunes. Terrestrial types are good colonizers, spreading by creeping rhizomes, often on the surface of the soil. This makes them excellent ground cover plants, especially in dry positions in sun or dappled shade, where they will provide greenery through the winter; they are also suitable for growing in mixed borders or rock gardens. Polypody ferns like a sharply drained but moisture-retentive soil. They are good architectural plants, with simple to pinnatifid or pinnate, occasionally more divided, fronds, with the sori arranged in rows either side of the midrib of each frond or pinna. They are borne along the rhizomes in double rows, seemingly at random.

Polypodium cambricum 'Omnilacerum Oxford' (Polypodiaceae)

Common names: None
Height: 2ft (60cm)
Spread: Indefinite
Aspect: Sun or half shade
Soil: Sharply drained, alkaline, humus-rich, fertile
Hardiness: Zone 6
Propagation: Spores, in warmth when ripe; division, in spring or autumn

A deciduous, terrestrial fern from Europe. Fronds tall, erect, lance-shaped to oblong, pinnate, pinnae lance-shaped, deeply cut, midgreen. Sori yellow in winter.

Polypodium vulgare 'Cornubiense' (Polypodiaceae)

Common name: Common polypody
Height: 16in (40cm)
Spread: Indefinite
Aspect: Sun or half shade
Soil: Sharply drained, humus-rich, fertile
Hardiness: Zone 3
Propagation: Spores, in warmth when ripe; division, in autumn or spring

An evergreen, terrestrial or epiphytic fern from Eurasia and Africa. Fronds thin, leathery, 3-pinnate, pinnae oblong to linear, dark green.

POLYSTICHUM (Dryopteridaceae)
Holly fern • Shield fern

A genus of some 200 or so terrestrial, usually evergreen, rhizomatous ferns from many and varied habitats all over the world. Shield ferns are generally regarded as some of the most desirable and garden-worthy ferns in cultivation. They are easy to grow and remarkably trouble-free plants, provided that their simple needs are met; they require good drainage and a moisture-retentive, fertile soil that is preferably neutral or acid, although they will tolerate slightly alkaline conditions. Due to their diverse natural ranges, they vary from hardy to tender. They are mostly shade-lovers (although *P. setiferum* 'Acutilobum' will grow in sun, and almost anywhere); they are even tolerant of dry conditions, making them a good choice for the notoriously difficult areas of dry shade under trees. Shield ferns are excellent subjects for a fernery, and also suit a mixed border. They bear handsome, often lance-shaped fronds, which are pinnate to 3-pinnate. The pinnae are hollylike, often with pointed lobes, giving rise to one of the common names. The old foliage should be removed in late spring as the new growth is about to unfold, to give the fronds space to develop when they appear in early summer.

Polystichum setiferum
A.G.M.
(Aspidaceae/Dryopteridaceae)

Common name: Soft shield fern
Height: 4ft (1.2m)
Spread: 3ft (90cm)
Aspect: Full or half shade
Soil: Well-drained, humus-rich, fertile
Hardiness: Zone 7
Propagation: Spores, when ripe; division, in spring; offsets, in autumn

A rhizomatous, terrestrial European fern. Fronds in "shuttlecocks," 2-pinnate, lance-shaped, midgreen. Lobes of pinnae ovate, toothed, angled obtusely from midrib.

Polystichum setiferum
'Pulcherrimum Bevis' A.G.M.
(Aspidaceae/Dryopteridaceae)

Common name: Soft shield fern
Height: 18in (45cm)
Spread: 3ft (90cm)
Aspect: Full or half shade
Soil: Well-drained, humus-rich, fertile
Hardiness: Zone 4
Propagation: Spores, when ripe; division, in spring; offsets, in autumn

Rhizomatous fern from North America. Fronds in a "shuttlecock," narrow, lance-shaped, pinnate, pinnae like holly, dark green. Fertile fronds narrow sharply to tip.

Polystichum setiferum
'Congestum'
(Aspidaceae/Dryopteridaceae)

Common name: Soft
shield fern
Height: 20in (50cm)
Spread: 2ft (60cm)
Aspect: Full or half shade
Soil: Well-drained, humus-
rich, fertile
Hardiness: Zone 7
Propagation: Spores, when ripe;
division, in spring; offsets, in autumn

Evergreen, rhizomatous, hardy fern. A
very compact, congested form of the
species; the congestion of the fronds is
often combined with cresting.

Pontederia cordata
A.G.M.
(Pontederiaceae)

Common name: Pickerel-
weed
Height: 4ft (1.2m)
Spread: 32in (80cm)
Aspect: Sun
Soil: Marginal aquatic
Hardiness: Zone 3
Propagation: Seed, when
ripe; division, in late spring

A marginal aquatic from the
Americas. Leaves broadly ovate, erect,
floating and submerged, glossy-green.
Flowers in closely packed spikes,
tubular, blue, late summer.

POTENTILLA (Rosaceae)
Cinquefoil

A genus of some 500 species of shrubs and clump-forming
subshrubs, as well as a few annuals and biennials. They come
from habitats across the northern hemisphere, ranging from
mountain to grassland. Cinquefoils have 3- to 7-palmate or
pinnate leaves, and saucer- or cup-shaped flowers in colors from
yellow to red, as well as some in white or pink. The shrubby
types, derived from *Potentilla fruticosa*, make good low
hedging. The clump-forming subshrubs are used extensively in
beds and borders because of their long flowering season, and
are hybrids derived from *P. nepalensis* and *P. atrosanguinea*
(Zone 5). They have attractive, 5-palmate leaves, which closely
resemble the leaves of strawberry plants. The flowers are the
typical saucer- or cup-shape, and are borne in panicles or cymes
over a long period from spring to autumn, in a range of colors.
They like a position in sun. The soil should be well-drained, and
poor to moderately fertile; if it is too rich, the plants will
produce foliage at the expense of flowers. They benefit from
being cut back hard in autumn. *P. anserina* is very invasive, and
should be avoided in the garden. Cinquefoils are low-allergen
plants; the flowers attract bees and are good for cutting.

Potentilla
'Blazeaway'
(Rosaceae)

Common name:
Cinquefoil
Height: 18in (45cm)
Spread: 2ft (60cm)
Aspect: Sun
Soil: Well-drained, poor
Hardiness: Zone 5
Propagation: Division, in
autumn or spring

Hybrid cultivar. Leaves pinnate; 5 to 7
mid-green, oblong leaflets. Flowers
large, single, orange with a red band
around a dark center, in cymes, early
to late summer.

Potentilla
'Flamenco'
(Rosaceae)

Common name:
Cinquefoil
Height: 18in (45cm)
Spread: 24in (60cm)
Aspect: Sun
Soil: Well-drained, poor
Hardiness: Zone 5
Propagation: Division, in
spring or autumn

A clump-forming hybrid. Leaves
palmate, leaflets narrow, elliptic,
midgreen. Flowers in cymes, single,
bright scarlet with a black center,
from late spring to midsummer.

Potentilla fruticosa
(Rosaceae)

Common name: Bush
cinquefoil
Height: 3ft (1m)
Spread: 5ft (1.5m)
Aspect: Sun
Soil: Well-drained, poor
Hardiness: Zone 2
Propagation: Seed, in
spring or autumn; greenwood
cuttings, in early summer

A deciduous subshrub. Leaves
pinnate; 5 to 7 narrow, oblong, dark
green leaflets. Flowers in cymes of up
to 3, yellow saucers, from spring to
autumn.

Potentilla fruticosa
'Abbotswood Silver'
(Rosaceae)

Common name: Bush
cinquefoil
Height: 3ft (1m)
Spread: 5ft (1.5m)
Aspect: Sun
Soil: Well-drained, poor
Hardiness: Zone 2
Propagation: Greenwood
cuttings, in early summer

A selected form of shrubby cinquefoil,
with pinnate leaves of dark blue-
green, and saucer-shaped, white
flowers from late spring to
midautumn.

369

Potentilla nepalensis
'Miss Willmott' A.G.M.
(Rosaceae)

Common name: Nepal
cinquefoil
Height: 18in (45cm)
Spread: 2ft (60cm)
Aspect: Sun
Soil: Well-drained, poor
Hardiness: Zone 5
Propagation: Division, in
autumn or spring

Hybrid cultivar. Leaves 5-palmate,
leaflets obovate, hairy, toothed,
midgreen. Flowers in loose cymes,
cherry with darker pink center, all
summer.

Potentilla recta
'Warrenii'
(Rosaceae)

Common name: Sulfur
cinquefoil
Height: 2ft (60cm)
Spread: 18in (45cm)
Aspect: Sun
Soil: Well-drained, poor
Hardiness: Zone 4
Propagation: Division, in
spring or autumn

A selected form of the species. Leaves
5- to 7-palmate, leaflets oblong,
toothed, midgreen. Flowers in loose
cymes, canary yellow, from early to
late summer.

Potentilla x tonguei
(Rosaceae)

Common name:
Tormentilla cinquefoil
Height: 4in (10cm)
Spread: 12in (30cm)
Aspect: Sun
Soil: Well-drained, poor
Hardiness: Zone 5
Propagation: Division, in
spring or autumn

Clump-forming garden hybrid. Leaves
3- to 5-palmate, leaflets obovate, dark
green. Flowers solitary or in cymes,
flat, apricot saucers with a red eye, in
summer.

Pratia pedunculata
'County Park'
(Campanulaceae)

Common names: None
Height: 1in (3cm)
Spread: Indefinite
Aspect: Full or deep shade
Soil: Humus-rich, fertile
Hardiness: Zone 7
Propagation: Division, at
any time

Creeping, mat-forming perennial from
Australia. Leaves ovate, midgreen.
Flowers almost stemless, small, deep
blue stars, in summer. Excellent
ground cover.

PRIMULA (Primulaceae)
Primrose • Primula

A large genus of over 400 species of perennials, mostly herbaceous, but some evergreen and woody. A few species are from the southern hemisphere, but the majority of them originate in the northern hemisphere; nearly half of those from the northern hemisphere are native to the Himalayas. Their range of habitats is very wide, from mountains to marshes, and their botanical classification is complex: the species have given rise to an abundance of cultivars. Of the large number of botanical groups, some are good rock-garden plants and a few have value as border plants; others require alpine house conditions, or a warm greenhouse or conservatory, and some are so difficult to cultivate that they are for the enthusiast only. All have basal rosettes of leaves that range from linear to ovate in shape. The flowers are usually salverform, but may be bell- or funnel-shaped or even tubular, and may be borne among the leaves or in whorls, umbels, or racemes on upright stalks. The color range in species includes yellow, orange, white, and shades of pink and purple; cultivars are often intensely colored or boldly patterned. Many members of the genus are highly allergenic, and contact with the foliage may cause skin irritation.

Primula auricula hort.
(B) A.G.M.
(Primulaceae)

Common name: Auricula primrose
Height: 8in (20cm)
Spread: 8in (20cm)
Aspect: Sun or half shade
Soil: Moist, well-drained, humus-rich, fertile
Hardiness: Zone 3
Propagation: Seed, when ripe or in spring; division, over winter

Evergreen hybrid. Leaves obovate, shiny, gray-green, white-mealy sometimes. Flowers in arched umbels, large, salverform, purple with a cream center, in spring.

Primula bulleyana
(4) A.G.M.
(Primulaceae)

Common name: Bulleys primrose
Height: 2ft (60cm)
Spread: 2ft (60cm)
Aspect: Half shade
Soil: Moist, acidic, deep, humus-rich
Hardiness: Zone 6
Propagation: Seed, when ripe or late winter to spring; division, in autumn or spring

Candelabra primula from China. Leaves ovate, toothed, midgreen. Flowers in whorls, salverform, red, aging quickly to orange, in summer.

Primula capitata
(5)
(Primulaceae)

Common names:
Purplehead primrose
Height: 16in (40cm)
Spread: 8in (20cm)
Aspect: Half shade
Soil: Moist, acidic, deep, humus-rich
Hardiness: Zone 5
Propagation: Seed, when ripe or late
winter to spring; division, in autumn
or spring

Short-lived perennial from India,
Tibet, and Bhutan. Leaves lance-
shaped, toothed, mealy, pale green.
Flowers in flat racemes, tubular, dark
purple, early to late summer.

Primula denticulata
(9) A.G.M.
(Primulaceae)

Common name:
Himalayan primrose
Height: 18in (45cm)
Spread: 18in (45cm)
Aspect: Sun or half shade
Soil: Moist, acidic, deep, humus-rich
Hardiness: Zone 5
Propagation: Seed, when ripe or late
winter to spring; division, in autumn
or spring

Vigorous primula from the
Himalayas. Leaves spoon-shaped,
white-mealy below. Flowers open
bells, purple, yellow-eyed, in tight,
globular umbels, in early summer.

Primula denticulata
var. alba (9)
(Primulaceae)

Common name: White
Himalayan primrose
Height: 18in (45cm)
Spread: 18in (45cm)
Aspect: Sun or half shade
Soil: Moist, well-drained, acidic, deep,
humus-rich
Hardiness: Zone 5
Propagation: Seed late winter to
spring; division, in autumn or spring

Pure white-flowered form of the
species. Tight, globular umbels of
flowers in early summer. Good for
lighting up a semishady corner.

Primula
'Inverewe' (4) A.G.M.
(Primulaceae)

Common name:
Candelabra primrose
Height: 30in (75cm)
Spread: 24in (60cm)
Aspect: Half shade
Soil: Moist, acidic, deep,
humus-rich
Hardiness: Zone 6
Propagation: Division, in autumn or
spring

A hybrid candelabra primula. Leaves
oval to lance-shaped, toothed, coarse,
midgreen. Flowers in whorls,
salverform, scarlet, in summer.

Primula japonica
(4) A.G.M.
(Primulaceae)

Common name: Japanese
primrose
Height: 18in (45cm)
Spread: 18in (45cm)
Aspect: Half shade
Soil: Moist, acidic, deep, humus-rich
Hardiness: Zone 5
Propagation: Seed, when ripe or late
winter to early spring; division, in
autumn or spring

Vigorous perennial from Japan.
Leaves obovate, toothed, midgreen.
Flowers in whorls of up to 25,
salverform, pink and purple, in late
spring and early summer.

Primula japonica
'Alba' (4)
(Primulaceae)

Common name: White
Japanese primrose
Height: 18in (45cm)
Spread: 18in (45cm)
Aspect: Half shade
Soil: Moist, acidic, deep, humus-rich
Hardiness: Zone 5
Propagation: Seed, when ripe or late
winter to early spring; division, in
autumn or spring

Flowers in whorls of up to 25,
salverform, white, in late spring and
early summer. Excellent for lighting
up a semishady corner, but must have
moisture at all times.

CLASSIFICATION OF PRIMULA
by Smith and Forrest (1928),
modified by Smith and Fletcher
(1941–49)

Of most interest as garden
perennials are those from Groups
2, 4, 5, 9, 17, 26, 30, and B.

Group 1 Amethystina

Group 2 Auricula

Group 3 Bullatae

Group 4 Candelabra

Group 5 Capitatae

Group 6 Carolinella

Group 7 Cortusoides

Group 8 Cuneifolia

Group 9 Denticulata

Group 10 Dryadifolia

Group 11 Farinosae

Group 12 Floribundae

Group 13 Grandis

Group 14 Malacoides

Group 15 Malvaceae

Group 16 Minutissimae

Group 17 Muscarioides

Group 18 Nivales

Group 19 Obconica

Group 20 Parryi

Group 21 Petiolares

Group 22 Pinnatae

Group 23 Pycnoloba

Group 24 Reinii

Group 25 Rotundifolia

Group 26 Sikkimensis

Group 27 Sinenses

Group 28 Soldanelloideae

Group 29 Souliei

Group 30 Vernales

Group A Alpine Auricula

Group B Border Auricula

Group D Double

Group Poly Polyanthus

Group Prim Primrose

Group S Show auricula

Primula juliae
(30)
(Primulaceae)

Common names: None
Height: 4in (10cm)
Spread: 10in (25cm)
Aspect: Sun or half shade
Soil: Moist, well-drained,
acidic, deep, humus-rich, fertile
Hardiness: Zone 5
Propagation: Seed, when ripe or
late winter to early spring; division,
in autumn or spring

A primula from the Caucasus. Leaves
in basal rosettes, round, scalloped,
dark green. Flowers solitary, magenta
saucers, on long stems, in spring and
summer.

Primula marginata
(2) A.G.M.
(Primulaceae)

Common name: Silveredge
primrose
Height: 6in (15cm)
Spread: 12in (30cm)
Aspect: Sun or half shade,
shaded from midday sun
Soil: Moist, sharply drained, alkaline
Hardiness: Zone 7
Propagation: Seed, when ripe or in
late winter to early spring

An auricula primula from the Alps.
Leaves obovate, toothed, midgreen.
Flowers in umbels, of up to 20,
perfumed, lavender-blue cups, with
white-mealy eyes.

Primula prolifera
(4) A.G.M.
(Primulaceae)

Common name:
Candelabra primrose
Height: 2ft (60cm)
Spread: 2ft (60cm)
Aspect: Half shade
Soil: Moist, acidic, deep, humus-rich
Hardiness: Zone 6
Propagation: Seed, when ripe or late
winter to early spring; division, in
autumn or spring

Primula from India, Myanmar, China
and Indonesia. Leaves dark green,
toothed, spoon-shaped. Flowers in
whorls, scented, white-mealy, yellow,
in early summer.

Primula pulverulenta
(4) A.G.M.
(Primulaceae)

Common name: Silverdust
primrose
Height: 3ft (90cm)
Spread: 2ft (60cm)
Aspect: Half shade
Soil: Moist, acidic, humus-rich, deep
Hardiness: Zone 6
Propagation: Seed, when ripe or late
winter to early spring; division, in
autumn or spring

A primula from wet areas of China.
Leaves obovate, toothed, midgreen.
Flowers in whorls, tubular, deep red
with dark eyes, in late spring and
early summer.

Primula rosea
(11) A.G.M.
(Primulaceae)

Common names: None
Height: 8in (20cm)
Spread: 8in (20cm)
Aspect: Half shade
Soil: Moist, acidic, deep,
humus-rich
Hardiness: Zone 6
Propagation: Seed, when ripe or in
late winter to early spring; division,
in autumn or spring

Perennial from wet Himalayan
meadows. Leaves obovate, toothed,
bronze turning midgreen. Flowers in
umbels of up to 12, pinkish-red with
a yellow eye, in spring.

Primula sikkimensis
(26)
(Primulaceae)

Common name: Sikkim
primrose
Height: 3ft (90cm)
Spread: 2ft (60cm)
Aspect: Half shade
Soil: Moist, acidic, deep, humus-rich
Hardiness: Zone 6
Propagation: Seed, when ripe or late
winter to early spring; division, in
autumn or spring

Perennial from wet Himalayan
meadows. Leaves oblong, toothed,
shiny green. Flowers in umbels,
pendent, funnel-shaped, yellow, white-
mealy, late spring and early summer.

Primula veris
(30) A.G.M.
(Primulaceae)

Common name: Cowslip primrose
Height: 10in (25cm)
Spread: 10in (25cm)
Aspect: Sun or half shade
Soil: Moist, well-drained,
acidic, humus-rich
Hardiness: Zone 5
Propagation: Seed, when ripe or late
winter to early spring; division, in
autumn or spring

A perennial from Eurasia, including
Britain. Leaves ovate, midgreen.
Flowers in umbels, perfumed,
pendent, salverform, deep yellow, in
mid- to late spring.

Primula vialii
(17) A.G.M.
(Primulaceae)

Common name: Littons
primrose
Height: 2ft (60cm)
Spread: 1ft (30cm)
Aspect: Half shade
Soil: Moist, acidic, deep, humus-rich
Hardiness: Zone 7
Propagation: Seed, in late winter to
early spring; division, in autumn or
spring

Perennial from wetlands in China.
Leaves broad, lance-shaped, toothed,
midgreen. Spikes of many, pendent,
tubular flowers, violet opening from
red buds, in summer.

Primula vulgaris
(30)
(Primulaceae)

Common name: English
primrose
Height: 8in (20cm)
Spread: 12in (30cm)
Aspect: Half shade
Soil: Moist, acidic, deep,
humus-rich
Hardiness: Zone 6
Propagation: Seed, in early spring;
division, in autumn or spring

Perennial from Europe and Turkey.
Leaves evergreen in mild areas,
obovate, toothed, veined, bright green.
Clusters of pale yellow, scented, saucer
flowers, early to late spring.

Prunella grandiflora
(Labiatae/Lamiaceae)

Common name: Bigflower
self-heal
Height: 6in (15cm)
Spread: 4ft (1.2m)
Aspect: Sun or half shade
Soil: Any
Hardiness: Zone 5
Propagation: Seed, in spring;
division, in spring or autumn

An invasive, ground-covering
perennial from Europe. Leaves ovate,
toothed, dark green. Flowers in
whorls, on upright leafy spikes,
purple, in summer.

Prunella grandiflora
'Pink Loveliness'
(Labiatae/Lamiaceae)

Common name: Bigflower
self-heal
Height: 6in (15cm)
Spread: 4ft (1.2m)
Aspect: Sun or half shade
Soil: Any
Hardiness: Zone 5
Propagation: Seed, in
spring; division, in spring
or autumn

Form of the species with clear pink
flowers in whorls on upright leafy
spikes, in summer. Invasive ground
cover, only for a wild or woodland
garden.

Pulmonaria angustifolia
A.G.M.
(Boraginaceae)

Common name: Cowslip
bungwort
Height: 12in (30cm)
Spread: 18in (45cm)
Aspect: Full or half shade
Soil: Moist, humus-rich,
fertile
Hardiness: Zone 3
Propagation: Seed, when ripe;
division, after flowering or in autumn

Rhizomatous European perennial;
excellent ground cover in shade.
Leaves lance-shaped, midgreen.
Flowers on erect stems, blue, funnel-
shaped, from early to late spring.

Pulmonaria officinalis
(Boraginaceae)

Common name: Common
lungwort
Height: 10in (25cm)
Spread: 2ft (60cm)
Aspect: Full or half shade
Soil: Moist, humus-rich,
fertile
Hardiness: Zone 6
Propagation: Seed, when ripe;
division, after flowering or in autumn

Rhizomatous, evergreen ground cover.
Leaves ovate, midgreen, spotted
white. Flowers tubular, pink, turning
violet, then blue, in terminal cymes,
early to late spring.

Pulmonaria rubra
'Bowles' Red'
(Boraginaceae)

Common name: Red
lungwort
Height: 16in (40cm)
Spread: 36in (90cm)
Aspect: Full or partial shade
Soil: Moist, humus-rich,
fertile
Hardiness: Zone 5
Propagation: Seed, when ripe;
division, after flowering or in autumn

Rhizomatous, evergreen ground cover.
Leaves elliptic, bright green with pale
green spots. Flowers in cymes, coral-
red, funnel-shaped, from late winter
to midspring.

Pulmonaria saccharata
(Boraginaceae)

Common name:
Bethlehem sage
Height 1ft (30cm)
Spread: 2ft (60cm)
Aspect: Full or half shade
Soil: Moist, humus-rich,
fertile
Hardiness: Zone 3
Propagation: Seed, when ripe;
division, after flowering or in autumn

Rhizomatous, evergreen ground cover
from Italy and France. Leaves elliptic,
spotted white. Flowers pink, turning
blue, funnel-shaped, in cymes, late
winter to late spring.

Pulsatilla alpina
subsp. *apiifolia* A.G.M.
(Ranunculaceae)

Common name: Alpine
anemone
Height: 12in (30cm)
Spread: 8in (20cm)
Aspect: Sun
Soil: Sharply drained,
acidic, humus-rich,
Hardiness: Zone 5
Propagation: Seed, as soon
as ripe; root cuttings, in winter

A clump-forming perennial. Leaves 2-
pinnate, hairy, midgreen. Flowers pale
yellow cups, petals silky-hairy, in
spring, followed by attractive seed
heads.

Pulsatilla vulgaris
A.G.M.
(Ranunculaceae)

Common name:
Pasqueflower
Height: 8in (20cm)
Spread: 8in (20cm)
Aspect: Sun
Soil: Sharply drained,
fertile
Hardiness: Zone 5
Propagation: Seed, as soon
as ripe; root cuttings, in winter

A clump-forming perennial. Leaves
pinnate, leaflets pinnatisect, lobes
linear, light green. Flowers solitary,
cup-shaped, silky-hairy, purple, in
spring. Dislikes transplantation.

Pulsatilla vulgaris
'Alba' A.G.M.
(Ranunculaceae)

Common name: White
pasqueflower
Height: 8in (20cm)
Spread: 8in (20cm)
Aspect: Sun
Soil: Sharply drained,
fertile
Hardiness: Zone 5
Propagation: Seed, as soon
as ripe

Differs from the species in its white,
silky-hairy, cup-shaped flowers.
Leaves pinnate, leaflets pinnatisect,
lobes linear, light green. Dislikes
transplantation.

Pulsatilla vulgaris rosea
(Ranunculaceae)

Common name: Pink
pasqueflower
Height: 8in (20cm)
Spread: 8in (20cm)
Aspect: Sun
Soil: Sharply drained,
fertile
Hardiness: Zone 5
Propagation: Seed, as soon
as ripe; root cuttings, in winter

Pink form of the pasque flower with
silky-hairy, cup-shaped flowers. Very
handsome leaves, pinnate, leaflets
pinnatisect, lobes linear, light green.
Dislikes transplantation.

Pulsatilla vulgaris
var. rubra
(Ranunculaceae)

Common name: Red
pasqueflower
Height: 8in (20cm)
Spread: 8in (20cm)
Aspect: Sun
Soil: Sharply drained,
fertile
Hardiness: Zone 5
Propagation: Seed, as soon
as ripe; root cuttings, in winter

Red form of the species. Leaves
pinnate, leaflets pinnatisect, lobes
linear, light green. Flowers solitary,
cup-shaped, silky-hairy, in spring.
Dislikes transplantation.

Puschkinia scilloides
var. *libanotica*
(Hyacinthaceae/Liliaceae)

Common name: Striped
squill
Height: 8in (20cm)
Spread: 2in (5cm)
Aspect: Sun or half shade
Soil: Well-drained
Hardiness: Zone 5
Propagation: Offsets, in
summer after foliage dies
down

Bulbous plant from the Lebanon and
Turkey. Leaves basal, paired,
semierect, linear, midgreen. Flowers
open bell-shaped, in dense racemes of
up to 10, white, spring.

Ramonda myconi
A.G.M.
(Gesneriaceae)

Common name: Rosette-
mullein
Height: 4in (10cm)
Spread: 6in (15cm)
Aspect: Half shade
Soil: Moist, well-drained,
humus-rich, fertile
Hardiness: Zone 6
Propagation: Seed, as soon
as ripe; leaf cuttings, in autumn

Slow-growing, rosette-forming
evergreen. Leaves spoon-shaped,
crinkled, hairy, dark green. Flowers in
cymes or solitary, lilac-blue, in late
spring and early summer.

RANUNCULUS (Ranunculaceae)
Buttercup

A genus of some 400 species of annuals, biennials, and
perennials from temperate regions of both hemispheres. They
come from very varied habitats, such that it is not possible to
generalize about their cultural requirements. They are variably
hardy, and may be evergreen or deciduous. The root system can
be fibrous, tuberous, rhizomatous, or fleshy and suckering.
Some are bog plants, some originate in high alpine conditions,
some are woodlanders, and some can be kept only in an alpine
house in wet countries because they need a dry summer
dormancy. A good number, however, are reliably hardy, easy to
cultivate, and suitable for a mixed border. Their foliage may be
basal or stem, and the leaf shape varies widely. They are grown
for their 5-petalled, cup-, bowl-, or saucer-shaped flowers,
which are usually yellow, but also orange, red, pink, or white,
and borne in spring or summer, or sometimes in autumn.
R. acris (Zone 5), *R. ficaria,* and *R. repens* are invasive weeds,
and best kept out of beds or borders, and reserved for the wild
or woodland garden. Some species are skin-irritant, whilst
others are poisonous, and all appear to be highly allergenic, so
allergic gardeners should treat them with caution.

Ranunculus acris 'Flore Pleno' (Ranunculaceae)

Common name: Tall buttercup
Height: 3ft (90cm)
Spread: 10in (25cm)
Aspect: Sun
Soil: Moist, well-drained, humus-rich
Hardiness: Zone 5
Propagation: Seed, when ripe; division, in spring or autumn

Leaves ovate, palmately 3- to 7-lobed, toothed. Flowers in panicles, double, dazzling yellow, in early and midsummer. Unlike the single form, this is not invasive.

Ranunculus aquatilis (Ranunculaceae)

Common name: Water buttercup
Height: Nil
Spread: Indefinite
Aspect: Sun
Soil: Marginal aquatic
Hardiness: Zone 5
Propagation: Seed, when ripe; division, in spring or autumn

Spreading, evergreen, aquatic plant. Leaves floating and submerged, round to reniform, deeply divided, midgreen. Flowers solitary white saucers, surface-borne, in summer.

Ranunculus bulbosus 'F.M. Burton' (Ranunculaceae)

Common name: Bulbous buttercup
Height: 30in (75cm)
Spread: 12in (30cm)
Aspect: Sun or half shade
Soil: Moist, well-drained, fertile
Hardiness: Zone 7
Propagation: Offsets, in spring or autumn

Selected form of a bulbous species. Leaves basal and stem, ovate, trilobed, dark green. Flowers in panicles of a few glossy, pale cream saucers, late spring and early summer.

Ranunculus cortusifolius (Ranunculaceae)

Common names: None
Height: 4ft (1.2m)
Spread: 2ft (60cm)
Aspect: Sun
Soil: Moist, well-drained, fertile
Hardiness: Zone 9
Propagation: Seed, when ripe; division, in spring or autumn

Tender perennial from the Canary Islands, the Azores, and Madeira. Leaves basal, leathery, rounded, toothed, midgreen. Flowers in corymbs, scented, yellow.

Ranunculus creticus
(**Ranunculaceae**)

Common name: Crete
buttercup
Height: 12in (30cm)
Spread: 6in (15cm)
Aspect: Half shade
Soil: Moist, well-drained,
fertile
Hardiness: Zone 8
Propagation: Seed, when ripe;
division, in spring or autumn

Pubescent perennial from Crete. Basal
leaves rounded, hairy, 5-lobed, stem
leaves midgreen. Flowers large,
several to a stem, yellow, in spring.

Ranunculus ficaria
(**Ranunculaceae**)

Common name: Lesser-
celandine
Height: 2in (5cm)
Spread: 18in (45cm)
Aspect: Full or half shade
Soil: Moist, humus-rich
Hardiness: Zone 5
Propagation: Seed, when
ripe; division, in spring or
autumn

A tuberous perennial with axillary
bulbils; highly invasive. Leaves broad,
heart-shaped, scalloped, dark green.
Flowers solitary, yellow or orange
cups, in spring.

Ranunculus gramineus
A.G.M.
(**Ranunculaceae**)

Common name: Grassy
buttercup
Height: 12in (30cm
Spread: 8in (20cm)
Aspect: Sun or half shade
Soil: Moist, well-drained,
fertile
Hardiness: Zone 7
Propagation: Seed, when ripe;
division, in spring or autumn

A clump-forming perennial. Leaves
basal, grassy, linear, glaucous green.
Flowers on branched stems, up to 3
on a stem, lemon-yellow, in late
spring and early summer.

Ranunculus lingua
(**Ranunculaceae**)

Common names: None
Height: 4ft (1.2m)
Spread: 6ft (2m)
Aspect: Sun
Soil: Marginal aquatic
Hardiness: Zone 4
Propagation: Seed, when
ripe; division, in spring or
autumn

A large aquatic marginal. Leaves on
non-flowering stems heart-shaped, on
flowering stems linear. Flowers yellow,
solitary or in few-flowered panicles, in
early summer.

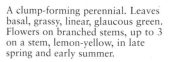

Ranunculus lyalii
(Ranunculaceae)

Common name: Lyall
buttercup
Height: 36in (1m)
Spread: 14in (35cm)
Aspect: Sun or half shade
Soil: Moist, well-drained,
fertile
Hardiness: Zone 6
Propagation: Seed, when ripe;
division, in spring or autumn

Rhizomatous perennial from New
Zealand. Leaves basal, rounded,
leathery, peltate, dark green,
evergreen in mild areas. Flowers in
panicles, white cups, in summer.

Ranunculus psilostachys
(Ranunculaceae)

Common names: None
Height: 12in (30cm)
Spread: 8in (20cm)
Aspect: Sun
Soil: Moist, well-drained,
fertile
Hardiness: Zone 6
Propagation: Seed, when
ripe; division, after flowering

Tuberous, spreading plant from
Turkey and the Balkans. Leaves basal,
3-lobed, segments obovate, toothed,
hairy below. Flowers upward-facing,
yellow, early summer.

Ratibida columnifera
(Asteraceae/Compositae)

Common name: Prairie
cone-flower
Height: 3ft (90cm)
Spread: 1ft (30cm)
Aspect: Sun
Soil: Dry, well-drained,
fertile
Hardiness: Zone 3
Propagation: Seed, in early spring;
division, in spring, when young

Perennial from North America and
Mexico. Leaves pinnate, hairy, gray-
green. Flowers daisylike, rays reflexed,
yellow, disc brown, columnar, early
summer to early autumn.

Rehmannia elata
(Scrophulariaceae)

Common name: Beverly-
bells rehmannia
Height: 4ft (1.2m)
Spread: 20in (50cm)
Aspect: Sun
Soil: Well-drained, humus-
rich, fertile
Hardiness: Zone 9
Propagation: Seed, in warmth in late
winter; separated runners, in spring

Rosette-forming perennial. Leaves
obovate, toothed, veined, hairy.
Flowers in leafy racemes, tubular,
semipendent, pink with spotted
throats, from summer to autumn.

Rehmannia glutinosa A.G.M. (Scrophulariaceae)

Common names: None
Height: 1ft (30cm)
Spread: 1ft (30cm)
Aspect: Sun
Soil: Well-drained, humus-rich, fertile
Hardiness: Zone 9
Propagation: Seed, in warmth in late winter; separated runners, in spring

Leaves in rosettes, obovate, scalloped, veined. Flowers pendent, tubular, reddish-brown with purple veins and pale brown lips, in racemes, midspring to summer.

Reineckea carnea (Convallariaceae/Liliaceae)

Common names: None
Height: 8in (20cm)
Spread: 2ft (60cm)
Aspect: Half shade
Soil: Moist, well-drained, acidic, humus-rich
Hardiness: Zone 7
Propagation: Seed, when ripe; division, in spring

Rhizomatous evergreen. Leaves arching, linear, glossy, bright green. Flowers shallow pink cups fading to white, in dense spikes, in late spring. Red berries in warm areas.

Rheum 'Ace of Hearts' (Polygonaceae)

Common name: Rhubarb
Height: 4ft (1.2m)
Spread: 4ft (1.2m)
Aspect: Sun or half shade
Soil: Moist, deep, humus-rich
Hardiness: Zone 7
Propagation: Seed, in autumn; division, in early spring

A rhizomatous, hybrid perennial. Leaves large, heart-shaped, dark green, veined red. Flowers in panicles, tiny, pink stars, in mid- and late summer.

Rheum palmatum var. *tanguticum* (Polygonaceae)

Common name: Rhubarb
Height: 6ft (2m)
Spread: 6ft (2m)
Aspect: Sun or half shade
Soil: Moist, humus-rich, fertile
Hardiness: Zone 7
Propagation: Seed, in autumn; division, in early spring

Rhizomatous perennial. Leaves large, jagged, reddish-green turning dark green and purple. Flowers in huge many-flowered panicles, white, red, or pink, in early summer.

Rhodanthemum gayanum
(Asteraceae/Compositae)

Common names: None
Height: 1ft (30cm)
Spread: 1ft (30cm)
Aspect: Sun
Soil: Sharply drained,
fertile
Hardiness: Zone 8
Propagation: Seed, in spring;
softwood cuttings, in early
summer

Leaves deeply 3-lobed, hairy, gray-green. Flowers solitary, daisylike, ray florets pale pink or white, disc florets brown, in summer. From Algeria and Morocco.

Rhodanthemum hosmariense A.G.M.
(Asteraceae/Compositae)

Common names: None
Height: 1ft (30cm)
Spread: 1ft (30cm)
Aspect: Sun
Soil: Sharply drained,
fertile
Hardiness: Zone 8
Propagation: Seed, in spring;
softwood cuttings, in early
summer

Spreading subshrub from Morocco. Leaves deeply 3-lobed, hairy, silver. Flowers single, solitary, white, daisylike with yellow centers, and surrounded by silver bracts.

Rhodiola wallichiana
(Crassulaceae)

Common names: None
Height: 16in (40cm)
Spread: 12in (30cm)
Aspect: Sun
Soil: Fertile
Hardiness: Zone 6
Propagation: Seed, in
spring or autumn; division,
in spring or early summer

Rhizomatous Himalayan perennial. Leaves linear to lance-shaped, toothed, midgreen. Flowers in dense terminal corymbs, pale or greenish-yellow stars, in early summer.

Rhodohypoxis baurii A.G.M.
(Hypoxidaceae)

Common names: None
Height: 4in (10cm)
Spread: 4in (10cm)
Aspect: Sun
Soil: Well-drained, humus-rich, fertile
Hardiness: Zone 8
Propagation: Seed, in
warmth when ripe; offsets,
in late autumn

A cormous perennial from South Africa. Leaves narrow, lance-shaped, keeled, grayish-green. Flowers solitary, flat, reddish-pink or white, all summer.

Ricinus communis
'Impala'
(Euphorbiaceae)

Rodgersia aesculifolia
A.G.M.
(Saxifragaceae)

Common name: Castor-
bean
Height: 4ft (1.2m)
Spread: 12ft (4m)
Aspect: Sun
Soil: Well-drained, humus-
rich, fertile
Hardiness: Zone 9
Propagation: Seed, after
soaking in late spring

Common names: None
Height: 6ft (2m)
Spread: 3ft (1m)
Aspect: Sun or half shade
Soil: Moist, humus-rich
Hardiness: Zone 5
Propagation: Seed or
division, both in spring

Tender subshrub, good in mixed
plantings. Leaves large, broad, ovate,
toothed, glossy, reddish-purple.
Flowers in spikes, females with red
stigma, males yellow, in summer.

Rhizomatous plant. Leaves basal,
palmate, 5- to 9-lobed, leaflets
obovate, toothed, midgreen, red-
veined. Tall panicles of many small,
starry, pink or white flowers, summer.

RODGERSIA (Saxifragaceae)

A genus of only some half-dozen species from the Far East, but
one which gives us very hardy and handsome architectural plants
for our gardens. They originate in the mountains of Burma,
Korea, China, and Japan, growing along streams in scrub and
woodlands. They are naturally moisture-lovers, but do not do
well in waterlogged soil, and will grow in sun or half shade; they
will tolerate drier soil in a partially shaded position better than
they will in a sunny site. *Rodgersia* are large plants, and not
really suitable for the very small garden, but do not usually require
staking. Their large, palmate or pinnate leaves are handsome,
although deciduous; some species have good autumn color. The
flowers are petalless and star-shaped, borne in summer in upright,
pyramidal panicles on tall stems, and are followed by attractive,
dark red or brown seed capsules. *Rodgersia* will build up into
quite large clumps requiring lots of room, and to prevent this,
the roots should be divided in a circle around the plant. They
are low-allergen plants and suit the allergic gardener. The young
leaves may be damaged by slugs, and since they are grown as
much for their foliage as their flowers, preventative measures
must be taken early or the plant will look untidy all season.

Rodgersia pinnata
'Alba'
(Saxifragaceae)

Common names: None
Height: 3ft (90cm)
Spread: 4ft (1.2m)
Aspect: Sun or half shade
Soil: Moist, humus-rich
Hardiness: Zone 5
Propagation: Seed or
division, both in spring

Clump-forming, rhizomatous plant.
Leaves large, palmate, 5- to 9-lobed,
obovate, glossy leaflets. Flowers small,
starry, white, in fluffy panicles, in
mid- and late summer.

Rodgersia pinnata
'Elegans'
(Saxifragaceae)

Common names: None
Height: 3ft (90cm)
Spread: 4ft (1.2m)
Aspect: Sun or half shade
Soil: Moist, humus-rich
Hardiness: Zone 5
Propagation: Seed or
division, both in spring

Cultivar with starry, pink flowers,
tinted cream. Leaves large, palmate,
5- to 9-lobed, obovate, glossy leaflets.
Lovely seed heads after flowering.

Rodgersia pinnata
'Superba' A.G.M.
(Saxifragaceae)

Common names: None
Height: 4ft (1.2m)
Spread: 30in (75cm)
Aspect: Sun or half shade
Soil: Moist, humus-rich
Hardiness: Zone 5
Propagation: Seed or
division, both in spring

Tall selected form; may be a separate
species. Leaves very large, palmate,
lobes fewer than in type, glossy,
veined, bronze-tinted. Large panicle of
salmon-pink flowers.

Rodgersia podophylla
A.G.M.
(Saxifragaceae)

Common name:
Bronzeleaf Rodger's-flower
Height: 5ft (1.5m)
Spread: 6ft (1.8m)
Aspect: Sun or half shade
Soil: Moist, humus-rich
Hardiness: Zone 5
Propagation: Seed or division, both in
spring

Rhizomatous plant from Japan and
Korea. Leaves huge, palmate, with 5
jagged, glossy midgreen, obovate
leaflets. Creamy-green flowers (*not
open here*) in panicles, summer.

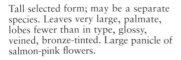

Romneya coulteri
A.G.M.
(Papaveraceae)

Common name: Matilija-
poppy
Height: 8ft (2.5m)
Spread: Indefinite
Aspect: Sun
Soil: Well-drained, fertile
Hardiness: Zone 7
Propagation: Seed or basal
cuttings, both in spring;
root cuttings, in winter

Suckering subshrub. Leaves glaucous
gray-green, rounded-pinnatifid, lobes
ovate to lance-shaped. Flowers
solitary, scented, large, yellow-
centered white cups, summer.

Romulea bulbocodium
(Iridaceae)

Common names: None
Height: 4in (10cm)
Spread: 2in (5cm)
Aspect: Sun
Soil: Well-drained, fertile
Hardiness: Zone 7
Propagation: Seed, in
autumn; offsets, when
dormant

Cormous perennial from the
Mediterranean and Africa. Leaves
basal, linear, channelled, arched. Up
to 5 flowers per stem, lilac funnels
with white centers, in spring.

Roscoea auriculata
(Zingiberaceae)

Common names: None
Height: 2ft (60cm)
Spread: 8in (20cm)
Aspect: Half shade
Soil: Moist, well-drained,
humus-rich, fertile
Hardiness: Zone 6
Propagation: Seed, when
ripe; division, in spring

Tuberous perennial from Nepal and
India. Leaves linear to lance-shaped,
dark green. Flowers axillary, hooded,
lips large, bracts overlapping, purple,
late summer to autumn.

Roscoea
'Beesiana'
(Zingiberaceae)

Common names: None
Height: 18in (45cm)
Spread: 12in (30cm)
Aspect: Half shade
Soil: Moist, well-drained,
humus-rich, fertile
Hardiness: Zone 6
Propagation: Seed, when
ripe; division, in spring

Hybrid perennial. Leaves lance-
shaped, arching, dark green. Flowers
hooded, with overlapping bracts,
yellow, striped mauve sometimes, in
late summer to autumn.

387

Roscoea cautleyoides A.G.M. (Zingiberaceae)

Common names: None
Height: 2ft (60cm)
Spread: 8in (20cm)
Aspect: Half shade
Soil: Moist, well-drained, humus-rich, fertile
Hardiness: Zone 6
Propagation: Seed, when ripe; division, in spring

Tuberous perennial from China. Leaves linear, midgreen. Flowers hooded, with overlapping bracts, on leafy stalks, yellow, purple, or white, late summer to autumn.

Roscoea purpurea (Zingiberaceae)

Common names: None
Height: 2ft (60cm)
Spread: 1ft (30cm)
Aspect: Half shade
Soil: Moist, well-drained, humus-rich, fertile
Hardiness: Zone 6
Propagation: Seed, when ripe; division, in spring

A tuberous perennial from the Himalayas. Leaves lance-shaped, dark green. Flowers hooded, purple, in late summer to early autumn. Appears late, so mark position.

Rosmarinus officinalis 'Severn Sea' A.G.M. (Labiatae/Lamiaceae)

Common names: Rosemary
Height: 3ft (90cm)
Spread: 5ft (1.5m)
Aspect: Sun
Soil: Well-drained, fertile
Hardiness: Zone 6
Propagation: Semiripe cuttings in summer

An aromatic, evergreen subshrub from the Mediterranean. Leaves linear, dark green, white-woolly below. Flowers in axillary whorls, blue, in late spring to summer.

Rosularia sedoides (Crassulaceae)

Common name: Himalayan houseleek
Height: 2in (5cm)
Spread: 8in (20cm)
Aspect: Sun
Soil: Sharply drained, humus-rich
Hardiness: Zone 7
Propagation: Separated offsets, in spring

Succulent, stoloniferous evergreen from the Himalayas. Leaves ovoid, hairy, green, red in sun, in rosettes like a houseleek. Flowers star-shaped, white, late summer to autumn.

Rudbeckia fulgida var. *sullivantii* 'Goldsturm' A.G.M. (Asteraceae/Compositae)

Common name: Showy coneflower
Height: 2ft (60cm)
Spread: 18in (45cm)
Aspect: Sun or half shade
Soil: Well-drained, humus-rich, fertile
Hardiness: Zone 4
Propagation: Division, in autumn or spring

Cultivar of a rhizomatous plant from the U.S.A. Leaves basal and stem, lance-shaped, midgreen. Flowers solitary, single, golden-yellow, daisylike, late summer to autumn.

Rudbeckia 'Herbstonne' (Asteraceae/Compositae)

Common name: Coneflower
Height: 1.8m (6ft)
Spread: 3ft (90cm)
Aspect: Sun or half shade
Soil: Well-drained, humus-rich, fertile
Hardiness: Zone 3
Propagation: Division, in spring or autumn

Hardy, rhizomatous, clump-forming, short-lived hybrid. Leaves ovate, toothed, glossy green. Flowers solitary, yellow, with a high, green boss, summer to early autumn.

Rudbeckia hirta (Asteraccae/Compositae)

Common name: Black-eyed Susan
Height: 36in (90cm)
Spread: 18in (45cm)
Aspect: Sun or half shade
Soil: Well-drained, humus-rich, fertile
Hardiness: Zone 4
Propagation: Seed, in spring; division, in spring or autumn

Rhizomatous, short-lived perennial. Leaves basal and stem, ovate, midgreen. Solitary, large, yellow, daisylike flowers with black, domed centers, summer to early autumn.

Rudbeckia subtomentosa (Asteraceae/Compositae)

Common name: Sweet coneflower
Height: 28in (70cm)
Spread: 2ft (60cm)
Aspect: Sun or half shade
Soil: Well-drained, humus-rich, fertile
Hardiness: Zone 5
Propagation: Seed, in spring; division, in spring or autumn

A short-lived perennial from the central U.S.A. Leaves ovate, midgreen. Flowers solitary, single, daisylike, yellow with dark purple-brown centers, in autumn.

Rumex sanguineus
(Polygonaceae)

Common names: Bloody
dock; red-veined dock
Height: 32in (80cm)
Spread: 12in (30cm)
Aspect: Sun
Soil: Well-drained, fertile
Hardiness: Zone 6
Propagation: Seed, sown
in situ in spring

Taprooted perennial. Leaves in
rosettes, oblong, dark green, boldly
red-veined. Flowers in panicles,
minute stars, green, turning brown, in
early to midsummer.

Ruta graveolens
(Rutaceae)

Common name: Common
rue
Height: 3ft (90cm)
Spread: 32in (80cm)
Aspect: Sun or half shade
Soil: Sharply drained,
fertile
Hardiness: Zone 5
Propagation: Seed, in spring;
semiripe cuttings, in summer

Evergreen subshrub. Leaves 2-
pinnatisect, ovate, lobes obovate,
glaucous blue-green, aromatic. Flowers
in cymes, yellow cups, in summer.
Irritant; poisonous in quantity.

Sagittaria latifolia
(Alismataceae)

Common name: Common
arrowhead
Height: 4ft (1.2m)
Spread: 3ft (90cm)
Aspect: Sun
Soil: Marginal aquatic
Hardiness: Zone 7
Propagation: Seed, as soon
as ripe; division or separated
runners, both in spring

A tuberous, aquatic marginal
perennial from the U.S.A. Leaves
aerial, arrow-shaped. Flowers in
whorled racemes, white, in summer.

Sagittaria sagittifolia
(Alismataceae)

Common name: Double
Oldworld arrowhead
Height: 3ft (90cm)
Spread: Indefinite
Aspect: Sun
Soil: Marginal aquatic
Hardiness: Zone 7
Propagation: Seed, as soon
as ripe; division or separated
runners, both in spring

Spreading, tuberous plant from
Eurasia. Leaves arrow-shaped,
midgreen, aerial. Flowers in racemes,
white with a purple spot at the base
of each petal, in summer.

SALVIA (Labiatae/Lamiaceae)
Sage

A very large and varied genus of about 900 species of annuals, biennials, perennials, and shrubs from grassland, scrub, or woodland habitats in tropical and temperate regions the world over. The perennials may be rhizomatous, tuberous, or fibrous-rooted, and evergreen or herbaceous, and they vary widely in hardiness from fully hardy to tender. The foliage is aromatic in many, hairy in some, and silvery in others. *Salvia* species all prefer light, alkaline soils that are well drained and moisture retentive. Almost all require full sun, especially the low-growing types with woolly or densely hairy leaves, but a few will tolerate light shade. The leaves are both basal and stem, and the two types often differ in form. The flowers are two-lipped; the upper petal arches forward to form a hood, and the lower petal is two-toothed. They are borne in panicles or in axillary whorls on upright stems. Many types attract bees, and some have culinary or medicinal use: *S. officinalis* is the common culinary sage. All sages are low-allergen, and suitable for the allergic gardener. Some of the taller varieties may need to be staked. The silvery-woolly types dislike winter wet and cold, drying winds, so should be either lifted and brought in or covered with a cloche.

Salvia africana-lutea
(Labiatae/Lamiaceae)

Common names: None
Height: 3ft (90cm)
Spread: 3ft (90cm)
Aspect: Sun
Soil: Moist, well-drained, humus-rich, fertile
Hardiness: Zone 9
Propagation: Basal or softwood cuttings, both in spring; semiripe cuttings, in autumn

A tender, evergreen subshrub from Africa. Leaves rounded, aromatic, hairy, white-woolly. Flowers in terminal racemes, red-brown, from summer to late autumn.

Salvia argentea
A.G.M.
(Labiatae/Lamiaceae)

Common name: Silver sage
Height: 3ft (90cm)
Spread: 2ft (60cm)
Aspect: Sun
Soil: Moist, well-drained, humus-rich, fertile
Hardiness: Zone 5
Propagation: Seed or division, both in spring

Short-lived perennial. Leaves large, in basal rosette, silky, silver-hairy. Flowers white or pale pink, in branched panicles, in summer; if cut down, will flower again in autumn.

Salvia azurea
(Labiatae/Lamiaceae)

Common name: Blue sage
Height: 4ft (1.2m)
Spread: 3ft (90cm)
Aspect: Sun or half shade
Soil: Moist, well-drained,
humus-rich, fertile
Hardiness: Zone 4
Propagation: Basal or
softwood cuttings, both in spring;
semiripe cuttings, in late summer

A straggly perennial from the U.S.A.
Leaves lance-shaped, softly hairy,
mid-green. Flowers in dense terminal
racemes, blue or white, from autumn
to winter.

Salvia buchananii
A.G.M.
(Labiatae/Lamiaceae)

Common names: None
Height: 1ft (30cm)
Spread: 1ft (30cm)
Aspect: Sun or half shade
Soil: Moist, well-drained,
humus-rich, fertile
Hardiness: Zone 9
Propagation: Basal or
softwood cuttings, both in spring;
semiripe cuttings, in late summer

Spreading evergreen. Leaves ovate,
toothed, leathery, glossy green.
Flowers in terminal racemes, red with
brown-purple calyces, from
midsummer to midautumn.

Salvia cacaliifolia
A.G.M.
(Labiatae/Lamiaceae)

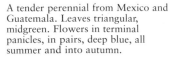

Common names: None
Height: 4ft (1.2m)
Spread: 1ft (30cm)
Aspect: Sun or half shade
Soil: Moist, well-drained,
humus-rich, fertile
Hardiness: Zone 9
Propagation: Basal or
softwood cuttings, both in spring;
semiripe cuttings, in late summer

A tender perennial from Mexico and
Guatemala. Leaves triangular,
midgreen. Flowers in terminal
panicles, in pairs, deep blue, all
summer and into autumn.

Salvia coccinea
(Labiatae/Lamiaceae)

Common name: Red
Texas sage
Height: 30in (75cm)
Spread: 12in (30cm)
Aspect: Sun or half shade
Soil: Moist, well-drained,
humus-rich, fertile
Hardiness: Zone 8
Propagation: Seed, in spring

A short-lived perennial from the
Americas. Leaves oval, hairy, toothed,
dark green. Flowers cherry-red, in
open spikes, from summer to autumn.

Salvia coccinea 'Coral Nymph' (Labiatae/Lamiaceae)

Common names: None
Height: 30in (75cm)
Spread: 12in (30cm)
Aspect: Sun or half shade
Soil: Moist, well-drained, humus-rich, fertile
Hardiness: Zone 8
Propagation: Division, in spring

A selected form of the species, with flowers having an upper lip of salmon-pink, and a lower lip of pale pink. Leaves oval, hairy, toothed, dark green.

Salvia confertiflora (Labiatae/Lamiaceae)

Common names: None
Height: 4ft (1.2m)
Spread: 2ft (60cm)
Aspect: Sun or half shade
Soil: Moist, well-drained, humus-rich, fertile
Hardiness: Zone 9
Propagation: Basal or softwood cuttings, both in spring; semiripe cuttings, in late summer

Leaves ovate, scalloped, green-yellow, woolly below, pungent. Flowers in terminal spikes, indigo-black with hairy, brown calyces, in late summer to midautumn.

Salvia darcyi (Labiatae/Lamiaceae)

Common names: None
Height: 1m (3ft)
Spread: 2ft (60cm)
Aspect: Sun or half shade
Soil: Moist, well-drained, humus-rich, fertile
Hardiness: Zone 8
Propagation: Basal or softwood cuttings, both in spring; semiripe cuttings, in late summer

Subshrub from Mexico. Leaves triangular, hairy, crenate, midgreen. Flowers in whorls of up to 6 on unbranched spikes, red, from summer to late autumn.

Salvia farinacea (Labiatae/Lamiaceae)

Common name: Mealycup sage
Height: 2ft (60cm)
Spread: 1ft (30cm)
Aspect: Sun or half shade
Soil: Moist, well-drained, humus-rich, fertile
Hardiness: Zone 9
Propagation: Seed, in spring

Bushy perennial from Mexico and the U.S.A. Leaves ovate, thin, glossy, midgreen, white below. Flowers in whorls of up to 16, in spikes, lavender-blue, summer to autumn.

Salvia forsskaolii
(Labiatae/Lamiaceae)

Common names: None
Height: 3ft (90cm)
Spread: 18in (45cm)
Aspect: Sun or half shade
Soil: Moist, well-drained,
humus-rich, fertile
Hardiness: Zone 7
Propagation: Seed, in
spring

Perennial from the Black Sea coast.
Leaves basal, broad, ovate, toothed,
midgreen. Flowers in spikes, tubes
white, lips violet, lower lip marked
yellow, all summer.

Salvia fulgens
A.G.M.
(Labiatae/Lamiaceae)

Common names: None
Height: 1m (3ft)
Spread: 1m (3ft)
Aspect: Sun or half shade
Soil: Moist, well-drained,
humus-rich, fertile
Hardiness: Zone 9
Propagation: Basal or
softwood cuttings, both in spring;
semiripe cuttings, in late summer

Tender, evergreen perennial from
Mexico. Leaves ovate, toothed, bright
green, white-woolly below. Flowers in
terminal racemes, red, lower lip
downy, in summer.

Salvia glutinosa
(Labiatae/Lamiaceae)

Common name: Jupiter's
distaff
Height: 3ft (90cm)
Spread: 2ft (60cm)
Aspect: Half shade
Soil: Moist, humus-rich,
fertile
Hardiness: Zone 5
Propagation: Seed, in
spring

Eurasian perennial. Leaves heart-
shaped, hairy, toothed. Flowers sticky,
in loose terminal racemes, pale yellow,
spotted maroon, from midsummer to
midautumn.

Salvia greggii
(Labiatae/Lamiaceae)

Common name: Autumn sage
Height: 30in (75cm)
Spread: 30in (75cm)
Aspect: Sun or half shade
Soil: Moist, well-drained,
humus-rich, fertile
Hardiness: Zone 9
Propagation: Basal or softwood
cuttings, both in spring; semi-ripe
cuttings, in late summer

Evergreen from Texas and Mexico.
Leaves elliptic, small, leathery.
Flowers in pairs in terminal racemes,
mauvish-red, pink, yellow, or violet,
late summer to autumn

Salvia greggii
'Peach' A.G.M.
(Labiatae/Lamiaceae)

Common name: Autumn sage
Height: 30in (75cm)
Spread: 30in (75cm)
Aspect: Sun or half shade
Soil: Moist, well-drained,
humus-rich, fertile
Hardiness: Zone 9
Propagation: Basal or softwood
cuttings, both in spring; semiripe
cuttings, in late summer

A selected form of the species, with
flowers in pairs, of a strong peach
color, from late summer to autumn.
Leaves elliptic, small, leathery,
midgreen.

Salvia hians
(Labiatae/Lamiaceae)

Common names: None
Height: 2ft (60cm)
Spread: 2ft (60cm)
Aspect: Sun or half shade
Soil: Moist, well-drained,
humus-rich, fertile
Hardiness: Zone 6
Propagation: Seed or
division, both in spring

Short-lived perennial from the
Himalayas. Leaves ovate, toothed,
veined, wrinkled, dark green. Flowers
in terminal spikes, purplish-blue,
lower lip white, all summer.

Salvia involucrata
'Bethellii'
(Labiatae/Lamiaceae)

Common names: None
Height: 5ft (1.5m)
Spread: 3ft (90cm)
Aspect: Sun or half shade
Soil: Moist, well-drained,
humus-rich, fertile
Hardiness: Zone 9
Propagation: Basal or softwood
cuttings, both in spring; semiripe
cuttings, in late summer

Selected form of a perennial from
Mexico. Leaves ovate, hairy, bright
green. Flowers in dense, terminal
racemes, purplish-crimson, bracts
pink, late summer to midautumn.

Salvia involucrata
'Boutin' A.G.M.
(Labiatae/Lamiaceae)

Common names: None
Height: 5ft (1.5m)
Spread: 3ft (90cm)
Aspect: Sun or half shade
Soil: Moist, well-drained,
humus-rich, fertile
Hardiness: Zone 9
Propagation: Basal or softwood
cuttings, both in spring; semiripe
cuttings, in late summer

Selected form of the species with
flowers in dense, terminal racemes,
dark pink with dark pink bracts, from
late summer to midautumn. Leaves
ovate, hairy.

Salvia leucantha A.G.M.
(Labiatae/Lamiaceae)

Common name: Mexican bush
Height: 3ft (90cm)
Spread: 3ft (90cm)
Aspect: Sun or half shade
Soil: Moist, well-drained,
humus-rich, fertile
Hardiness: Zone 10
Propagation: Basal or softwood
cuttings, both in spring; semiripe
cuttings, in late summer

Evergreen subshrub. Leaves ovate,
hairy, gray, white-tomentose below.
Flowers in terminal racemes, white
with bell-shaped, lavender calyces, in
autumn to winter.

Salvia microphylla
(Labiatae/Lamiaceae)

Common name: Myrtle sage
Height: 4ft (1.2m)
Spread: 4ft (1.2m)
Aspect: Sun or half shade
Soil: Moist, well-drained,
humus-rich, fertile
Hardiness: Zone 9
Propagation: Basal or softwood
cuttings, both in spring; semiripe
cuttings, in late summer

Evergreen perennial. Leaves small,
ovate, hairy, toothed, midgreen.
Flowers paired or whorled in terminal
racemes, crimson, in late summer and
autumn.

Salvia microphylla var. neurepia
(Labiatae/Lamiaceae)

Common names: Myrtle sage
Height: 4ft (1.2m)
Spread: 4ft (1.2m)
Aspect: Sun or half shade
Soil: Moist, well-drained,
humus-rich, fertile
Hardiness: Zone 9
Propagation: Basal or softwood
cuttings, both in spring; semiripe
cuttings, in late summer

A form of the species with shiny,
glabrous leaves of pale green, and red
flowers paired or whorled in terminal
racemes, from late summer to
autumn.

Salvia nemorosa 'Ostfriesland' A.G.M.
(Labiatae/Lamiaceae)

Common names: None
Height: 3ft (1m)
Spread: 2ft (60cm)
Aspect: Sun or half shade
Soil: Moist, well-drained,
humus-rich, fertile
Hardiness: Zone 5
Propagation: Basal or softwood
cuttings, both in spring; semiripe
cuttings, in late summer

A selected form of a species from
Eurasia. Leaves ovate, crenulate,
midgreen. Flowers in very dense,
terminal racemes, deep violet-blue,
from summer to autumn.

Salvia officinalis
(Labiatae/Lamiaceae)

Common name: Garden
sage
Height: 18in (45cm)
Spread: 18in (45cm)
Aspect: Sun or half shade
Soil: Moist, well-drained,
humus-rich, fertile
Hardiness: Zone 5
Propagation: Seed or
cuttings, both in spring

An evergreen, Mediterranean culinary
herb. Leaves aromatic, oblong,
woolly, gray-green. Flowers in
racemes, lilac, in early to midsummer.

Salvia officinalis
'Kew Gold' A.G.M.
(Labiatae/Lamiaceae)

Common name: Garden
sage
Height: 1ft (30cm)
Spread: 1ft (30cm)
Aspect: Sun or half shade
Soil: Moist, well-drained,
humus-rich, fertile
Hardiness: Zone 5
Propagation: Division, in
spring

A form of the common sage with
oblong, woolly, aromatic leaves of
pale green splashed with gold.
Flowers in racemes, lilac, in early to
midsummer.

Salvia officinalis
'Tricolor' A.G.M.
(Labiatae/Lamiaceae)

Common name: Garden
sage
Height: 12in (30cm)
Spread: 18in (45cm)
Aspect: Sun or half shade
Soil: Moist, well-drained,
humus-rich, fertile
Hardiness: Zone 5
Propagation: Division,
in spring

Form of the common sage with gray-
green leaves margined cream and
pink; young leaves have more pink
than cream. Flowers in racemes, lilac,
in early to midsummer.

Salvia patens
A.G.M.
(Labiatae/Lamiaceae)

Common name: Gentian
salvia
Height: 2ft (60cm)
Spread: 18in (45cm)
Aspect: Sun or half shade
Soil: Moist, well-drained,
humus-rich, fertile
Hardiness: Zone 8
Propagation: Seed or
division, both in spring

A tuberous perennial from Mexico.
Leaves ovate, hairy, toothed,
midgreen. Flowers in few-flowered
racemes, deep blue, from midsummer
to midautumn.

Salvia patens
'Cambridge Blue' A.G.M.
(Labiatae/Lamiaceae)

Common name: Gentian
salvia
Height: 2ft (60cm)
Spread: 18in (45cm)
Aspect: Sun or half shade
Soil: Moist, well-drained,
humus-rich, fertile
Hardiness: Zone 8
Propagation: Division,
in spring

A form of the species with flowers of
pale blue in few-flowered racemes,
from midsummer to midautumn.
Leaves ovate, hairy, toothed,
midgreen.

Salvia patens
'White Trophy'
(Labiatae/Lamiaceae)

Common name: Gentian
salvia
Height: 2ft (60cm)
Spread: 18in (45cm)
Aspect: Sun or half shade
Soil: Moist, well-drained,
fertile, humus-rich
Hardiness: Zone 8
Propagation: Division,
in spring

A white-flowered form of the species,
bearing few-flowered racemes from
midsummer to midautumn. Leaves
ovate, hairy, toothed, midgreen.

Salvia pratensis
Haematodes Group A.G.M.
(Labiatae/Lamiaceae)

Common name: Meadow
sage
Height: 1m (3ft)
Spread: 1ft (30cm)
Aspect: Sun or half shade
Soil: Moist, well-drained,
humus-rich, fertile
Hardiness: Zone 3
Propagation: Seed, in
spring

Also called *S. haematodes*. Leaves in
basal rosettes, large, ovate, dark
green. Flowers in panicles, bluish-
violet with pale throats, from early to
midsummer. Short-lived.

Salvia purpurea
(Labiatae/Lamiaceae)

Common names: None
Height: 6ft (1.8m)
Spread: 3ft (90cm)
Aspect: Sun
Soil: Moist, well-drained,
humus-rich, fertile
Hardiness: Zone 9
Propagation: Basal or
softwood cuttings, both in spring;
semiripe cuttings, in late summer

A tender perennial from Central
America. Leaves ovate, toothed,
midgreen. Flowers in short racemes,
pinkish-lilac, upper lip densely hairy,
from winter to spring.

Salvia roemeriana
A.G.M.
(Labiatae/Lamiaceae)

Common names: None
Height: 1ft (30cm)
Spread: 1ft (30cm)
Aspect: Sun or half shade
Soil: Moist, well-drained,
humus-rich, fertile
Hardiness: Zone 8
Propagation: Seed or basal
or softwood cuttings, all
in spring

A small perennial from Texas,
Arizona, and Mexico. Leaves
rounded, toothed, bright green.
Flowers in loose racemes, scarlet,
from midsummer to midautumn.

Salvia sclarea var.
turkestanica hort.
(Labiatae/Lamiaceae)

Common names: Clary;
clary sage
Height: 1m (3ft)
Spread: 1ft (30cm)
Aspect: Sun or half shade
Soil: Moist, well-drained,
humus-rich, fertile
Hardiness: Zone 5
Propagation: Softwood cuttings, in
spring; semiripe cuttings, in late summer

Unpleasant-smelling perennial. Leaves
in basal rosette, ovate, toothed,
wrinkled, midgreen. Flowers in
terminal panicles, white, edged pink,
from spring to summer.

Salvia spathacea
A.G.M.
(Labiatae/Lamiaceae)

Common names: None
Height: 1ft (30cm)
Spread: 3ft (90cm)
Aspect: Half shade
Soil: Moist, well-drained,
humus-rich, fertile
Hardiness: Zone 8
Propagation: Seed or basal
cuttings, both in spring

A rhizomatous, spreading perennial
from California. Leaves oblong,
sticky-hairy, light green. Flowers in
whorls, deep pink, surrounded by
bracts, in summer.

Salvia uliginosa
A.G.M.
(Labiatae/Lamiaceae)

Common names: None
Height: 5ft (1.5m)
Spread: 3ft (1m)
Aspect: Sun
Soil: Wet, humus-rich,
fertile
Hardiness: Zone 9
Propagation: Basal or
softwood cuttings, both in spring;
semiripe cuttings, in late summer

Rhizomatous perennial from swampy
areas of South America. Leaves
oblong, toothed, midgreen. Flowers in
terminal racemes, clear blue, late
summer to midautumn.

Salvia verticillata
(Labiatae/Lamiaceae)

Common names: None
Height: 32in (80cm)
Spread: 20in (50cm)
Aspect: Sun or half shade
Soil: Moist, well-drained,
humus-rich, fertile
Hardiness: Zone 6
Propagation: Basal or
softwood cuttings, both in spring;
semiripe cuttings, in late summer

A herbaceous perennial from Europe.
Leaves ovate, hairy, midgreen.
Flowers on branched stems, whorled,
in racemes, lilac, all summer.

Salvia verticillata
'Alba'
(Labiatae/Lamiaceae)

Common names: None
Height: 32in (80cm)
Spread: 20in (50cm)
Aspect: Sun or half shade
Soil: Moist, well-drained,
humus-rich, fertile
Hardiness: Zone 6
Propagation: Basal or
softwood cuttings, both in spring;
semiripe cuttings, in late summer

The white-flowered form of the
species. Flowers borne in whorled
racemes, on branched stems, all
summer. Leaves ovate, hairy,
midgreen.

Sanguinaria canadensis
'Plena' A.G.M.
(Papaveraceae)

Common name: Bloodroot
Height: 6in (15cm)
Spread: 12in (30cm)
Aspect: Full or deep shade
Soil: Moist, well-drained,
humus-rich, fertile
Hardiness: Zone 3
Propagation: Seed, in
autumn; division, just after
flowering

Hardy rhizomatous woodlander.
Leaves heart- or kidney-shaped, blue-
green. Flowers solitary, white, double,
very brief period in spring. Leaves
also vanish; mark position.

Sanguisorba albiflora
(Rosaceae)

Common name: Burnet
Height: 2ft (60cm)
Spread: 2ft (60cm)
Aspect: Sun or half shade
Soil: Moist, well-drained,
humus-rich, fertile
Hardiness: Zone 5
Propagation: Seed or
division, both in spring or
autumn

Short-lived, rhizomatous perennial.
Leaves pinnate, leaflets ovate, gray-
green. Flowers in arching, bottlebrush
spikes, small, fluffy, white, summer to
early autumn.

Sanguisorba canadensis
(Rosaceae)

Common name: American burnet
Height: 6ft (2m)
Spread: 3ft (1m)
Aspect: Sun or half shade
Soil: Moist, well-drained, humus-rich, fertile
Hardiness: Zone 4
Propagation: Seed or division, both in spring or autumn

Rhizomatous, invasive perennial. Leaves pinnate, leaflets oblong, gray-green. Flowers in bottlebrush spikes, small, white, fluffy, from midsummer to midautumn.

Sanguisorba menziesii
(Rosaceae)

Common name: Burnet
Height: 2ft (60cm)
Spread: 1ft (30cm)
Aspect: Sun
Soil: Moist, well-drained, humus-rich, fertile
Hardiness: Zone 5
Propagation: Seed or division, both in spring or autumn

A dwarf perennial. Leaves pinnate, leaflets obovate, toothed, light green. Flowers in bottlebrush spikes, small, maroon, over a few weeks in summer.

Sanguisorba obtusa
(Rosaceae)

Common name: Burnet
Height: 2ft (60cm)
Spread: 2ft (60cm)
Aspect: Sun or half shade
Soil: Moist, well-drained, humus-rich, fertile
Hardiness: Zone 5
Propagation: Seed or division, both in spring or autumn

Rhizomatous, spreading perennial from Japan. Leaves pinnate, leaflets oblong, gray-green. Flowers in bottlebrush spikes, small, fluffy, pink, summer to early autumn.

Sanguisorba officinalis 'Tanna'
(Rosaceae)

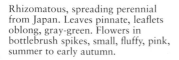

Common name: Burnet
Height: 10in (25cm)
Spread: 2ft (60cm)
Aspect: Sun or half shade
Soil: Moist, well-drained, humus-rich, fertile
Hardiness: Zone 4
Propagation: Division, in spring or autumn

Form of a rhizomatous, dwarf plant. Leaves basal, pinnate, leaflets elliptic, midgreen. Flowers maroon-purple, in short, bottle-brush spikes, late summer to early autumn.

401

Sanguisorba tenuifolia 'Rosea' (Rosaceae)

Common name: Burnet
Height: 4ft (1.2m)
Spread: 2ft (60cm)
Aspect: Sun or half shade
Soil: Wet, humus-rich, fertile
Hardiness: Zone 4
Propagation: Seed or division, both in spring or autumn

Rhizomatous perennial from the Far East. Leaves basal, large, pinnate, leaflets deeply divided, feathery. Flowers pink, in arching bottlebrushes, late summer to early autumn.

Santolina chamaecyparissus A.G.M. (Asteraceae/Compositae)

Common name: Lavender-cotton
Height: 18in (45cm)
Spread: 36in (1m)
Aspect: Sun
Soil: Well-drained, fertile
Hardiness: Zone 7
Propagation: Seed, in autumn or spring

Evergreen Mediterrenean subshrub. Leaves aromatic, pinnatisect, leaflets toothed, gray-white, deeply dissected. Flowers bright yellow buttons, in mid- to late summer.

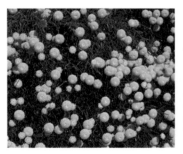

Santolina pinnata subsp. neapolitana 'Edward Bowles' (Asteraceae/Compositae)

Common name: Lavender-cotton
Height: 30in (75cm)
Spread: 36in (1m)
Aspect: Sun
Soil: Well-drained, fertile
Hardiness: Zone 7
Propagation: Seed, in autumn or spring

An evergreen subshrub from Italy. Leaves aromatic, pinnate, leaflets cylindrical, gray-green. Flowers on long stems, creamy-white buttons, in summer.

Santolina rosmarinifolia subsp. rosmarinifolia (Asteraceae/Compositae)

Common names: None
Height: 2ft (60cm)
Spread: 3ft (1m)
Aspect: Sun
Soil: Well-drained, fertile
Hardiness: Zone 7
Propagation: Seed, in spring or autumn

Evergreen subshrub from Europe. Leaves aromatic, pinnate, leaflets narrowly linear, toothed, bright green. Flowers on slim stems, pale yellow buttons, in midsummer.

Saponaria ocymoides
A.G.M.
(Caryophyllaceae)

Common name: Rock
soapwort
Height: 4in (10cm)
Spread: 18in (45cm)
Aspect: Sun
Soil: Well-drained, fertile,
alkaline
Hardiness: Zone 4
Propagation: Seed, in
autumn or spring

A creeping, mat-forming perennial.
Leaves ovate, hairy, bright green.
Flowers in loose cymes, pink, in
summer. Cut to the ground after
flowering to keep compact.

Saponaria officinalis
'Flore Pleno'
(Caryophyllaceae)

Common names: Bouncing
Bet
Height: 2ft (60cm)
Spread: 18in (45cm)
Aspect: Sun
Soil: Well-drained, fertile
Hardiness: Zone 4
Propagation: Seed or
division, both in autumn or
spring

Untidy, extremely invasive,
rhizomatous perennial. Leaves ovate,
veined, rough, midgreen. Flowers in
cymes, scented, pink, white, or red
from summer to autumn.

Sarracenia x catesbyi
A.G.M.
(Sarraceniaceae)

Common name: Pitcher-
plant
Height: 30in (75cm)
Spread: 36in (1m)
Aspect: Sun
Soil: Moist, sharply
drained, acidic, humus-rich
Hardiness: Zone 5
Propagation: Seed or
division, both in spring

Carnivorous, natural hybrid. Leaves
form vases, or "pitchers," which
secrete nectar and trap insects. Pitcher
erect, red. Flowers (*not shown*) large,
red, in spring.

Sarracenia flava
A.G.M.
(Sarraceniaceae)

Common name: Trumpet
pitcher-plant
Height: 3ft (1m)
Spread: 3ft (1m)
Aspect: Sun
Soil: Moist, well-drained,
acidic, humus-rich
Hardiness: Zone 7
Propagation: Seed or
division, both in spring

Carnivorous perennial. Leaves form
vases, or "pitchers," which secrete
nectar and trap insects. Pitchers
yellow-green. Flowers (*not shown*)
yellow, in spring.

Sauromatum venosum
(Araceae)

Saururus cernuus
(Saururaceae)

Common name: Monarch-
of-the-East
Height: 18in (45cm)
Spread: 8in (20cm)
Aspect: Half shade
Soil: Well-drained, acidic,
humus-rich, fertile
Hardiness: Zone 10
Propagation: Offsets, in
winter when dormant

Tuberous perennial. Spathe green,
spotted black, spadix long, arched,
foul-smelling, in spring to summer,
then a single leaf stem with a crown
of lance-shaped segments.

Common name: Swamp
lily
Height: 4ft (1.2m)
Spread: 2ft (60cm)
Aspect: Sun
Soil: Wet
Hardiness: Zone 5
Propagation: Seed, when
ripe

A rhizomatous perennial from the
U.S.A. Leaves heart-shaped, pointed,
midgreen. Flowers small, in arching
spikes, white, in early summer.

SAXIFRAGA (Saxifragaceae)
Saxifrage

A genus of over 400 species of perennials, biennials, and a few
annuals, found in mountain habitats, principally in the northern
hemisphere. The great majority of species are cushion-forming
or mat-forming alpine plants that are more suited to the rock
garden than the herbaceous border, but some make good
ground cover; *Saxifraga* x *urbium* is excellent for this, even in
the poorest of soils. The genus is a complex one botanically,
subdivided into sections as outlined below. The species vary
greatly in both their habit and their leaf form, but the leaves of
all are in rosettes, and many are evergreen. In a monocarpic
saxifrage, only the flowering rosette dies, not the plant; new
rosettes will replace the old. The flowers are small, cup-shaped
or star-shaped, and may be borne singly or in racemes, cymes,
or panicles; they are generally pink, white, or yellow. Saxifrages
are low-allergen plants. Many species are difficult to cultivate in
the open garden, as they must be completely protected from
winter wet, so must be given overhead cover. These types are
really only suitable for growing in an alpine house, and are
therefore not covered here. Slugs are the most common problem
with the saxifrages that can be grown outside.

Saxifraga fortunei
A.G.M. (4)
(Saxifragaceae)

Common name: Saxifrage
Height: 1ft (30cm)
Spread: 1ft (30cm)
Aspect: Full or half shade
Soil: Moist, well-drained,
humus-rich
Hardiness: Zone 7
Propagation: Seed, in
autumn; division, in spring

Clump-forming perennial. Leaves
rounded, scalloped, 7-lobed,
midgreen, red beneath. Flowers in
large, wide panicles, small, starry,
white, from early autumn to early
winter.

Saxifraga 'Flore Pleno'
(*granulata*) **(11)**
(Saxifragaceae)

Common name: Meadow
saxifrage
Height: 14in (35cm)
Spread: 12in (30cm)
Aspect: Sun or light shade
Soil: Moist, sharply
drained, humus-rich
Hardiness: Zone 5
Propagation: Seed, in
autumn; division, in spring

Bulbous perennial. Leaves in loose
rosettes, kidney-shaped, toothed,
midgreen. Flowers in panicles, on
sticky stems, double white, in late
spring; summer dormant.

Saxifraga
'Southside Seedling'
A.G.M. (7) (Saxifragaceae)

Common name: Saxifrage
Height: 1ft (30cm)
Spread: 1ft (30cm)
Aspect: Sun or half shade;
shaded from midday sun
Soil: Moist, sharply
drained, humus-rich
Hardiness: Zone 7
Propagation: Division, in
spring

A hybrid saxifrage. Leaves in rosettes,
spoon-shaped, light green. Flowers in
arched panicles, cup-shaped, white,
spotted red, in late spring and early
summer.

Saxifraga stolonifera
A.G.M. (4)
(Saxifragaceae)

Common name:
Strawberry saxifrage
Height: 1ft (30cm)
Spread: 1ft (30cm)
Aspect: Full or half shade
Soil: Moist, well-drained,
humus-rich
Hardiness: Zone 6
Propagation: Seed, in autumn;
division, in spring

A stoloniferous perennial from Japan
and China. Leaves in rosettes or tufts,
rounded, midgreen. Flowers in loose
panicles, tiny, white, spotted red or
yellow, in summer.

Saxifraga 'Tumbling Waters' A.G.M. (7) (Saxifragaceae)

Common name: Saxifrage
Height: 18in (45cm)
Spread: 12in (30cm)
Aspect: Sun
Soil: Sharply drained, fertile
Hardiness: Zone 7
Propagation: Division, in spring

Hybrid perennial. Leaves in large, tight rosettes, linear, silver-green, lime-encrusted. Flowers only after a few years, small, white cups, in dense, arched panicles, in spring.

CLASSIFICATION of SAXIFRAGE by G. Hegi, 1975

Classes 3, 4, 7, 8, 11, and 12 are of general horticultural interest.

Class 1 Micranthes

Class 2 Hirculus

Class 3 Gymnopera

Class 4 Diptera

Class 5 Trachyphyllum

Class 6 Xanthizoon

Class 7 Aizoonia

Class 8 Porophyllum

Class 9 Porophyrion

Class 10 Miscopetalum

Class 11 Saxifraga

Class 12 Trachyphylloides

Class 13 Cymbalaria

Class 14 Discogyne

Saxifraga × *urbium* A.G.M. (3) (Saxifragaceae)

Common names: None
Height: 1ft (30cm)
Spread: Indefinite
Aspect: Full or half shade
Soil: Moist, well-drained, humus-rich
Hardiness: Zone 6
Propagation: Seed, in autumn; division, in spring

Rampant ground cover. Leaves in large rosettes, leathery, toothed, midgreen spoons. Flowers in upright, loose panicles, small, white stars, flushed pink, in summer.

Saxifraga veitchiana (4) (Saxifragaceae)

Common name: Saxifrage
Height: 1ft (30cm)
Spread: Indefinite
Aspect: Full or half shade
Soil: Moist, well-drained, humus-rich
Hardiness: Zone 7
Propagation: Seed, in autumn; division, in spring

Stoloniferous, evergreen ground cover from China. Leaves rounded, crenate, matt green, red-brown below. Flowers in loose panicles, tiny, white, in late spring and early summer.

Scabiosa atropurpurea
(Dipsacaceae)

Common name: Sweet
scabious
Height: 36in (90cm)
Spread: 10in (25cm)
Aspect: Sun
Soil: Well-drained, fertile
Hardiness: Zone 7
Propagation: Seed, when
ripe or in spring; division,
in spring

A short-lived perennial from S
Europe. Leaves basal, spoon-shaped,
and stem, pinnatifid, midgreen.
Flowers solitary, perfumed, dark
purple, in summer.

Scabiosa caucasica
'Clive Greaves' A.G.M.
(Dipsacaceae)

Common name: Caucasian
scabious
Height: 2ft (60cm)
Spread: 2ft (60cm)
Aspect: Sun
Soil: Well-drained, fertile
Hardiness: Zone 4
Propagation: Seed, when
ripe or in spring; division,
in spring

A selected form of a hardy, clump-
forming perennial from the Caucasus.
Leaves lance-shaped, gray-green.
Flowers solitary, domed, double,
lavender, all summer if deadheaded.

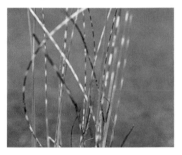

Scabiosa columbaria
var. *ochroleuca*
(Dipsacaceae)

Common name: Dove
scabious
Height: 30in (75cm)
Spread: 36in (90cm)
Aspect: Sun
Soil: Well-drained, fertile
Hardiness: Zone 6
Propagation: Seed, when
ripe or in spring; division,
in spring

Perennial from Eurasia. Leaves basal,
and stem, pinnatifid, grayish-green.
Flowers solitary, lemon-yellow, from
summer to early autumn. Superb for
flower-arranging.

Schoenoplectus lacustris
subsp. *tabernaemontani*
'Zebrinus'

Common names: None
Height: 3ft (1m)
Spread: 2ft (60cm)
Aspect: Sun
Soil: Wet, or marginal
aquatic
Hardiness: Zone 7
Propagation: Division, from
spring to summer

Rhizomatous perennial. Stems from
rhizome leafless, gray-green, banded
creamy-white. Flowers brown,
spikelets, in clusters, from early to
late summer.

Schizostylis coccinea
f. *alba*
(Iridaceae)

Common name: Crimson-
flag
Height: 2ft (60cm)
Spread: 1ft (30cm)
Aspect: Sun
Soil: Moist to wet, well-
drained, fertile
Hardiness: Zone 6
Propagation: Seed or
division, both in spring

Rhizomatous evergreen from southern
Africa. Leaves erect, narrow-linear,
pointed, midgreen. Flowers in spikes,
open cups, white, in autumn. Soon
becomes congested.

Schizostylis coccinea
'Major' A.G.M.
(Iridaceae)

Common name: Crimson-
flag
Height: 2ft (60cm)
Spread: 1ft (30cm)
Aspect: Sun
Soil: Moist to wet, well-
drained, fertile
Hardiness: Zone 6
Propagation: Seed or
division, both in spring

Rhizomatous evergreen from southern
Africa. Leaves erect, sword-shaped,
mid-green. Flowers in spikes, open
cups, red, in autumn. Becomes
congested rapidly.

Schizostylis coccinea
'Professor Barnard'
(Iridaceae)

Common name: Crimson-
flag
Height: 2ft (60cm)
Spread: 1ft (30cm)
Aspect: Sun
Soil: Moist to wet, well-
drained, fertile
Hardiness: Zone 6
Propagation: Seed or
division, both in spring

Rhizomatous evergreen. Flowers
large, deep dusky pink. Leaves erect,
sword-shaped, midgreen. Rapidly
becomes overcrowded; lift and divide
regularly.

Schizostylis coccinea
'Sunrise' A.G.M.
(Iridaceae)

Common name: Crimson-
flag
Height: 2ft (60cm)
Spread: 1ft (30cm)
Aspect: Sun
Soil: Moist to wet, well-
drained, fertile
Hardiness: Zone 6
Propagation: Division,
in spring

Selected form of rhizomatous
evergreen, with large, salmon-pink
flowers in autumn. Leaves evergreen,
erect, pointed, midgreen. Rapidly
becomes congested.

Scilla natalensis
(Hyacinthaceae/Liliaceae)

Scilla peruviana
(Hyacinthaceae/Liliaceae)

Common name: Natal
squill
Height: 4ft (1.2m)
Spread: 4in (10cm)
Aspect: Sun or half shade
Soil: Well-drained, fertile,
humus-rich
Hardiness: Zone 9
Propagation: Seed, when
ripe; offsets, when dormant

Bulbous perennial from South Africa.
Leaves basal, lance-shaped, midgreen.
Bears tall racemes of up to 100 small,
flat, lilac-blue, pink, or white flowers,
in summer.

Common name: Peruvian
squill
Height: 18in (45cm)
Spread: 12in (30cm)
Aspect: Sun or half shade
Soil: Well-drained, fertile,
humus-rich
Hardiness: Zone 8
Propagation: Seed, when
ripe; offsets, when dormant

Bulbous Mediterranean plant; named
for the ship it came to Britain on, the
Peru. Leaves in basal clusters, lance-
shaped. Flowers deep blue stars in
conical racemes.

Scopolia carniolica
(Solanaceae)

Scrophularia auriculata
'Variegata'
(Scrophulariaceae)

Common names: None
Height: 18in (45cm)
Spread: 24in (60cm)
Aspect: Half shade
Soil: Moist, well-drained,
humus-rich
Hardiness: Zone 5
Propagation: Seed, in
autumn or spring; division,
in spring

A poisonous, rhizomatous perennial
from Europe and the Caucasus.
Leaves ovate, veined, wrinkled,
midgreen. Flowers solitary, pendent,
brown-purple bells, spring.

Common name: Figwort
Height: 30in (75cm)
Spread: 2ft (60cm)
Aspect: Half shade
Soil: Moist to wet or
marginal aquatic
Hardiness: Zone 5
Propagation: Division, in
spring

Perennial from Europe. Leaves large,
ovate, wrinkled, toothed, pale green,
marked pink and cream. Flowers
insignificant, in cymes, yellowish-
green, in summer to autumn.

409

Scutellaria incana
(Labiatae/Lamiaceae)

Common name: Skullcap
Height: 4ft (1.2m)
Spread: 2ft (60cm)
Aspect: Sun or half shade
Soil: Sharply drained,
alkaline, fertile
Hardiness: Zone 5
Propagation: Seed, in
spring; division, in spring
or autumn

A perennial from the U.S.A. Leaves
ovate, toothed, hairy, crenate, sage-
gray. Flowers in corymbs, tubular, 2-
lipped, blue, in summer, and again
later if deadheaded.

Scutellaria integrifolia
(Labiatae/Lamiaceae)

Common name: Hyssop
skullcap
Height: 2ft (60cm)
Spread: 1ft (30cm)
Aspect: Sun or half shade
Soil: Sharply drained,
alkaline, fertile
Hardiness: Zone 5
Propagation: Seed, in spring; division,
in spring or autumn

A perennial from the eastern U.S.A.
Leaves ovate, hairy, midgreen.
Flowers tubular, 2-lipped, lilac-blue,
in racemes, in late spring to early
summer.

SEDUM (Crassulaceae)
Stonecrop

A wide genus of some 400 species, encompassing annuals,
biennials, deciduous, semievergreen, and evergreen perennials,
subshrubs, and shrubs from both hemispheres. Their habitats in
the wild vary from mountainous areas, where most are found,
to arid regions of South America. As a result, they vary widely
from dwarf, rock-garden plants (the predominant type) to fairly
tall plants, eminently suitable for beds or borders. Some of the
smaller species can be quite invasive. Stonecrops prefer sun, but
some will tolerate light shade. They are drought-tolerant, and
prefer light, well-drained soils; the border types will grow in
almost all soils, but become lush and need to be staked if grown
in over-fertile conditions. The foliage of stonecrops is of a thick,
fleshy, succulent nature, although the arrangement and form of
the leaves is very variable. The flowers appear in summer and
autumn. They are mostly 5-petalled and star-shaped, and borne
usually in terminal corymbs, panicles, or cymes. The flowers are
beloved of butterflies, especially those of *Sedum spectabile*.
Unfortunately, slugs and snails are also fond of the leaves. All
parts of the plants are poisonous, and contact with the sap may
cause skin irritation.

Sedum acre
(Crassulaceae)

Common name: Goldmoss
Height: 2in (5cm)
Spread: 32in (80cm)
Aspect: Sun
Soil: Sharply drained,
alkaline, fertile
Hardiness: Zone 5
Propagation: Seed, in
autumn; softwood cuttings
of blind shoots, in early summer

Creeping, evergreen perennial from
Turkey, North Africa, and Europe.
Leaves triangular, light green. Flowers
in cymes, yellow-green stars, over a
long period in summer.

Sedum acre
'Aureum'
(Crassulaceae)

Common name: Goldmoss
stonecrop
Height: 4in (10cm)
Spread: 8in (20cm)
Aspect: Sun
Soil: Well-drained,
alkaline, fertile
Hardiness: Zone 5
Propagation: Softwood cuttings
of blind shoots, in early summer

A form of the species in which the
leaves and flowers are bright yellow.
Very good for a scree garden or the
front of a border, and a superb
backdrop for butterflies.

Sedum aizoon
'Euphorbioides'
(Crassulaceae)

Common name: Aizoon
stonecrop
Height: 14in (35cm)
Spread: 12in (30cm)
Aspect: Sun
Soil: Well-drained, alkaline
Hardiness: Zone 7
Propagation: Softwood
cuttings of blind shoots,
in early summer

A rhizomatous, herbaceous perennial
from Japan and China. Leaves ovate,
toothed, dark green. Flowers in
terminal clusters, star-shaped, orange-
yellow, in summer.

Sedum alhoroseum
'Mediovariegatum'
(Crassulaceae)

Common name: Stonecrop
Height: 18in (45cm)
Spread: 12in (30cm)
Aspect: Sun
Soil: Well-drained, alkaline
Hardiness: Zone 4
Propagation: Softwood
cuttings of blind shoots, in
early summer

Also known as S. erythrostictum;
from Asia. Leaves ovate, cream,
margined green. Flowers in terminal
clusters, greenish-white stars, in late
summer.

411

Sedum populifolium
(Crassulaceae)

Common name: Poplar
sedum
Height: 12in (30cm)
Spread: 18in (45cm)
Aspect: Sun
Soil: Well-drained, alkaline
Hardiness: Zone 4
Propagation: Softwood
cuttings of blind shoots, in
early summer

A deciduous perennial from Siberia.
Leaves ovate, toothed, pale green.
Flowers scented, in many-flowered
cymes, pinkish-white, star-shaped, in
late summer and early autumn.

Sedum
'Ruby Glow' A.G.M.
(Crassulaceae)

Common name: Stonecrop
Height: 12in (30cm)
Spread: 18in (45cm)
Aspect: Sun
Soil: Well-drained, alkaline
Hardiness: Zone 7
Propagation: Softwood
cuttings of blind shoots, in
early summer

Hybrid perennial. Leaves elliptic,
toothed, purple-green. Flowers star-
shaped, ruby-colored, in loose, many-
flowered cymes, from summer to early
autumn.

Sedum rupestre
(Crassulaceae)

Common names: None
Height: 6in (15cm)
Spread: 2ft (60cm)
Aspect: Sun
Soil: Well-drained, alkaline
Hardiness: Zone 4
Propagation: Softwood
cuttings of blind shoots, in
early summer

An evergreen, mat-forming ground
cover from the mountains of Europe.
Leaves linear, gray-green. Flowers in
terminal cymes, star-shaped, yellow,
in summer.

Sedum spectabile
A.G.M.
(Crassulaceae)

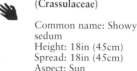

Common name: Showy
sedum
Height: 18in (45cm)
Spread: 18in (45cm)
Aspect: Sun
Soil: Well-drained, alkaline
Hardiness: Zone 4
Propagation: Softwood
cuttings of blind shoots, in
early summer

Clump-forming perennial from Japan
and China. Leaves fleshy, ovate,
toothed, light green. Flowers in dense,
flat-topped cymes, star-shaped, pink,
late summer to autumn.

Sedum telephium
'Abbeydore'
(Crassulaceae)

Common name: Orpine
Height: 2ft (60cm)
Spread: 1ft (30cm)
Aspect: Sun
Soil: Well-drained, alkaline
Hardiness: Zone 4
Propagation: Softwood
cuttings of blind shoots,
in early summer

Cultivar of a rhizomatous perennial.
Leaves oblong, toothed, gray-green.
Flowers star-shaped, dusky pink, in
dense cymes, in late summer to early
autumn.

Sedum telephium
'Arthur Branch'
(Crassulaceae)

Common name: Orpine
Height: 2ft (60cm)
Spread: 1ft (30cm)
Aspect: Sun
Soil: Well-drained, alkaline
Hardiness: Zone 4
Propagation: Softwood
cuttings of blind shoots,
in early summer

Cultivar of a rhizomatous perennial
from Eurasia and the Far East. Leaves
oblong, toothed, light green. Flowers
dusky red, in dense cymes, late
summer to early autumn.

***Sedum telephium* subsp.**
***maximum* 'Atropurpureum'**
A.G.M. (Crassulaceae)

Common name: Orpine
Height: 2ft (60cm)
Spread: 18in (45cm)
Aspect: Sun
Soil: Well-drained, alkaline
Hardiness: Zone 4
Propagation: Softwood
cuttings of blind shoots,
in early summer

A form of the species with dark
purple stems and glaucous, dark
purple leaves. Flowers in cymes, star-
shaped, purple-red, in late summer
and early autumn.

Sedum telephium
subsp. *ruprechtii*
(Crassulaceae)

Common name: Orpine
Height: 2ft (60cm)
Spread: 18in (45cm)
Aspect: Sun
Soil: Well-drained, alkaline
Hardiness: Zone 4
Propagation: Softwood
cuttings of blind shoots,
in early summer

A naturally occurring form of the
orpine with glaucous, blue-green
leaves and creamy-pink, star-shaped
flowers, in late summer and early
autumn.

Selaginella kraussiana
A.G.M.
(Selaginellaceae)

Common name: None
Height: 1in (2.5cm)
Spread: Indefinite
Aspect: Half shade
Soil: Well-drained, acidic,
humus-rich, fertile
Hardiness: Zone 9
Propagation: Spores, in
warmth as soon as ripe;
division, in spring

A tender, evergreen, mat-forming
perennial from the Azores and
southern Africa. Stems covered in
pinnatisect foliage of bright green.

Semiaquilegia ecalcarata
(Ranunculaceae)

Common names: None
Height: 12in (30cm)
Spread: 8in (20cm)
Aspect: Sun or half shade
Soil: Well-drained, acidic,
humus-rich
Hardiness: Zone 6
Propagation: Seed, when
ripe

A short-lived perennial from China.
Leaves 2-ternate, midgreen, purple
below. Flowers in loose panicles,
pendent, pink bells, in early summer.

Sempervivum
arachnoideum
A.G.M. (Crassulaceae)

Common name:
Spiderweb houseleek
Height: 4in (10cm)
Spread: 12in (30cm)
Aspect: Sun
Soil: Very sharply drained,
humus-rich
Hardiness: Zone 5
Propagation: Seed, in spring;
offsets, in spring to early summer

Evergreen, rosette-forming succulent
from the Alps. Leaves fleshy, obovate,
green or red, in cobwebbed rosettes.
Flowers in flat cymes, on leafy stems,
pink, in summer.

Senecio cineraria
(Asteraceae/Compositae)

Common name: Silver
groundsel
Height: 2ft (60cm)
Spread: 2ft (60cm)
Aspect: Sun
Soil: Well-drained, fertile
Hardiness: Zone 8
Propagation: Seed, in
spring; semiripe cuttings, in
summer

An evergreen, Mediterranean
subshrub. Leaves ovate, pinnatisect,
felted, silver-gray. Flowers in loose
corymbs, mustard yellow, in summer.

Senecio pulcher
(Asteraceae/Compositae)

Common name: Showy
groundsel
Height: 2ft (60cm)
Spread: 18in (45cm)
Aspect: Sun
Soil: Well-drained, fertile
Hardiness: Zone 8
Propagation: Seed, in
spring; semiripe cuttings, in
summer

Perennial from Argentina, Uruguay,
and Brazil. Leaves basal, elliptic, and
stem, lance-shaped, toothed. Flowers
in solitary corymbs, carmine-purple,
in late autumn.

Senecio viravira
A.G.M.
(Asteraceae/Compositae)

Common name: Argentine
groundsel
Height: 2ft (60cm)
Spread: 3ft (90cm)
Aspect: Sun
Soil: Well-drained, fertile
Hardiness: Zone 8
Propagation: Seed, in
spring; semiripe cuttings, in
summer

Evergreen subshrub from Argentina.
Leaves deeply pinnatisect, with 5 to 9
silver-white leaflets. Flowers of disc
florets only, in loose corymbs, off-
white, summer to autumn.

Serrratula seoanei
(Asteraceae/Compositae)

Common names: None
Height: 12in (30cm)
Spread: 8in (20cm)
Aspect: Sun
Soil: Well-drained
Hardiness: Zone 7
Propagation: Seed, in
autumn or spring; offsets,
in spring

Perennial from Europe. Leaves
pinnate, toothed, midgreen. Flowers
purple-pink, cornflowerlike, on
branched stems, solitary or in
panicles, in autumn to winter.

Seseli gummiferum
(Apiaceae/Umbelliferae)

Common names: None
Height: 3ft (1m)
Spread: 2ft (60cm)
Aspect: Sun
Soil: Well-drained, fertile
Hardiness: Zone 6
Propagation: Seed or
division, both in autumn
or spring

From the Crimea and Aegean. Leaves
2- or 3-pinnatisect, segments wedge-
shaped, hairy, glaucous-green. Flowers
in umbels of up to 60, pinkish-white
or red, in summer.

415

Sesleria glauca
(Graminae/Poaceae)

Common names: None
Height: 12in (30cm)
Spread: 8in (20cm)
Aspect: Sun or half shade
Soil: Well-drained, fertile
Hardiness: Zone 6
Propagation: Seed, in
spring or autumn; division,
in spring

An evergreen, perennial grass from
Eurasia. Leaves narrow, linear,
glaucous green. Flowers in dense,
cylindrical panicles, greenish-white.

Sidalcea
'Croftway Red'
(Malvaceae)

Common name: Checker-
mallow
Height: 3ft (90cm)
Spread: 18in (45cm)
Aspect: Sun
Soil: Moist, well-drained,
acidic, fertile
Hardiness: Zone 6
Propagation: Division, in
spring or autumn

A hybrid perennial. Leaves round,
lobed, midgreen. Flowers in racemes,
rich pinkish-red, in early and
midsummer. Good for flower
arrangements.

Sidalcea
'Elsie Heugh'
(Malvaceae)

Common name: Checker-
mallow
Height: 3ft (90cm)
Spread: 18in (45cm)
Aspect: Sun
Soil: Moist, well-drained,
acidic, fertile
Hardiness: Zone 6
Propagation: Division, in
spring or autumn

Hybrid perennial. Leaves round,
shallowly lobed, midgreen. Flowers in
racemes, large, satiny, lilac-pink, with
frilled petals, in early and midsummer.

Sidalcea
'William Smith' A.G.M.
(Malvaceae)

Common name: Checker-
mallow
Height: 3ft (90cm)
Spread: 18in (45cm)
Aspect: Sun
Soil: Moist, well-drained,
acidic, fertile
Hardiness: Zone 6
Propagation: Division, in
spring or autumn

A hybrid perennial. Leaves round,
shallowly lobed, midgreen. Flowers
borne in upright racemes, deep pink,
in early and midsummer.

Silene dioica
(Caryophyllaceae)

Common name: Red
campion
Height: 30in (75cm)
Spread: 18in (45cm)
Aspect: Sun or half shade
Soil: Well-drained,
alkaline, fertile
Hardiness: Zone 6
Propagation: Seed, in autumn;
basal cuttings, in spring

Clump-forming European perennial.
Leaves obovate, dark green. Flowers
in branched cymes, round, deep pink
with white base and notched petals, in
spring and summer.

Silene dioica
'Thelma Kay'
(Caryophyllaceae)

Common name: Red
campion
Height: 32in (80cm)
Spread: 18in (45cm)
Aspect: Sun or half shade
Soil: Well-drained,
alkaline, fertile
Hardiness: Zone 6
Propagation: Rooted offshoots,
from midsummer to autumn

Cultivar of the red campion with
variegated foliage and double flowers
in late spring to midsummer. Does not
self-seed as much as the single form.

Silene uniflora
'Druett's Variegated'
(Caryophyllaceae)

Common name: Bladder
campion
Height: 8in (20cm)
Spread: 8in (20cm)
Aspect: Sun
Soil: Well-drained,
alkaline, fertile
Hardiness: Zone 3
Propagation: Rooted offshoots,
from midsummer to autumn

Cultivar of a creeping, semievergreen,
coastal plant. Leaves lance-shaped,
fleshy, cream and green. Flowers
white, solitary or in clusters, petals
deeply cut, in summer.

Silene uniflora
'Robin Whitebreast'
(Caryophyllaceae)

Common name: Bladder
campion
Height: 8in (20cm)
Spread: 12in (30cm)
Aspect: Sun
Soil: Well-drained,
alkaline, fertile
Hardiness: Zone 3
Propagation: Rooted offshoots,
from midsummer to autumn

A sprawling, hybrid perennial. Leaves
lance-shaped, fleshy, green. Flowers
solitary or in clusters, white with a
green calyx, in summer.

Silphium laciniatum
(Asteraceae/Compositae)

Common name: Compass-plant
Height: 10ft (3m)
Spread: 2ft (60cm)
Aspect: Sun or half shade
Soil: Moist, fertile, deep, heavy
Hardiness: Zone 4
Propagation: Seed, when ripe; division, in spring

Ovate, bristly, toothed, midgreen leaves, pointing north-south to minimize exposure to sun. Terminal corymbs of dark-centered, yellow daisies, midsummer to early autumn.

Sisyrinchium angustifolium (Iridaceae)

Common name: Common blue-eyed grass
Height: 20in (50cm)
Spread: 6in (15cm)
Aspect: Sun
Soil: Well-drained, alkaline, fertile
Hardiness: Zone 3
Propagation: Seed, in spring; division, in spring or autumn

A clump-forming perennial from North America. Leaves linear, midgreen. Flowers solitary, single, blue with a yellow throat, in summer.

Sisyrinchium 'Californian Skies' (Iridaceae)

Common name: Blue-eyed grass
Height: 6in (15cm)
Spread: 4in (10cm)
Aspect: Sun
Soil: Well-drained, alkaline, fertile
Hardiness: Zone 8
Propagation: Division, in spring or autumn

Short-lived, rhizomatous hybrid. Leaves basal, sword-shaped, gray-green. Flowers large, flat, blue, dark-centered, in clusters, surrounded by bracts, spring and summer.

Sisyrinchium californicum Brachypus Group (Iridaceae)

Common name: Yellow-eyed grass
Height: 2ft (60cm)
Spread: 6in (15cm)
Aspect: Sun
Soil: Well-drained, alkaline, fertile
Hardiness: Zone 8
Propagation: Seed, in spring; division, in spring or autumn

A rhizomatous perennial from North America. Leaves sword-shaped, gray-green. Flowers small, solitary stars, yellow with dark veins, in succession, in summer.

Sisyrinchium idahoense 'Album'
(Iridaceae)

Common name: Idaho
blue-eyed grass
Height: 6in (15cm)
Spread: 6in (15cm)
Aspect: Sun
Soil: Well-drained,
alkaline, fertile
Hardiness: Zone 3
Propagation: Seed, in spring;
division, in spring or autumn

A rhizomatous perennial from the
U.S.A. Leaves narrowly linear,
midgreen. Flowers star-shaped, white
with yellow throats, in summer.

Sisyrinchium 'Quaint and Queer'
(Iridaceae)

Common name: Blue-eyed
grass
Height: 8in (20cm)
Spread: 8in (20cm)
Aspect: Sun
Soil: Well-drained,
alkaline, fertile
Hardiness: Zone 7
Propagation: Division, in
spring or autumn

A hybrid, rhizomatous perennial.
Leaves basal, narrowly linear,
midgreen. Flowers small, star-shaped,
yellow, brown, and purple, in
summer.

Sisyrinchium striatum
(Iridaceae)

Common names: None
Height: 3ft (90cm)
Spread: 1ft (30cm)
Aspect: Sun
Soil: Well-drained,
alkaline, fertile
Hardiness: Zone 8
Propagation: Seed, in
spring; division, in spring
or autumn

Rhizomatous evergreen from
Argentina and Chile. Leaves basal,
linear, stiff, gray-green. Flowers in
clusters, stemless, pale yellow cups,
early to midsummer. Black seed heads.

Sisyrinchium striatum 'Aunt May'
(Iridaceae)

Common names: None
Height: 3ft (90cm)
Spread: 1ft (30cm)
Aspect: Sun
Soil: Well-drained,
alkaline, fertile
Hardiness: Zone 8
Propagation: Division, in
spring or autumn

A form of the species with leaves
striped green and cream. Yellow,
stemless flowers in clusters in early to
midsummer, followed by attractive
seed heads.

419

Smilacina racemosa A.G.M. (Convallariaceae/Liliaceae)

Common names: False Solomon's seal; wild spikenard
Height: 1m (3ft)
Spread: 2ft (60cm)
Aspect: Full or half shade
Soil: Moist, well-drained, acidic, humus-rich, fertile
Hardiness: Zone 4
Propagation: Seed, in autumn; division, in spring

Rhizomatous woodlander. Leaves ovate to lance-shaped, midgreen. Flowers scented, creamy-white stars, in terminal racemes, in spring, sometimes followed by red berries.

Solenopsis axillaris (Campanulaceae)

Common names: None
Height: 1ft (30cm)
Spread: 1ft (30cm)
Aspect: Sun
Soil: Well-drained, fertile
Hardiness: Zone 9
Propagation: Seed, in warmth in spring; softwood cuttings, in summer

A tender perennial from Australia. Leaves ovate, pinnatisect, leaflets narrow, mid-green. Flowers small, star-shaped, pale blue, abundant, from spring to autumn.

Solidago 'Goldenmosa' A.G.M. (Asteraceae/Compositae)

Common name: Goldenrod
Height: 32in (80cm)
Spread: 18in (45cm)
Aspect: Sun
Soil: Sharply drained, fertile
Hardiness: Zone 4
Propagation: Division, in autumn or spring

Woody hybrid. Leaves wrinkled, midgreen, lance-shaped. Flowers tiny, yellow, in one-sided, conical panicles, late summer and autumn. Deadhead to prevent self-seeding.

x *Solidaster luteus* (Asteraceae/Compositae)

Common name: Hybrid goldenrod
Height: 3ft (1m)
Spread: 1ft (30cm)
Aspect: Sun
Soil: Well-drained, fertile
Hardiness: Zone 6
Propagation: Basal cuttings or division, both in spring

Intergeneric garden hybrid. Leaves lance-shaped to linear. Flowers small, yellow, daisylike, in panicles, midsummer to autumn. Deadhead to prevent self-seeding.

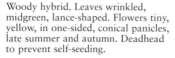

x *Solidaster luteus* 'Lemore' A.G.M. (Asteraceae/Compositae)

Common name: Hybrid goldenrod
Height: 32in (80cm)
Spread: 12in (30cm)
Aspect: Sun
Soil: Well-drained, fertile
Hardiness: Zone 6
Propagation: Division, in spring

Selected form of intergeneric garden hybrid, with panicles of small, daisylike flowers of pale lemon. Leaves lance-shaped to linear. Deadhead to prevent self-seeding.

Sparaxis elegans (Iridaceae)

Common name: Wand-flower
Height: 18in (45cm)
Spread: 4in (10cm)
Aspect: Sun
Soil: Well-drained, fertile
Hardiness: Zone 9
Propagation: Seed, when ripe; offsets, when dormant

Cormous perennial from South Africa. Leaves basal, in fans, sword-shaped, bright green. Flowers in spikes, wide funnels, red, orange, or white, in spring and summer.

Sphaeralcea fendleri (Malvaceae)

Common name: Prarie mallow
Height: 32in (80cm)
Spread: 24in (60cm)
Aspect: Sun
Soil: Sharply drained, fertile
Hardiness: Zone 8
Propagation: Seed, in spring; softwood cuttings, in summer

Sprawling subshrub from the U.S.A. Leaves ovate, 3-lobed, toothed, gray-green. Flowers in axillary panicles, pink saucers, in summer. Prune to keep compact.

Sphaeralcea munroana (Malvaceae)

Common name: Prarie mallow
Height: 32in (80cm)
Spread: 36in (90cm)
Aspect: Sun
Soil: Well-drained, fertile
Hardiness: Zone 8
Propagation: Seed, in spring; softwood cuttings, in summer

Sprawling perennial. Leaves ovate to diamond-shaped, 3- to 5-lobed, gray-green. Flowers in axillary panicles, salmon-pink saucers, over a very long period in summer.

421

Spiranthes gracilis
(Orchidaceae)

Stachys byzantina
(Labiatae/Lamiaceae)

Common name: Nodding
Ladies'-tresses
Height: 30in (75cm)
Spread: 4in (10cm)
Aspect: Half shade
Soil: Moist, well-drained,
humus-rich, fertile
Hardiness: Zone 3
Propagation: Division,
when dormant

Common names: Lamb's-
ears; woolly betony
Height: 18in (45cm)
Spread: 2ft (60cm)
Aspect: Sun
Soil: Well-drained, fertile
Hardiness: Zone 5
Propagation: Seed, in
autumn or spring; division,
in spring

A hardy, tuberous, terrestrial orchid
from North America. Leaves basal,
ovate, mid-green. Flowers in spiral
racemes, small, white, perfumed, in
autumn.

Mat-forming perennial. Leaves in
basal rosettes, oblong, veined, densely
white-woolly. Flowers in spikes, pink-
purple, woolly, from early summer to
autumn

Stachys macrantha
(Labiatae/Lamiaceae)

Stachys macrantha
'Superba'
(Labiatae/Lamiaceae)

Common names: None
Height: 2ft (60cm)
Spread: 1ft (30cm)
Aspect: Sun or half shade
Soil: Well-drained, fertile
Hardiness: Zone 5
Propagation: Seed, in
autumn or spring; division,
in spring

Common names: None
Height: 2ft (60cm)
Spread: 1ft (30cm)
Aspect: Sun or half shade
Soil: Well-drained, fertile
Hardiness: Zone 5
Propagation: Seed, in
autumn or spring; division,
in spring

Leaves ovate, scalloped, veined,
wrinkled, deep green. Flowers in
dense spikes, hooded, purplish-pink,
from early summer to early autumn.

A form of the species with dense
spikes of purplish, hooded flowers.
Leaves ovate, scalloped, veined,
wrinkled, deep green. Top-heavy,
especially in rain; needs staking.

Stachys monieri
(Labiatae/Lamiaceae)

Common names: None
Height: 20in (50cm)
Spread: 18in (45cm)
Aspect: Sun
Soil: Well-drained, fertile
Hardiness: Zone 5
Propagation: Seed, in
autumn or spring; division,
in spring

A perennial from the Alps and
Pyrenees. Leaves in basal rosette,
ovate, crinkled, glossy, dark green.
Flowers in spikes, pale pink, white, or
deep pink, in late summer.

Stachys officinalis
(Labiatae/Lamiaceae)

Common name: Common
betony
Height: 2ft (60cm)
Spread: 1ft (30cm)
Aspect: Sun or half shade
Soil: Well-drained, fertile
Hardiness: Zone 5
Propagation: Seed, in
autumn or spring; division,
in spring

Perennial from Europe. Leaves in
rosettes, ovate, veined, wrinkled,
scalloped, mid-green. Flowers in dense
spikes, purplish-red, white, or pink,
all summer.

Stipa gigantea
A.G.M.
(Graminae/Poaceae)

Common name: Giant
feather grass
Height: 8ft (2.5m)
Spread: 4ft (1.2m)
Aspect: Sun
Soil: Well-drained, fertile,
light
Hardiness: Zone 8
Propagation: Seed or
division, both in spring

Evergreen grass from the Iberian
peninsula. Leaves long, linear,
inrolled, midgreen. Flowers silvery,
green-purple spikes, turning gold, in
panicles in summer.

Stokesia laevis
(Asteraceae/Compositae)

Common name: Stokesia
Height: 2ft (60cm)
Spread: 18in (45cm)
Aspect: Sun
Soil: Moist, well-drained,
acidic, light, fertile
Hardiness: Zone 5
Propagation: Seed, in
autumn; division, in spring

Rosette-forming evergreen. Leaves
basal, lance-shaped, spiny, with white
midribs. Flowers solitary,
cornflowerlike, purplish-pink, center
paler, midsummer to autumn.

Stokesia laevis
'Alba'
(Asteraceae/Compositae)

Common name: White
Stokesia
Height: 2ft (60cm)
Spread: 18in (45cm)
Aspect: Sun
Soil: Moist, well-drained,
acidic, light, fertile
Hardiness: Zone 5
Propagation: Seed, in
autumn; division, in spring

Form of the species with
cornflowerlike, solitary, white flowers
from midsummer to autumn. Leaves
in basal rosette, evergreen, lance-
shaped, spiny, with white midribs.

Strobilanthes atropurpureus
(Acanthaceae)

Common names: None
Height: 4ft (1.2m)
Spread: 3ft (90cm)
Aspect: Sun or half shade
Soil: Sharply drained,
fertile
Hardiness: Zone 5
Propagation: Seed or basal
or softwood cuttings, all in
warmth in spring

A perennial from N India. Leaves
large, ovate, toothed, dark green.
Flowers tubular, indigo-blue, borne in
dense spikes, in summer.

Strelitzia reginae
A.G.M.
(Musaceae/Strelitziaceae)

Common name: Queen's
Bird-of-paradise
Height: 6ft (1.8m)
Spread: 3ft (90cm)
Aspect: Sun or half shade
Soil: Moist, well-drained,
humus-rich, fertile
Hardiness: Zone 9
Propagation: Seed or
division, both in spring

Evergreen from South Africa. Leaves
oblong to lance-shaped, midgreen.
Flowers have green spathes, flushed
purple-red, yellow calyces, blue
corollas, in winter to spring.

Stylophorum diphyllum
(Papaveraceae)

Common name: Celandine
poppy
Height: 1ft (30cm)
Spread: 1ft (30cm)
Aspect: Full or half shade
Soil: Moist, humus-rich,
fertile
Hardiness: Zone 7
Propagation: Seed, in
autumn; division, in spring

Perennial woodlander. Leaves
pinnatisect, with 5 to 7 hairy,
midgreen, obovate leaflets. Flowers
yellow, poppylike, in terminal umbels,
intermittently in summer.

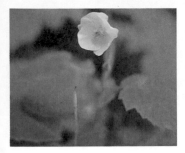

Stylophorum lasiocarpum
(Papaveraceae)

Common names: None
Height: 18in (45cm)
Spread: 12in (30cm)
Aspect: Full or half shade
Soil: Moist, humus-rich,
fertile
Hardiness: Zone 7
Propagation: Seed, in
autumn; division, in spring

Perennial woodlander from China.
Leaves pinnatifid, with 4 to 7 oblong,
toothed lobes, midgreen. Flowers in
terminal clusters, yellow, poppylike,
in summer.

Symphyandra armena
(Campanulaceae)

Common name: Ring
bellflower
Height: 18in (45cm)
Spread: 12in (30cm)
Aspect: Sun or half shade
Soil: Well-drained, fertile
Hardiness: Zone 7
Propagation: Seed, when
ripe or in spring

Rhizomatous plant from Turkey and
Iran. Leaves heart-shaped, velvety-
hairy, toothed, midgreen. Flowers in
corymbs, pendent, tubular, pale blue,
long period in summer.

Symphytum
'Goldsmith'
(Boraginaceae)

Common name: Comfrey
Height: 1ft (30cm)
Spread: 1ft (30cm)
Aspect: Sun or half shade
Soil: Moist, fertile
Hardiness: Zone 5
Propagation: Division,
in spring; root cuttings,
in early winter

Rhizomatous ground cover. Leaves
ovate to lance-shaped, dark green,
variegated cream and gold. Flowers in
cymes, pale blue, mid- and late spring.
Toxic and skin-irritant.

Symphytum ibericum
(Boraginaceae)

Common name: Comfrey
Height: 16in (40cm)
Spread: Indefinite
Aspect: Sun or half shade
Soil: Moist, fertile
Hardiness: Zone 5
Propagation: Seed, in
autumn or spring; division,
in spring

Invasive, rhizomatous plant. Leaves
ovate, wrinkled, veined, midgreen.
Flowers tubular, pendent, white or
pale yellow, in cymes, in late spring.
Toxic and irritant.

Symphytum ibericum
'Langthornes Pink'
(Boraginaceae)

Common name: Comfrey
Height: 16in (40cm)
Spread: 18in (45cm)
Aspect: Sun or half shade
Soil: Moist, fertile
Hardiness: Zone 5
Propagation: Division, in
spring; root cuttings, in
early winter

Form of the species with pendent,
tubular, pink flowers, in cymes, in late
spring. Leaves ovate, wrinkled, veined,
midgreen. Poisonous, skin-irritant, but
low-allergen.

Symphytum
'Lambrook Sunrise'
(Boraginaceae)

Common name: Comfrey
Height: 22in (55cm)
Spread: 12in (30cm)
Aspect: Sun or half shade
Soil: Moist, fertile
Hardiness: Zone 5
Propagation: Division, in
spring; root cuttings, in
early winter

A form which is non-invasive, and has
leaves of acid yellow. Flowers in
cymes, tubular, blue, in spring,
making a lovely contrast to the
foliage. Toxic and irritant.

Symphytum orientale
(Boraginaceae)

Common names: Comfrey
Height: 28in (70cm)
Spread: 18in (45cm)
Aspect: Sun or half shade
Soil: Moist, fertile
Hardiness: Zone 5
Propagation: Seed, in
autumn or spring; division,
in spring

Rhizomatous perennial from Europe.
Leaves ovate-oblong, densely hairy,
midgreen. Flowers in many-flowered
cymes, pendent, tubular, white, in
summer. Toxic, irritant.

Symphytum x
uplandicum
(Boraginaceae)

Common name: Comfrey
Height: 6ft (1.8m)
Spread: 4ft (1.2m)
Aspect: Sun or half shade
Soil: Moist, fertile
Hardiness: Zone 5
Propagation: Seed, in
autumn or spring; division,
in spring

A rhizomatous hybrid of garden
origin. Leaves basal, elliptic to lance-
shaped, midgreen. Flowers in cymes,
lilac-blue, from late spring to late
summer.

Symphytum × uplandicum 'Axminster Gold' (Boraginaceae)

Common name: Comfrey
Height: 6ft (1.8m)
Spread: 4ft (1.2m)
Aspect: Sun or half shade
Soil: Moist, well-drained
Hardiness: Zone 5
Propagation: Division, in spring; root cuttings, in early winter

A variegated and noninvasive form of this garden hybrid, with elliptic to lance-shaped leaves margined pale gold. Flowers white, in cymes, from late spring to late summer.

Symphytum × uplandicum 'Variegatum' A.G.M. (Boraginaceae)

Common name: Comfrey
Height: 6ft (1.8m)
Spread: 4ft (1.2m)
Aspect: Sun or half shade
Soil: Moist, fertile
Hardiness: Zone 5
Propagation: Division, in spring; root cuttings, in early winter

A noninvasive cultivar of this hybrid, with elliptic to lance-shaped leaves variegated heavily in yellow. Flowers in cymes, lilac, from late spring to late summer.

Tanacetum coccineum 'Brenda' A.G.M. (Asteraceae/Compositae)

Common names: Painted daisy; pyrethrum
Height: 30in (75cm)
Spread: 18in (45cm)
Aspect: Sun
Soil: Sharply drained
Hardiness: Zone 5
Propagation: Division or basal cuttings, both in spring

Clump-forming. Leaves basal, 2-pinnatisect, 10–14 lance-shaped, toothed leaflets. Single, solitary, yellow-centered, cerise daisies, early summer, again if deadheaded. Skin irritant.

Tanacetum coccineum 'Eileen May Robinson' A.G.M. (Asteraceae/Compositae)

Common names: Painted daisy; pyrethrum
Height: 30in (75cm)
Spread: 18in (45cm)
Aspect: Sun
Soil: Sharply drained
Hardiness: Zone 5
Propagation: Division or basal cuttings, both in spring

Clump-forming. Leaves pinnatisect, 10–14 lance-shaped, toothed segments. Solitary, single daisies, rich pink, yellow discs, early summer, again if deadheaded. Skin irritant.

Tanacetum coccineum 'James Kelway' A.G.M. (Asteraceae/Compositae)

Common names: Painted daisy; pyrethrum
Height: 30in (75cm)
Spread: 18in (45cm)
Aspect: Sun
Soil: Sharply drained
Hardiness: Zone 5
Propagation: Division or basal cuttings, both in spring

Short-lived. Leaves pinnatisect, 10–14 lance-shaped, toothed segments. Solitary, single daisies, deep crimson, yellow discs, in early summer, again if deadheaded. Skin irritant.

Tanacetum coccineum 'Snow Cloud' (Asteraceae/Compositae)

Common names: Painted daisy; pyrethrum
Height: 2ft (60cm)
Spread: 18in (45cm)
Aspect: Sun
Soil: Sharply drained
Hardiness: Zone 5
Propagation: Division or basal cuttings, both in spring

Short-lived. Leaves pinnatisect, 10–14 lance-shaped, toothed segments. Solitary, single white daisies, yellow centers, in early summer, again if deadheaded. Skin irritant.

Tanacetum parthenium 'Aureum' (Asteraceae/Compositae)

Common name: Feverfew
Height: 2ft (60cm)
Spread: 1ft (30cm)
Aspect: Sun
Soil: Sharply drained
Hardiness: Zone 6
Propagation: Seed or division, both in spring

Aromatic herb. Leaves basal and stem, hairy, ovate, pinnatisect, golden-yellow. Flowers in dense corymbs, small, single, white, daisylike, with yellow discs, summer.

Tanacetum vulgare (Asteraceae/Compositae)

Common name: Common tansy
Height: 3ft (90cm)
Spread: 18in (45cm)
Aspect: Sun
Soil: Sharply drained
Hardiness: Zone 4
Propagation: Seed or division, both in spring

Invasive perennial from Europe. Leaves aromatic, pinnate, up to 12 lance-shaped, toothed leaflets, midgreen. Flowers in flat corymbs, bright yellow buttons, in summer.

Telekia speciosa
(Asteraceae/Compositae)

Common names: None
Height: 6ft (1.8m)
Spread: 3ft (90cm)
Aspect: Half shade
Soil: Moist
Hardiness: Zone 6
Propagation: Seed, when
ripe; division, in spring

Woodlander. Leaves ovate, toothed,
midgreen, aromatic. Flowers in sprays,
single, with bracts, ray florets narrow,
yellow, late summer and early
autumn.

Tellima grandiflora
(Saxifragaceae)

Common name: Alaska
fringecup
Height: 30in (75cm)
Spread: 12in (30cm)
Aspect: Sun or half shade
Soil: Moist, humus-rich
Hardiness: Zone 6
Propagation: Seed or
division, both in spring

Rosette-forming ground cover for
shade. Leaves heart-shaped, hairy,
lobed, scalloped. Flowers greenish-
white, in terminal racemes on hairy
stems, late spring to midsummer.

Teucrium x lucidrys
(Labiatae/Lamiaceae)

Common name: Wall
germander
Height: 20in (50cm)
Spread: 12in (30cm)
Aspect: Sun
Soil: Well-drained,
alkaline, poor
Hardiness: Zone 5
Propagation: Seed, when ripe; softwood
or semi-ripe cuttings, in summer

Subshrub from Eurasia and North
Africa. Leaves aromatic, ovate-
obovate, toothed, dark green. Flowers
in racemes, in whorls, tubular,
purplish-pink, summer to autumn.

Teucrium x lucidrys
'Variegata'
(Labiatae/Lamiaceae)

Common name:
Variegated wall germander
Height: 20in (50cm)
Spread: 12in (30cm)
Aspect: Sun
Soil: Well-drained,
alkaline, poor
Hardiness: Zone 5
Propagation: Softwood or semi-ripe
cuttings, both in summer

Subshrub cultivar with aromatic,
ovate-obovate, toothed, cream and
green leaves. Flowers tubular,
purplish-pink, in whorled racemes.
Excellent ground cover.

Thalictrum aquilegiifolium 'White Cloud' (Ranunculaceae)

Common name: Meadow-rue
Height: 3ft (1m)
Spread: 18in (45cm)
Aspect: Half shade
Soil: Moist, humus-rich
Hardiness: Zone 6
Propagation: Seed, when ripe; division, in spring

Architectural, rhizomatous perennial. Leaves columbine-like, 2-pinnate, leaflets obovate, midgreen. Flowers in flat-topped panicles, in clusters, white, fluffy, in early summer.

Thalictrum delavayi A.G.M. (Ranunculaceae)

Common name: Meadow-rue
Height: 5ft (1.5m)
Spread: 2ft (60cm)
Aspect: Half shade
Soil: Moist, humus-rich
Hardiness: Zone 6
Propagation: Seed, when ripe or in spring

Rhizomatous perennial from Tibet to China. Leaves 2- or 3-pinnate, lobes 3-lobed. Pink, fluffy flowers on widely branching stems, in panicles, midsummer to early autumn.

Thalictrum delavayi 'Album' (Ranunculaceae)

Common name: Meadow-rue
Height: 5ft (1.5m)
Spread: 2ft (60cm)
Aspect: Half shade
Soil: Moist, humus-rich
Hardiness: Zone 6
Propagation: Division, in spring

Form of the species with white, fluffy flowers in panicles on widely branching stems, midsummer to early autumn. Leaves 2- or 3-pinnate.

Thalictrum delavayi 'Hewitt's Double' A.G.M. (Ranunculaceae)

Common name: Meadow-rue
Height: 5ft (1.5m)
Spread: 2ft (60cm)
Aspect: Half shade
Soil: Moist, humus-rich
Hardiness: Zone 6
Propagation: Division, in spring

Sterile form with flowers that lack stamens but have many sepals, making the flower a rounded pompon, rich mauve in color, from midsummer to early autumn.

Thalictrum flavum
(Ranunculaceae)

Common name: Yellow
meadow-rue
Height: 36in (90cm)
Spread: 18in (45cm)
Aspect: Half shade
Soil: Moist, humus-rich
Hardiness: Zone 6
Propagation: Seed, when
ripe or in spring

Rhizomatous perennial from Eurasia.
Leaves 2- or 3-pinnate, leaflets
obovate, midgreen. Flowers scented,
in panicles, with yellow sepals and
stamens, in summer.

Thalictrum flavum
subsp. _glaucum_ A.G.M.
(Ranunculaceae)

Common name: Yellow
meadow-rue
Height: 3ft (1m)
Spread: 2ft (60cm)
Aspect: Sun
Soil: Humus-rich
Hardiness: Zone 6
Propagation: Seed, when
ripe or in spring

Subspecies with 2- or 3-pinnate,
glaucous foliage. Bears large panicles
of pale lemon-yellow flowers in
summer. An excellent flower for
cutting.

Thalictrum minus
adiantifolium
(Ranunculaceae)

Common name: Meadow-
rue
Height: 32in (80cm)
Spread: 12in (30cm)
Aspect: Half shade
Soil: Moist, humus-rich
Hardiness: Zone 6
Propagation: Seed, when
ripe or in spring

Rhizomatous plant. Leaves 3- or 4-
pinnate, leaflets ovate, lobed,
glaucous, midgreen. Flowers in
panicles, insignificant, yellow, in
summer. Grown for its fernlike foliage.

Thermopsis lanceolata
(Leguminosae/Papilionaceae)

Common names: None
Height: 32in (80cm)
Spread: 12in (30cm)
Aspect: Sun or half shade
Soil: Well-drained, humus-
rich, fertile
Hardiness: Zone 3
Propagation: Seed, in
spring

Rhizomatous perennial from Siberia
to Japan. Leaves 3-palmate, leaflets
ovate, light green. Flowers in racemes,
lupinlike, yellow, from spring to
midsummer.

Thymus x *citriodorus*
'Silver Queen' A.G.M.
(Labiatae/Lamiaceae)

Common name: Lemon-
scented thyme
Height: 12in (30cm)
Spread: 18in (45cm)
Aspect: Sun
Soil: Well-drained, alkaline
Hardiness: Zone 7
Propagation: Division, in
spring

Evergreen subshrub of garden origin.
Leaves lance-shaped, lemon-scented
when bruised, midgreen, variegated
cream. Flowers in irregular heads,
pale pink, in summer.

Thymus serpyllum
var. *coccineus* A.G.M.
(Labiatae/Lamiaceae)

Common name: Mother-
of-thyme
Height: 4in (10cm)
Spread: 12in (30cm)
Aspect: Sun
Soil: Well-drained, alkaline
Hardiness: Zone 5
Propagation: Division, in
spring

Aromatic, evergreen subshrub from
Europe. Leaves aromatic, linear-
elliptic, dark green. Flowers crimson-
red, in summer. Excellent in a scree or
a raised bed.

Tiarella cordifolia
A.G.M.
(Saxifragaceae)

Common name: Allegheny
foam flower
Height: 1ft (30cm)
Spread: 2ft (60cm)
Aspect: Full or half shade
Soil: Any protected from
winter wet, but prefers
moist, humus-rich
Hardiness: Zone 3
Propagation: Seed, when ripe or in
spring; division, in spring

Rhizomatous, woodland perennial
from North America. Leaves ovate,
light green. Flowers in racemes, fluffy,
white, in summer. Spreads by stolons.

Tiarella wherryi
A.G.M.
(Saxifragaceae)

Common name: Foam
flower
Height: 8in (20cm)
Spread: 8in (20cm)
Aspect: Full or half shade
Soil: Any, but prefers
moist, humus-rich
Hardiness: Zone 6
Propagation: Seed, when ripe
or in spring; division, in spring

Rhizomatous perennial from the
U.S.A. Leaves ovate, hairy, 3-lobed,
light green. Flowers in racemes, white,
tinged pink, in late spring and early
summer.

Tolmeia menziesii
A.G.M.
(Saxifragaceae)

Common name: Piggy-
back plant
Height: 2ft (60cm)
Spread: 2m (6ft)
Aspect: Full shade
Soil: Moist, humus-rich
Hardiness: Zone 7
Propagation: Seed, in
autumn; division, in spring

Rhizomatous ground cover. Leaves
reniform, lobed, veined, toothed, light
green. Flowers small, purple-brown,
scented, in one-sided racemes, late
spring and early summer.

Tradescantia x
andersoniana 'Isis'
A.G.M. (Commelinaceae)

Common name:
Spiderwort
Height: 2ft (60cm)
Spread: 2ft (60cm)
Aspect: Sun or half shade
Soil: Moist, fertile
Hardiness: Zone 5
Propagation: Division, in
spring or autumn

Clump-forming hybrid. Leaves
narrow, lance-shaped, pointed,
midgreen. Flowers 3-petalled, dark
blue, in paired, terminal cymes, early
summer to early autumn.

TRADESCANTIA (Commelinaceae)
Spiderwort

A genus of some 60 or so species, all perennial, from North,
Central, and South America. The genus is well-known for the
tender species, often grown as house- or conservatory plants,
but there are also hardy types suitable for borders. Their natural
habitats are scrub or woodland, so they are fairly tolerant of
any soil as long as it is not waterlogged, and will do well in sun
or partial shade. The varieties in cultivation are hybrids, and go
by the name *Tradescantia* x *andersoniana*. Their leaves are green,
often flushed with purple, narrowly lance-shaped and slightly
fleshy, and they bear flowers in white and shades of pink, blue,
and purple. *Tradescantia* flowers are 3-petalled and saucer-
shaped. They are individually short-lived, but are borne in
succession over a long season from summer to autumn, especially
if deadheaded. They can be disappointing if not carefully
positioned, because the flowers nestle down in the leaves, and
may not be seen to their best advantage from any great
distance. Despite being quite dwarf, *Tradescantia* sometimes
need to be staked. They are fairly long-lived and become large
in time, and so benefit from regular division. They are low-
allergen plants, but contact with the sap may irritate the skin.

Tradescantia x *andersoniana*
'Karminglut'
(Commelinaceae)

Common name:
Spiderwort
Height: 2ft (60cm)
Spread: 2ft (60cm)
Aspect: Sun or half shade
Soil: Moist, fertile
Hardiness: Zone 5
Propagation: Division, in
spring or autumn

Clump-forming hybrid. Leaves
narrow, pointed, lance-shaped,
midgreen. Flowers 3-petalled,
carmine-red, in paired, terminal
cymes, early summer to early autumn.

Tradescantia x *andersoniana*
'Osprey' A.G.M.
(Commelinaceae)

Common name:
Spiderwort
Height: 2ft (60cm)
Spread: 2ft (60cm)
Aspect: Sun or half shade
Soil: Moist, fertile
Hardiness: Zone 5
Propagation: Division, in
spring or autumn

A hybrid, clump-forming perennial.
Leaves narrow, pointed, lance-shaped,
midgreen. Flowers in paired, terminal
cymes, large, white, from early
summer to early autumn.

Tradescantia x *andersoniana*
'Purewell Giant'
(Commelinaceae)

Common name:
Spiderwort
Height: 2ft (60cm)
Spread: 2ft (60cm)
Aspect: Sun or half shade
Soil: Moist, fertile
Hardiness: Zone 5
Propagation: Division, in
spring or autumn

Clump-forming hybrid. Leaves
narrow, lance-shaped, midgreen.
Flowers in paired, terminal cymes,
large, 3-petalled, purple-red, from
early summer to early autumn.

Tradescantia x *andersoniana*
'Zwanenburg Blue'
(Commelinaceae)

Common name: Spider
wort
Height: 2ft (60cm)
Spread: 2ft (60cm)
Aspect: Sun or half shade
Soil: Moist, fertile
Hardiness: Zone 5
Propagation: Division, in
spring or autumn

Clump-forming hybrid. Leaves
narrow, pointed, lance-shaped,
midgreen. Flowers in paired, terminal
cymes, 3-petalled, large, dark blue,
early summer to early autumn.

Tradescantia ohiensis
(Commelinaceae)

Common name: Ohio
spiderwort
Height: 3ft (90cm)
Spread 2ft (60cm)
Aspect: Sun or half shade
Soil: Moist, fertile
Hardiness: Zone 7
Propagation: Seed, when
ripe; division, in autumn or
spring

A perennial species from the U.S.A.
Leaves narrow, lance-shaped,
midgreen. Flowers in pairs in terminal
cymes, blue, white, purple or pink, in
spring.

Tricyrtis formosana
A.G.M.
(Convallariaceae/Liliaceae)

Common name: Toad-lily
Height: 30in (75cm)
Spread: 18in (45cm)
Aspect: Sun or half shade
Soil: Moist, well-drained,
humus-rich
Hardiness: Zone 7
Propagation: Seed, when
ripe; division, in early spring

Rhizomatous, stoloniferous plant.
Leaves inverse lance-shaped, veined,
glossy. Cymes of upward-facing,
pinkish stars, spotted purple, early
autumn. For a raised bed.

Tricyrtis hirta
(Convallariaceae/Liliaceae)

Common name: Hairy
toad-lily
Height: 30in (75cm)
Spread: 2ft (60cm)
Aspect: Sun or half shade
Soil: Moist, well-drained,
humus-rich
Hardiness: Zone 5
Propagation: Seed, when
ripe; division, in early spring

Rhizomatous plant. Leaves lance-
shaped, hairy, veined, light green.
Flowers white, purple-spotted stars,
late summer to midautumn. Seen at
best in a raised site.

Tricyrtis latifolia
(Convallariaceae/Liliaceae)

Common name: Toad-lily
Height: 30in (75cm)
Spread: 3ft (90cm)
Aspect: Sun or half shade
Soil: Moist, well-drained,
humus-rich
Hardiness: Zone 5
Propagation: Seed, when
ripe; division, in spring or
autumn

Rhizomatous, clump-forming plant.
Leaves ovate, veined, glossy green.
Branched cymes of yellow stars,
spotted brown, in early to
midsummer. Seen best in a raised site.

Tricyrtis ohsumiensis
(Convallariaceae/Liliaceae)

Common name: Toad-lily
Height: 8in (20cm)
Spread: 12in (30cm)
Aspect: Half or full shade,
protected from midday sun
Soil: Moist, well-drained,
humus-rich
Hardiness: Zone 5
Propagation: Seed, when ripe;
division, in spring or autumn

Rhizomatous, clump-forming plant.
Leaves lance-shaped, veined, glossy,
light green, scorched by hot sun.
Flowers yellow saucers, spotted
brown, in early autumn.

Trifolium pannonicum
(Leguminosae/Papilionaceae)

Common name:
Hungarian clover
Height: 3ft (90cm)
Spread: 3ft (90cm)
Aspect: Sun
Soil: Moist, well-drained,
fertile
Hardiness: Zone 5
Propagation: Seed, division or
separation of plantlets, all in spring

Perennial from E Europe. Leaves
palmate, basal leaves obovate, stem
leaves inverse lance-shaped, midgreen.
Flowers clover-like, creamy-yellow, in
summer.

Trifolium rubens
(Leguminosae/
Papilionaceae)

Common name: White
clover
Height: 12in (30cm)
Spread: 20in (50cm)
Aspect: Sun
Soil: Moist, well-drained,
fertile
Hardiness: Zone 4
Propagation: Seed, division or
separation of plantlets, all in spring

Selected form of the lawn weed, and
equally invasive. Leaves 3-foliate,
leaflets toothed, midgreen. Flowers
cloverlike, perfumed, pink, from
spring to autumn.

Trillium chloropetalum
var. *giganteum* A.G.M.
(Liliaceae/Trilliaceae)

Common name: Giant
trillium
Height: 16in (40cm)
Spread: 8in (20cm)
Aspect: Full or half shade
Soil: Moist, well-drained,
deep, acidic, humus-rich
Hardiness: Zone 6
Propagation: Seed, as soon as
ripe; division, after flowering

A rhizomatous perennial. Leaves
ovate to diamond-shaped, dark green,
marbled gray or maroon. Flowers
scented, brown-purple, among or
above the leaves, in spring.

TRILLIUM (Liliaceae/Ttrilliaceae)
Trinity flower • Wake-robin • Wood lily

A genus of some 30 species of rhizomatous woodland plants, the majority of them originating in North America, but some native to the Himalayas and northeast Asia. They bloom in the spring, and bear their leaves, tepals, and petals in threes, hence the name. The leaves, borne in an apical whorl, range from lance- to diamond-shaped, and are veined and often marbled with purple or silver. The flowers are cup- or funnel-shaped and often stalkless, growing directly above the leaves. All species like some degree of shade and an acidic soil, except for *Trillium rivale*, which prefers a sunny position and alkaline soil. All like a moisture-retentive, humus-rich, woodland type of soil, and should be mulched annually with leaf mold. They are extremely resentful of disturbance or damage to the roots, so site them carefully on first planting, and avoid digging around them. They require some patience: divisions may be slow to establish, and plants grown from seed take several years to reach flowering size. In all, these can be demanding plants, but the rewards are generous. They are soundly perennial, and would make good cut flowers, except that one has perforce to cut the leaves at the same time, and this is harmful to the plants, so best avoided.

Trillium chloropetalum
var. *giganteum* A.G.M.
(Liliaceae/Trilliaceae)

Common names: Giant
trillium
Height: 16in (40cm)
Spread: 8in (20cm)
Aspect: Full or half shade
Soil: Moist, well-drained,
deep, acidic, humus-rich
Hardiness: Zone 6
Propagation: Seed, as soon
as ripe; division, after flowering

This rhizomatous plant has a both a purple form (*left*) and this white form. Leaves ovate to diamond-shaped, dark green, marbled gray or maroon.

Trillium cuneatum
(Liliaceae/Trilliaceae)

Common name:
Whippoorwill flower
Height: 2ft (60cm)
Spread: 1ft (30cm)
Aspect: Full or half shade
Soil: Moist, well-drained,
deep, acidic, humus-rich
Hardiness: Zone 6
Propagation: Seed, as soon
as ripe; division, after flowering

Rhizomatous perennial from the southeast U.S.A. Leaves rounded, midgreen, marked silver. Flowers scented, maroon, borne above the leaves in spring.

Trillium erectum
A.G.M.
(Liliaceae/Trilliaceae)

Common names:
Berthroot, purple trillium
Height: 20in (50cm)
Spread: 12in (30cm)
Aspect: Full or half shade
Soil: Moist, well-drained,
deep, acidic, humus-rich
Hardiness: Zone 4
Propagation: Seed, as soon as
ripe; division, after flowering

A rhizomatous perennial from
E North America. Leaves ovate,
midgreen. Flowers deep red-purple,
borne above the leaves in spring.
Smell described as like a wet dog.

Trillium grandiflorum
A.G.M.
(Liliaceae/Trilliaceae)

Common name: Snow
trillium
Height: 16in (40cm)
Spread: 18in (45cm)
Aspect: Full or half shade
Soil: Moist, well-drained,
deep, acidic, humus-rich
Hardiness: Zone 5
Propagation: Seed, as soon as
ripe; division, after flowering

Rhizomatous perennial from E North
America. Leaves ovate, dark green.
Flowers pure white, fading to pink,
borne above the leaves in spring and
summer.

Trillium luteum
A.G.M.
(Liliaceae/Trilliaceae)

Common name: Yellow
trillium
Height: 16in (40cm)
Spread: 12in (30cm)
Aspect: Full or half shade
Soil: Moist, well-drained,
deep, acidic, humus-rich
Hardiness: Zone 5
Propagation: Seed, as soon as
ripe; division, after flowering

Rhizomatous perennial from the
southeast U.S.A. Leaves ovate,
midgreen. Flowers lemon-scented,
upright, yellow, borne above the
leaves in spring.

Trillium ovatum
A.G.M.
(Liliaceae/Trilliaceae)

Common name: Pacific
trillium
Height: 20in (50cm)
Spread: 8in (20cm)
Aspect: Full or half shade
Soil: Moist, well-drained,
deep, acidic, humus-rich
Hardiness: Zone 5
Propagation: Seed, as soon as
ripe; division, after flowering

Rhizomatous plant from western
North America. Leaves diamond-
shaped, deep green. Flowers upright,
pure white, petals ovate, borne above
the leaves in spring.

Trillium pusillum
(Liliaceae/Trilliaceae)

Trillium sessile
(Liliaceae/Trilliaceae)

Common name: Dwarf
trillium
Height: 6in (15cm)
Spread: 4in (10cm)
Aspect: Full or half shade
Soil: Moist, well-drained,
deep, acidic, humus-rich
Hardiness: Zone 6
Propagation: Seed, as soon as
ripe; division, after flowering

Rhizomatous perennial from eastern
North America. Leaves lance-shaped,
dark green. Flowers small, white,
borne among the leaves, in spring.

Common name: Toad
trillium
Height: 12in (30cm)
Spread: 8in (20cm)
Aspect: Full or half shade
Soil: Moist, well-drained,
deep, acidic, humus-rich
Hardiness: Zone 4
Propagation: Seed, as soon as
ripe; division, after flowering

Rhizomatous plant from the U.S.A.
Leaves rounded, dark green, marbled
gray, silver and maroon. Flowers
upright, maroon-red, petals lance-
shaped, above the leaves, spring.

Trillium vaseyi
(Liliaceae/Trilliaceae)

Tritonia disticha
subsp. *rubrolucens*
(Iridaceae)

Common name: Sweet
trillium
Height: 26in (65cm)
Spread: 12in (30cm)
Aspect: Full or half shade
Soil: Moist, well-drained,
deep, acidic, humus-rich
Hardiness: Zone 6
Propagation: Seed, as soon as
ripe; division, after flowering

A rhizomatous perennial from the
south-east U.S.A. Leaves rhombic,
dark green. Flowers held horizontally,
perfumed, dark red-purple, in spring.

Common names: None
Height: 3ft (90cm)
Spread 6in (15cm)
Aspect: Sun
Soil: Sharply drained
Hardiness: Zone 9
Propagation: Seed, in
warmth when ripe; offsets,
when dormant

Cormous perennial from southern
Africa. Leaves basal, linear, erect,
lance-shaped, midgreen. Flowers
open, pink funnels in one-sided spikes,
from mid- to late summer.

Trollius acaulis
(Ranunculaceae)

Common name:
Globeflower
Height: 12in (30cm)
Spread: 6in (15cm)
Aspect: Sun or half shade
Soil: Moist or wet, deep,
humus-rich, fertile
Hardiness: Zone 6
Propagation: Seed, as soon as ripe or
in spring; division, after flowering

Clump-forming waterside perennial.
Leaves 5- to 7-palmate, leaflets 3-
lobed, toothed, midgreen. Flowers
solitary, single, yellow saucers, in
spring. Poisonous.

Trollius chinensis
'Imperial Orange'
(Ranunculaceae)

Common name:
Globeflower
Height: 36in (90cm)
Spread: 18in (45cm)
Aspect: Sun or half shade
Soil: Moist or wet, deep,
humus-rich, fertile
Hardiness: Zone 5
Propagation: Seed, as soon as ripe or
in spring; division, after flowering

Cultivar of a clump-forming bog plant.
Leaves basal, large, 5 lance-shaped,
toothed lobes, and smaller stem.
Flowers solitary, bowl-shaped, orange,
in summer. Poisonous.

Trollius × cultorum
'Lemon Queen'
(Ranunculaceae)

Common name:
Globeflower
Height: 36in (90cm)
Spread: 18in (45cm)
Aspect: Sun or half shade
Soil: Moist or wet, deep,
humus-rich, fertile
Hardiness: Zone 5
Propagation: Seed, as soon as ripe or
in spring; division, after flowering

Hybrid cultivar. Leaves basal, large, 5-
lobed, lobes lance-shaped, toothed;
smaller stem leaves. Flowers large,
solitary, pale yellow, globular,
midspring to midsummer. Toxic.

Trollius × cultorum
'Orange Princess' A.G.M.
(Ranunculaceae)

Common name:
Globeflower
Height: 3ft (90cm)
Spread: 18in (45cm)
Aspect: Sun or half shade
Soil: Moist or wet, deep,
humus-rich, fertile
Hardiness: Zone 5
Propagation: Seed, as soon as ripe or
in spring; division, after flowering

Clump-forming hybrid. Leaves large
basal, smaller stem, 5-lobed, lobes
lance-shaped, toothed, glossy. Flowers
solitary, orange bowls, midspring to
midsummer. Poisonous.

Trollius europaeus
(Ranunculaceae)

Common name: Common
globeflower
Height: 3ft (90cm)
Spread: 18in (45cm)
Aspect: Sun or half shade
Soil: Moist or wet, deep,
humus-rich, fertile
Hardiness: Zone 5
Propagation: Seed, as soon as ripe or
in spring; division, after flowering

Clump-forming species. Leaves 5-
lobed, segments wedge-shaped,
toothed, midgreen. Flowers solitary,
spherical, yellow, early to midsummer.
Poisonous.

Trollius yunnanensis
(Ranunculaceae)

Common name:
Globeflower
Height: 28in (70cm)
Spread: 12in (30cm)
Aspect: Sun or half shade
Soil: Moist or wet, deep,
humus-rich, fertile
Hardiness: Zone 5
Propagation: Seed, as soon as ripe or
in spring; division, after flowering

A clump-forming bog plant. Leaves 3-
to 5-lobed, segments ovate, toothed,
glossy. Flowers solitary, yellow
saucers, from late spring to early
summer. Poisonous.

Tropaeolum polyphyllum
(Tropaeolaceae)

Common name: Wreath
nasturtium
Height: 4in (10cm)
Spread: 4ft (1.2m)
Aspect: Sun
Soil: Well-drained, humus-rich
Hardiness: Zone 8
Propagation: Division, in early spring;
basal or stem cuttings, in spring or
early summer

Trailing, rhizomatous, herbaceous
plant for a sunny wall. Leaves up to 9
lobes, glaucous. Flowers yellow, over a
long period in summer. Spreads a long
way underground.

Tuberaria lignosa
(Cistaceae)

Common names: None
Height: 1ft (30cm)
Spread: 3ft (90cm)
Aspect: Sun
Soil: Well-drained
Hardiness: Zone 8
Propagation: Seed, in early
spring

A spreading, rosette-forming
perennial from the Mediterranean.
Leaves ovate, hairy, dull green.
Flowers in loose cymes, bright yellow,
all summer.

441

Tulbaghia cepacea
(Alliaceae/Liliaceae)

Common names: None
Height: 24in (60cm)
Spread: 8in (20cm)
Aspect: Sun
Soil: Well-drained, humus-rich, fertile
Hardiness: Zone 8
Propagation: Seed, when ripe or in spring; division, in spring

Rhizomatous plant from southern Africa. Leaves narrow, linear, grayish-green. Flowers soft purple-pink, night-scented, tubular, in umbels, from late spring to summer.

Tulbaghia cominsii
(Alliaceae/Liliaceae)

Common names: None
Height: 10in (25cm)
Spread: 4in (10cm)
Aspect: Sun
Soil: Well-drained, humus-rich, fertile
Hardiness: Zone 8
Propagation: Seed, when ripe or in spring; division, in spring

Rhizomatous perennial from South Africa. Leaves narrowly linear, glaucous, midgreen. Flowers in terminal scapes, white, night-scented, in spring to summer.

Tulbaghia violacea
(Alliaceae/Liliaceae)

Common names: None
Height: 2ft (60cm)
Spread: 1ft (30cm)
Aspect: Sun
Soil: Well-drained, humus-rich, fertile
Hardiness: Zone 7
Propagation: Seed, when ripe or in spring; division, in spring

Rhizomatous perennial from South Africa. Leaves narrow, linear, grayish-green. Flowers in terminal umbels, scented, from summer to autumn.

Tulipa
'Apeldoorn' (4)
(Liliaceae)

Common names: None
Height: 2ft (60cm)
Spread: Nil
Aspect: Sun
Soil: Well-drained, fertile
Hardiness: Zone 5
Propagation: Offsets, after flowering

A Darwin hybrid tulip with flowers of cherry-red outside, signal-red with yellow-edged black marks inside, and with black anthers, in midspring.

TULIPA (Liliaceae)
Tulip

A genus of some 100 species from Europe, Asia and the Middle East, especially Central Asia. All are hardy, bulbous perennials. They prefer sun but will take light shade, and must have a well-drained soil but seem to prefer heavy soils to light ones. Tulips are grown for their showy flowers, which are usually terminal and upright, with six tepals. They vary from cup- or bowl-shaped to goblet-shaped, some with long, very narrow tepals, or lilylike or star-shaped; some are fringed. There is a wide range of colors and bicolors. The leaves are usually basal, broadly ovate, and sometimes wavy-edged or channeled. The bulbs should be planted 6in (15cm) deep in the autumn. Cultivars benefit from being lifted and ripened every year once the leaves have died down. The Greigii and Kaufmanniana groups and the species can be left in the ground all year; mark the position to avoid damaging the bulbs by infill planting. These also benefit from being lifted and divided every few years, and this should be done as soon as the foliage dies down; mice love tulip bulbs, so store lifted bulbs out of their reach and protect newly planted bulbs from disturbance. Contact with any part may cause skin irritation, and all parts are mildly poisonous if ingested.

Tulipa
'Bright Gem' (15)
(Liliaceae)

Common names: None
Height: 14in (35cm)
Spread: Nil
Aspect: Sun
Soil: Well-drained
Hardiness: Zone 5
Propagation: Offsets, after flowering

A Miscellaneous Group tulip with flowers of sulfur-yellow, flushed orange, and orange-bronze basal marks, in early and midspring.

Tulipa clusiana var.
chrysantha A.G.M (15)
(Liliaceae)

Common names: Clusius tulip
Height: 1ft (30cm)
Spread: Nil
Aspect: Sun
Soil: Well-drained, fertile
Hardiness: Zone 6
Propagation: Seed, in autumn; offsets, after flowering

A species from Iran to the Himalayas. Leaves linear, glaucous, gray-green. Flowers bowl-shaped, yellow, tinged red-brown outside, in early and midspring.

Tulipa
'Keizerskroon' A.G.M. (1)
(Liliaceae)

Common names: None
Height: 1ft (30cm)
Spread: Nil
Aspect: Sun
Soil: Well-drained, fertile
Hardiness: Zone 5
Propagation: Offsets, after
flowering

A Single Early Group tulip with cup-shaped, scarlet flowers with broad margins of bright yellow, in midspring. Leaves broadly ovate, midgreen.

Tulipa
'Fantasy' A.G.M. (10)
(Liliaceae)

Common names: None
Height: 22in (55cm)
Spread: Nil
Aspect: Sun
Soil: Well-drained, fertile
Hardiness: Zone 5
Propagation: Offsets, after
flowering

A Parrot Group tulip. Flowers cup-shaped, salmon-pink streaked green, with fringed edges, in late spring. Excellent border plant and a good cut flower.

CLASSIFIED LIST AND INTERNATIONAL REGISTER OF TULIP NAMES by Koninklijke Algemeene Vereening voor Bloembollenculture, 1996

Group 1 Single Early Group

Group 2 Double Early Group

Group 3 Triumph Group

Group 4 Darwin Hybrid Group

Group 5 Single late, including Darwin Group and Cottage Group

Group 6 Lily-Flowered Group

Group 7 Fringed Group

Group 8 Viridiflora Group

Group 9 Rembrandt Group

Group 10 Parrot Group

Group 11 Double Late Group

Group 12 Kaufmanniana Group

Group 13 Fosteriana Group

Group 14 Greigii Group

Group 15 Miscellaneous

Tulipa linifolia
A.G.M (15)
(Liliaceae)

Common names: None
Height: 8in (20cm)
Spread: Nil
Aspect: Sun
Soil: Well-drained, fertile
Hardiness: Zone 5
Propagation: Seed, in
autumn; offsets, after
flowering

Species from Afghanistan, Uzbekistan, and Iran. Leaves linear, sickle-shaped, grey-green. Flowers red with black-purple bases, bowl-shaped, in early and midspring.

Tulipa
'Monte Carlo' (2)
(Liliaceae)

Common names: None
Height: 1ft (30cm)
Spread: Nil
Aspect: Sun
Soil: Well-drained, fertile
Hardiness: Zone 5
Propagation: Offsets, after
flowering

A Double Early Group tulip with
bowl-shaped flowers of sulfur-yellow,
with small "feather" markings of red
at the tips of the tepals, in midspring.

Tulipa
'Oranje Nassau' A.G.M.
(2) (Liliaceae)

Common names: None
Height: 1ft (30cm)
Spread: Nil
Aspect: Sun
Soil: Well-drained, fertile
Hardiness: Zone 5
Propagation: Offsets, after
flowering

A Double Early Group tulip with
open, bowl-shaped flowers of blood-
red, flushed fiery-red, in midspring.
Good for growing in a container.

Tulipa praestans
'Fusilier' A.G.M. (15)
(Liliaceae)

Common name: Leather-
bulb tulip
Height: 1ft (30cm)
Spread: Nil
Aspect: Sun
Soil: Well-drained, fertile
Hardiness: Zone 5
Propagation: Offsets, after
flowering

Selected form of a species from
Kazakhstan and Tajikistan. Leaves
lance-shaped, keeled, downy grey-
green. Flowers in clusters, bright red,
in early to midspring.

Tulipa
'Red Riding Hood' A.G.M.
(14) (Liliaceae)

Common names: None
Height: 8in (20cm)
Spread: Nil
Aspect: Sun
Soil: Well-drained, fertile
Hardiness: Zone 5
Propagation: Offsets, after
flowering

A Greigii Group tulip. Leaves broad,
gray-green, spotted maroon-blue.
Flowers carmine red outside, scarlet-
red inside, with black bases, in early
spring.

445

Tulipa saxatilis
Bakeri Group (15)
(Liliaceae)

Common name: Cliff tulip
Height: 14in (35cm)
Spread: Nil
Aspect: Sun
Soil: Well-drained, fertile
Hardiness: Zone 6
Propagation: Offsets, after
flowering

Tulipa sprengeri
A.G.M. (15)
(Liliaceae)

Common names: None
Height: 20in (50cm)
Spread: Nil
Aspect: Sun or half shade
Soil: Well-drained
Hardiness: Zone 5
Propagation: Seed, in
autumn; offsets, after
flowering

Selection of a Mediterranean tulip.
Leaves linear, shiny, midgreen.
Flowers pink with yellow bases,
margined white, fragrant, mid- and
late spring. Spreads by runners.

Species from Turkey, but extinct in the
wild. Leaves linear, shiny, midgreen.
Flowers red or orange, in early
summer. Will naturalize, and has
attractive seed pods, shown here.

Tulipa tarda
A.G.M. (15)
(Liliaceae)

Common names: None
Height: 6in (15cm)
Spread: Nil
Aspect: Sun
Soil: Well-drained, fertile
Hardiness: Zone 5
Propagation: Seed, in
autumn; offsets, after
flowering

Tulipa
'Toronto' A.G.M. (14)
(Liliaceae)

Common names: None
Height: 8in (20cm)
Spread: Nil
Aspect: Sun
Soil: Well-drained, fertile
Hardiness: Zone 5
Propagation: Offsets, after
flowering

A species from Central Asia. Leaves
lance-shaped, arching, shiny, bright
green. Flowers in clusters, perfumed,
white, with yellow bases, in early and
midspring.

A Greigii Group tulip with broad,
ovate leaves, marked bluish-maroon.
Flowers pinkish-red, tinged vermilion
outside and tangerine inside, in
midspring.

Tulipa turkestanica
A.G.M. (15)
(Liliaceae)

Common names: None
Height: 1ft (30cm)
Spread: Nil
Aspect: Sun
Soil: Well-drained, fertile
Hardiness: Zone 5
Propagation: Seed, in
autumn; offsets, after
flowering

A species from Central Asia and
China. Leaves linear, gray-green.
Flowers star-shaped, white with
yellow centers, in early to midspring.

Tulipa urumiensis
A.G.M. (15)
(Liliaceae)

Common names: None
Height: 6in (15cm)
Spread: Nil
Aspect: Sun
Soil: Well-drained, fertile
Hardiness: Zone 5
Propagation: Seed, in
autumn; offsets, after
flowering

A Miscellanous Group tulip from
Iran. Leaves linear, midgreen. Flowers
star-shaped, yellow, flushed lilac or
brown outside, in pairs or solitary, in
early spring.

Tweedia caerulea
A.G.M.
(Asclepiadaceae)

Common names: None
Height: 36in (1m)
Spread: 8in (20cm)
Aspect: Sun
Soil: Moist, well-drained,
fertile
Hardiness: Zone 10
Propagation: Seed, in spring;
softwood cuttings, in
summer

A twining, evergreen subshrub from
Brazil. Leaves oblong, downy, pale
green. Flowers in 3- or 4-flowered
cymes, sky-blue aging to purple, from
summer to early autumn.

Umbilicus rupestris
(Crassulaceae)

Common names:
Navelwort; pennywort
Height: 16in (40cm)
Spread: 6in (15cm)
Aspect: Sun or half shade
Soil: Sharply drained
Hardiness: Zone 7
Propagation: Seed, in spring
or autumn

A perennial from Europe. Leaves
rounded, succulent, depressed in
center, midgreen. Flowers in spikes,
small, tubular, greenish-white, in
summer. Good wall plant.

Uncinia rubra

(Cyperaceae)

Common name: Hook
sedge
Height: 12in (30cm)
Spread: 16in (40cm)
Aspect: Sun or half shade
Soil: Moist, well-drained,
fertile
Hardiness: Zone 8
Propagation: Seed, in spring;
division, in early summer

An evergreen grass from New
Zealand. Leaves flat, linear, pointed,
rich red. Flowers dark brown to
black, in spikes, in mid- to late
summer.

Urospermum delachampii

(Asteraceae/Compositae)

Common names: None
Height: 16in (40 cm)
Spread: 24in (60cm)
Aspect: Sun
Soil: Sharply drained,
fertile
Hardiness: Zone 6
Propagation: Seed, in spring
or autumn; division, in
spring

A perennial from the Mediterranean.
Leaves obovate, toothed, gray-green.
Flowers dandelion-like, lemon-yellow,
in summer.

Uvularia grandiflora
A.G.M.
(Convallariaceae/Liliaceae)

Common name: Big
merrybells
Height: 32in (80cm)
Spread: 24in (60cm)
Aspect: Full or half shade
Soil: Moist, well-drained,
humus-rich, fertile
Hardiness: Zone 4
Propagation: Seed, when
ripe; division, in spring

Rhizomatous, spreading woodlander.
Ovate, perfoliate, leaves. Flowers
yellow, tubular, pendent, solitary or
paired, on arching stems, mid and late
spring. Red berries.

Valeriana officinalis
subsp. *sambucifolia*

(Valerianaceae)

Common name: Common
valerian
Height: 6ft (2m)
Spread: 30in (75cm)
Aspect: Sun or half shade
Soil: Moist
Hardiness: Zone 4
Propagation: Seed, division
or basal cuttings, all in
spring

Rhizomatous plant from Europe.
Leaves aromatic, pinnate; up to 9
pairs of lance-shaped, toothed,
leaflets. Flowers white, salverform, in
rounded cymes, all summer.

Valeriana phu
'Aurea'
(Valerianaceae)

Common name: Valerian
Height: 5ft (1.5m)
Spread: 2ft (60cm)
Aspect: Sun or half shade
Soil: Moist
Hardiness: Zone 6
Propagation: Seed,
division or basal cuttings,
all in spring

Rhizomatous perennial from the
Caucasus. Leaves aromatic, simple or
pinnatifid, first yellow, then lime- then
midgreen. Flowers in corymbs, white,
salverform, in spring.

Valeriana montana
(Valerianaceae)

Common name: Dwarf
valerian
Height: 16in (40cm)
Spread: 8in (20cm)
Aspect: Sun or half shade
Soil: Moist, alkaline,
fertile
Hardiness: Zone 5
Propagation: Seed, division
or basal cuttings, all in spring

Rhizomatous perennial from the
mountains of Europe. Leaves basal,
entire, elliptic, and stem, ovate.
Flowers in corymbs, white, salverform,
late spring or early summer.

Veratrum album
(Liliaceae/Melianthiaceae)

Common name: False
hellebore
Height: 6ft (2m)
Spread: 2ft (60cm)
Aspect: Sun or half shade
Soil: Moist, well-drained,
deep, fertile
Hardiness: Zone 5
Propagation: Seed, when ripe;
division, in autumn or spring

Rhizomatous plant. Leaves broad,
elliptic, pleated, shiny. Flowers in
many-branched panicles, white stars,
early and midsummer. Very
poisonous. Slugs can decimate it.

Veratrum nigrum
A.G.M.
(Liliaceae/Melianthiaceae)

Common name: False
hellebore
Height: 4ft (1.2m)
Spread: 2ft (60cm)
Aspect: Sun or half shade
Soil: Moist, well-drained,
deep, fertile
Hardiness: Zone 6
Propagation: Seed, when ripe;
division, in autumn or spring

Rhizomatous plant. Leaves broad,
elliptic, pleated, shiny, light green.
Flowers offensive-smelling, small,
brown-black, in panicles. Very toxic,
highly allergenic, and irritant.

VERBASCUM (Scrophulrriaceae)
Mullein

A genus of over 350 species, from Europe, Asia and North Africa. Most of the species are biennial, but there are also annuals, perennials, and some subshrubs; the perennial members are short-lived, often dying after flowering. Some are evergreen, but most are not. They grow for the most part in open scrubland or on dry hillsides, but a few are found in open woods. They like a sunny position and sharp drainage. They generally form a basal clump or rosette of large, soft, leaves, which may be simple, lobed, or toothed, and produce one or more dense spikes of saucer-shaped flowers. The flowers are individually short-lived, but they are borne in succession over a long season. The flowers of hybrid cultivars tend to be larger and more showy than those of species. Many mulleins are quite tall, and they may need to be staked. All self-sow freely, and the seedlings of the named varieties will not come true, so they should be deadheaded. The larger species can be left to naturalize in gravel or in wild gardens, where they make impressive architectural plants and benefit from the support of other plants. The smaller types are good for rock gardens, screes, or even walls. All mulleins are unfortunately prone to powdery mildew.

Verbascum bombyciferum
A.G.M.
(Scrophulariaceae)

Common name: Mullein
Height: 6ft (1.8m)
Spread: 3ft (90cm)
Aspect: Sun
Soil: Sharply drained, alkaline, poor
Hardiness: Zone 6
Propagation: Seed or division, both in spring; root cuttings, in winter

Short-lived evergreen from Turkey. Leaves basal, densely white-woolly, silky-hairy. Flowers sulfur-yellow, saucer-shaped, in spikes, in clusters, in summer.

Verbascum chaixii
(Scrophulariaceae)

Common name: Chaix mullein
Height: 3ft (90cm)
Spread: 18in (45cm)
Aspect: Sun
Soil: Sharply drained, alkaline, poor
Hardiness: Zone 5
Propagation: Seed or division, both in spring; root cuttings, in winter

Species from Europe. Leaves basal, ovate, hairy, and stem, rounded. Flowers in slim panicles on white-woolly stems, pale yellow saucers, from mid- to late summer.

Verbascum chaixii 'Album' (Scrophulariaceae)

Common name: Chaix mullein
Height: 3ft (90cm)
Spread: 2ft (60cm)
Aspect: Sun
Soil: Sharply drained, alkaline, poor
Hardiness: Zone 5
Propagation: Seed or division, both in spring; root cuttings, in winter

Leaves basal, ovate, hairy, midgreen, and stem, rounded. Flowers on white-woolly stems, in slim panicles, white saucers with mauve centres, from mid- to late summer.

Verbascum dumulosum A.G.M. (Scrophulariaceae)

Common name: Mullein
Height: 10in (25cm)
Spread: 16in (40cm)
Aspect: Sun
Soil: Sharply drained, alkaline, poor
Hardiness: Zone 8
Propagation: Seed or division, both in spring; root cuttings, in winter

Evergreen subshrub from Turkey. Leaves elliptic, hairy-felted, gray-green. Flowers on white-downy stems, in short racemes, yellow saucers, late spring to early summer.

Verbascum chaixii 'Gainsborough' A.G.M. (Scrophulariaceae)

Common name: Chaix mullein
Height: 4ft (1.2m)
Spread: 1ft (30cm)
Aspect: Sun
Soil: Sharply drained, alkaline, poor
Hardiness: Zone 6
Propagation: Division, in spring; root cuttings, in winter

A hybrid mullein. Leaves in basal rosettes, ovate, wrinkled, gray-green. Flowers in long panicles, soft yellow saucers, from early to late summer.

Verbascum 'Helen Johnson' A.G.M. (Scrophulariaceae)

Common name: Mullein
Height: 3ft (90cm)
Spread: 1ft (30cm)
Aspect: Sun
Soil: Sharply drained, alkaline, poor
Hardiness: Zone 7
Propagation: Division, in spring; root cuttings, in winter

Evergreen, hybrid mullein. Leaves ovate, wrinkled, downy, gray-green. Flowers in erect spikes, pinkish-brown saucers, from early to late summer.

Verbascum 'Jackie' (Scrophulariaceae)

Common name: Mullein
Height: 3ft (90cm)
Spread: 18in (45cm)
Aspect: Sun
Soil: Sharply drained, alkaline, poor
Hardiness: Zone 6
Propagation: Division, in spring; root cuttings, in winter

Rosette-forming, hybrid mullein. Leaves ovate, downy, gray-green. Flowers in erect spikes, buff-pink saucers with a purple eye, in summer.

Verbascum nigrum (Scrophulariaceae)

Common name: Dark mullein
Height: 3ft (90cm)
Spread: 2ft (60cm)
Aspect: Sun
Soil: Sharply drained, alkaline, poor
Hardiness: Zone 5
Propagation: Seed or division, both in spring; root cuttings, in winter

Rosette-forming species. Leaves basal, ovate, and stem, rounded, mid- to dark-green. Slim racemes of clustered flowers, dark yellow saucers, midsummer to early autumn.

Verbascum olympicum (Scrophulariaceae)

Common name: Olympic mullein
Height: 6ft (2m)
Spread: 2ft (60cm)
Aspect: Sun
Soil: Sharply drained, alkaline, poor
Hardiness: Zone 6
Propagation: Seed or division, both in spring; root cuttings, in winter

Rosette-forming species. Leaves broad, lance-shaped, gray-white woolly. Flowers in panicles, clustered, golden-yellow saucers, from early to late summer. May then die.

Verbena bonariensis (Verbenaceae)

Common names: None
Height: 6ft (2m)
Spread: 75cm (30in)
Aspect: Sun
Soil: Moist, well-drained, fertile
Hardiness: Zone 8
Propagation: Seed or division, both in spring

Clump-forming plant. Leaves few, oblong, wrinkled, stem-clasping, midgreen. Flowers in cymes, purple-lilac salvers, midsummer to early autumn. Excellent butterfly plant.

Verbena
'Alba'
(Verbenaceae)

Common name: White
blue vervain
Height: 4ft (1.2m)
Spread: 2ft (60cm)
Aspect: Sun
Soil: Moist, well-drained,
fertile
Hardiness: Zone 3
Propagation: Seed or
division, both in spring

Clump-forming plant from North
America. Leaves lance-shaped,
toothed, pointed, midgreen. Flowers
in stiff panicles, white, salverform,
early summer to early autumn.

Verbena
'Homestead Purple'
(Verbenaceae)

Common names: Hybrid
verbena
Height: 18in (45cm)
Spread: 20in (50cm)
Aspect: Sun
Soil: Moist, well-drained, fertile
Hardiness: Zone 8
Propagation: Division in spring
or autumn; stem-tip cuttings,
in late summer

Hybrid cultivar. Leaves ovate,
toothed, rough, dark green. Flowers
in tight panicles, tiny, salverform,
purple, all summer to autumn.

Verbena
'Sissinghurst' A.G.M.
(Verbenaceae)

Common name: Hybrid
verbena
Height: 18in (45cm)
Spread: (20in (50cm)
Aspect: Sun
Soil: Moist, well-drained,
fertile
Hardiness: Zone 8
Propagation: Division, in autumn or
spring; stem-tip cuttings, in late summer

A hybrid cultivar. Leaves ovate,
toothed, rough, midgreen. Flowers
tiny, salverform, cherry-red, in tight
panicles, from summer to autumn.

Veronica
'Blue Spire'
(Scrophulariaceae)

Common names: None
Height: 3ft (90cm)
Spread: 2ft (60cm)
Aspect: Sun or half shade
Soil: Moist, well-drained,
humus-rich, fertile
Hardiness: Zone 6
Propagation: Division, in
autumn or spring

A hybrid perennial. Leaves lance-
shaped, toothed, pointed, midgreen.
Flowers in dense, erect racemes,
tubular, deep blue, in late summer and
early autumn.

Veronica gentianoides A.G.M.
(Scrophulariaceae)

Common name: Gentian
speedwell
Height: 18in (45cm)
Spread: 18in (45cm)
Aspect: Sun or half shade
Soil: Moist, well-drained,
humus-rich, fertile
Hardiness: Zone 4
Propagation: Seed, in autumn;
division, in autumn or spring

Rosette-forming perennial from
Turkey and the Ukraine. Leaves
broad, lance-shaped, thick, dark
green. Flowers pale blue cups, in erect
racemes, in early summer.

Veronica 'Ray of Fire'
(Scrophulariaceae)

Common names: None
Height: 30in (75cm)
Spread: 2ft (60cm)
Aspect: Sun or half shade
Soil: Moist, well-drained,
humus-rich, fertile
Hardiness: Zone 5
Propagation: Division, in
autumn or spring

A hybrid, mat-forming perennial.
Leaves lance-shaped, pointed,
midgreen. Flowers in dense, terminal
panicles, pinkish-red, tubular, in late
summer and autumn.

Veronica spicata subsp. *incana* A.G.M.
(Scrophulariaceae)

Common name: Spike
speedwell
Height: 1ft (30cm)
Spread: 1ft (30cm)
Aspect: Sun or half shade
Soil: Moist, well-drained,
humus-rich, fertile
Hardiness: Zone 3
Propagation: Seed, in autumn;
division, in autumn or spring

A mat-forming perennial from Eurasia
and Turkey. Leaves linear, toothed,
silver-hairy. Flowers in dense, terminal
racemes, bright blue stars, from early
to late summer.

Veronica spicata 'Rotfuchs'
(Scrophulariaceae)

Common name: Spike
speedwell
Height: 1ft (30cm)
Spread: 1ft (30cm)
Aspect: Sun or half shade
Soil: Moist, well-drained,
humus-rich, fertile
Hardiness: Zone 3
Propagation: Division, in spring or
autumn; stem-tip cuttings, in summer

A hybrid, mat-forming perennial.
Leaves linear, toothed, midgreen.
Flowers in dense, terminal racemes,
deep pink stars, from early to late
summer.

Veronicastrum virginicum
f. *album*
(Scrophulariaceae)

Common name: Culver's
root
Height: 6ft (2m)
Spread: 18in (45cm)
Aspect: Sun or half shade
Soil: Moist, humus-rich,
fertile
Hardiness: Zone3
Propagation: Seed, in autumn;
division, in spring

Perennial from North America.
Leaves lance-shaped, toothed,
pointed, dark green. Flowers white,
tubular, in slim, dense racemes, from
midsummer to early autumn.

Veronicastrum virginicum
'Pink Glow'
(Scrophulariaceae)

Common name: Culver's-
root
Height: 6ft (2m)
Spread: 18in (45cm)
Aspect: Sun or half shade
Soil: Moist, humus-rich,
fertile
Hardiness: Zone 3
Propagation: Division, in
spring

Selected form of the species. Leaves
lance-shaped, toothed, pointed, dark
green. Soft pink, tubular flowers, in
dense racemes, from midsummer to
early autumn.

Vinca major
(Apocynaceae)

Common name: Big
periwinkle
Height: 18in (45cm)
Spread: Indefinite
Aspect: Sun or half shade
Soil: Moisture-retentive
Hardiness: Zone 7
Propagation: Division, from
autumn to spring

Evergreen, trailing, Mediterranean
ground-cover subshrub. Leaves ovate,
shiny, dark green. Flowers starry,
violet-blue, over long period from
mid-spring to autumn. Toxic.

Vinca major
'Variegata' A.G.M.
(Apocynaceae)

Common name:
Variegated big periwinkle
Height: 18in (45cm)
Spread: Indefinite
Aspect: Sun or half shade
Soil: Moisture-retentive
Hardiness: Zone 7
Propagation: Division, from
autumn to spring

Evergreen, trailing, Mediterranean
ground cover subshrub. Leaves ovate,
dark green margined cream; good for
cutting. Flowers lilac-blue, starry,
from spring to autumn.

Vinca minor
(Apocynaceae)

Common names: Myrtle;
periwinkle
Height: 8in (20cm)
Spread: Indefinite
Aspect: Sun or half shade
Soil: Moisture-retentive
Hardiness: Zone 4
Propagation: Division, from
autumn to spring

Trailing, evergreen subshrub from
Eurasia, not invasive like *V. major*.
Leaves ovate, dark green. Flowers
reddish-purple, blue or white, all
summer long.

Viola biflora
(Va)
(Violaceae)

Common name: Twin-
flowered violet
Height: 3in (8cm)
Spread: 8in (20cm)
Aspect: Half shade
Soil: Moist, humus-rich,
fertile
Hardiness: Zone 4
Propagation: Seed, as soon
as ripe or in spring

Dwarf, creeping, rhizomatous species
from Eurasia and North America.
Leaves heart-shaped, toothed, pale
green. Flowers pale yellow, dark-
veined, late spring and summer.

VIOLA (Violaceae)
Viola • Pansy • Violetta

A genus of some 500 species from habitats the world over. The
genus has given rise, by interbreeding, to three main types of
plant: garden pansies, violas and violettas. The garden pansies,
Viola x *wittrockiana*, have arisen from the crossing of several
species. They are biennial or at best a very short-lived perennial,
with unscented or only faintly scented flowers with a "face,"
and single-stemmed roots. The violas or tufted pansies are
perennial, with rounded, usually scented flowers with rays of a
contrasting, often deeper color, and multiple-stemmed roots.
The violettas are perennial, sweetly scented, with oval flowers
with a yellow center but no rays, and a multi-stemmed root
system. Other forms include South American species that have
rosettes of leaves like those of a sempervivum; these are very
difficult in cultivation, and best left to the enthusiast. There are
ten subdivisions in all, but only the violas (Va) and violettas
(Vtta) are of interest and covered here. All forms of *Viola* like
full sun or partial shade, and moist, well-drained but moisture-
retentive soil. They all have a long flowering season, and can be
made even more prolific by deadheading. Many of the species
violas are unfortunately short-lived.

Viola cornuta
A.G.M. (Va)
(Violaceae)

Common names: Horned
violet; tufted pansy
Height: 6in (15cm)
Spread: 16in (40cm)
Aspect: Sun or half shade
Soil: Moist, humus-rich,
fertile
Hardiness: Zone 7
Propagation: Division or stem-tip
cuttings, both in spring or autumn

A rhizomatous, evergreen species.
Leaves ovate, toothed, midgreen.
Flowers scented, lilac-blue, lower
petals marked white, from spring to
summer, twice if sheared over.

Viola cornuta
Alba Group A.G.M. (Va)
(Violaceae)

Common name: Tufted
pansy; white horned violet
Height: 6in (15cm)
Spread: 18in (45cm)
Aspect: Sun or half shade
Soil: Moist, humus-rich,
fertile
Hardiness: Zone 7
Propagation: Division or stem-tip
cuttings, both in spring or autumn

White form of evergreen, rhizomatous
species, flowering in spring and
summer, twice if sheared over.
Flowers pure white. Leaves ovate,
toothed, midgreen.

Viola
'Columbine' (Va)
(Violaceae)

Common names: None
Height: 8in (20cm)
Spread: 12in (30cm)
Aspect: Sun or half shade
Soil: Moist, well-drained,
fertile
Hardiness: Zone 7
Propagation: Division or
stem-tip cuttings, both in
spring or autumn

A compact, hybrid viola. Leaves
ovate, toothed, midgreen. Flowers
lilac and white, streaked purple, held
high above
the foliage, in spring and summer.

Viola
'Jackanapes' A.G.M. (Va)
(Violaceae)

Common names: None
Height: 8in (20cm)
Spread: 18in (45cm)
Aspect: Sun or half shade
Soil: Moist, well-drained,
fertile
Hardiness: Zone 7
Propagation: Division or
stem-tip cuttings, both in
spring or autumn

Vigorous, evergreen hybrid. Leaves
ovate, toothed, midgreen. Flowers
have upper 3 petals chocolate-colored,
lower 3 yellow, streaked purple, in
spring and summer.

Viola
'Jeannie Bellew' (Va)
(Violaceae)

Common names: None
Height: 8in (20cm)
Spread: 18in (45cm)
Aspect: Sun or half shade
Soil: Moist, well-drained,
fertile
Hardiness: Zone 7
Propagation: Division or
stem-tip cuttings, both in
spring or autumn

A hybrid viola cultivar. Leaves ovate,
toothed, midgreen. Flowers of pale
yellow are borne among the leaves in
spring and summer.

Viola
'Maggie Mott' A.G.M.
(Va) (Violaceae)

Common names: None
Height: 1ft (30cm)
Spread: 1ft (30cm)
Aspect: Sun or half shade
Soil: Moist, well-drained,
fertile
Hardiness: Zone 7
Propagation: Division or
stem-tip cuttings, both in
spring or autumn

Hybrid viola. Leaves ovate, toothed,
midgreen. Flowers perfumed, soft
silvery-mauve, with a pale cream
center, in spring and summer. A very
popular old variety.

Viola
'Rebecca' (Vtta)
(Violaceae)

Common names: None
Height: 6in (15cm)
Spread: 8in (20cm)
Aspect: Sun or half shade
Soil: Moist, well-drained,
fertile
Hardiness: Zone 7
Propagation: Division or
stem-tip cuttings, both in
spring or autumn

A hybrid violetta. Leaves ovate,
toothed, mid-green. Flowers scented,
creamy-white, flecked and streaked
with violet around the edges, in spring
and summer.

Viola tricolor (Va)
(Violaceae)

Common name: Johnny-
jump-up
Height: 5in (12cm)
Spread: 6in (15cm)
Aspect: Sun or half shade
Soil: Moist, well-drained,
fertile
Hardiness: Zone 4
Propagation: Seed, as soon
as ripe or in spring

Short-lived, evergreen species. Leaves
ovate, toothed, midgreen. Flowers
have dark purple upper petals and
yellow, streaked lower petals. Self-
seeds plentifully.

Viola
'Zoe' (Vtta)
(Violaceae)

Common names: None
Height: 6in (15cm)
Spread: 8in (20cm)
Aspect: Sun or half shade
Soil: Moist, well-drained,
fertile
Hardiness: Zone 7
Propagation: Division or
stem-tip cuttings, both in
spring or autumn

A hybrid violetta cultivar. Leaves
ovate, toothed, midgreen. Flowers
perfumed, mauve and white with a
yellow eye, in spring and summer.

Wachendorfia paniculata
(Haemodoraceae)

Common name: Redroot
Height: 6ft (1.8m)
Spread: 18in (45cm)
Aspect: Sun or half shade
Soil: Moist, well-drained,
humus-rich fertile
Hardiness: Zone 8
Propagation: Seed in
warmth or separated tubers,
both in spring

Tuberous, evergreen perennial from
South Africa. Leaves basal, broad,
linear, veined, midgreen. Flowers in
dense panicles, yellow, starry, in early
summer.

Watsonia borbonica
subsp. *ardernei*
(Iridaceae)

Common name: Bugle-lily
Height: 5ft (1.5m)
Spread: 4in (10cm)
Aspect: Sun
Soil: Well-drained, humus-
rich, fertile
Hardiness: Zone 9
Propagation: Seed, in
warmth in autumn; division,
in spring

A tender, cormous perennial from
South Africa. Leaves narrow, sword-
shaped, midgreen. Flowers in spikes
of up to 20, white, rarely pink, in
summer.

Watsonia densiflora
(Iridaceae)

Common name: Bugle-lily
Height: 5ft (1.5m)
Spread: 4in (10cm)
Aspect: Sun
Soil: Well-drained, humus-
rich, fertile
Hardiness: Zone 9
Propagation: Seed, in
warmth in autumn; division,
in spring

A tender, cormous perennial from
South Africa. Leaves narrow, sword-
shaped, midgreen. Flowers in spikes
of up to 30, red or orange-red, in
summer.

Watsonia marginata
(Iridaceae)

Common name: Bugle-lily
Height: 6ft (2m)
Spread: 6in (15cm)
Aspect: Sun
Soil: Well-drained, humus-
rich, fertile
Hardiness: Zone 9
Propagation: Seed, in
warmth in autumn; division,
in spring

A tender, cormous perennial from
South Africa. Leaves sword-shaped,
midgreen. Flowers in spikes, tubular,
mauve-pink, in spring and early
summer.

Woodsia polystichoides
A.G.M.
(Aspidiaceae/Dryopteridaceae)

Common name: Holly-
fern woodsia
Height: 12in (30cm)
Spread: 16in (40cm)
Aspect: Half shade
Soil: Moist, sharply
drained, fertile
Hardiness: Zone 4
Propagation: Spores, in warmth
when ripe; division, when dormant

A deciduous, rhizomatous, terrestrial
fern from high regions of East Asia.
Fronds lance-shaped, pinnate, with
15–30 pairs of oblong pinnae, pale
green.

Woodwardia radicans
A.G.M
(Blechnaceae)

Common name: European
chain fern
Height: 6ft (1.8m)
Spread: 10ft (3m)
Aspect: Half shade
Soil: Wet, fertile
Hardiness: Zone 8
Propagation: Bulbils or
spores, in warmth in early
autumn; division, in spring

Evergreen fern from Europe and
islands of the Atlantic. Fronds
pinnate, lance-shaped, dark green;
pinnae ovate, pinnatifid, with lance-
shaped, toothed segments.

Yucca filamentosa
A.G.M
(Agavaceae)

Common name: Adam's
needle
Height: 30in (75cm)
Spread: 5ft (1.5m)
Aspect: Sun
Soil: Well-drained
Hardiness: Zone 7
Propagation: Seed in warmth
or rooted suckers, both in
spring; root cuttings, in winter

Evergreen shrub. Leaves in basal
rosettes, inversely lance-shaped,
fringed, dark green. Flowers in short-
stemmed, upright panicles, nodding,
white bells, mid- to late summer.

Yucca flaccida
'Ivory' A.G.M.
(Agavaceae)

Common name: Spanish bayonet
Height: 2ft (60cm)
Spread: 5ft (1.5m)
Aspect: Sun
Soil: Well-drained
Hardiness: Zone 7
Propagation: Seed in warmth or rooted suckers, both in spring; root cuttings, in winter

Evergreen shrub. Leaves in basal rosettes, lance-shaped, dark blue-green, fringed. Flowers in panicles, nodding creamy-white bells, in mid- and late summer.

Yucca gloriosa
'Variegata' A.G.M.
(Agavaceae)

Common name: Mount-lily yucca
Height: 6ft (2m)
Spread: 6ft (2m)
Aspect: Sun
Soil: Well-drained
Hardiness: Zone 7
Propagation: Seed in warmth or rooted suckers, both in spring; root cuttings, in winter

Evergreen shrub. Leaves in basal rosettes, arching, lance-shaped, pointed, green, edged yellow. Flowers in panicles, white pendent bells, from late summer to autumn.

Zantedeschia aethiopica
A.G.M.
(Araceae)

Common name: Common calla
Height: 3ft (90cm)
Spread: 2ft (60cm)
Aspect: Sun
Soil: Moist or marginal aquatic, humus-rich
Hardiness: Zone 8
Propagation: Seed, in warmth when ripe; division, in spring

A rhizomatous perennial from southern Africa. Leaves arrow-shaped, glossy-green. Bears large, pure white spathes with yellow spadices from late spring to mid-summer.

Zantedeschia elliottiana
A.G.M.
(Araceae)

Common name: Golden calla
Height: 3ft (90cm)
Spread: 10in (25cm)
Aspect: Sun
Soil: Moist, humus-rich
Hardiness: Zone 9
Propagation: Seed, in warmth when ripe; division, in spring

Tender rhizomatous perennial of unknown source. Leaves basal, heart-shaped, dark green, spotted white. Spathes and spadices golden yellow, in summer.

461

Zantedeschia
Elliottiana hybrids
(Araceae)

Common name: Golden
calla
Height: 2ft (60cm)
Spread: 8in (20cm)
Aspect: Sun
Soil: Moist, humus-rich
Hardiness: Zone 9
Propagation: Division, in
spring

Tender, rhizomatous perennial hybrids
from *Z. elliottiana*. Leaves basal,
heart-shaped, dark green, unspotted.
Spathes in a variety of shades of red,
orange and yellow.

Zantedeschia rehmannii
A.G.M.
(Araceae)

Common name: Pink calla
Height: 16in (40cm)
Spread: 11in (28cm)
Aspect: Sun
Soil: Moist, humus-rich
Hardiness: Zone 9
Propagation: Seed, in
warmth when ripe; division,
in spring

A tender, rhizomatous perennial from
southern Africa. Leaves basal, lance-
shaped, dark green. Spathe pink,
spadix yellow, in summer.

Zauschneria californica
(Onagraceae)

Common name:
California- fuchsia
Height: 12in (30cm)
Spread: 20in (50cm)
Aspect: Sun
Soil: Well-drained, fertile
Hardiness: Zone 8
Propagation: Seed or basal
cuttings, both in spring

Rhizomatous evergreen from
California. Leaves lance-shaped, hairy,
gray-green. Flowers in racemes,
tubular, scarlet, long periods in late
summer and early autumn.

Zauschneria californica
subsp. *cana*
(Onagraceae)

Common name:
California- fuchsia
Height: 2ft (60cm)
Spread: 18in (45cm)
Aspect: Sun
Soil: Well-drained, fertile
Hardiness: Zone 8
Propagation: Seed or basal
cuttings, both in spring

Deciduous, rhizomatous perennial
from California. Leaves linear, gray
woolly-hairy. Flowers in racemes,
tubular, vermilion; long period from
late summer to early autumn.

Zephyranthes candida
(Amaryllidaceae)

Zephyranthes flavissima
(Amaryllidaceae)

Common name: Autumn
zephyr-lily
Height: 8in (20cm)
Spread: 3in (8cm)
Aspect: Sun
Soil: Moist, well-drained
Hardiness: Zone 9
Propagation: Seed, in warmth when
ripe; offsets, in spring

Tender, bulbous perennial from
Argentina. Leaves basal, grassy,
upright, midgreen. Flowers solitary,
crocus-like, white, over a long period
from summer to early autumn.

Common name: Autumn
zephyr-lily
Height: 8in (20cm)
Spread: 3in (8cm)
Aspect: Sun
Soil: Moist, well-drained
Hardiness: Zone 8
Propagation: Seed, in warmth when
ripe; offsets, in spring

A bulbous perennial from South
America. Leaves grassy, linear,
midgreen. Flowers solitary, crocus-
like, yellow goblets, from summer to
autumn.

Zigadenus elegans
(Liliaceae/Melianthaceae)

Common name: Mountain
deathcamus
Height: 28in (70cm)
Spread: 8in (20cm)
Aspect: Sun or half shade
Soil: Moist, well-drained
deep, fertile
Hardiness: Zone 3
Propagation: Seed, in warmth when
ripe; offsets, in spring

A bulbous perennial from North
America. Leaves basal, grassy, gray-
green. Flowers in many-flowered
spikes, small, greenish-white, starry,
in mid- and late summer.

APPENDICES

❧

THE APPENDICES BELOW list genera and species of perennials that share certain characteristics. These lists provide instant reference for the gardener looking for plants to suit specific growing conditions or plants with desirable attributes such as a long flowering season, perfumed flowers, or attractive seed heads. The selections also list plants to avoid if, for example, a child-friendly garden is required, free from poisonous plants, or if a household member is prone to allergies and therefore favors low-allergen plants. Detailed information on the plants in these appendices can be found by referring to the individual entry in the Plant Directory on pages 28–463.

Long-flowering perennials

Acanthus
Achillea
Aeonium
Alcea
Alchemilla
Alstroemeria
Althaea
Anchusa
Anemone x hybrida
Anemone multifida
Anisodontea capensis
Anthemis
Arctotis
Argyranthemum
Aster x frikartii 'Monch'
Astrantia
Begonia grandis
Bellis
Calceolaria
Campanula
Canna
Catananche
Centranthus
Chrysogonum
    virginianum
Commelina coelestis
Coreopsis
Corydalis ochroleuca
Cosmos atrpsanguineus
Crepis incana
Crocosmia
Dahlia
Dianthus deltoides
Diascia
Dicentra
Epilobium
Eremurus

Erigeron
Erodium
Erysimum
Eucomis
Fragaria
Fuchsia
Gaillardia
Gaura
Gazania
Geranium
Geum
Helenium
Helianthemum
Helichrysum italicum
Hieracium
Hemerocallis
Hosta
Iris japonica
Lavatera
Leucanthemum x
    superbum
Linaria purpurea
Linum perenne
Liriope
Lychnis coronaria
Lysimachia punctata
Lythrum
Malva moschata
Meconopsis cambrica
Melissa officinalis
Mertensia
Mimulus
Mirabilis jalapa
Monarda
Neirembergia
Nemesia denticulata
Nepeta

Nerine
Oenothera
Omphalodes
Origanum
Osteospermum
Pelargonium
Penstemon
Phlox 'Chattahoochee'
Phuopsis
Phygelius
Potentilla
Pratia
Pulmonaria
Rhodanthemum
Rhodohypoxis
Romneya
Roscoea
Rudbeckia
Salvia
Scabiosa
Senecio viravira
Solenopsis axillaris
Sphaeralcea
Stachys
Symphyandra
Symphytum armena
Teucrium
Tradescantia x
    andersoniana
Tuberaria lignosa
Tulbaghia
Verbascum
Verbena
Viola
Zauschneria

Evergreen perennials

Achillea (some)
Aciphylla
Agapanthus (some)
Agave
Alchemilla
Alyssum saxatile
Anthemis
Arabis
Armeria
Asarum
Asplenium
Astilbe glaberrima
Aubrieta
Bergenia
Blechnum
Campanla porschkiana
Carex
Celmisia
Cerastium
Chrysogonum
  virginianum
Cortaderia
Dianella
Dianthus
Dicksonia
Dierama
Draba
Dryopteris (some)
Epimedium (some)
Erigeron glaucus
Eryngium (some)

Erysimum
Euphorbia (most)
Fascicularia
Festuca (some)
Gazania
Geum
Helleborus
Heuchera (most)
x Heucherella
Iris douglasiana
Iris 'Holden Clough'
Iris innominata
Iris japonica
Iris pallida
Juncus
Kniphofia (some)
Lavandula
Lewisia
Libertia
Limonium
Liriope
Luzula
Mitchella repens
Moraea
Morina
Orthrosanthus
Parahebe
Pelargonium
Phlomis
Phormium
Plectranthus ciliatus

Polygala chamaebuxus
Polypodium (some)
Polystichium (some)
Pulmonaria (most)
Reineckia
Salvia africana-lutea
Salvia leucantha
Santolina
  chamaecyparissus
Saxifraga stolonifera
Saxifraga veitchiana
Sedum acre
Sedum rupestre
Selaginella
Sempervivum
  arachnoideum
Sesleria
Sisyrinchium
Stachys
Stipa gigantea
Strelitzia reginae
Tanacetum
Tellima
Tulbaghia
Tweedia caerulea
Uncinia
Valeriana
Vinca
Woodsia (some)
Woodwardia some
Yucca

Shade-loving perennials

Actaea
Ajuga
Alchemilla
Anemone x hybrida
Anemone nemorosa
Aquilegia
Arum italicum
Aruncus
Asplenium
  scolopodendrium
Aster macrophyllus
Astilbe
Athyrium filix-femina
Begonia grandis
Bergenia
Blechnum
Brunnera
Campanula latifolia
Cardamine
Cardiocrinum
Carex
Chaerophyllum
Chelidonium
Chrysogonum
Cicerbita
Cimicifuga
Clintonia
Codonopsis
Convallaria
Cortusa
Corydalis

Cyclamen
Cypripedium
Dactylorhiza
Davallia
Dicentra
Dicksonia
Digitalis
Diphylleia
Disporum
Dodecatheon
Doronicum
Dryopteris
Eomecon
Epimedium
Epipactis
Eupatorium
Euphorbia some
Gentiana aslepiadea
Geranium some
Helleborus
x Heucherella
Hosta
Hyacinthoides
Hylomecon
Iris foetidissima
Kirengeshoma palmata
Lamium
Leucojum
Lilium martagon
Liriope
Lunaria

Luzula
Meconopsis
Milium
Mitchella
Myrrhis
Nomocharis
Osmunda
Ourisia
Paeonia (some)
Paris
Podophyllum
Polygonatum
Polygonum
Polypodium
Polystichium
Primula
Pulmonaria
Saxifraga some
Scopolia
Selaginella
Sesleria
Smilacina
Spiranthes
Stipa
Stylophorum
Symphytum
Tellima
Tiarella
Trillium
Uvularia
Vinca

Drought-tolerant perennials

Acanthus
Achillea
Agapanthus
Agave
Aloe
Anemone nemorosa
Anisodontea
Anomatheca
Anthericum
Aristaea
Artemesia
Arthropodium
Arum
Asarina
Asphodelus
Asteriscus
Ballota
Begonia grandis
Buglossoides
Buphthalmum
Bupleurum
Camassia
Carex
Catananche
Centaurea
Chiastophyllum
Claytonia
Commelina
Convolvulus
Crambe
Crepis
Cynara
Dicentra
Dichelostemma
Digitalis
Diplarrhena
Dracunculus
Echinops
Echium
Elsholtzia
Elymus
Eranthis
Eremurus
Eriophyllum
Erodium
Eucomis
Francoa
Fritillaria
Galanthus
Galega
Galtonia
Geranium (most)
Gladiolus
Glaucium
Grindelia
Hedysarum
Hieracium
Hyacinthus
Ipheion
Iris (some)
Ixia
Knautia
Lamium
Lathyrus
Lavandula
Lavatera
Leonotis
Leptinella
Lewisia
Lilium (some)
Limonium
Linaria
Linum
Lotus
Luzula
Lychnis
Malvastrum
Marrubium
Megacarpaea
Melianthus
Melissa
Nepeta
Nerine
Oenothera (some)
Onosma
Ophiopogon
Origanum
Ornithogalum
Othonna
Oxalis
Papaver
Pentas
Perovskia
Phaenosperma
Phlomis
Phyteuma
Pilosella
Plantago
Polypodium
Polystichium
Pulsatilla
Puschkinia
Rehmannia
Reineckia
Rhodanthemum
Rhodiola
Rhodohypoxis
Rosularia
Scabiosa
Scilla
Sedum
Silene
Stachys
Stipa
Stokesia
Symphytum (some)
Thalictrum
Tiarella
Trifolium
Tritonia
Tulbaghia
Umbilicus
Verbascum
Verbena
Wachendorfia

Perennials for acid soils

Anemonopsis
   macrophylla
Blechnum
Celmisia
Cornus canadensis
Cypripedium
Dianella
Dodecatheon
Erythronium
Galax urceolata
Gentiana (autumn-
   flowering)
Hacquetia
Hylomecon
Iris 'Brighteyes'
Iris chrysographes
Iris douglasiana
Iris ensata
Iris graminea
Iris innominata
Iris laevigata
Iris missouriensis
Iris pallida
Iris pumila
Iris sibirica
Iris spuria
Iris tenax
Iris tridentata
Iris uromovii
Kirengeshoma palmata
Lilium formosanum
Lilium grayi
Lilium lancifolium
Lilium pumilum
Lilium speciosum
Lithodora diffusa
Maianthemum bifolium
Meconopsis
   betonicifolia
Meconopsis
   chelidoniifolia
Meconopsis grandis
Meconopsis napaulensis
Meconopsis punicea
Meconopsis regia
Meconopsis x sheldonii
Mitchella
Narcissus (some)
Ophiopogon
Osmunda
Plantago
Podophyllum
Primula bulleyana
Primula capitata
Primula denticulata
Primula japonica
Primula juliae
Primula prolifera
Primula pulverulenta
Primula rosea
Primula veris
Primula vialii
Reineckia carnea

Sarracenia	*Smilacina racemosa*	*Uvularia*
Sidalcea	*Trillium*	*Viola pedata*

Perennials for cut flowers

Achillea	*Dicentra*	*Paradisea*
Aconitum	*Digitalis*	*Phlox paniculata*
Agapanthus	*Doronicum*	*Platycodon*
Anaphalis	*Echinacea*	*Polemonium*
Anchusa	*Echinops ritro*	*Polygonatum* ×
Anemone × *hybrida*	*Gaillardia*	*hybridum*
Aquilegia	*Galanthus*	*Ranunculus*
Aster novae-angliae	*Gentiana*	*Rudbeckia*
Aster novae-belgii	*Gypsophila*	*Schizostylis*
Astilbe	*Helianthus*	*Solidago*
Astrantia major	*Helleborus*	*Stachys*
Bergenia	*Iris*	*Strelitzia*
Campanula	*Leucanthemum*	*Tanacetum*
Catananche	*Liatris*	*Tulipa*
Convallaria	*Lilium*	*Viola odorata*
Crocosmia	*Monarda*	*Zantedeschia*
Delphinium	*Narcissus*	
Dianthus	*Paeonia officinalis*	

Perennials with perfumed flowers

Asphodeline lutea	*Hosta* 'Sweet Susan'	*Mirabilis jalapa*
Begonia grandis	*Hyacinthoides non-*	*Muscari armeniacum*
Cardiocrinum	*scripta*	*Narcissus jonquilla*
giganteum	*Hyacinthus orientalis*	*Nymphaea*
Clematis heracleifolia	*Ipheion*	*Ornithogalum arabicum*
Convallaria majalis	*Iris chrysographes*	*Paeonia lactiflora*
Cosmos atrosanguineus	*Iris graminea*	*Paradisea*
Crambe	*Iris pallida*	*Phlox maculata*
Crinum × *powellii*	*Iris reticulata*	*Phlox paniculata* (some)
Cyclamen	*Lathyrus odoatus*	*Primula auricula*
Dianthus	*Lilium* 'African Queen'	*Primula vulgaris*
Dictamnus	*Lilium candidum*	*Romneya coulteri*
Erysimum	*Lilium formosanum*	*Sedum populifolium*
Filipendula	*Lilium grayi*	*Spiranthes*
Galanthus	*Lilium henryi*	*Tulbaghia*
Galtonia candicans	*Lilium monadelphum*	*Tulipa sylvestris*
Hedychium	*Lilium* Pink Perfection	*Verbena bonariensis*
Hemerocallis (some)	Group	*Verbena* × *hybrida*
Hesperis matrionalis	*Lilium pumilum*	*Viola odorata*
Hosta 'Honeybells'	*Lilium regale*	
Hosta plantaginea	*Lunaria rediviva*	

Aquatic and marginal perennials

Alisma plantago-	*Iris pseudacorus*	*Phormium tenax*
aquatica	*Iris sibirica*	*Pontederia cordata*
Butomus umbellatus	*Juncus spiralis*	*Ranunculus aquatilis*
Caltha palustris	*Lobelia cardinalis*	*Ranunculus lingua*
Carex	*Lythrum salicaria*	*Sagittaria*
Cyperus	*Mimulus*	*Saururus cernuus*
Houttuynia	*Myosotis scorpiodes*	*Schoenoplectus lacustris*
Iris ensata	*Nymphaea*	*Scirpus*
Iris 'Holden Clough'	*Nymphoides*	*Scrophularia auriculata*
Iris laevigata	*Peltiphyllum peltatum*	*Zantedeschia*

Bog garden perennials

Aruncus dioicus	*Caltha*	*Cardiocrinum*
Astilbe	*Cardamine*	*Cimicifuga simplex*

Eupatorium
Filipendula
Fritillaria meleagris
Geum rivale
Glyceria
Gunnera
Hemerocallis
Hosta
Houttuynia
Iris ensata
Iris laevigata
Iris pseudacorus
Iris sibirica
Kirengeshoma

Leucojum
Ligularia
Lobelia cardinalis
Lychnis flos-cuculi
Lysimachia
Lythrum
Mimulus
Monarda
Onoclea
Osmunda
Parnassia
Polygonum
Primula (many)
Ranunculus

    aconitifolius
Ranunculus lingua
Rheum
Rodgersia
Sanguisorba obtusa
Sarracenia
Schizostylis
Symphytum x
    uplandicum
Trollius
Uvularia
Woodsia
Woodwardia

Perennials with attractive seed heads

Acanthus
Achillea
Aconitum
Agapanthus
Alchemilla
Allium
Alstroemeria
Althaea
Anaphalis
Anemone x hybrida
Artemesia
Asphodeline
Asphodelus
Astilbe
Baptisia
Cardiocrinum
Catananche
Cautleya
Centaurea
Cimicifuga simplex
Clematis (some)

Crambe maritima
Dierama
Diplarrhena
Echinops
Eremurus
Eryngium
Eupatorium
Euphorbia some
Filipendula
Galtonia
Gillenia
Glaucium
Gypsophila
Hyacinthoides
Incarvillea
Iris (some)
Lathyrus vernus
Lychnis (some)
Malva
Monarda
Moraea

Morina
Nectaroscordum
    siculum
Paeonia (some)
Papaver orientale
Paradisea
Paris
Phlomis
Phormium
Pulsatilla
Rheum
Rodgersia
Rumex
Scabiosa (some)
Sedum (some)
Sisyrinchium striatum
Stokesia
Thalictrum
Veratrum
Veronicastrum

Perennials for ground cover

Acaena
Acanthus
Achillea
Adiantum
Aegopodium podagraria
Ajuga
Alchemilla
Alyssum
Anaphalis
Anemone x hybrida
Antennaria
Anthemis
Anthericum
Arabis
Arenaria
Arisarum
Armeria
Artemesia
Aruncus
Aster macrophyllus
Astilbe
Astrantia
Aubrieta
Ballota
Bergenia
Blechnum

Brunnera
Buphthalmum
Calamintha
Campanula carpatica
Campanula latiloba
Centaurea
Cerastium tomentosum
Chiastophyllum
    oppositifolium
Chrysanthemum
    yezoense
Claytonia sibirica
Convallaria
Corydalis
Crambe
Crocosmia
Cyclamen
Darmera
Dianthus
Dicentra
Dryopteris filix-mas
Epimedium
Erigeron glaucus
Eriogonum umbellatum
Eriophyllum lanatum
Erodium carviflorum

Erodium manescauii
Euphorbia polychroma
Euphorbia griffithii
Filipendula
Fragaria
Geranium (most)
Geum
Gypsophila
Helianthemum
Helleborus
Hemerocallis
Heuchera
x Heucherella
Hosta (all)
Houttuynia
Hypericum
Iberis
Iris (some)
Lamium
Limonium
Liriope
Lithodora diffusa
Lysimachia nummularia
Maianthemum
Mentha
Mitella

Nepeta
Omphalodes
Onoclea sensibilis
Ophiopogon
Osmunda
Othonna
Ourisia
Oxalis acetosella
Persicaria
Phlomis
Physalis
Polygonatum

Polygonum
Potentilla
Prunella grandiflora
Pulmonaria
Ranunculus aconitifolus
Rheum
Rodgersia
Saponaria
Saxifraga stolonifera
Saxifraga × urbium
Sedum
Smilacina

Stachys macrantha
Symphytum ibericum
Tellima
Teucrium × lucidrys
Thymus
Tiarella
Tolmiea
Trollius
Veronica
Vinca
Viola
Zauschneria

Perennials with aromatic foliage

Achillea filipendula
Achillea millefolium
Artemesia
Cedronella canariensis
Chamaemelum nobile
Dictamnus albus
Elsholtzia stauntonii
Filipendula ulmaria
Foeniculum vulgare
Geranium incanum
Geranium macorrhizum
Helichrysum italicum

Houttuynia cordata
Hyssopus officinalis
Lavandula
Leptinella dendyi
Malva moschata
Melissa officinalis
Mellitis melissophyllum
Mentha × gracilis
Monarda (all)
Morina longifolia
Myrrhis odorata
Nepeta

Origanum vulgare
Perovskia
Phuopsis stylosa
Rosmarinus
Ruta graveolens
Salvia oficinalis
Santolina
  chamaecyparissus
Tanacetum parthenium
Tanacetum vulgare
Teucrium × lucidrys
Thymus

Architectural perennials

Acanthus
Aciphylla
Aeonium
Amicia
Angelica archangelica
Cortaderia selloana
Crambe cordifolia
Cynara cardunculus
Darmera peltata
Dierama
Echinops
Echium
Eremurus

Eupatorium
Ferula
Hedychium
Helianthus
Heliopsis
Inula magnifica
Kniphofia
Leonotis
Ligularia
Macleaya
Meconopsis grandis
Meconopsis napaulensis
Meconopsis paniculata

Melianthus major
Nectaroscordum
  siculum
Ostrowskia magnifica
Paeonia (some)
Phormium tenax
Phygelius
Rheum
Ricinus
Rodgersia
Strelitzia
Telekia speciosa
Thalictrum

Perennials which have berries after flowering

Actaea alba
Actaea rubra
Arisaema ssp.
Arum italicum
Clintonia umbellulata
Convallaria majalis
Cornus canadensis
Dianella nigra
Dianella tasmanica
Diphyleia cymosa

Disporum smithii
Dracunculus vulgaris
Fragaria
Fuchsia
Iris foetidissima
Mitchella repens
Pachyphragma
  macrophyllum
Paeonia mascula subsp.
  triternata

Phytolacca americana
Phytolacca polyandra
Podophyllum
  hexandrum
Polygonatum ×
  hybridum
Smilacina racemosa
Uvularia grandiflora

Low-allergen perennials

Acanthus mollis
Aegopodium podagraria
Agapanthus
  campanulatus
Ajuga reptans
Alcea rosea

Alchemilla mollis
Allium
Anchusa azurea
Anemone × hybrida
Armeria maritima
Aquilegia

Aruncus dioicus
Asphodeline lutea
Astilbe
Astrantia
Baptisia australis
Bergenia

Brunnera
Camassia
Campanula persicifolia
Cardamine
Corydalis
Crambe
Crocosmia
Delphinium
Dicentra
Dierama
Digitalis
Dryas
Epilobium
Epimedium
Eremurus
Eryngium
Filipendula
Foeniculum
Galtonia
Gentiana asclepiadea
Geranium ssp.
Geum
Gladiolus
Glycyrrhiza
Helianthemum
Hemerocallis
Heuchera

x Heucherella
Houttuynia
Hyssopus
Iberis
Iris sibirica
Kirengeshoma palmata
Kniphofia
Lamium
Linum
Liriope
Lysimachia
Lythrum
Macleaya
Melissa
Mentha
Mertensia
    pulmonarioides
Monarda
Nepeta
Omphalodes
Origanum
Paeonia
Papaver
Penstemon
Phlox paniculata
Physostegia virginiana
Platycodon grandiflorus

Polemonium caeruleum
Potentilla
Prunella
Pulmonaria
Rodgersia
Rosmarinus
Salvia
Saxifraga
Scabiosa
Schizostylis
Scrophularia aquatica
Sidalcea
Sisyrinchium striatum
Stachys
Symphytum
Thalictrum
Tellima
Tiarella
Tradescantia x
    andersoniana
Trollius x cultorum
Valeriana
Verbena
Veronica
Vinca
Viola

High-allergen perennials

Achillea millefolium
Aconitum spp.
Alstroemeria spp.
Anaphalis spp.
Anemone nemorosa
Angelica archangelica
Arctotis
Argyranthemum
    frutesens
Armoracia rusticana
Arnica montana
Artemesia spp.
Arum spp.
Aster spp.
Bellis perennis
Caltha palustris
Catananche caerulea
Centurea spp.
Chamaemelum nobile
Chelidonum majus
Coreopsis spp.
Cortaderia selloana
Dactylis spp.
Dianthus spp.
Dictamnus albus
Echinacea purpurea

Echinops spp.
Elymus spp.
Erigeron spp.
Erysimum spp.
Euphorbia spp.
Festuca spp.
Gaillardia spp.
Gazania spp.
Gerbera
Hakonechloa spp.
Helenium autumnale
Helianthus spp.
Helictotrichon
    sempervirens
Helleborus spp.
Heracleum
    mantegazzanium
Holcus spp.
Hordeum jubatum
Imperata cylindrica
Lathyrus odoratus
Lavandula angustifolia
Ligularia spp.
Lilium spp.
Lupinus spp.
Microseris ringens

Milium spp.
Osteospermum spp.
Pennisetum orientale
Persicaria spp.
Phaenosperma
Phalaris arundinacea
Pilosella
Plantago spp.
Primula (many)
Pulsatilla vulgaris
Ranunculus spp.
Ruta graveolens
Rumex spp.
Santolina
    chamaecyparissus
Senecio jacobea
Sesleria
Solidago spp.
x Solidaster
Stipa gigantea
Stokesia laevis
Uncinia
Veratrum spp.
Zantedeschia aethiopica

Perennials which attract butterflies

Ajuga
Arabis
Armeria
Aubrieta
Aster
Aurinia
Calamintha
Centranthus

Cephalaria
Chrysanthemum
Coreopsis
Dahlia
Echinacea
Echinops
Erigeron
Eryngium

Helenium
Hesperis
Hyssopus
Iberis
Knautia
Lavandula
Lunaria
Melissa

Mentha
Nepeta
Phlox paniculata

Saponaria
Scabiosa
Sedum

Solidago
Thymus

Perennials which attract bees

Allium
Alstroemeria
Althaea
Anchusa
Anemone
Asclepias
Calamintha
Camassia
Campanula
Centaurea
Clematis
Colchicum
Coreopsis
Cosmos
Crocus
Dahlia
Doronicum
Echinacea
Echinops
Epilobium

Eranthis
Eryngium
Fuchsia
Galanthus
Galega
Galtonia
Gypsophila
Helenium
Helianthemum
Helianthus
Heliopsis
Hyacinthus
Hyssopus
Iberis
Inula
Lavandula
Ligularia
Lupinus
Lythrum
Malva

Mellitis
Mirabilis
Monarda
Nepeta
Oenothera
Origanum
Polemonium
Potentilla
Rudbeckia
Salvia
Scabiosa
Sedum
Senecio
Sidalcea
Stachys
Thymus
Verbascum
Veronica

Perennials for seaside gardens

Achillea
Acanthus
Alstroemeria
Amaryllis belladonna
Anaphalis
Anchusa
Anemone
Anthemis
Anthericum
Armeria
Artemesia
Aster (dwarf)
Bergenia
Campanula (dwarf)
Catananche
Celmisia
Centaurea
Centranthus
Crambe
Crocosmia
Cynoglossum
Dianthus
Dierama
Echinacea
Echinops
Erigeron

Erodium
Eryngium
Euphorbia
Fascicularia
Filipendula
Geranium
Glaucium
Gypsophila
Heuchera
Hieracium
Iris
Kniphofia
Lathyrus
Lavatera
Libertia
Limonium
Linaria
Lupinus
Lychnis flos-jovis
Melissa
Mertensia virginica
Mimulus
Morina
Myosotidium
Nerine
Oenothera

Origanum
Osteospermum
Penstemon
Perovskia
Phormium
Phygelius
Physostegia
Potentilla
Pulsatilla
Romneya coulteri
Salvia
Scabiosa
Schizostylis
Scrophularia
Sedum
Senecio
Sisyrinchium
Stachys
Stokesia
Tritonia
Veronica
Viscaria
Yucca
Zantedeschia

Rabbit-proof perennials

Acanthus
Aconitum
Agapanthus
Alchemilla
Anaphalis
Anemone
Aquilegia
Aster

Astilbe
Bergenia
Brunnera
Campanula lactiflora
Campanula latifolia
Cardiocrinum
Clematis
Colchicum

Convallaria
Cortaderia
Corydalis
Crinum
Crocosmia
Cyclamen
Cynara
Dahlia

Delphinium
Digitalis
Doronicum
Epimedium
Eranthis
Eupatorium
Euphorbia
Fuchsia
Galanthus
Gentiana asclepiadea
Geranium
Hedychium
Helenium
Helianthus
Helleborus
Hemerocallis
Hosta
Houttuynia
Iris
Kirengeshoma

Kniphofia
Lamium
Lavatera
Leucojum
Liriope
Lupinus
Luzula
Lysimachia
Malva
Melissa
Miscanthus
Narcissus
Nepeta
Omphalodes
Orchis
Paeonia
Papaver
Phormium
Phytolacca
Polygonatum

Polygonum
Pulmonaria
Rheum
Romneya
Rosmarinus
Ruta
Saxifraga geum
Saxifraga × umbrosa
Sedum
Stachys olympica
Tellima
Tradescantia
Trillium
Trollius
Tulipa
Verbena
Vinca
Yucca
Zantedeschia

Deer-resistant perennials

Acanthus
Aconitum
Agapanthus
Agave
Allium
Amaryllis
Aquilegia
Artemesia
Arum
Astilbe
Campanula
Carex
Centaurea
Ceratostigma
Clematis
Cortaderia
Crinum
Crocosmia
Delphinium
Dicentra
Digitalis
Epimedium
Euphorbia

Ferns
Festuca glauca
Filipendula
Gaillardia
Geranium
Helianthus
Helichrysum
Helleborus
Hosta
Iris
Kniphofia
Lavandula
Leucanthemum ×
     superbum
Leucojum
Liriope
Lupinus
Lychnis coronaria
Melianthus
Melissa
Melittis
Mentha
Mirabilis

Myosotis
Narcissus
Nepeta
Origanum
Paeonia
Papaver
Polygonatum
Potentilla
Pulmonaria
Romneya coulteri
Rudbeckia
Salvia
Satureja
Scabiosa
Sisyrinchium
Tellima
Thalictrum
Tiarella
Trillium
Veratrum
Vinca
Yucca

Poisonous perennials

All parts are poisonous,
unless specified

Aconitum
Actaea
Amaryllis
Anemone blanda
Anemone nemorosa
Anemone ranunculoides
Anemone rivularis
Aquilegia
Arisaema
Arnica
Arum
Asclepias
Calla palustris (fruits)
Chaerophyllum
     hirsutum 'Roseum'

Colchicum
Cyclamen persicum
Convallaria majalis
     (seeds)
Coriaria terminalis
     (fruits)
Crinum × powellii
Delphinium
Dendranthema
     weyrichii
Dendranthema yezoense
Dicentra
Dictamnus
Digitalis
Echium
Eranthis
Euphorbia
Galanthus

Helenium
Helleborus
Iris
Lathyrus (seeds)
Lupinus (seeds)
Narcissus (bulb)
Nuphar lutea
Ornithogalum
Paeonia
Paris quadrifolia (fruits)
Physalis alkengi
Phytolacca
Podophyllum
Polygonatum ×
     hybridum
Ranunculus ficaria
Ricinus (seeds)
Rumex

Scopolia (root)   Symphytum   Veratrum
Sedum   Trollius europaeus   Vinca
Senecio   Tulipa

Perennials which may cause skin irritation

Aconitum   Euphorbia   Phytolacca
Alstroemeria   Helenium   Podophyllum
Amsonia   Helianthus   Primula elatior
Aquilegia   Helleborus   Primula obconica
Arisaema   Heracleum   Pulmonaria
Arum   Hyacinthus   Ranunculus
Borago   Iris   Rumex
Caltha   Lobelia   Ruta
Chamaemelum   Macleaya   Symphytum
Chelidonum   Myosotis   Tanacetum
Cichorium   Narcissus   Tradescantia x
Clematis   Onosma   andersoniana
Delphinium   Ornithogalum   Tulipa
Dendranthema   Pelargonium   Veratrum
Dicentra   Pentaglottis
Echium   Persicaria

Perennials which seed freely

Achillea millefolium   Echinops   Marrubium supinum
Alchemilla mollis   Echium   Meconopsis cambrica
Allium christophii   Epilobium   Melissa officinalis
Anthericum   Erigeron compositus   Milium effusum
Antirrhinum   Erodium   Myrrhis odorata
Aquilegia (all)   Euphorbia characias   Nectaroscordum
Asphodeline   Galtonia   siculum
Asplenium   Geranium pratense   Oenothera fruticosa
Aster novae-belgii   Geranium pyrenaicum   Oxalis acetosella
Astrantia major   'Bill Wallis'   Papaver
Bellis   Glaucium   Parahebe
Brunnera   Helleborus orientalis   Pentaglottis
Bupleurum   Hesperis matrionalis   Phytolacca
Campanula latifolium   Hieracium   Pilosella
Campanula persicifolia Isatis tinctoria   Plantago
Campanula trachelium   Juncus   Polemonium
Centaurea montana   Lamium galeobdolon   Pulmonaria
Cephalaria   Lamium maculatum   Rumex
Chelidonum   Linaria   Senecio cineraria
Cicerbita   Lotus   Senecio uniflora
Cirsium   Lychnis chalcedonica   Sisyrinchium
Corydalis lutea   Lychnis coronaria   x Solidaster
Corydalis ochroleuca   Lychnis flos-cuculi   Telekia
Crepis   Lythrum salicaria   Valeriana
Cynara   Lythrum virgatum   Verbascum
Digitalis (most)   Malva   Verbena

Short-lived perennials

Achillea ptarmica   Belamcanda chinensis   Dianthus
Aethionema   Bupleurum falcatum   Diascia
Agastache   Calamintha nepeta   Dicentra spectabilis
Alcea   Campanula pulla   Dictamnus albus
Anagallis   Campanula pyramidalis   Erigeron
Anchusa   Carlina acaulis   Erinus
Antirrhinum   Catananche caerulea   Eryngium giganteum
Aquilegia   Claytonia   Erysimum
Arabis   Coreopsis   Gaillardia
Asarina procumbens   Crepis   Gaura
Baptisia australis   Delphinium Pacific   Glaucium
Begonia grandis   hybrids   Gypsophila

Hedysarum
Hesperis
Isatis tinctoria
Lavatera
Leontopodium
Linum
Lobelia
Lotus
Lupinus
Lychnis x arkwrightii
Lychnis coronaria
Malva
Matthiola
Meconopsis
    betonicifolia

Meconopsis grandis
Megacarpaea
Mimulus
Oenothera
Orthrosanthus
Papaver atlanticum
Papaver croceum
Papaver 'Fireball'
Papaver fourei
Papaver rupifragum
Polemonium
Primula capitata
Rehmannia
Rudbeckia
Salvia argentea

Salvia coccinea
Salvia pratensis
Sanguisorba albiflora
Scabiosa atropurpurea
Semiaquilegia ecalcarata
Senecio cineraria
Silene dioica
Silene uniflora
Sisyrinchium
Stylophorum
Symphyandra
Tanacetum
Verbascum
    bombiciferum
Viola

Invasive perennials

Acanthus hungaricus
Acanthus mollis
Acanthus spinosus
Achillea ptarmica
Aegopodium podagraria
Anemone x hybrida
Arisarum proboscideum
Arum italicum
Aruncus dioicus
Campanula persicifolia
Campanula pulla
Campanula rotundifolia
Campanula takesimana
Cardamine pentaphyllos
Cardamine pratensis
Ceratostigma
    plumbaginoides
Chamaemelum nobile
Cirsium rivulare
Commelina coelestis
Convallaria
Convolvulus altheoides
Cornus canadensis
Dicentra 'Pearl Drops'
Eomecon chionanthum
Epilobium
    angustifolium
Galium odoratum
Geranium himalayense
Gladiolus papilio
Glyceria maxima
Helianthus decapetalus

Helianthus doronicoides
Helianthus 'Lemon
    Queen'
Lamium galeobdolon
Houttuynia cordata
Hylomecon japonicum
Inula hookeri
Leonotis dysophyllus
Leonotis leonurus
Lilium bulbiferum
Linaria triornithophora
Lotus corniculatus
Lysimachia ciliata
Lysimachia nummularia
Lysimachia punctata
Maianthemum bifolium
Malvastrum lateritium
Mentha x gracilis
Mertensia implicissima
Mertensia
    pulmonarioides
Milium effusum
Muscari armeniacum
Myosotis scorpioides
Nectaroscordum
    siculum
Oenothera speciosa
Ornithogalum nutans
Ornithogalum
    thyrsoides
Ornithogalum
    tetraphylla

Oxalis acetosella
Oxalis pes-caprae
Oxalis tetraphylla
Persicaria affinis
Persicaria capitata
Petasites japonicus
Phygelius aequalis
Physalis alkengi
Physostegia virginiana
Plectranthus ciliatus
Pontederia cordata
Pratia pedunculata
Prunella grandiflora
Ranunculus acris
Ranunculus ficaria
Ranunculus repens
Sanguisorba canadensis
Sanguisorba obtusa
Sanguisorba officinalis
Sanguisorba tenuifolia
Saponaria officinalis
Saxifraga x urbium
Scopolia carniolica
Symphytum ibericum
Symphytum orientale
Symphytum x
    uplandicum
Telekia speciosa
Tiarella cordifolia
Tricyrtis formosana
Tricyrtis latifolia
Trifolium repens

Perennials which require to be lifted and divided regularly

Achillea
Aster amellus
Aster ericoides
Aster thomsonii
Astilbe
Bergenia
Camassia
Campanula persicifolia
Campanula pulla
Coreopsis
Crocosmia
Crocus
Doronicum

Dracunculus
Erigeron
Fritillaria imperialis
Geum
Gladiolus communis
Gladiolus papilio
Helenium
Helianthus
Heliopsis
Hemerocallis
Heuchera
Liatris
Muscari

Narcissus
Nerine
Ophiopogon
Ornithogalum
Phlox paniculata
Polygonatum x
    hybridum
Schizostylis
Sisyrinchium
Stachys byzantina
Tradescantia x
    andersoniana

Perennials which resent transplantation

Aciphylla
Aconitum
Agapanthus
Alstroemeria
Anemone x hybrida
Angelica
Anthemis
Aquilegia
Aristaea
Asclepias
Baptisia
Brunsvigia
Campanula lactiflora
Catananche
Centranthus
Cephalaria
Chaerophyllum
Claytonia
Clivia
Crambe
Crepis

Crinum
Cynara
Dictamnus
Dierama
Echinops
Echium
Eriogonum
Eryngium
Euphorbia
Fascicularia
Ferula
Foeniculum
Galega
Gentiana
Gerbera
Glaucium
Glycyrrhiza
Gypsophila
Hacquetia
Hedysarum
Hesperis

Isatis
Incarvillea
Lathyrus
Limonium
Linum
Lupinus
Megacarpaea
Mertensia
Myrrhis
Oenothera
Ostrowskia magnifica
Paeonia
Papaver orientale
Pentaglottis
Platycodon
Pulsatilla
Scabiosa
Thermopsis
Trillium
Tropaeolum
    polyphyllum

INDEX

❦

INDEX

Picture Credits

All photographs by Marshall Craigmyle, except:

Heather Angel 12, 13, 14, 15, 16, 20-21, 22-23, 28

Salamander Picture Library 1, 2, 3, 4, 9, 24, 25

Maps by Eugene Fleury © Salamander Books Ltd.